Network Consultants Handbook

Matthew Castelli

Cisco Press

Cisco Press
201 W 103rd Street
Indianapolis, IN 46290 USA

Network Consultants Handbook

Matthew Castelli

Copyright© 2002 (Cisco Press)

Published by:
Cisco Press
201 West 103rd Street
Indianapolis, IN 46290 USA

Printed in the United States of America 1 2 3 4 5 6 7 8 9 0

Library of Congress Cataloging-in-Publication Number: 2001-090431

ISBN: 1-58705-039-0

First Printing: December 2001

Warning and Disclaimer

This book is designed to provide information about network consulting. Every effort has been made to make this book as complete and as accurate as possible, but no warranty or fitness is implied.

The information is provided on an "as is" basis. The author, Cisco Press, and Cisco Systems, Inc. shall have neither liability nor responsibility to any person or entity with respect to any loss or damages arising from the information contained in this book or from the use of the discs or programs that may accompany it.

The opinions expressed in this book belong to the author and are not necessarily those of Cisco Systems, Inc.

Trademark Acknowledgments

All terms mentioned in this book that are known to be trademarks or service marks have been appropriately capitalized. Cisco Press or Cisco Systems, Inc. cannot attest to the accuracy of this information. Use of a term in this book should not be regarded as affecting the validity of any trademark or service mark.

Feedback Information

At Cisco Press, our goal is to create in-depth technical books of the highest quality and value. Each book is crafted with care and precision, undergoing rigorous development that involves the unique expertise of members from the professional technical community.

Readers' feedback is a natural continuation of this process. If you have any comments regarding how we could improve the quality of this book, or otherwise alter it to better suit your needs, you can contact us through e-mail at feedback@ciscopress.com. Please make sure to include the book title and ISBN in your message.

We greatly appreciate your assistance.

Publisher	John Wait
Editor-in-Chief	John Kane
Cisco Systems Management	Michael Hakkert
	Tom Geitner
	William Warren
Production Manager	Patrick Kanouse
Acquisitions Editor	Amy Lewis
Development Editors	Megan Crouch
	Melissa Thornton
Project Editor	Karen A. Gill
Copy Editor	Karen A. Gill
Technical Editors	Belinda Goldsmith
	Ron Milione
	Barb Nolley
	John Tiso
	Jeff Whittemore
Team Coordinator	Tammi Ross
Book Designer	Gina Rexrode
Cover Designer	Louisa Klucznik
Composition	Argosy
Indexer	Brad Herriman

CISCO SYSTEMS

Corporate Headquarters
Cisco Systems, Inc.
170 West Tasman Drive
San Jose, CA 95134-1706
USA
http://www.cisco.com
Tel: 408 526-4000
        800 553-NETS (6387)
Fax: 408 526-4100

European Headquarters
Cisco Systems Europe
11 Rue Camille Desmoulins
92782 Issy-les-Moulineaux
Cedex 9
France
http://www-europe.cisco.com
Tel: 33 1 58 04 60 00
Fax: 33 1 58 04 61 00

Americas Headquarters
Cisco Systems, Inc.
170 West Tasman Drive
San Jose, CA 95134-1706
USA
http://www.cisco.com
Tel: 408 526-7660
Fax: 408 527-0883

Asia Pacific Headquarters
Cisco Systems Australia, Pty.,
Ltd
Level 17, 99 Walker Street
North Sydney
NSW 2059 Australia
http://www.cisco.com
Tel: +61 2 8448 7100
Fax: +61 2 9957 4350

Cisco Systems has more than 200 offices in the following countries. Addresses, phone numbers, and fax numbers are listed on the Cisco Web site at www.cisco.com/go/offices

Argentina • Australia • Austria • Belgium • Brazil • Bulgaria • Canada • Chile • China • Colombia • Costa Rica • Croatia • Czech Republic • Denmark • Dubai, UAE • Finland • France • Germany • Greece • Hong Kong • Hungary • India • Indonesia • Ireland • Israel • Italy • Japan • Korea • Luxembourg • Malaysia • Mexico • The Netherlands • New Zealand • Norway • Peru • Philippines • Poland • Portugal • Puerto Rico • Romania • Russia • Saudi Arabia • Scotland • Singapore • Slovakia • Slovenia • South Africa • Spain • Sweden • Switzerland • Taiwan • Thailand • Turkey • Ukraine • United Kingdom • United States • Venezuela • Vietnam • Zimbabwe

About the Author

Matthew "Cat" Castelli has more than 13 years of experience in the telecommunications networking industry, starting as a cryptologic technician (communications) in the United States Navy. Cat has since been working as a principal consultant for a Cisco Professional Services partner and as a senior technical consultant/enterprise network design engineer for a global telecommunications integrator. Cat has broad exposure to LAN/WAN, Internet, and Alternative technologies (VoX) for service provider and enterprise networks of all sizes, including implementation, application, configuration, integration, network management, and security solutions. Cat currently holds CCNA, CCDA, CCNP, and CCDP certifications and recently completed Technical Review for Advanced MPLS Design and Implementation (Cisco Press).

When Cat is not involved with network design or engineering, he can be found pursuing his degree, reading, cheering for the Los Angeles Dodgers, or simply enjoying a cigar and scotch.

Cat is currently a network architect engineer for Global Crossing. He can be contacted at mjcastelli@earthlink.net.

About the Technical Reviewers

Belinda Goldsmith is a senior network engineer. She has 10 years of experience in the networking industry. She has worked in small/medium/enterprise environments supporting LAN/WAN/VOIP networks. She is a CCIE candidate, and currently holds the CCNP, CCDA, CCNA, and MCSE certifications.

Ron Milione, Ph.D., is one of the leading senior software staff developers at Computer Associates International, a Cisco developer partner and world-leading software company that develops eBusiness infrastructure software. Ron has MSEE and BSEE degrees from City College of New York with a major in telecommunications. Ron also holds CCDA, CCNA, CCDP, and CCNP certifications with Cisco. In addition to Cisco certification, Ron holds certifications in Compaq, Microsoft, and Novell and is an adjunct professor of computer science and telecommunications at St. John's University in New York. Ron has been published in several industry publications and other books. He can be reached via e-mail at ronald.milione@ca.com.

Barb Nolley is the president and principal consultant for BJ Consulting, Inc., a small consulting firm that specializes in networking education. Since starting BJ Consulting, Barb has developed and taught training courses for Novell's Master CNE certification, as well as several courses for Cisco Systems' Engineering Education group. Barb also likes to deliver high-energy presentations about networking technologies and recently started teaching the CCNA track for the University of California-Riverside Extension. Barb stays current on networking technologies by constantly reading published books and perusing more than 50 industry publications each month. Prior to starting her own company in 1993, Barb worked for Apple Computer, Tandem Computer, and Tymnet (now part of MCI), where she held positions in everything from technical support to project management.

John Tiso, CCIE #5162, is one of the senior technologists of NIS, a Cisco Systems silver partner. He has a BS degree from Adelphi University. John also holds the CCDP certification; the Cisco Security and Voice Access Specializations; and Sun Microsystems, Microsoft, and Novell certifications. John has been published in several industry publications. He can be reached via e-mail at johnt@jtiso.com.

Jeff Whittemore is the director of advanced technology for The Systems House, a supply chain software and data center services provider. Jeff has been involved in IT for 25 years and began his networking career in the early 1980s with the design of the first network server system in the Midwest to host a multiuser database. Recently, Jeff built a national network and central data center from the ground up for a multi-billion dollar office supply company. Jeff incorporates a special emphasis on fault tolerance and resiliency into his network and data center designs. He is UNIX AIX and Microsoft MCSE certified and can be reached via e-mail at jeff.whittemore@tsh.com.

Dedications

I am still learning.

    —Michelangelo (1475–1564)

Truth is what stands the test of experience.

    —Albert Einstein (1879–1955). Closing words, "The Laws of Science and the Laws of Ethics," *Out of My Later Years,* Rev. ed., 16, 1956 (1950).

I would like to thank the following people for their tireless support and encouragement in this endeavor.

Kim Graves, thank you for your encouragement, most notably in not letting me give up on the idea of this book. More importantly, thank you for your guidance, wisdom, and friendship. You've always brought out my best.

LJ Bur, I also say "thank you" for your guidance, insight, and friendship. May our "whiteboard" discussion never cease.

Jeff Wolfe, Jon Hage, Robert Douglas, and Joe Shannon, thank you for keeping the faith and continually demonstrating that "old school" is a "good school."

Jeff Whittemore, Randy Yeh, and Claude Hodges, you guys always kept me on my toes.

Michelle Cornell, my partner in crime furthering the plot for "world domination," thank you for your encouragement, support, friendship, and also for not letting me give up on the idea of this book. I look forward to our working together again.

Jeff Stevenson, John Steel II, Matt "Looch" Luetjen, Belinda Goldsmith, Andre Buckner, and Harrison McCoy: You are a phenomenal team and I look forward to working together again (for a bit longer this time).

To John, Lisa, Jim, Sean, Andy, and Cathy: You've always found ways to get my best work.

Thanks to Kenny Rodgers for all those times when it was up to you and me to figure things out, and we always did it together. We've been coworkers and friends for a long time now and it's been a lot of fun. "Who's your buddy?!"

Erin Barker, a great, true, and special friend, who showed me what such a friendship means. "May you live forever and I never die."

To "The Boys"—Spike, Zeke, Buzz and Keiser, for teaching me the value of the Undo option.

Most important and most notable of all is my family—my father, Jim, my mother, Jayne, and my brother, Dan. Thank you for your never-ending support, encouragement, guidance, wisdom, and friendship. I also say thanks to asking a young boy, many years ago, how to count to 10 in binary. It was that question that ultimately started me down this road of computers, networks, and telecommunications. You've always been there for me and for that I am eternally thankful.

Acknowledgments

I would like to thank the following individuals for their unending support in the making of this book. It is these individuals who had me sometimes wondering if writing the book wasn't the easiest part.

John Kane, your humor, good nature, encouragement, support, and friendship have been invaluable. It all started about a year ago when you asked if I had any ideas for a book. You've done it now and I thank you.

Amy Lewis, as much as any one person should have to work with me through combinations of caffeine and cotton candy, I say thank you because you deserve a medal. Your endless support, encouragement, motivation, and patience kept me going as deadlines loomed ever more intimidating. Your humor and friendship, however, may very well be one of the best things to come from this project.

To Jeff Whittemore, Belinda Goldsmith, John Tiso, Ron Millione and Barb Nolley, I say thank you for keeping my straight. It is through the efforts of these individuals that what you hold in your hands was verified as being "honest and true."

To Megan Crouch and Melissa Thornton, I say thank you for your hard work and determination, and our countless late nights as the deadline loomed near.

To Karen Gill, "What is she doing again?" . . . Thank you for your hard work and dedication to this book.

Contents at a Glance

Contents

Foreword

Many large projects in the networking industry, especially in the professional services or consulting arenas, have started with the statements: "There's something wrong in the network!" or the famous "The network is slow!" A large part of a networking consultant's working life can be devoted to identifying and resolving the underlying cause of those statements. When asked to resolve a networking issue, a consultant must grasp the problem (both actual and perceived), understand the environment of the problem (networking as well as organizational), and make intelligent guesses about the nature of the problem. The consultant must then drill down to find the exact nature of the problem, test the hypotheses, and then recommend or implement a solution.

The author of this book, Matt Castelli, and I have collaborated on a number of such projects. The challenge to the networking consultant is not only to have technical expertise, but to apply this expertise efficiently in an environment that is both complex and dynamic. Not only do today's networks entail transmission of data to and from a myriad of hosts, but also over a collection of different media, even within one network. If one looks at another network, many facets of the network will be different. Such is the result of the widespread application of standards in networks. There are now many ways to get a result. Matt not only understands the ins and outs of these complex issues, but he presents the issues in a manner that makes it more manageable for a consultant to apply the knowledge to the problem.

Cisco Press has numerous books on networking. What Matt offers in this book is something that I have not seen presented elsewhere. *Network Consultants Handbook* is a must-have for those professionals who need to solve various complex networking problems on a daily basis. The reader gets a general overview, followed by building blocks for bringing a consulting project to a successful resolution.

As a fellow networking professional, I am pleased to see Matt bring his years of experience in consulting and breadth of knowledge to bear on this book.

Jeffrey F. Stevenson
Director, Systems Engineering
Quarry Technologies, Inc.

Introduction

During the course of a typical day—if there is such a thing as a "typical" day—network consultants are bombarded with questions coming from all directions. These questions come from customers, peers, sales and marketing teams, network administrators, and so on, and the list seems neverending at times. Network consultants, designers, engineers, managers, and so on have developed an instinct over time and sometimes cringe or develop other nervous habits when the phrase, "You got a second?" is uttered.

To the uninitiated, this question seems innocent enough, but after a while they, too, develop the same cringe or nervous habit.

The reason is this: Networks are like snowflakes; no two are alike. This is the challenge that network consultants, engineers, managers, designers, and anyone else involved with a telecommunications network must face every day. The question "You got a second?" is often followed by the question's recipient researching through several volumes, Web sites, old e-mails, rolodexes of contacts, and so on in an effort to find the answer to that seemingly simple question. During this flurry of books, paper, Web sites, phone calls, and voice mails, the questioner sometimes says to himself, "I thought this person knew it all" or "What's the big deal?"

The big deal is that the telecommunications industry is in such a dynamic and fluid state that it is nearly impossible for someone to keep up with everything, leaving many individuals to become Subject Matter Experts, or SMEs, in one or several technologies. This specialization does not relieve the consultant (or whoever was the recipient of the "seemingly simple" question) of the responsibility of knowing something about everything. A "Jack of all trades, master of none" mentality begins to develop.

Not only do network consultants, engineers, managers, and so on face the everyday challenging task of managing and maintaining these networks and answering questions about past, current, or future (proposed) technology, but consultants and others must also document, review, analyze, and find ways to improve these networks. They are often looking for ways to cut costs, while maintaining the same, if not better, level of service to their users. Before a consultant or another can review a network, he must have a clear understanding of the network in question, whether it is a current or planned implementation. Just as no two networks are alike, documentation of such networks follows suit. Often networks are not so much documented as they are drawn—on white boards or with drawing software packages—with little supporting configuration information.

In the course of a single morning, I was the recipient of such questions including, but not limited to the following: Ethernet standards and limitations, Voice over Frame Relay, differences between and history of AMI and B8ZS line coding (and limitations of AMI), FRASI, and review of a customer's network document—and all this before lunch!

One of the questions asked was: "Isn't there a book or Web site that has all of this stuff?" That was the most poignant question of all, and one that caught my attention above all the others.

There was no single resource that I could read through and get what I needed, quickly and easily. Just as there was no single resource that helped me prepare documentation for my customer's current or proposed networks.

This same question further spawned an idea, an idea that was kicked around for a few years that resulted from my suffering through a "typical" day. I began to gather these books, Web sites, and old e-mails. I further created some document templates, and amassed what amounted to a labor of love: a collection of this information that, although organized in a fashion that would make Dewey Decimal cry, was still useful and served as my everyday resource.

What you hold in your hands, and can view on the Internet at www.ciscopress.com/ 1587050390, is the result of that fateful question "Isn't there a book or Web site that has all of this stuff?"

Purpose of This Book

The purpose of this book is to provide a resource to consultants and engineers to audit (assess), analyze, and evaluate any current or future network environment. Resources include form templates to complete during a network audit, necessary device commands to aid in obtaining necessary information, and consistent forms to aid in documentation.

This book is intended for anyone who designs, manages, sells, administrates, or desires to understand various internetworking technologies, without wading through the sometimes intense discussions, standards documents, books, or white papers involved.

This book is presented as a "greatest hits" of internetworking technologies, augmenting Cisco Press's *Internetworking Technologies Handbook: Third Edition,* with the addition of insight into some of the technology's infrastructure, as well as documentation templates and analysis guidelines.

How This Book Can Be Used

This book is intended to be used as a resource in whatever fashion the reader sees fit, either as a desktop reference resource or in the field where the tables and calculations help provide near-real time answers to internetworking issues and challenges.

The Twelve Networking Truths

One last note: I invite you to read the following, RFC 1925 by Ross Callon, perhaps ironically published April 1, 1996. Herein are the Twelve Networking Truths. Those in the know will nod silently, smirk, and perhaps chuckle. The uninitiated should consider themselves encouraged and shown the light.

The Twelve Networking Truths

Status of This Memo

This memo provides information for the Internet community. This memo does not specify an Internet standard of any kind. Distribution of this memo is unlimited.

Abstract

This memo documents the fundamental truths of networking for the Internet community. This memo does not specify a standard, except in the sense that all standards must implicitly follow the fundamental truths.

Acknowledgments

The truths described in this memo result from extensive study over an extended period of time by many people, some of whom did not intend to contribute to this work. The editor merely has collected these truths, and would like to thank the networking community for originally illuminating these truths.

1 Introduction

This Request For Comments (RFC) provides information about the fundamental truths underlying all networking. These truths apply to networking in general, and are not limited to TCP/IP, the Internet, or any other subset of the networking community.

2 The Fundamental Truths

(1) It Has To Work.

(2) No matter how hard you push and no matter what the priority, you can't increase the speed of light.

(2A) (corollary). No matter how hard you try, you can't make a baby in much less than 9 months. Trying to speed this up *might* make it slower, but it won't make it happen any quicker.

(3) With sufficient thrust, pigs fly just fine. However, this is not necessarily a good idea. It is hard to be sure where they are going to land, and it could be dangerous sitting under them as they fly overhead.

(4) Some things in life can never be fully appreciated nor understood unless experienced firsthand. Some things in networking can never be fully understood by someone who neither builds commercial networking equipment nor runs an operational network.

(5) It is always possible to agglutinate multiple separate problems into a single complex interdependent solution. In most cases, this is a bad idea.

(6) It is easier to move a problem around (for example, by moving the problem to a different part of the overall network architecture) than it is to solve it.

    (6A)   (corollary). It is always possible to add another level of indirection.

(7) It is always something.

    (7A)   (corollary). Good, Fast, Cheap: Pick any two (you can't have all three).

(8) It is more complicated than you think.

(9) For all resources, whatever it is, you need more.

    (9A)   (corollary) Every networking problem always takes longer to solve than it seems like it should.

(10) One size never fits all.

(11) Every old idea will be proposed again with a different name and a different presentation, regardless of whether it works.

    (11A)   (corollary). See rule 6a.

(12) In protocol design, perfection has been reached not when there is nothing left to add, but when there is nothing left to take away.

Feedback

Feedback, as always, is appreciated. This book is intended to be a living volume, with updates and modifications as current standards change and new standards are introduced. The templates herein are designed as a starting point, and I certainly encourage you to use these, create your own, or use some combination of the two. If you find a method or document design that works better than what is presented here and would like to share it, I wholeheartedly encourage you to do so.

I can be contacted either in care of Cisco Press, or directly at mjcastelli@earthlink.net.

CHAPTER 1

Open System Interconnection (OSI) Model

Although practically every networking book on the market today discusses the Open System Interconnection (OSI) model, its importance should not be taken for granted. For this reason, the OSI model will be discussed here as it pertains to local-area networks (LANs) and wide-area networks (WANs).

OSI Reference Model

The OSI reference model describes how information from a user or client application in one host or computer moves through an internetwork to an application on another host. The OSI model is a conceptual model composed of seven layers, each specifying particular network functions (see Figure 1-1).

Figure 1-1 *OSI Reference Model*

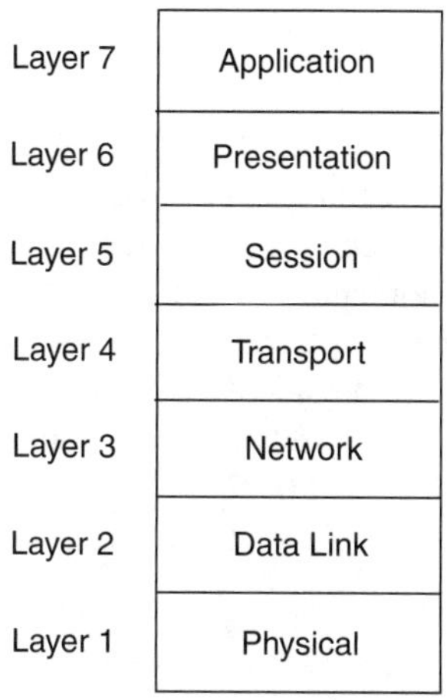

Layer 7	Application
Layer 6	Presentation
Layer 5	Session
Layer 4	Transport
Layer 3	Network
Layer 2	Data Link
Layer 1	Physical

The OSI model was developed by the International Organization for Standardization (ISO) in 1984, and is now considered the primary architectural model for internetwork communications. Each layer of the model is reasonably self contained, so that tasks assigned to each layer can be implemented independently. This design enables the solutions offered by one layer to be updated without adversely affecting the other layers, and is critical among internetwork vendors who want to focus their research and development on one particular function rather than the entire OSI model.

OSI Layer Characteristics

The seven layers of the OSI model can be divided into two categories:

- Upper layers—Deal with application issues and are implemented primarily in the client software. The highest layer, Layer 7 (application), is the closest layer to the end user. Both users and application-layer processes interact with software applications that contain a communications component. Sometimes the term "upper layer" is used to refer to any layer above another layer in the OSI model.

- Lower layers—Handle data transport across the internetwork. The physical and data link layers are implemented in both hardware and software environments. The other lower layers, network and transport, are generally implemented only in software environments. The lowest layer, physical, is closest to the physical network medium. It is responsible for placing information on the medium in the form of bits.

OSI Model Layers

The OSI reference model has seven layers. They are, starting from Layer 1, physical, data link, network, transport, session, presentation, and application.

Layer 1: Physical Layer

Physical layer (Layer 1) specifications, which are typically standards from other organizations to which OSI refers, deal with the physical characteristics of the physical medium. Connectors, pins, use of pins, electrical currents, encoding, and light modulation are all part of different physical layer specifications. Multiple specifications are sometimes used to complete all details of the physical layer. For example, RJ-45 defines the shape of the connector and the number of wires/pins in the cable. Ethernet and 802.3 define the use of wires/pins 1, 2, 3, and 6. To use a category 5 cable with an RJ-45 connector for an Ethernet connection, Ethernet and RJ-45 physical layer specifications are used.

Examples of Layer 1 (physical) protocol specifications include EIA/TIA-232, EIA/TIA-449, V.35, V.24, RJ-45, Ethernet, IEEE 802.3, IEEE 802.5, FDDI, NRZI, NRZ, and B8ZS (see Figure 1-2).

Figure 1-2   *OSI Model Layer 2: Sublayers*

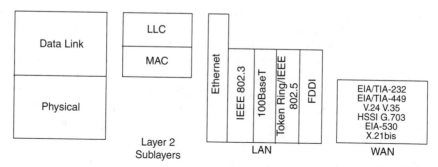

Layer 2: Data Link Layer

The data link (Layer 2) specifications involve getting data across one particular link or medium. The data link protocols define delivery across an individual link. These protocols are concerned with the type of media in question. For example, 802.3 and 802.2 are specifications from the IEEE, which are referenced by OSI as valid data link (Layer 2) protocols. These specifications define how Ethernet works. Other protocols, such as High-Level Data Link Control (HDLC) for a point-to-point WAN link, deal with the different details of a WAN link. OSI, like other networking models or architectures, often does not create original specifications for the data link layer, but instead relies on other standards bodies to create new data link and physical layer standards.

Examples of Layer 2 (data link) protocol implementations include Frame Relay, HDLC, PPP, IEEE 802.3/802.2, FDDI, ATM, and IEEE 802.5/802.2.

Layer 3: Network Layer

This layer defines end-to-end delivery of packets. To accomplish this delivery, the network layer defines logical addressing so that any endpoint can be identified. It also defines how routing works and how routes are learned so the packets can be delivered. In addition, the network layer defines how to fragment a packet into smaller packets to accommodate media with smaller maximum transmission unit (MTU) sizes. The network layer of OSI defines most of the details that a router considers when routing OSI. For example, IP that is running in a router is responsible for examining the destination IP address of a packet, comparing that address to the IP routing table, fragmenting the packet if the outgoing interface requires smaller packets, and queuing the packet to be sent out the interface.

Examples of Layer 3 (network) protocols include IP, IPX, and AppleTalk DDP.

Layer 4: Transport Layer

Layer 4 includes the choice of protocols that either do or do not provide error recovery. Reordering of the incoming data stream when segments arrive out of order is included within the Layer 4 mechanism. If the packet is fragmented during transmission, the data is reassembled at this layer. For example, TCP might give a 4200-byte segment of data to IP for delivery. IP will fragment the data into smaller sizes if a 4000-byte packet could not be delivered across some media. Each receiving TCP might get three different segments of 1400 bytes. The receiving TCP might receive these in a different order as well, so it reorders the received segments, compiles them into the original 4200-byte segment, and then is able to move on to acknowledging the data.

Examples of Layer 4 (transport) protocols include TCP, UDP, and SPX.

Layer 5: Session Layer

The session layer defines how to start, control, and end conversations, also called *sessions*. This includes the control and management of multiple bidirectional messages so that the application can be notified if only some of a series of messages are completed. For example, an Automated Teller Machine (ATM) transaction in which you get cash out of your checking account should not debit your account and fail before handing you the cash, and then record the transaction even though you did not receive money. The session layer creates ways to imply which flows are part of the same transaction and which flows must be completed before a transaction is considered complete.

Examples of Layer 5 (session) protocols include RPC, SQL, NetBIOS names, AppleTalk ASP, and DECnet SCP.

NOTE   NFS is an application layer protocol. It works with XDR (External Data Representation) at the presentation layer and NFS to provide the transparent access of remote data to users. The three-layer stack was developed by Sun Microsystems and is documented on the Internet in Request for Comments (RFCs).

Layer 6: Presentation Layer

This layer's main purpose is to define data formats, such as ASCII text, EBCDIC text, binary, BCD, and JPEG. OSI also defines encryption as a presentation layer service. For example, FTP allows you to choose binary or ASCII transfer. If binary is chosen, the sender and receiver do not modify the contents of the file. If ASCII is chosen, the sender translates the text from the sender's character set to a standard ASCII and sends the data. The receiver translates back from the standard ASCII to the character set used on the receiving computer.

Examples of Layer 6 (presentation) protocols include TIFF, GIF, JPEF, PICT, ASCII, EBCDIC, Encryption, MPEG, MIDI, and HTML.

NOTE   The presentation layer is the only layer that can manipulate or change user data. This change is brought about when data encryption is implemented.

Layer 7: Application Layer

An application that communicates with other computers is implementing OSI application layer concepts. The application layer refers to communications services to applications. For example, a word processor that lacks communications capabilities would not implement code for communications; therefore, a word processor programmer would not be concerned about OSI Layer 7. However, if an option for transferring a file were added, then the word processor would need to implement OSI Layer 7 (or the equivalent layer in another protocol stack).

Examples of Layer 7 (application) protocols include FTP, WWW browsers, Telnet, NFS, SMTP gateways (Eudora, cc:mail), SNMP, X.400 mail, and FTAM.

Layering Benefits and Concepts

The layering of protocol specifications has many benefits, which include the following:

- It is easier for humans to discuss and learn about the many details of a protocol specification.

- It standardizes interfaces between layers. This allows different products to provide functions of only some layers, such as routers with Layers 1 to 3. It also allows different products to supply parts of the functions of the protocol, such as Microsoft TCP/IP built into Windows 95, or Eudora Email providing TCP/IP application layer support. The reference of this capability to allow a package to implement only some layers of the protocol is called *Facilitates Modular Engineering*.

The layering of protocol specifications has many benefits, which include:

- It creates a better environment for interoperability.

- It reduces complexity, allowing easy programming changes and faster product evolution.

- Each layer, with the exception of Layer 1 (physical), creates headers only or headers and trailers around the data when sending, and interprets them when receiving. Anyone examining these headers or trailers for troubleshooting can find the header or trailer for Layer X and know what type of information should be found.

- The layer below another layer provides services to the higher layer, which makes remembering what each layer does easier. For example, the network layer needs to deliver data end-to-end. To do this task, the network layer uses data links to forward the data to the next successive device along that end-to-end path.

Layer Interactions

The following sequence outlines the basics of processing at each layer and explains how each lower layer is providing a service to the next higher layer:

1 The physical layer (Layer 1) ensures bit synchronization and places the received binary pattern into a buffer (transfer across a medium). It notifies the data link layer that a frame was received after decoding the incoming signal into a bit stream.

2 The data link layer examines the frame check sequence (FCS) in the trailer to determine whether errors occurred in transmission (error detection). If an error has occurred, the frame is discarded. Some data link protocols perform error recovery, and some do not. The data link address(es) are examined so the receiving host can decide whether to process the data further. If the address is the receiving node's MAC address, processing continues (physical addressing). The data between the Layer 2 header and trailer is given to the Layer 3 software on the receiving end. The data link layer delivers the data across the local link.

3 The network layer (Layer 3) destination address is examined. If the address is the receiving host's address, processing continues (logical addressing) and the data after the Layer 3 header is given to the transport layer (Layer 4) software, providing the service of end-to-end delivery.

4 If error recovery was an option chosen for the transport layer (Layer 4), the counters identifying this piece of data are encoded in the Layer 4 header along with acknowledgement information (error recovery). After error recovery and reordering of the incoming data, the data is given to the session layer.

5 The session layer (Layer 5) can be used to ensure that a series of messages is completed. For example, this data might be meaningless if the next four exchanges are not completed. The Layer 5 header includes fields that signify that this session flow is a middle flow, not an ending flow, in a transaction (transaction tracking). After the session layer ensures that all flows are completed, it passes the data after the Layer 5 header to the Layer 6 software.

6 The presentation layer (Layer 6) defines and manipulates data formats. For example, if the data is binary instead of character oriented, the header will state the fact. The receiver will not attempt to convert the data using the default ASCII character set of Host B. Typically, this type of header is included only for initialization flows and not

with every message being transmitted (data formats). After the data formats have been converted, the data (after the Layer 6 header) is then passed to the application layer (Layer 7) software.

7 The application layer (Layer 7) processes the final header and then examines the true end-user data. This header signifies agreement to operating parameters by the applications on the sending and receiving hosts. The headers are used to signal the values for all parameters; therefore, the header is typically sent and received at application initialization time only. For example, the screen size, colors supported, special characters, buffer sizes, and other parameters for terminal emulation are included in this header (application parameters).

Interaction Between Layers on Different Hosts

Layer *N* must interact with Layer *N* on another host to successfully implement its functions. For example, Layer 4 (transport layer) can send data, but if another host never acknowledges that data was received, the sender will not know when to perform error recovery. Likewise, the sending computer encodes a destination network layer (Layer 3) address in the network layer header. If the intervening network devices, such as routers, do not cooperate by performing their network layer tasks, the packet will not be delivered to the intended destination.

To interact with the same layer on another host, each layer defines either a header (Layers 5 to 7), or a header and a trailer (Layers 1 to 4). Headers and trailers are additional data bits created by the sending host's software or hardware that are placed before or after the data given to Layer *N* by Layer *N+1*. The information needed for the layer to communicate with the same layer process on the other computer is encoded in the header and trailer. The receiving host's Layer *N* software or hardware interprets the headers and trailers created by the other host's Layer *N*, learning how Layer *N*'s processing is being handled in this case.

Figure 1-3 provides a conceptual perspective on this concept of same-layer interactions. The application layer on the sending host communicates with the application layer on the receiving host. The presentation, session, and transport layers on both the sending host (Host A) and receiving host (Host B) communicate in a similar fashion. The bottom three layers of the OSI model—network, data link, and physical—are involved with delivery of the data. A network device, such as a router (demonstrated by *Router* 1), will interconnect the two host devices—in this case, Host A and Host B. Router 1 is involved in this process of data delivery because Router 1 is interconnected to both Host A's and B's network, data link, and physical layers.

Figure 1-3   *OSI Model Internetworking*

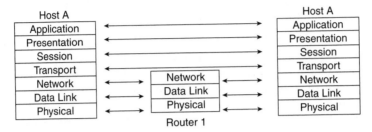

Data Encapsulation

The process by which data is handled layer-to-layer through the OSI model is referred to as *data encapsulation*. Following are the five steps of encapsulating data, according to Cisco, as data moves from Layer 7 (application) to Layer 1 (physical).

NOTE	OSI Layer 1 (physical) does not encapsulate data because it does not use headers or trailers.

1 User information creates the data (OSI Layers 5-7).

2 Data is converted to segments (OSI Layer 4).

3 Segments are converted to packets, or datagrams (OSI Layer 3).

4 Packets, or datagrams, are converted to frames (OSI Layer 2).

5 Frames are converted to bits (OSI Layer 1).

Some common terminology is necessary to discuss the data that a particular layer is processing. *Layer N protocol data unit (PDU)* is a term used to describe a set of bytes that include the Layer N header and trailer, all headers encapsulated, and the user data. From the perspective of Layer N, the higher layer headers and the user data forms one large *data* or *information* field. The Layer 2 PDU—including the data link header and trailer—is called a *frame*. The Layer 3 PDU is called a *packet*, or sometimes a *datagram*. The Layer 4 PDU is called a *segment*.

NOTE	The term "packet" has become a generic term for a piece of a data transmission. It is used, at times, to describe any of the other layers.

Summary

The importance of having a thorough and fundamental understanding of the OSI model and the interaction of its layers cannot be stressed enough.

The OSI model comprises seven layers: physical, data link, network, transport, session, presentation, and application.

As described by Cisco, data encapsulation goes through five steps as it moves through the OSI model from top (application layer) to bottom (physical layer):

1   User information creates the data (OSI Layers 5 to 7).

2   Data is converted to segments (OSI Layer 4).

3   Segments are converted to packets, or datagrams (OSI Layer 3).

4   Packets, or datagrams, are converted to frames (OSI Layer 2).

5   Frames are converted to bits (OSI Layer 1).

Each layer of the OSI model can be discussed in the form of Layer *N* PDU (Protocol Data Unit).

- Layer 5 to 7 PDU (application, presentation, and session): User data
- Layer 4 PDU (transport): Segments
- Layer 3 PDU (network): Packets
- Layer 2 PDU (data link): Frames
- Layer 1 PDU (physical): Bits

CHAPTER 2

LAN Topologies

The application in use, such as multimedia, database updates, e-mail, or file and print sharing, generally determines the type of data transmission.

LAN transmissions fit into one of three categories:

- Unicast
- Multicast
- Broadcast

Unicast

With unicast transmissions, a single packet is sent from the source to a destination on a network. The source-node addresses the packet by using the network address of the destination node. The packet is then forwarded to the destination network and the network passes the packet to its final destination. Figure 2-1 is an example of a unicast network.

Figure 2-1   *Unicast Network*

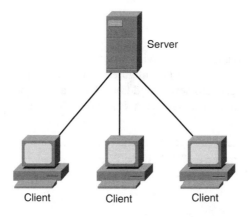

Multicast

With a multicast transmission, a single data packet is copied and forwarded to a specific subset of nodes on the network. The source node addresses the packet by using a multicast address. For example, the TCP/IP suite uses 224.0.0.0 to 239.255.255.255. The packet is then sent to the network, which makes copies of the packet and sends a copy to each segment with a node that is part of the multicast address. Figure 2-2 is an example of a multicast network.

Figure 2-2   *Multicast Network*

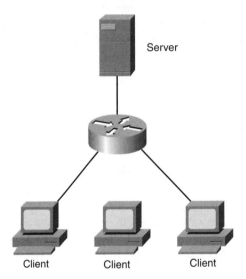

Broadcast

Broadcasts are found in LAN environments. Broadcasts do not traverse a WAN unless the Layer 3 edge-routing device is configured with a helper address (or the like) to direct these broadcasts to a specified network address. This Layer 3 routing device acts as an interface between the local-area network (LAN) and the wide-area network (WAN).

NOTE   Broadcasts will traverse a WAN if the WAN is bridged.

Figure 2-3   *Broadcast Network*

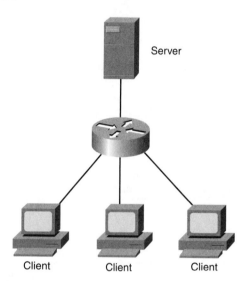

Multimedia broadcast traffic is a much more bandwidth-intensive broadcast traffic type. Multimedia broadcasts, unlike data broadcasts, typically are several megabits in size; therefore, they can quickly consume network and bandwidth resources. Broadcast-based protocols are not preferred because every network device on the network must expend CPU cycles to process each data frame and packet to determine if that device is the intended recipient. Data broadcasts are necessary in a LAN environment, but they have minimal impact because the data broadcast frames that are traversing the network are typically small. Broadcast storms can cripple a network in no time because the broadcasting device uses whatever available bandwidth is on the network.

An example of a data broadcast on a LAN could be a host searching for server resources, such as Novell's IPX GNS (Get Nearest Server) or AppleTalk's Chooser application.

Unlike data broadcasts, which are usually made up of small frames, multimedia broadcasts are typically several megabits in size. As a result, multimedia broadcasts can quickly consume all available bandwidth on a network, bringing a network and its attached devices to a crawl, if not render them inoperable.

Table 2-1 demonstrates the amount of bandwidth that multimedia applications can consume on a network.

Table 2-1 *Multimedia Bandwidth Impact on a LAN (1.5 Mbps* Stream)*

Link Type	Full-Screen, Full-Motion Client/Server Connections Supported (1.5 Mbps Stream)
10 Mbps	6 to 7
100 Mbps	50 to 60
1000 Mbps	250 to 300

*Mbps = megabits per second

For video-conferencing applications, 384 kilobits per second (Kbps) is the recommended maximum bandwidth for uncompressed data streams. Any bandwidth in excess of 384 Kbps typically will not be noticed by end users and could be considered a waste of bandwidth—and in some cases, money. Table 2-2 shows multimedia bandwidth impact on a LAN.

Table 2-2 *Multimedia Bandwidth Impact on a LAN (384 Kbps Stream)*

Link Type	Full-Screen, Full-Motion Client/Server Connections Supported (384 Kbps Stream)
10 Mbps	24 to 28
100 Mbps	200 to 240
1000 Mbps	1,000 to 1,200

LAN Addressing

LAN (or any internetwork) addresses identify individual or groups of devices. Addressing schemes vary depending on the protocol family and OSI layer.

MAC Addresses

Media Access Control (MAC) addresses identify network devices in LANs. MAC addresses are unique for each LAN interface on a device. MAC addresses are 48 bits in length and are expressed as 12 hexadecimal digits. The first six hexadecimal digits, which are administered by the IEEE, identify the manufacturer or vendor and comprise the organizational unique identifier (OUI). The last six hexadecimal digits comprise the interface serial number, or another value administered by the specific vendor. MAC addresses are sometimes referred to as burned-in addresses (BIAs) because they are burned into read-only memory (ROM) and are copied into random-access memory (RAM) when the interface card initializes.

MAC addresses are supported at the data link layer of the OSI model. According to the IEEE's specifications, Layer 2 comprises two components: the MAC sublayer and the logical link control (LLC) sublayer. The MAC sublayer interfaces with the physical layer (OSI model Layer 1), and the LLC sublayer interfaces with the network layer (OSI model Layer 3).

Network Layer Addresses

Network layer addresses identify a device at the OSI network layer (Layer 3). Network addresses exist within a hierarchical address space and sometimes are called *virtual* or *logical* addresses.

Network layer addresses have two parts: the *network* of which the device is a part and the device, or *host*, number of that device on that network. Devices on the same logical network must have addresses with the same network part; however, they will have unique device parts, such as network and host addresses in an IP or IPX network.

For example, an IP address is often expressed as a dotted decimal notation, such as *x.x.x.x*. Each *x* in the address indicates either a network or host number, demonstrated as *n.n.h.h*. The subnet mask determines where the network boundary ends and the host boundary begins.

LAN Topologies

Four LAN topologies exist:

- Star (Hub-and-Spoke)
- Ring
- Bus
- Tree

Star (Hub-and-Spoke) Topology

All stations are attached by cable to a central point, usually a wiring hub or other device operating in a similar function.

Several different cable types can be used for this point-to-point link, such as shielded twisted-pair (STP), unshielded twisted-pair (UTP), and fiber-optic cabling. Wireless media can also be used for communications links.

| NOTE | STP is not typically used in a point-to-point configuration. STP is used primarily in the Token Ring environment, where the hubs are called MAUs or MSAUs and the connections from the NIC to the MAU are not really point-to-point. This is because there is a transmit and a receive side, and the transmission is one way. In fact, this is sometimes called a "star-ring." |

The advantage of the star topology is that no cable segment is a single point of failure impacting the entire network. This allows for better management of the LAN. If one of the cables develops a problem, only that LAN-attached station is affected; all other stations remain operational.

The disadvantage of a star (hub-and-spoke) topology is the central hub device. This central hub is a single point-of-failure in that if it fails, every attached station is out of service.

These central hubs, or concentrators, have changed over the years. Today, it is common to deploy hubs with built-in redundancy. Such redundancy is designed to isolate a faulty or failed component, such as the backplane or power supply. Figure 2-4 is an example of a star (hub-and-spoke) topology.

Figure 2-4   *Star (Hub-and-Spoke) Topology*

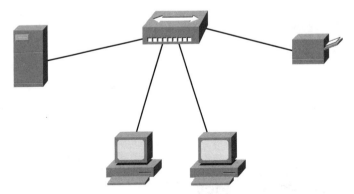

This example demonstrates a star topology with a file server, printer, and two workstations. If a cable to one of the workstations fails, the rest of the devices are unaffected unless they need to access resources from the "disconnected" device.

Ring Topology

All stations in a ring topology are considered repeaters and are enclosed in a loop. Unlike the star (hub-and-spoke) topology, a ring topology has no end points. The repeater in this case is a function of the LAN-attached station's network interface card (NIC).

Because each NIC in a LAN-attached station is a repeater, each LAN station will repeat any signal that is on the network, regardless of whether it is destined for that particular station. If a LAN-attached station's NIC fails to perform this repeater function, the entire network could come down. The NIC controller is capable of recognizing and handling the defective repeater and can pull itself off the ring, allowing the ring to stabilize and continue operating.

Token Ring (IEEE 802.5) best represents a ring topology. Although the physical cabling is considered to be a star topology, Token Ring is a ring in logical topology, as demonstrated by the following figures. Although physical topology is a physical layer attribute, the media access method used at the data link layer determines the logical topology. Token Ring defines a logical ring and contention, as Ethernet defines a logical bus. Even when attached to a hub, when one Ethernet device transmits, everyone hears the transmission, just as though on a bus. Figures 2-5 and 2-6 are examples of ring topologies.

Figure 2-5   *Ring Topology (Logical)*

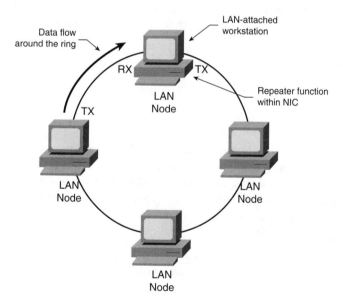

Figure 2-6   *Ring Topology*

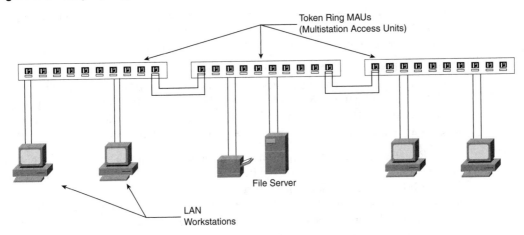

Fiber Data Distributed Interface (FDDI) is another example of a ring topology implementation. Like Token Ring, FDDI rings are physically cabled in a star topology. FDDI stations can be configured either as a single attachment station (SAS) or as a dual attachment station (DAS). SASs are connected to one of the two FDDI rings, whereas DASs are connected to both rings via an A and B port on the FDDI stations and concentrator.

Token Ring and FDDI LANs will be discussed in greater detail in Chapters 6, "Token Ring/ IEEE 802.5," and 7, "FDDI."

Bus Topology

Sometimes referred to as linear-bus topology, Bus is a simple design that utilizes a single length of cable, also known as the medium, with directly attached LAN stations. All stations share this cable segment. Every station on this segment sees transmissions from every other station on the cable segment; this is known as a *broadcast medium*. The LAN attachment stations are definite endpoints to the cable segment and are known as *bus network termination points*.

This single cable segment lends itself to being a single point of failure. If the cable is broken, no LAN station will have connectivity or the ability to transmit and receive.

Ethernet (IEEE 802.3) best represents this topology. Ethernet has the ability to utilize many different cable schemes. Further discussion of Ethernet and these cable schemes will be found in greater detail in Chapter 3. Figure 2-7 is an example of a bus topology.

Figure 2-7   *Bus Topology*

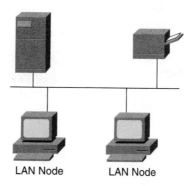

LAN Node   LAN Node

Tree Topology

The tree topology is a logical extension of the bus topology and could be described as multiple interconnected bus networks. The physical (cable) plant is known as a *branching tree* with all stations attached to it. The tree begins at the root, the pinnacle point, and expands to the network endpoints. This topology allows a network to expand dynamically with only one active data path between any two network endpoints.

A tree topology network is one that does not employ loops in its topology. An example of a tree topology network is a bridged or switched network running the spanning tree algorithm, usually found with Ethernet (IEEE 802.3) networks. The spanning tree algorithm disables loops in what would otherwise be a looped topology. Spanning tree expands through the network and ensures that only one active path exists between any two LAN-attached stations. Figure 2-8 is an example of a tree topology.

Figure 2-8 *Tree Topology*

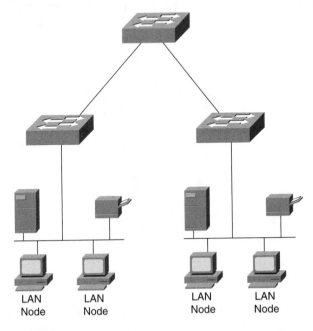

LAN Node   LAN Node   LAN Node   LAN Node

Network Devices

The four primary devices used in LANs are as follows:

- Hubs
- Bridges
- Switches
- Routers

Respective to the OSI model, these devices operate at the following layers:

- OSI Layer 1 (physical)—Hubs, repeaters (hubs are considered to be multiport repeaters)
- OSI Layer 2 (data link)—Bridges, switches
- OSI Layer 3 (network)—Routers

Hubs

Hubs operate at the physical layer (Layer 1) of the OSI model. A hub is used to connect devices so that they are on one shared LAN, as shown in Figure 2-9. Because only two devices can be directly connected with LAN cables, a hub is needed to interconnect two or more devices on a single LAN. The cable termination points are the hub and the LAN device (host).

Figure 2-9 *Hub-Based Network*

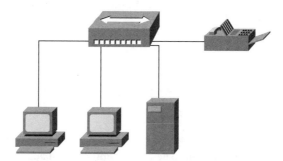

Ethernet hubs are not "smart" devices; hubs send all the data from a network device on one port to all other hub ports. When network devices are connected via a hub, LAN-attached devices will hear all conversations across the LAN. Each station then examines the message header to determine if it is the intended recipient. If more than one LAN station transmits at the same time, a collision occurs and both stations initiate a backoff algorithm before attempting retransmission. This type of operation is also known as *contention*. All devices attached to the hub are said to be in a *single collision domain*.

Backbone hubs are hubs deployed to connect other hubs to a single termination, or *root,* point. This is known as a *multitiered* design and is illustrated in Figure 2-10.

Figure 2-10 *Backbone, or Multitiered, Hub Network*

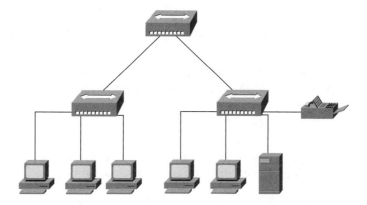

Several benefits can be derived from this multitiered design:

- It provides interdepartmental connections between hubs.
- It extends the maximum distance between any pair of nodes on the network.

Intelligent Hubs

Intelligent hubs contain logic circuits that will shut down a port if the traffic originating from that port indicates that bad, or malformed, frames are the rule rather than the exception.

Managed Hubs

Visit www.cisco.com for up-to-date product information and announcements.

Stackable Hubs

Visit www.cisco.com for up-to-date product information and announcements.

Bridges

This section focuses on transparent bridges, which can also be referred to as learning or Ethernet bridges. Bridges have a physical layer (Layer 1), but are said to operate at the data link layer (Layer 2) of the OSI model. Bridges forward data frames based on the destination MAC address.

Bridges also forward frames based on frame header information. Bridges create multiple collision domains and are generally deployed to provide more useable bandwidth. Bridges don't stop broadcast traffic; they forward broadcast traffic out every port of each bridge device. Each port on a bridge has a separate bandwidth (collision) domain, but all ports are on the same broadcast domain.

Bridges were also deployed in complex environments, which is where broadcast storms became such a problem.

Routers were added to the complex bridged environments to control broadcasts. Later, VLANs were devised when switches were deployed in enterprise environments and brought back the old problem of broadcast storms.

NOTE   Bridges, like repeaters, do not modify traffic. Unlike repeaters, bridges can originate traffic in the form of spanning tree bridge protocol data units (BPDUs).

Bridges maintain a MAC address table, sometimes referred to as a *content addressable memory (CAM)* or bridging table, which maintains the following information:

- MAC addresses
- Port assignment

NOTE   Bridges/switches can modify traffic. IP QoS and RIF are examples.

Bridge Operation

A learning bridge examines the source field of every frame it sees on each port and builds up a picture of which addresses are connected to which ports. This means that it will *not* retransmit a frame if it knows that the destination address is connected to the same port on which the bridge saw the frame.

A special problem arises if a bridge sees a frame addressed to a destination that is not in its address table. In this case, the frame is retransmitted on every port except the one on which it was received. This is known as *flooding*.

Bridges also age address table entries. If a given address has not been heard from in a specified period of time, then the address is purged from the address table.

The learning bridge concept works equally well with several interconnected networks, provided that no loops exist in the system. Consider the following simple configuration.

Suppose both stations A and B start up and A attempts to communicate with B (see Figure 2-11). At this point, the following process occurs:

1 A frame from A addressed to B reaches port 1 off bridge B1. B1 then learns that station A is connected to port 1, but it knows nothing about station B so it retransmits the frame destined for B on all available ports except port 1.

2 Bridge B2 receives the frame. Because Bridge B2 does not know where station B is, it retransmits on all available ports except port 1, causing the frame to reach B and generate a response.

3 By examining the incoming frame, bridge B2 knows that A is reachable via its port 1.

4 Station B's response reaches B2 on port 2 so that B2 can update its address table with information about the location of B.

5 B2 already knows how to get to A, so the response is transmitted on B2's port 1 and reaches B1.

6 B1 examines this incoming frame and determines that B is reachable via its port 2.

7 Both bridges now know how to send frames to both A and B.

Figure 2-11 *Simple Bridge Network*

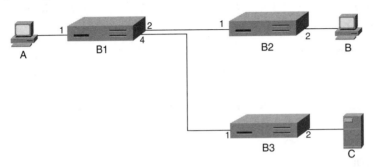

The original all-ports broadcast of A's first frame to B ensures that B3 knows how to send to frames to A. An attempt by C to communicate with B results in B3 broadcasting the frame on all ports (except number 2), so the frame reaches B1 on port 4. While B1 forwards this frame to B2, it also learns what to do with frames destined for C.

Unfortunately, this simple and elegant arrangement breaks down disastrously if loops are in the network. Consider the following arrangement. Figure 2-12 is an example of a looped bridge network.

Figure 2-12 *Looped Bridge Network*

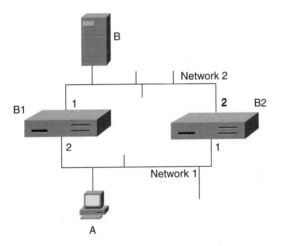

Suppose host A has just booted up and wants to communicate with B. A's initial frame will be seen on both Bridge 1's (B1) port 1 and Bridge 2's (B2) port 2, so both bridges know that host A is on network 1. The frame is then transmitted onto network 2 by B1 on port 2 and by B2 on port 1. One of the bridges will transmit it first—suppose it is B1—and then B2 will see a frame from A on its network 2 port 1. It will now update its table as to the location of A and retransmit the frame on network 1. B1 sees this frame and does not know that it's a duplicate, so it retransmits it on network 2. From there, B2 retransmits it on network 1, and so on indefinitely. Adding a third bridge to this two-network scenario makes things exponentially more complicated.

This is clearly unsatisfactory. Prohibiting loops is an unrealistic target. Practical bridges use a method known as the *spanning tree algorithm* to construct an effective non-looping topology by deciding not to use certain links in the network. It is also possible to reconfigure this network dynamically.

NOTE   Redundant bridges (bridge pairs), added for fault tolerance, cause bridging loops. The ability to reconfigure dynamically helps provide fault tolerance.

Bridges interchange special messages known as *configuration messages*. The spanning tree algorithm (IEEE 802.1) uses BPDUs. The bridge configuration message contains enough information to enable the bridges to do the following:

- Elect a single bridge from among all the connected bridges to be the "root" bridge.
- Calculate the least cost path to the "root" bridge from each bridge.
- For each LAN, identify a "designated bridge" on that LAN that will be used for forwarding frames toward the root.
- Choose a port on each bridge that gives the best path toward the root.
- Select ports to be included in the spanning tree.

The effective topology after construction of the spanning tree is loop free; this is achieved by effectively choosing not to use certain links between bridges. The links are still there and might come into use if the network is reconfigured.

Configuration messages are sent to a special multicast MAC address, meaning all bridges that use the binary SAP value 01000010. Configuration messages are autonomously originated by bridges, but they are *not* forwarded by bridges. A configuration message contains four pieces of information:

- The ID of the bridge assumed to be root.
- The ID of the bridge transmitting the message.
- The cost of the least cost-known path from the transmitting bridge to the assumed root.
- The port number on which the message was transmitted.

A bridge initially assumes itself to be the root, with a path cost of zero. For each bridge port, a bridge will receive incoming configuration messages from other bridges on the LAN connected to that same port. For each port, the bridge will remember the lowest cost configuration message. The following algorithm describes how a bridge would determine which of C_1 and C_2 is the better configuration message.

if(C_1.root_id < C_2.root_id) C_1 _is_BETTER

else if (C_1.root_id > C_2.root_id) C_2 _is_BETTER

else if (C_1.root_cost < C_2.root_cost) C_1 _is_BETTER

else if (C_1.root_cost > C_2.root_cost) C_2 _is_BETTER

else if (C_1.tx_id < C_2.tx_id) C_1 _is_BETTER

else if (C_1.tx_id > C_2.tx_id) C_2 _is_BETTER

else if (C_1.port_id < C_2.port_id) C_1 _is_BETTER

else if (C_1.port_id > C_2.port_id) C_2 _is_BETTER

If the bridge configuration message that a bridge receives on any port is better than the bridge configuration message it would transmit, the bridge stops transmitting configuration messages on that port. The bridge uses the new information to recalculate the spanning tree information in the BDPU configuration messages that it will transmit out ports other than the one from which the new information was learned.

This method details how a network starts up. It is also necessary for networks to be able to reconfigure automatically if a node or link fails or a new node or link comes online. To allow for reconfiguration updates, all stored configuration messages in a bridge are aged. After the age of a configuration message exceeds a certain value, it is discarded and the configuration is recalculated. In the normal course of events, the root bridge periodically transmits configuration messages with an age of zero; receipt of these by bridges causes the bridges to transmit their own configuration messages, also with an age of zero. The time between such messages is called the *Hello Time*.

After the network has stabilized, bridges will issue configuration messages only if they receive such messages or if the age of their internal messages has exceeded the maximum. Configuration messages with age zero can only be transmitted if a configuration message with age zero has been received.

Bridges might not attempt to forward data traffic while the spanning tree is being calculated. In fact, they should not even attempt the "learning" phase until the tree has been defined. This is called the *forward delay*. A special "topology change" flag in a configuration message forces a bridge into the spanning tree calculation mode.

Figure 2-13 illustrates the format of a bridge configuration message, and the following lists gives an explanation of each field.

Figure 2-13 *Configuration Message BPDU Frame Format*

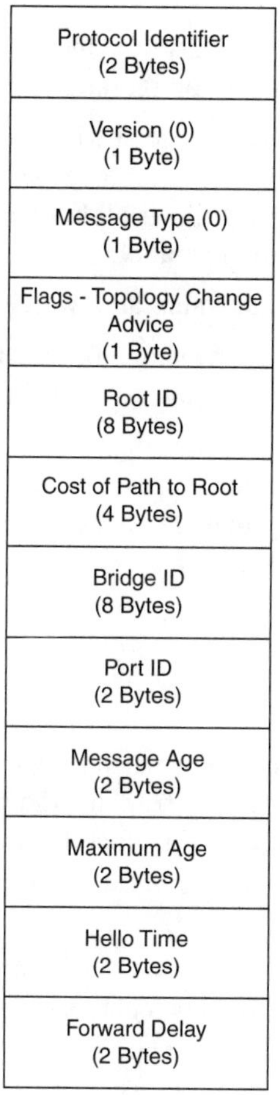

Protocol Identifier (2 Bytes)
Version (0) (1 Byte)
Message Type (0) (1 Byte)
Flags - Topology Change Advice (1 Byte)
Root ID (8 Bytes)
Cost of Path to Root (4 Bytes)
Bridge ID (8 Bytes)
Port ID (2 Bytes)
Message Age (2 Bytes)
Maximum Age (2 Bytes)
Hello Time (2 Bytes)
Forward Delay (2 Bytes)

- Protocol identifier—Contains the value zero.
- Version—Contains the value zero.
- Message type—Contains the value zero.
- Flags—Signifies one of two events: topology changes or acknowledgements to topology changes.
- Root ID—Defines the bridge that is at the top of the spanning tree.
- Cost of path to root—Defines the accumulated cost from the advertising bridge to the root bridge in the network.
- Bridge ID—Identifies the bridge that generated the BPDU and is used by the algorithm to build a spanning tree.

- Port ID—Defines from which port this BPDU message left the bridge. Other bridges use this to detect and remove loops in a network.

- Message age—Defines the last time the root bridge advertised a BPDU message on which the current network configuration is based.

- Maximum age—Defines the age at which the protocol will remove the information from its database and initiate a topology change by rerunning the spanning tree algorithm. This parameter allows all bridges to age uniformly and to rerun the spanning tree algorithm in parallel.

- Hello time—Serves as the interval in which a bridge advertises BPDUs.

- Forward delay—Defines the length of time that a port will remain in a port state. (Forward delay is discussed later in this chapter.)

A topology change can be advised using a type 128 message with only the first four fields present. Such messages are called topology change notification BPDUs and are defined by IEEE 802.1. They are encapsulated in normal LAN data link layer frames using SAP 01000010 (binary) and are sent to a special multicast MAC address that means "all bridges."

Latency

Bridges introduce latency, or delay, when forwarding traffic because of the overhead involved. This latency is measured from the moment that the first bit of a frame enters the input port on the device until the time that the first bit of the same frame is forwarded out of the exit port.

NOTE   Bridges introduce about 20 to 30 percent loss of throughput for some applications.

Latency has a severe negative impact with some time-dependent technologies, such as voice, video, or mainframe applications.

High levels of latency can result in loss of connections and noticeable video and voice degradation. Routers (OSI Layer 3 network devices) were introduced to overcome the inherent problems of bridging over multiple segments.

NOTE   Routers introduce more latency than a bridge does. Routers were introduced to contain broadcasts, one of the other problems associated with flat, bridged networks.

Types of Bridging

Following is a discussion of the four types of bridging:

- Transparent bridging
- Source-route bridging
- Source-route translational, or mixed-media, bridging
- Source-route transparent bridging

Transparent Bridging

Transparent bridging is so named because its operation is transparent to the network hosts. When a host on a remote LAN sends data to a specific destination, it does not look to see where on the bridging LAN the data is. The transparent bridge will read the source frames and forward the data, as discussed earlier.

The major difference between the tables built by bridges and the tables built by routers (Layer 3 devices) is that bridge tables are based on the MAC addresses, whereas routers build their tables based on the network addresses.

Transparent bridges build their tables independently of each other, rather than exchange information like routers. Each bridge learns different MAC addresses by associating the source addresses of transmitted frames with the port on which the frame arrived into the bridge. Each entry in this bridge table has a maximum age associated with it. If this maximum age timer is exceeded—meaning that no traffic has originated from that port within the defined timeframe—the entry is flushed out of the table.

A discussion of bridge states can be found later in this chapter, in the section "Spanning Tree Topology."

Source-Route Bridging

NOTE   IBM developed source-route bridging. It was later adopted into the IEEE 802.5 (Token Ring) standard.

In a source-route bridged (SRB) network, frames are sent with the complete source-to-destination path included. Source-route bridges check frames for destination information and store and forward as appropriate. The source will make the forwarding choice based on configurable source-route bridging metrics.

In an SRB network, end systems, or hosts, send an explorer frame to the network to find a path from source to destination prior to sending data. The source-route bridges are responsible for adding the path information to these explorer frames and making sure they are passed to and from the appropriate end systems. In addition to passing these explorer frames, source-route bridges also store this routing information in what is called a *RIF cache*. Source-route bridges look into a Token-Ring frame and determine whether routing information exists by checking the routing information indicator (RII) bit. The bridges then add the RII bit ring and bridge information to the routing descriptor (RD) field, also called the *routing information field* (*RIF*) or *RI field*.

Unlike transparent bridges, source-route bridges do not build and maintain tables of MAC addresses and associated ports. Instead, source-route bridges examine the contents of each Token-Ring frame as follows:

1 Source-route bridges start by examining the first bit of a Token-Ring frame's source address to see if the value is a zero or a one. This first bit is the RII. The source host of the frame sets the value of the RII.

2 If the RII is set to zero, no source-route information exists in the Token-Ring frame.

3 If the RII is set to one, source-route information exists within the Token-Ring frame and resides in the RIF.

Three types of explorer frames are found in a source-route bridged network: local explorers, all-routes explorers, and spanning tree explorers.

- Local explorers are used with local source-route bridged networks. Local source-route bridging directly connects two or more Token-Ring networks. Bridged traffic does not cross non-Token media.

- All-paths explorers, as the name implies, take all possible paths on their way to the destination. The amount of traffic generated by all-paths explorers could be considerable in a complex network, which is not good.

- Spanning tree explorers solve the problem of the all-paths explorer by sending packets only to branches in the spanning tree. The network administrator can statically assign which interfaces will forward spanning tree explorer frames and which interfaces will block them. The network administrator can also use the spanning tree algorithm to automatically set a single route explorer. (The spanning tree algorithm and the Spanning Tree Protocol will be discussed later in this chapter.)

Source-Route Translational, or Mixed-Media, Bridging

Source-route translational bridging (SR/TLB) is used when connecting two networks that are running different types of bridging technologies; the most common are Ethernet and Token-Ring. SR/TLB is implemented to perform several functions:

- Overcome MTU and frame format differences between Ethernet and Token Ring.

- Reconcile differences between Token-Ring frames (which contain RIFs) and Ethernet frames (which never contain RIFs) by using Source-route translational bridging.
- Resolve the formatting differences between Ethernet and Token Ring. Token Ring addresses are in non-canonical format; Ethernet addresses are in canonical format.

NOTE The MTU for Ethernet is 1,500 bytes. The MTU for 4 Mbps Token Ring is 4,550 bytes. 16 M and 100 M Token-Ring is 18.2 KB, or 18,200 bytes.

Source-route translational bridging assures that all these differences are resolved when forwarding frames from Token Ring to Ethernet and Ethernet to Token Ring.

NOTE The translational, transparent bridge translates only the frame format between many of the IEEE protocols and Fiber Distributed Data Interface (FDDI). It is transparent bridging on all ports.

Source-Route Transparent Bridging

Source-route transparent (SRT) bridging is a bridge that will either source-route bridge or transparent bridge a Token-Ring frame. The RII value makes this determination to either source-route or transparently bridge the frame.

- If the RII value is zero, the frame will be transparently bridged.
- If the RII value is one, the frame will be source-route bridged.

Cisco-Specific Bridging Solutions

Cisco has developed the following five alternative solutions to the previously discussed bridging options:

- Concurrent routing and bridging (CRB)—When CRB is implemented on a Cisco router, specific protocols can be bridged and routed to specific interfaces.
- Integrated routing and bridging (IRB)—Although CRB allows the concurrent routing and bridging of the same protocol on the same routing device, the two never mix. IRB allows bridged and routed traffic of the same protocol to be interchanged. By creating a logical interface, called the Bridge Virtual Identifier (BVI), bridged traffic of a given network layer protocol can be forwarded to a routed interface of the same protocol, and vice versa.

- Virtual rings for multiport source route bridges—Whereas standard Token-Ring bridges have only two ports, Cisco routers can be configured as a multiport source-route bridge by creating a virtual ring within the router. On a multiport source-route bridge, frames from physical interfaces are first forwarded to the virtual ring, and then to another physical interface.

- Remote source-route bridging (RSRB)—RSRB takes the concept of a virtual ring a step further. Instead of forwarding Token-Ring frames from one physical interface to another through a virtual ring, RSRB forwards Token-Ring frames from physical Token-Ring interfaces to interfaces connected to an IP cloud through a virtual ring. The benefit is that this provides a method for performing source-route bridging over a WAN, such as Frame Relay or ATM.

- Data-link switching plus (DLSw+)—DLSw+ is backward compatible with RSRB. DLSw+ performs the same functional tasks that RSRB does, with additional options supported. DLSw+ also supports interconnection of transparent bridging (TB), SRT bridging, SR/TLB, and SDLC-to-LAN conversion (SDLLC) over an IP backbone.

Switches

LAN switches are used to connect a common broadcast domain (a hub). They are also used to provide frame-level filtering as well as dedicated port speed to specific end users. Some switches have limited routing capabilities and can provide Layer 3 routing functions at the most basic level. Some of the major benefits of using switches in a network are higher bandwidth to the desktop and ease of configuration. Switches are being deployed more often to replace hubs and bridges as more bandwidth-intensive applications are being implemented at all levels of an organization.

Switch Operations

The following discussion focuses on Ethernet switches. The switches transfer data on a network by receiving data frames from a source port and forwarding them out to the destination through a different port on the switch based on the frame information. Like transparent bridges, Layer 2 Ethernet switching works by looking at the MAC addressing information in the data frame's header and forwarding the data according to the switch, or Content Addressable Memory (CAM), table information. If the switch looks at the MAC addressing information and still doesn't know from which port to send out the frames, it will broadcast the frames out all of the switch ports. This is known as *flooding*, and it is used to determine the destination. After the destination address is found, the information is added to the switching table.

Switches work by providing dedicated bandwidth per port to an end user or application. Switches allow fewer users in each network segment, and they provide dedicated bandwidth, which is increasingly important with graphics and multimedia applications.

Deploying LAN switches in an existing network environment requires minimal configuration and little or no changes to existing wiring closets, hubs, LAN cabling, or NICs.

Switches allow network users the ability to transfer data traffic in a network environment free of collisions and bandwidth contention. Several types of switching technologies enable quick and scalable network transmission.

Switching Modes

The switch can be configured in a variety of ways to allow certain network services and features to be available within the network.

The modes of LAN switching found today are store-and-forward, cut-through, runt-free, and adaptive cut-through. Some LAN switches can also support the router modes of fast switching and Layer-3 switching.

Store and Forward Switching

This is one of the two common modes of LAN switching. A store and forward switch works by reading and copying the entire data frame into its buffers. Error checking is performed, and the destination address is looked up in the MAC address table. After the switch has determined to which interface the frame should switch, the frame is forwarded to the appropriate destination.

Cut-Through Switching

The other common LAN switching mode is cut-through switching, which allows faster processing than store-and-forward switching. A switch using cut-through switching will copy the destination address and a small portion of the frame to its buffers before checking for the destination address interface in its MAC address table. As soon as the destination is found, the frame is sent out the appropriate port on the switch. Increased switching speed is realized because the cut-through switch does not copy the entire frame to the switch buffers. Cut-through switches enable faster processing by reducing the latency introduced by the switch to a small and constant value—the time it takes to read 6 bytes.

NOTE   Cut-through switching has an inherent danger to it in that the propagation of bad packets, such as runts or frames with an invalid CRC, can occur. To prevent this forwarding of "bad" frames runt-free (read 64 bytes before forwarding) or adaptive cut-through (fallback to store-and-forward if too many errors), modes might need to be implemented.

Fast Switching

Fast switching is the process of copying data frame headers into a memory buffer. You determine the path to the destination host by looking up the destination in the fast-switching cache, building a new frame header/trailer, and forwarding the frame out the appropriate interface. After you determine the destination host path, future data frames will use that switching path, reducing path determination time because the path and outgoing interface have already been established.

NOTE   This is more of a router function than a LAN switch function. Higher-end Cisco switches can perform this function with an installed router blade.

Layer 3 Switching

Layer 3 switching differs from traditional Layer 2 switching by enabling data frames to be switched based on network addressing information. Traditional Layer 2 switching will look at the frames for the MAC address information for the intended destination.

Layer 3 switching can use some routing functions, such as addressing and path determination. Switches can be configured like routers into an addressing mechanism, but they are still bound by a flat-network addressing scheme. Switches that operate at Layer 3 do not support features such as path optimization and load balancing because these features are based on routing processes.

Spanning Tree Algorithm

The spanning tree algorithm is based on the IEEE 802.1 standard, which specifies standards for network management at the hardware level. The spanning tree algorithm is used to ensure that only a single path is selected when using bridges or routers to pass messages—usually in the form of BPDUs between networks—and to find a replacement path if the selected path fails.

The Spanning Tree Protocol (STP) is based on this algorithm and is defined by the IEEE 802.1d standard.

Spanning Tree Protocol (IEEE 802.1d)

As stated earlier, when multiple bridges or switches are interconnected with multiple paths, a looped topology may be formed. A looped topology is often desirable to provide redundancy, but looped traffic is undesirable. Bridged traffic is especially vulnerable to broadcast loops. The Spanning Tree Protocol, IEEE 802.1d, was designed to prevent such loops from being formed. The Spanning Tree Protocol was originally developed for bridges. Today, it is also applied to LAN switch topologies. By applying the Spanning Tree Protocol to a looped bridged or LAN switch topology, all bridged segments will be reachable. However, any points where loops can occur will be blocked.

Spanning Tree Operation

The Spanning Tree Protocol has four phases of operation:

1 Electing a root bridge among a bridge/LAN group

2 Calculating the least-cost path to the root bridge/LAN switch by all non-root switches

3 Blocking higher cost paths to the root bridge/LAN switch by all non-root switches

4 Maintaining and recalculating the spanning tree with BPDUs

After a spanning tree is formed, all bridges and LAN switches know who the root bridge/LAN switch is, what direction the root bridge/LAN switch is in, and what the lowest path cost to the root of the spanning tree is.

When a bridge port or LAN switch port is first activated, it broadcasts BPDUs, with you as the root of the spanning tree. When a bridge or LAN switch receives BPDUs from other bridges or LAN switches, it conducts a spanning tree election to determine which bridge is the root of the spanning tree. Parameters used to determine this spanning tree root bridge include a spanning tree bridge/LAN switch priority number and a MAC address identifying the bridge or LAN switch. Only one root bridge exists in a single spanning tree at any given time.

Spanning Tree Topology

A spanning tree topology consists of the following basic components:

- Bridges/LAN switches
- Bridge/LAN switch segments

A spanning tree topology also consists of the following types of bridges:

- Root bridge/root LAN switches
- Designated bridges/LAN switches
- Non-root bridges/LAN switches
- Non-designated bridges/LAN switches

As previously stated, at any given time only one root bridge/LAN switch exists for the entire spanning tree. A spanning tree election process selects a root bridge/LAN switch.

A designated bridge/LAN switch is the device closest to the root bridge/LAN switch on a given segment. At any given time, only one designated bridge/LAN switch exists for each segment. A spanning tree election process selects a designated bridge/LAN switch. Each bridge segment must have a designated bridge.

NOTE	The non-designated bridge is called the *backup bridge*.

The root bridge/LAN switch is the designated bridge for all segments to which it is attached.

A spanning tree topology consists of the following types of ports:

- One designated port residing on each designated bridge for each bridge/LAN switch segment.

- One root port on every non-root bridge/LAN switch. The root port is the port that provides the most optimal path to the root bridge on a given bridge or LAN switch.

Port States

The IEEE 802.1d specification defines five port states for spanning tree:

1 Disabled—This is a unique state for a port. A port that is in a disabled state has either been disabled by the switch because of physical problems or security, or it has been manually disabled by the network administrator.

2 Blocking—When a port is in the blocking state, it only listens for BPDUs from other bridges. It does not listen to or save addresses or forward data frames.

NOTE	In this state, the bridge assumes that it is the root until it exchanges BPDUs with other bridges.

3 Listening—Passing from a blocking state, a port will then enter into a listening state. In this state, a port will listen for frames to detect available paths to the root bridge but will not take source MAC addresses of end stations and place them into the bridge's address table. Also in this state, the bridge will not forward user frames.

4 Learning—Upon completion of the listening state, a port will move into a learning state. In the learning state, a port will examine data frames for source MAC addresses and place these in the bridge's address table. Like the listening state, no user data frames are forwarded while the port is in this state.

5 Forwarding—After completing the learning state, a port will then be placed into a forwarding state where the bridge will perform its normal functioning. It will learn source MAC addresses and update the bridge's CAM table as well as forward frames through the bridge.

NOTE	Root bridge/LAN switch ports and designated ports are never in a blocking state.

When a bridge or LAN switch port is activated, it normally goes through three spanning tree states: listening, learning, and forwarding. If the port is the highest cost path to the root bridge in a looped topology, it enters the blocking state. By default, all bridge ports go through the first two states: learning and listening. Based on the information they obtain during these states, the interface attains a forwarding or blocking state.

Typically, the spanning tree algorithm takes 50 seconds to calculate a new topology. The transition time for each state is as follows:

- From blocking to listening—20 seconds
- From listening to learning—15 seconds
- From learning to forwarding—15 seconds

Latency, in addition to normal operation, is incurred when the ports go through the different states due to a network change, such as a failed path, addition of a new bridge or switch, or enabling a bridge or switch port. Cisco uses a default value of 15 seconds for the forward delay time, used to measure the time a port stays in a specific state.

CAUTION	In any bridged network, it is important to keep track of the number of times the Spanning Tree Protocol is run. As previously discussed, when each bridge runs the spanning tree algorithm, no user traffic is moved around the network, causing a disruption of service to the end users and their resources. Adding bridges to a network can lengthen the time it takes for the spanning tree algorithm to run its course.

Routers

Routers are not usually active in simple LAN environments because routers are WAN devices. Routers are typically found at the edge of a LAN, interfacing with a WAN. Routers operate at the network layer (Layer 3) of the OSI model. Broadcast containment and security are needed in more complex environments.

Whereas bridges and switches will use the spanning tree algorithm to determine the optimal path to a destination, routers use an algorithm based on the routing protocol that is implemented.

Summary

The three categories of LAN transmission are as follows:

- Unicast—One-to-one transmission
- Multicast—One-to-many transmission
- Broadcast—One-to-all transmission

LAN addressing uses the Layer 2 Media Access Control (MAC) burned-in address (BIA) on the network interface hardware. This address is 48 bits (12 hexadecimal) in length. The first 24 bits, or 6 hexadecimal digits, signify the organizational (vendor manufacturer) identifier as determined by the IEEE. The second 24 bits, or 6 hexadecimal digits, signify a value administered by the specific vendor.

The four primary LAN topologies are as follows:

- Star (hub-and-spoke)—All stations are attached by cable to a central point.
- Ring—All stations are considered repeaters and are enclosed in a loop. Logical configuration is a ring; physical configuration might be a ring or a star.
- Bus—All stations are directly attached to a shared cable segment.
- Tree—All stations are interconnected via several bus networks in a logical extension to the bus topology.

The four primary devices used in LANs include the following:

- Hubs—Hubs operate at the physical layer (Layer 1) of the OSI model and are essentially multiport repeaters, repeating signals out all hub ports.
- Bridges—Bridges create multiple collision domains. Bridges work at the physical layer (Layer 1) of the OSI model and operate at the data link layer (Layer 2). Bridges forward data frames based on the destination MAC address. Bridges utilize the spanning tree algorithm for path determination.
- Switches—LAN switches are essentially multiport bridges. LAN switches are used to connect common broadcast domains (hubs) and to provide frame-level filtering as well as dedicated port speed to end users. LAN switches are also used to create virtual LANs (VLANs). Like bridges, switches use the spanning tree algorithm for path determination.
- Routers—Routers are typically found at the edge of a LAN, interfacing with a WAN, or in more complex LAN environments. Routers operate at the network layer (Layer 3) of the OSI model.

The four types of bridges are as follows:

- Transparent bridges—These create two or more LAN segments (collision domains). They are transparent to end devices.

- Source-route bridging—Frames are sent from the source end device with the source-to-destination route, or path, included.

- Source-route translational, or mixed-media, bridging—These are used when connecting networks of two different bridging types (transparent and source-route) or media types, such as Ethernet and Token Ring.

- Source-route transparent bridging—This bridge will either source-route or transparently bridge a frame depending on the routing information indicator (RII) field.

CHAPTER 3

Ethernet/IEEE 802.3

Ethernet refers to the family of local-area networks (LANs) covered by the IEEE 802.3 standard. This standard also defines what is commonly known as the Carrier Sense Multiple Access/Collision Detect (CSMA/CD) protocol.

The Xerox Corporation Palo Alto Research Center (PARC) developed the original Ethernet as an experimental coaxial-cable network in the 1970s. This Ethernet operated with a data rate of 3 megabits per second (Mbps) using a carrier sense multiple access collision detect (CSMA/CD) protocol for LANs, and was designed for networks with intermittent heavy traffic requirements. Success with this project led to the 1980 joint development of the 10 Mbps Ethernet (Version 1.0) specification by the three-company consortium: Digital Equipment Corporation (DEC), Intel Corporation, and Xerox Corporation. In 1982, Ethernet II was jointly developed by DEC, Intel, and Xerox (DIX).

NOTE

Whereas Ethernet uses a frame length indicator in the frame header, Ethernet II uses a frame type.

The original IEEE 802.3 standard was based on and similar to the Ethernet Version 1.0 specification. The 802.3 working group approved the draft standard that was published as an official standard in 1985 (ANSI-IEEE Standard 802.3—1985). Since the release of this standard, a number of supplements have been defined to take advantage of improvements in newer technologies, support for additional network media, and higher data rate capabilities. These supplements also include several new optional network access control features, such as burst mode with IEEE 802.3z (Gigabit Ethernet).

Ethernet is a term with broad LAN implementation schemes and network access technologies. Table 3-1 demonstrates the different types of Ethernet networks.

Table 3-1 *Ethernet LANs*

Type	Description
10Base2	Thin Ethernet uses thin (3/16-inch), 50-ohm coaxial cable. Maximum segment length is 185 meters (m). Each segment is limited to 30 nodes.
10Base5	Thick Ethernet using thick (3/8-inch), 50-ohm coaxial cable. Maximum segment length is 500 m. Each segment is limited to 100 nodes.
10BaseT	Twisted-pair Ethernet using UTP cable. This configuration was adopted as the 802.3i standard in 1990 and is popular because UTP is inexpensive, easy to install, and easy to work with. Maximum cable segment length is 100 m.
1Base5	The StarLAN network developed by AT&T. StarLAN uses UTP cabling and a star topology. It was defined long before the 10BaseT standard was proposed.
10Broad36	The only broadband (analog uses FDM) network defined in the 802.3 standard. This network uses 75-ohm coaxial cable (CATV cable).
10BaseF	The only specification in the 802.3 standard that explicitly calls for fiber-optic cable. This type has three variations: 10BaseFB, 10BaseFP, and 10BaseFL.
10BaseFB	This network uses optical fiber for the backbone, or trunk, cable. Trunk segments can be up to 2 kilometers (km) in length.
10BaseFP	This specifies a network that uses optical fiber and a star topology. The coupler used to distribute the signal is passive, meaning that it does not regenerate the signal before distributing. This network needs no electronics except for those in the host. The maximum length for a piece of such cable is 500 m.
10BaseFL	This specifies a network that uses optical fiber to connect a node, or host, to a hub, or concentrator. Cable segments can be up to 2 km in length.
100VG-AnyLAN	A 100 Mbps network developed by Hewlett-Packard and AT&T Microelectronics as an alternative to CSMA/CD.
100BaseT	A 100 Mbps Ethernet network physical layer specification originally developed by Grand Junction Networks. This specification is a standard of the IEEE 802.3u study group. 100BaseT is also known as Fast Ethernet. Variations of this type are 100BaseT4, 100BaseT2, 100BaseTX, and 100BaseFX.
100BaseFX	A 100 Mbps network physical layer specification that uses a pair of either 50/125 microns or 62.5/125 microns optical fibers.

Table 3-1   *Ethernet LANs*

Type	Description
100BaseT2	A 100 Mbps network physical layer specification that uses two pairs of Category 3 or higher shielded twisted-pair (STP) or unshielded twisted-pair (UTP) wire.
100BaseT4	A 100 Mbps network Physical-layer specification that uses four pairs of Category 3 or higher STP or UTP wire. 100BaseT4 uses an 8B/6T data-translation scheme.
100BaseTX	A 100 Mbps network Physical-layer specification that uses two pairs of Category 5 STP or UTP wire.
1000BaseT	A physical layer specification for 1 gibabit per second (Gbps) Ethernet networks over four pairs of Category 5 UTP wire. 1000BaseT is also known as Gigabit Ethernet.
1000BaseX	A physical layer specification for 1 Gbps Ethernet networks. This specification is an IEEE 802.3z standard, with physical signaling based on the Fibre[*] Channel specifications. Variations of 1000BaseX include 1000BaseCX, 1000BaseLX, and 1000BaseSX.
1000BaseCX	A 1 Gbps network physical layer specification that uses two pairs of 150-ohm balanced copper cable (twinax). Used for short distance connections, such as between rooms, between wiring closets, or similar combinations. The maximum distance between nodes is 25 m.
1000BaseLX	A 1 Gbps network physical layer specification that uses long wavelength signals over a pair of optical fibers. Mainly used for horizontal cabling rather than the vertical cabling found in risers. Maximum distance between nodes is 3 kilometers with single-mode fiber (SMF), 440 meters with 62.5-micron multimode fiber (MMF), or 550 meters with 50-micron multimode fiber (MMF).
1000BaseSX	A 1 Gbps network physical layer specification that uses short wavelength signals over a pair of optical fibers. Mainly used for backbone cabling. Maximum distance between nodes is 260 m for 62.5-micron multimode fiber (MMF) or 525 m for 50-micron multimode fiber (MMF).

[*]The ANSI X3T11 committee is responsible for the Fibre Channel technology. ANSI decided to spell "Fibre" with "re" rather than "er" to differentiate it from the fiber-optic cable on which it is run.

The focus of this chapter will be three data rates that are currently defined for operation over optical fiber and twisted-pair cables:

- 10 Mbps—10BaseT Ethernet
- 100 Mbps—Fast Ethernet
- 1000 Mbps—Gigabit Ethernet

10-Gigabit Ethernet is under development and will likely be published as IEEE 802.3ae in late 2001 or early 2002.

Deployed in approximately 85 percent of the world's LANs, Ethernet has survived as the major LAN technology because its network architecture has the following characteristics:

- It is easy to understand, implement, manage, and maintain.
- It supports relatively low-cost network implementations.
- It provides extensive infrastructure flexibility for network implementation.
- It guarantees successful interconnection and operation of standards-compliant products.

Ethernet Network Elements

Ethernet LANs consist of two network elements: network nodes, or hosts, and interconnecting media. Network nodes fall into two major classes: data terminal equipment (DTE) and data communication equipment (DCE).

- DTE—Devices that are either the source or the destination of data frames. Examples of DTE are devices such as PCs, workstations, file servers, or print servers that, as a group, are often referred to as end hosts or LAN-attached hosts.
- DCE—Intermediate network devices that receive and forward frames across the network. Examples of DCE can be either standalone devices, such as repeaters, network switches, and routers, or communications interface units, such as network interface cards (NICs), multiplexers, channel service units (CSUs) and digital service units (DSUs), and modems (VF, xDSL, cable, and so on). (DCE can be defined as either data circuit-terminating equipment or data communication equipment; often the latter is the more common definition of the DCE acronym.)

NOTE   Depending on the conversation taking place, routers can be classified as DTE or DCE. The argument for a router being classified as DTE can be found in Cisco Press's *Interconnecting Cisco Network Devices* book, where DTE is classified as customer premise equipment (CPE) and DCE is a device used to convert user data from DTE to a form acceptable to the network service provider. By the definition of DTE originating or terminating user data, a router is classified as DCE because it is neither originating nor terminating user data transmission; instead, it is acting as a communications device carrying the data from origination to termination.

Ethernet Network Topologies and Structures

As discussed in Chapter 2, "LAN Topologies," LANs take on many topological configurations, but regardless of their size and complexity, all will be a combination of three basic network elements or building blocks. The three basic elements are as follows:

- DTE
- DCE
- Network link

The simplest network architecture is the point-to-point interconnection, as shown in Figure 3-1. Only two network devices are involved, and the connection can be DTE-to-DTE, DTE-to-DCE, or DCE-to-DCE. The cable in point-to-point interconnections is known as the *network link*. The maximum allowable length of the link depends on the type of cable and the transmission method that is used. A discussion of cable lengths can be found in Chapter 2.

Figure 3-1   *Point-to-Point Network Architecture*

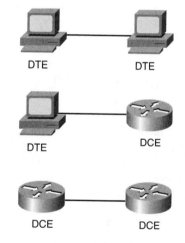

The original Ethernet networks were implemented with a coaxial bus structure. Segment lengths were limited to 500 m, and up to 100 hosts could be connected to a single segment. Individual segments could be interconnected with repeaters, as long as multiple paths did not exist between any two hosts on the network and the total number of DTE devices did not exceed 1024. The total path distance between the most-distant pair of hosts was also not allowed to exceed a maximum prescribed value as determined by network diameter calculations.

Since the early 1990s, the network configuration of choice has been the star-connected topology (see Figure 3-2). The central network unit is either a multiport repeater, also known as a *hub*, or it is a switch. All connections in this network are point-to-point links implemented with either twisted-pair or optical fiber cable.

Figure 3-2   *Ethernet Star Topology*

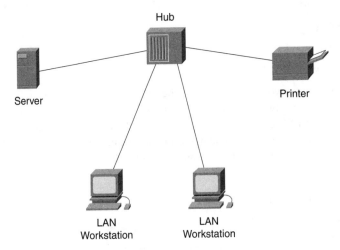

IEEE 802.3 Logical Relationship to the OSI Reference Model

Figure 3-3 illustrates the IEEE 802.3 logical layers and their relationship to the OSI reference model. As with all IEEE 802 protocols, the data link layer is divided into two IEEE 802 sublayers: the Media Access Control (MAC) sublayer and the MAC-client sublayer (logical-link control or bridge). The IEEE 802.3 physical layer corresponds to the OSI model physical layer (Layer 1).

Figure 3-3   *Ethernet and the IEEE 802.3 OSI Reference Model*

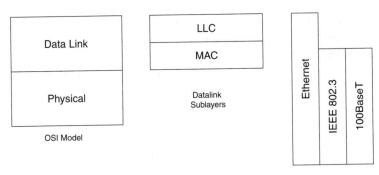

Above the MAC sublayer will be one of the following:

- Logical Link Control (LLC), if the device is DTE. This sublayer provides the interface between the Ethernet MAC and the upper layers in the protocol stack of the end host. The LLC sublayer is defined by the IEEE 802.2 standards.

- Bridge entity, if the device is a bridge (a DCE). Bridges can provide LAN-to-LAN interfaces between LANs that use the same protocol, such as Ethernet to Ethernet, or between different protocols, such as Ethernet to Token Ring. Bridges are defined by the IEEE 802.1 standards.

NOTE   Non-translating bridges are considered to be MAC sublayer bridges.

Because specifications for LLC and bridges are common for all IEEE 802 LAN protocols, network compatibility becomes the primary responsibility of the particular network (OSI Layer 3) protocol.

The MAC layer controls the network node's access to the network media and is specific to the individual protocol. All IEEE MACs must meet the same basic set of logical requirements, regardless of optional protocol extensions. The only requirement for basic communication between two network nodes is that both MACs must support the same transmission rate, for example, 10 Mbps half-duplex Ethernet.

The 802.3 physical layer is specific to the transmission data rate, the signal encoding, and the type of media interconnecting the two nodes. Gigabit Ethernet, for example, is defined to operate over twisted-pair or fiber cable, but each specific type of cable or signal-encoding procedure requires a different physical layer implementation.

The Ethernet MAC Sublayer

The MAC sublayer has two primary responsibilities:

- Data encapsulation—Frame assembly before transmission and frame parsing/error detection during and after reception.

- Media access control—Initiation of frame transmission and recovery from transmission failure.

The Basic Ethernet Frame Format

The IEEE 802.3 standard defines a basic data frame format that is required for all MAC implementations, plus several additional optional formats that are used to extend the protocol's basic capability. The discussion here will focus on the basic frame format because that is the commonality among all Ethernet implementations and calculations.

The basic data frame format contains seven fields, as shown in Figure 3-4.

Figure 3-4   *Ethernet Frame Format*

Preamble (7 Bytes)	SOF (1 Byte)	Destination Address (6 Bytes)	Source Address (6 Bytes)	Length (2 Bytes)	Data Payload (N Bytes)	FCS (4 Bytes)

- Preamble (PRE)—Consists of 7 bytes of 10101010. The preamble is an alternating pattern of ones and zeros that tells receiving hosts that a frame is coming. The preamble provides a means to synchronize the frame-reception portions of receiving physical layers with the incoming bit stream.
- Start-of-frame (SOF) delimiter—Consists of 1 byte of 10101011. The start-of-frame is an alternating pattern of ones and zeros, ending with two consecutive 1-bits indicating that the next bit in the data stream is the left-most bit in the left-most byte of the destination address.

NOTE   Regarding Ethernet implementations, the same eight bytes are considered a single field, called the *Preamble*. The IEEE 802.3 standard separated the eighth byte into its own field, the SOF delimiter.

- Destination address (DA)—Consists of 6 bytes. The destination address field identifies which host(s) should receive the frame. The left-most bit in the destination address field indicates whether the address is an individual, or unicast, address (indicated by a 0) or a group, or a multicast address (indicated by a 1). The second bit from the left indicates whether the destination address is globally administered (indicated by a 0) or locally administered (indicated by a 1). The remaining 46 bits are a uniquely assigned value that identifies a single host (unicast), a defined group of hosts (multicast), or all hosts on the network (broadcast).
- Source address (SA)—Consists of 6 bytes. The source address field identifies the sending host. The source address is always an individual address, and the left-most bit in the source address field is always 0.
    — Exception: This bit is the RI bit used in source-route bridging.
- Length/Type—Consists of 2 bytes. This field indicates either the number of LLC data bytes that are contained in the data field of the frame or the frame type ID if the frame is an Ethernet frame and not in 802.3 format. If the length/type field value is less than or equal to 1500, the number of LLC bytes in the data field is equal to the length/type

field value. If the length/type field value is greater than 1536, the frame is an Ethernet II frame, and the length/type field value identifies the particular type of frame being sent or received.

- Data—Is a sequence of *n* bytes of any value, where *n* is less than or equal to 1500 (1500 bytes = 12000 bits, or 12 Kb). If the length of the data field is less than 46, the data field must be extended by adding a filler, or pad, sufficient to bring the data field length to 46 bytes.

- Frame check sequence (FCS)—Consists of 4 bytes. This sequence contains a 32-bit cyclic redundancy check (CRC) value, which is created by the sending MAC and is recalculated by the receiving MAC to verify data integrity by checking for damaged frames. The FCS is generated over the DA, SA, length/type, and data fields.

Frame Transmission

Whenever an end host MAC adapter receives a transmit-frame request with the accompanying address and data information from the LLC sublayer, the MAC sublayer begins the transmission sequence by transferring the LLC information into the MAC frame buffer. This process is as follows:

- The preamble and start-of-frame delimiter are inserted into the PRE and SOF fields.

- The destination and source addresses are inserted into the address fields.

- The LLC data bytes are counted and the number of bytes is inserted into the length/type field.

- The LLC data bytes are inserted into the data field. If the number of LLC data bytes is less than 46, a pad is added to bring the data field length up to 46.

- An FCS value is generated over the DA, SA, length/type, and data fields and is appended to the end of the data field.

After the frame is assembled, frame transmission will depend on whether the MAC adapter is operating in half-duplex or full-duplex mode.

NOTE   Half-duplex transmission is a two-way operation, one way at a time, in which the MAC adapter must wait for the media to clear because the receiver is in use. Full-duplex transmission is a two-way operation, two ways at a time, where a transmission can begin immediately.

The IEEE 802.3 standard currently requires that all Ethernet MAC devices support half-duplex operation. Full-duplex operation is an optional capability if the MAC device supports full-duplex mode. Full-duplex allows the network devices to transmit and receive frames simultaneously. Full-duplex is used only when a single device is attached to each switch port.

Half-Duplex Transmission: The CSMA/CD Access Method

The Carrier Sense Multiple Access with Collision Detect (CSMA/CD) protocol was originally developed as a means by which two or more hosts could share a common media in a switchless environment. In this shared environment, the CSMA/CD protocol does not require central arbitration, access tokens, or assigned time slots to indicate when a host will be allowed to transmit. Based on sensing a data carrier on the network medium, each Ethernet MAC adapter determines for itself when it will be allowed to send a frame.

The CSMA/CD access rules are summarized by the protocol's acronym:

- Carrier sense (CS)—Each Ethernet LAN-attached host continuously listens for traffic on the medium to determine when gaps between frame transmissions occur.

- Multiple access (MA)—LAN-attached hosts can begin transmitting any time they detect that the network is quiet, meaning that no traffic is travelling across the wire.

- Collision detect (CD)—If two or more LAN-attached hosts in the same CSMA/CD network, or collision domain, begin transmitting at approximately the same time, the bit streams from the transmitting hosts will interfere (collide) with each other, and both transmissions will be unreadable. If that happens, each transmitting host must be capable of detecting that a collision has occurred before it has finished sending its respective frame. Each host must stop transmitting as soon as it has detected the collision and then must wait a random length of time as determined by a backoff algorithm before attempting to retransmit the frame. In this event, each transmitting host will transmit a 32-bit jam signal alerting all LAN-attached hosts of a collision before running the backoff algorithm.

CSMA/CD Operation

CSMA/CD operation, as defined by the IEEE 802.3 standard, is as follows:

1   The LAN-attached host listens to the Ethernet medium to see if any other node is transmitting by sensing the carrier signal on the bus. If a signal is detected on the wire, then a transmission is in progress. The host will continue listening until the channel is idle.

2   When no signal is detected across the medium, the host will start transmitting its data.

3   While data transmission is occurring, the LAN-attached host is still listening to the bus. This host compares the received message with what was transmitted. As long as these two remain the same, the host will continue to transmit. (Ethernet defines a

logical bus, which means all hosts, including the transmitting host, will see the data transmission. All hosts will look at the frame header and will make the determination, based on the MAC address, if that host is the intended recipient for that frame.)

4 If the transmitting host receives a frame other than what was transmitted, a collision is assumed and the transmitting host ceases data transmission.

5 A 32-bit jam signal is transmitted to all LAN-attached hosts alerting that a collision has been detected.

6 The transmitting host waits a random amount of time, as determined by the backoff algorithm, and then starts the transmission process again.

In a half-duplex Ethernet LAN, collisions are part of normal CSMA/CD operation. Collisions will occur more frequently in a heavily used network; consequently, network performance will decrease as traffic load increases.

CAUTION   Collisions will be discussed in greater detail later, but 40 percent congestion is the average maximum percentage you want to see on an Ethernet collision domain.

Network Diameter

CSMA/CD is subject to another potential network issue—the time it takes for the signal to travel across the medium between the two endpoints. If two LAN hosts were far enough apart, neither host would see traffic on the medium, and both could transmit at the same time, resulting in a collision. This anomaly is related to cable length and issues related to bit times.

The worst-case scenario occurs when the two most-distant hosts on the network both need to send a frame and when the second host does not begin transmitting until just before the frame from the first host arrives. The collision will be detected almost immediately by the second host, but it will not be detected by the first host until the corrupted signal has propagated all the way back to that host. The maximum time that is required to detect a collision (the collision window, or "slot time") is approximately equal to twice the signal propagation time between the two most-distant hosts on the network:

$$\text{CollisionDetectTime} = 2(H_1 - H_2)$$

where H_1 and H_2 are the two most distant hosts on the network.

Slot time is the maximum time that can elapse between the first and last network host's receipt of a frame. To ensure that a network host, or node, can determine whether the frame it transmitted has collided with another frame, a frame must be longer than the number of bits that can be transmitted in the slot time. In Ethernet networks, this time interval is about half a microsecond, which is long enough to transmit at least 512 bits.

This Collision Detect Time means that both the minimum frame length and the maximum collision diameter are directly related to the slot time. Longer minimum frame lengths translate to longer slot times and larger collision diameters; shorter minimum frame lengths correspond to shorter slot times and smaller collision diameters.

Table 3-2 demonstrates the different segment lengths allowed, based on the respective Ethernet implementation.

Table 3-2   *Ethernet/802.3 Collision Domain Distance Limitations*

	10Base5	10Base2	10BaseT	100BaseT
Topology	Bus	Bus	Star	Star
Maximum segment length (meters)	500	185	100 from hub to host	100 from hub to host
Maximum number of attachments per segment	100	30	2 (hub and host or hub-hub)	2 (hub and host or hub-hub)
Maximum collision domain	2500 meters of 5 segments and 4 repeaters; only 3 segments can be populated	2500 meters of 5 segments and 4 repeaters; only 3 segments can be populated	2500 meters of 5 segments and 4 repeaters; only 3 segments can be populated	See 100BaseT table

Table 3-3 demonstrates maximum distance allowed in 100BaseT, based on cabling technology used—for example, copper or fiber—and the number of repeaters, if any, that are implemented.

Table 3-3   *100BaseT Maximum Distance Table*

	Copper	Mixed Copper and Multimode Fiber	Multimode Fiber
DTE-DTE (or switch-switch)	100 m	—	412 m (2000 if full duplex)
One Class I repeater	200 m	260 m	272 m
One Class II repeater	200 m	308 m	320 m
Two Class II repeaters	205 m	216 m	228 m

CAUTION   The "5-4-3" rule is applicable to coaxial Ethernet segments with repeaters. The "5-4-3" rule states an Ethernet network has no more than five segments, four repeaters, and three active segments. This rule is enforced by network diameter and bit times.

In the IEEE 100BaseT specification, two types of repeaters are defined:

- Class I repeaters have a latency of 0.7 microseconds or less. Only one repeater hop is allowed.

- Class II repeaters have a latency of 0.46 microseconds or less. One or two repeater hops are allowed.

NOTE   The Cisco FastHub 316 is a Class II repeater.

A trade-off was necessary between network diameter and collision recovery. The trade-off was between the need to reduce the impact of collision recovery and the need for the network diameter to be large enough to accommodate reasonable network sizes. The compromise was to choose a maximum network diameter (approximately 2500 m) and then to set the minimum frame length long enough to ensure detection of all worst-case collisions.

This compromise worked well for 10 Mbps, but became a problem for higher data-rate Ethernet networks. Fast Ethernet (100 Mbps) was required to provide backward compatibility with earlier Ethernet networks, including the existing IEEE 802.3 frame format and error-detection processes. Additionally, all applications and networking software running on the 10 Mbps networks needed to be supported.

The time it takes for a signal to propagate across the network medium is essentially constant for all transmission rates. The time required to transmit a frame is inversely related to the transmission rate. At 100 Mbps, a minimum-length frame can be transmitted in approximately one-tenth of the defined slot time, and the transmitting hosts would not likely detect any collisions that could occur during this transmission. Therefore, the maximum network diameter specified for 10 Mbps networks could not be used for 100 Mbps (Fast Ethernet) networks. The solution for Fast Ethernet was to reduce the maximum network diameter by approximately a factor of 10, to a little more than 200 m.

This same problem of network diameter arose during specification development for Gigabit Ethernet; however, decreasing network diameters by another factor of 10, to approximately 20 meters, for 1000 Mbps operation was not practical. The developers decided to maintain approximately the same maximum collision domain diameters as Fast Ethernet (100 Mbps) networks and to increase the minimum frame size by adding a variable-length non user-data extension field to frames that are shorter than the minimum length. (The receiver removes the extension field from the frame.)

Table 3-4 demonstrates the variables relating to network diameter for 10 Mbps Ethernet, 100 Mbps (Fast) Ethernet, and 1000 Mbps (Gigabit) Ethernet.

Table 3-4 *Half-Duplex Operation Limits*

Parameter	10 Mbps	100 Mbps	1000 Mbps
Minimum frame size	64 bytes	64 bytes	520 bytes (with extension field added, if needed)
Maximum collision diameter, DTE-to-DTE	100 m UTP	100 m UTP	100 m UTP
		412 m fiber	316 m fiber
Maximum collision diameter with repeaters	2500 m	205 m	200 m
Maximum number of repeaters in network path	5	2	1

Cable Case Study

Copper and fiber-optic cable have a delay of between 0.5 and 0.6 microseconds/100 m. The formula used to calculate the maximum network diameter is as follows:

Network diameter = 25.6 microseconds / (0.6 microseconds/100 m) > 4,000 m

The minimum transmission time of 25.6 microseconds is divided by the cable delay. The minimum transmission time of 25.6 microseconds is derived from 51.2 microseconds/2 to account for round-trip delay.

CAUTION   To calculate the network diameter of a specific network and ensure that your Ethernet segment will function satisfactorily, use the following equation. The sum of the equation should not exceed half the minimum frame size. If it does, the network is too large and needs to be broken down into smaller segments.

(Repeated delays + cable delays + NIC delays) $\times$ *2* < maximum round-trip delay

- The maximum round-trip delay may be obtained from Table 3-5. It is 51.6 microseconds for 10 Mbps Ethernet, 5.12 microseconds for Fast Ethernet, and 4.096 microseconds for Gigabit Ethernet.

- The factor 2 in the equation accounts for round-trip delays. The frame needs to travel from the transmitter to the collision point and back to the transmitter again.

- Repeater and NIC delays can be obtained from the manufacturer.

  — Ethernet repeaters typically have latencies of 2 microseconds or less

  — Fast Ethernet Class I repeaters are less than 0.7 microseconds

  — Fast Ethernet Class II repeaters are less than 0.46 microseconds

  — A 10 Mbps NIC delay is about 1 microsecond

  — Fast Ethernet NIC delay is about 0.25 microsecond

- Cable delays can be obtained from Table 3-5. Cable delays have no dependence on Ethernet speed. Cable delays are usually measured as a fraction of the speed of light and mostly depend on the insulation material used. A 100 m UTP section takes about 0.55 microseconds one way.

Table 3-5 demonstrates the maximum delay time dependent on the associated network component.

Table 3-5   *Network Component Delays for Network Diameter Calculation*

Component	Maximum Delay Time in Microseconds
Two Fast Ethernet NICs or switch ports	0.5
Fast Ethernet MII (interface connector)	0.2
100 m Category 5 cable segment	0.556
1 m Category 5 cable segment	0.00556
100 m fiber-optic cable segment	0.5
1 m fiber-optic cable	0.005
Fast Ethernet Class I repeater	0.7
Fast Ethernet Class II repeater	0.46
Two Gigabit Ethernet NICs	0.864
Gigabit Ethernet repeater	0.488

Full-Duplex Transmission

Full-duplex operation is an optional MAC adapter capability that allows simultaneous two-way transmission over point-to-point links. Full duplex transmission is much simpler than half-duplex transmission because it involves no media contention, no collisions, no need to schedule retransmissions, and no need for extension bits on the end of short frames. The result is more time available for data transmission, effectively doubling the link bandwidth as each link can support simultaneous two-way transmission across the wire at the full bandwidth rate.

Table 3-6 demonstrates the maximum total data transfer rate for each Ethernet operational mode.

Table 3-6   *Ethernet Mode and Maximum Transfer Rate*

Operational Mode	Maximum Total Data Transfer Rate
1000BaseT full-duplex	2000 Mbps
1000BaseT half-duplex	1000 Mbps
100BaseT2 full-duplex	200 Mbps
100BaseT2 half-duplex	100 Mbps
100BaseTX full-duplex	200 Mbps
100BaseTX half-duplex	100 Mbps
100BaseT4 full-duplex	Not a supported implementation
100BaseT4 half-duplex	100 Mbps
10BaseT full-duplex	20 Mbps
10BaseT half-duplex	10 Mbps

Flow Control

Full-duplex operation requires concurrent implementation of the optional flow-control capability, allowing a receiving node that is becoming congested to request that the sending node stop sending frames for a selected short period of time. Control is MAC-to-MAC through the use of a pause frame that is automatically generated by the receiving MAC adapter. If the congestion is relieved before the requested wait has expired, a second pause frame with a zero time-to-wait value can be sent to request resumption of transmission.

The full-duplex operation and its companion flow control capability are both options for all Ethernet MACs and all transmission rates. Both options are enabled on a link-by-link state basis, assuming that the associated physical layers are also capable of supporting full-duplex operation.

Pause frames are identified as MAC control frames by an exclusive assigned (reserved) length/type value. Pause frames are also assigned a reserved destination address value to ensure that an incoming frame is never forwarded to upper protocol layers or to other ports in a switch.

Frame Reception

Frame reception is essentially the same for both half-duplex and full-duplex operations, except that full-duplex MACs must have separate frame buffers and data paths to allow for simultaneous frame transmission and reception.

Frame reception is the reverse of frame transmission. The destination address of the received frame is checked and matched against the host's address list (its MAC address, group address, and the broadcast address) to determine whether the frame is destined for that host. If an address match is found, the frame length is checked and the received FCS is compared to the FCS that was generated during frame reception. If the frame length is okay and there is an FCS match, the frame type is determined by the contents of the Length/Type field. The frame is then buffered and forwarded to the appropriate upper layer.

The Ethernet Physical Layers

Because Ethernet devices implement only the bottom two layers of the OSI protocol stack (OSI Layers 1 and 2), they are typically implemented as network interface cards (NICs) that plug into the host device. The different connectors are often identified by a three-part name that is based on the physical layer attributes.

These three parts specify LAN speed, signaling method, and an indication of either maximum distance (5 = 500 m, 2 = 185 m) per segment or physical media type (T = twisted pair). Table 3-7 demonstrates these differences.

Table 3-7   *IEEE 802.3 Comparison*

	IEEE 802.3 Values				
Characteristic	**10Base5**	**10Base2**	**10BaseT**	**10BaseFL**	**100BaseT**
Data rate (Mbps)	10	10	10	10	100
Signaling Method	Baseband	Baseband	Baseband	Baseband	Baseband
Maximum segment length (m)	500	185	100	2000	100
Media	50-ohm coax (thick)	50-ohm coax (thin)	Unshielded twisted-pair (UTP)	Fiber-optic	Unshielded twisted-pair (UTP)
Topology	Bus	Bus	Star	Point-to-point	Star

NOTE	All current Ethernet implementations use baseband transmission because broadband implementations were not successful in the marketplace.

10 Mbps Ethernet Operation

Ethernet segments are implemented on a coaxial cable up to 500 meters in length. This cable is similar to the type of cable found in the home for cable television; however, the impedance is different. Ethernet cable is 50 ohms, and cable TV cable is 75 ohms. Ethernet hosts attach to the segment by tapping into it; these taps must be at least 2.5 m apart. Directly attached to the tap is a small device called a *transceiver*. This transceiver detects when the line is idle. The transceiver transmits the signal when the host is transmitting and receives the signal when the host is receiving. The transceiver is connected to the Ethernet adapter, which in turn is plugged into the host.

NOTE	The Ethernet protocol operates within the adapter, not the transceiver. For 10BaseT and 10Base2, the transceiver is on the NIC.

Remember that multiple Ethernet segments can be joined together by *repeaters,* devices that forward, or repeat, digital signals. However, there are limitations. There can be no more than four repeaters between any pair of Ethernet hosts, and with the maximum four repeaters implemented, Ethernet has a maximum reach of 2,500 m.

NOTE	Ethernet is limited to supporting a maximum of 1024 hosts.

Bit Times

Ethernet has no centralized control; therefore, it is possible for two or more adapters to begin transmitting at the same time, either because both found the line to be idle or because both had been waiting for a busy line to become idle after running the backoff algorithm. When this situation occurs, the two or more frames are said to collide on the network. Because Ethernet supports collision detection, each sender is able to determine that a collision is in progress. At the moment an Ethernet MAC adapter detects that its frame is colliding with another, it transmits a 32-bit jam signal, and then stops transmission. A transmitter will send a minimum of 96 bits in the case of a collision—a 64-bit preamble plus the 32-48 bits jamming signal.

If two hosts are so close to each other that the adapter will only send 96 bits, a *runt frame* has occurred. If the two hosts had been farther apart, they would have had to transmit longer, and thus send more bits, before detecting the collision.

The worst-case scenario of collisions caused by network diameter "violations" occurs when two hosts are at opposite ends of the Ethernet. To know for sure that the frame it just sent did not collide with another frame, the transmitter might need to send as many as 512 bits. Not coincidentally, every Ethernet frame must be 512 bits (64 bytes) long: 14 bytes of header plus 46 bytes of data plus 4 bytes of CRC.

Ethernet frames must be 512 bits (64 bytes) in length because the farther apart that two nodes are, the longer it takes for a frame sent by one to reach the other. The network is vulnerable to a collision during this time.

Figure 3-5 illustrates the worst-case scenario where two hosts, A and B, are at opposite ends of the network.

Figure 3-5 *Hosts*

A   B

1   Suppose host A begins transmitting a frame at time *t* (see Figure 3-6).

Figure 3-6 *Host Transmission*

A   t   B

It takes one link latency, denoted as *d*, for the frame to reach host B. It could be stated that the first bit of A's frame arrives at B at time *t* + *d*, as shown in Figure 3-7.

Figure 3-7 *Calculation of Transmission Time*

A   t + d   B

2   Suppose an instant before host A's frame arrives, host B begins to transmit its own frame (see Figure 3-8), illustrated here as t_{-1}. Host B will see the segment as idle because there is no traffic on the wire.

Figure 3-8   *Multiple Transmissions*

B's frame will immediately collide with A's frame, and this collision will be detected by host B (see Figure 3-9).

Figure 3-9   *Collision*

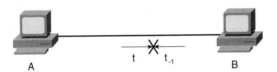

Host B will send the 32 to 48-bit jamming signal sequence (see Figure 3-10).

Figure 3-10   *Jamming Signal Sequence*

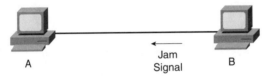

   3 Host A will not know that the collision occurred until host B's frame reaches it, which
      will happen one link latency later, at time *t + 2d (see Figure 3-11)*.

Figure 3-11   *Calculation of Collision Time*

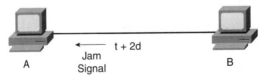

Host A must continue to transmit until this time to detect the collision. In other words, host A must transmit for *2d* to be sure that it detects all possible collisions.

Considering that a maximally configured Ethernet is 2,500 meters long, and that there can be up to four repeaters between any two hosts, the round-trip delay has been determined to be 51.2 microseconds, which on a 10 Mbps Ethernet corresponds to 512 bits. Another way to look at this situation is that Ethernet's maximum latency needs to be fairly small—for example, 51.2 microseconds—for this access algorithm to work. Therefore, Ethernet's maximum length must be something on the order of no more than 2,500 meters.

To calculate the time to transmit 1 bit for 10 Mbps Ethernet transmission, use the following formula:

> 1 bit-time = 1 bit/10Mhz = 0.1 microseconds or 100 ns

The minimum transmission time can be calculated from the minimum frame size.

> Minimum transmission time = Minimum frame size (512 bits) × Bit time (100 ns) = 51.2 microseconds

---

NOTE   Network diameter is directly related to frame size, as well as the bit time, as the following demonstrates:

> Network diameter = K × (Frame Size/Bit Time)

Backoff Algorithm

After a MAC adapter has detected a collision and stopped its transmission, it waits a certain amount of time and tries again. Each time the adapter tries to transmit and fails, the adapter doubles the amount of time it waits before trying again. This strategy of doubling the delay interval between each retransmission attempt is known as *exponential backoff.*

Exponential Backoff

The adapter first delays either 0 or 51.2 microseconds, selected at random. If this effort fails, it then waits 0, 51.2, 102.4, or 153.6 microseconds (selected randomly) before trying again, which can be expressed as $k \times 51.2$ for k=0,1..3. After the third collision, it waits $k \times 51.2$ for k=0..2^3-1, again selected at random.

In general, the algorithm randomly selects a k between 0 and 2^n-1 and waits $k \times 51.2$ microseconds, where n is the number of collisions experienced so far. The adapter gives up after a given number of tries, typically 16, and reports a transmit error to the host, although the backoff algorithm caps n in the previous formula at 10.

Table 3-8 demonstrates the parameters for 10 Mbps Ethernet implementations.

Table 3-8 *10 Mbps Ethernet Parameters*

Parameter	Ethernet/802.3
SlotTime	512 bit times (512 microseconds)
Minimum InterFrameGap	96 bit times (9.6 microseconds)
AttemptLimit	16
BackoffLimit	10 (exponential number)
JamSize	32-48 bits (4 bytes)
MaxFrameSize	12144 bits (1518 bytes)
MinFrameSize	512 bits (64 bytes)
AddressSize	48 bits (6 bytes)

Ethernet Case Study

Most Ethernet implementations are a bit more conservative than what the standards support, implementing fewer than 200 connected hosts (maximum 1024 allowed). Additionally, most Ethernet segment implementations are far shorter than the allowed 2,500 m, with a round-trip delay closer to 5 microseconds than 51.2 microseconds. Ethernet implementations are considered practical in that the Ethernet hosts typically provide end-to-end flow control because the Ethernet adapters do not implement link-level flow control. It is rare to find situations in which any one host is continually transmitting frames across the network.

Alternative Ethernet Technologies

Alternative Ethernet technologies have been introduced over the years. For example, rather than use the 50-ohm coaxial cable for Ethernet segments, a thinner cable might be used to build an Ethernet segment. The thick 50-ohm coaxial segment is called 10Base5 (maximum 500 m segment length), or thick-net, and the thinner cabling is called 10Base2 (maximum 200 m segment length), or thin-net.

New technology implemented 10BaseT, where T is twisted-pair cabling, typically Category 5, and is limited to 100 m in length. Both 100 Mbps and 1000 Mbps Ethernet can operate on Category 5 cabling at distances up to 100 m.

Because the cable is so thin, it is not necessary to tap into a 10Base2 or 10BaseT cable in the same fashion as required with a 10Base5 cable. With 10Base2, a T-joint is spliced into the cable, effectively daisy-chaining 10Base2 hosts together. With 10BaseT, the common configuration is to have several point-to-point segments spanning out of a multiport repeater, known as a hub. Multiple 10 or 100 Mbps Ethernet segments can be connected with a hub, whereas 1000 Mbps Ethernet segments cannot, instead requiring a switch.

Ethernet Applications

10 Mbps Ethernet is usually found in Small Office/Home Office (SOHO) environments due to its ease of implementation and minimal host configuration.

Organizations that do not require high-speed bandwidth to the desktop will also deploy 10 Mbps Ethernet. If users do not run multimedia, CAD/CAM, or other bandwidth intensive applications, 10 Mbps Ethernet can be deployed to conserve component costs, while laying the foundation for a migration path to 100 Mbps (Fast) Ethernet.

100 Mbps, or Fast Ethernet

100 Mbps Ethernet is a high-speed LAN technology that offers increased bandwidth to desktop users in the wiring center, as well as to servers and server clusters, or *server farms* as they are sometimes called, in data centers.

The IEEE Higher Speed Ethernet Study Group was formed to assess the feasibility of running Ethernet at speeds of 100 Mbps. At issue within the Study Group was whether 100 Mbps Ethernet would support CSMA/CD for network medium access or whether another access method would be available.

This IEEE study group was broken into two forums: the Fast Ethernet Alliance and the 100VG-AnyLAN Forum. Each group produced a specification for running Ethernet (100BaseT) and Token Ring (100VG-AnyLAN) at higher speeds.

100BaseT is the IEEE specification for 100 Mbps Ethernet implementations over UTP and STP cabling. The Media Access Control (MAC) layer is compatible with the IEEE 802.3 MAC layer. Fast Ethernet, standardized by the IEEE 802.3u specification, was developed by a part of the Cisco Systems Workgroup Business Unit, formerly Grand Junction.

100VG-AnyLAN is an IEEE specification for 100 Mbps Token Ring and Ethernet implementations over 4-pair UTP. The MAC layer is not compatible with the IEEE 802.3 MAC layer. 100VG-AnyLAN was developed by Hewlett-Packard (HP) to support newer time-sensitive applications, such as multimedia. A version of this implementation is standardized in the IEEE 802.12 specification.

100BaseT Overview

100BaseT uses the existing IEEE 802.3 CSMA/CD specification, retaining the IEEE 802.3 frame format, size, and error-detection mechanism. 100BaseT also supports all applications and networking software running on IEEE 802.3 networks. 100BaseT supports dual speeds of 10 and 100 Mbps using 100BaseT. 100BaseT hubs must be able to detect and support dual speeds, but adapter cards can support 10 Mbps, 100 Mbps, or both.

100BaseT Operation

100BaseT and 10BaseT use the same IEEE 802.3 MAC access and collision-detection methods. 100BaseT and 10BaseT also share the same frame format and length requirements. The main difference between 10BaseT and 100BaseT, other than the speed differential, is the network diameter.

NOTE	100BaseT can support a maximum network diameter of 205 m, whereas the 10BaseT network can support a maximum network diameter of approximately 2,000 m (with repeaters).

Reducing the 100BaseT network diameter is necessary because, like 10BaseT, 100BaseT uses the same collision-detection mechanism. With 10BaseT, distance limitations are defined so that a host knows while transmitting the smallest legal frame size (64 bytes) that a collision has taken place with another sending host that is located at the farthest point of the domain.

To achieve the increased throughput of 100BaseT, the size of the collision domain had to be reduced. This reduction was necessary because the propagation speed of the physical medium had not changed. A host transmitting 10 times faster must have a maximum distance that is 10 times less. As a result, any host knows within the first 64 bytes whether a collision has occurred with any other host.

Bit Times

Like Ethernet, Fast Ethernet has no centralized control. Therefore, it is possible for two or more adapters to begin transmitting at the same time, either because both found the line to be idle or because both had been waiting for a busy line to become idle after running the backoff algorithm. When this happens, the two or more frames are said to collide on the network. Because Fast Ethernet supports collision detection, each sender is able to determine that a collision is in progress. At the moment an Ethernet MAC adapter detects that its frame is colliding with another, it transmits a 32-bit jam signal, and then stops transmission. A transmitter will minimally send 96 bits in the case of a collision—64-bit preamble plus the 32-bit jamming signal.

One way that an adapter will send only 96 bits, sometimes called a *runt frame*, is if the two hosts are close to each other. Had the two hosts been farther apart, they would have had to transmit longer, and thus send more bits, before detecting the collision. In fact, the worst-case scenario happens when the two hosts are at opposite ends of the Ethernet. To know for sure that the frame it just sent did not collide with another frame, the transmitter might need to send as many as 512 bits. Not coincidentally, every Ethernet frame must be 512 bits (64 bytes) long: 14 bytes of header plus 46 bytes of data plus 4 bytes of CRC.

Considering that a maximally configured Ethernet is 2,500 m long, and that there can be up to four repeaters between any two hosts, the round-trip delay has been determined to be 5.12 microseconds, which on a 100 Mbps Ethernet corresponds to 512 bits. Another way to look at this situation is that Ethernet's maximum latency needs to be fairly small, such as 5.12 microseconds, for this access algorithm to work. Therefore, Fast Ethernet's maximum length must be something on the order of no more than 205 meters.

To calculate the time to transmit 1 bit for 100 Mbps Ethernet transmission, use the following formula:

> 1 bit-time = 1 bit/100Mhz = 0.01 microseconds or 10 ns

The minimum transmission time can be calculated from the minimum frame size.

> Minimum transmission time = Minimum frame size (512 bits) × Bit time (10 ns) = 5.12 microseconds

Backoff Algorithm

After a MAC adapter has detected a collision and stopped its transmission, it waits a certain amount of time and tries again. Each time the adapter tries to transmit and fails, the adapter doubles the amount of time it waits before trying again. This strategy of doubling the delay interval between each retransmission attempt is a general technique known as *exponential backoff*.

Exponential Backoff

The adapter first delays either 0 or 51.2 microseconds, selected at random. If this effort fails, it then waits 0, 51.2, 102.4, or 153.6 microseconds (selected randomly) before trying again; this can be expressed as $k \times 51.2$ for k=0,1..3. After the third collision, it waits $k \times 51.2$ for $k = 0..2^3 - 1$, again selected at random.

In general, the algorithm randomly selects a k between 0 and $2^n - 1$ and waits $k \times 51.2$ microseconds, where n is the number of collisions experienced so far. The adapter gives up after a given number of tries, typically 16, and reports a transmit error to the host, although the backoff algorithm caps n in the previous formula at 10.

Fast Ethernet's parameters are the same as Ethernet/IEEE 802.3, as demonstrated in Table 3-9.

Table 3-9   *100 Mbps Ethernet Parameters*

Parameter	Fast Ethernet/802.3u
SlotTime	512 bit times (512 microseconds)
Minimum InterFrameGap	96 bit times (9.6 microseconds)
AttemptLimit	16
BackoffLimit	10 (exponential number)
JamSize	32–48 bits (4 bytes)
MaxFrameSize	12144 bits (1518 bytes)
MinFrameSize	512 bits (64 bytes)
AddressSize	48 bits (6 bytes)

100BaseT FLPs

100BaseT uses fast link pulses, or FLPs, to check the link integrity between the hub and the 100BaseT device. FLPs are backward compatible with 10BaseT normal-link pulses (NLPs). FLPs contain more information than NLPs, and are used in the autonegotiation process between a hub and a network device on a 100BaseT network.

100BaseT Autonegotiation

100BaseT networks support autonegotiation as an optional feature. Autonegotiation enables a network device and a hub to exchange information (using 100BaseT FLPs) about their capabilities.

Autonegotiation supports a number of capabilities:

- Speed matching for network devices that support both 10 and 100 Mbps operation
- Full-duplex operation mode for network devices capable of supporting this mode
- Automatic signaling configuration for 100BaseT4 and 100BaseTX network hosts

Autonegotiation functions by proceeding through a list of supported configurations, each called a *level*. Table 3-10 shows the order of these autonegotiation levels, starting with number level nine (the first level attempted in the autonegotiation process).

Table 3-10   *Ethernet Autonegotiation Options*

Level	Operational Mode	Maximum Total Data Transfer Rate
9	1000BaseT full-duplex	2000 Mbps
8	1000BaseT half-duplex	1000 Mbps
7	100BaseT2 full-duplex	200 Mbps
6	100BaseTX full-duplex	200 Mbps
5	100BaseT2 half-duplex	100 Mbps
4	100BaseT4 half-duplex	100 Mbps
3	100BaseTX half-duplex	100 Mbps
2	10BaseT full-duplex	20 Mbps
1	10BaseT half-duplex	10 Mbps

100BaseT Media Types

Three media types are supported by 100BaseT at the OSI physical layer (Layer 1), as shown in Table 3-11.

- 100BaseTX—Based on the ANSI Twisted Pair-Physical Medium Dependent (TP-PMD) specification. The ANSI TP-PMD supports UTP and STP cabling. 100BaseTX uses the 100BaseX signaling scheme over 2-pair Category 5 UTP or STP cabling.

  The IEEE 802.3u specification for 100BaseTX networks allows a maximum of two repeater, or hub, networks and a total network diameter of approximately 200 m. A link segment, defined as a point-to-point connection between two Medium Independent Interface (MII) devices, can be up to 100 m.

- 100BaseFX—Based on the ANSI TP-PMD X3T9.5 specification for FDDI LANs. (FDDI LANs will be discussed in detail in Chapter 7, "FDDI.") 100BaseFX uses the 100BaseX signaling scheme over two-strand multimode fiber-optic (MMF) cable. The IEEE 802.3u specification for 100BaseFX networks allows DTE-to-DTE links of approximately 400 m, or one repeater network of approximately 400 m in length.

- 100BaseT4—Allows 100BaseT to run over existing Category 3 wiring, provided that all four pairs of cabling are installed to the desktop. 100BaseT4 uses the half-duplex 4T+ signaling scheme. The IEEE 802.3u specification for 100BaseT4 networks allows a maximum of two repeater, or hub, networks and a total network diameter of approximately 200 m. A link segment, defined as a point-to-point connection between two Medium Independent Interface (MII) devices, can be up to 100 m.

Table 3-11   *100BaseT Media Type Characteristics*

Characteristics	100BaseTX	100BaseFX	100BaseT4
Cable	Cat 5 UTP, or Types 1 and 2 STP	62.5/125 micron MMF	Cat 3, 4, or 5 UTP
Number of pairs or strands	2 pairs	2 strands	4 pairs
Connector	ISO 8877 (RJ-45)	Duplex media-interface connector (MIC)	ISO 8877 (RJ-45)
Maximum segment length	100 m	400 m	100 m
Maximum network diameter	200 m	400 m	200 m

Fast Ethernet Applications

Fast Ethernet is most often deployed to the desktop in large organizations with multimedia, CAD/CAM, or large data requirements, such as database updates. Fast Ethernet is also found in smaller data center implementations to provide faster access to server farms and other storage devices.

Fast Ethernet can also be deployed in Inter-Switch Link (ISL) implementations, where single (100 Mbps) or multiple (up to 800 Mbps) Fast Ethernet channels can be bundled to provide backbone trunking between 10/100 Mbps Ethernet switches.

100VG-AnyLAN

HP developed 100VG-AnyLAN as an alternative to CSMA/CD for newer time-sensitive applications, such as multimedia. The access method is based on host demand and was designed as an upgrade path from Ethernet and 16 Mbps Token Ring. 100VG-AnyLAN supports four cable types:

- 4-pair Category 3 UTP
- 2-pair Category 4 or 5 UTP
- STP
- Fiber optic

The IEEE 802.12 100VG-AnyLAN standard specifies the link-distance limitations, hub-configuration limitations, and maximum network-distance limitations.

Figure 3-12 illustrates the link distance limitations. Link distances from node-to-hub are 100 m (Cat 3 UTP) or 150 m (Cat 5 UTP).

Figure 3-12 *100VG-AnyLAN Distance Limitations*

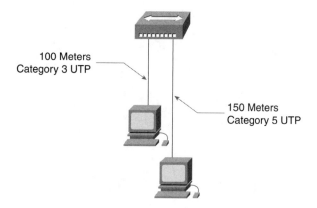

100VG-AnyLAN hubs are arranged in a hierarchical fashion, as shown in Figure 3-13. Each hub has at least one uplink port, and every other port can be a downlink port. Hubs can be cascaded three-deep if uplinked to other hubs, and cascaded hubs can be 100 m apart (Cat 3 UTP) or 150 m apart (Cat 5 UTP).

Figure 3-13 *100VG-AnyLAN Hierarchy*

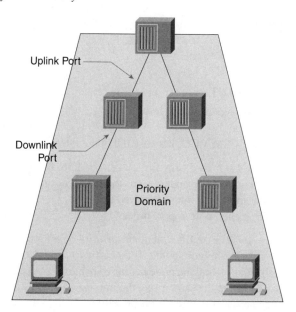

In Figure 3-14, end-to-end network-distance limitations are 600 m (Cat 3 UTP) or 900 m (Cat 5 UTP). If hubs are located in the same wiring closet, end-to-end distances shrink to 200 m (Cat 3 UTP) and 300 m (Cat 5 UTP).

Figure 3-14 *100VG-AnyLAN End-to-End Distance Limitations*

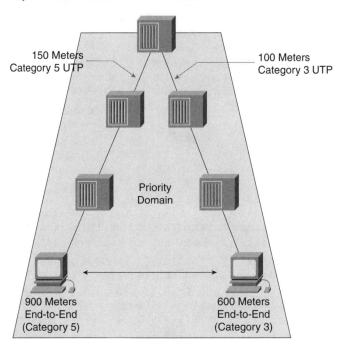

100VG-AnyLAN Operation

100Vg-AnyLAN uses a demand-priority access method that eliminates collisions and can, therefore, be more heavily loaded than 100BaseT. The demand-priority access method is deterministic, unlike CSMA/CD, because the hub controls access to the network.

The 100Vg-AnyLAN standard calls for a level-one hub, or repeater, that acts as the root. This root repeater controls the operation of the priority domain. Hubs can be cascaded three-deep in a star topology. Interconnected hubs act as a single large repeater, with the root repeater polling each port in port order.

In general, under 100VG-AnyLAN demand-priority operation, a node wanting to transmit signals its request to the hub or switch. If the network is idle, the hub immediately acknowledges the request and the node begins transmitting a packet to the hub. If more than one request is received at the same time, the hub uses a round-robin technique to acknowledge each request in turn. High-priority requests, such as time-sensitive videoconferencing applications, are serviced ahead of normal-priority requests. To ensure fairness to all hosts, a hub does not grant priority access to a port more than twice in a row.

100VG-AnyLAN supports a network diameter of up to 4,000 m, versus the 2,500 m supported by 10BaseT and the 200 to 370 m supported by 100BaseT. 100VG-AnyLAN supports both IEEE 802.3 and IEEE 802.5 frame formats.

100VG-AnyLAN Applications

100VG-AnyLAN's chief benefit is as a migration point while upgrading to a higher transmission speed, as well as a single network infrastructure supporting both Ethernet (IEEE 802.3) and Token Ring (IEEE 802.5) frame formats.

100VG-AnyLAN is a collision-free domain, supporting easier migration to ATM LAN emulated network implementations.

1000 Mbps, or Gigabit (Gbps) Ethernet

The IEEE ratified the Gigabit Ethernet standard in 1998 as IEEE 802.3z. Gigabit Ethernet is much like Fast Ethernet with an extra zero added.

Gigabit Ethernet uses the same 802.3 frame format as that of 10 Mbps and 100 Mbps Ethernet and operates in the same half- or full-duplex modes. When small frames are transmitted in a half-duplex environment, many carrier extension bits will be added. This environment makes Gigabit Ethernet inefficient for small frames because large amounts of useless carrier extension bits are transmitted.

Suppose a host was to transmit only 64-byte minimum size frames. The carrier extension would add 438 bytes to meet the specification of a 512-byte slot time. To calculate the overall efficiency, the interframe gap (IFG) overhead of 12 bytes is added, yielding the following equation and result: $64/(512+12)=12\%$ efficiency, or 122 Mbps, marginally better than a Fast Ethernet implementation.

Small frames are quite common, so this issue was addressed by the IEEE 802.3z standard with the implementation of *burst mode* in the Gigabit Ethernet MAC adapter.

Burst Mode

Burst mode is a change to the Ethernet CSMA/CD transmission specification for gigabit operation. Burst mode is a feature that allows a MAC adapter to send a short sequence, or burst, of frames equal to approximately 5.4 maximum-length frames (8192 bytes of data) without having to relinquish control of the medium. The transmitting MAC adapter fills each interframe interval with extension bits so that other hosts on the network will see that the network is busy and will not attempt transmission during the burst until the sending host is finished.

If the length of the frame is less than the minimum frame length, an extension field is added to extend the frame length to the values indicated in Table 3-12. Subsequent frames in a frame-burst sequence do not need extension fields, and a frame burst might continue as long as the burst limit has not been reached. If the burst limit is reached after a frame transmission has begun, transmission is allowed to continue until the entire frame has been sent.

Table 3-12 *Gigabit Ethernet Parameters*

Parameter	Gigabit Ethernet/802.3z
SlotTime	4096 bit times (4.096 microseconds)
Minimum InterFrameGap	96 bit times (9.6 microseconds)
AttemptLimit	16
BackoffLimit	10 (exponential number)
JamSize	32-48 bits (4 bytes)
MaxFrameSize	12144 bits (1518 bytes)
MinFrameSize	512 bits (64 bytes)
AddressSize	48 bits (6 bytes)

NOTE   Frame extension fields are not defined, and burst mode is not allowed for 10 Mbps and 100 Mbps transmission rates.

Gigabit Ethernet CSMA/CD

The Gigabit Ethernet MAC adapter uses the same Ethernet MAC algorithm, operating at 10 times the speed of 100BaseT. Running Gigabit Ethernet created some challenges for CSMA/CD implementation. To make CSMA/CD work at 1 GHz (Gbps), a minor modification to the slot time was required. The slot time was increased from 512 bits (64 bytes) for 10/100 Mbps to 4096 bits (512 bytes) for 1000 Mbps.

NOTE   The slot time is the allocated time during which the complete frame needs to be transmitted. During the slot time, the transmitter retains control of the media.

In a Gigabit Ethernet implementation (refer to Table 3-12), if the transmitted frame is smaller than 512 bytes, an extra carrier extension is added. The carrier extension is added at the end of the completed frame to make it meet the new slot time of 512 bytes.

1000 Mbps, or 1 Gbps Ethernet Applications

Gigabit Ethernet is most often deployed to the desktop in larger organizations with multimedia, CAD/CAM, or large data requirements, such as database updates, where Fast Ethernet will not provide enough bandwidth. Gigabit Ethernet is also found in larger data center implementations to provide faster access to server farms and other storage devices.

Gigabit Ethernet can also be deployed in Inter-Switch Link (ISL) implementations where Gigabit Ethernet channels of 2 Gbps to 8 Gbps can be bundled to provide backbone trunking between 10/100 Mbps Ethernet switches.

10 Gbps, or 10 Gigabit Ethernet

10 Gigabit Ethernet uses the IEEE 802.3 Ethernet MAC protocol, frame format, and frame size. In short, 10 Gigabit Ethernet is still Ethernet. 10 Gigabit Ethernet is full-duplex only, operating like full-duplex Fast Ethernet and Gigabit Ethernet; therefore, 10 Gigabit Ethernet has no additional inherent distance limitations.

The IEEE 802.3ae Task Force, a subcommittee of the larger 802.3 Ethernet Working Group, is currently developing 10 Gigabit Ethernet. As of this writing, a 10 Gigabit Ethernet standard is expected to be completed as of March 2002.

10 Gigabit Ethernet enables Ethernet to match the speed of the fastest WAN backbone technology today, OC-192. (OC-192 runs at approximately 9.5 Gbps.)

NOTE   CyOptics Inc., a semiconductor firm in Los Angeles, has developed a chip that supports OC-768 (40 Gbps) networks.

The IEEE 802.3ae 10 Gigabit Ethernet Task Force has specified an optional interface that delivers Ethernet data at a rate compatible with SONET/SDH. This WAN physical layer (PHY) interface enables the attachment of packet-based IP/Ethernet switches to SONET/SDH access equipment.

The 10 Gigabit Ethernet Alliance supports the standards set forth by the 10 Gigabit Ethernet Task Force. This Alliance was formed February 8, 2000 and comprises Cisco, 3Com, Extreme Networks, Intel, Nortel Networks, Sun Microsystems, and World Wide Packets. The Alliance's mission is to promote 10 Gigabit Ethernet for LAN, MAN, and WAN implementations.

Because the 10 Gigabit Ethernet standard is still Ethernet, it requires no change to the Ethernet MAC protocol or frame format. 10 Gigabit Ethernet supports all upper-layer services. These services include all of the Cisco Intelligent Network Services that operate at OSI Layers 2 and 3 and higher, including high availability, Multiprotocol label switching (MPLS), quality of service (QoS) including voice over IP (VoIP) services, security and policy enforcement, server load balancing (SLB), and Web caching. 10 Gigabit Ethernet will support all standard Layer 2 functions including 802.1p, 802.1q (VLANs), EtherChannel, and spanning tree.

10 Gigabit Ethernet Applications

10 Gigabit Ethernet has applications across local-area networks (LANs), metropolitan-area networks (MANs), and wide-area networks (WANs).

LAN Applications

10 Gigabit Ethernet would serve well in the following network environments:

- Server interconnect for clusters of servers
- Aggregation of multiple 1000BaseX or 1000BaseT segments into 10 Gigabit Ethernet links
- Switch-to-switch links for very high-speed connections between switches in the same data center, in an enterprise backbone, or in different buildings

The cable medium supporting 10 Gigabit Ethernet in a LAN environment will be single-mode fiber (SMF), FDDI-grade multimode fiber, or the new higher-bandwidth multimode fiber (MMF) (see Figure 3-15).

Figure 3-15 *10-Gigabit Ethernet LAN Application*

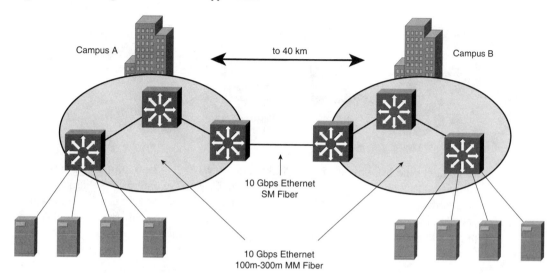

10 Gigabit Ethernet will most likely be found in service provider and enterprise data centers and LANs. It is anticipated that network managers will initially deploy 10 Gigabit Ethernet to provide high-speed interconnection between large-capacity switches inside the data center or computer room, or between buildings in a campus environment. As bandwidth needs increases, 10 Gigabit Ethernet will most likely be deployed throughout the entire LAN, including switch-to-server and MAN and WAN access applications.

MAN Applications

The Gigabit Ethernet space has seen significant growth in the deployment of long-distance Gigabit Ethernet using long wavelength optics (1000BaseLX and 1000BaseZX) on dark fiber links. Cisco helps customers build these links, ranging up to 100 km, with the use of pluggable transceivers called *gigabit interface converters,* or GBICs.

10 Gigabit Ethernet will likely be deployed in MAN applications, as shown in Figure 3-16, over *dark fiber*, dark wavelength, and as a fundamental transport for facility services. *Dark fiber* refers to unused single-mode fiber (SMF) capacity from fiber that has been installed for long-distance applications that usually reach up to 100 km without amplifiers or optical repeaters. This fiber is not "lit," meaning that it is not carrying traffic and it is not terminated.

Figure 3-16 *10-Gigabit Ethernet MAN Application*

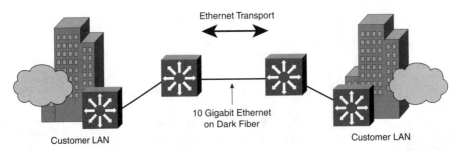

10 Gigabit Ethernet will be a natural fit with dense wave division multiplexing (DWDM) equipment as more DWDM-based systems are deployed. For enterprise solutions, 10 Gigabit Ethernet services over DWDM will enable serverless buildings, remote backup, and disaster recovery. For service provider solutions, 10 Gigabit Ethernet will enable the provisioning of dark wavelength gigabit services to customers at a competitive cost structure.

NOTE   Dark wavelength, or dark lambda, refers to unused capacity on a DWDM system.

WAN Applications

10 Gigabit Ethernet WAN applications look similar to MAN applications because they also support dark fiber, dark wavelength, and SONET infrastructures (see Figure 3-17). Multilayer switches and terabit routers will be attached via 10 Gigabit Ethernet to the SONET optical network, which includes add drop multiplexers (ADMs) and DWDM devices. When dark wavelengths are available, 10 Gigabit Ethernet can be transmitted directly across the optical infrastructure, reaching distances from 70 to 100 km.

NOTE   SONET is the dominant transport protocol in the WAN backbone today and most MAN service offerings supporting SONET OC-3 (155 Mbps) or OC-12 (622 Mbps).

Figure 3-17 *10-Gigabit Ethernet WAN Application*

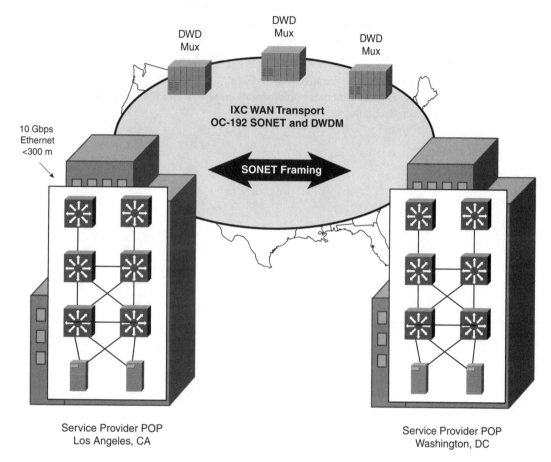

Summary

The term *Ethernet* refers to the family of local-area networks (LANs) standardized by the IEEE 802.3 Working Group. This standard also defines what is commonly known as the CSMA/CD (Carrier Sense Multiple Access with Collision Detect) protocol.

Ethernet is a broad term in its own right. It has several subsets ranging from 10Base2 (10 Mbps Ethernet with a maximum segment length of 185 meters over thin coaxial cable) to 1000BaseT (1000 Mbps Ethernet or Gigabit Ethernet with a maximum segment length in excess of 500 m over fiber-optic cable). Anticipated in Spring 2002 is the standardization of 10-Gigabit Ethernet, supporting distances up to 40 km over single-mode fiber.

Ethernet started off as a shared-media technology, using repeaters to increase network size. As Ethernet speeds have increased, the network diameter has shrunk proportionately. Whereas 10 Mbps Ethernet supports up to four repeater hops, 100 Mbps (Fast) Ethernet supports only one or two repeater hops. Gigabit Ethernet had to be modified a bit by the use of carrier extensions in the frame to make one repeater hop possible.

Over time, especially with the advent of 10 Gigabit Ethernet, the CSMA/CD algorithm will be utilized less as more Ethernet implementations will utilize the full-duplex features with LAN switching technology.

CHAPTER 4

Ethernet Documentation

Chapter 3, "Ethernet/IEEE 802.3," discussed the underlying technology for Ethernet LAN networks; this chapter will discuss some recommendations and guidelines to follow to document an Ethernet network.

Most networking discussions today include the topic of documentation at some point, whether the mention is a statement advising that you should document your network assets or a statement advising that network documentation is a good tool to have when troubleshooting a network issue. The challenge here is what network information should be documented and later reviewed and analyzed for any potential network-related issues.

Network documentation should be both easy to complete and easy to understand. In an effort to make the network documentation process easier to manage for Ethernet LAN implementations, templates have been prepared and presented here for use. These templates are preceded by relevant console commands, a case study, and a sample completed template serving as a guide.

NOTE

The templates presented here are also available for download from the Cisco Press Web site (www.ciscopress.com/1587050390).

An introduction or case study precedes each template, with suggestions regarding template completion. These templates are not all encompassing, nor are they designed to be. Rather, these templates are designed to help the consultant, engineer, or anyone involved with a network gather the vital information pertaining to a network and its related segments.

Case Study: Naming Conventions

A naming convention, or scheme, that is easy to use should be employed in any network for which you are responsible. A naming convention should scale with the network as it grows. The purpose behind a naming convention is to make network documentation easier to prepare, and assist with network maintenance and troubleshooting. For example, a network engineer new to the company's operations would be able to easily recognize the function and purpose of a device so named HQ_7500Router_WAN rather than the same device referred to as Sprint Router.

A good naming scheme would incorporate the geographic location of the device. Use the following design:

Geographic location_Network Device Division or Segment_Miscellaneous Identifier

For example, a switch located at an organization's corporate headquarters could be named in one of the following fashions:

- Chicago_Switch
- HQ_Switch

This reflects a network switch located at corporate headquarters, in this case located in Chicago, Illinois.

A network device being used by a particular division or building floor might use the following scheme:

- Chicago_Switch_Marketing
- HQ_Switch_IT
- Dallas_5509_Floor4 (Dallas_5509_4thFloor)

The *Miscellaneous Identifier* gives flexibility in identifying the network device in question.

For example, NewYork_Router_IT_Backup, clearly identifies where and what the network device in question is (Router in New York), the network segment (IT), and the devices function (Backup).

A naming convention should be easy and comfortable to use, and a single naming convention cannot work with every network. These are examples of what can be called a "generic" convention, but one that certainly is useful and flexible. If you have found a different scheme that works, then please continue to use it. The idea is that if someone else looks at your network documentation, that person can easily determine the topology.

This same naming convention can be globally deployed and supported across the organization by the use of a domain name server (DNS). By deploying the naming scheme across the domain with DNS, administration and inventory are easier to manage. Troubleshooting is also facilitated in a more manageable fashion than without the use of naming.

For example, the following *trace route* command would not be of much help to an engineer without the names (unless the engineer was fortunate to know to which device each network address was assigned):

```
1    WashingtonDC.MCIRouter.Engineering [207.69.220.81]
2    cisco-f0-1-0.norva3.mindspring.net [207.69.220.65]
3    s10-0-1.vienna1-cr3.bbnplanet.net [4.1.5.237]
4    p4-2.vienna1-nbr2.bbnplanet.net [4.0.1.133]
5    p4-0.washdc3-br2.bbnplanet.net [4.0.1.97]
6    p3-0.washdc3-br1.bbnplanet.net [4.24.4.145]
7    p2-0.chcgil1-br2.bbnplanet.net [4.24.6.93]
8    p4-0.chcgil1-br1.bbnplanet.net [4.24.5.225]
9    so-4-1-0.chcgil2-br1.bbnplanet.net [4.24.9.69]
10   p1-0.chcgil2-cr11.bbnplanet.net [4.24.6.22]
11   p7-1.paloalto-nbr1.bbnplanet.net [4.24.6.98]
12   p1-0.paloalto-cr1.bbnplanet.net [4.0.6.74]
13   h1-0.cisco.bbnplanet.net [4.1.142.238]
14   pigpen.cisco.com [192.31.7.9]
15   www.cisco.com [198.133.219.25]
```

Small Ethernet (Hub-Based) Networks

Hub-based networks are generally found in the Small Office/Home Office (SOHO) environment. Generally, these networks have a central 10/100 megabits per second (Mbps) hub interconnecting workstations, servers, and printers. For connectivity to an external network, such as the Internet, a wide-area network (WAN) device, such as a router or modem (for example, ISDN, xDSL, and cable modem), is attached to this central hub.

Figure 4-1 illustrates a basic SOHO Ethernet LAN implementation.

Figure 4-1 *Basic SOHO Ethernet (Hub-Based) LAN*

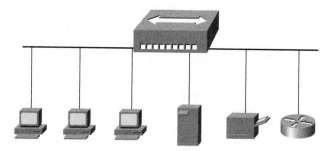

The following IOS commands might be used to collect Ethernet LAN information.

Commands

Following are the relevant router commands (for the Cisco 2505, 2507, or 2516) used to gather the necessary information. Keep in mind there are other commands that can provide this same information, such as **show config**.

show hub

The **show hub** command is used to display information about the built-in hub on an
Ethernet interface of a Cisco 2505, Cisco 2507, or Cisco 2516.

```
show hub [ether number [port [end-port]]]
```

Syntax Description:

ether—(Optional) Indication that this is an Ethernet hub.

number—(Optional) Hub number, starting with 0. Since there is currently only one hub,
this number is 0.

port—(Optional) Port number on the hub. On the Cisco 2505, port numbers range from 1
through 8. On the Cisco 2507, port numbers range from 1 through 16. On the Cisco 2516,
Ethernet ports number 1 to 14. If a second port number follows, then this port number
indicates the beginning of a port range.

end-port—(Optional) Ending port number of a range.

The following is sample output from the **show hub** command for hub 0, port 2 only:

```
Router# show hub ethernet 0 2
Port 2 of 16 is administratively down, link state is down
0 packets input, 0 bytes
0 errors with 0 collisions
(0 FCS, 0 alignment, 0 too long,
0 short, 0 runts, 0 late,
0 very long, 0 rate mismatches)
0 auto partitions, last source address (none)
Last clearing of "show hub" counters never
Repeater information (Connected to Ethernet0)
2792429 bytes seen with 18 collisions, 1 hub resets
Version/device ID 0/1 (0/1)
Last clearing of "show hub" counters never
```

The following is sample output from the **show hub** command for hub 0, all ports:

```
Router# show hub ethernet 0
Port 1 of 16 is administratively down, link state is up
2458 packets input, 181443 bytes
3 errors with 18 collisions
(0 FCS, 0 alignment, 0 too long,
0 short, 3 runts, 0 late,
0 very long, 0 rate mismatches)
0 auto partitions, last source address was 0000.0cff.e257
Last clearing of "show hub" counters never
.
.
.
```

```
Port 16 of 16 is down, link state is down
0 packets input, 0 bytes
0 errors with 0 collisions
(0 FCS, 0 alignment, 0 too long,
0 short, 0 runts, 0 late,
0 very long, 0 rate mismatches)
0 auto partitions, last source address (none)
Last clearing of "show hub" counters never
Repeater information (Connected to Ethernet0)
2792429 bytes seen with 18 collisions, 1 hub resets
Version/device ID 0/1 (0/1)
Last clearing of "show hub" counters never
Internal Port (Connected to Ethernet0)
36792 packets input, 4349525 bytes
0 errors with 14 collisions
(0 FCS, 0 alignment, 0 too long,
0 short, 0 runts, 0 late,
0 very long, 0 rate mismatches)
0 auto partitions, last source address (none)
Last clearing of "show hub" counters never
```

Documentation Case Study

Figure 4-2 depicts a LAN with three fixed workstations, a file server, a network printer, and a router for WAN connectivity. This network is used to support a small sales office with about 10 users.

Figure 4-2   *Small Ethernet Hub Network (Example)*

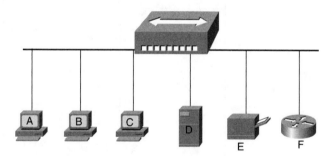

This network is used to demonstrate the following documentation template for a small Ethernet (hub) network.

Table 4-1 *Ethernet Documentation Template for Hubbed Segments [Example]*

Organization:	Sales		
LAN Segment Name:	Sales_Cincy		
LAN Segment Description:	Cincinnati Office (Remote)		
LAN Backbone Speed [10/100 Mbps]:	10 Mbps		
Hub Device [Vendor and Model]:	Cisco 1524 M	**Mgmt Address:**	
Number of Users:	10	**Primary Network Apps:**	E-Mail, Intranet, WWW
ID	**Host Name**	**MAC Address**	**Network Address**	**Description**
---	---	---	---	---
A	LocalUser_1	00-00-86-5c-7a-3a	10.124.173.25/24	Workstation
B	LocalUser_2	00-aa-00-62-c6-09	10.124.173.26/24	Workstation
C	LocalUser_3		10.124.173.27/24	
D	Sales_Server		10.124.173.10/24	File Server
E	LAN_Printer		10.124.173.242/24	Network Printer
F	Cincy_Router	00-aa-84-51-a3-07	10.124.173.2/24	WAN Router
G				
H				
I				
J				
K				
L				
M				
N				
O				
P				
Q				
R				
S				
T				

Notes: Any miscellaneous information pertaining to the network environment, such as users, pending changes, and so on would be entered here.

NOTE Not every field requires completion as long as the document reader is able to ascertain the topology, components, and function of the network.

- Organization—The organization(s) that this LAN segment supports
- LAN Segment Name—A unique identifying name for this LAN segment.
- LAN Segment Description—The purpose of this LAN segment
- LAN Backbone Speed [10/100]—10 Mbps or 100 Mbps
- Hub Device [Vendor and Model]—Not necessary, but useful if vendors' technical support organization assistance is needed
- Management Address—Used if the hub is capable of being remotely managed.
- Number of Users—The total number of users on the segment; identified as active, inactive, or both.
- Primary Network Apps—The applications that this segment primarily supports
- ID—An alpha-character ID used to easily identify a network device. This ID can also serve as a reference point for network review and analysis.
- Host Name—It is recommended that you use a unique name, although it is not necessary. The advantages of a unique host name are that the features and advantages of DNS implementation can be realized.
- MAC Address—This is the OSI Layer 2 physical address of the device. This address is useful for network troubleshooting, but is not necessary if the Network Address is known.
- Network Address—This is the OSI Layer 3 logical (network) address of the device. This address is useful for network troubleshooting, but is not necessary if the MAC Address is known.
- Description—This is a miscellaneous field used for descriptive or other comments regarding the device. This field could be optional but is worth using because any information makes for more efficient network management and planning.

NOTE The Network Addressing scheme is dependent on the network protocol in use, such as the TCP/IP suite, Novell's IPX implementation, or Apple Computer's AppleTalk implementation.

Table 4-2 *Ethernet Documentation Template for Hubbed Segments*

Organization:				
LAN Segment Name:				
LAN Segment Description:				
LAN Backbone Speed [10/100 Mbps]:				
Hub Device [Vendor and Model]:		Mgmt Address:		
Number of Users:		Primary Network Apps:		

ID	Host Name	MAC Address	Network Address	Description
A				
B				
C				
D				
E				
F				
G				
H				
I				
J				
K				
L				
M				
N				
O				
P				
Q				
R				
S				
T				
Notes:				

Small Ethernet (Bridge-Based) Networks

Bridge-based networks are generally found in the SOHO and medium-sized networking environments. Generally these networks have a central 10/100 Mbps bridge interconnecting workstations, servers, and printers. For connectivity to an external network, such as the Internet, a wide-area network (WAN) device, such as a router or modem (for example, ISDN, xDSL, or cable modem) is attached to this central bridge. Bridges are often deployed when it is necessary for the LAN to span a greater distance than what would normally be supported by a hub, although the deployment of repeaters is more cost effective. Bridges also provide separation of collision domains by filtering and forwarding data traffic based on the MAC address.

Figure 4-3 illustrates a basic Ethernet LAN implementation utilizing a bridge for interconnectivity.

Figure 4-3 *Basic Ethernet (Bridge-Based) LAN*

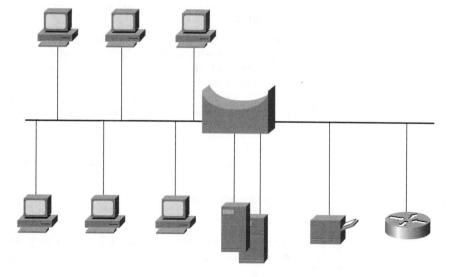

Commands

Following is the relevant router command used to gather the necessary information. Keep in mind there are other commands that can provide this same information, such as **show config**.

show bridge

The Cisco router command **show bridge** provides interface and subinterface information
(if applicable) of each MAC address available.

For example, the **show bridge** command on the router would yield the following output,
and would be described as shown in Table 4-3.

```
Total of 300 station blocks, 280 free
Codes: P - permanent, S - self

Bridge Group 32:Bridge Group 32:

        Address      Action   Interface      Age   RX count   TX count
    0180.c200.0000   forward  Ethernet1/1     S        0          0
    ffff.ffff.ffff   forward  Ethernet1/1     S        0          0
    0900.2b01.0001   forward  Ethernet1/1     S        0          0
    0300.0c00.0001   forward  Ethernet1/1     S        0          0
    0000.0c05.1000   forward  Ethernet1/1     4        1          0
```

Table 4-3   *show bridge Field Descriptions*

Field	Description
Total of 300 station blocks	Total number of forwarding database elements in the system. The memory to hold bridge entries is allocated in blocks of memory sufficient to hold 300 individual entries. When the number of free entries falls below 25, another block of memory sufficient to hold another 300 entries is allocated. Therefore, the size of the bridge-forwarding database is limited to the amount of free memory in the router.
280free	Number in the free list of forwarding database elements in the system. The total number of forwarding elements is expanded dynamically, as needed.
Bridge Group	Bridging group to which the address belongs.
Address	Canonical (Ethernet ordered) MAC address.
Action	Action to be taken when that address is looked up; choices are to discard or forward the datagram.
Interface	Interface, if any, on which that address was seen.
Age	Number of minutes since a frame was received from or sent to that address. The letter "P" indicates a permanent entry. The letter "S" indicates the system as recorded by the router (self). On the modular systems, this is typically the broadcast address and the router's own hardware address; on the IGS, this field will also include certain multicast addresses.
RX count	Number of frames received from that address.
TX count	Number of frames forwarded to that address.

Documentation Case Study

Figure 4-4 depicts a LAN with six fixed workstations, two servers, a network printer, and a router for WAN connectivity. This network is used for a small enterprise full-time network operations center (NOC) located in Philadelphia, Pennsylvania with a staff of about 50 personnel. The bridge functions here are actually implemented in the Cisco 2611 router. To illustrate and document the logical topology, the routing and bridging functions have been separated.

Figure 4-4   *Ethernet Bridged Network (Example)*

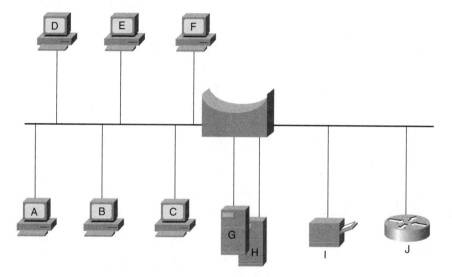

This network is used to demonstrate the documentation template for an Ethernet [transparent] bridged network.

Table 4-4   *Ethernet Documentation Template for Bridged Segments [Example]*

Organization:		Network Operations			
LAN Segment Name:		NOC_EastCoast			
LAN Segment Description:		East Coast NOC in Philadelphia, PA			
LAN Backbone Speed [10/100 Mbps]:		100 Mbps			
Hub Device [Vendor and Model]:		Cisco 2611	**Mgmt Address:**		10.142.16.1
Number of Users:		~50	**Primary Network Apps:**		E-Mail and SNMP Traffic
ID	**Port**	**Host Name**	**MAC Address**	**Network Address**	**Description**
A	1	NOC_WS1	00-31-0d-c1-f1-16	10.142.16.10/24	
B	2	NOC_WS2	00-37-00-e3-00-21	10.142.16.11/24	
C	3	NOC_WS3	00-41-00-ab-d1-f1	10.142.16.14/24	
D	6	NOC_SUPE1	00-31-0c-d1-f0-1c	10.142.16.17/24	
E	8	NOC_SUPE2	09-00-2b-01-00-01	10.142.16.22/24	NOC_SUPE1 Backup
F	9	NOC_WS4	03-00-0c-00-00-01	10.142.16.23/24	
G	4	NOC_MAILSVR	00-40-0b-b2-f4-00	10.142.16.15/24	E-mail Server
H	5	NOC_AGENTSVR	00-40-0b-d4-f1-0c	10.142.16.16/24	SNMP Agent Server
I	7	NOC_Printer	00-00-0c-05-10-00	10.142.16.43/24	Network Printer
J	10	NOC_WAN_Router	00-42-a1-31-ff-01	10.142.16.8/24	Interface E1
K					
L					
M					
. . .					
AD					
AE					
AF					
Notes: Any miscellaneous information pertaining to the network environment, such as users, pending changes, and so on would be entered here. Such as noted previously, the bridging functions in this network are implemented within the Cisco router.					

- Organization—The organization(s) that this LAN segment supports.
- LAN Segment Name—A unique identifying name for this LAN segment.
- LAN Segment Description—The purpose of this LAN segment.
- LAN Backbone Speed [10/100]—10 Mbps or 100 Mbps.
- Bridge Device [Vendor and Model]—Not necessary, but useful if vendors' technical support organization assistance is needed.
- Management Address—Used if the bridge is capable of being remotely managed.
- Number of Users—The total number of users on the segment; identified as active, inactive, or both.
- Primary Network Apps—The applications that this segment primarily supports.
- ID—An alpha-character ID used to easily identify a network device. This ID can also serve as a reference point for network review and analysis.
- Port—The bridge port ID. Although not necessary, this information can be useful for network troubleshooting.
- Host Name—It is recommended that this be a unique name, although it is not necessary. The advantage of a unique host name are the features and advantages of DNS implementation that can be realized.
- MAC Address—The OSI Layer 2 physical address of the device. This address is useful for network troubleshooting, but is not necessary if the Network Address is known.
- Network Address—This is the OSI Layer 3 logical (network) address of the device. This address is useful for network troubleshooting, but is not necessary if the MAC Address is known.
- Description—This is a miscellaneous field used for descriptive or other comments regarding the device. This field could be optional but is worth using because any information makes for more efficient network management and planning.

NOTE   The Network Addressing scheme is dependent on the network protocol in use, such as the TCP/IP suite, Novell's IPX implementation, or Apple Computer's AppleTalk implementation.

Table 4-5   *Ethernet Documentation Template for Bridged Segments*

Organization:				
LAN Segment Name:				
LAN Segment Description:				
LAN Backbone Speed [10/100 Mbps]:				
Bridge Device [Vendor and Model]:		Mgmt Address:		
Number of Users:		Primary Network Apps:		

ID	Port	Host Name	MAC Address	Network Address	Description
A					
B					
C					
D					
E					
F					
G					
H					
I					
J					
K					
L					
M					
N					
O					
P					
Q					
R					
S					
T					

Notes:

Small Ethernet (Layer 2 Switch-Based) Networks

Layer 2 switch-based networks are generally found in the medium- and larger-sized networking environments. Generally, these networks have a central 10/100 Mbps or Gigabit switch interconnecting workstations, servers, and printers. For connectivity to an external network, such as the Internet, a wide-area network (WAN) device, such as a router or modem (for example, ISDN, xDSL, or cable modem) is attached to this central switch. Switches are often deployed when it is necessary for the LAN to break up a collision domain or to support multiple VLANs. Layer 2 switches provide separation of collision domains by filtering and forwarding data traffic based on the MAC address.

NOTE   Although Layer 3 switching uses routing principles, an external routing device, or, in some cases, a Route Switch Module (RSM), it is still necessary for routing between VLANs or WAN connectivity.

Figure 4-5 illustrates a basic Ethernet LAN implementation utilizing a Layer 2 switch for interconnectivity.

Figure 4-5   *Basic Ethernet (Switch-Based) LAN*

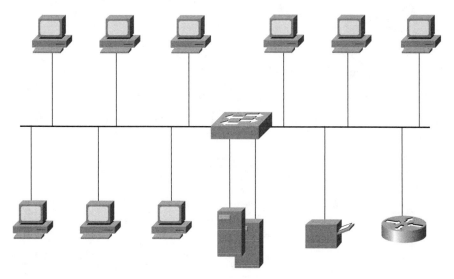

Commands

Following are the relevant switch commands used to gather the necessary information. Keep in mind that other commands can provide this same information, such as **show config**.

show module

The **show module** command is used to display module status and information.

The following example shows how to display module status and information:

```
Console> show module
Mod Module-Name            Ports Module-Type          Model    Serial-Num Status
--- -------------------- ----- -------------------- -------- --------- -------
1                          2     100BaseTX Supervisor WS-X2900 002477455 ok
2                          12    100BaseTX Ethernet   WS-X2902 002567322 ok


Mod MAC-Address(es)                              Hw     Fw     Sw
--- ------------------------------------------- ------ ------ ----------------
1   00-40-0b-b2-f4-00 thru 00-40-0b-b2-f7-ff  1.81   2.112  2.126
2   00-40-0b-d5-04-8c thru 00-40-0b-d5-04-97  1.4    1.2    2.126
```

show port

The **show port** command is used to display port status and counters:

```
show port
show port mod_num
show port mod_num/port_num
```

Syntax Description:

mod_num—The number of the module.

port_num—The number of the port on the module.

The following example shows how to display the status and counters for all ports on module 2:

```
Console> show port
Port Name                 Status     Vlan      Level  Duplex Speed Type
---- -------------------- ---------- --------- ------ ------ ----- -----------
1/1                        connected  trunk     normal half   100   100BaseTX
1/2                        notconnect 1         normal half   100   100BaseTX
2/1                        notconnect 1         normal half   100   100BaseTX
2/2                        notconnect 1         normal half   100   100BaseTX
2/3                        notconnect 1         normal half   100   100BaseTX
2/4                        notconnect 1         normal half   100   100BaseTX
2/5                        notconnect 1         normal half   100   100BaseTX
2/6                        notconnect 1         normal half   100   100BaseTX
2/7                        notconnect 1         normal half   100   100BaseTX
2/8                        notconnect 1         normal half   100   100BaseTX
2/9                        notconnect 1         normal half   100   100BaseTX
2/10                       notconnect 1         normal half   100   100BaseTX
2/11                       notconnect 1         normal half   100   100BaseTX
2/12                       notconnect 1         normal half   100   100BaseTX
Port Align-Err  FCS-Err    Xmit-Err   Rcv-Err
---- ---------- ---------- ---------- ----------
```

```
1/1        0         0         0          0
1/2        0         0         0          0
2/1        0         0         0          0
2/2        0         0         0          0
2/3        0         0         0          0
2/4        0         0         0          0
2/5        0         0         0          0
2/6        0         0         0          0
2/7        0         0         0          0
2/8        0         0         0          0
2/9        0         0         0          0
2/10       0         0         0          0
2/11       0         0         0          0
2/12       0         0         0          0
Port Single-Col Multi-Coll Late-Coll  Excess-Col Carri-Sens Runts      Giants
----  ---------- ---------- ---------- ---------- ---------- ---------- ----------
1/1        0         0         0          0          0         0          -
1/2        0         0         0          0          0         0          -
2/1        0         0         0          0          0         0          -
2/2        0         0         0          0          0         0          -
2/3        0         0         0          0          0         0          -
2/4        0         0         0          0          0         0          -
2/5        0         0         0          0          0         0          -
2/6        0         0         0          0          0         0          -
2/7        0         0         0          0          0         0          -
2/8        0         0         0          0          0         0          -
2/9        0         0         0          0          0         0          -
2/10       0         0         0          0          0         0          -
2/11       0         0         0          0          0         0          -
2/12       0         0         0          0          0         0          -
Last-Time-Cleared
- - - - - - - - - - - - - - - - - - - - - - - - -
Sun Apr 21 1996, 11:51:37
```

show spantree

The **show spantree** command is used to display spanning-tree information for a VLAN:

```
show spantree [ vlan ]
show spantree mod_num/port_num
```

Syntax Description:

Vlan—(Optional) The number of the VLAN. If the VLAN number is not specified, the default is VLAN 1.

Mod_num—The number of the module.

Port_num—The number of the port on the module.

The following example shows how to display the spantree syntax structure and options:

```
Console>  show spantree ?

Usage: show spantree [vlan]
       show spantree
```

The following example shows how to display the spantree configuration:

```
Console> (enable) show spantree 1
VLAN 1
Spanning tree enabled
Designated Root                  00-40-0b-ac-80-00
Designated Root Priority     32768
Designated Root Cost         10
Designated Root Port         1/1
Root Max Age    20 sec    Hello Time 2  sec   Forward Delay 15 sec
Bridge ID MAC ADDR           00-40-0b-b2-f4-00
Bridge ID Priority           32768
Bridge Max Age 20 sec    Hello Time 2  sec   Forward Delay 15 sec
Port     Vlan  Port-State      Cost   Priority Fast-Start
-------- ----  ------------    -----  -------- ----------
1/1      1     forwarding       10        32   disabled
1/2      1     not-connected    10        32   disabled
2/1      1     not-connected    10        32   disabled
2/2      1     not-connected    10        32   disabled
2/3      1     not-connected    10        32   disabled
2/4      1     not-connected    10        32   disabled
2/5      1     not-connected    10        32   disabled
2/6      1     not-connected    10        32   disabled
2/7      1     not-connected    10        32   disabled
2/8      1     not-connected    10        32   disabled
2/9      1     not-connected    10        32   disabled
2/10     1     not-connected    10        32   disabled
2/11     1     not-connected    10        32   disabled
2/12     1     not-connected    10        32   disabled
```

The following example shows how to display the spantree configuration for module 1, ports 1 and 2, and module 2, ports 1 through 4:

```
Console> show spantree 1/1-2,2/1-4
Port     Vlan  Port-State      Cost   Priority Fast-Start
-------- ----  ------------    -----  -------- ----------
1/1      1     forwarding       10        32   disabled
1/1      3     forwarding       10        32   disabled
1/1      44    forwarding       10        32   disabled
1/1      55    forwarding       10        32   disabled
1/1      66    not-connected    10        32   disabled
1/1      77    forwarding       10        32   disabled
1/1      88    not-connected    10        32   disabled
1/1      99    not-connected    10        32   disabled
1/2      1000  inactive         10        32   disabled
2/1      1000  inactive        100        32   disabled
2/2      1000  inactive        100        32   disabled
2/3      1     not-connected   100        32   disabled
2/4      1     not-connected   100        32   disabled
```

Documentation Case Study

The NOC in the previous case study has now expanded its mission from monitoring the East Coast enterprise network (WAN) to monitoring and managing the nationwide enterprise WAN. The new network consists of an Ethernet LAN with nine fixed workstations, two servers, a network printer, and a router for WAN connectivity. The number of personnel has increased from 50 to 100. The bridge has been replaced with a Cisco Catalyst 5509 10/100 Ethernet Switch, with the user workstations in one VLAN, the supervisor workstations in another VLAN, the file servers and printer in a third VLAN, and the WAN router in a fourth VLAN.

This network is used to demonstrate the documentation template for an Ethernet Layer-2 switched network.

Figure 4-6   *Ethernet Switched Network (Example)*

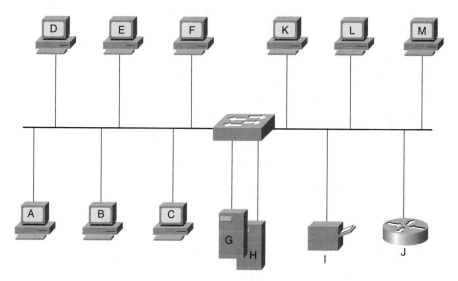

Table 4-6   *Ethernet Documentation Template for Switch Segments [Example]*

Organization:			Network Operations		
LAN Segment Name:			NOC_National		
LAN Segment Description:			National NOC in Philadelphia, PA		
LAN Backbone Speed [10/100 Mbps]:			100 Mbps		
Bridge Device [Vendor and Model]:			Catalyst 5509	**Mgmt Address:**	10.142.16.2
Number of Users:			100	**Primary Network Apps:**	E-Mail and SNMP Traffic

ID	Mod/ Port	Host Name	MAC Address	Network Address	VLAN	Description
A	1/ 1	NOC_WS1	00-31-0d-c1-f1-16	10.142.16.10/24	2	
B	1/ 2	NOC_WS2	00-37-00-e3-00-21	10.142.16.11/24	2	
C	1/ 3	NOC_WS3	00-41-00-ab-d1-f1	10.142.16.14/24	2	
D	1/ 4	NOC_SUPE1	00-31-0c-d1-f0-1c	10.142.16.17/24	50	
E	1/ 5	NOC_SUPE2	09-00-2b-01-00-01	10.142.16.22/24	50	NOC_SUPE1 Backup
F	1/ 6	NOC_WS4	03-00-0c-00-00-01	10.142.16.23/24	2	
G	2/ 2	NOC_MAILSVR	00-40-0b-b2-f4-00	10.142.16.15/24	85	E-Mail Server
H	2/ 3	NOC_AGENTSVR	00-40-0b-d4-f1-0c	10.142.16.16/24	85	SNMP Agent Server
I	2/ 4	NOC_Printer	00-00-0c-05-10-00	10.142.16.43/24	85	Network Printer
J	2/ 1	NOC_WAN_Router	00-42-a1-31-ff-01	10.142.16.8/24	100	Interface E1
K	2/ 5	NOC_WS5	05-22-f1-a0-d1-c1	10.142.16.121/24	2	
L	2/ 6	NOC_WS6	00-40-b1-c0-f1-36	10.142.16.143/24	2	
M	1/ 7	NOC_WS7	04-40-b0-d1-32-25	10.142.16.144/24	2	
.						
.						
.						
BJ						
BK						
BL						

Notes: Any miscellaneous information pertaining to the network environment, such as users, pending changes, and so on, would be entered here.

- Organization—The organization(s) that this LAN segment supports.
- LAN Segment Name—A unique identifying name for this LAN segment.
- LAN Segment Description—The purpose of this LAN segment.
- LAN Backbone Speed [10/100]—10 Mbps or 100 Mbps.
- Hub Device [Vendor and Model]—Not necessary, but useful if vendors' technical support organization assistance is needed.
- Management Address—Used if the switch is capable of being remotely managed.
- Number of Users—The total number of users on the segment; identified as active, inactive, or both.
- Primary Network Apps—The applications that this segment primarily support.
- ID—An alpha-character ID used to easily identify a network device. This ID can also serve as a reference point for network review and analysis.
- Port—The switch port ID that is usually annotated as "module/port"; for example, port 2/5 indicates module 2, port 5.
- Host Name—It is recommended that this be a unique name although it is not necessary. The advantages of a unique host name are the features and advantages that DNS implementation can be realized.
- MAC Address—The OSI Layer 2 physical address of the device. This address is necessary if any port level filtering or blocking is to be applied to the switch configuration.
- Network Address—The OSI Layer 3 logical (network) address of the device. This address is useful for network troubleshooting, but is not necessary if the MAC Address is known.
- VLAN—This is used to identify what VLAN this host is a member of. VLAN 1 is used for management purposes with regard to Catalyst Switches.
- Description—This is a miscellaneous field used for descriptive or other comments regarding the device. This field could be optional, but is worth using because any information makes for more efficient network management and planning.

NOTE   The Network Addressing scheme is dependent on the network protocol in use, such as the TCP/IP suite, Novell's IPX implementation, or Apple Computer's AppleTalk implementation.

Table 4-7 *Ethernet Documentation Template (Sample)*

Organization:							
LAN Segment Name:							
LAN Segment Description:							
LAN Backbone Speed [10/100 Mbps]:							
Bridge Device [Vendor and Model]:			Mgmt Address:				
Number of Users:			Primary Network Apps:				
ID	Mod/ Port	Host Name	MAC Address	Network Address	VLAN	Description	
A							
B							
C							
D							
E							
F							
G							
H							
I							
J							
K							
L							
M							
N							
O							
P							
Q							
R							
S							
T							
U							
Notes:							

Summary

Several network auto-discovery tools are available on the market today that can expedite the network discovery and documentation process. These tools generally use Simple Network Management Protocol (SNMP) implementations to collect and correlate network information for presentation.

Up-to-date documentation is paramount in troubleshooting any network issue. Due to a network troubleshooter's reliance on current documentation, the importance of keeping this documentation current cannot be stressed enough.

CHAPTER 5

Ethernet Network Review and Analysis

After an Ethernet network has been documented, the next step is to review the physical and logical topology for any performance-impacting issues.

The physical topology review ensures that the standards and practices for Ethernet and IEEE 802.3 networks, such as the "5-4-3" repeater rule and cable lengths, are followed.

The logical topology review looks at the "soft" side of the Ethernet network segment, analyzing traffic patterns, network thresholds, and possible network issues such as congestion.

This chapter examines the information provided by the Cisco router interface and the different types of errors that can be found on an Ethernet segment, what these errors indicate, and what corrective action might be required.

Cisco Router Interface Commands

The router interface commands discussed include the following:

- **show interfaces ethernet**
- **show buffers ethernet**
- **show processes cpu**

Each of these commands provides unique and useful information, which when combined, present a clear picture of how the network segment is performing.

show interfaces ethernet

show interfaces ethernet is entered from the privileged EXEC command interface on the Cisco router. It displays information about the specified Ethernet interface.

The syntax for this command is as follows:

> **show interface ethernet number**
>
> **show interface ethernet number accounting**

show interfaces ethernet number

Following is a sample of the output produced by this command:

```
Router# show interfaces ethernet 0

Ethernet 0 is up, line protocol is up
    Hardware is MCI Ethernet, address is aa00.0400.0134 (bia 0000.0c00.4369)
    Internet address is 131.108.1.1, subnet mask is 255.255.255.0
    MTU 1500 bytes, BW 10000 Kbit, DLY 1000 usec, rely 255/255, load 1/255
    Encapsulation ARPA, loopback not set, keepalive set (10 sec)
    ARP type: ARPA, PROBE, ARP Timeout 4:00:00
    Last input 0:00:00, output 0:00:00, output hang never
    Output queue 0/40, 0 drops; input queue 0/75, 2 drops
    Five minute input rate 61000 bits/sec, 4 packets/sec
    Five minute output rate 1000 bits/sec, 2 packets/sec
        2295197 packets input, 305539992 bytes, 0 no buffer
        Received 1925500 broadcasts, 0 runts, 0 giants
        3 input errors, 3 CRC, 0 frame, 0 overrun, 0 ignored, 0 abort
        0 input packets with dribble condition detected
        3594664 packets output, 436549843 bytes, 0 underruns
        8 output errors, 1790 collisions, 10 interface resets, 0 restarts
        0 output buffer failures, 0 output buffers swapped out
```

Table 5-1 explains each output field.

Table 5-1   *show interface ethernet Port Field Descriptions*

Field	Description
Ethernet is up	Indicates whether the interface hardware is currently active.
Ethernet is administratively down	Indicates whether an administrator has taken down the current active interface.
Ethernet is disabled	Indicates whether the router has received more than 5,000 errors in a (default) 10-second keepalive interval.
Line protocol is [up | down | administratively down]	Indicates whether the line protocol software processes believe the interface is usable or if an administrator has taken it down.
Hardware	Indicates the hardware type and (MAC) address.
Internet address	Indicates the configured Internet address and associated subnet mask.
MTU	Indicates the interface's maximum transmission unit (MTU).
BW	Indicates the interface's bandwidth in kilobits per second (kbps).
DLY	Indicates the interface's delay in microseconds.
Rely	Indicates the interface's reliability as a fraction of 255 (100 percent reliability is expressed as 255/255), calculated as an exponential average over 5 minutes.

Table 5-1   *show interface ethernet Port Field Descriptions*

Field	Description
Load	Indicates the interface's load as a fraction of 255 (255/255 is completely saturated), calculated as an exponential average over 5 minutes.
Encapsulation	Indicates the interface's assigned encapsulation method: • Ethernet version II (ARPA) • Novell-specific framing (Novell-ether) • Ethernet 802.3/802.2 without SNAP (sap) • Ethernet 802.3/802.2 with SNAP (snap)
ARP type	Indicates the type of assigned Address Resolution Protocol (ARP).
Loopback	Indicates whether loopback is set.
Keepalive	Indicates whether keepalives are set.
Last input	Indicates the number of hours, minutes, and seconds since the last packet was successfully received by an interface. This is useful for knowing when a dead interface failed.
Output	Indicates the number of hours, minutes, and seconds since the last packet was successfully transmitted by an interface. This is useful for knowing when a dead interface failed.
Output hang	Indicates the number of hours, minutes, and seconds (or never) since the interface was last reset because of a transmission that took too long. When the number of hours in any of the "last" fields exceeds 24 hours, the number of days and hours is printed. If that field overflows, asterisks are printed.
Last clearing	Indicates the time at which the counters that measure cumulative statistics (such as number of bytes transmitted and received) shown in this report were last reset to zero. Note that variables that might affect routing (for example, load and reliability) are not cleared when the counters are cleared. Asterisks indicate the elapsed time because the last counter clearing is too large to be displayed.
Output queue, input queue, drops	Indicates the number of packets in output and input queues. Each number is followed by a slash (/), the maximum size of the queue, and the number of packets dropped due to a full queue.

(continues)

Table 5-1 *show interface ethernet Port Field Descriptions (Continued)*

Field	Description
Five minute input rate, Five minute output rate	Indicates the average number of bits and packets transmitted per second in the past 5 minutes. If the interface is not in promiscuous mode, it senses the network traffic it sends and receives (rather than all network traffic).
	The 5-minute input and output rates should be used only as an approximation of traffic per second during a given 5-minute period. These rates are exponentially weighted averages with a time constant of 5 minutes.
Packets input	Indicates the total number of error-free packets received by the system.
Bytes input	Indicates the total number of bytes, including data and MAC encapsulation, in the error-free packets that are received by the system.
No buffers	Indicates the number of received packets that are discarded because the main system had no buffer space. Compare this with ignored count. Broadcast storms on Ethernet are often responsible for no input buffer events.
Received..broadcasts	Indicates the total number of broadcast or multicast packets received by the interface.
Runts	Indicates the total number of frames that are discarded because they are smaller than the medium's minimum frame size. Ethernet frames less than 64 bytes in length are considered runts.
Giants	Indicates the total number of frames that are discarded because they exceed the medium's maximum frame size. Ethernet frames greater than 1,518 bytes are considered giants.
Input error	Includes runts, giants, no buffer, CRC, frame, overrun, and ignored counts. Other input-related errors can also cause the input errors count to be increased, and some datagrams might have more than one error; therefore, this sum might not balance with the sum of enumerated input error counts.
CRC	Indicates that the cyclic redundancy checksum generated by the originating LAN host does not match the checksum calculated from the data received on the interface. On a LAN, this usually indicates noise, transmission problems on the LAN interface, or the LAN bus. A high number of CRCs is usually the result of collisions or a station transmitting bad data. CRC errors are generally indicative of a physical layer (OSI Layer 1) issue.

Table 5-1   *show interface ethernet Port Field Descriptions*

Field	Description
Frame	Indicates the number of frames received incorrectly that have a CRC error or a non-integer number of octets. On a LAN, this error usually results from collisions or a malfunctioning Ethernet device.
Overrun	Indicates the number of times that the receiver hardware was unable to hand received data to a hardware buffer because the input rate exceeded the receiver's ability to handle the data.
Ignored	Indicates the number of received frames that were ignored by the interface because the interface hardware ran low on internal buffers. These buffers are different from the system buffers mentioned previously in the buffer description. Broadcast storms and noise bursts can cause the ignored count to be increased.
Input packets with dribble condition detected	Indicates that a frame is slightly longer than expected for the media type. This frame error counter is incremented for informational purposes, as the router accepts the frame.
Packets output	Indicates the total number of packets that were transmitted by the system.
Bytes	Indicates the total number of bytes, including data and MAC encapsulation, that was transmitted by the system.
Underruns	Indicates the number of times that the transmitter has been running faster than the router can handle. This might never be reported on some interfaces.
Output errors	Indicates the sum of all errors that prevented the final transmission of datagrams out of the interface being examined. Note that this might not balance with the sum of the enumerated output errors. This is because some datagrams might have more than one error, and others might have errors that do not fall into any of the specifically tabulated categories.
Collisions	Indicates the number of frames retransmitted due to an Ethernet collision. Collisions are usually the result of an overextended LAN, such as an Ethernet or transceiver cable being too long, more than two repeaters being between hosts, or too many cascaded multiport repeaters. A frame that collides is counted only once in output packets. Collisions are also the likely result of layer 1 problems or duplex mismatch (in switched networks).

(continues)

Table 5-1 *show interface ethernet* Port Field Descriptions (Continued)

Field	Description
Interface resets	Indicates the number of times an interface has been completely reset. This can happen if frames queued for transmission were not sent within several seconds. Interface resets can also occur when an interface is looped back or shut down.
Restarts	Indicates the number of times that a Type 2 Ethernet controller was restarted because of errors.
Output buffer failures	Indicates the number of times that a frame was not output from the output hold queue because of a shortage of MEMD shared memory.
Output buffers swapped out	Indicates the number of frames that are stored in the main memory when the output queue is full. Swapping buffers to the main memory prevents frames from being dropped when output is congested. This number is high when traffic is bursty.

Some important "early warning" information can be obtained by the output displayed from the **show interface ethernet** *port* command.

The following output is used to demonstrate these early warning signs of potential network issues:

```
Ethernet 0 is up, line protocol is up
    Hardware is MCI Ethernet, address is aa00.0400.0134 (bia 0000.0c00.4369)
    Internet address is 131.108.1.1, subnet mask is 255.255.255.0
    MTU 1500 bytes, BW 10000 Kbit, DLY 1000 usec, rely 255/255, load 1/255
    Encapsulation ARPA, loopback not set, keepalive set (10 sec)
    ARP type: ARPA, PROBE, ARP Timeout 4:00:00
    Last input 0:00:00, output 0:00:00, output hang never
    Output queue 0/40, 0 drops; input queue 0/75, 2 drops
    Five minute input rate 61000 bits/sec, 4 packets/sec
    Five minute output rate 1000 bits/sec, 2 packets/sec
        2295197 packets input, 305539992 bytes, 0 no buffer
        Received 1925500 broadcasts, 0 runts, 0 giants
        3 input errors, 34215 CRC, 0 frame, 0 overrun, 0 ignored, 0 abort
        0 input packets with dribble condition detected
        3594664 packets output, 436549843 bytes, 0 underruns
        8 output errors, 1790 collisions, 10 interface resets, 0 restarts
        0 output buffer failures, 0 output buffers swapped out
```

CRC Errors

No segments should have more than one CRC error per million bytes of data, or 0.0001 percent CRC errors on each segment.

This can be represented by the following formula:

$$(CRCs / total bytes) \times 100 \leq 0.0001\%$$

NOTE   The term *CRCs* is often used for brevity when discussing CRC errors.

In the following code, the total amount of data is 742089835 bytes [Input Bytes (305539992) + Output Bytes (436549843) = Total Bytes (742089835)]. The total number of CRCs indicated is 34215.

```
.
.
 2295197 packets input, 305539992 bytes, 0 no buffer
 Received 1925500 broadcasts, 0 runts, 0 giants
 3 input errors, 34215 CRC, 0 frame, 0 overrun, 0 ignored, 0 abort
 0 input packets with dribble condition detected
 3594664 packets output, 436549843 bytes, 0 underruns
.
.
```

Using the previous formula, (CRCs / total bytes) $\times$ 100, you can determine the following:

$$(34215/742089835) \times 100 = 0.0046\%$$

This is an unacceptable amount of CRC errors because the total here (0.0046 percent) is greater than 0.0001 percent of all CRCs. An acceptable threshold would be 742 CRC errors (742,089,835 $\times$ 0.0001 percent = 742.089).

A case in which the number of CRC errors is high, but the number of collisions is not proportionately high, is usually an indication of excessive noise. In this case, the following actions should be taken:

1   Check the cables to determine whether any are damaged.

2   Look for badly spliced taps, causing reflections.

3   If using 100BaseTX, make sure Category 5 cabling is being used and not another type, such as Category 3.

Ethernet Collisions

On Ethernet segments, less than 0.1 percent of the frames that are identified as packets in the **show interface** output are collisions.

This can be represented by the following formula:

$$(Collisions / (Input packets + Output packets)) \times 100 \leq 0.1\%$$

The following code explains the output from Ethernet segments from the **show interface** command:

```
.
.
.
2295197 packets input, 305539992 bytes, 0 no buffer
Received 1925500 broadcasts, 0 runts, 0 giants
3 input errors, 34215 CRC, 0 frame, 0 overrun, 0 ignored, 0 abort
0 input packets with dribble condition detected
3594664 packets output, 436549843 bytes, 0 underruns
8 output errors, 1790 collisions, 10 interface resets, 0 restarts
0 output buffer failures, 0 output buffers swapped out
.
.
.
```

Using the previous formula, (Collisions / (Input packets + Output packets)) $\times$ 100, you can determine the following:

(1790/(2295197 + 3594664)) $\times$ 100 = 0.03%

This is an acceptable amount of collision errors because this is less than 0.1 percent of collisions. An acceptable maximum threshold would be 5890 collisions (2295197 + 3594664 $\times$ 0.1 percent = 5889.861).

Collisions are part of normal operation for Ethernet and IEEE 802.3 (CSMA/CD) networks. Excessive collisions could be caused by a number of factors. If an excessive number of collisions is detected on the interface, the following steps should be taken to correct them:

1 Use a TDR to find any unterminated Ethernet cables.

2 Look for a jabbering transceiver attached to a host. (This might require host-by-host inspection or the use of a protocol analyzer.)

3 Use a class 1 cable scanner to make sure cabling certifies from end to end. (Category 3, 5, and so on are end-to-end specs, and a poor punch-down can cause cabling systems to be out of spec.)

A network analyzer is necessary to determine the type of collision that is detected on the network segment. Three types of collisions can usually be found on an Ethernet segment:

- Local collisions
- Remote collisions
- Late collisions

Local Collisions

On a coaxial cable segment (10Base2 and 10Base5), the signal traverses the cable until it encounters the signal from the other host. The signals then overlap, canceling some parts of the signal out and reinforcing (doubling) other parts. The "doubling" of the signal pushes the voltage level of the signal beyond the maximum-allowed transmit voltage level. All of the hosts then sense this over-voltage condition on the cable segment as a local collision. On unshielded twisted-pair (UTP) cable (10Base-T), a local collision is detected only when a host detects a signal on the receive (RX) pair at the same time that it is transmitting on the transmit (TX) pair.

Although local collisions are part of normal operation on a CSMA/CD network, they could be caused by a number of factors:

- Overloaded network segment
- Faulty or marginal network interface card (NIC)
- Ethernet transceiver fault
- Ethernet repeater fault
- Illegal hardware configuration
- Ethernet cable fault
- Bad or poor host termination
- Bad grounding
- Induced noise on the segment (improperly shielded cabling)

Remote Collisions

If a collision occurs on the far side of a repeater, the over-voltage state is not observed on the near side of the repeater; what is seen is the beginning of an incomplete message. This shortened message does not have a proper FCS checksum, and is not long enough to meet the 64-byte (after the preamble) minimum requirement for CSMA/CD networks. This message is likely so short that the entire header block (with source and destination address) cannot be seen. Also seen is the "jam" signal occupying the last four octets of the shortened message.

Because a 10Base-T hub is essentially a multiport repeater with a segment dedicated to each station, or host, collisions on 10Base-T are nearly always detected as remote collisions. (A host on the network segment would have to be transmitting to sense a local collision.)

Like local collisions, remote collisions are a part of normal operation on a CSMA/CD network. Remote collisions could be caused by a number of factors:

- Overloaded network segment
- Faulty or marginal NIC
- Ethernet transceiver fault
- Ethernet repeater fault
- Illegal hardware configuration

- Ethernet cable fault
- Bad or poor host termination
- Bad grounding
- Induced noise on the segment (improperly shielded cabling)

Late Collisions

Late collisions occur after the first 64 bytes in a frame, but only when the other symptoms of a "local" collision are present at the same time (over-voltage or simultaneous transmit and receive). Late collisions are detected the same as a local collision; however, the detection of the collisions happens too far into the frame. Generally, late collisions are seen only on a coaxial segment. (In 10Base-T networks, the monitoring station must be transmitting simultaneously to see a late collision.) Late collisions are caused by duplex mismatches, a faulty NIC or network that is too long, or exceeding the parameters as identified by network diameter calculations. One of the most probable causes of late collisions is marginal or failed hardware. In 10Base-T networks, late collisions are often detected simply as FCS errors.

The issue with late collisions is that they do not cause the NIC card to automatically attempt to retransmit the collided frame. As far as the NIC is concerned, everything went out fine, and the upper layers of the protocol stack must determine that the frame was lost.

Late collisions register on the Cisco router's Ethernet interface as collisions and are generally the result of extended cable lengths in the network. To summarize, late collisions might be caused by a number of factors, including the following:

- Duplex mismatches
- Faulty or marginal NIC
- Ethernet transceiver fault
- Ethernet repeater fault
- Too many repeaters on the segment (violation of the "5-4-3" rule or number of Class I/II repeaters in use)
- Illegal hardware configuration or cable length
- Ethernet cable fault
- Bad or poor host termination
- Bad grounding
- Induced noise on the segment (improperly shielded cabling)

The following steps should be taken to correct issues with regard to late collisions:

1 Use a protocol analyzer to check for late collisions.

 Late collisions should never occur in a properly designed Ethernet network.

 Late collisions usually occur when Ethernet cables are too long or when too many repeaters are in the network, violating the "5-4-3" rule.

2 Check the diameter of the network and make sure it is within specifications.

Output Queue Drops

On a Cisco router, the number of output queue drops should not exceed 100 in any hour.

No formula exists to determine this number. The output from the **show interface ethernet** **port** clearly provides this information, as the following demonstrates.

```
.
.
Last input 0:00:00, output 0:00:00, output hang never
Output queue 0/40, 0 drops; input queue 0/75, 2 drops
Five minute input rate 61000 bits/sec, 4 packets/sec
Five minute output rate 1000 bits/sec, 2 packets/sec
.
.
```

Output queue drops are registered if the interface is not able to clear up the queue as fast as the router is sending (queuing) the packets.

NOTE   The IOS 10.0 and higher code has two output processes. The 9.1 (9.14) and lower code has only one output process.

Drops indicate that the router is overpowering the interface. On a LAN, this would likely be a busy or congested LAN segment, preventing frames from getting out on the wire. These frames usually carry data packets that would be mainly process-switched in the router, such as routing updates, Novell SAPs, access list control, and helpers.

NOTE   *Process-switching* is defined as an operation that provides full route evaluation and per-packet load balancing across parallel WAN links, with the router making a route selection for each packet. Process-switching is the most resource-intensive switching operation that the CPU can perform. Process-switching is contrasted by *fast-switching*, which is a Cisco feature whereby a route cache is used to expedite packet switching through a router.

If many SAPs need to be sent out, the output process is busy just sending SAPs. This can result in poor performance of other applications on the router.

The output queue can be modified using the interface subcommand **hold-queue *xx* out**, where *xx* is a value. The default for *xx* is 40. The command path to change this configuration is as follows:

```
Router>enable
Password:
Router#:config t
Router(config)#interface en [Where n is the Ethernet interface number]
Router(config-if)#hold-queue xx out
```

Input Queue Drops

On a Cisco router, the number of input queue drops should not exceed 50 in any hour.

No formula is available to determine this number; however, the output from the **show interface ethernet *port*** clearly provides this information, as the following code demonstrates:

```
  .
  .
  .
Last input 0:00:00, output 0:00:00, output hang never
Output queue 0/40, 0 drops; input queue 0/75, 2 drops
Five minute input rate 61000 bits/sec, 4 packets/sec
Five minute output rate 1000 bits/sec, 2 packets/sec
  .
  .
  .
```

Input queue drops are registered if the incoming frame rate is faster than the outgoing frame rate; when the frame rate is faster, the queue is filled up. Incoming data from an interface gets into the input queue for further processing. Looking at an Ethernet interface, data is coming *from* the Ethernet segment, not going *out* to it. After the queue is full, all the subsequent incoming frames are dropped.

Drops indicate that the interface is overpowering the router. On a LAN, this would likely be a busy or congested LAN segment; most likely, frames are being flooded onto the wire into the router's interface.

The input queue can be modified using the interface subcommand **hold-queue *xx* in**, where *xx* is a value. Where *xx* in the previous example is configured for 75, the default for *xx* is 40. The command path to change this configuration is as follows:

```
Router>enable
Password:
Router#:config t
Router(config)#interface en [Where n is the Ethernet interface number]
Router(config-if)#hold-queue xx in
```

Ignored Packets

On a Cisco router, the number of ignored packets on any interface should not exceed more than (approximately) 10 in an hour.

No formula is available to determine this number. However, the output from the **show interface ethernet *port*** clearly provides this information, as the following demonstrates:

```
.
.
.
2295197 packets input, 305539992 bytes, 0 no buffer
Received 1925500 broadcasts, 0 runts, 0 giants
3 input errors, 34215 CRC, 0 frame, 0 overrun, 0 ignored, 0 abort
0 input packets with dribble condition detected
3594664 packets output, 436549843 bytes, 0 underruns
.
.
.
```

Ignores are caused when the Ethernet interface cannot place a packet into an incoming hardware buffer pool. This means that the router does not have enough hardware buffers to accept a packet.

If the ignores are due to bursty traffic, nothing can be done for the ignore issue in the configuration. If this is normal behavior on the network segment, upgrading to a more powerful router, such as a Cisco 7xxx Series, should be considered.

If upgrading is not an option, it is recommended that you open a case with the Cisco TAC to have the issue further evaluated.

show interface ethernet *number* accounting

This command is entered from the **privileged EXEC** command interface on the Cisco router. It displays information about protocol distribution with regard to the specified Ethernet interface.

The syntax for this command is as follows:

```
show interface ethernet number accounting
```

accounting is an optional parameter that displays the number of packets of each protocol type that has been sent through the interface. The syntax for this command is as follows:

```
Router#show interfaces ethernet 0 accounting
Ethernet0
           Protocol  Pkts In   Chars In  Pkts Out  Chars Out
                 IP    15613     346578    231435     533413
            DEC MOP        0          0         2        154
                ARP        3        180         0          0
                CDP       14        704         9       2388
                IPX    72715    1315681     15134      45116
```

To determine the protocol distribution percentage, divide the packets (input, output, or total) for the protocol in question by the same parameter from the **show interfaces *port*** *number* output. For example, examine the distribution for IP traffic using the previous output from a **show interfaces ethernet 0 accounting**, combined with the earlier output from a **show interfaces ethernet 0**, shown here:

```
.
.
2295197 packets input, 305539992 bytes, 0 no buffer
Received 1925500 broadcasts, 0 runts, 0 giants
3 input errors, 34215 CRC, 0 frame, 0 overrun, 0 ignored, 0 abort
0 input packets with dribble condition detected
3594664 packets output, 436549843 bytes, 0 underruns
.
.
```

The information in the following sections can be determined by using the embedded formula.

Input Distribution Percentage

The percentage of incoming IP packets is determined by the following formula:

$$(Protocol_{INPUT}/Total_{INPUT}) \times 100 = Protocol_{DISTRIBUTION}\%$$

$(15613/2295197) \times 100 = 0.68$ percent. Therefore, 68 percent of the total traffic input into this interface is IP traffic.

Output Distribution Percentage

The percentage of outgoing IP packets is determined by the following formula:

$$(Protocol_{OUTPUT}/Total_{OUTPUT}) \times 100 = Protocol_{DISTRIBUTION}\%$$

$(231435/3594664) \times 100 = 6.44$ percent. Therefore, 6.44 percent of the total traffic output from this interface is IP traffic.

Total Distribution Percentage

The percentage of total IP packets is determined by the following formula:

$$(Protocol_{INPUT+OUTPUT}/Total_{INPUT+OUTPUT}) \times 100 = Protocol_{DISTRIBUTION}\%$$

$(247048/5889861) \times 100 = 4.19$ percent. Therefore, 4.19 percent of the total traffic input to and output from this interface is IP traffic.

show buffers ethernet

This command is entered from the privileged EXEC command interface on the Cisco router. It displays information about the specified Ethernet interface.

The syntax for this command is as follows:

```
show buffers interface number
```

This command displays utilization statistics for the network packet buffer allocator. For each pool, the network server keeps counts of the number of buffers outstanding, the number of buffers in the free list, and the maximum number of buffers allowed in the free list. Buffer failures are one of the most common reasons for packet drops. When packet drops occur because of buffer failure, the following things happen:

1   After a buffer failure, the router processor (RP) has an outstanding request to "create" more buffers of the appropriate size for the particular pool.

2   During the time it takes for the RP to service the "create buffers" request, the pool might contain additional failures.

3   The RP might even fail to create more buffers because of memory constraints in the system at the time the extra buffers are required.

4   Essentially, the "create" buffers operation could take several microseconds in which packets are continually dropped because of the buffer shortage.

5   In addition, if buffers are used as quickly as they are created, the RP could be forced to spend more time creating buffers than processing packets.

This can cause the RP to begin dropping packets so quickly that performance degrades and sessions are lost.

The optional arguments *interface* and *number* cause a search of all buffers that have been associated with that interface for longer than one minute:

```
show buffers ethernet 0
```

Following is sample output without the optional arguments:

```
Router#show buffers

Buffer elements:
     250 in free list (250 max allowed)
     10816 hits, 0 misses, 0 created
Small buffers, 104 bytes (total 120, permanent 120):
     120 in free list (0 min, 250 max allowed)
     26665 hits, 0 misses, 0 trims, 0 created
Middle buffers, 600 bytes (total 90, permanent 90):
     90 in free list (0 min, 200 max allowed)
     5468 hits, 0 misses, 0 trims, 0 created
Big buffers, 1524 bytes (total 90, permanent 90):
     90 in free list (0 min, 300 max allowed)
     1447 hits, 0 misses, 0 trims, 0 created
Large buffers, 5024 bytes (total 0, permanent 0):
     0 in free list (0 min, 100 max allowed)
     0 hits, 0 misses, 0 trims, 0 created
Huge buffers, 12024 bytes (total 0, permanent 0):
     0 in free list (0 min, 30 max allowed)
     0 hits, 0 misses, 0 trims, 0 created
0 failures (0 no memory)
```

Table 5-2 describes the output from the **show buffers** command.

NOTE	The number of buffers "in free list" is the number of available buffers. When a buffer request comes in, a buffer from the "in free list" is allocated.

Table 5-2 *show buffers Field Description*

Field	Description
Buffer elements	Blocks of memory used in internal operating system queues.
Small buffers Middle buffers Big buffers Large buffers Huge buffers	Blocks of memory used to hold network packets.
Hits	Count of successful attempts to allocate a buffer when needed.
Misses	Count of allocation attempts that failed for lack of a free buffer in the pool.
Created	Count of new buffers created. Buffers are created when the number of buffers created in the pool "in free list" was less than "min."
Trims	Count of buffers destroyed. Trims are the number of buffers that have been trimmed from the pool when the number of buffers "in free list" exceeds the number of "max allowed" buffers.
in free list	Number of buffers of a given type that are not currently allocated and are available for use.
max allowed	Maximum number of buffers of a given type allowed in the system.
Failures	Total number of allocation requests that have failed for lack of a free buffer. The number of "failures" represents the number of packets that have been dropped due to buffer shortage.
no memory	Number of failures due to a lack of memory to create a new buffer.

If no buffers are available and fast switching is enabled, the buffer fails and the packet is dropped. When the buffer pool manager process detects a buffer failure, it "creates" a new buffer to avoid future failures.

The router does not create a new buffer if the number "in free list" equals the "max allowed" value. If the router does not have enough memory to create a new buffer, this is recorded as "no memory." If the number "in free list" is greater than the "permanent" number, the router "trims" some excess buffers.

The number of "failures" and "no memory" are the only areas worth concern. Failures can occur, but these should stabilize after a while. The router creates or trims buffers as necessary to stabilize the number of failures. If the number of failures continues to increase, then buffer tuning might be necessary.

If not enough memory is available to create new buffers, a buffer leak or a more general memory problem is likely the cause. Buffers are not created in the fast-switching path. If the router tries to fast-switch a packet and no buffer is available, the packet is dropped and a failure is reported. The next time the buffer pool manager runs, a new buffer is created.

Buffer Misses

On any Cisco router, the number of buffer misses should not be more than (approximately) 25 in a given hour.

No formula is necessary to determine the number of misses. The output from the **show buffers** *interface* clearly provides this information, as the following code demonstrates:

```
Buffer elements:
     250 in free list (250 max allowed)
     10816 hits, 0 misses, 0 created
Small buffers, 104 bytes (total 120, permanent 120):
     120 in free list (0 min, 250 max allowed)
     26665 hits, 0 misses, 0 trims, 0 created
Middle buffers, 600 bytes (total 90, permanent 90):
     90 in free list (0 min, 200 max allowed)
     5468 hits, 0 misses, 0 trims, 0 created
Big buffers, 1524 bytes (total 90, permanent 90):
     90 in free list (0 min, 300 max allowed)
     1447 hits, 0 misses, 0 trims, 0 created
Large buffers, 5024 bytes (total 0, permanent 0):
     0 in free list (0 min, 100 max allowed)
     0 hits, 0 misses, 0 trims, 0 created
Huge buffers, 12024 bytes (total 0, permanent 0):
     0 in free list (0 min, 30 max allowed)
     0 hits, 0 misses, 0 trims, 0 created
0 failures (0 no memory)
```

Although not more than 25 buffer misses should occur in an hour, misses are usually okay as long as "failures" shown at the bottom of the **show buffers** display is not incrementing.

A buffer miss identifies the number of times that a system buffer has been requested, but no more buffers were available in the free list for that buffer type. A buffer failure identifies the number of failures to grant a buffer to a requester under interrupt time. (The router can create new buffers at process switching level; consequently, a failure does not exist unless there is no memory.) The number of "failures" represents the number of packets that have been dropped due to buffer shortage.

Sometimes, the corrective action is the addition of router memory. Other times, the corrective action might be more extensive, such as tuning the buffer parameters. Before performing any type of buffer tuning action, it is recommended that you open a case with the Cisco TAC to have the issue further evaluated.

show processes cpu

The **show processes cpu** command displays information about the active processes in the router and their corresponding CPU utilization statistics. Following is an example of the output, although this is not a complete list, and the processes that are running vary for each system:

```
CPU utilization for five seconds: 8%/4%; one minute: 6%; five minutes: 5%

PID  Runtime(ms)  Invoked  uSecs    5Sec    1Min    5Min TTY Process
  1          384    32789     11   0.00%   0.00%   0.00%   0 Load Meter
  2         2752     1179   2334   0.73%   1.06%   0.29%   0 Exec
  3       318592     5273  60419   0.00%   0.15%   0.17%   0 Check heaps
  4            4        1   4000   0.00%   0.00%   0.00%   0 Pool Manager
  5         6472     6568    985   0.00%   0.00%   0.00%   0 ARP Input
  6        10892     9461   1151   0.00%   0.00%   0.00%   0 IP Input
  7        67388    53244   1265   0.16%   0.04%   0.02%   0 CDP Protocol
  8       145520   166455    874   0.40%   0.29%   0.29%   0 IP Background
  9         3356     1568   2140   0.08%   0.00%   0.00%   0 BOOTP Server
 10           32     5469      5   0.00%   0.00%   0.00%   0 Net Background
 11        42256   163623    258   0.16%   0.02%   0.00%   0 Per-Second Jobs
 12       189936   163623   1160   0.00%   0.04%   0.05%   0 Net Periodic
 13         3248     6351    511   0.00%   0.00%   0.00%   0 Net Input
 14          168    32790      5   0.00%   0.00%   0.00%   0 Compute load avgs
 15       152408     2731  55806   0.98%   0.12%   0.07%   0 Per-minute Jobs
 16            0        2      0   0.00%   0.00%   0.00%   0 HyBridge Input
 17         6352   163952     38   0.00%   0.00%   0.00%   0 Spanning Tree
 18            4        2   2000   0.00%   0.00%   0.00%   0 Tbridge Monitor
 19         7696     2745   2803   0.16%   0.01%   0.00%   0 IP-RT Background
 20        18484   330791     55   0.00%   0.00%   0.00%   0 BGP Router
 21         2824     9266    304   0.00%   0.00%   0.00%   0 BGP I/O
 22          520     2771    187   0.00%   0.03%   0.00%   0 BGP Scanner
 23            0        1      0   0.00%   0.00%   0.00%   0 OSPF Hello
 24            8        6   1333   0.00%   0.02%   0.00%   0 OSPF Router
```

Table 5-3 describes the fields in the **show processes cpu** output.

Table 5-3   *show processes cpu Field Description*

Field	Description
CPU utilization for five seconds	CPU utilization for the past five seconds. The first number indicates the total, and the second number indicates the percent of CPU time spent at the interrupt level.
one minute	CPU utilization for the past minute.
five minutes	CPU utilization for the past five minutes.
PID	Process ID.
Runtime (ms)	CPU time that the process has used, expressed in milliseconds (ms).
Invoked	Number of times that the process has been invoked.
uSecs	Microseconds of CPU time for each process invocation.
5Sec	CPU utilization by task in the past five seconds.
1Min	CPU utilization by task in the past minute.

Table 5-3 *show processes cpu Field Description*

Field	Description
5Min	CPU utilization by task in the past five minutes.
TTY	Terminal that controls the process.
Process	Name of the process.

CPU Utilization

On any Cisco router, the 5-minute CPU utilization rate should be under 75 percent.

No formula is available to determine 5-minute CPU utilization rate. The output from the **show processes cpu** clearly provides this information, as the following demonstrates:

CPU utilization for five seconds: 8%/4%
one minute: 6%
five minutes: 5%

If the CPU utilization is continually over 75 percent, you might want to consider getting a router upgrade or dividing the traffic between multiple routers. Prior to making these changes, it is necessary to get an assessment of what is causing the CPU load. It might be a particular protocol or other process. The output from the **show processes cpu** command lists all active processes on the router and the load that each process is placing on the CPU. If the router is not that busy, then what might be seen are some abnormalities in the network (broadcast storms, flapping routes).

Ethernet Network Analysis

Before raw data analysis can begin, it is necessary to review the formulae that are used to determine thresholds and measurements for 10 Mbps, 100 Mbps (Fast), and 1000 Mbps (Gigabit) Ethernet network segments.

Ethernet Frame Transmission

Following are formulae used to determine the amount of time it takes for a single Ethernet frame (10 Mbps, 100 Mbps, or 1000 Mbps) to traverse the network segment. These formulae are used to determine this time based on both the minimum and maximum supported frame size for the respective technology.

10 Mbps Ethernet

Using the minimum Ethernet frame size (72 bytes), the following is true for the transmission time for one frame (72 bytes) across a 10 Mbps Ethernet network segment:

9.6 microseconds + (72 bytes × (8 bits/1 byte) × (100 ns/1 bit)) = 0.06 ms

NOTE | The minimum Ethernet frame size of 72 bytes comprises just the Preamble/SOF and the minimum 64-byte payload. Ns stands for nanoseconds.

9.6 microseconds + (72 bytes × (8 bits/1 byte) × (100 ns/1 bit)) = 0.06 ms

NOTE | 9.6 microseconds is the dead time between frames as defined by Ethernet and IEEE 802.3 standards.

Because it takes one 72-byte frame 0.06 ms to traverse a 10 Mbps Ethernet segment, approximately 16667 (minimum-sized) frames are transmitted per second [(1/0.06 ms) × 1000 = 16667].

Using the maximum Ethernet frame size (1526 bytes), the following is true for the transmission time for one frame (1526 bytes) across a 10 Mbps Ethernet network segment:

9.6 microseconds + (1526 bytes × (8 bits/1 byte) × (100 ns/1 bit)) = 1.22 ms

NOTE | The maximum Ethernet frame of 1526 bytes includes the Preamble/SOF, MAC Header, payload, and CRC value.

NOTE | 9.6 microseconds is the dead time between frames as defined by Ethernet and IEEE 802.3 standards.

It takes one 1526-byte frame 1.22 ms to traverse a 10 Mbps Ethernet segment; therefore, approximately 819 (maximum-sized) frames are transmitted per second [(1/1.22 ms) × 1000 = 819].

100 Mbps (Fast) Ethernet

Using the minimum Ethernet frame size (72 bytes), the following is true for the transmission time for one frame (72 bytes) across a 100 Mbps (Fast) Ethernet network segment:

9.6 microseconds + (72 bytes × (8 bits/1 byte) × (10 ns/1 bit)) = 0.006 ms

---

NOTE   9.6 microseconds is the dead time between frames as defined by Ethernet and IEEE 802.3 standards.

It takes one 72-byte frame 0.006 ms to traverse a 100 Mbps (Fast) Ethernet segment. Therefore, approximately 166667 (minimum-sized) frames are transmitted per second [(1/0.006 ms) × 1000 = 166667].

Using the maximum Ethernet frame size (1526 bytes), the following is true for the transmission time for one frame (1526 bytes) across a 100 Mbps (Fast) Ethernet network segment:

9.6 microseconds + (1526 bytes × (8 bits/1 byte) × (10 ns/1 bit)) = .122 ms

---

NOTE   9.6 microseconds is the dead time between frames as defined by Ethernet and IEEE 802.3 standards.

Because it takes one 1526-byte frame .122 ms to traverse a 100 Mbps (Fast) Ethernet segment, approximately 8196 (maximum-sized) frames are transmitted per second [(1/.122ms) × 1000 = 8196].

1000 Mbps (Gigabit) Ethernet

The parameters for Gigabit Ethernet are a bit different from 10 Mbps and 100 Mbps Ethernet, especially with regard to minimum frame size. The minimum frame size for Gigabit Ethernet is 520 bytes, versus the 72-byte minimum of 10 Mbps and 100 Mbps (Fast) Ethernet. The dead time interval between frames for Gigabit Ethernet is also different from that of 10 Mbps and 100 Mbps (Fast) Ethernet. Gigabit Ethernet uses a dead time interval of 0.096 microseconds and a bit duration of 1 ns:

0.096 microseconds + ((520 bytes × (8 bits/1 byte)) × 1 ns/bit) = 4.160 microseconds

NOTE	The minimum Gigabit Ethernet frame size of 520-bytes includes the Preamble/SOF and the minimum slot size of 512 bytes.

In one second, a maximum of 1/4.160 microseconds or 240385 minimum-sized (520-byte) frames can exist.

Using the maximum Ethernet frame size (1526 bytes), the following is true for the transmission time for one frame (1526 bytes) across a 1000 Mbps (Gigabit) Ethernet network segment:

0.096 microseconds + ((1526 bytes × (8 bits/1 byte)) × 1 ns/bit) = 0.0122 microseconds

In one second, a maximum of 1/0.0122 microseconds or 81967 maximum-sized (1526-byte) frames can exist.

Ethernet Baseline

This information can be used to establish an approximate baseline for frame processing with regards to 10 Mbps, 100 Mbps (Fast), and 1000 Mbps (Gigabit) Ethernet networks, as Table 5-4 demonstrates.

Table 5-4   *Ethernet Baseline Processing Parameters*

		Frames Per Second	
Network Type	Frame Size	50 Percent Network Load	100 Percent Network Load
10 Mbps Ethernet	Maximum: 1526	409	819
	Minimum: 72	8333	16667
100 Mbps (Fast) Ethernet	Maximum: 1526	4098	8196
	Minimum: 72	83333	166667
1000 Mbps (Gigabit) Ethernet	Maximum: 1526	40983	81967
	Minimum: 520	120192	240385

Table 5-5 demonstrates expected values regarding the number of frames per second with regard to 10 Mbps, 100 Mbps (Fast), and 1000 Mbps (Gigabit) Ethernet network segments.

NOTE   Remember: The minimum frame size for Gigabit Ethernet is not 72 bytes, as with 10 Mbps and 100 Mbps (Fast) Ethernet, but rather 520 bytes.

Table 5-5   *Ethernet Frames Per Second*

Average Frame Length (Bytes)	10 Mbps Ethernet Frames Per Second		100 Mbps Ethernet Frames Per Second		1000 Mbps Ethernet Frames Per Second	
	50 Percent Load	100 Percent Load	50 Percent Load	100 Percent Load	50 Percent Load	100 Percent Load
72	7440.48	14880.95	74404.76	148809.52	116390.05	232780.09
80	6793.48	13586.96	67934.78	135869.57	116390.05	232780.09
100	5580.36	11160.71	55803.57	111607.14	116390.05	232780.09
125	4562.04	9124.09	45620.44	91240.88	116390.05	232780.09
150	3858.02	7716.05	38580.25	77160.49	116390.05	232780.09
175	3342.25	6684.49	33422.46	66844.92	116390.05	232780.09
200	2948.11	5896.23	29481.13	58962.26	116390.05	232780.09
225	2637.13	5274.26	26371.31	52742.62	116390.05	232780.09
250	2385.50	4770.99	23854.96	47709.92	116390.05	232780.09
275	2177.70	4355.40	21777.00	43554.01	116390.05	232780.09
300	2003.21	4006.41	20032.05	40064.10	116390.05	232780.09
325	1854.60	3709.20	18545.99	37091.99	116390.05	232780.09
350	1726.52	3453.04	17265.19	34530.39	116390.05	232780.09
375	1614.99	3229.97	16149.87	32299.74	116390.05	232780.09
400	1516.99	3033.98	15169.90	30339.81	116390.05	232780.09
425	1430.21	2860.41	14302.06	28604.12	116390.05	232780.09
450	1352.81	2705.63	13528.14	27056.28	116390.05	232780.09
475	1283.37	2566.74	12833.68	25667.35	116390.05	232780.09
500	1220.70	2441.41	12207.03	24414.06	116390.05	232780.09
525	1163.87	2327.75	11638.73	23277.47	116390.05	232780.09
550	1112.10	2224.20	11121.00	22241.99	111212.44	222424.88
575	1064.74	2129.47	10647.36	21294.72	106475.86	212951.72
600	1021.24	2042.48	10212.42	20424.84	102126.27	204252.54

(continues)

Table 5-5   *Ethernet Frames Per Second (Continued)*

Average Frame Length (Bytes)	10 Mbps Ethernet Frames Per Second		100 Mbps Ethernet Frames Per Second		1000 Mbps Ethernet Frames Per Second	
	50 Percent Load	100 Percent Load	50 Percent Load	100 Percent Load	50 Percent Load	100 Percent Load
625	981.16	1962.32	9811.62	19623.23	98118.09	196236.19
650	944.11	1888.22	9441.09	18882.18	94412.66	188825.32
675	909.75	1819.51	9097.53	18195.05	90976.91	181953.82
700	877.81	1755.62	8778.09	17556.18	87782.44	175564.88
725	848.03	1696.07	8480.33	16960.65	84804.69	169609.39
750	820.21	1640.42	8202.10	16404.20	82022.34	164044.69
775	794.16	1588.31	7941.55	15883.10	79416.76	158833.53
800	769.70	1539.41	7697.04	15394.09	76971.63	153943.26
825	746.71	1493.43	7467.14	14934.29	74672.56	149345.12
850	725.06	1450.12	7250.58	14501.16	72506.85	145013.70
875	704.62	1409.24	7046.22	14092.45	70463.23	140926.45
900	685.31	1370.61	6853.07	13706.14	68531.64	137063.28
925	667.02	1334.04	6670.22	13340.45	66703.13	133406.26
950	649.69	1299.38	6496.88	12993.76	64969.66	129939.32
975	633.23	1266.46	6332.32	12664.64	63324.00	126648.01
1000	617.59	1235.18	6175.89	12351.78	61759.66	123519.31
1025	602.70	1205.40	6027.00	12054.00	60270.74	120541.47
1050	588.51	1177.02	5885.12	11770.24	58851.92	117703.83
1075	574.98	1149.95	5749.77	11499.54	57498.36	114996.72
1100	562.05	1124.10	5620.50	11241.01	56205.67	112411.34
1125	549.69	1099.38	5496.92	10993.84	54969.82	109939.64
1150	537.87	1075.73	5378.66	10757.31	53787.15	107574.31
1175	526.54	1053.07	5265.37	10530.75	52654.30	105308.61
1200	515.68	1031.35	5156.77	10313.53	51568.19	103136.38
1225	505.25	1010.51	5052.55	10105.09	50525.98	101051.95
1250	495.25	990.49	4952.46	9904.91	49525.05	99050.11
1275	485.63	971.25	4856.25	9712.51	48563.02	97126.04

Table 5-5   *Ethernet Frames Per Second*

Average Frame Length (Bytes)	10 Mbps Ethernet Frames Per Second		100 Mbps Ethernet Frames Per Second		1000 Mbps Ethernet Frames Per Second	
	50 Percent Load	100 Percent Load	50 Percent Load	100 Percent Load	50 Percent Load	100 Percent Load
1300	476.37	952.74	4763.72	9527.44	47637.65	95275.30
1325	467.46	934.93	4674.64	9349.29	46746.88	93493.77
1350	458.88	917.77	4588.84	9177.68	45888.82	91777.64
1375	450.61	901.23	4506.13	9012.26	45061.69	90123.38
1400	442.63	885.27	4426.35	8852.69	44263.85	88527.70
1425	434.93	869.87	4349.34	8698.68	43493.77	86987.53
1450	427.50	854.99	4274.97	8549.93	42750.02	85500.05
1475	420.31	840.62	4203.09	8406.19	42031.29	84062.58
1500	413.36	826.72	4133.60	8267.20	41336.32	82672.64
1526	406.37	812.74	4063.72	8127.44	40637.52	81275.04

Ethernet MTU

The MTU value for Ethernet is 1500 bytes. This value is presented via the **show interface Ethernet** *port* command at the EXEC interface.

```
Ethernet 0 is up, line protocol is up
    Hardware is MCI Ethernet, address is aa00.0400.0134 (bia 0000.0c00.4369)
    Internet address is 131.108.1.1, subnet mask is 255.255.255.0
    MTU 1500 bytes, BW 10000 Kbit, DLY 1000 usec, rely 255/255, load 1/255
    Encapsulation ARPA, loopback not set, keepalive set (10 sec)
    .
    .
```

The administrator can change this value at the EXEC prompt, using the following command structure:

```
Router(config-if)#mtu value
```

where *value* is any number from **<64-18000>**.

NOTE   It is not recommended that you change the MTU size unless it is necessary because routing metrics and application services can be negatively impacted. It is recommended that you work with the Cisco TAC to evaluate the actions and results of manually changing the MTU size.

Ethernet Throughput

Table 5-6 demonstrates expected values regarding the number of bits-per-second with regard to 10 Mbps, 100 Mbps (Fast), and 1000 Mbps (Gigabit) Ethernet network segments.

Table 5-6   *Ethernet Bits Per Second*

Average Frame Length (Bytes)	10 Mbps Ethernet Bits Per Second		100 Mbps Ethernet Bits Per Second		1000 Mbps Ethernet Bits Per Second	
	50 Percent Load	100 Percent Load	50 Percent Load	100 Percent Load	50 Percent Load	100 Percent Load
72	2738095	5476190	27380952	54761905	464629065	929258130
80	2934783	5869565	29347826	58695652	464629065	929258130
100	3303571	6607143	33035714	66071429	464629065	929258130
125	3613139	7226277	36131387	72262774	464629065	929258130
150	3827160	7654321	38271605	76543210	464629065	929258130
175	3983957	7967914	39839572	79679144	464629065	929258130
200	4103774	8207547	41037736	82075472	464629065	929258130
225	4198312	8396624	41983122	83966245	464629065	929258130
250	4274809	8549618	42748092	85496183	464629065	929258130
275	4337979	8675958	43379791	86759582	464629065	929258130
300	4391026	8782051	43910256	87820513	464629065	929258130
325	4436202	8872404	44362018	88724036	464629065	929258130
350	4475138	8950276	44751381	89502762	464629065	929258130
375	4509044	9018088	45090439	90180879	464629065	929258130
400	4538835	9077670	45388350	90776699	464629065	929258130
425	4565217	9130435	45652174	91304348	464629065	929258130
450	4588745	9177489	45887446	91774892	464629065	929258130
475	4609856	9219713	46098563	92197125	464629065	929258130
500	4628906	9257813	46289063	92578125	464629065	929258130
525	4646182	9292365	46461825	92923650	464629065	929258130
550	4661922	9323843	46619217	93238434	466202540	932405080
575	4676320	9352641	46763203	93526405	467641986	935283971
600	4689542	9379085	46895425	93790850	468963827	937927654
625	4701727	9403454	47017268	94034537	470181911	940363822

Table 5-6   *Ethernet Bits Per Second*

Average Frame Length (Bytes)	10 Mbps Ethernet Bits Per Second		100 Mbps Ethernet Bits Per Second		1000 Mbps Ethernet Bits Per Second	
	50 Percent Load	100 Percent Load	50 Percent Load	100 Percent Load	50 Percent Load	100 Percent Load
650	4712991	9425982	47129909	94259819	471307993	942615986
675	4723435	9446870	47234352	94468705	472352117	944704234
700	4733146	9466292	47331461	94662921	473322916	946645833
725	4742198	9484396	47421981	94843962	474227853	948455707
750	4750656	9501312	47506562	95013123	475073410	950146820
775	4758577	9517154	47585769	95171537	475865246	951730491
800	4766010	9532020	47660099	95320197	476608322	953216644
825	4772999	9545998	47729988	95459976	477307009	954614018
850	4779582	9559165	47795824	95591647	477965168	955930335
875	4785795	9571590	47857948	95715896	478586226	957172452
900	4791667	9583333	47916667	95833333	479173234	958346469
925	4797225	9594450	47972252	95944504	479728918	959457837
950	4802495	9604990	48024948	96049896	480255721	960511441
975	4807497	9614995	48074975	96149949	480755835	961511671
1000	4812253	9624506	48122530	96245059	481231241	962462481
1025	4816779	9633558	48167792	96335583	481683723	963367447
1050	4821092	9642185	48210923	96421846	482114902	964229805
1075	4825207	9650414	48252070	96504140	482526248	965052496
1100	4829137	9658273	48291367	96582734	482919098	965838195
1125	4832894	9665787	48328936	96657872	483294671	966589342
1150	4836489	9672978	48364888	96729776	483654084	967308168
1175	4839933	9679865	48399326	96798652	483998357	967996714
1200	4843234	9686469	48432343	96864686	484328427	968656855
1225	4846403	9692805	48464026	96928052	484645156	969290312
1250	4849445	9698891	48494453	96988906	484949336	969898672
1275	4852370	9704740	48523699	97047397	485241698	970483396
1300	4855183	9710366	48551829	97103659	485522918	971045837

(continues)

Table 5-6   *Ethernet Bits Per Second (Continued)*

Average Frame Length (Bytes)	10 Mbps Ethernet Bits Per Second		100 Mbps Ethernet Bits Per Second		1000 Mbps Ethernet Bits Per Second	
	50 Percent Load	100 Percent Load	50 Percent Load	100 Percent Load	50 Percent Load	100 Percent Load
1325	4857891	9715782	48578908	97157816	485793622	971587244
1350	4860499	9720999	48604993	97209985	486054387	972108775
1375	4863014	9726027	48630137	97260274	486305753	972611505
1400	4865439	9730878	48654391	97308782	486548217	973096433
1425	4867780	9735560	48677801	97355602	486782244	973564488
1450	4870041	9740082	48700410	97400821	487008268	974016536
1475	4872226	9744452	48722260	97444519	487226692	974453383
1500	4874339	9748677	48743386	97486772	487437892	974875784
1526	4876463	9752926	48764629	97529259	487650257	975300514

Ethernet Effective Utilization

As is demonstrated by Tables 5-4, 5-5, and 5-6, as the size of the frame approaches the maximum allowable frame size, the effective throughput increases. The reason for this is that more data can be carried in the payload of a larger frame, which in turn means less overhead.

The effective data throughput rate for 10 Mbps Ethernet, when the maximum frame size is transmitted, is as follows:

10 Mbps – ((9.6 microseconds/100 ns) × 819) = 9999921 bps

The effective data throughput rate for 100 Mbps (Fast) Ethernet, when the maximum frame size is transmitted, is as follows:

100 Mbps – ((.96 microseconds/10 ns) × 8196) = 99999213 bps

The effective data throughput rate for 1000 Mbps (Gigabit) Ethernet, when the maximum frame size is transmitted, is as follows:

1000 Mbps – ((.096 microseconds/1 ns) × 81967) = 999992131 bps

The formula used to determine maximum possible utilization across any network connection is as follows:

Utilization (U) Percentage = (Throughput/Data Rate) × 100

Using the previously established values for 10 Mbps, 100 Mbps (Fast), and 1000 Mbps (Gigabit) Ethernet, it is determined that the maximum possible network utilization, with minimum Ethernet frame overhead, is consistently at 99.999213 percent.

This number is created in a pure Ethernet environment, without collisions, CRC errors, dropped frames due to full buffers, and so on. Additional protocol and application overhead (OSI Layers 3 through 7) also need to be taken into account when determining the effective throughput for a specific application or service.

Ethernet with IP Networking

Sometimes it might be necessary to adjust the MTU size for transmission across wide-area networks (WAN) when fragmentation can become an issue. The MTU size should be set the same as on the Ethernet if you want to avoid fragmentation. It is not beneficial to increase the MTU by a few bytes to handle Ethernet LAN traffic because only for wide-area networked traffic does MTU size matter. Broadcasts that are associated with IP are going to be sourced from the router, not the LAN segments from where they come; therefore, from this perspective, MTU size is independent.

If adjusting the frame MTU is the selected course of action, Table 5-7 demonstrates expected throughput values in bits per second for 10 Mbps, 100 Mbps (Fast), and 1000 Mbps (Gigabit) Ethernet network segments operating with the TCP/IP Suite. (The OSI Layer 3 [Network] protocol is IP.)

Table 5-7   *Ethernet with IP Throughput (Bits Per Second)*

Average Frame Length (Bytes)	10 Mbps Ethernet Bits Per Second		100 Mbps Ethernet Bits Per Second		1000 Mbps Ethernet Bits Per Second	
	50 Percent Load	100 Percent Load	50 Percent Load	100 Percent Load	50 Percent Load	100 Percent Load
72	1309524	2619048	13095238	26190476	442282176	884564352
80	1630435	3260870	16304348	32608696	442282176	884564352
100	2232143	4464286	22321429	44642857	442282176	884564352
125	2737226	5474453	27372263	54744526	442282176	884564352
150	3086420	6172840	30864198	61728395	442282176	884564352
175	3342246	6684492	33422460	66844920	442282176	884564352
200	3537736	7075472	35377358	70754717	442282176	884564352
225	3691983	7383966	36919831	73839662	442282176	884564352
250	3816794	7633588	38167939	76335878	442282176	884564352
275	3919861	7839721	39198606	78397213	442282176	884564352

(continues)

Table 5-7 *Ethernet with IP Throughput (Bits Per Second) (Continued)*

Average Frame Length (Bytes)	10 Mbps Ethernet Bits Per Second		100 Mbps Ethernet Bits Per Second		1000 Mbps Ethernet Bits Per Second	
	50 Percent Load	100 Percent Load	50 Percent Load	100 Percent Load	50 Percent Load	100 Percent Load
300	4006410	8012821	40064103	80128205	442282176	884564352
325	4080119	8160237	40801187	81602374	442282176	884564352
350	4143646	8287293	41436464	82872928	442282176	884564352
375	4198966	8397933	41989664	83979328	442282176	884564352
400	4247573	8495146	42475728	84951456	442282176	884564352
425	4290618	8581236	42906178	85812357	442282176	884564352
450	4329004	8658009	43290043	86580087	442282176	884564352
475	4363450	8726899	43634497	87268994	442282176	884564352
500	4394531	8789063	43945313	87890625	442282176	884564352
525	4422719	8845438	44227188	88454376	442282176	884564352
550	4448399	8896797	44483986	88967972	444849752	889699504
575	4471891	8943782	44718910	89437819	447198620	894397240
600	4493464	8986928	44934641	89869281	449355583	898711166
625	4513344	9026688	45133438	90266876	451343237	902686473
650	4531722	9063444	45317221	90634441	453180762	906361525
675	4548763	9097525	45487627	90975255	454884550	909769101
700	4564607	9129213	45646067	91292135	456468688	912937376
725	4579376	9158752	45793758	91587517	457945352	915890704
750	4593176	9186352	45931759	91863517	459325120	918650240
775	4606099	9212198	46060991	92121982	460617227	921234454
800	4618227	9236453	46182266	92364532	461829770	923659539
825	4629630	9259259	46296296	92592593	462969877	925939754
850	4640371	9280742	46403712	92807425	464043852	928087704
875	4650507	9301015	46505073	93010147	465057287	930114573
900	4660088	9320175	46600877	93201754	466015159	932030318
925	4669157	9338314	46691569	93383138	466921917	933843835
950	4677755	9355509	46777547	93555094	467781546	935563092

Table 5-7   *Ethernet with IP Throughput (Bits Per Second)*

Average Frame Length (Bytes)	10 Mbps Ethernet Bits Per Second		100 Mbps Ethernet Bits Per Second		1000 Mbps Ethernet Bits Per Second	
	50 Percent Load	100 Percent Load	50 Percent Load	100 Percent Load	50 Percent Load	100 Percent Load
975	4685917	9371834	46859169	93718338	468597627	937195253
1000	4693676	9387352	46936759	93873518	469373387	938746773
1025	4701061	9402122	47010608	94021215	470111742	940223484
1050	4708098	9416196	47080979	94161959	470815334	941630669
1075	4714811	9429623	47148114	94296228	471486563	942973125
1100	4721223	9442446	47212230	94424460	472127609	944255219
1125	4727353	9454705	47273527	94547054	472740465	945480931
1150	4733219	9466437	47332186	94664372	473326951	946653901
1175	4738837	9477675	47388374	94776748	473888731	947777462
1200	4744224	9488449	47442244	94884488	474427335	948854671
1225	4749394	9498787	47493937	94987874	474944169	949888338
1250	4754358	9508716	47543582	95087163	475440525	950881051
1275	4759130	9518260	47591298	95182595	475917598	951835197
1300	4763720	9527439	47637195	95274390	476376490	952752980
1325	4768138	9536275	47681376	95362752	476818220	953636440
1350	4772394	9544787	47723935	95447871	477243734	954487468
1375	4776496	9552992	47764960	95529921	477653908	955307816
1400	4780453	9560907	47804533	95609065	478049558	956099116
1425	4784273	9568546	47842728	95685456	478431441	956862882
1450	4787962	9575923	47879617	95759234	478800263	957600527
1475	4791527	9583053	47915266	95830531	479156684	958313368
1500	—	—	—	—	—	—
1526	—	—	—	—	—	—

NOTE   The maximum sized IP datagram that can be carried within an Ethernet frame is 1476 bytes because IP adds 24 bytes of overhead.

Table 5-8 demonstrates expected throughput values in megabits per second for 10 Mbps, 100 Mbps (Fast), and 1000 Mbps (Gigabit) Ethernet network segments operating with the TCP/IP Suite (OSI Layer 3 [network] Protocol is IP).

Table 5-8   *Ethernet with IP Throughput (Megabits Per Second)*

Average Frame Length (Bytes)	10 Mbps Ethernet Bits Per Second		100 Mbps Ethernet Bits Per Second		1000 Mbps Ethernet Bits Per Second	
	50 Percent Load	100 Percent Load	50 Percent Load	100 Percent Load	50 Percent Load	100 Percent Load
72	1.31	2.62	13.10	26.19	442.28	884.56
80	1.63	3.26	16.30	32.61	442.28	884.56
100	2.23	4.46	22.32	44.64	442.28	884.56
125	2.74	5.47	27.37	54.74	442.28	884.56
150	3.09	6.17	30.86	61.73	442.28	884.56
175	3.34	6.68	33.42	66.84	442.28	884.56
200	3.54	7.08	35.38	70.75	442.28	884.56
225	3.69	7.38	36.92	73.84	442.28	884.56
250	3.82	7.63	38.17	76.34	442.28	884.56
275	3.92	7.84	39.20	78.40	442.28	884.56
300	4.01	8.01	40.06	80.13	442.28	884.56
325	4.08	8.16	40.80	81.60	442.28	884.56
350	4.14	8.29	41.44	82.87	442.28	884.56
375	4.20	8.40	41.99	83.98	442.28	884.56
400	4.25	8.50	42.48	84.95	442.28	884.56
425	4.29	8.58	42.91	85.81	442.28	884.56
450	4.33	8.66	43.29	86.58	442.28	884.56
475	4.36	8.73	43.63	87.27	442.28	884.56
500	4.39	8.79	43.95	87.89	442.28	884.56
525	4.42	8.85	44.23	88.45	442.28	884.56
550	4.45	8.90	44.48	88.97	444.85	889.70
575	4.47	8.94	44.72	89.44	447.20	894.40
600	4.49	8.99	44.93	89.87	449.36	898.71
625	4.51	9.03	45.13	90.27	451.34	902.69

Table 5-8   *Ethernet with IP Throughput (Megabits Per Second)*

Average Frame Length (Bytes)	10 Mbps Ethernet Bits Per Second		100 Mbps Ethernet Bits Per Second		1000 Mbps Ethernet Bits Per Second	
	50 Percent Load	100 Percent Load	50 Percent Load	100 Percent Load	50 Percent Load	100 Percent Load
650	4.53	9.06	45.32	90.63	453.18	906.36
675	4.55	9.10	45.49	90.98	454.88	909.77
700	4.56	9.13	45.65	91.29	456.47	912.94
725	4.58	9.16	45.79	91.59	457.95	915.89
750	4.59	9.19	45.93	91.86	459.33	918.65
775	4.61	9.21	46.06	92.12	460.62	921.23
800	4.62	9.24	46.18	92.36	461.83	923.66
825	4.63	9.26	46.30	92.59	462.97	925.94
850	4.64	9.28	46.40	92.81	464.04	928.09
875	4.65	9.30	46.51	93.01	465.06	930.11
900	4.66	9.32	46.60	93.20	466.02	932.03
925	4.67	9.34	46.69	93.38	466.92	933.84
950	4.68	9.36	46.78	93.56	467.78	935.56
975	4.69	9.37	46.86	93.72	468.60	937.20
1000	4.69	9.39	46.94	93.87	469.37	938.75
1025	4.70	9.40	47.01	94.02	470.11	940.22
1050	4.71	9.42	47.08	94.16	470.82	941.63
1075	4.71	9.43	47.15	94.30	471.49	942.97
1100	4.72	9.44	47.21	94.42	472.13	944.26
1125	4.73	9.45	47.27	94.55	472.74	945.48
1150	4.73	9.47	47.33	94.66	473.33	946.65
1175	4.74	9.48	47.39	94.78	473.89	947.78
1200	4.74	9.49	47.44	94.88	474.43	948.85
1225	4.75	9.50	47.49	94.99	474.94	949.89
1250	4.75	9.51	47.54	95.09	475.44	950.88
1275	4.76	9.52	47.59	95.18	475.92	951.84
1300	4.76	9.53	47.64	95.27	476.38	952.75

(continues)

Table 5-8   *Ethernet with IP Throughput (Megabits Per Second) (Continued)*

Average Frame Length (Bytes)	10 Mbps Ethernet Bits Per Second		100 Mbps Ethernet Bits Per Second		1000 Mbps Ethernet Bits Per Second	
	50 Percent Load	100 Percent Load	50 Percent Load	100 Percent Load	50 Percent Load	100 Percent Load
1325	4.77	9.54	47.68	95.36	476.82	953.64
1350	4.77	9.54	47.72	95.45	477.24	954.49
1375	4.78	9.55	47.76	95.53	477.65	955.31
1400	4.78	9.56	47.80	95.61	478.05	956.10
1425	4.78	9.57	47.84	95.69	478.43	956.86
1450	4.79	9.58	47.88	95.76	478.80	957.60
1475	4.79	9.58	47.92	95.83	479.16	958.31
1500	—	—	—	—	—	—
1526	—	—	—	—	—	—

NOTE   The maximum effective data throughput of IP operating over 10 Mbps, 100 Mbps (Fast), and 1000 Mbps (Gigabit) Ethernet is approximately 95.83 percent.

Ethernet with IPX Networking

As mentioned in the previous section, broadcasts that are associated with IPX are going to be sourced from the router, not the LAN segments where they came from; therefore, this perspective MTU size is independent of the LAN media.

NOTE   IPX does not support fragmentation.

If adjusting the frame MTU is the selected course of action, Table 5-9 demonstrates expected throughput values regarding the number of bits per second for 10 Mbps, 100 Mbps

(Fast), and 1000 Mbps (Gigabit) Ethernet network segments operating with the Novell NetWare Suite. (The OSI Layer 3 [Network] protocol is IPX.)

Table 5-9   *Ethernet with IPX Throughput (Bits Per Second)*

Average Frame Length (Bytes)	10 Mbps Ethernet Bits Per Second		100 Mbps Ethernet Bits Per Second		1000 Mbps Ethernet Bits Per Second	
	50 Percent Load	100 Percent Load	50 Percent Load	100 Percent Load	50 Percent Load	100 Percent Load
72	952381	1904762	9523810	19047619	436695454	873390908
80	1304348	2608696	13043478	26086957	436695454	873390908
100	1964286	3928571	19642857	39285714	436695454	873390908
125	2518248	5036496	25182482	50364964	436695454	873390908
150	2901235	5802469	29012346	58024691	436695454	873390908
175	3181818	6363636	31818182	63636364	436695454	873390908
200	3396226	6792453	33962264	67924528	436695454	873390908
225	3565401	7130802	35654008	71308017	436695454	873390908
250	3702290	7404580	37022901	74045802	436695454	873390908
275	3815331	7630662	38153310	76306620	436695454	873390908
300	3910256	7820513	39102564	78205128	436695454	873390908
325	3991098	7982196	39910979	79821958	436695454	873390908
350	4060773	8121547	40607735	81215470	436695454	873390908
375	4121447	8242894	41214470	82428941	436695454	873390908
400	4174757	8349515	41747573	83495146	436695454	873390908
425	4221968	8443936	42219680	84439359	436695454	873390908
450	4264069	8528139	42640693	85281385	436695454	873390908
475	4301848	8603696	43018480	86036961	436695454	873390908
500	4335938	8671875	43359375	86718750	436695454	873390908
525	4366853	8733706	43668529	87337058	436695454	873390908
550	4395018	8790036	43950178	87900356	439511555	879023110
575	4420784	8841567	44207836	88415673	442087779	884175557
600	4444444	8888889	44444444	88888889	444453522	888907045
625	4466248	8932496	44662480	89324961	446633568	893267136
650	4486405	8972810	44864048	89728097	448648955	897297910

(continues)

Table 5-9 *Ethernet with IPX Throughput (Bits Per Second) (Continued)*

Average Frame Length (Bytes)	10 Mbps Ethernet Bits Per Second		100 Mbps Ethernet Bits Per Second		1000 Mbps Ethernet Bits Per Second	
	50 Percent Load	100 Percent Load	50 Percent Load	100 Percent Load	50 Percent Load	100 Percent Load
675	4505095	9010189	45050946	90101892	450517659	901035317
700	4522472	9044944	45224719	90449438	452255131	904510262
725	4538670	9077341	45386703	90773406	453874727	907749453
750	4553806	9107612	45538058	91076115	455388048	910776095
775	4567980	9135959	45679797	91359593	456805222	913610445
800	4581281	9162562	45812808	91625616	458135131	916270263
825	4593787	9187575	45937873	91875747	459385594	918771188
850	4605568	9211137	46055684	92111369	460563523	921127047
875	4616685	9233371	46166855	92333709	461675052	923350104
900	4627193	9254386	46271930	92543860	462725640	925451281
925	4637140	9274280	46371398	92742796	463720167	927440334
950	4646570	9293139	46465696	92931393	464663002	929326005
975	4655522	9311044	46555218	93110436	465558074	931116149
1000	4664032	9328063	46640316	93280632	466408923	932817846
1025	4672131	9344262	46721311	93442623	467218747	934437493
1050	4679849	9359699	46798493	93596987	467990442	935980885
1075	4687213	9374425	46872125	93744250	468726641	937453283
1100	4694245	9388489	46942446	93884892	469429737	938859475
1125	4700967	9401935	47009675	94019349	470101914	940203828
1150	4707401	9414802	47074010	94148021	470745167	941490334
1175	4713564	9427127	47135636	94271272	471361324	942722649
1200	4719472	9438944	47194719	94389439	471952062	943904124
1225	4725141	9450283	47251415	94502829	472518922	945037844
1250	4730586	9461173	47305864	94611727	473063323	946126645
1275	4735820	9471639	47358197	94716395	473586573	947173147
1300	4740854	9481707	47408537	94817073	474089883	948179765
1325	4745699	9491399	47456993	94913987	474574370	949148739

Table 5-9   *Ethernet with IPX Throughput (Bits Per Second)*

Average Frame Length (Bytes)	10 Mbps Ethernet Bits Per Second		100 Mbps Ethernet Bits Per Second		1000 Mbps Ethernet Bits Per Second	
	50 Percent Load	100 Percent Load	50 Percent Load	100 Percent Load	50 Percent Load	100 Percent Load
1350	4750367	9500734	47503671	95007342	475041070	950082141
1375	4754867	9509733	47548666	95097332	475490947	950981894
1400	4759207	9518414	47592068	95184136	475924893	951849786
1425	4763396	9526792	47633960	95267919	476343740	952687480
1450	4767442	9534884	47674419	95348837	476748262	953496524
1475	—	—	—	—	—	—
1500	—	—	—	—	—	—
1526	—	—	—	—	—	—

NOTE   The maximum sized IPX datagram that can be carried within an Ethernet frame is 1470 bytes because IPX adds 30 bytes of overhead.

Table 5-10 demonstrates expected throughput values regarding the number of megabits per second for 10 Mbps, 100 Mbps (Fast), and 1000 Mbps (Gigabit) Ethernet network segments operating with the Novell NetWare Suite. (The OSI Layer 3 [Network] protocol is IPX.)

Table 5-10   *Ethernet with IPX Throughput (Megabits Per Second)*

Average Frame Length (Bytes)	10 Mbps Ethernet Bits Per Second		100 Mbps Ethernet Bits Per Second		1000 Mbps Ethernet Bits Per Second	
	50 Percent Load	100 Percent Load	50 Percent Load	100 Percent Load	50 Percent Load	100 Percent Load
72	0.95	1.90	9.52	19.05	436.70	873.39
80	1.30	2.61	13.04	26.09	436.70	873.39
100	1.96	3.93	19.64	39.29	436.70	873.39
125	2.52	5.04	25.18	50.36	436.70	873.39
150	2.90	5.80	29.01	58.02	436.70	873.39
175	3.18	6.36	31.82	63.64	436.70	873.39

(continues)

Table 5-10 *Ethernet with IPX Throughput (Megabits Per Second) (Continued)*

Average Frame Length (Bytes)	10 Mbps Ethernet Bits Per Second		100 Mbps Ethernet Bits Per Second		1000 Mbps Ethernet Bits Per Second	
	50 Percent Load	100 Percent Load	50 Percent Load	100 Percent Load	50 Percent Load	100 Percent Load
200	3.40	6.79	33.96	67.92	436.70	873.39
225	3.57	7.13	35.65	71.31	436.70	873.39
250	3.70	7.40	37.02	74.05	436.70	873.39
275	3.82	7.63	38.15	76.31	436.70	873.39
300	3.91	7.82	39.10	78.21	436.70	873.39
325	3.99	7.98	39.91	79.82	436.70	873.39
350	4.06	8.12	40.61	81.22	436.70	873.39
375	4.12	8.24	41.21	82.43	436.70	873.39
400	4.17	8.35	41.75	83.50	436.70	873.39
425	4.22	8.44	42.22	84.44	436.70	873.39
450	4.26	8.53	42.64	85.28	436.70	873.39
475	4.30	8.60	43.02	86.04	436.70	873.39
500	4.34	8.67	43.36	86.72	436.70	873.39
525	4.37	8.73	43.67	87.34	436.70	873.39
550	4.40	8.79	43.95	87.90	439.51	879.02
575	4.42	8.84	44.21	88.42	442.09	884.18
600	4.44	8.89	44.44	88.89	444.45	888.91
625	4.47	8.93	44.66	89.32	446.63	893.27
650	4.49	8.97	44.86	89.73	448.65	897.30
675	4.51	9.01	45.05	90.10	450.52	901.04
700	4.52	9.04	45.22	90.45	452.26	904.51
725	4.54	9.08	45.39	90.77	453.87	907.75
750	4.55	9.11	45.54	91.08	455.39	910.78
775	4.57	9.14	45.68	91.36	456.81	913.61
800	4.58	9.16	45.81	91.63	458.14	916.27
825	4.59	9.19	45.94	91.88	459.39	918.77
850	4.61	9.21	46.06	92.11	460.56	921.13

Table 5-10   *Ethernet with IPX Throughput (Megabits Per Second)*

Average Frame Length (Bytes)	10 Mbps Ethernet Bits Per Second		100 Mbps Ethernet Bits Per Second		1000 Mbps Ethernet Bits Per Second	
	50 Percent Load	100 Percent Load	50 Percent Load	100 Percent Load	50 Percent Load	100 Percent Load
875	4.62	9.23	46.17	92.33	461.68	923.35
900	4.63	9.25	46.27	92.54	462.73	925.45
925	4.64	9.27	46.37	92.74	463.72	927.44
950	4.65	9.29	46.47	92.93	464.66	929.33
975	4.66	9.31	46.56	93.11	465.56	931.12
1000	4.66	9.33	46.64	93.28	466.41	932.82
1025	4.67	9.34	46.72	93.44	467.22	934.44
1050	4.68	9.36	46.80	93.60	467.99	935.98
1075	4.69	9.37	46.87	93.74	468.73	937.45
1100	4.69	9.39	46.94	93.88	469.43	938.86
1125	4.70	9.40	47.01	94.02	470.10	940.20
1150	4.71	9.41	47.07	94.15	470.75	941.49
1175	4.71	9.43	47.14	94.27	471.36	942.72
1200	4.72	9.44	47.19	94.39	471.95	943.90
1225	4.73	9.45	47.25	94.50	472.52	945.04
1250	4.73	9.46	47.31	94.61	473.06	946.13
1275	4.74	9.47	47.36	94.72	473.59	947.17
1300	4.74	9.48	47.41	94.82	474.09	948.18
1325	4.75	9.49	47.46	94.91	474.57	949.15
1350	4.75	9.50	47.50	95.01	475.04	950.08
1375	4.75	9.51	47.55	95.10	475.49	950.98
1400	4.76	9.52	47.59	95.18	475.92	951.85
1425	4.76	9.53	47.63	95.27	476.34	952.69
1450	4.77	9.53	47.67	95.35	476.75	953.50
1475	—	—	—	—	—	—
1500	—	—	—	—	—	—
1526	—	—	—	—	—	—

NOTE	The maximum effective data throughput of IPX operating over 10 Mbps, 100 Mbps (Fast), and 1000 Mbps (Gigabit) Ethernet is approximately 95.35 percent.

Case Study: Ethernet Network Analyzers

Several analysis tools are available on the market, and it is up to the individual or organization to make the decision which to use. The purpose of this discussion is to review what information is provided by these, and other, network analysis tools. Two such tools are EtherPeek by WildPackets (www.wildpackets.com, formerly AG Group) and SnifferPro (www.snifferpro.com). The Ethernet interface on the Cisco router can also provide information that can be used to perform some basic network analysis.

Ethernet network analyzers are a specific function of a protocol analyzer. Whereas a protocol analyzer can monitor and analyze data for multiple LAN technologies and protocols, an Ethernet analyzer functions only with Ethernet networks.

Ethernet and other network analyzers are useful when you need to dissect a network issue, such as identify the source(s) of collisions or identify the "top talkers" on a network segment. Network analyzers are also useful for breaking down the traffic flow by protocol, and identifying what percentage of the total traffic flow each protocol occupies.

Ethernet Network Analysis

Figure 5-1 is a SnifferPro screenshot breaking down the IP protocol distribution during a defined period.

Figure 5-1   *SnifferPro IP Protocol Distribution*

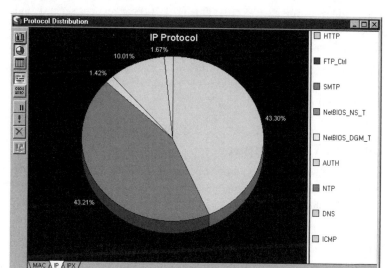

Figure 5-2 illustrates the network utilization for another network segment by category over a 10-minute period.

Figure 5-2   *Network Utilization Ranges*

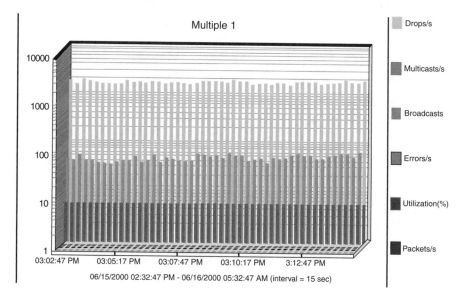

This illustrates the utilization ranges from a low of 6 percent to a high of 10 percent. Packets per second levels range between 1,000 and 1,100 packets per second, and Layer 3 broadcasts are non-existent. Significant here are the errors/second levels, ranging from 30 to 70 per second.

Because these errors have been identified as being significant, the next step would be to drill down with the network analyzer and other network test equipment to determine the source of these network errors.

Ethernet Network Throughput

Measuring network throughput usually requires the use of a network analyzer; however, some rudimentary estimates can be determined by using the formulae and tools discussed earlier in this chapter.

Network Transfer Rate (Effective Throughput)

Given the transfer rate, or effective throughput, of a LAN segment (H_T), where H_1 is the maximum frames per second on a single LAN segment, the following can be derived:

$$H_T = (1/(1/H_1))$$

It was determined earlier in this chapter that the frame transmission rate for a 10 Mbps Ethernet segment yielded 819 maximum-sized (1,526 byte) frames. Therefore,

$$H_T = (1/(1/819)) = 819$$

If the LAN comprises multiple segments bridged together, an adjusted formula is derived:

$$H_T = (1/(1/H_1)+(1/H_2)+(1/H_3)+...(1/H_X))$$

For example, if two 10 Mbps Ethernet LAN segments (819 frames per second) and one 100 Mbps Ethernet LAN segment (8,196 frames per second) are bridged, the following would be used to calculate the transfer rate, or throughput, of the LAN as a whole:

$$H_T = (1/((1/819)+(1/819)+(1/8196))) = 390$$

To correlate the [maximum] frames per second to a bits per second result, multiply the result of H_T by the number of bytes per frame (1526), and again multiply by 8 bits per byte:

$$H_T = 390 \text{ frames per second} \times (1526 \text{ bytes/frame}) \times (8 \text{ bits/byte}) = 4761120 \text{ bps, or}$$
47.6 Mbps.

Average Bandwidth Per User

After the effective throughput rate has been determined, determining the average bandwidth (X) per user is relatively simple using the following formula, where X is the number of users:

$$X = (H_T/X) \times ((\text{maximum bytes/frame}) \times (8 \text{ bits/byte}))$$

Using the maximum bytes for a 10 Mbps Ethernet frame (1,526) and approximately 50 users on the same network segment, the following is derived:

$$X = (819/50) \times ((1526/\text{frame}) \times (8 \text{ bits/byte})) = 199967 \text{ bps, or } 0.20 \text{ Mbps}$$

The average amount of bandwidth per user on a 50-user, 10 Mbps Ethernet segment is approximately 0.20 Mbps (199.99 Kbps). It can be safely assumed that each user has access to more than his respective 0.20 Mbps of bandwidth, unless each user attempts to transmit data at the same time.

Ethernet with IP and IPX Network Throughput

To measure the throughput of an Ethernet network that is operating with IP or IPX as its networking protocol, the same formulae apply, bearing in mind the maximum frame size is reduced due to protocol overhead.

For example, the maximum frame size for IP over Ethernet is 1476 bytes; therefore, on a 50-user, 10 Mbps Ethernet segment, the average bandwidth per user is 0.19 Mbps (193.4 Kbps), as derived by the following:

$$X = (819/50) \times ((1,476/\text{frame}) \times (8 \text{ bits/byte})) = 193415 \text{ bps} = 0.19 \text{ Mbps}$$

For example, the maximum frame size for IPX over Ethernet is approximately 1,450 bytes; therefore, on a 50-user, 10 Mbps Ethernet segment, the average bandwidth per user is 0.19 Mbps (190.0 Kbps), as derived by the following formula:

$$X = (819/50) \times ((1450/\text{frame}) \times (8 \text{ bits/byte})) = 190008 \text{ bps} = 0.19 \text{ Mbps}$$

Summary

After an Ethernet network has been documented, the next step is to review the physical and logical topology for any performance-impacting issues.

Although several third-party Ethernet network analyzers are available on the market today, you can garner substantial information from the router interface.

The three primary Cisco router interface commands that are used to gather information about the state and health of the network are as follows:

- **show interfaces ethernet**
- **show buffers ethernet**
- **show processes cpu**

Each of these commands provides useful information, that when combined, presents a clear picture of how the network segment is performing.

Several "early warning" signs indicate current or predictable network issues that can be derived from the Cisco router.

No segments should have more than one CRC error per million bytes of data, or 0.0001 percent CRC errors (CRCs) on each segment.

$$(\text{CRCs} / \text{total bytes}) \times 100 \le 0.0001\%$$

On Ethernet segments, less than 0.1 percent of the frames (identified as packets in the show interface output) are collisions.

$$(\text{Collisions} / (\text{Input packets} + \text{Output packets})) \times 100 \le 0.1\%$$

On a Cisco router, the number of output queue drops should not exceed 100 in any hour, and the number of input queue drops should not exceed 50 in any hour.

On a Cisco router, the number of ignored packets on any interface should not exceed more than (approximately) 10 in an hour.

On any Cisco router, the number of buffer misses should not be more than (approximately) 25 in a given hour.

On any Cisco router, the 5-minute CPU utilization rate should be under 75 percent.

The following formulae are used to determine the amount of time it takes for a single Ethernet frame (10 Mbps, 100 Mbps or 1000 Mbps) to traverse the network segment.

For 10 Mbps Ethernet segments, using the maximum Ethernet frame size (1,526 bytes), the following is true for the transmission time for one frame (1,526 bytes):

$$9.6 \text{ microseconds} + (1526 \text{ bytes} \times (8 \text{ bits}/1 \text{ byte}) \times (100 \text{ ns}/1 \text{ bit})) = 1.22 \text{ ms} = 819$$
frames per second

For 10 Mbps Ethernet segments, using the minimum Ethernet frame size (72 bytes), the following is true for the transmission time for one frame (72 bytes):

$$9.6 \text{ microseconds} + (72 \text{ bytes} \times (8 \text{ bits}/1 \text{ byte}) \times (100 \text{ ns}/1 \text{ bit})) = 0.06 \text{ ms} = 16667$$
frames per second

For 100 Mbps (Fast) Ethernet segments, using the maximum Ethernet frame size (1526 bytes), the following is true for the transmission time for one frame (1526 bytes):

9.6 microseconds + (1526 bytes × (8 bits/1 byte) × (10 ns/1 bit)) = .122 ms = 8196 frames per second

For 100 Mbps (Fast) Ethernet segments, using the minimum Ethernet frame size (72 bytes), the following is true for the transmission time for one frame (72 bytes):

9.6 microseconds + (72 bytes × (8 bits/1 byte) × (10 ns/1 bit)) = 0.006 ms = 166667 frames per second

For 1000 Mbps Ethernet segments, using the minimum Gigabit Ethernet frame size (520 bytes), the following is true for the transmission time for one frame (520 bytes):

0.096 microseconds + ((520 bytes × (8 bits/1 byte)) × 1 ns/bit) = 4.160 microseconds = 240385 frames per second

Using the maximum Ethernet frame size (1526 bytes), the following is true for the transmission time for one frame (1526 bytes) across a 1000 Mbps (Gigabit) Ethernet network segment:

0.096 microseconds + ((1,526 bytes × (8 bits/1 byte)) × 1 ns/bit) = 0.0122 microseconds = 81967 frames per second

The frame size is determined by the maximum transmission unit (MTU). This value can be changed at the EXEC prompt, using the **mtu *value*** command, where ***value*** is any number between 64 and 18000.

The effective throughput for 10 Mbps, 100 Mbps (Fast), and 1000 Mbps (Gigabit) Ethernet network segments is approximately 99.999213 percent. This does not take into account any upper-layer protocol (such as IP or IPX) overhead or requested retransmissions.

The effective throughput of a specific LAN segment (H_T) can be determined using the following formula, where H_1 is the maximum frames per second on a single LAN segment.

$$H_T = (1/(1/H_1))$$

If the LAN comprises multiple segments bridged together, an adjusted formula is derived:

$$H_T = (1/(1/H_1)+(1/H_2)+(1/H_3)+...(1/H_X))$$

After the effective throughput rate has been determined, determining the average bandwidth (X) per user is relatively simple using the following formula, where X is the number of users:

$$X = (H_T/X) × ((maximum\ bytes/frame) × (8\ bits/byte))$$

CHAPTER 6

Token Ring/IEEE 802.5

Two standard LANs use Token Ring: IEEE 802.5 and FDDI. This chapter discusses the IEEE 802.5-based implementations.

Token Ring

The term *Token Ring* is generally used to refer to both IBM's Token Ring and IEEE 802.5 network implementations. IBM originally developed the Token Ring network in the 1970s, and it is still IBM's primary local-area network (LAN) technology. The related IEEE 802.5 specification is almost identical and completely compatible with IBM's Token Ring network implementations. The IEEE 802.5 specification was modeled after IBM's Token Ring specification, and the IEEE 802.5 specification continues to follow IBM's research and developmental work with Token Ring.

Although the Token Ring and IEEE 802.5 network specifications differ slightly, the network implementations are basically compatible. IBM's Token Ring network implementations specify a star topology, with all end hosts, or hosts, attached to a multistation access unit (MSAU or MAU). The IEEE 802.5 specification does not specify a topology, although practically all IEEE 802.5 implementations are based on a star topology.

Token Ring is considered a half-duplex network implementation because only one host can transmit at any given time. Token Ring's full-duplex network implementation is known as *Dedicated Token Ring (DTR)*. Token Ring hosts connect, point-to-point, to a DTR concentrator or switch and have all available link bandwidth to use for data transmission and reception. Dedicated Token Ring will be discussed later in this chapter.

NOTE Unless Early Token Release is implemented, Token Ring networks will have no collisions in a deterministic Token Ring network environment.

Table 6-1 demonstrates key differences between the IBM Token Ring and the IEEE 802.5 network implementation specifications.

Table 6-1   *IBM Token Ring and IEEE 802.5 Specification Differences*

	IBM Token Ring	**IEEE 802.5**
Data Rates	4, 16 megabits per second (Mbps)	4, 16 Mbps
Hosts Per Segment	260 (shielded twisted pair)	250
	72 (unshielded twisted pair)	
Topology	Star	Not specified
Media	Twisted-pair	Not specified
Signaling	Baseband	Baseband
Access Method	Token passing	Token passing
Encoding	Differential Manchester	Differential Manchester
Routing Information Field (RIF) Size	2 to 30 bytes	2 to 30 bytes
Maximum Frame Size	4 Mbps = 4,550 bytes	4 Mbps = 4,550 bytes
	16 Mbps = 18,200 bytes	16 Mbps = 18,200 bytes

NOTE   100 Mbps 802.5 was standardized in 1998 as 802.5t.

The High-Speed Token Ring Alliance (HSTRA) wrote a specification for 100 Mbps full-duplex Token Ring to meet the challenge by Fast and Gigabit Ethernet.

16 Mbps (half-duplex) and 32 Mbps (full-duplex) Token Ring implementations currently seem to offer sufficient bandwidth for desktop applications requiring networking functions. When the requirement for a higher-speed network infrastructure needs to be met, some organizations will deploy 100 Mbps Token Ring, whereas others will upgrade to 100 Mbps (Fast) Ethernet, 1000 Mbps (Gigabit) Ethernet, or ATM LAN Emulation network implementations.

NOTE   100VG-AnyLAN implementations were designed to help smooth the migration path from Token Ring to Fast Ethernet implementations as 100VG-AnyLAN can interconnect with both Token Ring and Ethernet networking environments. However, 100VG-AnyLANs were unsuccessful in gathering vendor support, despite standardization as IEEE 802.12. Networking vendors opted to support Ethernet instead of 100VG-AnyLAN.

Physical Connections

IBM Token Ring network hosts, or hosts, are directly connected to MAUs, which can be wired together to form one large ring. Patch cables connect MAUs to adjacent MAUs to build these rings, and lobe cables connect MAUs to end hosts. Token Ring MAUs include bypass relays for removing hosts from the ring if a problem is detected with a particular host.

Although Token Ring and IEEE 802.5 networks are physically cabled in a star topology, they operate in a logical ring topology, as illustrated by Figures 6-1 and 6-2.

Figure 6-1   *Token Ring Physical Topology*

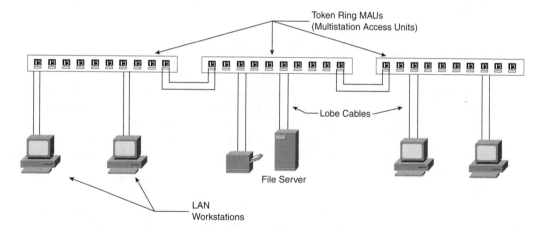

Figure 6-2 *Token Ring Logical Topology*

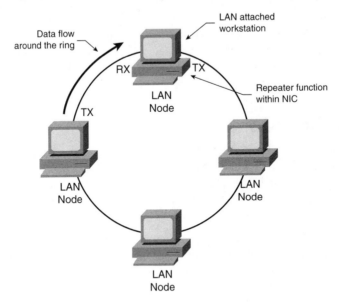

Token Ring Operation

Token Ring and IEEE 802.5 are two of the three principal examples of token-passing network implementations, the third being Fiber Distributed Data Interface (FDDI). Token passing networks move a small frame, called a *token*, around the network. Possession of the token by a host grants the right to transmit. If a host, or node, receiving the token has no information to send, it passes the token to the next host in the ring. Each host can hold the token for a maximum period of time, called the Token Holding Time (THT), and the default is 10 milliseconds (ms).

NOTE Traditional Token Ring network implementations operate in half-duplex mode. Full-duplex mode is supported through the implementation of Dedicated Token Ring (discussed later in this chapter).

If a host that is possessing the token does have information to transmit, it seizes the token. The host then alters 1 bit of the token, turning the token into a start-of-frame sequence; appends the information the host wants to transmit; and sends this information to the next host on the ring, known as the *downstream neighbor*.

While the data information frame is circling the ring, no token is on the network, unless the ring supports early token release. If the ring does not support early token release, other hosts wanting to transmit must wait. If early token release is supported, a new token can be released when frame transmission is completed. If early token release is not supported on the ring, collisions cannot occur in Token Ring network implementations.

The data information frame circulates the ring until it reaches the intended destination host, which copies the information for further processing. The data information frame continues to circle the ring and is removed when it reaches the originating host. When the destination host receives the frame, it modifies the frame by setting a bit so that the originating host will know that the intended destination has read it. The originating host will then check the returning frame to determine if the frame was seen and subsequently copied by the destination.

The direction in which data is transmitted is known as the *downstream direction* and the direction from which the data is received is known as the *upstream direction*. The immediate upstream neighbor that transmits to a host is called the *nearest active upstream neighbor (NAUN)*.

Figure 6-3 illustrates the following:

* Host B is the downstream neighbor of host A.
* Host A is the downstream neighbor of host D.
* Host A is the nearest active upstream neighbor of host B.

Figure 6-3   *Token Ring Neighbors*

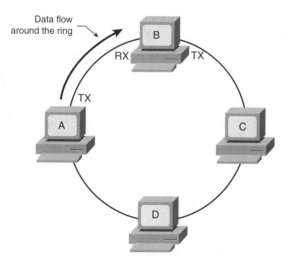

Unlike CSMA/CD networks (broadcast), such as Ethernet, token passing networks are deterministic, meaning that it is possible to calculate the maximum time that will pass before any host will be capable of transmitting. This feature and several reliability features, discussed later in this chapter in the section "Token Ring Fault Management," make Token Ring networks the ideal for applications in which delay must be predictable and stable and reliable network operation is important, such as with legacy SNA or mainframe-based environments.

Joining a Ring

When a host is inactive on the ring, its lobe cable is bypassed by the MAU. A host must actively perform an insertion procedure before it can participate in the ring. Five steps are involved in this process:

1 Test the cable—The host sends a series of Lobe Media Test frames onto its cable, addressed to the null address (hex: 00-00-00-00-00-00), and they are wrapped back to the host by the concentrator. This enables the host to determine whether its cable is faulty or good. If this test passes, the host places a DC current on its cable that causes the concentrator to open its bypass relay and insert the host onto the ring.

2 Determine presence of active monitor—The host sets a timer and watches for indications of an active monitor on the ring. Specifically, the host looks for an Active Monitor Present, Standby Monitor Present, or Ring Purge frame. If none of these arrive during the host's timeout period, the host initiates an active monitor election process by sending Claim Token frames.

3 Verify duplicate addresses—The host will make sure that no other host on the ring has the same address by sending a Duplicate Address Test frame. If a duplicate address exists, then the host will remove itself from the ring.

NOTE   Token Ring networks support locally administered MAC addresses as an option to globally administered, unique, manufacturer-assigned MAC addresses. The duplicate address test is a necessary precaution when locally administered addresses are used.

---

4 Learn upstream neighbor's address—After the host has verified that its address on the ring is unique, it then starts to participate in the nearest upstream neighbor notification process.

5 Obtain configuration parameters—This function is rarely used. The host might transmit a Request Initialization frame to the Ring Parameter Server functional multicast address. If there is a Ring Parameter Server, it responds with an Initialize Host or Change Parameters frame.

NOTE	Token Ring network implementations support locally administered addressing. IBM recommends from 40-00-00-00-00-00 to 40-00-FF-FF-FF-FF. IBM also provides further recommendations regarding station assignment.

Ring Operation Frames

Several special Token Ring MAC frames are essential to the operation of a Token Ring network:

- LLC frames—These are frames that carry user data and carry an LLC header.

- MAC frames—These are frames that carry various types of Token Ring protocol messages.

- Active Monitor Present (AMP) frames—These are frames that the Active Monitor periodically sends out to announce that it is still doing its job of monitoring ring operations. If these messages cease, the standby monitors (any other host attached to the ring) initiate an election process to select the new active monitor.

- Ring Purge frames—These are the first frames that a newly elected active monitor will transmit onto the ring to clean out all old data. Each host that receives a Ring Purge frame resets all its timers and becomes quiet, simply repeating the bit stream it receives across the ring. When the active monitor receives back its Ring Purge frame after it has circled the ring, the active monitor removes the Ring Purge frame and initiates normal operation by transmitting a token.

- Claim Token frames—These are frames sent by a host that detects that the active monitor is not functioning properly. Claim Token frames initiate the election process for a new active monitor on the ring.

Ring Special Servers

Three server options are supported in a Token Ring network implementation:

- Ring Parameter Server—When a host first joins a ring, it sends a request for parameter values, maintained by the Ring Parameter Server. If no answer comes back to the host, default parameters are used.

- Configuration Report Server—When a host detects that its nearest active upstream neighbor (NAUN) MAC address has changed, it sends a message to the Configuration Report Server. The Configuration Report Server can send a message to a host to perform one of the following:

  — Change its parameters.

  — Ask the host to remove itself from the ring.

  — Ask the host to provide status information.

- Ring Error Monitor—This collects periodic error counts from hosts on the ring network.

Error Types

Two types of errors are found in Token Ring network implementations:

- Hard errors—Faults that prevent frames or tokens from circulating around the ring. The beaconing process immediately handles hard errors (discussed later in this chapter).

- Soft errors—Faults that cause data corruption but do not prevent frames or tokens from circulating around the ring. Each host maintains a set of soft error counters and will occasionally report these error counts to the Ring Error Monitor.

NOTE   On Token Ring segments, an indication that network issues are present is if more than 0.1 percent of the frames are soft errors and are not related to ring insertion.

Token Priority

Token Ring and IEEE 802.5 networks use a priority system that permits certain user-designated, high-priority hosts to use the network more frequently.

Only hosts with a priority equal to or higher than the priority value contained within a token can seize that token. After the token is seized and changed to an information frame, only hosts with a priority value higher than that of the transmitting host can reserve the token for the next pass around the network. When the next token is generated, it includes the higher priority of the reserving host. Hosts that raise a token's priority level must reinstate the previous priority after their transmission is complete.

Eight levels of priority are supported by providing each data frame and token two 3-bit fields: a priority field and a reservation field.

Given the following

- Pf = Priority of frame to be transmitted by host
- Ps = Service priority: priority of current token
- Pr = Value of Ps as contained in the last token received by this host
- Rs = Reservation value in current token
- Rr = Highest reservation value in the frames received by this host during the last token rotation

The Token Ring priority scheme works as follows:

1 A host wanting to transmit must wait for a token where Ps ≤ Pf. (The priority of the current token is less than or equal to the priority of the frame to be transmitted by the host.)

2 While waiting, a host can reserve a future token at its priority level, Pf. If a data frame goes by the host on the ring, and the reservation field is less than its priority (Rs < Pf), then the host can set the reservation field of the frame to its priority (Rs ← Pf). If a token frame goes by, and if (Rs < Pf and Pf < Ps), then the host sets the reservation field of the frame to its priority, Rs ← Pf. This has the effect of preempting any lower-priority reservation.

3 When a host seizes a token, the following actions occur:

   — The token bit is set to 1 to indicate the start of a data frame.

   — The reservation field of the data frame is set to 0.

   — The priority field is unchanged (the same as that of the incoming token frame).

4 Following transmission of one or more data frames, a host issues a new token with the priority and reservation fields set appropriately.

Token Holding Time (THT)

Token Holding Time (THT) addresses the issue of how much data a given host is allowed to transmit each time it possesses the token, or stated differently, how long a given host on the network is allowed to hold the token.

THT is based on the following premise: If it is assumed that most hosts on the network do not have data to send at any given time, then a case could be made for letting a host that possesses the token transmit as much data as it has before passing the token on to the next host. This would set the THT to infinity (∞), effectively disallowing any other host on the ring to seize the token and subsequently transmit its data. In this case, it is not practical to limit a host to sending a single message and to force it to wait until the token circulates all the way around the ring before getting a chance to send another message. The "as much data as it has" model would be dangerous because a single host could keep the token for an arbitrarily long time, but the THT could be set to significantly more than the time to send one frame.

The more bytes of data a host can send each time it has the token, the better the ring utilization can be achieved in the situation in which only a single host has data to send. This methodology does not work when multiple hosts have data to send; it favors hosts that have a lot of data to send over hosts that only have a small amount of data to send, regardless of the importance of this data.

Before putting each frame onto the ring, the sending host must check that the amount of time it would take to transmit the frame would not cause it to exceed the token holding time. This means keeping track of how long the host has already held the token, and looking at the length of the next frame that it wants to send.

From the THT, another useful quantity can be derived: the Token Rotation Time (TRT). The TRT is the amount of time it takes a token to circle around the ring as viewed by a given host.

The TRT is less than or equal to the number of active hosts multiplied by the THT, plus the latency of the ring network.

Token Ring Fault Management

Token Ring networks employ several mechanisms for detecting and adjusting to network faults. For example, one host in the Token Ring network is selected to be the active monitor. The active monitor host, which potentially can be any host on the network, acts as a centralized source of timing information for other ring hosts and performs a variety of ring-maintenance functions. One of these functions is the removal of continuously circulating frames from the ring. When a sending device fails, its frame can continue to circle the ring. This can prevent other hosts from transmitting their own frames and essentially lock up the network. The active monitor can detect such frames, remove them from the ring, and generate a new token.

The monitor's job is to ensure the health of the ring. Any host on the ring can become the monitor, and defined procedures exist whereby the monitor is elected when the ring is first connected or on the failure detection of the current monitor. A healthy monitor periodically announces its presence with a special control frame: the Active Monitor Present (AMP) frame. If a host fails to see such a message for some period of time, it will assume that the monitor has failed and will try to become the monitor. The procedures for electing a monitor are the same whether the ring has just come up or the active monitor has just failed.

When a host decides that a new monitor is needed, it transmits a "Claim Token" frame, announcing its intent to become the new monitor. If that token circulates back to the originator, it can assume that it is okay for it to become the monitor. If some other host is also trying to become the monitor at the same instant, the sender might see a Claim Token message from that other host first. In this case, it will be necessary to break the tie with the well-defined rule of "highest address wins," in this case, the highest MAC address.

Monitor Election Process

The Claim Token election process determines active monitors. When hosts detect no active monitor, a host that detects that the active monitor is not functioning will participate in a monitor election by sending a Claim Token frame. The originating host, or transmitter, repeats its Claim Token frame periodically, sending interframe gap filler—1 byte for 4 Mbps Token Ring and 5 bytes for 16 Mbps Token Ring—between the Claim Token frames.

Several hosts might detect the issue and become transmitters at the same time. Furthermore, other hosts that find out what is happening by receiving a Claim Token frame might have been configured to contend the election by becoming transmitters. These hosts will start to send their own Claim Token frames, with any remaining hosts staying out of the contest, repeating the Claim Token frames as they are received.

The transmitter with the highest MAC address wins the active monitor election. The election procedure is clear-cut; a transmitter that receives the Claim Token frame originating from a host with a higher MAC address is knocked out of the active monitor contest and becomes a repeater. This process is repeated until one transmitter is left. When this transmitter starts receiving its own Claim Token frames, it knows it has won the election and becomes the active monitor.

Active Monitor

After the monitor is agreed upon, it plays a number of roles. The monitor might need to insert additional delay into the ring by instituting *delayed release* on the token. The monitor is also responsible for making sure that a token is always somewhere in the ring, either circulating or currently held by a host. A token might disappear for several reasons, such as bit error or the host holding onto the token crashing. To detect a missing token, the monitor watches for a passing token and maintains a timer equal to the maximum possible token rotation time, as demonstrated by the following formula:

$$TRT_{Max} = \# \text{ of Hosts} \times THT + Latency_{Ring}$$

NOTE   *Early release* is when the sender inserts the token back onto the ring immediately following its frame. *Delayed release* is when the sender inserts the token back onto the ring after the frame it transmitted has gone all the way around the ring and been removed.

The monitor also checks for corrupted or orphaned frames. Corrupted frames have checksum errors or invalid formats, and without monitor intervention, they could circle the ring forever. The monitor cleans these frames off the ring before reinserting the token. An orphaned frame is one that was transmitted correctly onto the ring, but whose "parent host" died, meaning that the sending host went down before it could remove the frame from the ring. The monitor detects corrupted and orphaned frames by using the "monitor" bit in the token frame header. This bit is set to 0 upon initial transmission and is set to 1 the first time it passes the monitor. If the monitor sees a frame with this bit set, it knows the frame is going around the ring a second time and it clears the frame off the ring.

The IBM Token Ring network's star topology also contributes to overall network reliability by the detection of dead hosts on the ring. Because all information in a Token Ring network is seen by active MAUs, these devices can be configured to check for problems and selectively remove hosts from the ring as necessary.

A Token Ring algorithm called *beaconing* detects and tries to repair certain network faults.

Beaconing

Whenever a host detects a serious problem with the network, such as a cable break, it sends a beacon frame, which defines a failure domain. This domain includes the host reporting the failure, its nearest active upstream neighbor (NAUN), and everything in between. Beaconing initiates a process called auto-reconfiguration, in which hosts within the failure domain automatically perform diagnostics in an attempt to reconfigure the network around the failed areas. Physically, the MAU can accomplish this through electrical reconfiguration.

All active hosts participate in the beaconing process. The beacon process identifies the location of a fault and starts to send periodic beacon MAC frames in response to any of the following events:

- A signal loss occurs, and the host receives no information from its upstream link.

- The host is receiving bits, but the data does not conform to the expected protocol (for example, a long stream of interframe gaps).

- The upstream neighbor has been sending a string of Claim Tokens for an extended period of time.

NOTE   Remember: An active host intending to become the active monitor on the ring sends Claim Tokens.

Beacon frames contain the following:

- The cause of the beacon

- The originating host's upstream neighbor's MAC address

If the upstream neighbor receives these beacons pointing to its own MAC address, the host removes itself from the ring and tests its network interface card (NIC) to determine if there is a problem.

If the transmitting host's NIC receives its own beacon frame, it means the frames are being delivered around the ring and whatever issue was present has since been resolved. The host then initiates the Claim Token process to elect an active monitor on the ring. If the issue has not been resolved when a timeout expires, the host that started the beaconing process will remove itself from the ring and test its own NIC.

A failure caused by a faulty link or NIC that cannot recognize the need to remove itself from the ring requires administrative action. An administrator monitoring the beaconing process can isolate the fault domain. The fault domain consists of three parts:

- The downstream host, which reports the issue
- The upstream host (of the fault)
- The equipment between the upstream and downstream hosts, such as cables, concentrators, repeaters, and so on

Frame Format

Token Ring and IEEE 802.5 support two basic frame types: tokens and data/command frames. Tokens are 3 bytes in length and consist of a start delimiter, an access control byte, and an end delimiter (see Figure 6-4). Data/command frames vary in size, depending on the size of the Information field, where the data is carried. Data frames carry information for upper-layer protocols, whereas command frames contain control information and have no data for upper-layer protocols.

Figure 6-4   *Token Frame*

Starting Delimiter (1 Byte)	Access Control (1 Byte)	Ending Delimiter (1 Byte)

Token Frame Fields

The three token frame fields are as follows:

- Start Delimiter (SD)—Alerts each host of the arrival of a token, or data/command frame.

- Access Control (AC) byte—As Figure 6-5 shows, the Access Control byte contains the Priority field (the most significant 3 bits) and the Reservation field (the least significant 3 bits). It also contains a token bit (used to differentiate a token from a data/command frame) and a monitor bit (used by the active monitor to determine whether a frame is circling the ring endlessly).

Figure 6-5   *Access Control Byte Breakdown*

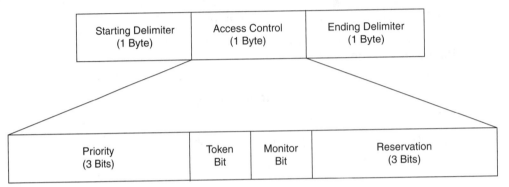

- End Delimiter (ED)—Signals the end of the token or data/command frame. This field also contains bits to indicate a damaged frame or identify the frame that is the last in a logical sequence.

Data/Command Frame Fields

Data/command frames have the same three fields as Token Frames, plus several others, as demonstrated by the following, and detailed in Figures 6-6 and 6-7:

- Start Delimiter—Alerts each host of the arrival of a token or data/command frame.
- Access Control byte—Contains the Priority field (the most significant 3 bits) and the Reservation field (the least significant 3 bits). It also contains a token bit (used to differentiate a token from a data/command frame) and a monitor bit (used by the active monitor to determine whether a frame is circling the ring endlessly). See Figure 6-7.
- Frame Control bytes—Indicates whether the frame contains data or control information. In control frames, this byte specifies the type of control information.
- Destination and Source Addresses—Consists of two 6-byte address fields that identify the destination and source host addresses.
- Data—Indicates that the length of the field is limited by the ring token holding time, which defines the maximum time a host can hold the token.

- Frame Check Sequence (FCS)—Is filled by the source host with a calculated value dependent on the frame contents. The destination recalculates the value to determine whether the frame was damaged in transit. If the frame was damaged, it is discarded. Cyclic Redundancy Check (CRC) is used here.

- End Delimiter—Signals the end of the token or data/command frame. The end delimiter also contains bits to indicate a damaged frame or identify the frame that is the last in a logical sequence.

- Frame Status—Is a 1-byte field terminating a command/data frame. The Frame Status field includes the address-recognized indicator and frame-copied indicator.

Figure 6-6   *Token Ring Data/Command Frame*

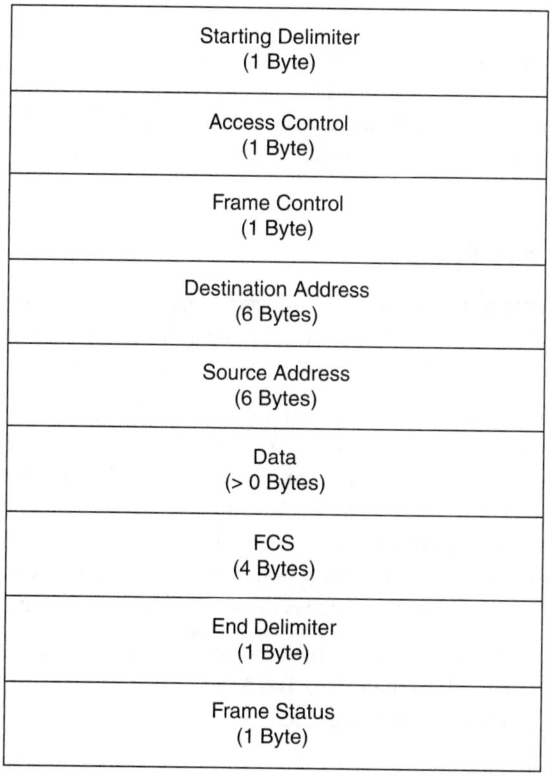

Starting Delimiter (1 Byte)
Access Control (1 Byte)
Frame Control (1 Byte)
Destination Address (6 Bytes)
Source Address (6 Bytes)
Data (> 0 Bytes)
FCS (4 Bytes)
End Delimiter (1 Byte)
Frame Status (1 Byte)

Figure 6-7 *Access Control Byte Breakdown*

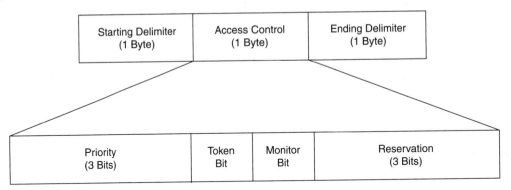

After the data/command is an Interframe Gap, which is essentially a gap between the end of one frame and the beginning of the next. For 4 Mbps Token Ring network implementations, the Interframe Gap is at least 1 byte. For 16 Mbps Token Ring network implementations, the Interframe Gap is at least 5 bytes.

Dedicated Token Ring

The 1997 update to IEEE 802.5 introduced a new access control technique known as *Dedicated Token Ring* (DTR). In a traditional Token Ring configuration, the network utilizes a star topology by the use of a hub, or concentrator.

However, it is possible to have this central hub function as a concentrator or switch, so that the connection between each host and the switch functions as a full-duplex point-to-point link, effectively doubling the available bandwidth on the link; for example, 16 Mbps half-duplex effectively becomes 32 Mbps full-duplex. The DTR specification defines the use of hosts and concentrators in this switched mode. The DTR concentrator acts as a frame-level relay rather than a bit-level repeater, or hub, so that each link from concentrator to host is a dedicated link with immediate access possible; token passing is not used.

DTR can be used in 4 Mbps and 16 Mbps implementations as an alternative to the original token passing method. In the newer 100 Mbps Token Ring implementations, DTR is the only medium access method supported.

The DTR protocol supports backward compatibility with half-duplex Token Ring operation. This backward compatibility means that you could expect to see an implementation where older half-duplex compatible equipment is in use in a DTR environment.

Full-duplex DTR is a point-to-point protocol implementation. Data is not passed around a ring as it is with the traditional Token Ring implementation, and no token exists.

NOTE   Full-duplex Token Ring operates in what is known as *transmit immediate (TXI) mode*. Half-duplex Token Ring operates in what is known as *token passing (TKP) mode*.

Dedicated Token Ring Concentrators/Switches

A DTR Concentrator/Switch performs both concentrating and switching functions. The concentrating function also provides the capability to connect a set of half-duplex hosts into a virtual ring.

A DTR Concentrator/Switch usually has support for SNMP management variables, including RMON (Remote Monitoring). This functionality makes the Concentrator/Switch an ideal network management tool because it accumulates information from several Token Rings.

C-Ports

C-Ports, or Concentrator Ports, are defined for use with DTR Concentrators/Switches to support full-duplex DTR hosts. C-Ports are also backward compatible and can behave like a traditional half-duplex Token Ring port.

Whereas Ethernet ports are always ready and available for use, Token Ring ports passively wait until a Token Ring host terminates the end of the lobe cable, which then initiates the ring insertion process (as described earlier).

NOTE   Dedicated Token Ring Concentrator/Switches usually support both source-routing and transparent bridging capabilities.

The C-Port's behavior depends on network implementation and configuration:

- A DTR host can connect in full-duplex mode, linking the host to the Concentrator/Switch's bridging function.
- Multiple C-Ports can be combined to create a shared logical, or virtual, ring. The Concentrator/Switch's bridging function interconnects these logical rings with each other and with DTR-switched hosts.

Full-Duplex Operation

In full-duplex mode, data does not circle a ring and there is no active or standby monitor functionality on the ring. The priority, monitor, and reservation bits in the frame access control (AC) field are all set to 0 because these functions are not necessary in full-duplex mode.

Detecting a cable or host fault is handled differently in full-duplex operations. Traditional (half-duplex) Token Ring implementations rely on long silences detected by the receivers to indicate an upstream fault. Full-duplex operation does not have the continuous data stream as that of a ring. Frames are sent/received by hosts on an as-needed basis, and the frames do not circle back to the originating host.

To avoid this lull of incoming traffic into a host, a Heartbeat MAC frame was introduced. Heartbeats are periodically sent by both end points of the lobe cable: the DTR host and the C-port on the concentrator/switch. A long silence on the wire in this scenario indicates a hard fault on the line, initiating the beaconing process.

NOTE   The heartbeat frame also replaces the neighbor notification method of providing an ongoing check of the neighboring host's MAC address.

High-Speed Token Ring

As mentioned in the beginning of this chapter, a specification for 100 Mbps full-duplex Token Ring was written by the High-Speed Token Ring Alliance (HSTRA) to meet the challenge of Fast and Gigabit Ethernet. High-Speed Token Ring (HSTR) is a 100 Mbps implementation of DTR.

NOTE   High-Speed Token Ring's official title is 100 Mbps Dedicated Token Ring and was standardized in 1998 as IEEE 802.5t.

High-Speed Token Ring operates only in full-duplex mode and uses the full-duplex DTR protocol for MAC operation.

High-Speed Token Ring Applications

Aside from providing 100 Mbps link speed to the desktop, High-Speed Token Ring has been deployed as switch-to-switch links between 16 Mbps Token Ring concentrator/switches.

Summary

The term *Token Ring* is generally used to refer to both IBM's Token Ring and IEEE 802.5 network implementations. IBM originally developed the Token Ring network in the 1970s and it is still IBM's primary local-area network (LAN) technology. The related IEEE 802.5 specification is almost identical and completely compatible with IBM's Token Ring network implementations.

Token Ring networks do not suffer from collisions like Ethernet networks because only one host at any given time can transmit across the wire. Collisions are possible only if Early Token Release is supported and implemented by all Token Ring hosts.

Traditional Token Ring implementation supports either 4 Mbps or 16 Mbps in half-duplex mode. With the addition of a Dedicated Token Ring (DTR) concentrator/switch, full-duplex operation is available, effectively doubling the half-duplex bandwidth link speeds.

High-Speed Token Ring (HSTR) is officially known as 100 Mbps DTR, and is only supported in full-duplex mode, with a concentrator/switch implemented. The IEEE standardized HSTR as 802.5t in 1998.

Traditional (half-duplex) Token Ring implementations use a beaconing process to determine network faults on the ring. Dedicated (full-duplex) Token Ring implementations use a Heartbeat MAC between the C-port (concentrator/switch port) and the LAN host to determine network health.

Traditional Token Ring implementations utilize an active monitoring station on the ring to monitor network health. This active monitor station is elected by all hosts on the ring via the Claim Token election process. If more than one host contends for active monitor status, the host with the highest MAC address wins, and all other hosts become standby monitors.

High-Speed Token Ring network implementations do not use the active monitor process because each host is on a point-to-point link with the concentrator/switch, and no token passing takes place.

Token Ring and IEEE 802.5 support two basic frame types: tokens and data/command frames. Tokens are 3 bytes in length and consist of a start delimiter, an access control byte, and an end delimiter. Data/command frames vary in size, depending on the size of the Information field where the data is carried. Data frames carry information for upper-layer protocols, whereas command frames contain control information and have no data for upper-layer protocols.

CHAPTER 7

FDDI

The American National Standards Institute (ANSI) introduced Fiber Distributed Data Interface (FDDI) LANs in the mid-1980s as ANSI standard X3T9.5. FDDI LANs operate in a similar fashion to Token Ring LAN implementations.

FDDI LANs are a popular choice for LAN backbones for the following reasons:

- They operate at high speeds—Data is transmitted around a FDDI ring at 100 Mbps.

- They are reliable—Servers, workstations, or other network devices can be connected to dual rings. After a ring failure, a usable path on both rings is automatically available.

- They support a large network diameter—Dual fiber-optic rings can have a network diameter of up to 100 kilometers (km) each.

Fiber-Optic Transmission Modes

In discussions of fiber-optic transmission, a *mode* is a ray of light that enters the fiber-optic strand at a particular angle. The FDDI standard defines two types of optical fiber: single-mode and multimode. Single-mode transmissions generally use lasers, whereas multimode transmissions use light emitting diodes (LEDs) as the light-generating device.

Multimode fiber (MMF) allows multiple modes, or rays, of light to propagate through the fiber-optic strand. These modes of light enter the strand at different angles; consequently, they will arrive at the terminating end at different times. This phenomenon is known as *modal dispersion*, which is the limitation of the bandwidth and distances supportable by MMF. Because of these distance and bandwidth limitations, multimode fiber is usually implemented for connectivity within a building or a campus environment.

Single-mode fiber (SMF) allows one mode of light to propagate through the fiber-optic strand. Modal dispersion is not present with single-mode implementations because only a single mode of light is used. Because only a single mode of light is used, SMF is capable of delivering higher performance connectivity over much larger distances. This performance value is why SMF is generally used for connectivity between buildings and within environments that are more geographically dispersed.

NOTE FDDI implementations over copper wiring are standardized as Copper Distributed Data
Interface (CDDI), and are discussed in the next section, "FDDI Topology."

FDDI Topology

In a FDDI LAN, the hosts that can be the source or destination endpoints of data frames are
referred to as *stations*. A station has a MAC layer, one or more MAC addresses, and one or
more FDDI ports. These stations attach to the FDDI ring, or trunk, either directly or through
a concentrator. Concentrators can be cascaded in a tree topology supporting access to the
trunk for multiple stations.

FDDI LANs operate like Token Ring LANs in that they are made up of a series of point-to-
point links that connect a station to a station, a station to a concentrator, or a concentrator
to a concentrator. FDDI specifies the use of fiber-optic cabling for its infrastructure, but
later copper specifications were introduced and are supported by the CDDI specifications.

Figure 7-1 illustrates a FDDI LAN topology with both single attachment stations (SAS) and
dual attachment stations (DAS). Also illustrated is the use of FDDI concentrators, used to
connect multiple stations to the FDDI LAN. To provide external access to a wide-area
network (WAN), a router with dual attachment FDDI ports (ports A and B) is attached to
the FDDI ring. DAS offer a distinct advantage over SAS in that if the primary path fails, the
attached station will converge on the secondary path.

Separate fibers are used in both transmit and receive directions, providing both an input and
output point on each FDDI station.

Figure 7-1   *FDDI Topology*

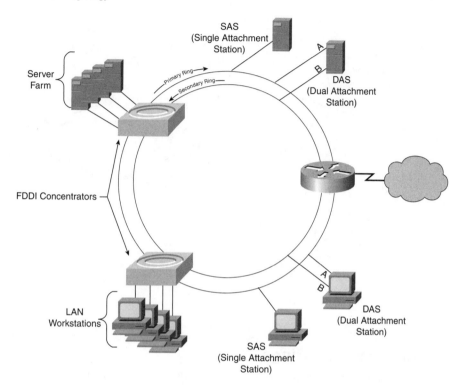

Dual Homing

Dual homing is a fault-tolerant technique used for critical network devices, such as mainframes, server farms, or other organization-identified mission-critical devices. Dual homing provides additional redundancy to help guarantee fault-tolerant operation. In a dual-homed topology, as illustrated in Figure 7-2, the critical device is attached to two FDDI concentrators. The deployment of a DAS on a FDDI ring has a drawback: If the DAS loses power, the FDDI ring is adversely impacted. This situation is avoidable if the DAS is equipped with an Optical Bypass switch.

Figure 7-2 *FDDI Dual Homing Topology*

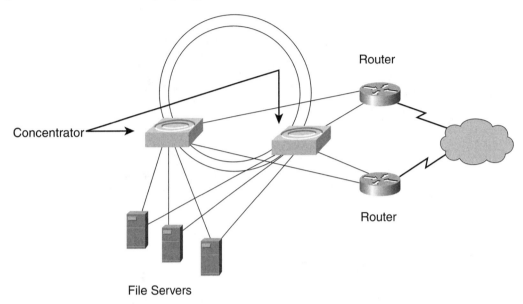

Primary and Secondary Rings

The FDDI trunk consists of two rings, called a *dual ring*. During normal operation, traffic flows on the primary ring of the dual ring. The secondary ring is the backup ring if the primary ring fails. If primary ring failure occurs, the systems that are adjacent to the break automatically reconfigure the ring path and create a new path that is a combination of both the primary and secondary rings.

The total path length around the ring is limited to 200 km. It is this limitation that restricts the LAN circumference of the dual ring to 100 km. If one of the rings fails, the dual ring becomes a single large ring, combining the circumference distances of both the primary and secondary rings.

Although the FDDI standard does not dictate the maximum number of stations that can attach to a FDDI ring, the standard does recommend a default maximum of 1000 port attachments, equating to 500 stations. (Each station has two ports.)

NOTE	The maximum time it takes for a single bit to circle the maximum-length fiber ring that is loaded with the maximum amount of stations is about 2 milliseconds (ms).

FDDI is made up of a primary and secondary ring, which are said to be counter-rotating. Traffic flow direction on the secondary ring is in the opposite direction of the traffic flow on the primary ring. For example, if traffic on the primary ring is flowing in a clockwise direction, the traffic flow on the secondary ring is flowing in a counterclockwise direction.

Single Attachment Stations (SAS): The S Port

A port that is used for a single attachment connection to one of the FDDI rings is called an *S Port*, illustrated in Figure 7-3. Data flows into the port on one line and out on the other line.

Figure 7-3   *FDDI Single Attachment Station Ports*

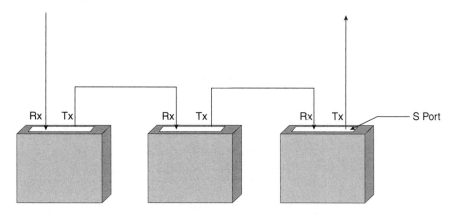

The S Port is a single-ring termination point on the FDDI station, with one receive line and one transmission line. Figure 7-4 illustrates S Port station implementations. S Port stations are single attachment stations, in which no ring redundancy is available to these stations if the ring that these stations are attached to fails.

Figure 7-4 *FDDI Single Attachment Stations (SAS)*

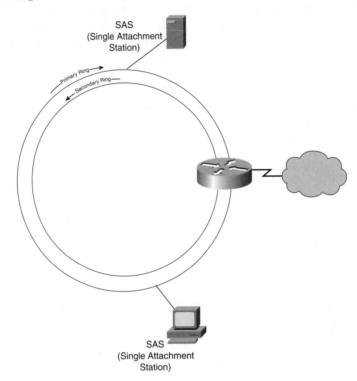

Dual Attachment Stations (DAS): The A and B Ports

Figure 7-5 illustrates the ports of two stations that are attached to both the primary and secondary rings.

Dual attachment stations have two ports:

- A Port—The receive line is attached to the primary ring, and the transmit line is attached to the secondary ring. In short, primary means in and secondary means out.
- B Port—The transmit line is attached to the primary ring and the receive line is attached to the secondary ring. In short, secondary means in and primary means out.

Figure 7-5   *FDDI Dual Attachment Station Ports*

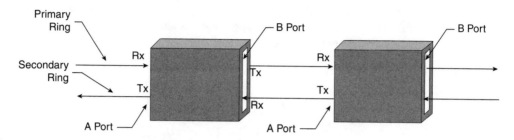

Figure 7-6 illustrates a dual-trunk ring infrastructure in which all stations are dual attachment stations. The primary ring enters each station on the A port and exits on the B port, whereas the secondary ring enters each station on the B port and exits on the A port.

Figure 7-6   *FDDI Dual-Trunk Ring*

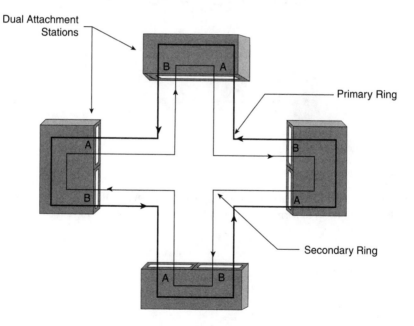

Concentrator M Ports

FDDI concentrators are usually deployed to connect several single attachment stations to the dual FDDI rings. These single attachment stations attach to the M-port on the concentrator, as illustrated in Figure 7-7.

Figure 7-7 *FDDI Concentrator M Ports*

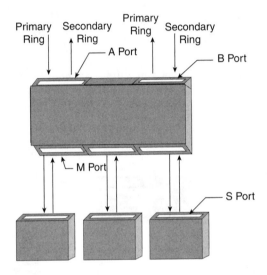

FDDI Ring Failure

When either the primary or secondary ring fails on a FDDI LAN, the stations adjacent to the failure wrap to form a single larger ring, as illustrated in Figure 7-8.

Figure 7-8   *FDDI Wrapped Ring (Around Failed Link)*

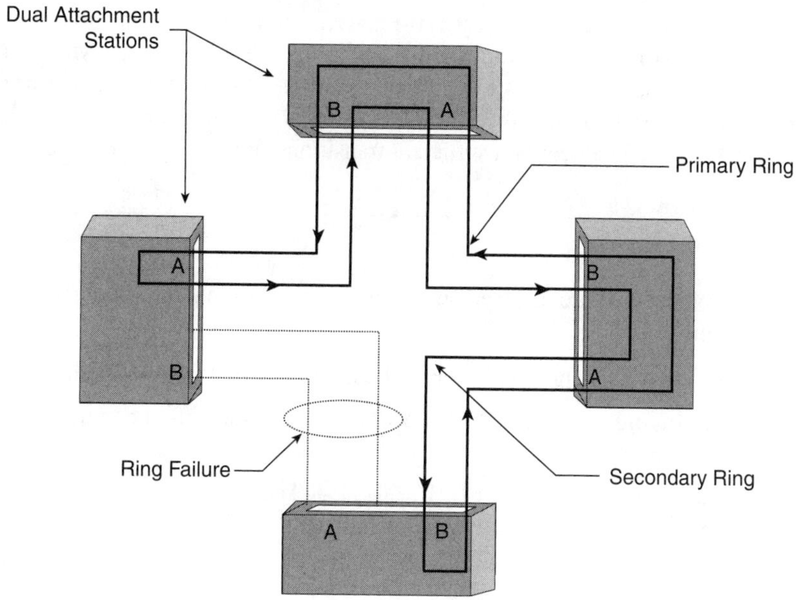

NOTE

NOTE   As previously stated, the path length around the ring is limited to 200 km; therefore, the circumference of each ring is limited to 100 km.

FDDI Media and Encoding

Originally, single-mode and multimode fiber optics were used for FDDI node-to-node implementations. Since then, the introduction of a copper implementation brought about CDDI.

The data-encoding mechanism for FDDI is a scheme called 4B/5B. Data is transformed before it is sent to a FDDI or CDDI link, with each byte broken down into two 4-bit nibbles. Each nibble is subsequently translated into a 5-bit pattern, hence the name 4B/5B.

NOTE	This encoding was chosen because, at the time, protocols such as Ethernet and Token Ring used a clock that was twice as fast as the bit rate, with the extra transitions used for Physical Layer timing (bit synchronization). It was felt that a 200-megahertz (MHz) clock for FDDI would make the components too expensive. Instead, the 4B/5B scheme was devised: It maps each 4-bits to 5, such that the 16-bit patterns used (4 bits worth out of the 32 possible with 5 bits) would all contain sufficient transitions from 0 to 1 and 1 to 0 for timing purposes.

Extra 5-bit patterns are used, either alone or combined in pairs, as special control codes, such as the following:

- Idle (11111)—The idle pattern is continuously sent between frames.
- Start-of-stream delimiter (11000 10001)—The start-of-stream delimiter introduces a new frame.
- End-of-stream delimiter (01101 00111)—The end-of stream delimiter is sent at the end of a frame.

FDDI Operation

As with Token Ring, hosts, or stations, on a FDDI ring pass a token around each ring. The holder of the token has the right to transmit data for a period of time. The token is then passed to the next (downstream) station on the ring.

FDDI allocates bandwidth to each station in a different manner than Token Ring LAN operation. Each FDDI station is guaranteed a reserved time quota and is permitted to transmit frames for that time period when that station receives the token. This use of reserved time is known as *synchronous transmission.*

FDDI stations also loosely share an extra amount of time on the ring. During ring initialization, the stations agree on a Target Token Rotation Timeout (TTRT). The TTRT is the average time any station can expect to wait before it receives use of the token.

During normal operation, the longest time any station will have to wait to receive the token is twice the Target Token Rotation Timeout, or 2 × TTRT.

If a token arrives before the TTRT time, the extra slack time can be used by that station—in addition to its reserved time—to transmit data. This extra time is used for asynchronous transmission. This asynchronous transmission time is unpredictable, unlike the synchronous transmission time.

Two types of tokens are found on a FDDI ring:

- Unrestricted token—This token is an ordinary token.

- Restricted token—A station uses a restricted token when it wants to have an uninterrupted data flow with another station during time currently available for asynchronous transmission. The restricted token enables the station to pass control back and forth to its communications partner, enabling the two stations to send frames back and forth to one another.

Claim Frames

FDDI stations must perform the following actions to prepare a FDDI ring for operational use:

- Decide which station will transmit the first token

- Determine the value of the TTRT

The stations elect an initial token transmitter and choose the TTRT winner by the use of *claim frames*. Each claim frame includes the following:

- The value that the station would like to use as the TTRT. This parameter is preconfigured at each FDDI station.

- The sending FDDI station's MAC address.

If a station receives a claim frame whose target timeout is larger than its own, it discards the frame and transmits its own claim frame. If the timeout values are the same, the sender with the biggest MAC address wins the tie. Eventually, this process winds down until only one winning station is transmitting claim frames and the lowest target timeout value has been discovered. This lowest value becomes the operational TTRT for the FDDI ring. The winning station then transmits a token onto the ring, enabling data operation to begin.

Station Management

Whereas a Token Ring LAN implementation utilizes MAC frames and an active monitor to watch for errors and initiate necessary recovery processes, FDDI LAN implementations operate differently.

FDDI LAN implementations do not utilize an active monitor. Instead, every FDDI station participates in ring management and recovery using a component called station management (SMT).

The station management component performs the following tasks:

- It completes steps required to initialize FDDI functions at the station.
- It controls the optical bypass of an inactive station.
- It tests the integrity of the link to an adjacent node and performs ongoing monitoring of link errors.
- It checks whether the other end of a station port's line is compatible:
  — An M Port must connect to an S Port.
  — An A Port must connect to a B Port.
  — A B Port must connect to an A Port.
- It inserts an active station into the ring and removes it from the ring.
- It initiates the sending of claim frames.
- It wraps and unwraps functions, as necessary, and changes the port used to transmit or receive as needed.
- It manages the station's management information database, which contains configuration parameters, status values, and performance statistics.

Beacon Frames

Beacon frames are used to recover from serious link faults, such as link failures, reconfigured rings, or failed claim processes. Any FDDI station that detects a fault transmits a continuous stream of beacon frames to its downstream neighbor.

If the downstream neighbor is sending its own beacons, it stops and instead repeats incoming beacons. Eventually, only the station that is immediately downstream from the fault is initiating beacons. This station sends beacons that carry their upstream neighbor's MAC address.

These beacons will propagate around the ring to the station that is upstream from the identified fault. This station will remove itself from the FDDI ring and perform self tests. If the station passes these tests, it will reinsert itself into the ring.

Station management operates the recovery processes based on these beacon frames. If a ring wrap is necessary, station management will initiate and supervise the required path change.

FDDI Frames

FDDI frames come in four types:

- LLC frames—Carry user data.

- MAC frames—Perform initialization and recovery actions.

- Station management (SMT) frames—Identify upstream neighbors and perform test and management functions.

- Void frames—Cause receivers to reset their timers to startup values. Void frames circulate the ring before the ring is reinitialized with claim frames. Void frames contain no payload.

MAC frames come in two types:

- Claim frames—Elect the station that will send the first token and establish the TTRT for the ring

- Beacon frames—Announce a ring fault and identify the stations that are upstream and downstream of the fault

Station management (SMT) frames come in six types:

- Neighbor Information frames—Enable each MAC to determine its upstream neighbor's MAC address. These frames are also used to detect duplicate MAC addresses. Neighbor information SMT frames are transmitted every 2 to 30 seconds.

- Echo frames—Used for loopback testing. Echo SMT frames are also used to check the operational status of the target port, MAC layer, and SMT function.

- Status Information frames—Used for Request and Response frames that retrieve basic status information.

- Parameter Management frames—Used to set or get station management (SMT) parameters.

- Request Denied frames—Indicate if a request is inappropriate or in an incorrect format.

- Status Reporting frames—Notify FDDI managers of station events and conditions via a status report protocol.

FDDI Token Frame Format

A FDDI token must be preceded by four or more idle symbols. The starting and ending delimiters of the token are made up of pairs of special symbols, represented by 5-bit code groups that are never used to represent data bytes. Figure 7-9 illustrates the FDDI Token Frame format.

Figure 7-9 *FDDI Token Frame*

Starting Delimiter (JK Code Groups) (1 Byte)	Frame Control (1 Byte)	Ending Delimiter (TT Code Groups) (1 Byte)

- The starting delimiter code groups are always called J and K and are transmitted as '11000 10001'.

- The ending delimiter repeats the T code group twice, transmitted as '01101 01101'.

- The Frame Control byte can be one of the following:

  — '10000000'—Identifies an ordinary token

  — '11000000'—Identifies a restricted token

FDDI Frame Format

The FDDI frame format is almost identical to the frame format used for Token Ring LAN implementations, including the maximum frame length of 4500 bytes.

The sending station will transmit a preamble of at least 16 idles before the start of a frame. Because of delay differences between nodes, the number of idle symbols might shrink as the frame is repeated around the ring. Figure 7-10 illustrates the FDDI frame format.

The FDDI frame is constructed as follows:

- Preamble—A unique sequence preparing each station for an upcoming frame.

- Starting Delimiter—The beginning of a FDDI frame; indicated by the use of a signaling pattern that is different from the rest of the frame.

- Frame Control—Identification of the frame's type, such as LLC or MAC. Frame Control is also an indication of whether the frame contains synchronous or asynchronous data.

- Destination Address—Identification of a unicast, multicast, or broadcast address (6 bytes in length).

- Source Address—Identification of the single station responsible for frame transmission (6 bytes in length).

- Data—Payload for upper-layer protocols or control information. User data frames start with an LLC header.

- Frame Check Sequence (FCS)—A cyclic redundancy check (CRC) based on the frame contents. The receiving station runs the FCS and discards the frame if the calculated CRC values do not match.

- Ending Delimiter—A single T group, instead of the repeated pair found in FDDI tokens.

- Frame Status—Three special symbols that are used like the status bits at the end of a Token Ring frame. These symbols are used to report error status, address recognized, and frame-copied conditions.

Figure 7-10 *FDDI Frame*

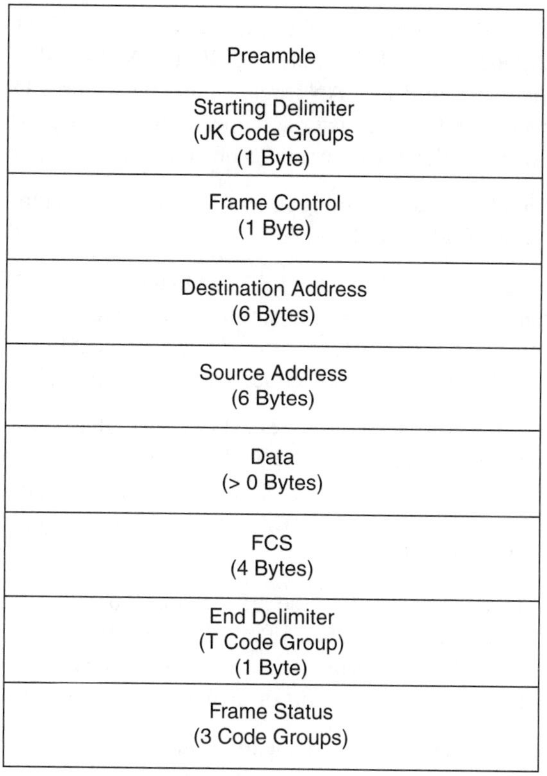

Preamble
Starting Delimiter (JK Code Groups (1 Byte)
Frame Control (1 Byte)
Destination Address (6 Bytes)
Source Address (6 Bytes)
Data (> 0 Bytes)
FCS (4 Bytes)
End Delimiter (T Code Group) (1 Byte)
Frame Status (3 Code Groups)

FDDI LAN Applications

FDDI LANs are often used for building or campus LAN backbones because of their high speed (100 Mbps) and inherent support for fault-tolerant operation. FDDI LANs are ideal for high-bandwidth applications to the desktop, such as multimedia or CAD/CAM.

FDDI LANs are being phased out and replaced with Gigabit, and soon 10-Gigabit, Ethernet LAN implementations. FDDI LANs currently support only 100 Mbps operation.

Summary

Fiber Distributed Data Interface (FDDI) LANs were introduced in the mid-1980s by the American National Standards Institute (ANSI) as ANSI standard X3T9.5 and operate in a similar fashion to Token Ring LAN implementations. Copper Distributed Data Interface (CDDI) LANs were introduced later and operate in the same fashion as FDDI LANs, with the notable exception that CDDI operates on copper rings rather than fiber-optic rings.

FDDI is a technology that is waning in its usefulness and deployment with the advent of Gigabit, and soon 10-Gigabit, Ethernet.

FDDI LANs operate like Token Ring LANs in that they are made up of a series of point-to-point links that connect a station to a station, a station to a concentrator, or a concentrator to a concentrator. FDDI specifies the use of fiber-optic cabling for its infrastructure, but later copper specifications were introduced and are supported by the CDDI specifications.

The FDDI trunk consists of two rings, also known as a dual ring. During normal operation, traffic flows on the primary ring of the dual ring, with the secondary ring acting as the backup ring if the primary ring fails. The implementation of single attachment stations (SAS) and dual attachment stations (DAS) is the determining factor regarding the availability of the fault tolerance.

SAS attach via the S Port to either the primary or secondary ring of the dual trunk. The S Port of the SAS will connect to the M Port of the FDDI concentrator. DAS attach via both the A and B Ports to both the primary and secondary rings of the dual trunk. The A Port on one station will connect to the B Port of the next downstream station on the link.

Unlike Token Ring, FDDI LANs do not utilize an active monitor; rather, every FDDI station participates in ring management and recovery using a station management (SMT) capability.

Any station on a FDDI LAN that detects a fault transmits a continuous stream of beacon frames to its downstream neighbor. These beacon frames are used to recover from serious link faults, such as link failures, reconfigured rings, or failed claim processes.

FDDI uses a 4B/5B data-encoding mechanism. Data is transformed before it is sent onto a FDDI or CDDI link, with each byte broken down into two 4-bit nibbles. Each nibble is subsequently translated into a 5-bit pattern.

The FDDI frame format is almost identical to the frame format used for Token Ring LAN implementations, including the maximum frame length of 4500 bytes.

CHAPTER 8

Token Ring and FDDI LAN Documentation

Chapter 5, "Ethernet Network Review and Analysis," discussed the underlying technology for Token Ring and FDDI LAN networks; this chapter discusses some recommendations and guidelines to follow when documenting these networks.

Most networking discussions today include the topic of documentation at some point, whether the mention is a statement advising that you should document your network assets or a statement advising that network documentation is a good tool to have when troubleshooting a network issue. The challenge here is what network information you should document and later review and analyze for potential network-related issues.

The theme to network documentation is that it should be both easy to complete and easy to understand. In an effort to make the network documentation process easier to manage for Token Ring LAN implementations, templates have been prepared and presented here for use. These templates are preceded by relevant console commands, a case study, and a sample completed template serving as a guide.

NOTE The templates presented here are also available electronically on the Cisco Press Web site (www.ciscopress.com/1587050390).

Each template will be preceded by an introduction or case study with suggestions regarding template completion. These templates are not all encompassing, nor are they designed to be. Rather, these templates are designed to help the consultant, engineer, or anyone involved with a network gather the vital information pertaining to a network and its related segments.

Because Token Ring and FDDI LAN topologies are similar (they are ring topologies defined by a token-passing access method), both documentation templates will be presented here.

Case Study: Naming Conventions

A naming convention, or scheme, that is easy to use should be employed in any network for which you are responsible. A naming convention should scale with the network as it grows. The purpose behind a naming convention is to make network documentation easier to prepare and assist with network maintenance and troubleshooting. For example, a network engineer new to the company's operations would be able to easily recognize the function and purpose of a device named HQ_7500Router_WAN rather than the same device referred to as Sprint Router.

A good naming convention to use would incorporate the geographic location of the device, using the following design:

Geographic-location_Network-device | Division_Network-device

For example, a switch located at an organization's corporate headquarters could be named in one of the following fashions:

- Chicago_Switch
- HQ_Switch

This reflects a network switch located at corporate headquarters, in this case located in Chicago, Illinois.

A network device, used for a particular division or building floor, could use the following scheme:

- Chicago_Switch_Marketing
- HQ_Switch_IT
- Dallas_5509_Floor4 (Dallas_5509_4thFloor)

The *miscellaneous identifier* gives flexibility in identifying the network device in question. This can be used for any comment.

NOTE   Some would view such a descriptive naming convention as a security concern. Like so many things, there are trade-offs involved: descriptive naming versus security. These trade-offs need to be addressed prior to a naming convention. In some instances, the use of internal codes is used, satisfying both network management and security concerns.

For example, NewYork_Router_IT_Backup clearly identifies where and what the network device in question is (router in New York), what the network segment is (IT), and what the device's function is (backup).

A naming convention should be easy and comfortable to use, and a single naming convention cannot work with every network. These are examples of what might be called a "generic" convention, but one that certainly is useful and flexible. If you have a different scheme that works, then please continue to use it. The idea is that if someone else looks at your network documentation, that person can easily determine the topology.

This same naming convention can be globally deployed and supported across the organization by the use of a domain name server (DNS). By deploying the naming scheme across the domain with DNS, administration and inventory are easier to manage. Troubleshooting is also facilitated in a more manageable fashion than without the use of naming.

For example, the **trace route** command in Example 8-1 would not be much help to an engineer without the names (unless the engineer was fortunate to know to which device each network address was assigned).

Example 8-1 *trace route* Command

```
 1   WashingtonDC.MCIRouter.Engineering [207.69.220.81]
 2   cisco-f0-1-0.norva3.mindspring.net [207.69.220.65]
 3   s10-0-1.vienna1-cr3.bbnplanet.net [4.1.5.237]
 4   p4-2.vienna1-nbr2.bbnplanet.net [4.0.1.133]
 5   p4-0.washdc3-br2.bbnplanet.net [4.0.1.97]
 6   p3-0.washdc3-br1.bbnplanet.net [4.24.4.145]
 7   p2-0.chcgil1-br2.bbnplanet.net [4.24.6.93]
 8   p4-0.chcgil1-br1.bbnplanet.net [4.24.5.225]
 9   so-4-1-0.chcgil2-br1.bbnplanet.net [4.24.9.69]
10   p1-0.chcgil2-cr11.bbnplanet.net [4.24.6.22]
11   p7-1.paloalto-nbr1.bbnplanet.net [4.24.6.98]
12   p1-0.paloalto-cr1.bbnplanet.net [4.0.6.74]
13   h1-0.cisco.bbnplanet.net [4.1.142.238]
14   pigpen.cisco.com [192.31.7.9]
15   www.cisco.com [198.133.219.25]
```

Case Study: Simple Token Ring LAN

Figure 8-1 represents a Token Ring LAN and is used to complete the documentation template.

Figure 8-1 *Token Ring Logical Topology*

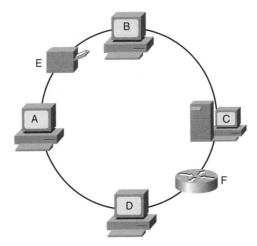

Table 8-1   *Token Ring Documentation (Sample)*

Organization:			JeanneNet		
LAN Segment Name:			CorpHQ LAN	Ring Number:	3
LAN Segment Description:					
LAN Segment Location:					
LAN Backbone Speed [4/16 Mbps]:			16		
MAU Device [Vendor and Model]:				Mgmt Address:	
Number of Users:			10	Primary Network Apps:	E-Mail, Intranet, WWW
ID	**Host Name**	**MAC Address**	**Network Address**	**Description**	
A	LocalUser_1	00-00-86-5c-7a-3a	10.124.173.25/24	Workstation	
B	LocalUser_2	00-aa-00-62-c6-09	10.124.173.26/24	Workstation	
C	Sales_Server		10.124.173.27/24		
D	LocalUser_3		10.124.173.10/24	File Server	
E	LAN_Printer		10.124.173.242/24	Network Printer	
F	Denver_Router	00-aa-84-51-a3-07	10.124.173.2/24	WAN Router	
G					
H					
I					
. . .					
BX					
BY					
BZ					
Notes:					

Table 8-2 *Token Ring Documentation*

Organization:				
LAN Segment Name:		Ring Number:		
LAN Segment Description:				
LAN Segment Location:				
LAN Backbone Speed [4/16 Mbps]:				
MAU Device [Vendor and Model]:		Mgmt Address:		
Number of Users:		Primary Network Apps:		

ID	Host Name	MAC Address	Network Address	Description
A				
B				
C				
D				
E				
F				
G				
H				
I				
J				
K				
L				
M				
N				
O				
P				
Q				
R				
S				
T				
U				
Notes:				

Case Study: Simple FDDI LAN

Figure 8-2 represents a FDDI LAN and will be used to complete the documentation template. Note the single (SAS) and dual attachment stations (DAS).

Figure 8-2   *FDDI Logical Topology*

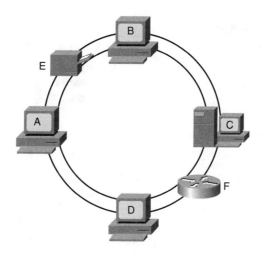

Table 8-3   *FDDI Documentation (Sample)*

Organization:			JackieNet		
LAN Segment Name:			CorpHQ	**Ring Number:**	5
LAN Segment Description:					
LAN Segment Location:					
LAN Backbone Speed [100 Mbps]:			100		
MAU Device [Vendor and Model]:				**Mgmt Address:**	
Number of Users:			10	**Primary Network Apps:**	E-Mail, Intranet, WWW

ID	Host Name	MAC Address	Network Address	Description	SAS/ DAS
A	LocalUser_1	00-00-86-5c-7a-3a	10.124.173.25/24	Workstation	SAS
B	LocalUser_2	00-aa-00-62-c6-09	10.124.173.26/24	Workstation	SAS
C	Sales_Server		10.124.173.27/24		DAS
D	LocalUser_3		10.124.173.10/24	File Server	DAS
E	LAN_Printer		10.124.173.242/24	Network Printer	SAS
F	Denver_Router	00-aa-84-51-a3-07	10.124.173.2/24	WAN Router	DAS
G					
H					
I					
J					
K					
L					
M					
N					
. . .					
BX					
BY					
BZ					
Notes:					

Table 8-4   *FDDI Documentation*

Organization:						
LAN Segment Name:			**Ring Number:**			
LAN Segment Description:						
LAN Segment Location:						
LAN Backbone Speed [100 Mbps]:						
MAU Device [Vendor and Model]:			**Mgmt Address:**			
Number of Users:			**Primary Network Apps:**			
ID	**Host Name**	**MAC Address**	**Network Address**	**Description**	**SAS/ DAS**	
A						
B						
C						
D						
E						
F						
G						
H						
I						
J						
K						
L						
M						
N						
O						
P						
Q						
R						
S						
T						
Notes:						

Summary

This chapter discussed some recommendations and guidelines to follow when documenting Token Ring and FDDI LAN networks.

The tables found in this chapter can be downloaded from www.ciscopress.com/ 1587050390 for your use.

CHAPTER 9

Token Ring and FDDI Network Review and Analysis

After a Token Ring or Fiber Distributed Data Interface (FDDI) network has been documented, the next step is to review the physical and logical topology for any performance-impacting issues.

Token Ring and FDDI network review and analysis concepts are similar because they are both token passing, which means they are deterministic network technologies. This means that it is possible to calculate the maximum time that passes before a host is capable of transmitting, unlike contention-based networks, such as CSMA/CD networks (Ethernet is one example).

The physical topology review ensures that the standards and practices for Token Ring (IEEE 802.5) and FDDI (ANSI standard X3T9.5) networks, such as cable lengths, are followed.

The logical topology review looks at the "soft" side of the Token Ring network segment, analyzing traffic patterns, network thresholds, and possible network issues, such as congestion.

This chapter examines the information provided by the Cisco router interface and the different types of errors that can be found on a Token Ring or FDDI LAN segment, what these errors indicate, and what corrective action can be required.

Token Ring LANs

As discussed in Chapter 5, "Ethernet Network Review and Analysis," token-passing networks (such as Token Ring and FDDI) are deterministic. This feature and several reliability features make Token Ring networks ideal for applications in which delay must be predictable and stable and network operation must be reliable.

The functionality of 4 megabits per second (Mbps) and 16 Mbps Token Ring LANs is identical, with the variable difference being the operating speed of the ring segment and the default early token release with 16 Mbps implementations.

Because Token Ring LANs use a token-passing–based system to control network access, it is a bit easier to predict network operation and the effective throughput of a Token Ring LAN than it is to predict the network operation and effective throughput of a contention-based LAN, such as Ethernet.

NOTE   Deterministic networks such as Token Ring and FDDI typically achieve 80 to 85 percent of wire speed as an average sustained throughput—the rest being the somewhat higher overhead associated with these protocols. In other words, throughput increases with load—up to wire speed minus overhead. With probabilistic (contention) networks, such as Ethernet, throughput quickly drops with load, achieving a typical throughput of 40 to 45 percent of wire speed.

Cisco Router Interface Commands

The router interface commands discussed here are as follows:

- **show interfaces tokenring**
- **show controllers tokenring**
- **show buffers tokenring**
- **show processes cpu**

Each of these commands provides unique and useful information, that when combined presents a clear picture of how the network segment is performing.

show interfaces tokenring

This command is entered from the privileged EXEC command interface on the Cisco router. It displays information about the specified Token Ring interface.

The syntax for this command is as follows:

```
show interfaces tokenring number
show interfaces tokenring number accounting
```

show interfaces tokenring *number*

Following is an example of the output produced by this command, and Table 9-1 presents the field descriptions:

```
Router# show interfaces tokenring 0

TokenRing 0 is up, line protocol is up
Hardware is 16/4 Token Ring, address is 5500.2000.dc27 (bia 0000.3000.072b)
    Internet address is 150.136.230.203, subnet mask is 255.255.255.0
    MTU 8136 bytes, BW 16000 Kbit, DLY 630 usec, rely 255/255, load 1/255
```

```
       Encapsulation SNAP, loopback not set, keepalive set (10 sec)
       ARP type: SNAP, ARP Timeout 4:00:00
       Ring speed: 16 Mbps
       Single ring node, Source Route Bridge capable
       Group Address: 0x00000000, Functional Address: 0x60840000
       Last input 0:00:01, output 0:00:01, output hang never
       Output queue 0/40, 0 drops; input queue 0/75, 0 drops
       Five minute input rate 0 bits/sec, 0 packets/sec
       Five minute output rate 0 bits/sec, 0 packets/sec
       16339 packets input, 1496515 bytes, 0 no buffer
            Received 9895 broadcasts, 0 runts, 0 giants
              0 input errors, 0 CRC, 0 frame, 0 overrun, 0 ignored, 0 abort
          32648 packets output, 9738303 bytes, 0 underruns
      0 output errors, 0 collisions, 2 interface resets, 0 restarts
            5 transitions
```

Table 9-1   *show interfaces tokenring Field Description*

Field	Description
Token Ring is up | down	Interface is either currently active and inserted into ring (up) or inactive and not inserted (down).
	On the Cisco 7xxx series, token ring gives the interface processor type, slot number, and port number.
	"Disabled" indicates the router has received more than 5,000 errors in a keepalive interval, which is 10 seconds by default.
Token Ring is Reset	A hardware error has occurred.
Token Ring is Initializing	The hardware is up and in the process of inserting into the ring.
Token Ring is Administratively Down	An administrator has taken down the hardware.
Line protocol is {up | down | administratively down}	This indicates whether the software processes that handle the line protocol believe the interface is usable (that is, whether keepalives are successful).
Hardware	This indicates the hardware type. Hardware is Token Ring indicates that the board is a CSC-R board.
	Hardware is 16/4 Token Ring indicates that the board is a CSC-R16 board, whereas the CSC-R card is a 4 megabit (Mb) card.
	The interface (MAC) address is also shown here.
Internet address	This lists the Internet address followed by the subnet mask.
MTU	This is the maximum transmission unit of the interface.

(continues)

Table 9-1 *show interfaces tokenring* Field Description (Continued)

Field	Description
BW	This represents the bandwidth of the interface in kilobits per second. Note: The bandwidth command sets an informational-only parameter for higher-level protocols. For example, IGRP uses this value in determining the metrics.
DLY	This is the delay of the interface in microseconds.
rely	This is the reliability of the interface as a fraction of 255 (255/255 is 100 percent reliability), calculated as an exponential average over 5 minutes.
load	This is the load on the interface as a fraction of 255 (255/255 is completely saturated), calculated as an exponential average over 5 minutes.
Encapsulation	This is an encapsulation method assigned to interface.
loopback	This indicates whether loopback is set.
keepalive	This indicates whether keepalives are set.
ARP type	This is the type of Address Resolution Protocol assigned.
Ring speed	This indicates the speed of Token Ring—4 or 16 Mbps.
{Single ring/multi-ring node}	This indicates whether a node is enabled to collect and use source routing information (RIF) for routable Token Ring protocols.
Group Address	This represents the interface's group address, if any. The group address is a multicast address; any number of interfaces on the ring can share the same group address. Each interface can have at most one group address.
Last input	This is the number of hours, minutes, and seconds since an interface successfully received the last packet. This is useful for knowing when a dead interface failed.
Last output	This indicates the number of hours, minutes, and seconds since the last packet was successfully transmitted by an interface.
output hang	This is the number of hours, minutes, and seconds (or never) since the interface was last reset because of a transmission that took too long. When the number of hours in any of the "last" fields exceeds 24 hours, the number of days and hours is printed. If that field overflows, asterisks are printed.

Table 9-1   *show interfaces tokenring Field Description*

Field	Description
Last clearing	This is the time at which the counters that measure cumulative statistics (such as number of bytes transmitted and received) shown in this report were last reset to zero. Note that variables that might affect routing (for example, load and reliability) are not cleared when the counters are cleared.
	Asterisks (***) indicate that the elapsed time is too large to be displayed.
	0:00:00 indicates that the counters were cleared between 2^{31} and 2^{32} milliseconds (ms) ago.
Output queue, drops Input queue, drops	This indicates the number of packets in output and input queues. Each number is followed by a slash, the maximum size of the queue, and the number of packets dropped due to a full queue.
Five minute input rate, Five minute output rate	This is the average number of bits and packets transmitted per second in the past 5 minutes.
	The 5-minute input and output rates should be used only as an approximation of traffic per second during a given 5-minute period. These rates are exponentially weighted averages with a time constant of 5 minutes. A period of four time constants must pass before the average is within 2 percent of the instantaneous rate of a uniform stream of traffic over that period.
packets input	This is the total number of error-free packets received by the system.
bytes input	This is the total number of bytes, including data and MAC encapsulation, in the error-free packets received by the system.
no buffers	This is the number of received packets that were discarded because the main system had no buffer space. Compare this with ignored count. LAN broadcast storms and bursts of noise on serial lines are often responsible for no input buffer events.
broadcasts	This is the total number of broadcast or multicast packets that the interface receives.
runts	This is the number of packets that are discarded because they are smaller than the medium's minimum packet size.

(continues)

Table 9-1 *show interfaces tokenring Field Description (Continued)*

Field	Description
giants	This is the number of packets that are discarded because they exceed the medium's maximum packet size.
Input errors	This is an indication that the interface received a bad packet, which could be caused by CRC, frame, overrun, ignored, or abort errors.
CRC	This is calculated from the data received.
	On a local-area network (LAN), this usually indicates noise or transmission problems on the LAN interface or the LAN bus. A high number of CRCs is usually the result of a station that is transmitting bad data.
frame	This is the number of packets received incorrectly that have a CRC error and a non-integer number of octets.
overrun	This is the number of times that the serial receiver hardware was unable to hand received data to a hardware buffer because the input rate exceeded the receiver's ability to handle the data.
ignored	This indicates that the interface hardware ran low on internal buffers. These buffers are different from the system buffers mentioned previously in the buffer description.
	Broadcast storms and bursts of noise can cause the ignored count to be increased.
packets output	This is the total number of messages that the system transmits.
bytes output	This is the total number of bytes, including data and MAC encapsulation, that are transmitted by the system.
underruns	This is the number of times that the far-end transmitter has been running faster than the near-end router's receiver can handle. This might never be reported on some interfaces.
output errors	This is the sum of all errors that prevented the final transmission of datagrams out of the interface from being examined.
	Note that this might not balance with the sum of the enumerated output errors. Some datagrams might have more than one error, and others might have errors that do not fall into any of the specifically tabulated categories.

Table 9-1 *show interfaces tokenring Field Description*

Field	Description
collisions	Because a Token Ring cannot have collisions, this statistic is nonzero only if an unusual event occurs when the system software queues or de-queues frames.
	Collisions might be present if early token release is implemented in the LAN environment.
interface resets	This can be reset by the administrator or automatically when an internal error occurs.
Restarts	This should always be zero for Token Ring interfaces.
transitions	This is the number of times that the ring made a transition from up to down, or vice versa. A large number of transitions indicate a problem with the ring or the interface.

You can obtain some important "early warning" information by the output displayed from the **show interfaces tokenring** *number* command.

The following output is used to demonstrate these early warning signs of potential network issues.

```
TokenRing 0 is up, line protocol is up
Hardware is 16/4 Token Ring, address is 5500.2000.dc27 (bia 0000.3000.072b)
    Internet address is 150.136.230.203, subnet mask is 255.255.255.0
    MTU 8136 bytes, BW 16000 Kbit, DLY 630 usec, rely 255/255, load 1/255
    Encapsulation SNAP, loopback not set, keepalive set (10 sec)
    ARP type: SNAP, ARP Timeout 4:00:00
    Ring speed: 16 Mbps
    Single ring node, Source Route Bridge capable
    Group Address: 0x00000000, Functional Address: 0x60840000
    Last input 0:00:01, output 0:00:01, output hang never
    Output queue 0/40, 0 drops; input queue 0/75, 0 drops
    Five minute input rate 0 bits/sec, 0 packets/sec
    Five minute output rate 0 bits/sec, 0 packets/sec
    16339 packets input, 1496515 bytes, 0 no buffer
        Received 9895 broadcasts, 0 runts, 0 giants
        1425 input errors, 21564 CRC, 0 frame, 0 overrun, 0 ignored, 0 abort
      32648 packets output, 9738303 bytes, 0 underruns
 0 output errors, 0 collisions, 2 interface resets, 0 restarts
        5 transitions
```

CRC Errors

No segments should have more than one CRC error per million bytes of data, or 0.0001% CRC errors on each segment.

This can be represented by the following formula:

$$(\text{CRCs} / \text{total bytes}) \times 100 \leq 0.0001\%$$

In this example, the total amount of data is 11234818 bytes [Input Bytes (1496515) + Output Bytes (9738303) = Total Bytes = (11234818)]. The total number of CRCs as indicated by the following output is 21564.

```
        .
        .
   16339 packets input, 1496515 bytes, 0 no buffer
        Received 9895 broadcasts, 0 runts, 0 giants
        1425 input errors, 21564 CRC, 0 frame, 0 overrun, 0 ignored, 0 abort
    32648 packets output, 9738303 bytes, 0 underruns
        .
        .
```

Using the previous formula (CRCs / total bytes) × 100), you can determine the following:

$(21564/11234814) \times 100 = 0.19\%$

This is an unacceptable amount of CRC errors because the total (0.19 percent) is greater than 0.0001 percent of CRCs. An acceptable threshold would be 11 CRC errors (11234814 × 0.0001 percent = 11.23).

A high number of CRC errors is usually an indication of excessive noise. In this case, the following actions should be taken:

1 Check cables to determine whether any are damaged.

2 Look for badly spliced taps that cause reflections.

3 Verify NIC connections, and, if necessary, use a network analyzer to determine the source of the bad data. A high number of CRCs can be the result of a station that is transmitting bad data.

Token Ring Soft Errors

On a Token Ring segment, less than 0.1 percent of the packets should be soft errors that are not related to ring insertion.

Token Ring soft errors are faults that cause corruption of the data, but do not prevent frames and tokens from circulating around the ring.

Token Ring hard errors are faults that prevent tokens or frames from circulating around the ring; usually these are hardware-related errors, such as a faulty network interface card (NIC).

To display information about memory management, error counters, and the CSC-R, CSC-1R, CSC-2R, C2CTR, and CSC-R16 (or CSC-R16M) Token Ring interface cards or Cisco Token Ring Interface Processor (TRIP), in the case of the Cisco 7xxx series, use the **show controllers tokenring** privileged EXEC command. Depending on the board being used, the output can vary. This command also displays information that is proprietary to Cisco Systems.

Following is sample output from a Cisco 7xxx Series router:

```
Router#show controllers tokenring

Tokenring4/0: state administratively down
  current address: 0000.3040.8b4a, burned in address: 0000.3040.8b4a
  Last Ring Status: none
    Stats: soft: 0/0, hard: 0/0, sig loss: 0/0
           tx beacon: 0/0, wire fault 0/0, recovery: 0/0
           only station: 0/0, remote removal: 0/0
  Monitor state: (active), chip f/w: '000000........', [bridge capable]
    ring mode: 0"
    internal functional: 00000000 (00000000), group: 00000000 (00000000)
    internal addrs: SRB: 0000, ARB: 0000, EXB 0000, MFB: 0000
                    Rev: 0000, Adapter: 0000, Parms 0000
    Microcode counters:
      MAC giants 0/0, MAC ignored 0/0
      Input runts 0/0, giants 0/0, overrun 0/0
      Input ignored 0/0, parity 0/0, RFED 0/0
      Input REDI 0/0, null rcp 0/0, recovered rcp 0/0
      Input implicit abort 0/0, explicit abort 0/0
      Output underrun 0/0, tx parity 0/0, null tcp 0/0
      Output SFED 0/0, SEDI 0/0, abort 0/0
      Output False Token 0/0, PTT Expired 0/0
    Internal controller counts:
      line errors: 0/0,  internal errors: 0/0
      burst errors: 0/0,  ari/fci errors: 0/0
      abort errors: 0/0, lost frame: 0/0
      copy errors: 0/0, rcvr congestion: 0/0
      token errors: 0/0, frequency errors: 0/0
    Internal controller smt state:
      Adapter MAC:     0000.0000.0000, Physical drop:    00000000
      NAUN Address:    0000.0000.0000, NAUN drop:        00000000
      Last source:     0000.0000.0000, Last poll:        0000.0000.0000
      Last MVID:       0000,           Last attn code:   0000
      Txmit priority:  0000,           Auth Class:       0000
      Monitor Error:   0000,           Interface Errors: 0000
      Correlator:      0000,           Soft Error Timer: 0000
      Local Ring:      0000,           Ring Status:      0000
      Beacon rcv type: 0000,           Beacon txmit type: 0000
      Beacon type:     0000,           Beacon NAUN:      0000.0000.0000
      Beacon drop:     00000000,       Reserved:         0000
      Reserved2:       0000
```

The soft error counter is available in the first segment of the **show controllers token** output, as demonstrated here:

```
      .
      .
      .
  Last Ring Status: none
    Stats: soft: 0/0, hard: 0/0, sig loss: 0/0
           tx beacon: 0/0, wire fault 0/0, recovery: 0/0
           only station: 0/0, remote removal: 0/0
      .
      .
      .
```

Soft Errors

Soft errors allow the ring-recovery protocols to restore normal token operation, but they cause performance degradation due to a disruption in the network operation. Soft errors include the following:

- Line errors
- Lost frames
- Lost tokens
- Lost active monitor
- Corrupted tokens
- Circulation of priority tokens or frames
- Frame delimiter errors
- Multiple monitors on the ring
- List delimiters
- Wiring issues (loose or faulty)
- Line noise or jitter

Soft errors are of four types:

- Type 1—These require no ring recovery function to be executed.
- Type 2—These require the ring-purge process to be executed.
- Type 3—These require the monitor contention and ring-purge processes to be executed.
- Type 4—These require the beacon, monitor contention, and ring-purge functions to be executed.

The upper-layer protocols perform the detection and recovery of lost frames caused by soft error conditions.

Output Queue Drops   On a Cisco router, the number of output queue drops should not exceed 100 an hour.

You can collect this information in two ways:

- Clear the counters and observe the values after an hour.
- Make note of the current count and make another observation after an hour.

No formula exists to determine this number as the output. The **show interfaces tokenring** *number* provides this information, as the following demonstrates.

```
.
.
Last input 0:00:01, output 0:00:01, output hang never
Output queue 0/40, 0 drops; input queue 0/75, 0 drops
Five minute input rate 0 bits/sec, 0 packets/sec
Five minute output rate 0 bits/sec, 0 packets/sec
.
.
```

Output queue drops are registered if the interface is not able to clear up the queue as fast as the router is sending them.

NOTE   The IOS 10.0 and higher code has two output processes; in the 9.1 (9.14) and lower code, only one output process exists.

Drops indicate that the router is overpowering the interface. On a LAN, this would likely be a busy or congested LAN segment, preventing frames from getting out on the wire. These frames usually carry data packets that would be mainly processed-switched in the router, like routing updates, Novell SAPs, access list control, and helpers.

NOTE   If a large number of SAPs need to be sent out, the output process is busy just sending SAPs. This can result in poor performance of other applications running on the router.

The output queue can be modified using the interface configuration subcommand **hold-queue** *xx* **out**, where *xx* is a numeric value. The default for *xx* is 40. The command path to change this configuration is as follows:

```
Router>enable
Password:
Router#:config t
Router(config)#interface ton [Where n is the Token Ring interface number]
Router(config-if)#hold-queue xx out
```

Input Queue Drops   On a Cisco router, the number of input queue drops should not exceed 50 in any hour.

No formula is available to determine this number. The output from the **show interfaces tokenring** *number* provides this information, as the following code demonstrates.

```
.
.
Last input 0:00:01, output 0:00:01, output hang never
Output queue 0/40, 0 drops; input queue 0/75, 0 drops
```

```
Five minute input rate 0 bits/sec, 0 packets/sec
Five minute output rate 0 bits/sec, 0 packets/sec
.
.
```

Input queue drops are registered if the incoming frame rate is faster than the outgoing frame rate; when this happens, the queue is filled up. Incoming data from an interface gets into the input queue for further processing. Looking at a Token Ring interface, data is coming from the Token Ring segment, not going out to it. After the queue is full, all the subsequent incoming frames are dropped.

Drops indicate that the interface is overpowering the router. On a LAN, this would likely by a busy or congested LAN segment. Most likely, frames are being flooded onto the wire into the router's interface.

The input queue can be modified using the interface subcommand **hold-queue *xx* in**, where *xx* is a numeric value. The default for *xx* is **40**. The command path to change this configuration is as follows:

```
Router>enable
Password:
Router#:config t
Router(config)#interface ton [Where n is the Token Ring interface number]
Router(config-if)#hold-queue xx in
```

Ignored Packets   On a Cisco router, the number of ignored packets on any interface should not exceed more than (approximately) 10 in an hour.

No formula is available to determine this number. The output from the **show interfaces tokenring** *number* clearly provides this information, as the following code demonstrates:

```
    .
    .
   16339 packets input, 1496515 bytes, 0 no buffer
      Received 9895 broadcasts, 0 runts, 0 giants
        1425 input errors, 21564 CRC, 0 frame, 0 overrun, 0 ignored, 0 abort
     32648 packets output, 9738303 bytes, 0 underruns
 0 output errors, 0 collisions, 2 interface resets, 0 restarts
    .
    .
```

Ignores are caused when the Token Ring interface cannot place a packet into an incoming hardware buffer pool. In this case, the router does not have enough hardware buffers to accept a packet.

If the ignores are due to bursty traffic, nothing can be done for the ignore issue in the configuration. If this is normal behavior on the network segment, consider upgrading to a more powerful router, such as a Cisco 7xxx Series.

If upgrading is not an option, open a case with the Cisco TAC (http://www.cisco.com/kobayashi/support/tac/home.shtml) to have the issue further evaluated.

show interfaces tokenring *number* accounting

You enter this command from the privileged EXEC command interface on the Cisco router. The command displays information about protocol distribution with regard to the specified Token Ring interface.

The syntax for this command is as follows:

```
show interfaces tokenring number accounting
```

accounting is an optional parameter that displays the number of packets and characters of each protocol type that has been sent through the interface, as shown next:

```
Router#show interfaces tokenring 0 accounting
TokenRing 0
Protocol       Pkts In  Chars In      Pkts Out     Chars Out
IP             7344              4787842      1803        1535774
AppleTalk      33345    4797459       12781    1089695
DEC MOP        0                 0            127         9779
ARP            7                 420          39          2340
```

To determine the protocol distribution percentage, divide the packets (input, output, or total) for the protocol in question by the same parameter from the **show interfaces** *port number* output. For example, examine the distribution for IP traffic using the previous output from **show interfaces tokenring 0 accounting**, combined with the earlier output from a **show interfaces tokenring 0**, shown here:

```
       .
       .
    16339 packets input, 1496515 bytes, 0 no buffer
       Received 9895 broadcasts, 0 runts, 0 giants
         1425 input errors, 21564 CRC, 0 frame, 0 overrun, 0 ignored, 0 abort
       32648 packets output, 9738303 bytes, 0 underruns
  0 output errors, 0 collisions, 2 interface resets, 0 restarts
       .
       .
```

Input Distribution Percentage   You can determine the percentage of incoming IP packets by using the following formula:

$$(\text{Protocol}_{INPUT}/\text{Total}_{INPUT}) \times 100 = \text{Protocol}_{DISTRIBUTION}\%$$

Therefore, $(7344/16339) \times 100 = 44.9$ percent. 44.9 percent of the total traffic input into this interface is IP traffic.

Output Distribution Percentage   You can determine the percentage of outgoing IP packets by using the following formula:

$$(\text{Protocol}_{OUTPUT}/\text{Total}_{OUTPUT}) \times 100 = \text{Protocol}_{DISTRIBUTION}\%$$

Therefore, $(1803/32648) \times 100 = 5.52$ percent. 5.52 percent of the total traffic output from this interface is IP traffic.

Total Distribution Percentage   You can determine the percentage of total IP packets by using the following formula:

$$(\text{Protocol}_{INPUT+OUTPUT}/\text{Total}_{INPUT+OUTPUT}) \times 100 = \text{Protocol}_{DISTRIBUTION}\%$$

Therefore, $(9147/48987) \times 100 = 18.7$ percent. 18.7 percent of the total traffic input to and output from this interface is IP traffic.

Buffer Misses

On any Cisco router, the number of buffer misses should not be more than (approximately) 25 in a given hour.

No formula is available to determine the number of misses. The output from the **show buffers** *interface* provides this information, as the following code demonstrates:

```
Buffer elements:
     250 in free list (250 max allowed)
     10816 hits, 0 misses, 0 created
Small buffers, 104 bytes (total 120, permanent 120):
     120 in free list (0 min, 250 max allowed)
     26665 hits, 0 misses, 0 trims, 0 created
Middle buffers, 600 bytes (total 90, permanent 90):
     90 in free list (0 min, 200 max allowed)
     5468 hits, 0 misses, 0 trims, 0 created
Big buffers, 1524 bytes (total 90, permanent 90):
     90 in free list (0 min, 300 max allowed)
     1447 hits, 0 misses, 0 trims, 0 created
Large buffers, 5024 bytes (total 0, permanent 0):
     0 in free list (0 min, 100 max allowed)
     0 hits, 0 misses, 0 trims, 0 created
Huge buffers, 12024 bytes (total 0, permanent 0):
     0 in free list (0 min, 30 max allowed)
     0 hits, 0 misses, 0 trims, 0 created
0 failures (0 no memory)
```

Although the number of buffer misses in an hour should not exceed 25, as a rule, misses are okay as long as "failures" shown at the bottom of the **show buffers** display is not incrementing.

A buffer miss identifies the number of times a buffer has been requested but there were no more buffers available in the free list. A buffer failure identifies the number of failures to grant a buffer to a requester under interrupt time (the router can create new buffers at process switching level; consequently, there is no failure unless there is no memory). The number of "failures" represents the number of packets that have been dropped due to buffer shortage.

Sometimes the corrective action here is adding router memory, and other times the corrective action might be more extensive, such as tuning the buffer parameters. Before performing any type of buffer tuning action, open a case with the Cisco TAC to have the issue further evaluated.

show processes CPU

The **show processes cpu** command displays information about the active processes in the router and their corresponding CPU utilization statistics. Following is an example of the output. Keep in mind that this is not a complete list, and the processes that are running vary for each system:

```
CPU utilization for five seconds: 8%/4%; one minute: 6%; five minutes: 5%

PID  Runtime (ms)  Invoked  uSecs    5Sec    1Min    5Min  TTY Process
  1           384    32789     11    0.00%   0.00%   0.00%   0 Load Meter
  2          2752     1179   2334    0.73%   1.06%   0.29%   0 Exec
  3        318592     5273  60419    0.00%   0.15%   0.17%   0 Check heaps
  4             4        1   4000    0.00%   0.00%   0.00%   0 Pool Manager
  5          6472     6568    985    0.00%   0.00%   0.00%   0 ARP Input
  6         10892     9461   1151    0.00%   0.00%   0.00%   0 IP Input
  7         67388    53244   1265    0.16%   0.04%   0.02%   0 CDP Protocol
  8        145520   166455    874    0.40%   0.29%   0.29%   0 IP Background
  9          3356     1568   2140    0.08%   0.00%   0.00%   0 BOOTP Server
 10            32     5469      5    0.00%   0.00%   0.00%   0 Net Background
 11         42256   163623    258    0.16%   0.02%   0.00%   0 Per-Second Jobs
 12        189936   163623   1160    0.00%   0.04%   0.05%   0 Net Periodic
 13          3248     6351    511    0.00%   0.00%   0.00%   0 Net Input
 14           168    32790      5    0.00%   0.00%   0.00%   0 Compute load avgs
 15        152408     2731  55806    0.98%   0.12%   0.07%   0 Per-minute Jobs
 16             0        2      0    0.00%   0.00%   0.00%   0 HyBridge Input
 17          6352   163952     38    0.00%   0.00%   0.00%   0 Spanning Tree
 18             4        2   2000    0.00%   0.00%   0.00%   0 Tbridge Monitor
 19          7696     2745   2803    0.16%   0.01%   0.00%   0 IP-RT Background
 20         18484   330791     55    0.00%   0.00%   0.00%   0 BGP Router
 21          2824     9266    304    0.00%   0.00%   0.00%   0 BGP I/O
 22           520     2771    187    0.00%   0.03%   0.00%   0 BGP Scanner
 23             0        1      0    0.00%   0.00%   0.00%   0 OSPF Hello
 24             8        6   1333    0.00%   0.02%   0.00%   0 OSPF Router
```

Table 9-2 describes the fields in the **show processes cpu** output.

Table 9-2   *show processes cpu Field Description*

Field	Description
CPU utilization for five seconds	This indicates the CPU utilization for the past five seconds. The first number indicates the total, and the second number indicates the percentage of CPU time spent at the interrupt level.
one minute	This indicates the CPU utilization for the past minute.
five minutes	This indicates the CPU utilization for the past five minutes.
PID	This indicates the process ID.

(continues)

Table 9-2   *show processes cpu Field Description (Continued)*

Field	Description
Runtime (ms)	This indicates the CPU time that the process has used, expressed in milliseconds.
Invoked	This indicates the number of times that the process has been invoked.
uSecs	This indicates microseconds of CPU time for each process invocation.
5Sec	This indicates CPU utilization by task in the past five seconds.
1Min	This indicates CPU utilization by task in the past minute.
5Min	This indicates CPU utilization by task in the past five minutes.
TTY	This indicates the terminal that controls the process.
Process	This indicates the name of the process.

CPU Utilization

On any Cisco router, the 5-minute CPU utilization rate should be under 75 percent.

No formula is available to determine 5-minute CPU utilization rate. The output from the **show processes cpu** provides this information, as the following demonstrates:

```
CPU utilization for five seconds: 8%/4%; one minute: 6%; five minutes: 5%
```

If the CPU utilization is continually greater than 75 percent, it might be worthwhile to consider a router upgrade or a division of the traffic between multiple routers. Prior to making these changes, get an assessment of what is causing the CPU load because it might be a particular protocol or other process. The output from the **show processes cpu** command lists all active processes on the router, and the load that each process is placing on the CPU. If the router is not that busy, then what might be seen are some abnormalities in the network (broadcast storms, flapping routes).

Token Ring Network Analysis

Before beginning raw data analysis, review the formulae that are used to determine thresholds and measurements for 4 Mbps and 16 Mbps Token Ring LANs.

Token Ring Bit Times [Propagation Delay]

The bit duration for 4 Mbps Token Ring is 1/4000000, or 2.5×10^{-7} seconds. For 16 Mbps Token Ring networks, the bit duration is 1/16000000, or 6.25×10^{-8} seconds. As derived from the speed of light, the time it takes for electrons to traverse 1,000 feet of cable is

1.64×10^{-6} seconds. The propagation delay of a cable segment can be converted into bit times by using the following formula:

(Electron Speed)/(Token Ring Bit Time) = Propagation Delay (measured in bit times)

For 4 Mbps Token Ring LANs with 1,000 feet of cable, the propagation delay can be determined as follows:

$(1.64 \times 10^{-6})/(2.5 \times 10^{-7}) = 6.56$ bit times

For 16 Mbps Token Ring LANs with 1000 feet of cable, the propagation delay can be determined as follows:

$(1.64 \times 10^{-6})/(6.25 \times 10^{-8}) = 26.24$ bit times

NOTE   The speed of light in a vacuum, which is without impedance, is 186,000 miles per second. The speed of electrons across twisted-pair cable has been proven to be 62 percent of the speed of light. Therefore, electrons travel approximately 115,320 miles per second (62 percent of 186,000 miles per second).

With 5,280 feet in a mile, the speed of electrons is equivalent to 608,889,600 feet per second (115,320 miles per second × 5,280 feet per mile), or approximately 609 feet per microsecond. It would take 1.64×10^{-6} seconds for an electron to travel 1,000 feet of cable $(1000/609 \times 10^{6})$.

Token Ring Network Performance

To approximately model and predict the performance of a Token Ring LAN, you need to account for certain variables:

- Number of hosts on the LAN segment
- Total cabling length
- Data frame size

Following is the process used to determine the effective operating throughput of a 4 Mbps Token Ring LAN. These formulae do not include protocol overhead from upper-layer protocols because these are considered part of the data payload in the Token Ring frame.

Token Ring Propagation Delay Equation   Given a Token Ring LAN with N hosts, a free token circulates around the ring an average of $N/2$ hosts until it is seized and turned into a start-of-frame delimiter.

Each host adds a 2.5 bit-time delay to examine the token. A bit time on a 4 Mbps Token Ring LAN equates to 2.5×10^{-7} seconds; therefore, each host introduces a delay of $(2.5) \times (2.5 \times 10^{-7})$, or 6.25×10^{-7} seconds.

A token consists of three bytes (24 bits), requiring 60×10^{-7} seconds for the token to be placed onto the ring, as follows:

$$[(24) \times (2.5 \times 10^{-7} \text{ seconds/bit}) = 60 \times 10^{-7} \text{ seconds}]$$

The time it takes for the token to be placed onto the ring and to circulate half the ring until it is seized by another host is the sum of the product of the steps. The time it takes is the result of the following equation:

$$[(N/2 \times (6.25 \times 10^{-7})) + (60 \times 10^{-7})]$$

After the token has been seized and converted into a start-of-frame delimiter, on the average it travels $N/2$ hosts to its intended destination. A frame that contains 64 bytes of application data is in actuality 85 bytes because 21 bytes are Token Ring protocol-related overhead. The time necessary to place the frame onto the ring is then represented by the following formula:

$$[(85 \text{ bytes}) \times (8 \text{ bits/byte}) \times (2.5 \times 10^{-7} \text{ seconds/bit}) = 1.7 \times 10^{-4} \text{ seconds}]$$

If the Token Ring network contains N hosts, the frame must pass through an average of $N/2$ hosts to reach its intended destination. The time required for the frame to be placed onto and circulate half the ring can be derived from the following:

$$[(1.7 \times 10^{-4}) + (N/2 \times (6.25 \times 10^{-7} \text{ seconds}))]$$

The total token and frame time then becomes the following:

$$[(N/2 \times (6.25 \times 10^{-7})) + (60 \times 10^{-7}) + (N/2 \times (6.25 \times 10^{-7})) + (1.7 \times 10^{-4} \text{ seconds})]$$

or

$$[(N) \times (6.25 \times 10^{-7})) + (60 \times 10^{-7}) + (1.7 \times 10^{-4} \text{ seconds})]$$

After the data frame has reached its intended destination, it must circulate through another (on average) $N/2$ hosts to return to the originating host, which then removes the frame from the network. When this occurs, the originating station then generates a new token onto the network. The time it takes for the frame to circulate through half of the network is then represented as $[(N/2) \times (6.25 \times 10^{-7} \text{ seconds})]$. This time is then added to the time determined from the previous step, deriving the following:

$$[(N \times (9.375 \times 10^{-7})) + (60 \times 10^{-7}) + (1.7 \times 10^{-4} \text{ seconds})]$$

To consider the effect of propagation delay time as tokens and frames flow in the network cabling, you must also consider the sum of the ring length and twice the sum of all the lobe distances. You must double the lobe distances because the tokens flow to and from each host on the lobe. Given that C is the cable length (in thousands of feet), the time (in seconds) that it takes to travel across the ring is derived from the following:

$$[(N \times (9.375 \times 10^{-7})) + (60 \times 10^{-7}) + (1.7 \times 10^{-4}) + ((1.64 \times 10^{-6}) \times C)]$$

or

$$[(N \times (9.375 \times 10^{-7})) + (1.76 \times 10^{-4}) + ((1.64 \times 10^{-6}) \times C)]$$

where N = the number of hosts and C = cable length (measured in thousands of feet).

Token Ring LAN Effective Throughput   To demonstrate how the previous equation can be applied, assume a 4 Mbps Token Ring LAN with 80 hosts and 5,000 total feet of cabling, where $N = 80$ and $C = 5$. Therefore, $[(80 \times (9.375 \times 10^{-7})) + (1.76 \times 10^{-4}) + ((1.64 \times 10^{-6}) \times 5)] = 0.00259$, or 2.59×10^{-4} seconds.

In one second ($1/(2.59 \times 10^{-4}$ seconds$) = 3861$), 3,861 information frames (64 bytes each) can move around the network.

The effective operating throughput of this Token Ring LAN can be measured as follows:

$$(3861 \times (64 \text{ bytes} \times (8 \text{ bits/byte})) = 1.98 \text{ Mbps}$$

It is a safe assumption that the frame rate on a Token Ring LAN is larger than 64 bytes. In these instances, the formulae are processed as follows, first determining the time it takes to place the frame onto the wire, and then determining the effective operating throughput of the Token Ring LAN:

$$((\text{Frame size in bytes}) \times (8 \text{ bits/byte}) \times (2.5 \times 10^{-7} \text{ seconds/bit})$$

NOTE   The maximum transmission unit (MTU) of the interface derives the frame size. The MTU can be found by reviewing the output from the **show interfaces tokenring** *number* command in the privileged EXEC mode.

Using the example of 3,000 data bytes in a frame, plus the additional 21 bytes due to Token Ring protocol overhead, the following is derived:

$$((3021) \times (8) \times (2.5 \times 10^{-7})) = 60.42 \times 10^{-4} \text{ seconds}$$

Furthering the example, assume 80 hosts and 4,000 feet of cabling:

$$[(80 \times (9.375 \times 10^{-7})) + (60.42 \times 10^{-4}) + ((1.64 \times 10^{-6}) \times 4)] = 3946723 \text{ bps, or } 3.95$$
Mbps effective operating throughput

A Microsoft Excel spreadsheet is provided on www.ciscopress.com/1587050390, so that the variables N (Number of hosts), C (Cable length in thousands of feet), and *Frame Length* can be adjusted to model a specific Token Ring LAN environment.

Token Ring Performance Model

To determine the bit time on a Token Ring LAN, divide 1 by the total bandwidth on the ring. Therefore, the bit time for a 4 Mbps Token Ring LAN is 1/4000000, or 2.5×10^{-7}. The bit time for a 16 Mbps Token Ring LAN is 1/16,000,000, or 6.25×10^{-8}.

As stated previously, each host adds a delay of 2.5 bit times. Given that B_T is the bit time as determined by the ring speed, and B_H is the bit time delay for each host, the following can be derived:

$$B_{HOSTDELAY} = (2.5 \times B_{TIME})$$

The next step in the process is determining the amount of time it takes to place a token (24 bits) onto the ring. Therefore:

$$TOKEN_{RINGPLACE} = (24 \times B_{TIME})$$

First determine the amount of time to place a token on the ring and circulate the token around (on average) half the ring ($N/2$, where N is the number of hosts on the ring), represented as $TOKEN_{FLOW} = ((N/2) \times B_{HOSTDELAY}) + TOKEN_{RINGPLACE}$. Then you can determine how long it takes a data frame to circulate (on average) half the ring:

$$FRAME_{TIME} = ((FRAME_{LENGTH}) + 21) \times (8 \times B_{TIME}), \text{ where } FRAME_{LENGTH} \text{ is}$$
measured in bytes

Given on average that a Token Ring frame must circulate through half the ring to reach its intended destination, the time it takes ($FRAME_{TRAVEL}$) can be represented as follows:

$$FRAME_{TRAVEL} = ((N/2) \times (B_{HOSTDELAY})) + FRAME_{TIME}, \text{ where } FRAME_{TIME} \text{ is}$$
measured in seconds

Given the amount of time it takes for a frame to circulate around half the ring, the next step is to determine the propagation delay of the network. Propagation delay is directly relational to the length of the network cabling (C, in thousands of feet):

$$TIME_{CABLE} = ((C) \times (1.64 \times 10^{-6})), \text{ where C is measured in thousands of feet}$$

The frame rate of the Token Ring LAN segment can then be computed as follows:

$$\text{Frames per second} = (1/TIME_{TOTAL} + TIME_{CABLE})$$

where $TIME_{TOTAL}$ is derived from the following: $[((FRAME_{TRAVEL}) + (FRAME_{TRAVEL}) + (N/2)) \times (B_{HOSTDELAY})]$, where N is the number of hosts on the Token Ring LAN segment.

Consequently, you can determine the effective throughput by multiplying the frames per second by the number of bits per frame (bytes multiplied by 8):

$$\text{Effective Throughput} = \text{Frames per second} \times (\text{Bytes per frame} \times 8 \text{ bits/byte})$$

The Token Ring Performance model is available as a Microsoft Excel spreadsheet on www.ciscopress.com/1587050390, where the variables N (Number of hosts), C (Cable length in thousands of feet), and *Frame Length* can be adjusted to model both 4 Mbps and 16 Mbps Token Ring LAN environments.

Token Ring Fault Management

Token Ring networks employ several mechanisms for detecting and compensating for network faults. For example, one station in the Token Ring network is selected to be the active monitor. This station, potentially any station on the LAN, acts as a centralized source of timing information for other ring stations and performs a variety of ring maintenance functions. One of these functions is the removal of continuously circulating frames from the ring. When a sending device fails, its frame might continue to circle the ring. This can prevent other stations from transmitting their own frames and essentially lock up the network. The active monitor can detect such frames, remove them from the ring, and generate a new token.

IBM's Token Ring network star topology contributes to overall network reliability. Because active multistation access units (MAUs) see all information in a Token Ring network, these devices can be programmed to check for problems and selectively remove "trouble" stations from the ring.

A Token Ring algorithm called *beaconing* detects and attempts to repair certain network faults. When a station detects a serious fault with the network (such as a cable break), it sends a beacon frame, defining a failure domain. This beacon frame includes the station that is reporting the failure, its nearest active upstream neighbor (NAUN), and everything in between. Beaconing initiates a process called *autoreconfiguration*, in which nodes within the failure domain automatically perform diagnostics in an attempt to reconfigure the network around the failed areas. Physically, the MAU can accomplish this through electrical reconfiguration, bypassing the MAU port identified as the source of the "fault."

FDDI LANs

As discussed in Chapter 6, "Token Ring/IEEE 802.5," token-passing networks (such as Token Ring and FDDI) are deterministic. This means that it is possible to calculate the maximum time that passes before a host is capable of transmitting, unlike CSMA/CD (contention-based) networks, such as Ethernet. The high bandwidth relative to Token Ring LANs, the deterministic feature, and several reliability features make FDDI networks ideal for applications in which delay must be predictable and network operation must be high speed, stable, and reliable.

Because FDDI LANs use a token-passing–based system to control network access, it is a bit easier to predict network operation and the effective throughput of a FDDI LAN than it is to predict the network operation and effective throughput of a CSMA/CD-based LAN, such as Ethernet.

Cisco Router Interface Commands

The router interface commands discussed here include the following:

- **show interfaces fddi**
- **show buffers fddi**
- **show processes cpu**

Each of these commands provides unique and useful information, that when combined, presents a clear picture of how the network segment is performing.

show interfaces FDDI

When you enter this command from the privileged EXEC command interface on the Cisco router, it will display information about the specified Token Ring interface.

The syntax for this command is as follows:

```
show interfaces fddi number
show interfaces fddi number accounting
```

show interfaces fddi *number*

Following is an example of the output produced by this command that is detailed in Table 9-3:

```
Router# show interfaces fddi 0

Fddi0 is up, line protocol is up
  Hardware is cBus Fddi, address is 0000.0c06.8de8 (bia 0000.0c06.8de8)
  Internet address is 131.108.33.9, subnet mask is 255.255.255.0
  MTU 4470 bytes, BW 100000 Kbit, DLY 100 usec, rely 255/255, load 1/255
  Encapsulation SNAP, loopback not set, keepalive not set
  ARP type: SNAP, ARP Timeout 4:00:00
  Phy-A state is active, neighbor is B, cmt signal bits 008/20C, status ILS
  Phy-B state is connect, neighbor is unk, cmt signal bits 20C/000, status QLS
  ECM is insert, CFM is c_wrap_a, RMT is ring_op
  token rotation 5000 usec, ring operational 1d01
  Upstream neighbor 0000.0c06.8b7d, downstream neighbor 0000.0c06.8b7d
  Last input 0:00:08, output 0:00:08, output hang never
  Last clearing of "show interface" counters never
  Output queue 0/40, 0 drops; input queue 0/75, 0 drops
  Five minute input rate 5000 bits/sec, 1 packets/sec
  Five minute output rate 76000 bits/sec, 51 packets/sec
     852914 packets input, 205752094 bytes, 0 no buffer
     Received 126752 broadcasts, 0 runts, 0 giants
     0 input errors, 0 CRC, 0 frame, 0 overrun, 0 ignored, 0 abort
     8213126 packets output, 616453062 bytes, 0 underruns
     0 output errors, 0 collisions, 4 interface resets, 0 restarts
     5 transitions, 0 traces
```

Table 9-3   *show interfaces fddi* Field Description

Field	Description
FDDI is up I down I administratively down	This gives the interface processor unit number and tells whether the interface hardware is currently active and can transmit and receive, or if it has been taken down by an administrator.
	"Disabled" indicates that the router has received more than 5,000 errors in a keepalive interval, which is 10 seconds by default.
line protocol is {up I down I administratively down}	This indicates whether the software processes that handle the line protocol believe that the interface is usable (that is, whether keepalives are successful).
Hardware	This provides the hardware type, followed by the hardware (MAC) address.
Internet address	This lists the Internet address followed by subnet mask.
MTU	This lists the maximum transmission unit of the interface.
BW	This lists the bandwidth of the interface in kilobits per second.
	Note: The bandwidth command sets an informational-only parameter for higher-level protocols. For example, IGRP uses this value in determining the metrics.
DLY	This is the delay of the interface in microseconds.
rely	This is the reliability of the interface as a fraction of 255 (255/255 is 100 percent reliability), calculated as an exponential average over 5 minutes.
load	This is the load on the interface as a fraction of 255 (255/255 is completely saturated), calculated as an exponential average over 5 minutes.
Encapsulation	This is the encapsulation method assigned to the interface.
loopback	This indicates whether loopback is set.
keepalive	This indicates whether keepalives are set.
ARP type:	This is the type of Address Resolution Protocol that is assigned.
Phy- {A I B}	This lists the state that the Physical A or Physical B connection is in. This state can be off, active, trace, connect, next, signal, join, verify, or break.

(continues)

Table 9-3 *show interfaces fddi Field Description (Continued)*

Field	Description
neighbor	This is the state of the neighbor:
	• A—Indicates that the CMT process has established a connection with its neighbor. The bits that are received during the CMT signaling process indicate that the neighbor is a Physical A type dual attachment station (DAS) or concentrator that attaches to the primary ring IN and the secondary ring OUT when attaching to the dual ring.
	CMT is defined as connection management. CMT is the FDDI process that handles the transition of the ring through its various states (off, active, connect, and so on), as defined by the ANSI X3T9.5 specification.
	• S—Indicates that the CMT process has established a connection with its neighbor. The bits that are received during the CMT signaling process indicate that the neighbor is one Physical type in a single attachment station (SAS).
	• B—Indicates that the CMT process has established a connection with its neighbor. The bits that are received during the CMT signaling process indicate that the neighbor is a Physical B dual attachment station or concentrator that attaches to the secondary ring IN and the primary ring OUT when attaching to the dual ring.
	• M—Indicates that the CMT process has established a connection with its neighbor. The bits received during the CMT signaling process indicate that the router's neighbor is a Physical M-type concentrator that serves as a Master to a connected station or concentrator.
	• unk—Indicates that the network server has not completed the CMT process, and as a result, does not know about its neighbor.
cmt signal bits	This shows the transmitted/received CMT bits. The transmitted bits are 0x008 for a Physical A type and 0x20C for a Physical B type. The number after the slash (/) is the received signal bits. If the connection is not active, the received bits are zero (0).

Table 9-3   *show interfaces fddi* Field Description

Field	Description
status	The status value displayed is the actual status on the fiber. The FDDI standard defines the following values:
	• LSU—Line state unknown is the criteria for entering or remaining in any other line state that has not been met.
	• NLS—Noise line state is entered upon the occurrence of 16 potential noise events without satisfying the criteria for entry into another line state.
	• MLS—Master line state is entered upon the reception of eight or nine consecutive HQ or QH symbol pairs.
	• ILS—Idle line state is entered upon receipt of four or five idle symbols.
	• HLS—Halt line state is entered upon the receipt of 16 or 17 consecutive H symbols.
	• QLS—Quiet line state is entered upon the receipt of 16 or 17 consecutive Q symbols or when carrier-detect goes low.
	• ALS—Active line state is entered upon receipt of a JK symbol pair when carrier-detect is high.
	• OVUF—This is elasticity buffer overflow/underflow. The normal states for a connected Physical type are ILS or ALS. A report that displays the QLS status indicates that the fiber is disconnected from Physical B, that it is not connected to another Physical type, or that the other station is not running.
Off	This indicates that the CMT is not running on the Physical sublayer. The state is off if the interface has been shut down or if the cmt disconnect command has been issued for Physical A or Physical B.
Brk	Break state is the entry point in the start of a physical connection management (PCM) connection.
Tra	Trace state localizes a stuck beacon condition.
Con	Connect state is used to synchronize the ends of the connection for the signaling sequence.
Nxt	Next state separates the signaling performed in the signal state and transmits protocol data units (PDUs) while MAC Local Loop is performed.
Sig	Signal state is entered from the next state when a bit is ready to be transmitted.

(continues)

Table 9-3 *show interfaces fddi* *Field Description (Continued)*

Field	Description
Join	Join state is the first of three states in a unique sequence of transmitted symbol streams that are received as line states—the halt line state, master line state, and idle line state, or HLS-MLS-ILS—that leads to an active connection.
Vfy	Verify state is the second state in the path to the active state and is reached by a connection that is synchronized.
Act	Active state indicates that the CMT process has established communications with its physical neighbor.
	The transition states are defined in the X3T9.5 specification. (Refer to the X3T9.5 specification for details about these states.)
ECM	ECM is the SMT entity coordination management, which overlooks the operation of CFM and PCM. The ECM state can be one of the following:
	• out—The router is isolated from the network.
	• in—The router is actively connected to the network. This is the normal state for a connected router.
	• trace—The router is trying to localize a stuck beacon condition.
	• leave—The router is allowing time for all the connections to break before leaving the network.
	• path_test—The router is testing its internal paths.
	• insert—The router is allowing time for the optical bypass to insert.
	• check—The router is making sure optical bypasses are switched correctly.
	• deinsert—The router is allowing time for the optical bypass to deinsert.

Table 9-3   *show interfaces fddi* *Field Description*

Field	Description
CFM	This contains information about the current state of the MAC connection.
	The Configuration Management (CFM) state can be one of the following:
	• isolated—The MAC is not attached to a Physical type.
	• wrap_a—The MAC is attached to Physical A. Data is received on Physical A and transmitted on Physical A.
	• wrap_b—The MAC is attached to Physical B. Data is received on Physical B and transmitted on Physical B.
	• wrap_s—The MAC is attached to Physical S. Data is received on Physical S and transmitted on Physical S. This is the normal mode for a single attachment stations (SAS).
	• thru—The MAC is attached to Physical A and B. Data is received on Physical A and transmitted on Physical B. This is the normal mode for a DAS with one MAC. The ring has been operational for 1 minute and 42 seconds.
RMT	RMT (Ring Management) is the SMT MAC-related state machine.
	The RMT state can be one of the following:
	• isolated—The MAC is not trying to participate in the ring. This is the initial state.
	• non_op—The MAC is participating in ring recovery and the ring is not operational.
	• ring_op—The MAC is participating in an operational ring. This is the normal state while the MAC is connected to the ring.
	• detect—The ring has been non-operational for longer than normal. Duplicate address conditions are being checked.
	• non_op_dup—Indications have been received that the address of the MAC is a duplicate of another MAC on the ring. Ring is not operational.
	• ring_op_dup—Indications have been received that the address of the MAC is a duplicate of another MAC on the ring. The ring is operational in this state.
	• directed—The MAC is sending beacon frames notifying the ring of the stuck condition.
	• trace—A trace has been initiated by this MAC, and the RMT state machine is waiting for its completion before starting an internal path test.

(continues)

Table 9-3 *show interfaces fddi* Field Description (Continued)

Field	Description
token rotation	Token rotation value is the default or configured rotation value as determined by the **fddi token-rotation-time** command. All stations on the ring use this value. The default is 5,000 microseconds.
ring operational	When the ring is operational, the displayed value is the negotiated token rotation time of all stations on the ring.
	Operational times are displayed by the number of hours:minutes:seconds that the ring has been up. If the ring is not operational, the message "ring not operational" is displayed.
Upstream | downstream neighbor	This displays the canonical MAC address of outgoing upstream and downstream neighbors. If the address is unknown, the value is the FDDI unknown address (0x00 00 f8 00 00 00).
Last input	This is the number of hours, minutes, and seconds since the last packet was successfully received by an interface. Last input is useful for knowing when a dead interface failed.
output	This is the number of hours, minutes, and seconds since the last packet was successfully transmitted by an interface.
output hang	This is the number of hours, minutes, and seconds (or never) since the interface was last reset because of a transmission that took too long.
	When the number of hours in any of the "last" fields exceeds 24 hours, the number of days and hours is printed. If that field overflows, asterisks are printed.
Last clearing	This is the time at which the counters that measure cumulative statistics (such as number of bytes transmitted and received) shown in this report were last reset to zero. Note that variables that might affect routing (for example, load and reliability) are not cleared when the counters are cleared.
	Asterisks (***) indicate that the elapsed time is too large to be displayed.
	0:00:00 indicates that the counters were cleared more than 2 31 ms (and less than 2 32 ms) ago.
Output queue, input queue, drops	This is the number of packets in output and input queues. Each number is followed by a slash, the maximum size of the queue, and the number of packets dropped due to a full queue.

Table 9-3   *show interfaces fddi* Field Description

Field	Description
Five-minute input rate Five-minute output rate	This is the average number of bits and packets transmitted per second in the past 5 minutes.
	The five-minute input and output rates should be used only as an approximation of traffic per second during a given 5-minute period.
	These rates are exponentially weighted averages with a time constant of 5 minutes. A period of four time constants must pass before the average is within 2% of the instantaneous rate of a uniform stream of traffic over that period.
packets input	This is the total number of error-free packets received by the system.
bytes	This is the total number of bytes, including data and MAC encapsulation, in the error-free packets received by the system.
no buffer	This is the number of received packets discarded because the main system has no buffer space. Compare with ignored count.
	LAN broadcast storms and bursts of noise on serial lines are often responsible for no input buffer events.
broadcasts	This is the total number of broadcast or multicast packets received by the interface.
runts	This is the number of packets discarded because they are smaller than the medium's minimum packet size.
giants	This is the number of packets discarded because they exceed the medium's maximum packet size.
CRC	This is the cyclic redundancy checksum that is generated by the originating LAN station or far-end device that does not match the checksum calculated from the data received.
	On a LAN, this usually indicates noise or transmission problems on the LAN interface or the LAN bus. A high number of CRCs is usually the result of collisions or a station transmitting bad data. Because collisions do not occur on a FDDI LAN during normal operation, and FDDI does not support early token release, CRC errors are usually caused by faulty equipment or stations that transmit bad data.
frame	This is the number of packets received incorrectly that have a CRC error and a non-integer number of octets.
	On a FDDI LAN, this can be the result of a failing fiber (cracks) or a hardware malfunction.
overrun	This is the number of times that the serial receiver hardware was unable to hand received data to a hardware buffer because the input rate exceeded the receiver's ability to handle the data.

(continues)

Table 9-3   *show interfaces fddi* Field Description *(Continued)*

Field	Description
ignored	This is the number of received packets ignored by the interface because the interface hardware ran low on internal buffers. These buffers are different from the system buffers mentioned previously in the buffer description. Broadcast storms and bursts of noise can cause the ignored count to be increased.
packets output	This is the total number of messages transmitted by the system.
bytes	This is the total number of bytes, including data and MAC encapsulation, transmitted by the system.
underruns	This is the number of transmit aborts (when the router cannot feed the transmitter fast enough).
output errors	This is the sum of all errors that prevented the final transmission of datagrams out of the interface being examined. Note that this might not balance with the sum of the enumerated output errors. Some datagrams can have more than one error, and others can have errors that do not fall into any of the specifically tabulated categories.
collisions	This statistic is always zero because a FDDI ring cannot have collisions.
interface resets	This is the number of times that an interface has been reset. The interface can be reset by the administrator or automatically when an internal error occurs.
restarts	This should always be zero for FDDI interfaces.
transitions	This is the number of times that the ring made a transition from ring operational to ring non-operational, or vice versa. A large number of transitions indicates a problem with the ring or the interface.
traces	Trace count applies to FCI, FCIT, and FIP. Traces indicates the number of times that this interface started a trace.
claims	This pertains to FCIT and FIP only. Claims indicates the number of times that this interface has been in claim state.
beacons	This pertains to FCIT and FIP only. It indicates the number of times that the interface has been in beacon state.
Protocol	This is the protocol that is operating on the interface.
Pkts In	This is the number of packets received for that protocol.
Chars In	This is the number of characters received for that protocol.
Pkts Out	This is the number of packets transmitted for that protocol.
Chars Out	This is the number of characters transmitted for that protocol.

Some important "early warning" information can be obtained by the output displayed from the **show interface fddi** *port* command.

The following output is used to demonstrate these early warning signs of potential network issues:

```
Fddi0 is up, line protocol is up
  Hardware is cBus Fddi, address is 0000.0c06.8de8 (bia 0000.0c06.8de8)
  Internet address is 131.108.33.9, subnet mask is 255.255.255.0
  MTU 4470 bytes, BW 100000 Kbit, DLY 100 usec, rely 255/255, load 1/255
  Encapsulation SNAP, loopback not set, keepalive not set
  ARP type: SNAP, ARP Timeout 4:00:00
  Phy-A state is active, neighbor is B, cmt signal bits 008/20C, status ILS
  Phy-B state is connect, neighbor is unk, cmt signal bits 20C/000, status QLS
  ECM is insert, CFM is c_wrap_a, RMT is ring_op
  token rotation 5000 usec, ring operational 1d01
  Upstream neighbor 0000.0c06.8b7d, downstream neighbor 0000.0c06.8b7d
  Last input 0:00:08, output 0:00:08, output hang never
  Last clearing of "show interface" counters never
  Output queue 0/40, 0 drops; input queue 0/75, 0 drops
  Five minute input rate 5000 bits/sec, 1 packets/sec
  Five minute output rate 76000 bits/sec, 51 packets/sec
    852914 packets input, 205752094 bytes, 0 no buffer
    Received 126752 broadcasts, 0 runts, 0 giants
    0 input errors, 124823 CRC, 0 frame, 0 overrun, 0 ignored, 0 abort
    8213126 packets output, 616453062 bytes, 0 underruns
    0 output errors, 0 collisions, 4 interface resets, 0 restarts
    5 transitions, 0 traces
```

CRC Errors   No segments should have more than one CRC error per million bytes of data, or 0.0001 percent CRC errors on each segment.

This can be represented by the following formula:

$$(\text{CRCs} / \text{total bytes}) \times 100 \le 0.0001\%$$

In this example, the total amount of data is 11234818 bytes [Input Bytes (205752094) + Output Bytes (616453062) = Total Bytes = (822205156)]. The total number of CRCs indicated is 124823.

```
  .
  .
    852914 packets input, 205752094 bytes, 0 no buffer
    Received 126752 broadcasts, 0 runts, 0 giants
    0 input errors, 124823 CRC, 0 frame, 0 overrun, 0 ignored, 0 abort
    8213126 packets output, 616453062 bytes, 0 underruns
    0 output errors, 0 collisions, 4 interface resets, 0 restarts
  .
  .
```

Using the previous formula (CRCs / total bytes) × 100), you can determine the following:

$$(124823/822205156) \times 100 = 0.015\%$$

This is an unacceptable amount of CRC errors because the total here (0.015 percent) is greater than 0.0001 percent of CRCs. An acceptable threshold would be 822 CRC errors (822205156 × 0.0001 percent = 822.2).

A high number of CRS errors is usually an indication of excessive noise. In this case, the following actions should be taken:

1 Check cables to determine whether any are damaged.

2 Look for badly spliced taps causing reflections.

3 Verify NIC connections, and if necessary, use a network analyzer to determine the source of the bad data. A high number of CRCs can also be the result of a station transmitting bad data.

FDDI Ring Operations   On a FDDI segment, no more than one ring operation should occur per hour that is unrelated to ring insertion.

Although ring insertion statistics are not readily apparent, the number of ring transitions might derive the impact on the FDDI LAN.

```
    .
    .
    .
0 output errors, 0 collisions, 4 interface resets, 0 restarts
5 transitions, 0 traces
    .
    .
```

Transitioning is not bad. The FDDI ring implements the link error monitor (LEM) that monitors each link for errors and, if the rates of errors cross the threshold as determined by the CRC calculations, it is time to take the FDDI ring down for out-of-service testing.

Also, the TVX (Valid Transmission Timer) times out in 2.5 ms or 3.4 ms, depending on implementation, if it does not see tokens or valid frames on the ring. Therefore, the ring goes down and comes back up. Because the claim resolution typically takes the order of milliseconds, transitioning does not affect upper layer operation because those protocols take the order of seconds to timeout. If the ring has a persistent problem, one of the FDDI LAN station's beacons or the link upstream to that station has a problem.

A marginal link could be causing one station to time out after claiming the ring is stable for a while. If these transitions occur several times per minute, the upper protocols would be affected. A FDDI network analyzer would also be useful at this point to isolate the source of the frequent transitions. Some of the more common analyzers are Tekelec CHAM100, Digital Technology, Inc. LANHawk, Network General SNIFFER, HP Network Advisor, and Wandel/Goltermann DA-30.

If out-of-service testing or network analysis yields inconclusive results, it is recommended that you open a case with the Cisco TAC to have the issue further evaluated.

Output Queue Drops   On a Cisco router, the number of output queue drops should not exceed 100 in any hour.

No formula is available to determine this number. The output from the **show interfaces fddi** *number* provides this information, as the following code demonstrates:

```
.
.
Last clearing of "show interface" counters never
Output queue 0/40, 0 drops; input queue 0/75, 0 drops
Five minute input rate 5000 bits/sec, 1 packets/sec
Five minute output rate 76000 bits/sec, 51 packets/sec
.
.
```

Output queue drops are registered if the interface is not able to clear up the queue as fast as the router is queuing them for transmission.

NOTE   The IOS 10.0 and higher code has two output processes, and the 9.1 (9.14) lower code has only one output process.

Drops indicate that the router is overpowering the interface. On a LAN, this would likely be a busy or congested LAN segment, preventing frames from getting out on the wire. These frames usually carry data packets that would be mainly processed-switched in the router, such as routing updates, Novell SAPs, access list control, and helpers.

NOTE   If many SAPs need to be sent out, the output process is busy just sending SAPs. This can result in poor performance of other applications of the router.

The output queue can be modified using the interface subcommand **hold-queue** *xx* **out**, where *xx* is a numeric value. The default for *xx* is 40. The command path to change this configuration is as follows:

```
Router>enable
Password:
Router#:config t
Router(config)#interface fn [Where n is the FDDI interface number]
Router(config-if)#hold-queue xx out
```

Input Queue Drops   On a Cisco router, the number of input queue drops should not exceed 50 in any hour.

No formula is available to determine this number. The output from the **show interfaces fddi** *number* provides this information, as the following code demonstrates:

```
.
.
.
Last clearing of "show interface" counters never
Output queue 0/40, 0 drops; input queue 0/75, 0 drops
Five minute input rate 5000 bits/sec, 1 packets/sec
Five minute output rate 76000 bits/sec, 51 packets/sec
.
.
.
```

Input queue drops are registered if the incoming frame rate is faster than the outgoing frame rate; when this happens, the queue is filled up. Incoming data from an interface gets into the input queue for further processing. Looking at a FDDI interface, data is coming from the FDDI segment, not going out to it. After the queue is full, all the subsequent incoming frames are dropped.

Drops indicate that the interface is overpowering the router. On a LAN, this would probably be the result of a busy or congested LAN segment. Most likely, frames are being flooded onto the wire into the router's interface.

The input queue can be modified using the interface subcommand **hold-queue *xx* in**, where *xx* is a numeric value. The default for *xx* is 40. The command path to change this configuration is as follows:

```
Router>enable
Password:
Router#:config t
Router(config)#interface fn [Where n is the FDDI interface number]
Router(config-if)#hold-queue xx in
```

Ignored Packets   On a Cisco router, the number of ignored packets on any interface should not exceed more than (approximately) 10 in an hour.

No formula is available to determine this number. The output from the **show interfaces fddi** *number* provides this information, as the following code demonstrates:

```
.
.
.
852914 packets input, 205752094 bytes, 0 no buffer
Received 126752 broadcasts, 0 runts, 0 giants
0 input errors, 124823 CRC, 0 frame, 0 overrun, 0 ignored, 0 abort
8213126 packets output, 616453062 bytes, 0 underruns
0 output errors, 0 collisions, 4 interface resets, 0 restarts
.
.
.
```

Ignores are caused when the FDDI interface cannot place a packet into an incoming hardware buffer pool because the router does not have enough hardware buffers to accept a packet.

If the ignores are due to bursty traffic, nothing can be done for the ignore issue in the configuration. If this is normal behavior on the network segment, consider upgrading to a more powerful router, such as a Cisco 7xxx Series.

If upgrading is not an option, open a case with the Cisco TAC to have the issue further evaluated.

show interfaces FDDI *number* accounting

This command is entered from the privileged EXEC command interface on the Cisco router, and displays information about protocol distribution with regard to the specified Token Ring interface.

The syntax for this command is as follows:

```
show interfaces fddi number accounting
```

where accounting is an optional parameter that displays the number of packets of each protocol type that has been sent through the interface.

```
Router#show interfaces fddi 0 accounting

Router# show interfaces fddi 0 accounting

Fddi 0
Protocol       Pkts In      Chars In      Pkts Out     Chars Out
IP             7344    4787842      1803    1535774
Appletalk 33345      4797459      12781    1089695
DEC MOP        0            0            127          9779
ARP            7            420          39           2340
```

To determine the protocol distribution percentage, divide the packets (input, output, or total) for the protocol in question by the same parameter from the **show interfaces** *fddi number* output. For example, examine the distribution for IP traffic using the previous output from a **show interfaces fddi 0 accounting**, combined with the earlier output from **show interfaces fddi 0**, shown here:

```
    .
    .
    .
2295197 packets input, 305539992 bytes, 0 no buffer
Received 1925500 broadcasts, 0 runts, 0 giants
3 input errors, 34215 CRC, 0 frame, 0 overrun, 0 ignored, 0 abort
0 input packets with dribble condition detected
3594664 packets output, 436549843 bytes, 0 underruns
    .
    .
    .
```

Input Distribution Percentage   Input distribution percentage is the percentage of incoming IP packets as determined by the following formula:

$$(Protocol_{INPUT}/Total_{INPUT}) \times 100 = Protocol_{DISTRIBUTION}\%$$

Therefore, $(7344/2295197) \times 100 = 0.32$ percent. 0.32 percent of the total traffic input into this interface is IP traffic.

Output Distribution Percentage   Output distribution percentage is the percentage of outgoing IP packets as determined by the following formula:

$$(Protocol_{OUTPUT}/Total_{OUTPUT}) \times 100 = Protocol_{DISTRIBUTION}\%$$

Therefore, $(1803/3594664) \times 100 = 0.05$ percent. 0.05 percent of the total traffic output from this interface is IP traffic.

Total Distribution Percentage   Total distribution percentage is the percentage of total IP packets as determined by the following formula:

$$(\text{Protocol}_{\text{INPUT+OUTPUT}}/\text{Total}_{\text{INPUT+OUTPUT}}) \times 100 = \text{Protocol}_{\text{DISTRIBUTION}}\%$$

Therefore, $(9147/5889861) \times 100 = 0.16$ percent. 0.16 percent of the total traffic input to and output from this interface is IP traffic.

Buffer Misses

On any Cisco router, the number of buffer misses should not be more than (approximately) 25 in a given hour.

No formula is available to determine the number of misses. The output from the **show buffers** *interface* provides this information, as the following code demonstrates:

```
Buffer elements:
      250 in free list (250 max allowed)
      10816 hits, 0 misses, 0 created
Small buffers, 104 bytes (total 120, permanent 120):
      120 in free list (0 min, 250 max allowed)
      26665 hits, 0 misses, 0 trims, 0 created
Middle buffers, 600 bytes (total 90, permanent 90):
      90 in free list (0 min, 200 max allowed)
      5468 hits, 0 misses, 0 trims, 0 created
Big buffers, 1524 bytes (total 90, permanent 90):
      90 in free list (0 min, 300 max allowed)
      1447 hits, 0 misses, 0 trims, 0 created
Large buffers, 5024 bytes (total 0, permanent 0):
      0 in free list (0 min, 100 max allowed)
      0 hits, 0 misses, 0 trims, 0 created
Huge buffers, 12024 bytes (total 0, permanent 0):
      0 in free list (0 min, 30 max allowed)
      0 hits, 0 misses, 0 trims, 0 created
0 failures (0 no memory)
```

Although the number of buffer misses per hour should not exceed 25, as a rule, misses are okay as long as "failures" shown at the bottom of the **show buffers** display is not incrementing.

A buffer miss identifies the number of times that a buffer has been requested but no more buffers were available in the free list. A buffer failure identifies the number of failures to grant a buffer to a requester under interrupt time. (The router can create new buffers at process-switching level; consequently, a failure only occurs if no memory exists.) The number of "failures" represents the number of packets that have been dropped due to buffer shortage.

Sometimes, the corrective action is adding router memory, and other times the corrective action might be more extensive, such as tuning the buffer parameters. Before you perform any type of buffer-tuning action, open a case with the Cisco TAC to have the issue further evaluated.

show processes cpu

The **show processes cpu** command displays information about the active processes in the router and their corresponding CPU utilization statistics. Following is an example of the output. Note, however, that this is not a complete list, and the processes that are running vary for each system:

```
CPU utilization for five seconds: 8%/4%; one minute: 6%; five minutes: 5%

PID  Runtime(ms)  Invoked  uSecs    5Sec    1Min    5Min  TTY  Process
  1         384     32789     11   0.00%   0.00%   0.00%    0  Load Meter
  2        2752      1179   2334   0.73%   1.06%   0.29%    0  Exec
  3      318592      5273  60419   0.00%   0.15%   0.17%    0  Check heaps
  4           4         1   4000   0.00%   0.00%   0.00%    0  Pool Manager
  5        6472      6568    985   0.00%   0.00%   0.00%    0  ARP Input
  6       10892      9461   1151   0.00%   0.00%   0.00%    0  IP Input
  7       67388     53244   1265   0.16%   0.04%   0.02%    0  CDP Protocol
  8      145520    166455    874   0.40%   0.29%   0.29%    0  IP Background
  9        3356      1568   2140   0.08%   0.00%   0.00%    0  BOOTP Server
 10          32      5469      5   0.00%   0.00%   0.00%    0  Net Background
 11       42256    163623    258   0.16%   0.02%   0.00%    0  Per-Second Jobs
 12      189936    163623   1160   0.00%   0.04%   0.05%    0  Net Periodic
 13        3248      6351    511   0.00%   0.00%   0.00%    0  Net Input
 14         168     32790      5   0.00%   0.00%   0.00%    0  Compute load avgs
 15      152408      2731  55806   0.98%   0.12%   0.07%    0  Per-minute Jobs
 16           0         2      0   0.00%   0.00%   0.00%    0  HyBridge Input
 17        6352    163952     38   0.00%   0.00%   0.00%    0  Spanning Tree
 18           4         2   2000   0.00%   0.00%   0.00%    0  Tbridge Monitor
 19        7696      2745   2803   0.16%   0.01%   0.00%    0  IP-RT Background
 20       18484    330791     55   0.00%   0.00%   0.00%    0  BGP Router
 21        2824      9266    304   0.00%   0.00%   0.00%    0  BGP I/O
 22         520      2771    187   0.00%   0.03%   0.00%    0  BGP Scanner
 23           0         1      0   0.00%   0.00%   0.00%    0  OSPF Hello
 24           8         6   1333   0.00%   0.02%   0.00%    0  OSPF Router
```

Table 9-4 describes the fields in the **show processes cpu** output.

Table 9-4 *show processes cpu Field Description*

Field	Description
CPU utilization for five seconds	The CPU utilization for the past five seconds. The first number indicates the total; the second number indicates the percent of CPU time spent at the interrupt level.
one minute	The CPU utilization for the past minute.
five minutes	The CPU utilization for the past five minutes.
PID	The process ID.
Runtime (ms)	The CPU time that the process has used, expressed in milliseconds.
Invoked	The number of times that the process has been invoked.

(continues)

Table 9-4   *show processes cpu Field Description (Continued)*

Field	Description
uSecs	The microseconds of CPU time for each process invocation.
5Sec	The CPU utilization by task in the past five seconds.
1Min	The CPU utilization by task in the past minute.
5Min	The CPU utilization by task in the past five minutes.
TTY	The terminal that controls the process.
Process	The name of the process.

CPU Utilization

On any Cisco router, the 5-minute CPU utilization rate should be less than 75 percent.

No formula is available to determine the 5-minute CPU utilization rate. The output from the **show processes cpu** provides this information, as the following code demonstrates:

CPU utilization for five seconds: 8%/4%; one minute: 6%; five minutes: 5%

If the CPU utilization is continually over 75 percent, you might want to consider upgrading your router dividing the traffic between multiple routers. Prior to making these changes, it is necessary to get an assessment of what is causing the CPU load. It might be a particular protocol or other process. The output from the **show processes cpu** command lists all active processes on the router and the load that each process is placing on the CPU. If the router is not busy, then what can be seen are some abnormalities in the network (broadcast storms, flapping routes).

If CPU utilization is greater than 75 percent, Cisco recommends checking for an IOS bug.

NOTE   You can use Cisco's online software center to verify the status of an IOS release (http://www.cisco.com/kobayashi/releases/Release_notes.html).

FDDI Network Analysis

Before raw data analysis can begin, it is necessary to review the formulae that are used to determine thresholds and measurements for 100 Mbps FDDI LANs.

FDDI Bit Times (Propagation Delay)

The bit duration for 100 Mbps FDDI is 1/100000000, or 1×10^{-8} seconds. As derived from the speed of light, the time it takes for electrons to traverse 1,000 feet of cable is

1.02×10^{-6} seconds. The propagation delay of a cable segment can be converted into bit times by using the following formula:

(Electron Speed)/(FDDI Bit Time) = Propagation Delay (measured in bit times)

For 100 Mbps FDDI LANs with 1,000 feet of cable, the propagation delay can be determined as follows:

$(1.02 \times 10^{-6})/(1 \times 10^{-8}) = 102$ bit times

NOTE The speed of light in a vacuum, which is without impedance, is 186,000 miles per second. With 5,280 feet in a mile, the speed of electrons is equivalent to 982,080,000 feet per second (186,000 miles per second × 5,280 feet per mile), or approximately 982 feet per microsecond. It would take 1.02×10^{-6} seconds for an electron to travel 1,000 feet of cable $(1000/982 \times 10^{6})$.

FDDI Network Performance

To approximately model and predict the performance of a FDDI LAN, you must account for certain variables:

- Number of hosts on the LAN segment
- Total cabling length
- Data frame size

Following is the process used to determine the effective operating throughput of a 100 Mbps FDDI LAN. These formulae do not include protocol overhead from upper-layer protocols because these are considered part of the data payload in the FDDI frame.

FDDI Propagation Delay Equation   Given a FDDI LAN with N hosts, a free token circulates around the ring an average of $N/2$ hosts until it is seized and turned into a start-of-frame delimiter.

Each host adds a 2.5 bit-time delay to examine the token. A bit time on a 100 Mbps FDDI LAN equates to 1×10^{-8} seconds; therefore, each host introduces a delay of $(2.5) \times (1 \times 10^{-8})$, or 2.5×10^{-8} seconds.

A token consists of four bytes (32 bits), requiring 32×10^{-8} seconds for the token to be placed onto the ring.

$[(32) \times (1 \times 10^{-8} \text{ seconds/bit}) = 32 \times 10^{-8} \text{ seconds}]$

The time it takes for the token to be placed onto the ring and to circulate half the ring until it is seized by another host is the sum of the product of steps 2 and 3. The time it takes is the result of the following equation:

$$[(N/2 \times (2.5 \times 10^{-8})) + (32 \times 10^{-8})]$$

After the token has been seized and converted into a start-of-frame delimiter, on the average it travels $N/2$ hosts to its intended destination. A frame that contains 64 bytes of application data is in actuality 108 bytes because 44 bytes are FDDI protocol-related overhead. The time necessary to place the frame onto the ring is then represented by the following formula:

$$[(108 \text{ bytes}) \times (8 \text{ bits/byte}) \times (1 \times 10^{-8} \text{ seconds/bit}) = 8.64 \times 10^{-6} \text{ seconds}$$

If the FDDI network contains N hosts, the frame must pass through an average of $N/2$ hosts to reach its intended destination. The time required for the frame to be placed onto and circulate half the ring can be derived from the following:

$$[(8.64 \times 10^{-6}) + (N/2 \times (2.5 \times 10^{-8} \text{ seconds}))]$$

The total token and frame time then becomes:

$$[(N/2 \times (2.5 \times 10^{-8})) + (32 \times 10^{-8}) + (N/2 \times (2.5 \times 10^{-8})) + (8.64 \times 10^{-6} \text{ seconds})]$$

or

$$[(N) \times (2.5 \times 10^{-8})) + (32 \times 10^{-8}) + (8.64 \times 10^{-6} \text{ seconds})]$$

After the data frame has reached its intended destination, it must circulate through another (on average) $N/2$ hosts to return to the originating host, which then removes the frame from the network. When this occurs, the originating station generates a new token onto the network. The time it takes for the frame to circulate through half of the network is then represented as $[(N/2) \times (2.5 \times 10^{-8} \text{ seconds})]$. This time is then added to the time determined from the previous step, deriving the following:

$$[(N \times (9.375 \times 10^{-7})) + (32 \times 10^{-8}) + (8.64 \times 10^{-6} \text{ seconds})]$$

To consider the effect of propagation delay time as tokens and frames flow in the network cabling, you must also consider the sum of the ring length and twice the sum of all the lobe distances. The lobe distances must be doubled because the tokens flow to and from each host on the lobe. Given that C is the cable length (in thousands of feet), the time (in seconds) that it takes to travel across the ring is derived from the following:

$$[(N \times (9.375 \times 10^{-7})) + (32 \times 10^{-8}) + (8.64 \times 10^{-6}) + ((1.02 \times 10^{-6}) \times C)]$$

or

$$[(N \times (9.375 \times 10^{-7})) + (1.76 \times 10^{-4}) + ((1.02 \times 10^{-6}) \times C)], \text{ where N = the number of}$$
hosts and C = cable length (measured in thousands of feet).

FDDI LAN Effective Throughput   To demonstrate how the previous equation can be applied, assume a [100 Mbps] FDDI LAN with 80 hosts and 5,000 total feet of cabling, $N = 80$ and $C = 5$. Therefore, $[(80 \times (9.375 \times 10^{-7})) + (8.64 \times 10^{-6}) + ((1.02 \times 10^{-6}) \times 5)] = 0.00008874$ or 8.874×10^{-5} seconds.

Therefore, in one second ($1/(8.874 \times 10^{-5}$ seconds$) = 11269$), 11269 information frames (64 bytes each) can move around the network.

The effective operating throughput of this FDDI LAN can be measured as follows:

$(11269 \times (64$ bytes $\times (8$ bits/byte$)) = 5.77$ Mbps

It is a safe assumption that the frame rate on a FDDI LAN is larger than 64 bytes. In these instances, the formulae are processed by first determining the time it takes to place the frame onto the wire, and then determining the effective operating throughput of the FDDI LAN:

$((\text{Frame size in bytes}) \times (8$ bits/byte$) \times (1 \times 10^{-8}$ seconds/bit$)$

NOTE   The MTU of the interface determines the frame size. The MTU can be found by reviewing the output from the **show interfaces fddi** *number* command in the privileged EXEC mode.

Using the example of 4470 data bytes in a frame, plus the additional 42 bytes due to FDDI protocol overhead, the following is derived:

$((4492) \times (8) \times (1 \times 10^{-8})) = 3.576 \times 10^{-4}$ seconds [to transmit a data frame, resolving into an approximate throughput of 99.98 Mbps]

Furthering the example, assume 80 hosts and 4,000 feet of cabling:

$[(80 \times (9.375 \times 10^{-7})) + (3.576 \times 10^{-4}) + ((1.02 \times 10^{-6}) \times 4)] = 3946723$ bps, or 3.95 Mbps effective operating throughput

A Microsoft Excel spreadsheet is provided on the Cisco Press Web site (www.ciscopress.com/1587050390) so that the variables N (Number of hosts), C (Cable length in thousands of feet), and *Frame Length* can be adjusted to model a specific FDDI LAN environment.

FDDI Performance Model

To determine the bit time on a FDDI LAN, divide 1 by the total bandwidth on the ring; therefore, the bit time for a 100 Mbps FDDI LAN is 1/100000000 or 1×10^{-8}.

As stated previously, each host adds a delay of 2.5 bit times. Given that B_T is the bit time as determined by the ring speed and B_H is the bit time delay for each host, the following can be derived:

$$B_{HOSTDELAY} = (2.5 \times B_{TIME})$$

The next step in the process is determining the amount of time it takes to place a token (32 bits) onto the ring. Therefore:

$$TOKEN_{RINGPLACE} = (32 \times B_{TIME})$$

After the amount of time to place a token on the ring is determined and the token has circulated around (on average) half the ring N/2, where N is the number of hosts on the ring, represented as:

$$TOKEN_{FLOW} = ((N/2) \times B_{HOSTDELAY}) + TOKEN_{RINGPLACE}$$

then it can be determined how long it takes a data frame to circulate (on average) half the ring:

$$FRAME_{TIME} = ((FRAME_{LENGTH}) + 42) \times (8 \times B_{TIME}),$$ where $FRAME_{LENGTH}$ is measured in bytes

Given on average that a FDDI frame must circulate through half the ring to reach its intended destination, the time it takes ($FRAME_{TRAVEL}$) can be represented as follows:

$$FRAME_{TRAVEL} = ((N/2) \times (B_{HOSTDELAY})) + FRAME_{TIME},$$ where $FRAME_{TIME}$ is measured in seconds

Given the amount of time it takes for a frame to circulate around half the ring, the next step is to determine the propagation delay of the network. Propagation delay is directly relational to the length of the network cabling (C, in thousands of feet):

$$TIME_{CABLE} = ((C) \times (1.02 \times 10^{-6})),$$ where C is measured in thousands of feet

The frame rate of the FDDI LAN segment can then be computed as follows:

Frames per second $= (1/TIME_{TOTAL} + TIME_{CABLE})$, where $TIME_{TOTAL}$ is derived from $[((FRAME_{TRAVEL}) + (FRAME_{TRAVEL}) + (N/2)) \times (B_{HOSTDELAY})]$, where N is the number of hosts on the FDDI LAN segment.

Consequently, you can determine the effective throughput by multiplying the frames per second by the number of bits per frame (bytes multiplied by 8):

Effective Throughput = Frames per second × (Bytes per frame × 8 bits/byte)

The FDDI performance model is available as a Microsoft Excel spreadsheet on www.ciscopress.com/1587050390, where the variables N (Number of hosts), C (Cable length in thousands of feet), and *Frame Length* can be adjusted to model both 100 Mbps FDDI LAN environments.

Summary

This chapter has discussed Token Ring and FDDI network review and analysis.

After a Token Ring or FDDI network has been documented, the next step is to review the physical and logical topology for any performance-impacting issues.

As discussed in Chapter 5, "Ethernet Network Review and Analysis," token-passing networks (such as Token Ring and FDDI) are deterministic.

CHAPTER 10

ATM LAN Emulation (LANE)

LAN emulation (LANE) is one method used to extend broadcast domains across an ATM wide-area network (WAN), regardless of the upper-layer protocols in use. LANE extends VLANs (virtual LANs) through the ATM WAN cloud in what is known as an Emulated LAN (ELAN).

ATM LANs do not operate in the traditional way that other LAN implementations do, where a LAN host sends data frames at any time to one or multiple hosts on the LAN. Hosts on an ATM LAN must initiate a call setup process prior to data transmission.

With this major difference among LAN architectures, the ATM Forum wanted to integrate ATM switches into the conventional LAN architecture. This solution is known as LAN emulation, or LANE.

LANE meets these ATM Forum requirements:

- LANE enables a set of systems that have ATM network interfaces (NICs) and are connected to ATM switches to emulate a traditional LAN environment.

- LANE enables Ethernet or Token Ring systems connected to traditional hubs and switches to interact with ATM implementations as if they all belong to a single conventional LAN.

- LANE also provides backward compatibility with existing higher-layer protocols and applications, making it possible for existing network implementations to run across an ATM implementation without making software changes. This implementation is possible because to the higher layers (OSI Layer 3, network layer, and above), the LAN environment appears to be Ethernet or Token Ring.

NOTE   As of this writing, LANE does not support FDDI LAN implementations.

It is possible to build a high-performance LAN that spans multiple sites. Wide-area ATM can run at speeds that meet or exceed the bandwidth available by these local-area networks.

Figure 10-1 illustrates Ethernet LANs, interconnected by ATM switches across an ATM WAN. Also depicted are servers directly connected to each ATM switch.

Figure 10-1 *Emulated LAN Spanning Across a WAN*

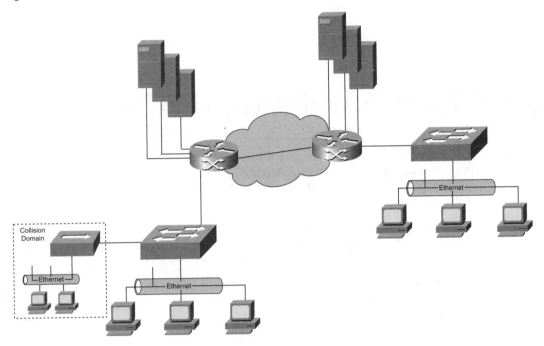

Emulated LAN Environments

The following two components are essential to LANE functionality with ATM:

- LAN Emulation Client (LEC) software resides on the end system.
- LAN Emulation Server (LES) software resides on the switch.

The following list details the process of an LEC being added to an existing emulated LAN environment:

1 During the initial boot sequence, the ATM adapter registers with the local switch and exchanges management information.

2 The local switch provides a prefix to the ATM adapter, which in combination with the MAC address of the adapter, becomes the ATM address of the adapter. The local switch also provides its ATM address.

3 The two ATM addresses are known, so the LEC establishes a virtual circuit connection (VCC) with the LES.

4 The LEC registers its ATM/IP/MAC address with the LES and joins the emulated LAN.

5 The LES then adds the new LEC to the ARP distribution tree.

6 The LEC now queries the LES for the broadcast/unknown server (BUS) for multicast receiving the BUS address from the LES.

7 The LEC establishes a VCC with the BUS and registers its ATM/IP/MAC address to the multicast distribution tree.

8 The LEC can now "talk" to other end systems by ARPing for the ATM address to the LES.

9 The LES does a lookup and one of the following occurs:

— Upon a hit, the LES returns the address to the LEC.

— On a miss, the LES broadcasts the ARP with the expectation that an LEC will answer.

10 The response is then returned by the LES to the originating LEC.

11 At this point, a VCC is established between the two LECs and data traffic begins flowing.

LANE is used to create an emulated LAN. An emulated LAN (ELAN) comprises PCs, LAN switches, routers, and bridges that have ATM interfaces and are directly connected to ATM switches. One ELAN can span several interconnected ATM switches, and the same set of switches can support several ELANs, each identified by a unique name.

ELANs and VLANs share a close similarity. An ELAN can be part of a larger VLAN that spans multiple ATM systems and traditional LAN implementations. In a VLAN environment, network administrators can configure an ELAN to be a part of a particular VLAN.

Like Ethernet and Token Ring NICs, an ATM NIC is assigned a unique 6-byte MAC LAN address, which is essential for participating in an emulated LAN.

ATM's virtual circuit-based environment is molded into a LAN-like environment through the implementation of three special emulation servers. These emulation servers make it possible for a MAC frame to get from source to its intended destination(s).

Figure 10-2 demonstrates how an existing application and LAN implementation can interconnect with another application riding an ATM LANE implementation.

Figure 10-2   *Existing LAN Host and ATM Host Interconnection*

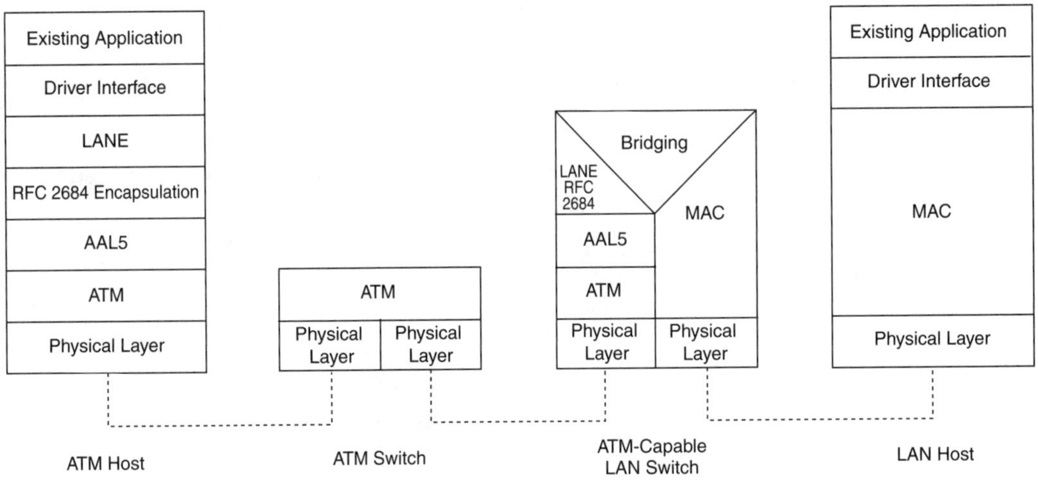

Ethernet Emulated LAN Environments

Figure 10-3 illustrates an Ethernet LAN implementation that has ATM ELAN components. In this figure, each Ethernet switch, as well as a pair of application servers, is connected to a backbone ATM switch. The hosts attached to the Ethernet switches and to the hubs in the Ethernet collision domain can communicate with each other and with the application servers directly connected to the ATM switch.

The Ethernet switches relay traffic between the Ethernet and ATM LAN environments. These switches are referred to as *proxies* because they relay traffic to and from ATM systems on behalf of the traditional LAN hosts.

Figure 10-3   *Emulated Ethernet LAN*

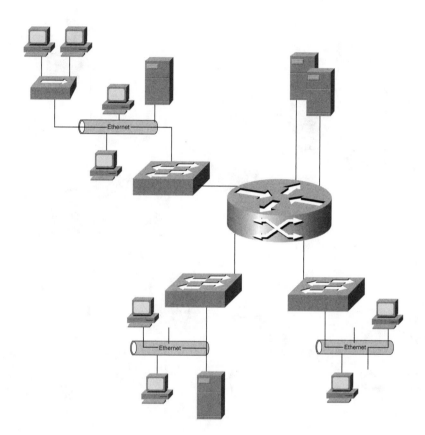

Token Ring-Emulated LAN Environments

Figure 10-4 illustrates a Token Ring LAN implementation that has ATM ELAN components. The Token Ring bridges are source-route bridges, directly connected to the ATM switch, as are the two application servers depicted here. The traditional Token Ring LAN implementations, and LAN-attached hosts, are attached to the Token Ring switches or source-route bridges. These hosts can communicate with each other or with the ATM-attached application servers.

Figure 10-4   *Emulated Token Ring LAN*

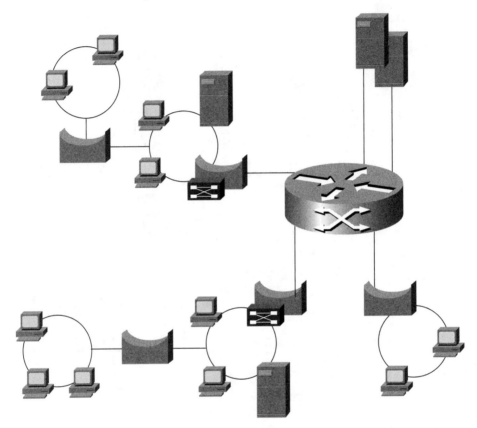

As with emulated Ethernet LANs, the Token Ring switches are known as proxies because they relay traffic between the Token Ring LAN and ATM environments.

LAN Emulation Clients (LECs)

A LANE hides the underlying ATM layers from higher-layer protocols. A device driver known as the LAN emulation client (LEC) or LANE client performs this function.

NOTE   Every major operating system has device drivers for LANE clients.

To the upper layers (Layers 3 through 7) of the OSI model, the LANE client looks and acts like a traditional Ethernet or Token Ring MAC operation. However, the LANE client sends its data through an ATM interface rather than the broadcast medium of Ethernet or the token-based medium of Token Ring LAN implementations.

The LANE client performs several functions apart from data transmission:

- It enrolls its associated system into an ELAN, tying the client to two emulation servers. One server handles unicast operations and the other handles broadcast and multicast operations.

- It queries the emulation server, asking for the ATM address(es) of the client's intended destination(s).

- It opens the ATM circuit to the destination(s).

- It exchanges frames from the destination(s) peer system(s).

When an upper layer protocol tells the LANE client to send a broadcast or multicast frame, the client forwards the frame to the second emulation server, the BUS server. The BUS server relays the data frame(s) to the other (intended) members of the ELAN.

LAN Emulation Servers (LESs)

Three LAN emulation servers are used in the ATM LANE environment:

- LANE configuration server (LECS)—Assigns a LAN emulation client to a specific ELAN (emulated LAN).

- LANE or LAN emulation server (LES)—Responsible for one emulated LAN and keeps track of both MAC and ATM addresses of its ELAN members. A LANE client stays connected to this server so that the client can ask for MAC-to-ATM address translations whenever necessary.

- Broadcast/unknown server (BUS)—Delivers broadcast and multicast frames to hosts in the emulated LAN. A client stays connected to this server so that broadcast and multicast frames can be sent and received at any time.

Figures 10-5 and 10-6 illustrate both and Ethernet and Token Ring emulated LAN with LANE clients and servers.

Figure 10-5 *Ethernet ELAN with Clients and Servers*

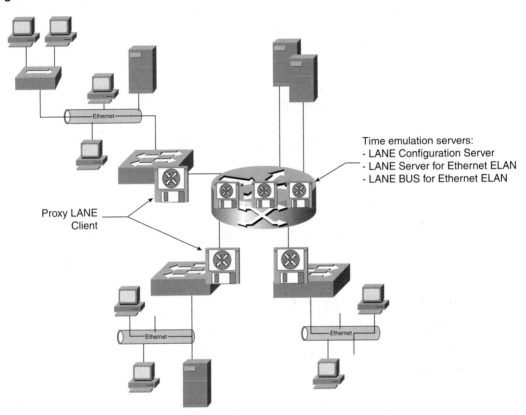

Time emulation servers:
- LANE Configuration Server
- LANE Server for Ethernet ELAN
- LANE BUS for Ethernet ELAN

Proxy LANE
Client

Figure 10-6   *Token Ring ELAN with Clients and Servers*

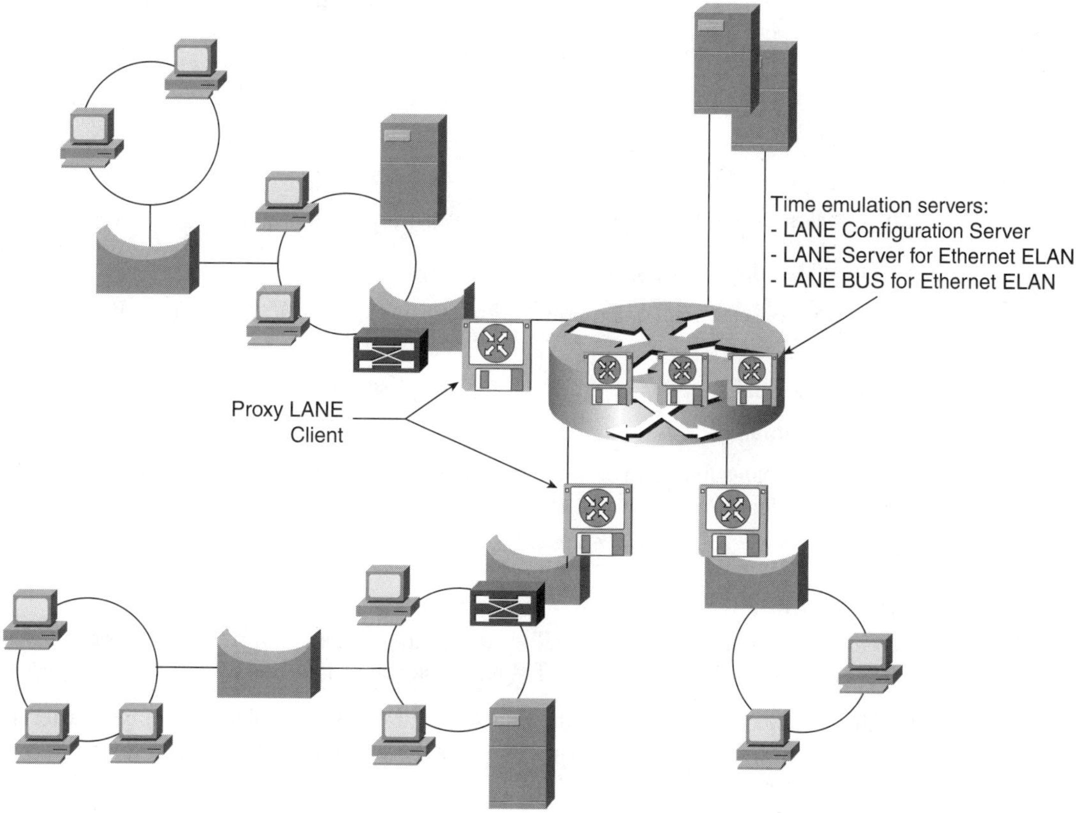

The three emulation servers are depicted here as being located in the ATM switch. These three servers can be located in a switch or router system, or spread across different network environments. Each ELAN host knows how to reach each of these servers when necessary.

LAN Emulation Configuration Server (LECS)

The manner in which the LANE client interacts with the configuration server is simple. The client opens an ATM circuit to the server and announces its ATM address. The client can also provide additional parameters that the server can use to determine to which ELAN the client should be assigned.

The additional parameters include the following:

- The type of ELAN the client wants to join, such as Ethernet or Token Ring
- The name of ELAN the client wants to join
- The maximum frame size the client can support
- The client's MAC address
- The Layer 3 address

The LECS will respond to the client with the following configuration information:

- The ATM address of a specified LANE server
- The ELAN type, such as Ethernet or Token Ring, to which the client has been assigned
- The ELAN name to which the client has been assigned
- The maximum ELAN-supported frame size

A single LECS can support an entire network; however, from a redundancy standpoint, it is advisable to deploy at least two LECS to share tasks.

Configuration Server Implementation

When implementing an LECS server, the administrator must perform several tasks, based on the pairing of the ELAN and the ATM address of the ELAN server.

After the pairing of the ELAN and the ELAN server (LES), the client assignment criteria must be entered into the LECS configuration database. Following is a list of some recommendations:

- Enter one ELAN name, and assign all clients to this ELAN by default.
- Assign a client to an ELAN when the client requests that specific ELAN.
- Assign a client to an ELAN based on the client's ATM address. If this recommendation is implemented, the ATM address for each client and its respective ELAN must be configured.
- Implement two ELANS: an Ethernet implementation and a Token Ring implementation. Clients are then assigned based on the type of requested ELAN.

Configuration Server Location

Prior to operation, the client must determine which one of the following three methods it can use to contact its configuration server.

- Use a well-known ATM group address that has been reserved for configuration servers:

    — Hexadecimal address:

        470079000000000000000000-00A09E000001-00

- Obtain the configuration server's address during client system initialization. This address acquisition is accomplished using the integrated local management interface (ILMI) protocol.

- When the client system is implemented, a permanent virtual circuit (PVC) is set up that is automatically activated when the client comes online. This PVC must have the following address parameters: VPI=0, VCI=17.

This last method is the preferred method for client configuration. When the client contacts the configuration server, the ATM address of its LANE server is retrieved.

LAN Emulation or LANE Server (LES)

After the client has the address of its LANE server, it is prepared to join an ELAN. First, the client must open a connection with the LANE server. This connection is known as the client's control-direct virtual channel connection.

The client and LANE server exchange a join request and response. The client has the option of including its MAC address with its join request, or it can announce its MAC address via a separate register request after the join has been completed.

Some clients are configured with more than one MAC address. These clients can announce multiple MAC addresses in a series of register requests.

If the client is connected via Ethernet or Token Ring bridge or switch, the bridge or switch will indicate that it is a proxy. The bridge or switch will register its own address but will also indicate that it represents other clients whose MAC addresses will not be registered. Data traffic to these clients will be relayed via an ATM connection to the identified proxy.

In a Token Ring LAN environment, the source route bridge can register its route descriptor in lieu of, or in addition to, its MAC address. In this case, the LANE server maintains a list of source route descriptors in addition to the MAC and ATM addresses.

The following is accomplished upon completion of the client and server "join and register" steps:

- The server knows the ATM and MAC addresses of the client.
- The client has been given authoritative values of the ELAN name, LAN type, and maximum frame sizes supported.
- The client might have been assigned a LAN emulation client ID (LECID), a unique 2-byte identifier. The client includes this identifier in all its information frames. Some LAN servers do not assign LECIDs.
- The server knows whether the client acts as an end system or as a proxy (bridge or switch).

Address Resolution (LE ARP)

LANE servers build a database that contains the MAC-to-ATM address translation tables for systems that have joined its ELAN. This database construction puts the LANE server in an ideal position to assist LANE clients who need a map for a destination MAC address to a destination ATM address, to initiate an ATM connection, and subsequently, to exchange data frames across this connection. This MAC-to-ATM address discovery process is known as *address resolution*.

After a client has joined an ELAN, it maintains its initial connection to its LANE server. The client will send address resolution requests, known as *LAN emulation ARP requests* (LE ARP requests), across the connection and receive the appropriate LE ARP responses from the server on the same connection. This connection is known as the *control-distribute virtual channel connection*.

Although this virtual connection might be point-to-point, implementing a point-to-multipoint, or multicast, operation might be more efficient than a separate point-to-point connection between each client.

Broadcast/Unknown Server (BUS)

A client sends broadcasts and multicasts by linking to the broadcast/unknown server (BUS). To get the ATM address of the BUS, the client sends an LE ARP query to its LANE server. This query asks for the ATM address of the system(s) corresponding to the broadcast MAC address.

NOTE   The broadcast MAC address, represented in hexadecimal, is FF-FF-FF-FF-FF-FF.

Upon receipt of the BUS's ATM address, the client opens an ATM connection and uses this connection to send its broadcast and multicast frames. This connection is known as the *multicast-send virtual channel connection*.

If the local LANE server does not have a destination MAC address in its database, it will not be able to complete the MAC-to-ATM address translation. In this case, the client can ask the BUS to flood the frame out all connections.

After the client has connected to the BUS, the BUS will open a separate connection used to deliver broadcast, multicast, or flooded frames to the client. This connection, illustrated in Figure 10-7, is known as the *multicast-forward virtual channel connection*.

Figure 10-7   *ATM BUS Multicast Operation*

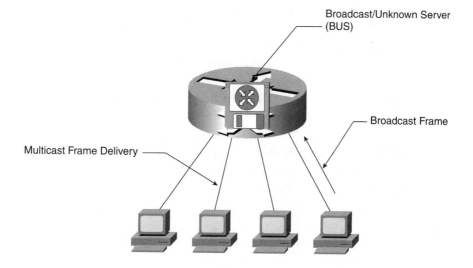

ATM LANE Protocol

The LANE protocol comprises four elements:

- ATM addresses
- Integrated local management interface (ILMI) for ATM address initialization
- LANE data frame format
- LANE protocol control frame functions and formats

NOTE   ATM addresses and ILMI are elements of the ATM protocol found in both LANE and WAN implementations.

ATM Addresses

Several formats are defined for ATM addressing. Despite this variation in formats, a common trait can be found. ATM addressing is hierarchical, meaning that the address defines a network range and a host on that defined network. ATM addresses, as illustrated in Figure 10-8, are known as E.164, or NSAP, addresses.

Figure 10-8   *E.164 Address Format*

Address Type (1 Byte)	E.164 Address (8 Bytes)	High-Order Domain-Specific Part (4 Bytes)	End System Identifier (ESI) (MAC Address) (6 Bytes)	Selector (1 Byte)

ATM address frames are 20 bytes in length, and are broken down as follows:

- Address type—The initial byte indicates the type of address used. In this instance of using E.164 addressing, this byte will be represented as 01000101.

- E.164 address—The next 8 bytes are the E.164 address. This address is a standard E.164 number and is generally used to reach the destination site across the wide-area network (WAN).

- High-order domain-specific part—The next 4 bytes are used to identify a specific switch at the destination site.

- End system identifier (ESI)—These 6 bytes identify the end system, or host, and typically use the MAC address.

- Selector (SEL)—This byte at the end plays no role in the routing of an ATM call. The use of this byte has not been standardized and is often used by ATM vendors for proprietary implementations, such as differentiating among multiple LANE servers at the same site.

The ATM Forum defined an address format based on the structure of the OSI network service access point (NSAP) addresses.

The 20-byte NSAP-format ATM addresses are designed for use within private ATM networks. Public networks typically use E.164 addresses, which are formatted as defined by ITU-T. The ATM Forum has specified an NSAP encoding for E.164 addresses, which is used for encoding E.164 addresses within private networks, but this address can also be used by some private networks.

Such private networks can base their own (NSAP format) addressing on the E.164 address of the public UNI to which they are connected and can take the address prefix from the E.164 number, identifying local nodes by the lower-order bits.

All NSAP-format ATM addresses consist of three components: the authority and format identifier (AFI), the initial domain identifier (IDI), and the domain specific part (DSP). The AFI identifies the type and format of the IDI. The IDI, in turn, identifies the address allocation and administrative authority. The DSP contains actual routing information.

Three formats of private ATM addressing differ by the nature of the AFI and IDI. In the NSAP-encoded E.164 format, the IDI is an E.164 number. In the DCC format, the IDI is a data country code (DCC), which identifies particular countries, as specified in ISO 3166. (See Appendix C, "List of ITU-TX.121 Data Country or Geographical Codes," for more information.) The ISO National Member Body administers such addresses in each country. In the ICD format, the IDI is an international code designator (ICD), which is allocated by the ISO 6523 registration authority (the British Standards Institute). ICD codes identify particular international organizations.

The ATM Forum recommends that organizations or private-network service providers use either the DCC or ICD formats to form their own numbering plan.

ILMI Initialization

ATM uses SNMP messages to implement integrated local management interface (ILMI) procedures. ILMI procedures are general ATM procedures and are not specific to ATM LANE.

The following occurs during ILMI initialization:

- The endpoint system obtains the first 13 bytes of its ATM address from its associated switch (address type, E.164 address, and domain-specific part).

- The system completes its own ATM address by registering its MAC address at the ATM switch.

- The system and its associated switch exchange configuration settings and select a common set of parameters that both systems are capable of supporting.

- A system can also determine the addresses of the LANE configuration server via ILMI.

ATM switches continually use ILMI to periodically poll their connections and verify that the link's distant end stations are still functioning.

NOTE   ILMI messages are SNMP requests that are carried as AAL5 payloads, not needing UDP or IP as traditional SNMP requests require.

LANE Data Frames

Figure 10-9 illustrates the format of an Ethernet frame that is carried via an AAL5 frame. The Ethernet frame does not include a frame check sequence (FCS) because the AAL5 Trailer's CRC value provides error checking.

Figure 10-9   *LANE Ethernet Frame*

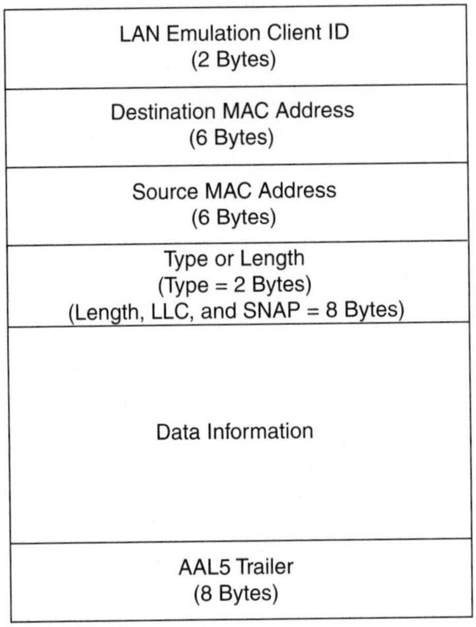

Ethernet frames sent between a pair of ATM clients can be larger than traditional Ethernet frames, up to the size of Token Ring frames.

Using large frames with ATM-to-ATM communication is an efficient use of the link; however, these same large frames cannot be supported when an ATM client communicates with a traditional Ethernet LAN client.

LANE Control Frames

The configuration-direct connection between an ATM LANE client and a LANE configuration server, and the control-direct and control-distribute connections between an ATM LANE client and its LANE server, are used to set up and maintain the ATM LANE environment. Ordinary data frames are not carried across these connections because they carry special control frames that contain a variety of requests and responses.

Table 10-1 lists these special control frames, along with a brief description.

Table 10-1   *LANE Control Frames (LE = LAN Emulation)*

Control Frame	Description
LE Configure Request	Sent by a client wanting to join an ELAN that needs to determine the ATM address of its LANE server.
LE Configure Response	Provides the address of a LANE server, along with any predefined optional parameters.
LE Join Request	Sent to a LANE server by a client that wants to join an ELAN.
LE Join Response	Sent by a LANE server. If the client has been accepted, the server provides the name of the ELAN, the ELAN type, the maximum frame size, and if predefined, the optional client's LANE identifier.
LE Register Request	Sent by a client to register a MAC address or a Token Ring route descriptor.
LE Register Response	Acknowledges the registration.
LE Unregister Request	Sent by a client to withdraw a registration, such as when detaching from a network.
LE Unregister Response	Acknowledges the unregistration.
LE ARP Request	Sent by a client that wants to know the ATM address corresponding to a given MAC address. If the LANE server does not know this information, it will forward the request out all interfaces to all clients (known as *flooding*).
LE ARP Response	Provides the ATM address corresponding to a given MAC address.
Ready Indication	Sent by a caller as soon as it is ready to receive data frames on a newly established connection.
Ready Query	Sent by a called party if it has not yet received an expected Ready Indication.
LE Flush Request	Sent by a client to clear a connection. The client waits for a response before sending more data frames over the connection.
LE Flush Response	Sent in response to a Flush Request.
LE NARP Request	Sent by a client to announce that its MAC-to-ATM address pairing has changed.
LE Topology Request	Sent by a LANE client in a transparent bridge to its LANE server. It announces that the client has sent a Configuration BPDU to the BUS and indicates whether a Spanning Tree topology change is occurring. The server forwards the message to other clients.

LANE Control Frame Format

Figure 10-10 illustrates the construction of the LANE control frame.

Figure 10-10 *LANE Control Frame Format*

Control Frame Marker	
Protocol	Version
Op-Code: Type of Control Frame (2 Bytes)	
Status	
Transaction Identifier (4 Bytes)	
Requester LAN Emulation Client ID (2 Bytes)	
Flags (2 Bytes)	
Source MAC Address or Token Ring Route Descriptor (8 Bytes)	
Destination MAC Address or Token Ring Route Descriptor (8 Bytes)	
Source ATM Address (20 Bytes)	
LAN Type (1 Byte)	Max Frame Size (1 Byte)
Number of TLV Fields (1 Byte)	Size of ELAN Name (1 Byte)
Destination ATM Address (20 Bytes)	
ELAN Name (32 Bytes)	
Sequemce of Type-Length-Value (TLV) Fields	

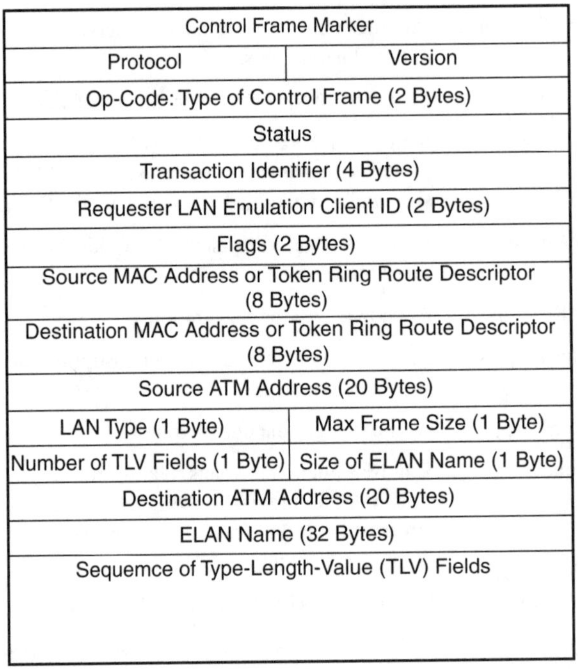

The LANE control frame comprises the following fields:

- Control Frame Marker—Hexadecimal FF-00 indicates that this item is a control frame.
- Protocol—Hexadecimal 01 is used to identify the ATM LANE protocol.
- Version—Identifies ATM LANE protocol version 1 or version 2.
- Op-Code—Identifies the type of control frame, such as a configuration, join, or ARP request.
- Status—Usually set to Hexadecimal 00-00 in successful request and response messages; otherwise, this field reports a problem.
- Transaction ID—Used to match a response to its associated request.
- Requester-LECID—The LAN emulation client ID of the client making a request. If the client's identifier is unknown, the value is set to Hexadecimal 00-00.
- Flags—Indicates miscellaneous facts, such as whether the sender of the frame is a LAN switch or a router proxy client.

- Source—The source MAC address associated with the message or the Token Ring route descriptor that identifies a client that is a source route bridge.
- Destination (Target)—The destination MAC address associated with the message or the Token Ring route descriptor that identifies a client that is a source route bridge.
- Source ATM Address—The ATM address of the frame source.
- Destination (Target) Address—The ATM address of the frame destination, or target.
- LAN Type—Hexadecimal values specify the following:
  - 00—Unspecified
  - 01—Ethernet
  - 02—Token Ring

LANE Version 2

LANE Version 2 adds some features to version 1:

- Quality of service (QoS) parameters
- Capability to implement multiple instances of each server type for redundancy (accomplished via the server cache synchronization protocol, or SCSP)
- Improved handling of multicast traffic

The introduction of QoS allows a LANE client to register the service categories it is willing to accept for incoming calls. Callers can set up multiple connections to a destination system with a different QoS on each connection, supporting different applications, such as multimedia, voice, or traditional data.

LANE Version 2 defines standard protocols that support communication between servers to coordinate their activities. LANE Version 1 suffers from the fact that the configuration, LANE, and BUS servers are single points of failure. Some widely distributed ELAN systems must maintain long-haul connections to support the participation of the server in an ELAN. This long-haul connection can become costly if the carrier is billing on a usage rate (for example, cost per MB) rather than a fixed rate.

NOTE   Multiple LANE servers that coordinate their MAC- and ATM-address databases with one another can support Version 2 ELANs.

LANE Version 2 BUSes have access to the LANE server's address database. Multiple BUSes can be connected, with each BUS responsible for flooding frames to connected systems. The LANE server database maintains a list of all BUSes for the LAN. When a

BUS floods a frame to all network hosts, it sends the frame to its connected clients and to the other BUSes.

Version 2 BUSes can be considered "intelligent" in that if the BUS receives a client frame, it will forward the frame to the intended receiver rather than flood the frame to all clients (as a Version 1 BUS would behave).

LANE Version 1 multicast traffic is forwarded to all clients, leaving the client to determine if it should act on the frame. LANE Version 2 multicast traffic is forwarded to a multicast group. LANE Version 2 clients can register their membership to this multicast group and be assigned to a selective multicast server (SMS). SMSs open and maintain a point-to-multipoint connection to their clients and forward the multicast frames to the members of those multicast groups.

Server Cache Synchronization Protocol (SCSP)

The server cache synchronization protocol (SCSP) is used to accomplish server redundancy with LANE Version 2 implementations. SCSP is defined by RFC 2334 and is responsible for the synchronization of the databases across multiple LANE servers. The ATM Forum specification AF-LANE-0112.000 specifies SCSP's relation to LNNI.

NOTE	LNNI is LANE NNI, or LANE network-to-network interface, which is the interface between two LANE servers, such as LES-LES, BUS-BUS, LECS-LECS, or LES-LECS.

Class of Service (CoS)

ATM virtual circuit connections comprise two components: a virtual path and a virtual channel. Two channels exist for each virtual circuit—one channel for each direction, or flow, of traffic.

Virtual path identifiers (VPIs) identify ATM virtual paths, and virtual channel identifiers (VCIs) identify virtual channels.

Figure 10-11 illustrates the support of multiple virtual channels over a single virtual path.

Figure 10-11 *ATM Virtual Path and Virtual Channels*

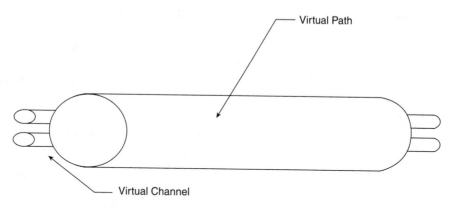

ATM supports five QoS modes across virtual circuit connections, as shown in Table 10-2.

Table 10-2 *ATM Class of Service (CoS) Categories*

Class of Service (CoS)	Description
Constant bit rate (CBR)	Provides constant bandwidth, delay, and jitter across the virtual connection. Typically used for private line emulated services, such as that needed by multimedia, CAD/CAM, or medical imaging. CBR is sometimes referred to as a circuit emulation service (CES).
	An ATM VC configured as CBR can send cells at peak cell rate (PCR) at any time and for any duration. Cisco encapsulation configuration is "all."
Variable bit rate real-time (VBR-rt)	Provides a specified average bandwidth across the virtual connection. Used to support delay-sensitive applications, such as voice or video. Voice or video is usually associated with the isochronous services of CBR and compressed voice or video with this class.
	Cisco encapsulation configuration is "aal5mux voice."
Variable bit rate near-real-time (VBR-nrt)	Provides a specified average bandwidth across the virtual connection. Used to support non-delay-sensitive applications, such as data information or bursty LAN traffic.
	Cisco encapsulation configuration is "aal5snap" (with traffic-shaping parameters) or "aal5muxframe-relay."

(continues)

Table 10-2   *ATM Class of Service (CoS) Categories (Continued)*

Class of Service (CoS)	Description
Unspecified bit rate (UBR)	This is a best-effort service, meaning that no bandwidth is specified across the connection or delivery of service guaranteed. Cisco encapsulation configuration is "aal5snap" (without traffic-shaping parameters).
Available bit rate (ABR)	This is a best-effort service implemented in a different fashion from UBR. ABR service provides continual feedback indicating how much bandwidth is available for use. By throttling back as necessary, sending hosts avoid network congestion, preventing traffic from being sent, but thrown away before it reaches its intended destination. Typically, ABR service is used to support data applications where delivery is important, but not necessarily in a near-real-time (nrt) environment.

VPI and VCI

VPI and VCI numbers are used to identify a circuit or path between two ATM switches. The VPI and VCI identifiers have no impact, nor are they impacted, by an E.164 address. VPI and VCI numbers are used as a matter of convenience when implementing permanent or switched virtual circuits across a WAN.

VPI and VCI numbers are used as a matter of convenience when implementing permanent or switched virtual circuits across a WAN.

More will be discussed regarding VPIs and VCIs in Chapter 18, "ATM Wide-Area Networking (WAN) and MPOA."

LAN Emulation Applications

LANE can be deployed to connect Ethernet or Token Ring LANs via ATM, supporting connectivity requirements for multimedia or other high-bandwidth applications across a wide-area ATM network.

ATM LAN emulation network implementations can also be considered an alternative to Gigabit Ethernet deployment, depending on the application requirements, including the need for wide-area connectivity.

LANE can also be used to create emulated LANs, or ELANs, that operate in the same fashion as virtual LANs (VLANs). With the implementation of ELANs, broadcast domains can be larger than otherwise supported by the native protocol, supporting applications that might otherwise be hindered by Ethernet's distance constraints.

Summary

As stated earlier, LAN emulation (LANE) is one method used to extend broadcast domains across an ATM wide-area network (WAN), regardless of the upper-layer protocols in use. LANE extends virtual LANS (VLANs) through the ATM WAN cloud in what is known as an emulated LAN (ELAN).

ATM LANs do not operate in the traditional way that other LAN implementations do, where a LAN host sends data frames at any time to one or multiple hosts on the LAN.

LANE is used to create an emulated LAN. An emulated LAN (ELAN) comprises PCs, LAN switches, routers, and bridges that have ATM interfaces and are directly connected to ATM switches. One ELAN can span several interconnected ATM switches, and the same set of switches can support several ELANs, each identified by a unique name.

ELANs and VLANs share a close similarity. An ELAN can be part of a larger VLAN that spans multiple ATM systems and traditional LAN implementations. In a VLAN environment, network administrators can configure an ELAN to be a part of a particular VLAN.

The LAN emulation client (LEC) hides the underlying ATM layers from the higher-layer protocols (OSI Layers 3 through 7). A device driver known as the LAN emulation client (LEC) or LANE client performs this function.

Three LAN emulation servers are used in the ATM LANE environment:

- LANE configuration server (LECS)—Assigns a LAN emulation client to a specific ELAN (emulated LAN).
- LANE or LAN emulation server (LES)—Responsible for one emulated LAN and keeps track of both MAC and ATM addresses of its ELAN members. A LANE client stays connected to this server so that the client can ask for MAC-to-ATM address translations whenever necessary.
- Broadcast/unknown server (BUS)—Delivers broadcast and multicast frames to hosts in the emulated LAN. A client stays connected to this server so that broadcast and multicast frames can be sent and received at any time.

The ATM LANE protocol comprises four elements:

- ATM addresses
- Integrated local management interface (ILMI) for ATM address initialization
- LANE data frame formats
- LANE protocol control frame functions and formats

Two versions of LANE are supported today, appropriately identified as LANE Version 1 and LANE Version 2. LANE Version 2 adds some features not found in LANE Version 1:

- Class of Service (CoS) parameters: CBR, VBR-rt, VBR-nrt, UBR, ABR
- Capability to implement multiple instances of each server type for redundancy (accomplished via the server cache synchronization protocol, or SCSP)
- Improved handling of multicast traffic

CHAPTER 11

ATM LANE Documentation, Review, and Analysis

After an Asynchronous Transfer Mode (ATM) LAN Emulation (LANE) network has been documented, the next step is to review the physical and logical topology for any performance-impacting issues.

This chapter will also review the information provided by the Cisco router interface for any possible error indications and corrective actions that might be required.

Effective Operating Rate

The *effective operating rate* is the total amount of bandwidth supported by the ATM service. The effective operating rate is often confused with the *effective throughput*, which is the total amount of bandwidth available for data transport.

Every twenty-seventh ATM cell is used for operational, administrative, and maintenance (OAM) activity and is not available for data transport. This OAM overhead must be accounted for when determining the effective operating rate for each ATM service.

Given the line-operating rate of the ATM service, such as 45 Mbps, 155 Mbps, or 622 Mbps, the OAM overhead must first be accounted for. This is accomplished by the following formula:

[(Line Rate, or RateLINE / 27)] = OAM overhead

[(RateLINE – OAM overhead)] = Effective line operating rate (RateEFFECTIVE)

For example, given the following line rates, the effective operating rate is shown in Table 11-1.

Table 11-1 *ATM Service Effective Operating Rate*

ATM Line Rate (Rate$_{LINE}$)	OAM Overhead	Effective Line Operating Rate (Rate$_{EFFECTIVE}$)
45 Mbps	1.67 Mbps	43.3 Mbps
155 Mbps	5.74 Mbps	149.26 Mbps
622 Mbps	23.03 Mbps	598.97 Mbps

ATM LANE Traffic Classes

As discussed in Chapter 7, "FDDI," four defined ATM adaptation layers (AAL) exist, each using a predefined cell format for data segmentation. Table 11-2 maps these AALs to their respective class-of-service/quality-of-service (CoS/QoS) and payload capacity.

Table 11-2 *ATM Adaptation Layer (AAL) Traffic Classes*

AAL	CoS/QoS	AAL Payload Capacity Mbps	Description
AAL-1	Constant bit rate (CBR)	132.81	Emulates TDM (isochronous) service as it provides constant bandwidth across the virtual connection. Typically used for private line emulated services, such as multimedia, CAD/CAM, or medical imaging.
AAL-2	Variable bit rate real-time (VBR-rt)	129.98	Provides a specified average bandwidth across the virtual connection. Used to support delay-sensitive applications, such as voice or video.
AAL-3/4,5	Variable bit rate near-real-time (VBR-nrt)	AAL3/4; 124.33 AAL5; _128.10	Provides a specified average bandwidth across the virtual connection. Used to support non-delay-sensitive applications, such as data applications.
Unspecified	Unspecified bit rate (UBR)		Is a best-effort service, meaning that no bandwidth is specified across the connection or delivery of service guaranteed.
AAL-3/4	Available bit rate (ABR)	124.33	Is a best-effort service implemented in a different fashion from UBR. ABR service provides continuing feedback to the sending device advising how much bandwidth is available for use. ABR is used to support data applications where delivery is important, but not necessarily required in near-real-time.

AAL-1 / CBR

AAL-1 enables a CBR connection with source and destination timing relationships.

Effective Throughput of AAL1

AAL-1 uses a one-byte header within the cell payload, reducing the amount of available payload for data transport from 48 bytes to 47 bytes.

The effective data throughput is determined by using the following formula. (See Table 11-3 for throughput descriptions.)

- $[(RateEFFECTIVE) \times (48$ available bytes/53 total bytes)*] = Effective Line Throughput (LineEFFECTIVE)

    *48/53 = 0.90566038

- $[(Line_{EFFECTIVE}) \times (47$ available bytes/48 total bytes)*] = Effective Data Throughput
    *47/48 = 0.97916667

Table 11-3 *AAL-1 Effective Data Throughput*

ATM Line Rate (Rate$_{LINE}$)	OAM Overhead	Effective Line Operating Rate (Rate$_{EFFECTIVE}$)	Effective Line Throughput Rate	Effective Data Throughput
45 Mbps	1.67 Mbps	43.3 Mbps	39.22 Mbps	38.40 Mbps
155 Mbps	5.74 Mbps	149.26 Mbps	135.18 Mbps	132.36 Mbps
622 Mbps	23.03 Mbps	598.97 Mbps	542.46 Mbps	531.15 Mbps

AAL-2 / VBR-rt

AAL-2 enables time-dependent VBR-rt data to be transmitted between source and destination points.

Effective Throughput of AAL2

AAL-1 uses a two-byte header within the cell payload, reducing the amount of available payload for data transport from 48 bytes to 46 bytes.

The effective data throughput is determined by using the following formula. (See Table 11-4 for throughput descriptions.)

- $[(RateEFFECTIVE) \times (48$ available bytes/53 total bytes)*] = Effective Line Throughput (LineEFFECTIVE)

    *48/53 = 0.90566038

- [(LineEFFECTIVE) × (46 available bytes/48 total bytes)*] = Effective Data Throughput

  *46/48 = 0.95833333

Table 11-4 *AAL-2 Effective Data Throughput*

ATM Line Rate (Rate$_{LINE}$)	OAM Overhead	Effective Line Operating Rate (Rate$_{EFFECTIVE}$)	Effective Line Throughput Rate	Effective Data Throughput
45 Mbps	1.67 Mbps	43.3 Mbps	39.22 Mbps	37.59 Mbps
155 Mbps	5.74 Mbps	149.26 Mbps	135.18 Mbps	129.55 Mbps
622 Mbps	23.03 Mbps	598.97 Mbps	542.46 Mbps	519.86 Mbps

AAL-3/4 / VBR-nrt

AAL-3/4 enables time-independent VBR-nrt data to be transmitted between source and destination points.

Effective Throughput of AAL3/4

AAL-3/4 uses a four-byte header within the cell payload, reducing the amount of available payload for data transport from 48 bytes to 44 bytes.

NOTE   Compared to the traditional 48-byte payload, the 44-byte payload capacity of AAL-3/4 has a distinct adverse affect on user data transfer in that less payload is available for user data, impacting the effective throughput.

The effective data throughput is determined by using the following formula. (See Table 11-5 for throughput descriptions.)

- [(RateEFFECTIVE) × (48 available bytes/53 total bytes)*] = Effective Line Throughput (LineEFFECTIVE)

  *48/53 = 0.90566038

- [(LineEFFECTIVE) × (44 available bytes/48 total bytes)*] = Effective Data Throughput

  *44/48 = 0.91666667

Table 11-5 *AAL-3/4 Effective Data Throughput*

ATM Line Rate (Rate$_{LINE}$)	OAM Overhead	Effective Line Operating Rate (Rate$_{EFFECTIVE}$)	Effective Line Throughput Rate	Effective Data Throughput
45 Mbps	1.67 Mbps	43.3 Mbps	39.22 Mbps	35.95 Mbps
155 Mbps	5.74 Mbps	149.26 Mbps	135.18 Mbps	123.92 Mbps
622 Mbps	23.03 Mbps	598.97 Mbps	542.46 Mbps	497.26 Mbps

AAL5 / VBR-nrt

AAL5 is a simplified version of AAL-3/4. AAL5 assumes the user sequences the data, eliminating the requirement for sequence numbering and length indication fields.

Effective Throughput for AAL-5

Because AAL5 places an 8-byte trailer in the cell payload of the last cell in a sequence, the effective throughput varies depending on the number of cells in the transmission sequence. This range leads to three values for AAL5 payload capacity (for a 155 Mbps line rate):

* Average: 128.10 Mbps

* Best Case (65535 cell sequence): 135.63 Mbps

* Worst Case (1 cell sequence) 113.03 Mbps

IOS Commands

The following Cisco IOS commands are used to gather configuration information regarding an ATM LANE network environment.

show lane

The **show lane** command is used to display global and per-VCC LANE information for all the LANE components configured on an interface or any of its subinterfaces, on a specified subinterface, or on an emulated LAN. See Table 11-6 for the syntax and descriptions.

```
show lane [interface atm card/subcard/port[.subinterface-number] ¦ name
elan-name] [brief]
```

Table 11-6   *show lane Syntax and Description*

Syntax	Description
card/subcard/port	Card, subcard, and port number for the ATM interface.
subinterface-number	Subinterface number.
elan-name	Name of emulated LAN. Maximum length is 32 characters.
brief	Displays the global information, but not the per-VCC information.

Entering the **show lane** command is equivalent to entering the **show lane config, show lane server, show lane bus,** and **show lane client** commands. The **show lane** command shows all LANE-related information except the **show lane database** information.

Example

The following is sample output of the **show lane** command. (See Table 11-7 for output descriptions.)

```
Switch# show lane

LE Client ATM0  ELAN name: alpha  Admin: up  State: operational
Client ID: 2
HW Address: 0041.0b0a.2c82  Type: ethernet          Max Frame Size: 1516
ATM Address: 47.00918100000000410B0A2C81.001122334455.00

VCD  rxFrames  txFrames  Type      ATM Address
  0         0         0  configure 47.33330000000000000000000.000111222333.00
255         1         2  direct    47.33330000000000000000000.001122334455.00
256         1         0  distribute 47.33330000000000000000000.001122334455.00
257         0         0  send      47.33330000000000000000000.000000111111.00
258         0         0  forward   47.33330000000000000000000.000000111111.00

LE Client ATM0.5  ELAN name: alpha5  Admin: up  State: operational
Client ID: 2
HW Address: 0041.0b0a.2c82  Type: ethernet          Max Frame Size: 1516
ATM Address: 47.00918100000000410B0A2C81.001122334455.05

VCD  rxFrames  txFrames  Type      ATM Address
  0         0         0  configure 47.33330000000000000000000.000111222333.00
259         1         5  direct    47.33330000000000000000000.001122334455.05
260         7         0  distribute 47.33330000000000000000000.001122334455.05
261         0        13  send      47.33330000000000000000000.000000111111.05
262        19         0  forward   47.33330000000000000000000.000000111111.05
VCD  rxFrames  txFrames  Type      ATM Address
264        22        12  data      47.33330000000000000000000.000011112222.05
```

Table 11-7 *show lane Command Field Descriptions*

Field*	Description
LE Client	Interface on which the LANE configuration server is configured.
	LE Client identifies the following lines as applying to the LANE configuration server. These lines are also displayed in output from the **show lane lecs** command.
config table	Name of the database associated with the LANE configuration server.
State	State of the configuration server: down or operational. If down, a "down reasons" field indicates why it is down. The reasons include the following: NO-config-table, NO-nsap-address, NO-config-pvc, and NO-interface-up.
ATM Address	ATM address or addresses of this configuration server.
LE Server	Identifies the following lines as applying to the LANE server. These lines are also displayed in output from the **show lane server** command.
ATM x/x/x.x	Interface or subinterface that this LANE server is on.
ELAN name	Name of the emulated LAN (ELAN) served by this LE server.
State	Status of this LANE server. Possible states for a LANE server include down, waiting_ILMI, waiting_listen, up_not_registered, operational, and terminating.
Type	Type of emulated LAN.
Max Frame Size	Maximum frame size on this type of LAN.
ATM Address	ATM address of this server.
Config Server ATM addr	ATM address used to reach the LANE configuration server.
control distribute: VCD 20, 2 members, 6 packets	Virtual circuit descriptor of the Control Distribute VCC.
proxy/ (ST: Init, Conn, Waiting, Adding, Joined, Operational, Reject, Term)	Status of the LANE client at the other end of the Control Distribute VCC.
lecid	Identifier for the LANE client at the other end of the Control Distribute VCC.
ST	Status of the LANE client at the other end of the Control Distribute VCC. Possible states are Init, Conn, Waiting, Adding, Joined, Operational, Reject, and Term.
VCD	Virtual channel descriptor used to reach the LANE client.

(continues)

Table 11-7   *show lane* Command Field Descriptions (Continued)

Field*	Description
pkts	Number of packets sent by the LANE server on the Control Distribute VCC to the LANE client.
Hardware Addr	MAC-layer address of the LANE client.
ATM Address	ATM address of the LANE client.
LE BUS	Identification of the following lines as applying to the LANE broadcast/unknown server. These lines are also displayed in output from the **show lane bus** command.
ATM x/x/x.x	Interface or subinterface that this LANE broadcast/unknown server is on.
ELAN name	Name of the emulated LAN served by this broadcast/unknown server.
State	Status of this LANE client. Possible states include down and operational.
Type	Type of emulated LAN.
Max Frame Size	Maximum frame size on this type of LAN.
ATM Address	ATM address of this LANE broadcast/unknown server.
data forward: vcd 22, 2 members, 10 packets	Virtual channel descriptor of the Data Forward VCC, number of LANE clients attached to the VCC, and number of packets transmitted on the VCC.
lecid	Identifier assigned to each LANE client on the Data Forward VCC.
VCD	Virtual channel descriptor used to reach the LANE client.
Pkts	Number of packets sent by the broadcast/unknown server to the LANE client.
ATM Address	ATM address of the LANE client.
LE Client	Identification of the following lines as applying to a LANE client. These lines are also displayed in output from the **show lane client** command.
ATM x/x/x.x	Interface or subinterface that this LANE client is on.
ELAN name	Name of the emulated LAN to which this client belongs.
State	Status of this LANE client. Possible states include initialState, lecsConnect, configure, join, busConnect, and operational.
HW Address	MAC address, in dotted hexadecimal notation, which is assigned to this LANE client.
Type	Type of emulated LAN.
Max Frame Size	Maximum frame size on this type of LAN.

Table 11-7   *show lane Command Field Descriptions*

Field*	Description
ATM Address	ATM address of this LANE client.
VCD	Virtual channel descriptor for each of the VCCs established for this LANE client.
rxFrames	Number of frames received on the VCC.
txFrames	Number of frames transmitted on the VCC.
Type	Type of VCC; same as the SVC and PVC types. Possible VCC types are configure, direct, distribute, send, forward, and data.
ATM Address	ATM address of the LANE component at the other end of the VCC.

*The Configure Direct VCC is shown in this display as *configure*. The Control Direct VCC is shown as *direct*. The Control Distribute VCC is shown as *distribute*. The Multicast Send VCC and Multicast Forward VC are shown as *send* and *forward*, respectively. The Data Direct VCC is shown as *data*.

show lane bus

The **show lane bus** command is used to display detailed LANE information for the broadcast/unknown server that is configured on an interface or any of its interfaces, on a specified subinterface, or on an ELAN. (See Table 11-8 for syntax descriptions.)

```
show lane bus [interface atm card/subcard/port[.subinterface-number] ¦ name
elan-name] [brief]
```

Table 11-8   *show lane bus Syntax and Description*

Syntax	Description
card/subcard/port	Card, subcard, and port number for the ATM interface.
Subinterface-number	Subinterface number.
elan-name	Name of the emulated LAN. Maximum length is 32 characters.
Brief	Keyword used to display the global information but not the per-VCC information.

Example

The following is sample output from the **show lane bus** command. (See Table 11-7 for field descriptions.)

```
Switch# show lane bus interface atm 3/0/0.1

interface atm 3/0/0.1
type Ethernet       name: pubs     AAL5-SDU length:1516
max frame age: 2 seconds   relayed frames/sec: 116
NSAP: 45.000001415555121f.yyyy.zzzz.0800.200c.1002.01
lecid  vcd    cnt    NSAP
```

```
*     80    659   45.000001415555121f.yyyy.zzzz.0800.200c.1002.01
1     81    99    45.000001415555121f.yyyy.zzzz.0800.200c.1000.01
5     89    41    45.000001415555122f.yyyy.zzzz.0800.200c.1100.01
6     99    101   45.000001415555124f.yyyy.zzzz.0800.200c.1300.01
```

Table 11-9　*show lane bus Command Field Descriptions*

Field*	Description
Interface	Interface or subinterface for which information is displayed.
type	Type of emulated LAN interface.
name	Name of the emulated LAN.
MTU	Maximum transmission unit (packet) size on the emulated LAN.
AAL5-SDU	Maximum number of bytes in a LANE segment data unit (SDU) encapsulated in an ATM AAL5 frame. This length includes a 2-byte marker and a full Ethernet-like frame from the destination MAC address field through the last byte of data. It does not include the Ethernet CRC or FRC, which is not present on emulated LAN frames. The number does not include the 8-byte AAL5 trailer in the last ATM cell of the frame or the padding between the last data byte and the 8-byte trailer.
max frame age	After receiving a frame over Multicast Send VCC, the broadcast/unknown server must transmit the frame to all relevant Multicast Forward VCCs within this number of seconds. When the time expires, the server discards the frame.
NSAP	ATM address of this broadcast/unknown server.
Lecid	Unique identifier of the LANE client at the other end of this VCC.
Vcd	Virtual circuit descriptor that uniquely identifies this VCC.
Cnt	For Multicast Send VCC, the number of packets sent from the client to the broadcast/unknown server.
	For Multicast Forward VCC, the number of packets sent from the broadcast/unknown server clients.
NSAP	For Multicast Send VCC, the ATM address of the LANE client at the other end of this VCC.
	For Multicast Forward VCC, the ATM address of the broadcast/unknown server.

*The Configure Direct VCC is shown in this display as *configure*. The Control Direct VCC is shown as *direct*. The Control Distribute VCC is shown as *distribute*. The Multicast Send VCC and Multicast Forward VC are shown as *send* and *forward*, respectively. The Data Direct VCC is shown as *data*.

show lane client

The **show lane client** command is used to display global and per-VCC LANE information for all the LANE clients configured on an interface or any of its subinterfaces, on a specified subinterface, or on an ELAN. (See Table 11-10 for syntax descriptions.)

```
show lane client [interface atm card/subcard/port[.subinterface-number] ¦ name
elan-name] [brief ¦ detail]
```

Table 11-10 *show lane client Syntax and Description*

Syntax	Description
card/subcard/port	Card, subcard, and port number for the ATM interface.
Subinterface-number	Subinterface number.
elan-name	Name of the emulated LAN. Maximum length is 32 characters.
Brief	Keyword used to display the global information but not the per-VCC information.
Detail	Keyword used to display backup server connection information.

Examples

The following is sample output from the **show lane client** command. (See Table 11-11 for field descriptions.)

```
Switch# show lane client
LE Client ATM0  ELAN name: alpha  Admin: up  State: operational
Client ID: 2
HW Address: 0041.0b0a.2c82   Type: ethernet         Max Frame Size: 1516
ATM Address: 47.00918100000000410B0A2C81.001122334455.00

VCD  rxFrames  txFrames  Type      ATM Address
  0         0         0  configure 47.33330000000000000000000.000111222333.00
255         1         2  direct    47.33330000000000000000000.001122334455.00
256         1         0  distribute 47.33330000000000000000000.001122334455.00
257         0         0  send      47.33330000000000000000000.000000111111.00
258         1         0  forward   47.33330000000000000000000.000000111111.00

LE Client ATM0.5  ELAN name: alpha5  Admin: up  State: operational
Client ID: 2
HW Address: 0041.0b0a.2c82   Type: ethernet         Max Frame Size: 1516
ATM Address: 47.00918100000000410B0A2C81.001122334455.05

VCD  rxFrames  txFrames  Type      ATM Address
  0         0         0  configure 47.33330000000000000000000.000111222333.00
259         1         5  direct    47.33330000000000000000000.001122334455.05
260         7         0  distribute 47.33330000000000000000000.001122334455.05
261         0        13  send      47.33330000000000000000000.000000111111.05
262        20         0  forward   47.33330000000000000000000.000000111111.05
VCD  rxFrames  txFrames  Type      ATM Address
264        22        12  data      47.33330000000000000000000.000011112222.05
```

Table 11-11 *show lane client Command Field Descriptions*

Field*	Description
Interface	Interface or subinterface for which information is displayed.
Name	Name of the emulated LAN.
MAC	MAC address of this LANE client.
type	Type of emulated LAN, Ethernet, or Token Ring.
MTU	Maximum transmission unit (packet) size on the emulated LAN.
AAL5-SDU length	Maximum number of bytes in a LANE SDU that is encapsulated in an AAL5 frame. This length includes a 2-byte marker and a full Ethernet-like frame from the destination MAC address field through the last byte of data. It does not include an Ethernet CRC (or FRC), which is not present on emulated LAN frames. The number does not include the 8-byte AAL5 trailer in the last ATM cell of the frame or the padding between the last data byte and the 8-byte trailer.
NSAP	ATM address of this LANE client.
VCD	Virtual channel descriptor that uniquely identifies this VCC.
rxFrames	Number of packets received.
txFrames	Number of packets transmitted.
Type	Type of VCC. This is the same as the SVC and PVC types. Possible VCC types are configure, direct, distribute, send, forward, and data.
NSAP	ATM address of the LANE component at the other end of this VCC.

*The Configure Direct VCC is shown in this display as *configure*. The Control Direct VCC is shown as *direct*. The Control Distribute VCC is shown as *distribute*. The Multicast Send VCC and Multicast Forward VC are shown as *send* and *forward*, respectively. The Data Direct VCC is shown as *data*.

show lane config

The **show lane config** command is used to display global LANE information for the ATM LANE configuration server that is configured on a router interface (see Table 11-12 for syntax descriptions).

```
show lane config [interface atm card/subcard/port] [brief]
```

Table 11-12 *show lane config Syntax and Description*

Syntax	Description
card/subcard/port	Card, subcard, and port number for the ATM interface.
Brief	Keyword used to display the global information, but not the per-VCC information.

Examples

The following is sample output from the **show lane config** command on a configuration server with two ATM addresses:

```
Switch# show lane config

LE Config Server ATM 1/0/0 config table: table State: operational
ATM Address: 39.000000000000000000000000.000000000500.00
ATM Address: 39.000000000000000000000000.000000000500.01
cumulative total number of unrecognized packets received so far:0
cumulative total number of config requests received so far: 10
cumulative total number of config failures so far: 0
```

The following code shows an operational server, even though the addresses are not completely registered. The first address is not registered with the ILMI, as indicated by the ilmi-state. The second address is not registered with either the ILMI or the ATM signaling subsystem, as indicated by the atmsig-state.

```
Switch# show lane config

LE Config Server ATM 1/0/0 config table: table State: operational
ATM Address: 39.000000000000000000000000.000000000500.00 ilmi-
ATM Address: 39.000000000000000000000000.000000000500.01 ilmi- atmsig-
cumulative total number of unrecognized packets received so far:0
cumulative total number of config requests received so far: 10
cumulative total number of config failures so far: 0
```

The following code displays some physical connectivity problems, resulting in the configuration server ATM address being undetermined. Either the prefix was not obtained or it is not available. As a result, the address cannot be computed and the message "EXACT ADDRESS NOT YET SET (NO PREFIX?)" is displayed. (See Table 11-13 for command field descriptions.)

```
Switch# show lane config

LE Config Server ATM 1/0/0 config table: table State: operational
ATM Address: EXEACT ADDRESS NOT YET SET (NO PREFIX ?) ilmi- atmsig-
   actual user specified form:...
cumulative total number of unrecognized packets received so far:0
cumulative total number of config requests received so far: 0
cumulative total number of config failures so far: 0
```

Table 11-13 *show lane config Command Field Descriptions*

Field	Description
LE Config Server	Major interface on which the LANE configuration server is configured.
config-table	Name of the database associated with the LANE configuration server.
State	State of the configuration server: down or operational.
	If down, the reasons field indicates why it is down. The reasons include the following:
	NO-config
	NO-nsap-address
	No-interface-up
ATM address	ATM address of this configuration server.

show lane database

The **show lane database** command is used to display the database of the configuration server.

Example

The following is sample output from the **show lane database** command. (See Table 11-14 for the command field descriptions.)

```
Switch# show lane database

config-table: engandmkt - bound to interface/s: atm 1/0/0
default ELAN: none
ELAN eng: les NSAP 45.000001415555121f.yyyy.zzzz.0800.200c.1001.01
  LEC MAC 0800.200c.1100
  LEC NSAP 45.000001415555121f.yyyy.zzzz.0800.200c.1000.01
  LEC NSAP 45.000001415555121f.yyyy.zzzz.0800.200c.1300.01
ELAN mkt: les NSAP 45.000001415555121f.yyyy.zzzz.0800.200c.1001.02
  LEC MAC 0800.200c.1100
  LEC NSAP 45.000001415555121f.yyyy.zzzz.0800.200c.1000.02
  LEC NSAP 45.000001415555121f.yyyy.zzzz.0800.200c.1300.02
```

Table 11-14 *show lane database Command Field Descriptions*

Field	Description
config-table	Name of current database and interface to which it is bound.
default ELAN	Default name, if one is established.
ELAN	Name of the emulated LAN whose data is reported in this line and the next three lines.
LEC MAC	MAC addresses of an individual LANE client in the emulated LAN. This display includes a separate line for every LANE client in this emulated LAN.
LEC NSAP	ATM addresses of all LANE clients in the emulated LAN.

ATM LANE Documentation

The **show lane** command is recommended for use in completing the following template example (see Table 11-15).

The following output will be used for this template example:

```
LE Client ATM0.5  ELAN name: alpha5  Admin: up  State: operational
Client ID: 2
HW Address: 0041.0b0a.2c82   Type: ethernet          Max Frame Size: 1516
ATM Address: 47.00918100000000410B0A2C81.001122334455.05

    VCD  rxFrames  txFrames  Type      ATM Address
    0         0         0  configure  47.33330000000000000000000.000111222333.00
    259       1         5  direct     47.33330000000000000000000.001122334455.05
    260       7         0  distribute 47.33330000000000000000000.001122334455.05
    261       0        13  send       47.33330000000000000000000.000000111111.05
    262      20         0  forward    47.33330000000000000000000.000000111111.05
    VCD  rxFrames  txFrames  Type      ATM Address
    264      22        12  data       47.33330000000000000000000.000011112222.05
```

Table 11-15 *ATM LAN Documentation Template (Example)*

ELAN Name	Alpha5		
LEC Interface	ATM0.5		
Configuration Server Address	47.00918100000000410B0A2C81.001122334455.05		
Client Address	Client VC	Description	Comments
47.333300000000000000000000.000111222333.00	0	Configuration Direct VCC	
47.333300000000000000000000.001122334455.05	259	Control Direct VCC	
47.333300000000000000000000.001122334455.05	260	Control Distribution	
47.333300000000000000000000.000000111111.05	261	Multicast Sending	
47.333300000000000000000000.000000111111.05	262	Multicast Forwarding	
47.333300000000000000000000.000011112222.05	264	Data	

Table 11-16 *ATM LAN Documentation Template*

ELAN Name			
LEC Interface			
Configuration Server Address			
Client Address	Client VC	Description	Comments

The following **show lane bus** output will be used for the template example (see Table 11-17).

```
Switch# show lane bus interface atm 3/0/0.1

interface atm 3/0/0.1
type Ethernet        name: pubs    AAL5-SDU length:1516
max frame age: 2 seconds   relayed frames/sec: 116
NSAP: 45.000001415555121f.yyyy.zzzz.0800.200c.1002.01
lecid  vcd   cnt   NSAP
*      80    659   45.000001415555121f.yyyy.zzzz.0800.200c.1002.01
1      81    99    45.000001415555121f.yyyy.zzzz.0800.200c.1000.01
5      89    41    45.000001415555122f.yyyy.zzzz.0800.200c.1100.01
6      99    101   45.000001415555124f.yyyy.zzzz.0800.200c.1300.01
```

Table 11-17 *Broadcast/Unknown Server (BUS) Document Template (Example)*

ELAN Name	Pubs		
BUS Interface	ATM 3/0/0.1		
BUS Server Address	45.000001415555121f.yyyy.zzzz.0800.200c.1002.01		
BUS Client Address	**Client ID**	**VCD**	**Comments/Description**
45.000001415555121f.yyyy.zzzz.0800.200c.1002.01		80	
45.000001415555121f.yyyy.zzzz.0800.200c.1000.01	1	81	
45.000001415555122f.yyyy.zzzz.0800.200c.1100.01	5	89	
45.000001415555124f.yyyy.zzzz.0800.200c.1300.01	6	99	

Table 11-18 *Broadcast/Unknown Server (BUS) Document Template*

ELAN Name			
BUS Interface			
BUS Server Address			
BUS Client Address	Client ID	VCD	Comments/Description

Summary

ATM LANE networks can be difficult at times to document because of the many types of services, such as multicast, broadcast, and connection paths across the emulated LAN (ELAN). Do not be disheartened at what can be considered a deluge of configuration information. As is the underlying theme, the goal of a good network document is to provide the necessary information needed for maintenance and troubleshooting, not all the information within a configuration.

The more useful Cisco IOS commands include the following:

- **show lane**
- **show lane config**
- **show lane client**
- **show lane database**
- **show lane bus**

These Cisco IOS commands will give the network manager an understanding of how the ATM LANE network is constructed.

CHAPTER 12

Telecommunications and Telephony

Telecommunications is defined as the transmission of a voice or data signal from one point to another over short or long distances.

Voice switching and routing within the telecommunications network is based on the automatic number identification (ANI). ANIs are constructed per the North American Numbering Plan (NANP). Data switching and routing within the telecommunications switched network are usually in the form of dedicated, ISDN, or xDSL connections. Dedicated connections are discussed in Chapter 13, "Private Line WANs." ISDN and xDSL are discussed later in this chapter.

Voice Signaling

Three types of signaling are used to establish a voice call:

- Supervisory—Informs the telephone switch port of the local loop status and of any connected trunks between switches and private branch exchanges (PBXs).

- Address—Provides the telephone number (ANI) that enables the call to be routed to its destination.

- Informational or Call Progress—Informs the originator as to the status of a dialed call.

Supervisory Signaling

The six types of supervisory signaling are as follows:

- Loop-start
- Ground-start
- Wink-start
- Immediate-start
- Tone-start

- E&M
  - Type I
  - Type II
  - Type III
  - Type IV
  - Type V

Loop-Start Signaling

The operation of loop-start signaling is dependent on the actions of the telephone handset. When the telephone handset is lifted (off-hook), the switch hook closes, resulting in current flowing across the local loop between the telephone handset and the telephone switch (or PBX). The switch (or PBX) responds to this current with a dial tone, enabling the calling party to place an outbound, or dialed, call.

Placing the telephone handset back in the cradle (on-hook) terminates the call, resulting in an opening of the connection to the switch hook and terminating any current across the local loop.

NOTE	Loop-start signaled lines are susceptible to a condition known as *cross-talk*, or *glare*. Glare occurs when both sides of the local loop seize, or go "off-hook," at the same time, and two calls "collide" across the local loop.

Ground-Start Signaling

Ground-start signaling is a modification of loop-start signaling. Ground-start signaling eliminates the potential for glare (both ends of a local loop seizing the line at the same time) across the local loop.

Figure 12-1 illustrates the steps (listed after Figure 12-1) involved in handling a ground-start call:

Figure 12-1   *Ground-Start Signaling*

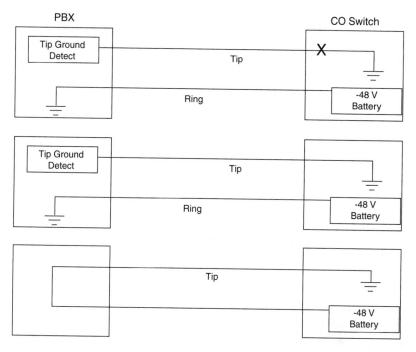

1 The PBX grounds the ring lead, causing current to flow across the local loop from the PBX to the telephone (central office) switch.

2 At the central office (CO), the switch module/port senses the current on the line and recognizes it as a trunk-seizure request from the distant-end (of the local loop).

3 Depending on trunk availability, the switch module/port acknowledges the request by closing its tip switch, generating a ground on the tip lead.

4 The flow of current across this tip lead acts as the acknowledgement to the requesting PBX.

5 The PBX closes the loop by holding a coil across the ring and tip leads, removing the ring ground. At this point, the circuit acts like a loop-start [signaled] circuit.

When a CO switch initiates a ground-start signaled call, it requests the trunk (local loop) by closing the tip switch, generating a ringing voltage across the ring lead. The PBX must recognize this seizure within 100 milliseconds (ms) to prevent glare (both ends of the loop seizing the trunk at the same time) on the trunk.

Responding to this ring lead voltage, the PBX places a holding coil across the tip and ring leads. The PBX closes the loop, removes the ringing voltage, and establishes the call in a fashion similar to loop-start signaled calls.

Wink-Start Signaling

Wink-start signaling operates by having the originating trunk placed in an off-hook condition, resulting in the remote switch responding by transmitting an off-hook pulse of 140 to 290 ms in duration. After this off-hook pulse is transmitted, the switch returns to an idle (on-hook) condition. This off-hook pulse is known as *wink-back*. When the originating switch station detects the wink-back, the switch waits 210 ms before transmitting digits that the remote switch will use to address the call. The remote switch returns to an off-hook condition to answer (receive) this call.

Immediate-Start Signaling

Immediate-start signaling operates by having the originating switch place the trunk in an off-hook condition and maintain this condition for a minimum of 150 ms. After this 150 ms interval, the switch outputs the address, or called, digits. In contrast to wink-start signaling, immediate-start signaling has no direct handshake, making immediate-signaling appropriate only when dedicated trunks (logical or physical) are used between switches.

Tone-Start Signaling

Tone-start signaling operates by leaving the originating trunk circuit in an off-hook condition. The receiving switch recognizes this condition and generates a dial tone. The switch can use this dial tone to output previously stored digits. If the switch is operating in a cut-through mode, the distant dial tone is passed to the user for outbound dialing. Tone-start signaling is commonly used in private voice networks that are constructed by PBX interconnection and not the public switched telephone network (PSTN).

E&M Signaling

E&M signaling is the most common method used for trunk signaling. The letters "E&M" are derived from the words "Ear" and "Mouth." The E-lead is used to receive signaling information, and the M-lead is used to send signaling information. With E&M signaling, separate paths are used for voice and signaling. The voice path consists of either two wires or four wires, and the signaling path uses one of five standards, referred to as Types I through V.

- Type I—The PBX provides the battery for both E and M leads. An on-hook condition at the PBX results in the M-lead being grounded and the E-lead being open. In contrast, an off-hook condition results in the M-lead providing the battery and the E-lead being grounded.

  Type I signaling can cause a high return current through the grounding system. If both PBXs are improperly grounded, this can result in false trunk seizures.

E&M Type I signaling is the most commonly used interface in North America for 4-wire trunk interfaces.

- Type II—To address the ground issues with Type I signaling, Type II signaling added two additional leads: signal battery (SB) and signal ground (SG). The E-lead is strapped to the SG-lead, whereas the M-lead is strapped to the SB-lead. This strapping results in the grounding of the trunk at each end and eliminates grounding problems. In Type II signaling, the M-lead states are "open" and "battery."

- Type III—This is similar to Type I signaling. The difference between Type III signaling and Type I signaling is in the use of transmission equipment that supplies the battery and ground sources. Type III signaling was primarily used with old telephone central office (CO) equipment and is rarely used in modern day deployments. This older CO equipment has been replaced.

- Type IV—This is similar to Type II signaling. The difference between Type IV and Type II signaling is in the M-leads. Whereas the M-lead states in Type II signaling are "open" and "battery," the M-lead states in Type IV signaling are "ground" and "open." A significant advantage of Type IV signaling is that accidental shorting of the signal battery (SB) lead will not result in excessive current flow.

- Type V—Both the switch and transmission equipment supply a battery. The battery for the M-lead is located in the signaling equipment, and the battery for the E-lead is in the PBX.

  Type V signaling is the ITU E&M signaling standard and is the most common method of E&M signaling outside of North America.

NOTE   In the United Kingdom, the British Telecom uses their own standard: Type VI signaling.

Address Signaling

Address signaling provides the telephone number, or ANI, that enables the call to be routed to its intended destination. Two common methods of address signaling are used:

- Dial pulse—Digits are transmitted from the originating, or sending, telephone set by the opening and closing of the local loop. Each dialed digit is generated at a specific rate with each pulse consisting of two parts: make and break.

  — Make—This segment represents the period when the circuit is closed.

  — Break—This segment represents the period when the circuit is open during a dialed-digit period.

- Tone dialing—More formally known as *dual-tone multifrequency (DTMF)*. DTMF signaling results in the use of a 12-key keypad that has two frequencies associated with each key, as illustrated in Figure 12-2. Each row and column of keys is associated with a predefined frequency, with the pressing of a key resulting in the generation of a low- and high-frequency pair of tones. This resulting tone pair informs the connected telephone switch or PBX that a certain digit was dialed.

Figure 12-2   *DTMF Keypad*

	1209 Hz	1336 Hz	1477 Hz	1633 Hz
697 Hz	1	ABC 2	DEF 3	A
770 Hz	GHI 4	JKL 5	MNO 6	B
852 Hz	PRS 7	TUV 8	WXY 9	C
941 Hz	*	oper 0	#	D

NOTE   In North America, the make/break ratio is 39/61—39 percent make to 61 percent break. In the United Kingdom, the make/break ratio is 33/67—33 percent make to 67 percent break.

Informational Signaling

Informational signaling informs the originator, or calling party, as to the status of a dialed call and also rings the called party to advise of a call presence. Informational signaling is often referred to as *call-progress signaling* and includes the following five types of signaling conditions.

- Dial tone—Certain predefined frequency pairs are used to convey informational signaling. A dial tone results from the generation of a continuous 350 and 440 Hz frequency pair by the telephone company switch or local PBX.

- Ringing signal—When a call is routed to its intended destination, the service switch or PBX sends a 20 Hz 86-VAC (volts alternating current) ringing signal that cycles for 2 seconds on and 4 seconds off.

- Ringback signal—When a call is in a ringing state, the ringback tone informs the caller as such. The ringback tone consists of a 400 and 48 Hz frequency pair. Like the ringing signal, it cycles on for 2 seconds and off for 4 seconds.

- Busy signal—When a call cannot be completed because the intended, or called, destination line is in use, the local PBX or switch generates a busy signal back to the calling party. The busy signal cycles between the frequency pair of 480 and 620 Hz for 1/2 second (0.5) on followed by a 1/2 second off.

- Fast busy signal—When a call cannot be completed because of trunks between switches being busy, a fast busy signal is sent. The fast busy signal consists of the same frequency pair as a regular busy, 480 and 620 Hz, but is cycled on for 0.2 seconds and off for 0.3 seconds. The local telephone company switch or corporate PBX generates the fast busy signal upon indications that it cannot find a trunk to carry the call beyond the local switch/PBX.

ANI

ANI, or *automatic number identification*, is a service that provides the telephone number of an incoming call. ANI is used for a variety of functions. By receiving the incoming telephone number, telephone companies can direct a call to the proper long-distance carrier's equipment, help identify the caller's address for 911 calls, and route 800 number calls to the nearest vendor. Call centers can also use ANI to identify the calling party to better service a customer.

ANI numbers, sometimes referred to as ANIs, are constructed per the NANP.

NANP

The NANP was designed to allow for quick and discreet connection to any phone in North America. The NANP comprises three elements:

- Area Code (NPA)
- Central Office Code (NXX)
- Station Subscriber Number (XXXX)

Area Code (NPA)

The Area Code, or Numbering Plan Assignment (NPA), identifies the calling destination area. The first number of an NPA is 2 to 9, with 0 and 1 reserved. Zero is reserved for operator access or operator services. One is reserved for the local switching office so they can immediately set up a tandem switch connection for a long-distance toll call.

Certain NPAs have been set up for predefined or specific functions:

- 456 NXX
- 900/976 NXX
- 500 NXX
- 8XX (800/888/877/866/855)

456 NXX

Numbers within the 456 NPA are used to identify carrier-specific services. Carrier identification is provided within the dialed digits of the E.164 number; the prefix following 456 (456-NXX) identifies the carrier. Use of these numbers enables the proper routing of inbound international calls destined for these services into and between North American Numbering Plan area countries.

Current 456-NXX assignments are as follows:

NXX	CARRIER
226	Teleglobe Canada
288	AT&T
289	AT&T
333	Startec, Inc.
624	MCI
640	Sprint
741	STSJ
808	Hawaiian Tel

900/976 NXX

900 numbers are used to identify premium services. The cost of calls to these services is billed to the calling party.

900 numbers are in the format 900-NXX-XXXX. 900 service is not portable; the identity of the service provider is embedded in the number. The prefix (NXX) indicates the 900 service provider, and the line number (XXXX) indicates the particular premium service.

500 NXX

500 numbers are used for "follow me" personal communication services.

500 numbers are in the format 500-NXX-XXXX. 500 service is not portable. The identity of the service provider is embedded in the number. The prefix (NXX) indicates the 500 service provider, and the line number (XXXX) indicates the particular premium service.

Exchange Code (NXX)

This is the central office (CO) designator listing the possible number of central office codes within each area code (NPA).

Certain NXXs have been set up for predefined or specific functions. These include the following:

- 555-XXXX
- 800-855-XXXX

555-Numbers

555 numbers are used to reach a wide variety of information services. For example, NPA-555-1212 will provide directory assistance information for the specified NPA.

555 numbers are in the format 555-XXXX. The line number (XXXX) indicates the particular information service. The ATIS-sponsored Industry Numbering Committee assigns these 555 numbers.

555 numbers can be assigned for either national or local use. A national assignment requires that the 555 number be implemented in at least 30% of all NPAs or states or provinces in the NANP area. A local assignment is made for implementation in certain NPAs specified at assignment time.

800-855

800-855 numbers, in the format 800-855-XXXX, are used to access PSTN services intended for use by the deaf, hard of hearing, or speech impaired. Such services include telecommunications relay service and message relay service.

Subscriber Extension (XXXX)

This number identifies the service subscriber of the central office identified by the NXX. No special or reserved XXXX numbers are available.

Lines and Trunks

A line is an end point from a CO or a PBX and carries a single conversation. A trunk interconnects two switching systems, such as between LEC central offices, or a LEC CO switch and a customer PBX. Trunks bundle several lines, carrying multiple simultaneous conversations, and are used for call switching and routing.

Direct Inward Dialing (DID)

Direct inward dialing (DID) refers to a service whereby a caller can dial a 10-digit number from outside a switch and reach a specific individual without operator intervention (either live automated). In the context of a PBX, DID is a feature that must be configured to enable the direct dialing of an extension.

Direct Outward Dialing (DOD)

Similar to DID, direct outward dialing enables a caller behind a switch or PBX to place outbound calls without operator or automated attendant assistance. This was necessary in the early days of corporate telephone systems when operators screened incoming and outgoing calls to prohibit employees from making international long-distance personal calls. These limits can now be configured on a corporate switch or PBX.

Telephone companies offer a service in which the last few (typically three or four) digits that a caller dials are forwarded to the called party (destination) on a special DID trunk. This forwarding usually takes place by dial pulse (just as if the caller had a rotary phone), multifrequency tones (MF tones are different from the DTMF tones and are usually used only within telephone networks), or by DTMF (dual-tone multifrequency) tones.

For example, all phone numbers from 555-1000 to 555-1999 could be assigned to a customer with 20 DID trunks. When a caller dials any number in this range, the call is forwarded on any available trunk of the 20 (that is, the trunks are *equivalent*, which is also called being in a *hunt group* or a *rotary*). If the caller dialed 555-1234, then the digits 2, 3, and 4 (assuming three-digit outpulsing was used) would be forwarded. These DID trunks could be terminated on the following:

- A private branch exchange (PBX)—Knows which number was called and rings that phone extension. This makes it look as though 555-1234 and the other 999 lines all have direct outside lines, while only requiring 20 trunks to service the 1,000 telephone extensions.

- A fax server—Can provide routing for inbound faxes. Each fax user is assigned a unique telephone number. When the fax server gets the number dialed from the DID trunk, it forwards the subsequent fax to the specified (according to the phone number dialed) person's PC (where it can be viewed, printed, or stored).

Tie Lines

Tie lines, or tie trunks, are dedicated private line, point-to-point, circuits used to connect two voice facilities. A dedicated trunk between two organization's PBXs, in different locations, is an example of a tie line. There are no geographical limits to implementing tie lines; however, cost needs to be a consideration because most network service provider private line services are distance sensitive with a billable cost per mile.

Telephone Network

Figure 12-3 illustrates a typical point of presence (POP) or CO infrastructure for a network service provider.

Figure 12-3   *Typical Service Provider POP/CO Infrastructure*

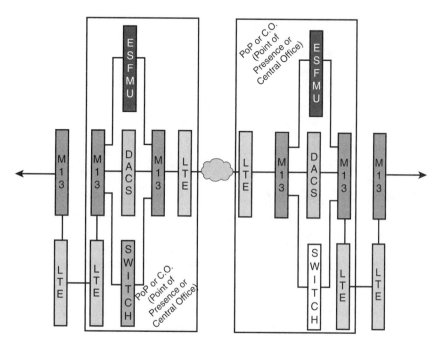

The equipment illustrated here is identified as follows:

- Light termination equipment (LTE)—Fiber-optic transmission terminate here, usually in the form of fiber or lightwave multiplexers (muxes). LTE is used to support OC-x services between service provider POPs/COs, between LEC POPs/COs, or interconnecting between service provider and LEC POPs/COs.

- Multiplexer DS1/DS3 (M13)—Pronounced "M-One-Three," it performs both multiplexing and demultiplexing functions. M13 multiplexes 28 DS1 signals into a single DS3 signal for transmission, usually terminating to the LTE. It demultiplexes DS3 signals into 28 DS1 signals, usually terminating into an ESFMU, DACS (DXC), or voice/data switch.

- Digital cross connect system (DXC or DACS)—This electronically switches the DS0s within each DS1. DACS can also be used to provide network for dedicated T1 service, provided they are configured to do so. DACS are usually groomed as "T1 Intact" to provide network timing.

- Switch—This could be a voice or data (ATM or Frame Relay) switch. The switch acts as an interface to the respective network to which it is providing service, such as voice or data.

- Extended superframe monitoring unit (ESFMU)—ESFMU is used to provide in-band monitoring of T1 services. Typically, ESFMUs are provisioned as part of a dedicated private line service offering; however, they can be placed anywhere in the path of a T1 service.

  For more information regarding ESFMUs and other facets of dedicated T1 service, please refer to Chapter 13.

NOTE   ESFMUs have two sides: East and West. The East side always faces the network, and the West side always faces the customer.

Pulse Code Modulation (PCM)

For voice (analog) and data (digital) to share the same digital transmission media, the voice analog signals must be converted into digital signals. This digitizing of the analog signals is known as *Pulse Code Modulation* (*PCM*). PCM is a sampling process that compresses a voice signal into a 64 Kbps standard digital service rate, known as a DS0.

PCM involves two steps:

1 The incoming analog signal is sampled 8,000 times per second. These sampled values are converted to pulses using the pulse amplitude modulation (PAM) process.

2 The height of each pulse is assigned a representative 8-bit binary value resulting in a digital representation of the pulse and ultimately the sampled analog waveform.

Figure 12-4 illustrates both PAM and PCM. (The 8-bit binary values are for illustration purposes only and are not actual values).

Figure 12-4   *Pulse Amplitude Modulation (PAM) and Pulse Code Modulation (PCM)*

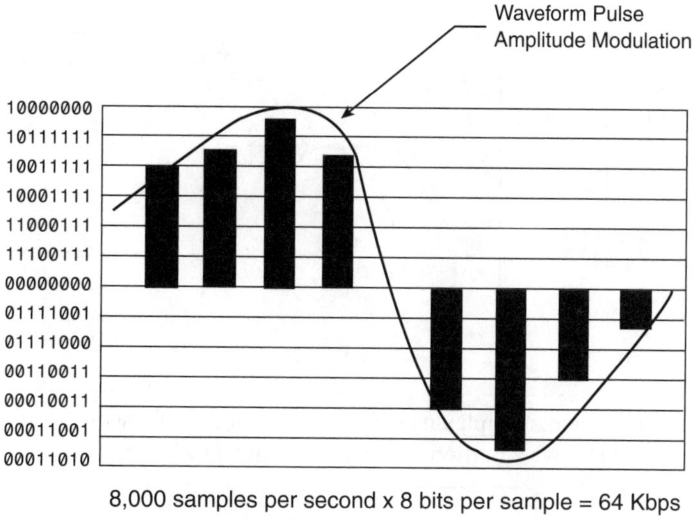

Waveform Pulse
Amplitude Modulation

10000000
10111111
10011111
10001111
11000111
11100111
00000000
01111001
01111000
00110011
00010011
00011001
00011010

8,000 samples per second x 8 bits per sample = 64 Kbps

PCM is the underlying principle behind T1 services and time division multiplexing (TDM).

TDM

TDM is the foundation behind network service provider services, the most common being T1/T3. TDM was designed on the premise that each user, or channel, will have the total bandwidth for a portion of time.

After the voice/data signals have been digitized, they are then multiplexed and transmitted over the T1 (E1, T3, and so on) link. This multiplexing process is called TDM.

TDM divides the T1 link into 24 discrete timeslots, or channels. Each timeslot, or channel, is a DS0 signal (64 Kbps), as illustrated in Figure 12-5.

Figure 12-5 *T1 TDM Timeslots (64 Kbps each)*

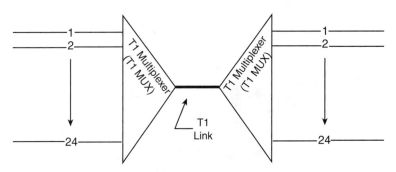

NOTE Frequency division multiplexing (FDM) is similar to TDM with the exception that a user, or channel, will have a portion of the bandwidth all the time.

Local Loop and Transmission Media

Four media types are used for transmission:

- Copper cable
- Coaxial cable
- Fiber-optic cable
- Wireless

Copper Cable

Copper cabling is technically known as unshielded twisted-pair (UTP). The lack of a shield allows the high-frequency part of a signal to leak, limiting its support for high-speed data transmission.

Copper cabling is subjected to two unique scenarios:

- Loading coils—Loading coils are often deployed to local loops longer than 18,000 feet. Loading coils are basically low frequency pass-through filters. These pass-through filters block frequencies above voiceband (VF, 300 to 3400 Hz), which essentially blocks data transmission, most notably in the higher frequencies.

- Bridge taps—Bridge taps are unterminated portions of a loop that are not directly in the transmission path. Bridge taps can be used on a cable pair that is connected at an intermediate point or on an extension beyond a customer premise. For example, a drop wire that provides a second line to a residence is left in place after the customer premise equipment (CPE), such as a telephone set, is removed.

Coaxial Cable

Coaxial cable, or "coax," consists of a single copper strand running down the axis of the cable. Contrast this to the strand that is being twisted[md[like copper cabling. The copper strand is separated from the outer shielding of the cable by an insulator, usually made of foam, which is then wrapped with an insulating cover, completing the cable "shield". Coax can carry high frequencies with no concerns regarding signal seepage. Coax cable is used to carry several cable TV signals to homes, with each television signal being ~6 megahertz (MHz) wide.

Fiber-Optic Cable

Whereas copper and coax cabling carry transmission frequencies in the megahertz range, fiber-optic cabling carries frequencies at a much higher band, approximately a million times higher. Whereas copper and coax cabling carry transmission signals in the form of electromagnetic waves, fiber-optic cabling carries signals in the form of light waves. Fiber-optic cabling can carry signals as high as 10 Gigahertz (GHz).

Fiber-optic cabling is deployed in one of two modes:

- Single-mode—Uses a single glass strand with a smaller core than that of multimode fiber. Because single-mode fiber uses a smaller core of 8 to 10 micrometer, single-mode fiber enables only one mode of light travel over the fiber.

- Multimode—Comprises multiple strands of glass fibers and has a larger core than single-mode fiber. Multimode fiber-optic cables have a combined diameter of 50 to 100 microns, with each cable carrying independent signals. Multimode fiber has greater bandwidth capabilities than single-mode fiber.

NOTE   Multimode fiber is primarily used for applications in which the distance limitation of 2 kilometers (km) is not an issue, such as in a campus environment.

Wireless

Wireless transmission media can take several forms: microwave, digital radio, infrared, low-earth-orbit (LEO) satellites, geosynchronous satellites, cellular, and PCS. Wireless media has both advantages and disadvantages. The most notable advantage is the mobility of cellular and the disregard for cable plant construction. The most notable disadvantage is the signal attenuation effects (often due to atmospheric conditions) and coverage areas with regard to mobile implementations.

ISDN

Integrated Services Digital Network (ISDN) is a system of digital phone connections that enable data to be transmitted digitally end to end.

With ISDN, voice and data are carried by bearer channels (B-channels) at a bandwidth of 64 Kbps (kilobits per second). The data channel (D-channel) handles signaling at 16 Kbps (BRI) or 64 Kbps (PRI), depending on the service type.

NOTE   In ISDN terminology, "K" means 1000, not 1024. A 64 Kbps channel carries data at a rate of 64,000 bps. Under this schema, "K" (Kilo) means 1,000, and "M" (Mega) means 1,000,000.

ISDN service are of two basic types:

- Basic rate interface (BRI)—BRI consists of two 64 Kbps B-channels and one 16 Kbps D-channel; 2B + D.
- Primary rate interface (PRI)—PRI consists of 23 64 Kbps B-channels and one 64 Kbps D-channel; 23B + D or 30B + D.

ISDN Standards

A number of international standards define ISDN. I.430 describes the physical layer and part of the data link layer for BRI. The Q.921 standard documents the data link protocol used over the D-channel. The Q.931 standard documents the network layer user-to-network interface, providing call setup and breakdown and channel allocation. Variants of Q.931 are used in both ATM and voice-over-IP (VoIP). The G.711 standard documents the standard 64 kbps audio encoding used by LECs throughout the world.

ITU I.430

ITU I.430 documents the physical layer and lower data link layers of the ISDN BRI interface. The specification defines a number of *reference points* between the LEC switch and the end system.

Q.921

Q.921, also referred to as Link Access Protocol (LAPD) D-channel, is a close cousin of HDLC. Q.921 is the Data Link Protocol used over ISDN's D-channel. It operates at Layer 2 of the OSI model.

Q.931

Q.931 is ISDN's connection control protocol, operating at Layer 3 of the OSI model. Q.931 is comparable to TCP in the Internet protocol stack, managing connection setup and breakdown. Q.931 does not provide flow control or perform retransmission.

G.711

G.711 is the international standard for encoding audio on 64 kbps channels. G.711 is a pulse code modulation (PCM) scheme operating at an 8 kHz sample rate, with 8 bits per sample. According to the Nyquist theorem, G.711 can encode frequencies between 0 and 4 kHz. LECs can select between two different variants of G.711: A-law and mu-law. A-law is the standard for international circuits, and mu-law is the standard for domestic circuits.

The Nyquist theorem states that a signal must be sampled at twice its highest frequency component. Simply stated, Nyquist's theorem states that, when sampling at a given rate, the highest frequency that can appear in the sampled signal is half of the sampling frequency.

If the sampled signal contains frequencies higher than half of the sampling frequency (higher than 4 kHz when sampling at 8 kHz, as is the case for u-law), these higher frequencies will appear folded down to below half the sampling frequency when the signal is reconstructed. This is known as "the aliasing problem."

A visual example of the same phenomenon is when you see wheels turning backward, like a train in a movie.

You can find the mathematic details of the Nyquist Sampling Theorem at http://ptolemy.eecs.berkeley.edu/eecs20/week13/nyquistShannon.html.

ISDN BRI

BRI service consists of the same twisted pair of wires traditionally used for analog telephones. BRI provides two types of ISDN communications channels: two "bearer service" B-channels, carrying data services at 64 Kbps each, and a 16 Kbps D-channel, carrying signaling and administrative information used to set up and terminate calls.

Up to eight ISDN devices can be connected to a single BRI line and can share the B- and D-channels. Two B-channels are available at any given time for use. Other calls can be put "on hold" via D-channel signaling, a process known as *multiple call appearances*. Figure 12-6 illustrates a BRI configuration.

Figure 12-6   *ISDN Basic Rate Interface (BRI)*

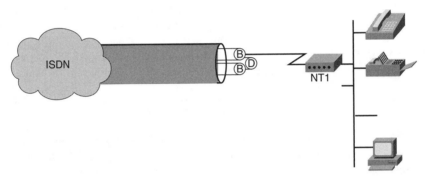

ISDN Primary Rate Interface (PRI)

ISDN PRI includes 23 B-channels in North America and Japan and 30 B-channels in Rest of World (ROW), plus one 64 Kbps D-channel. The number of B-channels is limited by the size of the standard trunk line, which is T1 in North America, J1 in Japan, and E1 elsewhere. PRI does not support a multiple subscriber configuration such as BR. Only one device can be connected to a PRI line. Figure 12-7 illustrates a PRI configuration.

Figure 12-7   *ISDN Primary Rate Interface (PRI)*

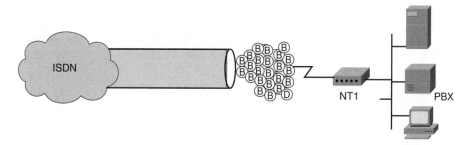

The primary benefit of PRI is that its bandwidth can be dynamically allocated among applications. For example, certain channels can be allocated for voice calls, but as those calls are terminated, the unused B-channels can be reallocated to such high-bandwidth applications as videoconferencing. This is usually accomplished via a PBX or a server capable of distributing the T1/E1 bandwidth on a PRI link.

B-channels are logical "pipes" in a single ISDN line. Two or more B-channels can be combined, or bonded together, usually with ISDN bonding or multilink PPP. Each B-channel provides a 64 Kbps clear channel whose entire bandwidth is available for voice or data because call setup and other signaling is done through a separate D-channel. B-channels form circuit-switched connections, resembling analog telephone connections in that they are end-to-end physical circuits temporarily dedicated to transfer between two devices.

PRI is intended for users with greater capacity requirements. Typically the channel structure is 23 B-channels plus one 64 kbps D-channel for a total of 1536 kbps. In Europe, PRI consists of 30 B-channels plus one 64 kbps D-channel for a total of 1984 kbps. It is also possible to support multiple PRI lines with one 64 kbps D-channel using non-facility associated signaling (NFAS).

H channels provide a way to aggregate B-channels. They are implemented as follows:

- H0=384 kbps (6 B-channels)
- H10=1472 kbps (23 B-channels)
- H11=1536 kbps (24 B-channels)
- H12=1920 kbps (30 B-channels)—international (E1) only

NOTE   Customer sites must be within 18,000 feet (about 3.4 miles or 5.5 km) of the LEC CO for BRI service. Beyond that, repeaters are required, or ISDN service might not be available.

Signaling

Instead of the phone company sending a ring voltage signal to ring the bell in a phone set ("in-band signal"), it sends a digital packet on a separate channel ("out-of-band signal"). The out-of-band signal does not disturb established connections, and call setup time is fast. The signaling indicates who is calling, what type of call it is (data/voice), and what number was dialed.

NOTE A V.34 modem typically takes 30 to 60 seconds to establish a connection, whereas an ISDN call usually takes less than 2 seconds.

In the U.S., the telephone company provides a U interface for its BRI subscribers. The U interface is a two-wire (single pair) interface from the phone switch, supporting full-duplex data transfer over a single pair of wires. This device is called a network termination 1 (NT-1). International ISDN implementations are a bit different because the phone company is allowed to supply the NT-1; therefore, the customer is given an S/T interface.

The NT-1 is a device that converts the 2-wire U interface into the 4-wire S/T interface. The S/T interface supports up to 7 devices.

ISDN devices must go through a Network Termination 2 (NT-2) device, which converts the T interface into the S interface. (Note: The S and T interfaces are electrically equivalent.) Virtually all ISDN devices include an NT-2 in their design. The NT-2 communicates with terminal equipment and handles the Layer 2 and 3 ISDN protocols. Devices most commonly expect either a U interface connection (these have a built-in NT-1) or an S/T interface connection.

All other devices that are not ISDN capable but that have a plain old telephone service (POTS) telephone interface (also called the R interface)—including ordinary analog telephones, FAX machines, and modems—are designated Terminal Equipment 2 (TE2). A terminal adapter (TA) connects a TE2 to an ISDN S/T bus.

ISDN Reference Points

As stated previously, ITU I.430 documents the physical layer and lower data link layers of the ISDN BRI interface. ITU I.430 also defines the ISDN reference points between the LEC switch and the end system.

Figure 12-8 illustrates each interface point.

Figure 12-8   *ISDN Interfaces*

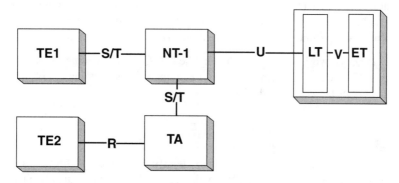

ISDN functional identifiers include the following:

- Terminal Equipment 1 (TE1)—A device that is ISDN compatible.

- Terminal Equipment 2 (TE2)—A device that is not ISDN compatible and requires a terminal adapter (TA).

- Terminal Adapter (TA)—A device that converts non-ISDN signals into ISDN compatible signals so that non-ISDN devices can connect to an ISDN network.

- Network Termination Type 1 (NT1)—A device that connects 4-wire ISDN subscriber units to the conventional 2-wire local loop facility. In the U.S. the NT1 is part of the CPE; in Europe and Japan, it is part of the local exchange facility.

- Network Termination Type 2 (NT2)—A device that performs switching and concentration of non-ISDN signals, often a PBX. Requires a TA to interconnect with the ISDN network.

- Line Termination (LT)—A device that is located on the local exchange carrier (LEC) side of the subscriber line that functions as an NT1.

- Exchange Termination (ET)—Subscriber cards in the ISDN exchange.

ISDN reference points include the following:

- User reference point (U)—Located between the NT1 and LT. Corresponds to a subscriber line.

- Terminal reference point (T)—Located between the NT1 and NT2 or between the NT1 and TE1 or TA, if no NT2 device exists. Same characteristics as the S reference point.

- System reference point (S)—Located between the NT2 and TE1 or T1 connecting the terminal to the ISDN network. Same characteristics as the T reference point.

- Rate reference point (R)—Located between TA and TE2. The TE2 connects to the TA via a standard physical interface, such as EIA/TIA-232, V.24, X.21, and V.35.

The ITU I-series and G-series documents specify the ISDN physical layer. The U interface that the LEC provides for BRI is a 2-wire, 160 kbps digital connection. Echo cancellation is used to reduce noise and data encoding schemes (2B1Q in North America, 4B3T in Europe) and permit this relatively high data rate over ordinary single-pair local loops.

The ISDN network layer is specified by the ITU Q-series documents Q.930 through Q.939. Layer 3 is used for the establishment, maintenance, and termination of logical network connections between two devices.

ISDN SPIDs

Service Profile IDs (SPIDs) are used to identify the services and features that the LEC switch provides to the attached ISDN device. SPIDs are optional; when used, they are accessed at device initialization time, before call setup. The format of the SPID is usually the 10-digit phone number of the ISDN line. A prefix and a suffix are sometimes used to identify additional line features. If an ISDN line requires a SPID, but the SPID is not implemented or configured properly, then Layer 2 initialization will take place, but Layer 3 will not, and the device will not be able to place or accept calls.

ISDN Call Setup

The following process details what occurs when an ISDN call is established. In the following example, messages are sent and received at three points:

- The Caller
- The ISDN Switch
- The Receiver

Following is the process:

1 The Caller sends a SETUP to the Switch.

2 If the SETUP is okay, the Switch sends a CALL PROCeeding to the Caller, and then a SETUP to the Receiver.

3 The Receiver gets the SETUP. If it is okay, then it rings the phone and sends an ALERTING message to the Switch.

4 The Switch forwards the ALERTING message to the Caller.

5 When the receiver answers the call, is sends a CONNECT message to the Switch.

6 The Switch forwards the CONNECT message to the Caller.

7 The Caller sends a CONNECT ACKnowledge message to the Switch.

8 The Switch forwards the CONNECT ACK message to the Receiver.

9 The connection is now up.

DSL

Digital subscriber line (DSL) is fundamentally another name for ISDN-BRI, in which each 64 K channel can carry voice and data in both directions simultaneously. xDSL refers to various arrangements where modulation techniques implemented differ to achieve higher throughput in either direction across a loop facility.

xDSL is a modem-like technology in that it requires an xDSL terminating device at each end of the cable pair. The terminating device accepts a data stream, usually in digital format, and overlays it onto a high-speed analog signal.

The current Public Switched Telephone Network (PSTN) and supporting local access networks have been designed with guidelines that limit transmissions to a 3,400 Hertz analog voice channel. For example, telephones, dial modems, fax modems, and private line modems limit their transmissions over the local access phone lines to the frequency spectrum that exists between DC or 0 Hertz and 3,400 Hertz. The highest achievable information rate using that 3,400 Hertz frequency spectrum is less than 56 kbps.

DSL eliminates the 3,400 Hertz boundary, which limits the rate at which data can be transmitted. DSL, much like traditional T1 or E1, uses a much broader range of frequencies than the voice channel. Such an implementation requires transmission of information over a wide range of frequencies from one end of the copper wire loop to another complementary device that receives the wide frequency signal at the far end of the copper loop.

Attenuation

When electrical signals are transmitted over a copper wire line, the use of higher frequencies to support higher speed services results in shorter loop reach. This is because high frequency signals transmitted over metallic loops attenuate energy more quickly than the lower frequency signals.

One way to minimize attenuation is to use lower resistance wire. Thick wires have less resistance than thin wires. This, in turn, means less signal attenuation, enabling the signal to travel a longer distance. Conversely, thicker gauge wire means more copper, which also means higher per-foot plant costs.

In the U.S., wire thickness is represented by the denominator composed of the fraction of an inch in wire size, assuming a numerator of 1. Therefore, a wire that is 1/24 inch in diameter is referred to as 24 American Wire Gauge (AWG). Wire gauges of 24 and, more often, 26 are present in most North American cable plants. The design rules used by nearly all telephone companies provided for a change in wire gauge with a thinner gauge used near the entrance of a central office to minimize physical space requirements and a change to thicker gauges over long loops to maximize loop reach.

DSL Modulation Techniques

BRI-ISDN provides up to two 64 kbps bearer, or B-channels, plus a 16 kbps D-channel used for signaling and packet data. The information payload plus other overhead associated with implementation results in 160 kbps in total transmitted information. A key requirement of ISDN was to reach the customers over existing non-loaded copper wire loops, equating to 18,000 feet. However, an Alternate Mark Inversion (AMI) implementation of Basic Rate ISDN would require use of the lower 160,000 Hertz. This would result in too much signal attenuation and would fall short of the required 18,000 feet loop reach on 26 gauge wire.

Some vendors encouraged using two-binary/1-qurarternary (2B1Q) signaling at higher speeds as an alternative way to provision T1 and E1 services, without repeaters. The technique consisted of splitting the 1,544,000 bit per second service into two pairs (four wires), which each ran at 784,000 bits per second. By splitting the service across two lines, line speed and resulting need for frequency spectrum could be reduced to allow longer loop reach. This technique was referred to as high bit-rate digital subscriber line (HDSL). The result was that an HDSL-based DS-1 service could be implemented over specified loops of up to 12,000 feet long (assuming 24 gauge, or 9,000 feet with 26 gauge wire), with no repeaters. Some network service providers have begun to deploy HDSL service over dedicated T1 local loops through the LEC facility.

Crosstalk

The electrical energy transmitted across the copper wire line as a modulated signal also radiates energy onto adjacent copper wire loops, which are located in the same wire bundle. This cross coupling of electromagnetic energy is called *crosstalk*.

In the telephone network, multiple insulated copper pairs are bundled together into a cable called a *cable binder*. Adjacent systems within a cable binder that transmit or receive information in the same range of frequencies can create significant crosstalk interference. This is because crosstalk-induced signals combine with the signals that were originally intended for transmission over the copper wire loop. The result is a slightly different shaped waveform than was originally transmitted.

Crosstalk can be categorized in one of two forms. Near-end crosstalk, commonly referred to as NEXT, is the most significant because the high-energy signal from an adjacent system can induce relatively significant crosstalk into the primary signal. The other form is Far-end crosstalk, or FEXT. FEXT is typically less of an issue because the far-end interfering signal is attenuated as it traverses the loop. Figure 12-9 illustrates the NEXT/FEXT model.

Figure 12-9   *NEXT/FEXT Model*

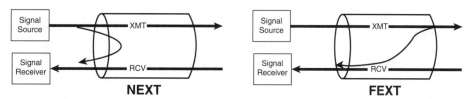

NEXT   **FEXT**

Crosstalk is a dominant factor in the performance of many systems. As a result, DSL system performance is often stated relative to "in the presence of other systems," which might introduce crosstalk. For example, the loop reach of a DSL system can be stated as in the presence of 49 ISDN disturbers, or 24 HDSL disturbers. As you can imagine, it is rather unlikely that you will deploy a DSL service in a 50-pair cable that happens to have 49 (2-wire) ISDN circuits or 24 (4-wire) HDSL circuits concurrently running in the same bundle. Therefore, these performance parameters typically represent a conservative performance outlook.

Transmitting and receiving information using the same frequency spectrum creates interference within the single loop system. This interference differs from crosstalk because the offending transmit waveform is known to the receiver and can effectively be subtracted from the attenuated receive signals. Eliminating the effects of the transmitter is referred to as *echo cancellation*.

Minimizing Crosstalk

If the effects of the attenuation and crosstalk are insignificant, the DSL systems can reconstruct the signal back into a digital format. However, when one or both of these phenomena becomes significant, the signals are misinterpreted at the far end and bit errors occur.

Some DSL systems actually use different frequency spectrum for transmit and receive signals. This frequency-separated implementation is referred to as *frequency division multiplexing (FDM)*. The advantage of FDM-based systems over echo-canceled systems is that NEXT is eliminated. This is achieved because the system is not receiving in the same range of frequencies in which the adjacent system is transmitting. FEXT is present, and the FEXT signal is substantially attenuated and less of an interferer because the origin of the FEXT signal is at the distant end of the loop. FDM-based systems often provide better performance than echo-canceled systems, relative to crosstalk from similar adjacent systems.

ADSL

The American National Standards Institute (ANSI) working group T1E1.4 published an ADSL standard at rates up to 6.1 Mbps (ANSI Standard T1.413). The European Technical Standards Institute (ETSI) contributed an Annex to T1.413 to reflect European requirements.

NOTE   The ATM forum has recognized ADSL as a physical layer transmission protocol for copper, or UTP, media.

ADSL depends on advanced digital signal processing and creative algorithms to squeeze so much information through twisted-pair telephone lines. Long telephone lines generally attenuate signals at 1 MHz (the outer edge of the band used by ADSL) by as much as 90 decibels (dB), forcing analog sections of ADSL modems to compensate to realize large dynamic ranges, separate channels, and maintain low noise figures.

To create multiple channels, ADSL modems divide the available bandwidth of a telephone line in one of two ways: frequency division multiplexing (FDM) or echo cancellation. FDM assigns one band for upstream data and another band for downstream data. The downstream path is then divided by time division multiplexing into one or more high-speed channels, each carrying one or more low-speed channels. The upstream path is also multiplexed into corresponding low-speed channels. Echo cancellation assigns the upstream band to overlap the downstream and separates the two by means of local echo cancellation, a technique using V.32 and V.34 modems. With either technique, ADSL splits off a 4 kHz region for POTS at the DC end of the band.

An ADSL modem organizes the aggregate data stream created by multiplexing downstream channels, duplex channels, and maintenance channels together into blocks, and attaches an error correction code to each block. The receiver then corrects errors that occur during transmission up to the limits implied by the code and the block length.

ADSL modems provide data rates consistent with North American and European digital hierarchies and can be purchased with various speed ranges and capabilities. The minimum configuration provides 1.5 or 2.0 Mbps downstream and a 16 kbps duplex channel; others provide rates of 6.1 Mbps and 64 kbps duplex. Products with downstream rates up to 8 Mbps and duplex rates up to 640 kbps are available today. ADSL modems will accommodate ATM transport with variable rates and compensation for ATM overhead, as well as IP protocols.

The receiver then corrects errors that occur during transmission up to the limits implied by the code and the block length. The unit can, at the user's option, also create superblocks by interleaving data within subblocks. This allows the receiver to correct any combination of errors within a specific span of bits and allows for effective transmission of both data and video signals alike.

Downstream data rates depend on a number of factors, including the length of the copper line, its wire gauge, presence of bridged taps, and cross-coupled interference. Line attenuation increases with line length and frequency and decreases as wire diameter increases.

Ignoring bridged taps, ADSL will perform as shown in Table 12-1.

Table 12-1   *ADSL Data Rates*

Data Rate	Wire Gauge	Distance	Wire Size	Distance
1.5 or 2 Mbps	24 AWG	18,000 ft	0.5 mm	5.5 km
1.5 or 2 Mbps	26 AWG	15,000 ft	0.4 mm	4.6 km
6.1 Mbps	24 AWG	12,000 ft	0.5 mm	3.7 km
6.1 Mbps	26 AWG	9,000 ft	0.4 mm	2.7 km

ANSI working group T1E1.4 approved the first ADSL in 1995. It supported data rates up to 6.1 Mbps (ANSI Standard T1.413). ETSI contributed an annex to T1.413 to reflect European requirements. T1.413 (Issue I) was limited to a single terminal interface at the premise end. Issue II (T1.413i2), approved in 1998, expanded the standard to include a multiplexed interface at the premise end, protocols for configuration and network management, and other improvements.

Work toward an Issue III was ultimately submitted to the international standards body, the ITU-T, to develop the international standards for ADSL. The ITU-T standards for ADSL are most commonly referred to as G.lite (G.992.2) and G.dmt (G.992.1), both of which were approved in June 1999. Having an international standard has aided in moving toward vendor interoperability and service provider acceptance, increased deployment, and better availability for the consumer.

The ATM Forum has recognized ADSL as a physical layer transmission protocol for unshielded twisted-pair media.

RADSL

ANSI's T1E1.4 working group has established a RADSL Ad Hoc Standards working group to develop a rate-adaptive DSL standard that is optimized around data communications, as opposed to the original ADSL standard that was optimized around fixed speeds to support bit synchronous video services.

RADSL systems are implemented in FDM, resulting in an upstream channel of up to 1 Mbps occupying the midband above POTS and the downstream channel occupying the upper band.

SDSL

For symmetric applications, multirate SDSL (MSDSL) builds on the single pair SDSL technology. MSDSL supports changing operating line rates of the transceiver and the operating distance of the transceiver. MSDSL supports eight distinct rates, allowing 64 kbps/128 kbps service to reach 29,000 ft (8.9 km) on 24 gauge (.5 mm) cable and stepping down to 15,000 ft (4.5 km) at a full 2 Mbps rate. MSDSL deploys autorate abilities similar to RADSL.

DSL-Based Services and Components

DSL Access Multiplexers, or DSLAMs, are located at the CO and a DSL Remote Transceiver Unit (XTU-R) located at the home or the remote office. Transmission speeds of 7 Mbps and beyond are possible depending on a number of factors including equipment, loop length, and condition of the loop.

Figure 12-10 illustrates a typical xDSL infrastructure.

Figure 12-10   *xDSL Infrastructure*

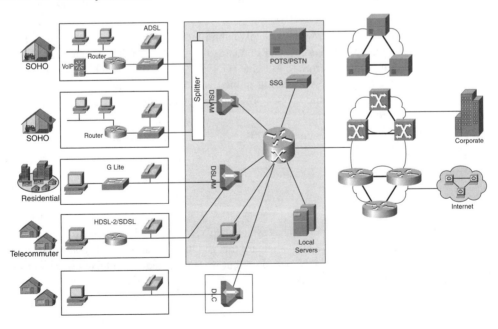

Transport System

This component provides the carrier backbone transmission interface for the DSLAM system. This device can provide service-specific interfaces, such as T1/E1, T3/E3, OC-1/3, and STS-1/3.

Local Access Network

The Local Access Network utilizes the local carrier Inter-CO network as a foundation. To provide connectivity between multiple service providers and multiple service users, additional equipment might be required. Frame Relay switches, ATM switches and routers can be provisioned within the access network for this purpose.

The AN (Access Node) is where switches and routing equipment are physically located. Depending on the scale of the desired access network and the costs associated with transport, you can expect to find one or more ANs per Local Access Network, thus creating an overlay structure on top of the Inter-CO network. In some cases, the AN is integrated within the DSLAM.

Digital Subscriber Line Access Multiplexer (DSLAM)

Residing within the CO environment, the DSLAM concentrates the data traffic from multiple DSL loops onto the backbone network for connection to the rest of the network. The DSLAM provides back-haul services for packet, cell, and circuit-based applications through concentration of the DSL lines onto 10Base-T, 100Base-T, T1/E1, T3/E3, or ATM outputs.

In addition to concentration functions and depending on the specific service being provisioned, a DSLAM will provide added functions. The DSLAM might, in some cases, be required to open data packets to take some action. For example, to support dynamic IP address assignment using the Dynamic Host Control Protocol (DHCP), each packet must be viewed to direct packets to the proper destination (referred to as a *DHCP-relay function*).

DSL Transceiver Unit (xTU-R)

The remote transceiver unit is the customer site equipment for the service user's connection to the DSL loop. The xTU-R connection is typically 10Base-T, V.35, ATM-25, or T1/E1.

XTU-Rs are available in a number of different configurations depending on the specific service being provisioned. In addition to providing basic DSL modem functionality, many XTU-Rs contain additional functionality, such as bridging, routing, TDM, or ATM multiplexing.

Protocol transparent endpoints behave very much like a DSU/CSU. They provide an interface to the DSL link for existing routers and FRADS. The routers and FRADs handle all of the connected LAN's traffic management, whereas the XTU-R passes all traffic to the upstream DSL link.

Channelized TDM endpoints can operate like DSU/CSUs for traditional T1/E1 service. They also provide an interface to routers, FRADs, multiplexers, PBXs, or any other device accustomed to a traditional service.

POTS Splitters

This optional device resides at both the CO and service user locations, allowing the copper loop to be used for simultaneous high-speed DSL data transmission and single-line telephone service. POTS splitters usually come in two configurations: a single splitter version designed for mounting at the residence and a multiple splitter version designed for mass termination at the CO.

NOTE   Not all DSL line-coding schemes support a single channel of POTS service.

POTS splitters can be either passive or active. Active POTS splitters require an external power source for voice and DSL to operate over a single copper pair. Passive POTS splitters require no power and will typically have a higher Mean-Time-Between-Failure (MTBF) than their active counterpart. Whereas the passive POTS splitter supports lifeline services such as 911 in the event of a DSLAM or ATU-R power loss, the active POTS splitter must have power backup to provide these critical services in the event of a power loss.

Summary

Telecommunications is defined as the transmission of a voice or data signal from one point to another over short or long distances.

Voice switching and routing within the telecommunications network is based on the automatic number identification (ANI). ANIs are constructed per the North American Numbering Plan (NANP). Data switching and routing within the telecommunications switched network is usually in the form of dedicated, ISDN, or xDSL connections.

ANI is a service that provides the telephone number of an incoming call. ANI numbers, sometimes referred to as ANIs, are constructed per the NANP.

For voice (analog) and data (digital) to share the same digital transmission media, the voice analog signals must be converted into digital signals. This digitizing of the analog signals is known as Pulse Code Modulation, or PCM. PCM is a sampling process that compresses a voice signal into a 64 Kbps standard digital service rate, known as a DS0.

PCM involves two steps:

1 The incoming analog signal is sampled 8,000 times per second. These sampled values are converted to pulses using the pulse amplitude modulation (PAM) process.

2 The height of each pulse is assigned a representative 8-bit binary value, resulting in a digital representation of the pulse and ultimately the sampled analog waveform.

Time division multiplexing (TDM) is the foundation behind network service provider services, the most common being T1/T3. TDM is designed on the premise that each user, or channel, will have the total bandwidth for a portion of time.

Four media types are used for telecommunication transmission facilities:

- Copper cable
- Coaxial cable
- Fiber-optic cable
- Wireless

Integrated Services Digital Network, or ISDN, is a system of digital phone connections that enable data to be transmitted digitally end-to-end.

With ISDN, voice and data are carried by bearer channels (B-channels) at a bandwidth of 64 kilobits per second (Kbps). The data channel (D-channel) handles signaling at 16 Kbps (BRI) or 64 Kbps (PRI), depending on the service type.

Two basic types of ISDN service exist:

- Basic rate interface (BRI)—BRI consists of two 64 Kbps B-channels and one 16 Kbps D-channel; 2B + D.
- Primary rate interface (PRI)—PRI consists of 23 64 Kbps B-channels and one 64 Kbps D-channel; 23B + D or 30B + D.

Digital Subscriber Line (DSL) is fundamentally another name for ISDN-BRI, where each 64 K channel can carry voice and data in both directions simultaneously. xDSL refers to various arrangements where modulation techniques implemented differ to achieve higher throughput in either direction across a loop facility.

xDSL is a modem-like technology in that it requires an xDSL-terminating device at each end of the cable pair, which accepts a data stream, usually in digital format, and overlays it onto a high-speed analog signal.

DSL eliminates the 3,400 hertz boundary, which limits the rate at which data can be transmitted across the public switched telephone network (PSTN). DSL, much like traditional T1 or E1, uses a much broader range of frequencies than the voice channel. Such an implementation requires transmission of information over a wide range of frequencies from one end of the copper wire loop to another complementary device, which receives the wide frequency signal at the far end of the copper loop.

CHAPTER 13

Private Line WANs

Private Line WANs can comprise dedicated DS1/T1, DS3/T3, or DS0/DDS data services.

T1 Basics

T1 is a digital communications link that enables the transmission of voice, data, and multimedia application signals at a rate of 1.544 Mbps. T1 is the "productized" version of the BellLabs Digital Service Level 1 (DS1) format.

Figure 13-1 illustrates life before the advent of T1 services. Each end-to-end service required a dedicated service to be provisioned by the network service provider. This mechanism led to costly network configurations, especially over long distances. The network service provider's tariff services typically charged a flat rate per mile, regardless of actual bandwidth usage. (Imagine paying for a long-distance phone call that was operational 24 hours a day, 7 days a week, regardless of whether anyone was actually speaking on the line.)

Figure 13-1   *Telecommunications Network Configuration Prior to T1 Service*

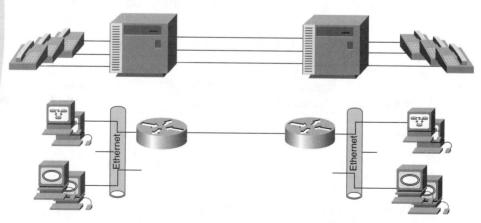

Figure 13-2 illustrates life after the advent of T1 services. Each end-to-end service still required a dedicated service to be provisioned by the network service provider; however, these services could be shared over a single line, the T1 link. This mechanism reduced what were costly network configurations. The long-distance long-haul charges remained from the service provider; however, customers were only paying for a single long-haul line, not several.

Figure 13-2 *Telecommunications Network Configuration After T1 Service*

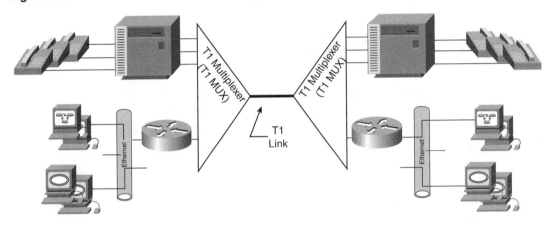

Time Division Multiplexing (TDM) Hierarchy

North America and Canada identify the digital time division multiplexing (TDM) hierarchy as "T," as in T1, T3, and so on. Japan identifies the digital TDM hierarchy as "J," as in J1, J3, and so on. International identification of the digital TDM hierarchy is "E," as in E1, E3, and so on.

Table 13-1 details the number of [DS0] channels and data rates for each TDM hierarchy level.

Table 13-1 *North American, Canadian, Japanese, and International TDM Carrier Standards[*]*

North America (Canada, Japan)			International (ITU-T)		
Designation	Number of Channels (DS0s)	Data Rate (Mbps)	Level	Number of Channels (DS0s)	Data Rate (Mbps)
DS-1	24	1.544	1	30	2.048
DS-1C	48	3.152	2	120	8.448
DS-2	96	6.312	3	480	34.368
DS-3	672	44.736	4	1920	139.264
DS-4*	4032	274.176	5	7680	565.148

[*]At the time AT&T BellLabs introduced the DS-4, the Optical Carrier (OC) was developed, which enabled the bundling of several DS-3s to be transmitted via fiber-optic cable.

Pulse Code Modulation (PCM)

For voice (analog) and data (digital) to share the same digital transmission media, the analog signals of voice must be converted into digital signals. This digitizing of analog signals is known as *pulse code modulation* (PCM). PCM is a sampling process that compresses a voice signal into a 64 kilobits per second (Kbps) standard digital service rate, known as a DS0.

PCM involves two steps:

1 The incoming analog signal is sampled 8,000 times per second. These sampled values are converted to pulses using the pulse amplitude modulation (PAM) process.

2 The height of each pulse is assigned a representative 8-bit binary value resulting in a digital representation of the pulse and ultimately the sampled analog waveform.

Figure 13-3 illustrates both PAM and PCM. (The 8-bit binary values are for illustration purposes only and are not actual values).

Figure 13-3   *Pulse Amplitude Modulation (PAM) and Pulse Code Modulation (PCM)*

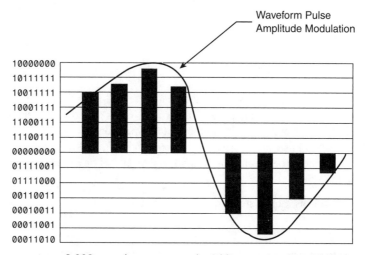

8,000 samples per second x 8 bits per sample = 64 Kbps

TDM

TDM is the foundation behind T1 services. It is designed on the premise that each user, or channel, will have the total bandwidth for a portion of time.

After the voice/data signals have been digitized, they are then multiplexed and transmitted over the T1 (E1, T3, and so on) link. This multiplexing process is called TDM.

TDM divides the T1 link into 24 discrete timeslots, or channels. Each timeslot, or channel, has a DS0 signal (64 Kbps), as illustrated in Figure 13-4.

Figure 13-4   *T1 TDM Timeslots (64 Kbps Each)*

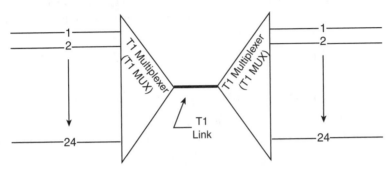

NOTE   Frequency division multiplexing (FDM) is similar to TDM with the exception that a user, or channel, will have a portion of the bandwidth all the time.

1.544 Mbps

In T1, the eight-bit digital samples created in the PCM (voice only) are grouped into 24 discrete DS0 timeslots. Each group of 24 timeslots is called a T1 frame. Because each timeslot contains eight bits, the number of information bits within each frame equals 192 (24 frames × 8 bits/frame = 192 bits/frame). An additional framing bit, the 193rd bit, is added to delineate between frames, marking the end of one frame and the beginning of the next frame.

Figure 13-5 illustrates a standard T1 (D4) frame.

Figure 13-5   *Standard T1 (D4) Frame*

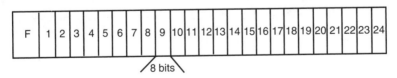

Because DS0 signals are sampled 8,000 times/second, 8,000 192-bit data frames are created each second, totaling 1536 Kbps, or 1.536 megabits per second (Mbps).

Figure 13-6 illustrates a data stream consisting of consecutive 193-bit (192 data bits + 1 framing bit) frames.

Figure 13-6   *T1 D4 Frames*

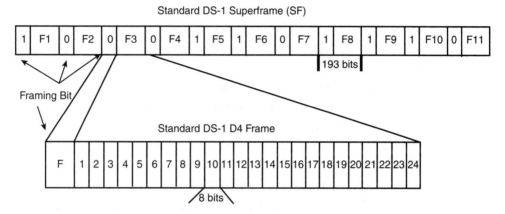

The additional framing bits add 8 Kbps to the total, yielding a 1.544 Mbps digital signal rate, also known as a *digital signal level 1 (DS1)*.

NOTE   *Multiplexing* is defined as the combining, or aggregation, of multiple analog or digital signals over a single line or media. The most common type of multiplexing combines several low-speed signals for transmission over a single high-speed connection, such as 24 DS0s (64 Kbps each) over a single DS1 (1.536 Mbps) line.

The following are examples of different multiplexing methods:

- FDM—Each signal is assigned a different frequency.

- TDM—Each signal is assigned a fixed time slot in a fixed rotation.

- Statistical time division multiplexing (STDM)—Time slots are assigned to signals dynamically to make better use of bandwidth.

- Wavelength division multiplexing (WDM)—Each signal is assigned a particular wavelength; used on optical fiber.

T1/DS1 service has two framing formats:

- D4, or Superframe (SF)
- Extended Superframe (ESF)

D4, or Superframe (SF)

With D4 framing, the following specifications apply:

- Twenty-four 64 Kbps channels plus a single-frame synchronization bit (at the beginning) per frame (193 total bits per frame), as previously discussed.

- Twelve of the individual (D4) frames are grouped together to form an SF.

- Framing bits always use 100011011100 as the standard pattern to identify the frame number and the start of the frame and to provide synchronization.

- Line level is at a +/-3 Volt and 0-Volt nominal transmission level.

Figure 13-7 illustrates a D4 (Superframe) T1 frame.

Figure 13-7 *D4 Framing*

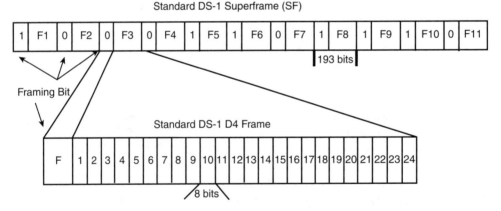

In the sixth ("A" bits) and twelfth frames ("B" bits), the seventh bit (numbered 0 to 7 and representing the least significant bits) of every byte (channel) is "robbed" to encode control signal information such as answer supervision, off-hook notification, status of E&M leads, and busy signals. This is known as *in-band signaling*.

Extended Superframe (ESF)

ESF comprises 24 individual frames grouped together to form one ESF frame. These frames comprise and perform the following functions:

- ESF frame sync bit pattern is reduced to six bits 001011 at the head of frames 4, 8, 12, 16, 20, and 24.

- Robbed bit signaling is extended to frames 18 ("C" bits) and 24 ("D" bits) in addition to frames 6 and 12, as in SF.

- Six bits at the head of frames 2, 6, 10, 14, 18, and 22 are used as a cyclic redundancy check code (CRC-6) for detection of errors.

- Twelve bits in the odd-numbered frames form a synchronous 4 Kbps data link (DL) channel. This DL channel is used for such functions as the following:

  — Protection switching

  — Alarm transmission

  — Loopback commands

  — Received line performance reports (ESFMUs)

  — Supervisory or switching command facility

  — Network control configurations

ESF framing offers significant advantages over D4 framing, including the following:

- Sixteen possible ABCD signaling states

- False alarm protection if CRC-6 code is checked before certifying frame sync

- Non-intrusive network-monitoring capability

- Data link bits available for network control purposes

The non-intrusive monitoring is performed with a device called an extended superframe monitoring unit (ESFMU). ESFMUs are provisioned by the network service provider on the path of the T1 link across the backbone and are usually placed close to the customer's access to the network on each side of the link.

Figure 13-8 illustrates the use of ESFMUs within a network service provider's network.

Figure 13-8   *Network Service Provider ESFMUs*

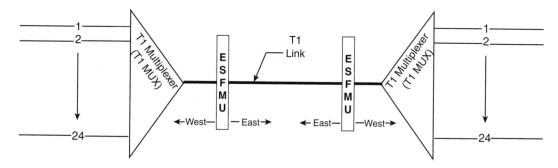

As illustrated in Figure 13-8, ESFMUs have two directions: east and west. The west side always faces the local customer, whereas the east side always faces the network. This allows for quick isolation and troubleshooting of T1 link issues without taking the link out of service.

The ESF frame format is illustrated in Figure 13-9, and is described in detail in the following bulleted list.

Figure 13-9   *T1 ESF Frame Format*

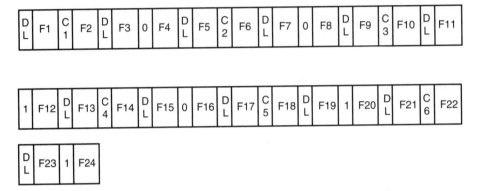

- DL—4 Kbps data link channel
- C 1 to 6—Cyclic redundancy check code (CRC-6)
- Sync bits—001011 at head of frames 4, 8, 12, 16, 20, 24
- F 1 to 24—Individual frames 1 through 24, 24 channels each

Table 13-2 demonstrates the T1 statistics and testing that ESF enables and the methodology for obtaining the measurement.

Table 13-2   *T1 Measurements*

Measurement	Description	Method
Bit errors	The basic performance evaluator counting the number of logical errors in the bit stream, such as 1s and 0s that should be 0s and 1s.	Out-of-service testing only
Bi-polar violations (BPVs)	Measurement of the number of times that consecutive pulses of the same polarity were transmitted across the T1 link.	In-service via ESFMU or out-of-service testing
Frame errors	Measurement of the number of times an incorrect bit value appeared in a position reserved for frame (193rd bit).	In-service via ESFMU or out-of-service testing
Cyclic redundancy check (CRC) errors	Measurement of one or more bit errors in a data block.	In-service via ESFMU or out-of-service testing (usually with 98.4% accuracy of bit error detection)

T1/DS1 Signaling/Line Coding

The DS1 signal transmitted across a T1 link is signaled, or encoded, in one of two formats:

- Alternate mark inversion (AMI)
- Bi-polar with 8-zero substitution (B8ZS)

T1 signals are bi-polar, meaning that the electrical waveform consists of positive (+), negative (-), and zero voltage levels. Positive and negative voltage levels represent a mark or a 1. All marks or 1s must be of opposite polarity (+ or - voltage) of the preceding mark. If not, a BPV will occur. Zero voltage levels represent a space or a 0.

Figure 13-10 illustrates a bi-polar signal with no bi-polar violations.

Figure 13-10   *Bi-Polar Signal*

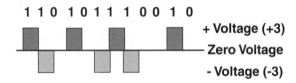

Alternate Mark Inversion (AMI)

Alternate mark inversion (AMI) is the T1 line coding format whereby successive 1s (marks) are alternately inverted (sent with opposite electrical voltage polarity) from that of the preceding mark or 1.

No more than 15 consecutive 0s are permitted to be output on the T1 carrier. Otherwise, synchronization can be lost because no alternate voltage is available to which to clock.

NOTE   The standard for 1s density in a bit stream is 12.5 percent, or a single 1 for every eight bits in the stream.

To prevent violation of the 12.5 percent zero density rule, the seventh bit (least significant) of any 8-bit byte (channel within frame) must be altered. (This has no consequence to voice, but it effectively restricts data to 7/8 of 64 Kbps, or 56 Kbps, as discussed next.)

Long periods (15 consecutive 0s) of no voltage (mark or a 1) present on the T1 circuit can cause equipment to lose its reference point, thereby causing framing and synchronization errors. This is known as the *zero density rule* and is illustrated in Figure 13-11.

Figure 13-11   *1s Density*

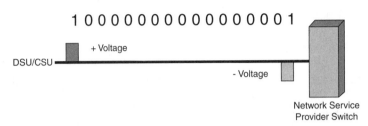

This is why the seventh bit (least significant) is altered to force a 1 (voltage) onto the circuit in AMI line coding systems.

Because the seventh bit of every T1 frame is altered to meet the 1s density requirement (12.5 percent), that bit is not available for user data to be transmitted. Therefore, a T1 with AMI line coding is only capable of supporting N × 56 Kbps channels, not N × 64 Kbps channels. AMI encoded T1s have a maximum bandwidth of 1.344 Mbps (24 channels × 56 Kbps/channel).

NOTE   BPVs do not get carried across the network. If BPVs are detected in a link between two network service provider multiplexers, the BPVs do not get transmitted beyond the multiplexer (mux) in each direction.

Bi-Polar with 8-Zero Substitution (B8ZS)

B8ZS line coding methodology examines the T-1 composite data stream on its way to or in the CSU and replaces any sequence of eight consecutive 0s with a 1s polarity violation sequence. When the receiver detects such a sequence, it is replaced by an all zero bit sequence.

B8ZS line coding is illustrated in Figure 13-12 and works as follows:

- When the receiving CSU sees two BPVs (consecutive 1s or marks of the same voltage polarity), it interprets the consecutive BPVs as consecutive 0s.

- The B8ZS algorithm is looking at the fourth and seventh bit of every octet.

- If the fourth bit is of the same electrical polarity as the last 1 bit of the preceding octet, and the seventh bit has the same electrical polarity as the fifth bit, two BVPs have occurred. The data is then interpreted as 8 consecutive 0s and output as such out its DTE port.

Figure 13-12 *B8ZS Line Coding*

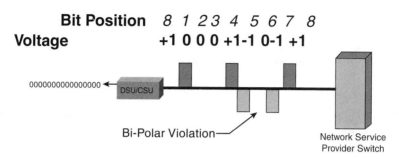

B8ZS offers certain advantages over AMI line coding:

- B8ZS allows data and voice channels to operate more efficiently at the full DS0 64 Kbps rate without triggering alarms.

- Use of the B8ZS coding option requires that the customer premise CSU, local exchange carrier's digital cross connect (DXC) equipment. In addition, the network service provider terminal equipment must be capable and optioned for this feature.

- B8ZS is essential to support ISDN, B-ISDN, ATM, or any clear-channel based services.

NOTE   DS1 is not the only service for which line coding is afforded. The following details other examples where line coding mechanisms are implemented:

- The DS-2 line coding technique known as B6XS—When the network detects six consecutive 0s, it replaces them with a BPV algorithm (0VB0VB). The receiving network equipment translates these two BPVs into the original six 0s.

- The DS-3 line coding technique known as B3ZS—When the network detects three consecutive 0s on the bit stream, it replaces them with a 3-bit BPV algorithm, which is translated back to the three consecutive 0s by the receiving DS3 equipment.

NOTE   BPVs do not get carried across the network. If BPVs are detected on a link between two network service provider multiplexers, the BPVs are not transmitted beyond the multiplexer in each direction.

AMI/B8ZS Mismatches

An AMI/B8ZS mismatch occurs when the T1 equipment is configured for one-line coding and it receives another for transmission. For example, an AMI-configured multiplexer receives a B8ZS signal, including the BPVs associated with B8ZS encoding. It then turns around and transmits across an AMI encoded line, BPVs and all.

NOTE   Line coding is configured on the transmit interface of the T1 multiplexer.

AMI encoded T1s can be transmitted across B8ZS links because the B8ZS rule will never be invoked. AMI forces the 7th bit to be set high, or to a 1; therefore, an AMI encoded bit stream will never have eight consecutive 0s unless the equipment malfunctions.

B8ZS encoded T1s can not be transmitted across AMI links because the B8ZS algorithm will be induced if eight consecutive 0s are in the bit stream.

Figure 13-13 is an example of a T1 link encoded B8ZS from end to end across the network service provider.

Figure 13-13   *End-to-End B8ZS Encoding*

Figure 13-14 illustrates a T1 link that is configured with mismatched line coding. In this example, Terminal B would receive BPVs from the Multiplexer DS1/DS3 (M13), receiving the T1 signal from Terminal A.

Figure 13-14   *AMI/B8ZS Mismatch*

T1 Documentation

T1 links are generally found in one of two configurations:

- End to end across the network service provider's backbone
- Dedicated access to the network service provider's edge devices, where the T1 timeslots, or channels, are then switched to accommodate the provisioned services, such as voice, data, and so on.

End-to-End T1 Links

Illustrated in Figure 13-15 and Table 13-3 is a typical end-to-end T1 link carrying both voice and data traffic between two end nodes.

Figure 13-15   *Long-Haul Dedicated T1 Link Between KimCo and BicAislNet*

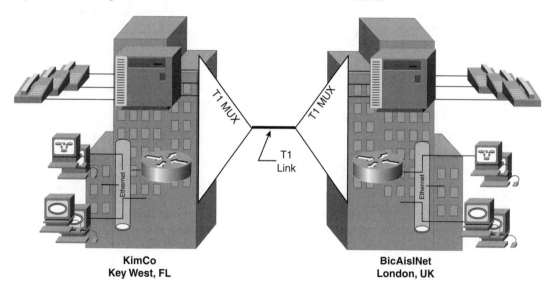

KimCo
Key West, FL

BicAislNet
London, UK

Table 13-3 *Documentation Between KimCo and BicAislNet*

T1 Carrier	Global Crossing	IXC Circuit ID		
Site A	KimCo		Site B	BicAislNet
Site A LEC ID			Site B LEC ID	
T1 Framing (SF/ESF)	ESF	T1 Line Coding (AMI/B8ZS)		B8ZS

Channel Number	Service	Site A In-House Termination Point	Site B In-House Termination Point	Comments
1	Voice	3rd Floor PBX	Basement SWX	Interoffice Tie Line
2	Voice	3rd Floor PBX	Basement SWX	Interoffice Tie Line
3	Voice	3rd Floor PBX	Basement SWX	Interoffice Tie Line
4	Voice	3rd Floor PBX	Basement SWX	Interoffice Tie Line
5	Voice	3rd Floor PBX	Basement SWX	Interoffice Tie Line
6	Voice	3rd Floor PBX	Basement SWX	Interoffice Tie Line
7	Voice	3rd Floor PBX	Basement SWX	Interoffice Tie Line
8	Voice	3rd Floor PBX	Basement SWX	Interoffice Tie Line
9 to 20	OPEN			
21	256 K LAN	7th Floor IT	3rd Floor IT	Channels 21 to 24 are providing a 256 K LAN interconnect link
23	256 K LAN			
24	256 K LAN			
22	256 K LAN			

Some T1 channel service units (CSUs), or Multiplexers (Muxes), allow the end user to map channels to different timeslots on the DTE, or equipment, side of the device. For instance, in the previous example, KimCo could have voice services provisioned on channels 1 to 8. BicAislNet could map those channels to different timeslots on the DTE side of the T1 CSU/Mux. In these cases, the significance of proper documentation by both parties cannot be stressed enough.

Tables 13-4 and 13-5 provide a guide for these scenarios.

Table 13-4   *Template for DTE Mapped T1 Links*

T1 Carrier		IXC Circuit ID	

Site A		Site B	

Site A LEC ID		Site B LEC ID	

T1 Framing (SF/ESF)		T1 Line Coding (AMI/B8ZS)	

Site A Channel Number	Site B Channel Number	Service	Site A In-House Termination Point	Site B In-House Termination Point	Comments
1					
2					
3					
4					
5					
6					
7					
8					
9					
10					
11					
12					
13					
14					
15					
16					
17					
18					
19					
20					

Table 13-5 *Long-Haul Dedicated T1 Link Documentation Template*

T1 Carrier		IXC Circuit ID		
Site A			Site B	
Site A LEC ID			Site B LEC ID	
T1 Framing (SF/ESF)		T1 Line Coding (AMI/B8ZS)		

Channel Number	Service	Site A In-House Termination Point	Site B In-House Termination Point	Comments
1				
2				
3				
4				
5				
6				
7				
8				
9				
10				
11				
12				
13				
14				
15				
16				
17				
18				
19				
20				

T1 Access

T1 links can be deployed as dedicated links between an end node and the serving network service provider, either LEC or IXC. In instances where an end node does not require dedicated long-haul services, but has several services from the network service provider, T1 links can be used to carry these multiple services to the end node.

Figure 13-16 illustrates a dedicated T1 access link between the network service provider and an end node customer. The T1 link is carrying voice and data traffic that The network service provider is demultiplexing and subsequently electronically switching the voice channels to the PSTN switch and the data channels to. This is usually done with a digital cross-connect system—in this case, a Frame Relay WAN edge router.

Figure 13-16 *Dedicated T1 Access to the Network Service Provider*

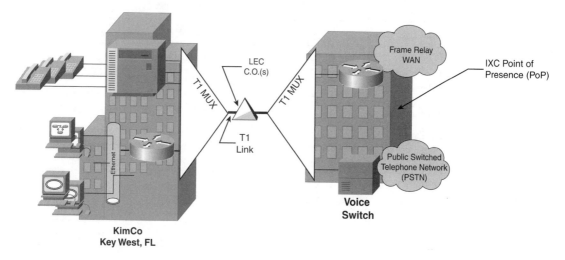

NOTE	The LEC facilities treat the T1 as a high-capacity (hi-cap) link and generally do not channelize the T1 out in any of the LEC COs without special arrangements with the end node customer.

Tables 13-6 and 13-7 provide a guide for the T1 access.

Table 13-6   *Template for T1 Access Configuration*

T1 Carrier	MCIW	IXC Access Circuit ID		LEC Circuit ID	36/HCGS/275156
T1 Framing (SF/ESF)	ESF	**T1 Line Coding (AMI/B8ZS)**			B8ZS

Channel Number	Service	IXC Circuit ID	Comments
1	Voice		Long-distance
2	Voice		Long-distance
3	Voice		Long-distance
4	Voice		Long-distance
5	Voice		Long-distance
6	Voice		Long-distance
7	Voice		Long-distance
8	Voice		Long-distance
9	OPEN		
10	OPEN		
11	OPEN		
12	OPEN		
13	OPEN		
14	OPEN		
15	OPEN		
16	OPEN		
17	OPEN		
18	OPEN		
19	OPEN		
20	OPEN		
21	256 K	ZABCAEDG0001-0004	256 K Frame Relay WAN link
22	256 K		

Table 13-7   *T1 Access Configuration Template*

T1 Carrier		IXC Access Circuit ID		LEC Circuit ID	
T1 Framing (SF/ESF)			T1 Line Coding (AMI/B8ZS)		
Channel Number	Service	IXC Circuit ID		Comments	
1					
2					
3					
4					
5					
6					
7					
8					
9					
10					
11					
12					
13					
14					
15					
16					
17					
18					
19					
20					
21					
22					

T1 Testing and Analysis

Several defined test patterns can be used to test T1 links, each pattern testing for a specific issue. These test patterns are outlined in Table 13-8.

Table 13-8   *T1 Link Test Patterns*

Test Pattern	Description
T1-1 (72 octet)	Stress testing of the repeater preamplifier and automatic line build-out (ALBO) circuitry. Detects marginal equipment using rapid transitions from a low 1s density to a high 1s density.
T1-2 (96-octet)	Empirical stress testing of T1 circuits and equipment.
T1-3 (54-octet)	Empirical stress testing of T1 circuits and equipment.
T1-4 (120 octet)	Empirical stress testing of T1 circuits and equipment.
T1-5 (53 octet)	Empirical stress testing of T1 circuits and equipment.
T1-6 (55 octet)	Empirical stress testing of T1 circuits and equipment. Often used to detect AMI/B8ZS mismatches.
T1-mW	T1 milliwatt. Digitized 1004 Hz tone with a 0dBm0 level on one DS0 channel. Standard tone (u-law) used in voice frequency (VF) testing.
QRSS	Quasi-random signal state. Similar to a ps2e20 test pattern.
3 in 24	Fixed pattern generating 3 bits in 24 bits, meeting 1s density rule (12.5 percent) with a string of 15 consecutive 0s in the stream. Used to identify AMI/B8ZS line coding mismatches. Test Pattern appears as 100010001000000000000000
1:7	Fixed pattern generating one mark (1) for every seven spaces (0). This pattern is used to stress the 12.5 percent 1s density requirement for T1s.
$2^{15}-1$, or ps2e15	32,767-bit pseudorandom pattern generating a maximum of 14 sequential 0s and 15 sequential 1s. Provides for maximum number of 0s for framed, non-B8ZS testing.
$2^{20}-1$, or ps2e20	1,048,575-bit pseudorandom pattern generating a maximum of 19 sequential 0s and 20 sequential 1s. Used to stress T1 circuits with excess 0s.
$2^{23}-1$, or ps2e23	8,388,607-bit pseudorandom pattern generating a maximum of 22 sequential 0s and 23 sequential 1s.
All 1s	This pattern is a continuing stream of marks, or 1s. It is used to stress test the T1 equipment's ability to handle sustained power output. This pattern should be run "framed" because some T1 equipment will recognize an "unframed" all 1s pattern as an alarm.
All 0s	This pattern is a continuing stream of spaces, or 0s, and is used to test the T1 equipment's line-coding configuration. If this pattern encounters errors, it is often an indication of an AMI/B8ZS mismatch.

Table 13-9 provides the parameters for T1 error thresholds.

Table 13-9   *T1 Errored Seconds (ES) and Severely Errored Seconds (SES) Thresholds*

Parameter	Per 15 Minutes	Per 4 Hours
ES (0-50 miles)	≤ 1	≤ 20
ES (> 50 miles)	Add .02 ES per mile	Add .02 ES per mile
SES	0	0

Table 13-10 provides the threshold formulae for Errored Seconds (ES), % Error Free Seconds (%EFS), and Severely Errored Seconds (SES) based on mileage between end points.

Table 13-10   *Threshold Formulae for Errored Seconds (ES), % Error Free Seconds (%EFS), and Severely Errored Seconds (SES)*

Route Mileage	ES	%EFS	SES
500	1	99.999	0
1500	1	99.999	0
4000	2	99.998	1

```
Mileage used is based on actual one-way route mileage.

The formulae are as follows:
Mileage = 1 - 1500
((mileage x .005) + 2) x .1 = ES
((mileage x .002) + 1) x .1 = SES

Mileage = 1501 - 4000
((mileage x .003) + 3) x .1 = ES
((mileage x .001) + 2) x .1 = SES
```

DS0 Basics

DS0s by definition are 64 Kbps bit streams, but they are often provisioned in sub-64 Kbps rates, such as 56 Kbps.

Figure 13-17 illustrates a typical DS0/DDS configuration from an end node.

Figure 13-17 *DS0/DDS Circuit Layout*

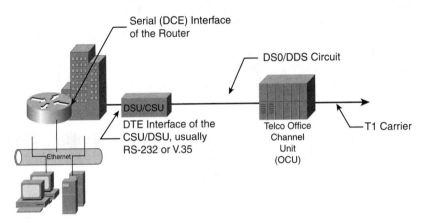

The documentation of DS0 links is similar to that of T1 links (see Table 13-11).

Table 13-11 *DS0 Point-to-Point Template*

Site A			Site B		
Site A LEC ID			Site B LEC ID		
Circuit ID	Service	Site A In-House Termination Point	Site B In-House Termination Point	Comments	
1					
2					
3					
4					
5					
6					
7					
8					
9					
10					

Table 13-12 details the test patterns and descriptions of DS0/DDS.

Table 13-12 *Test Pattern Descriptions*

Test Pattern	Description
2^{15}-1, or ps2e15	32,767-bit pseudorandom pattern generating a maximum of 14 sequential 0s and 15 sequential 1s.
2^{20}-1, or ps2e20	1,048,575-bit pseudorandom pattern generating a maximum of 19 sequential 0s and 20 sequential 1s.
2^{23}-1, or ps2e23	8,388,607-bit pseudorandom pattern generating a maximum of 22 sequential 0s and 23 sequential 1s.
DDS1	Pattern of 100 octets with all 1s (11111111), followed by 100 octets with all 0s (00000000). Stresses any DS0/DDS circuit's minimum and maximum power requirements for signal recovery.
DDS2	Pattern of 100 octets of 0111110, followed by 100 octets of all 0s. Simulation of an HDLC packet frame.
DDS3	Fixed pattern of 01001100. Minimum stress of clock recovery on DDS circuits.
DDS4	Fixed pattern of 00000010. Moderate stress of DDS clock recovery.
DDS5	Pattern is a combination of DDS1-4. Useful as a quick test of a DDS circuit.
DDS6	A 7-octet fixed pattern of 11111110 followed by one octet of 11111111; simulates a DDS signal transition from idle to data mode. Useful in detecting marginal equipment in multipoint circuits, such as those found with legacy SNA applications.

DS0/DDS Alarm Codes

Table 13-13 presents alarm codes that the network service provider can detect during out-of-service testing. Knowing these codes can sometimes greatly reduce troubleshooting and isolation time.

Table 13-13 *Alarm Code Descriptions*

Code	Description
ASC	Abnormal Station Code. Indicates that there is an open on the circuit between the Telco Office channel unit and the end node CSU/DSU. Possible Causes: • Disconnected CSU/DSU • No power to the CSU/DSU • Cable cut on the "last mile" • Flipped cable pairs—This can lead to false conditions because loopback testing to the CSU will prove successful, yet this condition will resume when testing is completed.
CMI	Channel (or Control) Mode Idle. Indicates the Request to Send (RTS) is low on the CSU/DSU. Usually means the DTE is offline.
MOS	Mux-out-of-sync. Indicates the local carrier has a "mux," or T-carrier, out-of-service.
UMC	Unassigned mux code. Digital cross-connect or Telco Office channel unit is missing.

DS3

DS3s comprise 28 DS1/T1s. DS3s are encoded with B3ZS, where three 0s are substituted with BPVs.

DS3/T3 service is implemented like that of DD1/T1 service, with the exception of being channelized into 28 DS1/T1s. DS1/T1s are channelized into 24 DS0/DDS timeslots.

Tables 13-14 and 13-15 can be used to document end-to-end T3 service between two end nodes.

Table 13-14 *DS3/T3 End-to-End Template*

Channel Number	Service	Site A In-House Termination Point	Site B In-House Termination Point	Comments
T3 Carrier		**IXC Circuit ID**		
Site A			**Site B**	
Site A LEC ID			**Site B LEC ID**	
1				
2				
3				
4				
5				
6				
7				
8				
9				
10				
11				
12				
13				
14				
15				
16				
17				
18				
19				
20				
21				

Table 13-15 *DS3/T3 Access Template*

T3 Carrier		IXC Access Circuit ID		LEC Circuit ID	
Channel Number	Service	IXC Circuit ID		Comments	
1					
2					
3					
4					
5					
6					
7					
8					
9					
10					
11					
12					
13					
14					
15					
16					
17					
18					
19					
20					
21					
22					
23					

Summary

Private Line WANs can comprise dedicated DS1/T1, DS3/T3, or DS0/DDS data services.

T1 is a digital communications link that enables the transmission of voice, data, and multimedia application signals at a rate of 1.544 Mbps. T1 is the "productized" version of the BellLabs Digital Service Level 1 (DS1) format.

For voice (analog) and data (digital) to share the same digital transmission media, the analog signals of voice must be converted into digital signals. This digitizing of the analog signals is known as pulse code modulation (PCM). PCM is a sampling process that compresses a voice signal into a 64 Kbps standard digital service rate, known as a DS0.

PCM involves two steps:

1 The incoming analog signal is sampled 8,000 times per second. These sampled values are converted to pulses using the pulse amplitude modulation (PAM) process.

2 The height of each pulse is assigned a representative 8-bit binary value resulting in a digital representation of the pulse and ultimately the sampled analog waveform.

Time division multiplexing (DTM) is the foundation behind T1 services. TDM is designed on the premise that each user, or channel, will have the total bandwidth for a portion of time.

After the voice/data signals have been digitized, they are multiplexed and transmitted over the T1 (E1, T3, and so on) link. This multiplexing process is called TDM.

T1/DS1 service has two framing formats:

- D4, or Superframe (SF)
- Extended Superframe (ESF)

The DS1 signal transmitted across a T1 link is signaled, or encoded, in one of two formats:

- Alternate mark inversion (AMI)
- Bi-polar with 8-zero substitution (B8ZS)

Both formats are designed to ensure the 1s density rule is followed. The 1s density rule states that no more than 15 consecutive 0s (12.5 percent, or one 1 for every eight bits) are permitted to be output on the T1 carrier or synchronization can be lost (no alternate voltage to which to clock).

T1 links can be deployed as dedicated links between an end node and the serving network service provider, either LEC or IXC. In instances where an end node does not require dedicated long-haul services but has several services from the network service provider, T1 links can be used to carry these multiple services to the end node.

DS0s by definition are 64 Kbps bit streams, but they are often provisioned in sub-64 Kbps rates, such as 56 Kbps.

DS3s comprise 28 DS1/T1s. DS3s are encoded with B3ZS, in which three 0s are substituted with BPVs.

DS3/T3 service is implemented like that of DD1/T1 service, with the exception of being channelized into 28 DS1/T1s. DS1/T1s are channelized into 24 DS0/DDS timeslots.

CHAPTER 14

Fiber-Optic Technology

The foundation of any optical system is the fiber-optic cabling. Basic fiber cables consist of the following components:

- Silica core—This is located at the center of the cable. This object and the cladding are used for carrying the optic, or lightwave, signal.

- Cladding—This is also located at the center of the cable. This object and the silica core are used for carrying the optic, or lightwave, signal.

- Coating, strength members, and a plastic jacket—This encloses the fiber, providing the necessary tinsel and scratch resistance to protect the fibers.

- Transceivers—This is attached to both ends of the core for emitting and receiving the light pulses that form the information bits in the optical network. The ability of clear glass to contain light is the key behind optical transmissions and is based around the principle of total internal reflection.

Fiber-optic transmission operates by injecting light at a specific angle, where the glass cladding acts as a mirror reflecting light within the silica. The refractive index (RI), or the change in the speed of light in a substance (in this case silica) relative to the speed of light in a vacuum, is significant.

Light normally travels at about 300,000 kilometers (km) per second in a vacuum. When light moves from a substance of lower density to one of higher density, such as between air and water, the light changes and is refracted. Refraction is the phenomenon used to explain why a stick appears to bend when one half of the stick is placed in water.

The "bending" of the light beam depends on two things: the angle at which light strikes the water and the RI. At some point, an angle is reached so that the light reflects off the water like a mirror. This angle is called the *critical angle* and the reflection of all the light is known as the *total internal reflection*.

Total internal reflection determines how light propagates down a clear fiber. Fibers are manufactured so that the core contains a slightly higher RI than the surrounding cladding. If light travels through the core and hits the cladding at a particular angle, it will stay in the fiber. The exact size of the angle depends on the difference in RIs; however, if a typical RI difference of 1 percent is assumed, all light striking the cladding at 8 degrees or less will continue on through the fiber.

Optic Bands and Transmission Windows

The light used in fiber-optic transmission is not the same as the light in a flashlight. Optical network light sources are more precise. The International Telecommunications Union (ITU) has specified six transmission bands for fiber-optic transmission. These bands are measured and represented in terms of wavelength sizes measured in nanometers (nm), one billionth of a meter, or microns, one thousandth of a meter.

The six bands, or transmission windows, are as follows:

- O-Band (1,260 nm to 1,310 nm)
- E-Band (1,360 nm to 1,460 nm)
- S-Band (1,460 nm to 1,530 nm)
- C-Band (1,530 nm to 1,565 nm)
- L-Band (1,565 nm to 1,625 nm)
- U-Band (1,625 nm to 1,675 nm)

A seventh band, not defined by the ITU but used in private networks, runs around 850 nm.

NOTE   The human hair is about 100 microns wide.

Typically, the higher the transmission window, the lower the attenuation or signal degradation and the more expensive the electronics.

The earliest fibers operated in the first transmission window of 850 nm. These standard multimode, or step-index, fibers contained a relatively large core of 50.5 microns or 62.5 microns, depending on the cable. The term *multimode* is derived from the makeup of the light taking multiple paths or modes through the fiber. These modes cause many issues for step-index fiber, resulting in limited distances.

Modal dispersion is a significant issue. As modes extend through the fiber at different angles, their lengths are slightly different. This difference results in light that takes less time to travel down the shorter modes than the longer ones, dispersing, or spreading out, the light pulse. Short fiber spans have little dispersion of the pulse; however, on distances longer than a kilometer, the light pulse disperses so much that it is unreadable by the receiver.

Multimode Fiber

Multimode fiber-optic cable comprises multiple strands of glass fibers and has a larger core than single-mode fiber. Multimode fiber-optic cables have a combined diameter of 50 to 100 microns, with each cable carrying independent signals. Multimode fiber has greater bandwidth capabilities than single-mode fiber because of its larger core size, which leads to ease of coupling and interconnecting.

Multimode fiber is primarily used for specific applications in which the distance limitation of 2 km is not an issue.

To increase the range, manufacturers developed graded index (GI) fiber. GI fiber is an improved multimode fiber that operates in the second transmission window (band) at around 1,300 nm. Graded index fiber nearly eliminates modal dispersion by gradually decreasing the RI out toward the cladding where the modes are longest. Waves on the long modes travel faster than waves on the short modes; therefore, the entire pulse arrives at the receiver at about the same time.

NOTE   With GI fiber, manufacturers can extract 200 MHz of bandwidth over 2 km.

On distances greater than 2 km, GI fibers need high-powered lasers, introducing the issue of modal noise. With modal noise, the fiber and connectors interact so that power fluctuations exist at the receivers. This modal noise increases the signal-to-noise ratio in a link, limiting the length of the fiber.

Single-Mode Fiber

Single-mode fiber uses a single glass strand with a smaller core than that of multimode fiber. Because single-mode fiber uses a smaller core of 8 to 10 microns, it enables only one mode of light travel over the fiber. With a single mode, many multimode problems, such as modal noise and modal dispersion, are no longer an issue. Single-mode fiber can reach as far as 100 to 200 km before a fiber-optic repeater, or amplifier, is required.

However, cost is an issue. The minute size of these cores demands that components have much tighter tolerance, increasing costs for the user. However, the increased bandwidth and increased distances of 80 km and longer easily outweigh the cost.

The following are the two main types of single-mode fiber and the two types of dispersion:

- Non-dispersion shifted fiber (NDSF)
- Dispersion-shifted fiber (DSF)
    - Zero-dispersion shifted fiber (ZDSF)
    - Non-zero dispersion shifted fiber (NZDF)

Non-Dispersion Shifted Fiber (NDSF)

Like GI fibers, the earliest single-mode fiber, non-dispersion shifted fiber (NDSF), also carries signals in the second transmission window at 1,310 nm. NDSF, like all single-mode fiber, greatly improves on a GI fiber's range; however, chromatic dispersion is an issue. Any light pulse, no matter the laser precision, contains a range of waves at different frequencies. Because the impact of the RI varies with the wave's frequency, the waves propagate down the fiber at different velocities and the pulse disperses until the signal becomes unintelligible.

Waveguide dispersion affects wavelength velocity. As waves move down the wire, parts of the electric and magnetic fields extend into the cladding, where the RI is lower. The longer the wavelength, the more energy carried in the cladding and the faster the wave travels. At the second band, or transmission window (around 1,310 nm), chromatic dispersion and waveguide dispersion cancel each other. Outside of that window, dispersion increases, limiting the length of the fiber.

The third and fourth transmission windows, or bands, are better suited for longer distances than the second transmission window. They have lower attenuation and can work with the best optical amplifiers, Erbium-Doped Fiber Amplifiers (EDFAs).

Dispersion-Shifted Fiber (DSF)

Dispersion-shifted fiber (DSF) moves optimal dispersion points to higher frequencies by altering the core-cladding interface. Zero Dispersion Shifted Fiber (ZDSF) moves the zero-dispersion frequency from 1,310 nm by increasing the waveguide dispersion until it cancels out chromatic dispersion at 1,550 nm.

NOTE   Dense wavelength division multiplexing (DWDM) gear and EDFAs operate in this window.

Zero-Dispersion Shifted Fiber (ZDSF)

Signals traveling over zero-dispersion shifted fiber (ZDSF) can combine to create additional signals that can be amplified by EDFAs and superimposed onto DWDM channels, causing noise in a problem known as "four-wave mixing."

Non-Zero Dispersion Shifted Fiber (NZDF)

Non-zero dispersion shifted fiber (NZDF) avoids four-wave mixing by moving the zero-dispersion point above the range of EDFAs. The signal continues to operate in the third or fourth transmission window with a moderate dispersion. This helps because it provides a minimal level of interference needed to separate DWDM channels from one another. Therefore, NZDF is the preferred cable for new optic installations.

Manufacturers have reduced the attenuation and the transmission window restriction on NZDF cables. Cisco Systems, Inc. implements NZDF dispersion at the 1550 nm window.

SONET/SDH

Synchronous Optical Networking, or SONET, specifications define optical carrier (OC) interfaces and their electrical equivalents, which enable the transmission of lower-rate signals at a common synchronous rate. SONET enables multiple vendors to provide compatible transmission equipment in the same span. SONET also enables dynamic drop and insert (DRI) capabilities on the data payload without the delay and additional hardware associated with multiplexing and demultiplexing the higher rate signal. Because SONET's overhead is independent of the data payload, SONET is able to integrate new services, such as Asynchronous Transfer Mode (ATM), Fiber Distributed Data Interface (FDDI), DS3, and DS1. Furthermore, SONET's operations, administration, maintenance, and provisioning (OAM&P) capabilities are built directly into the SONET signal overhead to enable maintenance of the network without taking the SONET infrastructure out of service.

SONET multiplexing combines low-speed digital signals such as DS1, DS1C, E1, DS2, and DS3 with required overhead to form a building block called Synchronous Transport Signal Level One (STS-1).

Table 14-1 reflects the bandwidth rates that SONET supports.

Table 14-1 *SONET Hierarchy*

Frame Format	Optical Carrier	SONET Transport	Bit Rate	DS0s	DS1s	DS3s
STS-1	OC-1	—	51.84 Mbps	672	28	1
STS-3	OC-3	STM-1	155.52 Mbps	2,016	84	3
STS-12	OC-12	STM-4	622 Mbps	8,064	336	12
STS-48	OC-48	STM-16	2.488 Gbps	32,256	1344	48
STS-192	OC-192	STM-64	9.953 Gbps	129,024	5376	192

NOTE The average efficiency of SONET can be computed as a percentage in the following formula:

$$(\%) = 1/[1.008 + (9/N)] \times 100$$

where N refers to the multiplexing scheme as in STS-N.

SONET Synchronization

SONET functionality is based heavily on three digital signal concepts:

- Synchronous—Digital signal transitions occur at exactly the same rate. A phase difference might exist between the two signals within specified limits. The phase difference here could be due to propagation delay or jitter. All clocks are traceable to one primary reference clock (PRC), which is derived from a cesium atomic standard clock.

- Plesiochronous—Digital signal transitions occur at almost the same rate, with variations being constrained by tight limits. Plesiochronous synchronization often occurs when two networks are internetworked, each with its own primary reference clock (PRC). Although these two PRCs are accurate in their own right, they are slightly different. This difference is known as a *plesiochronous difference*.

- Asynchronous—Digital signal transition does not occur at the same rate. Regarding SONET, asynchronous means that the difference between the two clocks, or PRCs, is greater than the plesiochronous difference. Asynchronous signals here could be described as two transceivers each running off an internal quartz clock, rather than a PRC.

SONET Standards

SONET was originally developed by BellCore Labs and standardized by ANSI, listed by the following standards:

- T1.105-199x dpANS for Telecommunications—Digital hierarchy-optical interface rates and formats specifications (SONET).

- T1.105-01-1994 ANS for Telecommunications—SONET automatic protection switching.

- T1-105.02-199x dpANS for Telecommunications—SONET payload mappings.

- T1.105.03-1994 ANS for Telecommunications—SONET jitter at network interfaces.

- T1.105-04-199x dpANS for Telecommunications—SONET date communications channel protocols and architectures.

- T1.105.05-1994 ANS for Telecommunications—SONET tandem connection maintenance.

- T1.105.06-199x dpANS for Telecommunications—SONET physical layer specifications.

- T1.105.07-199x dpANS for Telecommunications—SONET sub STS-1 interface rates and formats specifications.

- T1.105.08-199x dpANS Directory Service for Telecommunications Management Network (TMN) and SONET—When published, this standard might carry a T1.2xx number.

- T1.105.09-199x dpANS for Telecommunications—SONET timing and synchronization.

The ITU-T published a compatible version in Recommendation G.707 as the Synchronous Digital Hierarchy (SDH).

SONET Frames

The STS-1 frame is the basic building block of SONET transmission. The STS-1 frame consists of 810 bytes, or octets, and is transmitted every 125 microseconds, providing an overall data rate of 51.84 Mbps. The STS-1 frame can be logically viewed as a matrix of 9 rows, 90 bytes (or octets) per row. One row is transmitted at a time, from top left to bottom right.

Figure 14-1 illustrates the basic STS-1 frame format.

Figure 14-1 *STS-1 Frame Format*

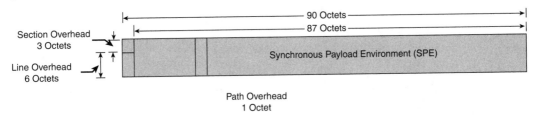

The first three columns (3 octets × 9 rows = 27 octets) are devoted to frame overhead. Nine octets are devoted to section-related overhead, and the remaining 18 octets are devoted to line overhead. The remainder of the frame is the payload. The frame payload includes a column of path overhead, not necessarily in the beginning of the frame, as illustrated in Figure 14-1.

SONET Frame Overhead

Figure 14-2 illustrates the construction of the SONET transport overhead frames.

Figure 14-2 *SONET STS-1 Transport and Path Overhead Octets*

Section Overhead	Framing A1	Framing A2	STS-ID C1		Trace J1
	BIP-8 B1	Orderwire E1	User F1		BIP-8 B3
	DataCom D1	DataCom D2	DataCom D3		Signal Label C2
Line Overhead	Pointer H1	Pointer H2	Pointer Action H3		Path Status G1
	BIP-8 B2	APS K1	APS K2		User F2
	DataCom D4	DataCom D5	DataCom D6		Multiframe H4
	DataCom D7	DataCom D8	DataCom D9		Growth Z3
	DataCom D10	DataCom D11	DataCom D12		Growth Z4
	Growth Z1	Growth Z2	Orderwire E2		Growth Z5

Section Overhead

Table 14-2 describes the STS-1 octets used in the section overhead portion of the transport overhead octet group.

Table 14-2 *STS-1 Octets: Section Overhead Portion*

Octet Name	Description
A1, A2	Framing bytes = F6, 28 hex; used to synchronize frame start
C1	STS-1 ID that identifies the STS-1 number (N) within an STS-N multiplexed carrier
B1	Bit-interleaved parity byte providing even parity over previous STS-N frame after scrambling
E1	Section level 64 Kbps PCM orderwire; optional 64 Kbps voice channel that can be used between section terminating equipment
F1	64 Kbps channel for user purposes
D1–D3	192 Kbps data channel for alarms, maintenance, control, and administration between sections

Line Overhead

Table 14-3 describes the STS-1 octets used in the line overhead portion of the transport overhead octet group.

Table 14-3 *STS-1 Octets: Line Overhead Portion*

Octet Name	Description
H1–H3	Pointer octets used in frame and frequency alignment adjustment of payload data
B2	Bit-interleaved parity for line-level error monitoring
K1, K2	Two octets used for signaling between line-level automatic-protection switching equipment
D4–D12	576 Kbps data channel for alarms, maintenance, control, monitoring, and administration at the line level
Z1, Z2	Reserved for future use
E2	64 Kbps PCM voice channel for line-level orderwire

Path Overhead

Table 14-4 describes the STS-1 octets used in the path overhead portion of the transport overhead octet group.

Table 14-4   *STS-1 Octets: Path Overhead Portion*

Octet Name	Description
J1	64 Kbps channel used to repeatedly send a 64-octet fixed-length string for a receiving terminal to continually verify path integrity against
B3	Bit-interleaved parity at the path level, calculated over all bits from the previous synchronous payload environment (SPE)
C2	STS path signal label designating equipped and unequipped STS signals
	Equipped—Label indicates specific STS payload mapping
	Unequipped—Line connection is complete, but no path data for transmission exists
G1	Status byte sent between path-termination equipment
F2	64 Kbps channel for path user
H4	Multiframe indicator for payloads needing frames longer than a single STS frame payload (87 octets)
Z3–Z5	Reserved for future use

Packet Over SONET (PoS)

Packet over SONET (PoS) technology efficiently transports data over SONET/SDH. PoS is a flexible solution that can be used to enable a variety of transport applications. For example, some transport applications include network backbone infrastructure and data aggregation or distribution on the network edge and in the metropolitan area. Router PoS interfaces are frequently connected to add drop multiplexers (ADMs), terminating point-to-point SONET/SDH links. Direct connections over dark fiber or via dense wave-division multiplexing (DWDM) systems are also becoming increasingly popular.

PoS line cards are popular Cisco gigabit switch routers (GSRs). Other Cisco products such as the Cisco 7500 and 7200 series routers also feature PoS interfaces. The Catalyst 6500 and 8500 series enterprise switches are potential candidates for PoS interfaces in the future.

Cisco currently deploys the ONS 15190 IP Transport and the GSR 12000 Series router for PoS applications.

The current Internet Engineering Task Force (IETF) PoS specification is RFC 2615 (PPP over SONET), which makes RFC 1619 obsolete. PoS provides a method for efficiently carrying data packets in SONET/SDH frames. High-bandwidth capacity, coupled with efficient link utilization, makes PoS the preference for the core layer of data network topologies. PoS overhead, which averages about 3 percent, is significantly lower than the 15 percent average for the ATM cell tax.

PoS Frame Format

PoS uses PPP in high-level data link control (HDLC)-like framing (as specified in RFC 1662) for data encapsulation at the data link layer of the OSI model (Layer 2). This mechanism provides packet delineation and error control. The frame format for PPP in HDLC-like framing is shown in Figure 14-3.

Figure 14-3 *PoS Frame Format*

RFC 2615 specifies the use of PPP encapsulation over SONET/SDH links. PPP was designed for use on point-to-point links and as such is suitable for SONET/SDH links, which are provisioned as point-to-point circuits, even in ring topologies.

PoS specifies STS-3c/STM-1 (155 Mbps) as the basic data rate, and has a usable data bandwidth of 149.760 Mbps. PoS frames are mapped into the payload envelope of SONET/SDH frames. RFC 2615 recommends payload scrambling as a safeguard against bit sequences, which might disrupt timing.

PoS Synchronization

PoS interfaces are typically connected over carrier SONET/SDH networks, where timing is synchronized to a reference Layer 1 clock running at 0.000001 parts per minute (ppm). The PoS interface derives timing information from the incoming data stream. This timing information is then distributed and synchronized throughout the rest of the network. A PoS interface retrieving timing in this fashion is said to be loop (or line) timed.

When PoS interfaces are not connected to carrier SONET/SDH networks, the links are independently timed by 20 ppm internal clock sources built into the Cisco PoS interfaces. This type of timing, referred to as *internal*, is sufficient for simple point-to-point connections in which network timing distribution is not required. Internal timing is suitable for situations with less rigorous timing requirements, including connectivity over DWDM systems. Cisco Systems has demonstrated the feasibility of 20 ppm internal timing in numerous field deployments and in interoperability testing.

DWDM

DWDM allows service providers to enable customer services such as e-mail, video, and multimedia to be carried as IP data over ATM and voice carried over SONET/SDH. Despite the fact that these formats utilize unique bandwidth-management techniques, all three can be transported over the optical layer using DWDM.

DWDM increases the capacity of existing fiber by assigning incoming optical signals to specific frequencies, wavelengths, or lambdas within a designated frequency band and then multiplexing these signals out onto a single fiber. Because incoming signals are never terminated in the optical layer, the interface is bit-rate and format independent.

DWDM contains multiple optical signals so that they can be amplified as a group and transported over a single fiber to increase capacity. Each signal can carry different rates—such as OC-x (OC-3, OC-12, OC-48)—and in a different format, such as SONET or ATM. Current DWDM systems can achieve a capacity of more than 40 Gbps. Future developments will be able to carry 80 wavelengths of OC-48 (2.5 Gbps), totaling 200 Gbps, or 40 wavelengths of OC-192 (10 Gbps), totaling 400 Gbps.

The ITU has standardized channel separation of DWDM wavelengths at 100 GHz. However, more vendors today are using 50 GHz or less to separate the wavelengths, yielding more capacity across the fiber.

DWDM Technology

High-speed, high-volume transmission is achieved by optical amplifiers. Optical amplifiers operate in a specific band of the frequency spectrum and are optimized for operation with existing fiber, making it possible to boost lightwave signals, extending their reach without converting them back to electrical form.

Optical amplifiers have two significant elements:

- Optical fiber doped with the element erbium—When a pump laser is used to energize the erbium with light at a specific wavelength, the erbium acts as a gain medium that amplifies the incoming optical signal. If a connector is used instead of a splice, slight amounts of surface dirt might cause the connector to become damaged.

- Amplifier—Both silica-based and fluoride-based fiber amplifiers are used. In the 1530 to 1565 nm range, both perform about the same. Fluoride-based optical amplifiers are more expensive to implement because immediate testing of their long-range reliability is not available, making implementation a costly and risky venture.

DWDM systems consist of multiple input lasers, light termination equipment (LTE) multiplexers, transport fibers, LTE demultiplexers, and receiving laser diodes. Each channel is separated by a 100 GHz spacing to avoid nonlinearities, or lightwave "bleedover" due to the scattering of refracted light wavelengths. Some newer systems enable 50 GHz spacing between wavelengths.

NOTE	The DWDM spectrum ranges from 191.1 Terahertz (THz) to 196.5 THz, centering around 193.1 THz.

DWDM Capacity

Table 14-5 demonstrates the current and future trends of DWDM and available fiber rates.

Table 14-5   *DWDM Technology Timeline*

Wavelength	Timeline	Capacity
DWDM at OC-192 and 40	Current	40 wavelengths at 100 GHz spacing, at 10 Gbps each, totaling 400 Gbps.
DWDM at OC-192 and 80	Current	80 wavelengths at 50 GHz spacing, at 10 Gbps each, totaling 800 Gbps.
DWDM at OC-768 and 40	Current	This information is current because developmental work is still being performed. 40 wavelengths, at 40 Gbps per wavelength, totaling 1.6 Terabits-per-second (Tbps).
DWDM at OC-768 and 80	Future	(2002) 80 wavelengths totaling 3.2 Tbps.
DWDM at OC-192 and 160	Future	(2005) 160 wavelengths (with closer spacing) at 10 Gbps, totaling 1.6 Tbps.
DWDM at OC-768 and 160	Future	(2008 through 2009) 160 wavelengths at 40 Gbps, totaling 6.4 Tbps.

Optical Switching

Optical switching is a light-based form of a digital cross-connect. The digital cross-connect system, sometimes referred to as a DACS or DXC, is a switch designed to establish long-term "nailed-up" circuit paths.

Traditional electronic-based switching systems convert the wavelengths from an optical signal, to an electronic signal, back to an optical signal (optical-electronic-optical). This conversion system is not an ideal scenario because the electronic conversion process presents limitations to the bandwidth capacity.

Micro electrical mechanical systems (MEMS) is the switching technology that lambda-based systems use when deploying optical-based switching and routing devices. Figure 14-4 illustrates how MEMS performs optical switching. MEMS relies on micron-mirrors, which can be configured at various angles to ensure that incoming lambdas hit one fixed mirror, reflect to a movable mirror (reflector), then reflect back to another fixed mirror, and finally reflect back out to another lambda.

Figure 14-4 *Micro Electrical Mechanical Systems (MEMS)*

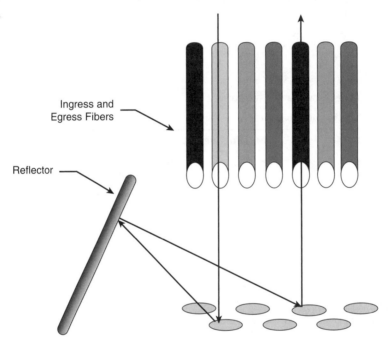

Ingress and Egress Fibers

Reflector

Summary

The foundation of any optical system is the fiber-optic cabling. Basic fiber cables consist of the following components:

- Silica core—At the center of the cable. This object and the cladding are used for carrying the optic, or lightwave, signal.

- Cladding—Also at the center of the cable. This object and the silica core are used for carrying the optic, or lightwave, signal.

- Coating, strength members, and a plastic jacket—This encloses the fiber, providing the necessary tinsel and scratch resistance to protect the fibers.

- Transceivers—This is attached to both ends of the core for emitting and receiving the light pulses that form the information bits in the optical network. The ability of clear glass to contain light is the key behind optical transmissions and is based around the principle of total internal reflection.

Fiber-optic transmission operates by injecting light at a specific angle, where the glass cladding acts as a mirror reflecting light within the silica. The refractive index (RI), or the change in the speed of light in a substance (in this case silica) relative to the speed of light in a vacuum, is significant.

Two modes of fiber optic exist: multimode and single-mode.

Multimode fiber-optic cable is comprised of multiple strands of glass fibers and has a larger core than single-mode fiber. Multimode fiber-optic cables have a combined diameter of 50 to 100 microns, with each cable carrying independent signals. Multimode fiber has greater bandwidth capabilities than single-mode fiber because of its larger core size, which leads to ease of coupling and interconnecting.

Multimode fiber is primarily used for specific applications where the distance limitation of 2 km is not an issue.

Single-mode fiber uses a single glass strand with a smaller core than that of multimode fiber. Because single-mode fiber uses a smaller core of 8 to 10 microns, single-mode fiber enables only one mode of light travel over the fiber. With a single mode, many multimode problems, such as modal noise and modal dispersion, are no longer an issue. Single-mode fiber can reach as far as 100 to 200 km before a fiber-optic repeater, or amplifier, is required.

As a technology layered on top of multimode or single-mode fiber, SONET, Packet over SONET (PoS), and DWDM enable available bandwidth in the magnitudes of Gigabits-per-second (Gbps).

Synchronous Optical Networking, or SONET, specifications define optical carrier (OC) interfaces and their electrical equivalents, enabling transmission of lower-rate signals at a common synchronous rate. SONET enables multiple vendors to provide compatible transmission equipment in the same span. SONET also enables dynamic drop and insert (DRI) capabilities on the data payload without the delay and additional hardware associated with multiplexing and demultiplexing the higher rate signal.

Because SONET's overhead is independent of the data payload, SONET is able to integrate new services, such as Asynchronous Transfer Mode (ATM), Fiber Distributed Data Interface (FDDI), DS3, and DS1 services. Furthermore, SONET's operations, administration, maintenance, and provisioning (OAM&P) capabilities are built directly into the SONET signal overhead to enable maintenance of the network without taking the SONET infrastructure out of service.

Packet over SONET (PoS) technology efficiently transports data over SONET/SDH. PoS is a flexible solution that can be used to enable a variety of transport applications. For example, some transport applications include network backbone infrastructure and data aggregation or distribution on the network edge and in the metropolitan area. Router PoS interfaces are frequently connected to add drop multiplexers (ADMs), terminating point-to-point SONET/SDH links. Direct connections over dark fiber or via dense wave-division multiplexing (DWDM) systems are also becoming increasingly popular.

DWDM systems consist of multiple input lasers, light termination equipment (LTE) multiplexers, transport fibers, LTE demultiplexers, and receiving laser diodes. Each channel is separated by a 100 GHz spacing to avoid nonlinearities, or lightwave "bleedover" due to the scattering of refracted light wavelengths. Some newer systems enable 50 GHz spacing between wavelengths.

Micro electrical mechanical systems (MEMS) is the switching technology that lambda-based systems use when deploying optical-based switching and routing devices. MEMS relies on micron-mirrors, which can be configured at various angles to ensure that incoming lambdas hit one fixed mirror, reflect to a movable mirror (reflector), then reflect back to another fixed mirror, and finally reflect back out another lambda.

CHAPTER 15

Frame Relay

Frame Relay is a Layer 2 (data link) wide-area networking (WAN) protocol that operates at both Layer 1 (physical) and Layer 2 (data link) of the OSI networking model. Although Frame Relay internetworking services were initially designed to operate over Integrated Services Digital Network (ISDN), the more common deployment today involves dedicated access to WAN resources.

NOTE   ISDN and Frame Relay both use the signaling mechanisms specified in ITU-T Q.933 (Frame Relay Local Management Interface [LMI] Type Annex-A) and American National Standards Institute (ANSI) T1.617 (Frame Relay LMI Type Annex-D).

Frame Relay is considered to be a more efficient version of X.25 because it does not require the windowing and retransmission features found with X.25. This is primarily due to the fact that Frame Relay services typically are carried by more reliable access and backbone facilities.

Frame Relay networks are typically deployed as a cost-effective replacement for point-to-point private line, or leased line, services. Whereas point-to-point customers incur a monthly fee for local access and long-haul connections, Frame Relay customers incur the same monthly fee for local access, but only a fraction of the long-haul connection fee associated with point-to-point private line services. The long-haul charges are typically usage-based across the virtual circuit (VC).

NOTE   The long-haul fee associated with point-to-point private (leased) line services is sometimes known as the inter-office connection fee. Service providers generally file a tariff with the FCC regarding these fees, comprising a base cost plus a per-mile charge.

NOTE   X.25 was designed for use over less reliable transmission medium than what is available in the marketplace today. Due to this unreliable nature, X.25 took on the error detection and correction (windowing and retransmission) mechanisms within the protocol stack. This resulted in higher overhead on the network, yielding less available bandwidth for data throughput.

NOTE   Frame Relay is a packet-switched technology, enabling end nodes to dynamically share network resources.

Frame Relay was standardized by two standards bodies—internationally by the International Telecommunication Union Telecommunication Standardization Sector (ITU-T) and domestically by ANSI.

Frame Relay Terms and Concepts

Frame Relay is a frame-switched technology, meaning that each network end user, or end node, will share backbone network resources, such as bandwidth. Connectivity between these end nodes is accomplished with the use of Frame Relay virtual circuits (VCs). Figure 15-1 illustrates the components of a Frame Relay WAN.

Figure 15-1   *Frame Relay WAN*

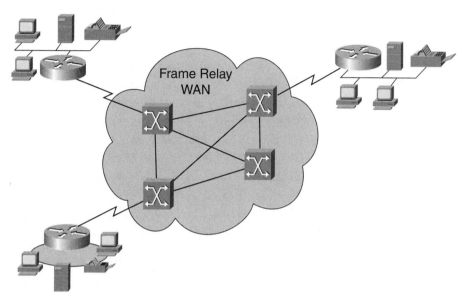

Table 15-1 defines the common and relevant Frame Relay terms.

Table 15-1   *Frame Relay Terms and Definitions*

Acronym	Definition
B_c	Committed burst. Negotiated tariff metric in Frame Relay internetworks. The maximum amount of data (measured in bits) that a Frame Relay internetwork is committed to accept and transmit at the committed information rate (CIR). B_c can be represented by the formula $B_c = CIR \times T_c$.
B_e	Excess burst. Negotiated tariff metric in Frame Relay internetworks. The number of bits that a Frame Relay internetwork will attempt to transfer after B_c is accommodated. B_e data is generally delivered with a lower probability than B_C data because B_e data is marked as discard eligible (DE) by the network.
BECN	Backward explicit congestion notification. A Frame Relay network in frames traveling in the opposite direction of frames that are encountering a congested path sets this bit. Data terminal equipment (DTE) receiving frames with the BECN bit set can request that higher-level protocols take flow control action as appropriate, such as the throttling back of data transmission.
CIR	Committed information rate. Rate at which a Frame Relay network agrees to transfer information under normal conditions, averaged over a minimum increment of time. CIR, measured in bits per second (bps), is one of the key negotiated tariff metrics.
DCE	Data communications equipment. The DCE provides a physical connection to the network, forwards traffic, and provides a clocking signal used to synchronize data transmission between DCE and DTE.

(continues)

Table 15-1 *Frame Relay Terms and Definitions (Continued)*

Acronym	Definition
DE	Discard eligible. If the Frame Relay network is congested, DE-marked frames can be dropped to ensure delivery of higher-priority traffic—in this case, CIR-marked frames.
DLCI	Data-link connection identifier. Values used to identify a specific PVC or SVC. In Frame Relay internetworks, DLCIs are locally significant. In a Frame Relay LMI extended environment, DLCIs are globally significant because they indicate end devices.
DTE	Data terminal equipment. Device at the end of a User-Network Interface (UNI) that serves as either a data source or destination.
FECN	Forward explicit congestion notification. Bit set by a Frame Relay network to inform the DTE receiving the frame that congestion was experienced in the path from origination to destination. The DTE that is receiving frames with the FECN bit set can request that higher-level protocols take flow control action as appropriate, such as throttling back data transmission.
LMI	Local Management Interface. Set of enhancements to the basic Frame Relay specification. LMI includes support for keepalive mechanisms, verifying the flow of data; multicast mechanisms, providing the network server with local and multicast DLCI information; global addressing, giving DLCIs global rather than local significance; and status mechanisms, providing ongoing status reports on the switch-known DLCIs.
NNI	Network-to-Network Interface. Standard interface between two Frame Relay switches that are both located in either a private or public network.
PVC	Permanent virtual circuit. Frame Relay virtual circuit that is permanently established (does not require call-setup algorithms).
SVC	Switched virtual circuit. Frame Relay virtual circuit that is dynamically established via call-setup algorithms. Usually found in sporadic data transfer environments.
T_c	T_c is a periodic interval. This interval is triggered anew when data is incoming to the network. When there is no data traffic when time T_c has elapsed, a new interval does not begin until new data traffic is sent to the network.
UNI	User-Network Interface. Frame Relay interface between a Frame Relay switch in a private network (such as a customer premise) and a public network (such as a service provider). Sometimes referred to as a Subscriber Network Interface (SNI).

Figure 15-2 illustrates some of the Frame Relay terminology used. The remainder of the terms will be illustrated where appropriate throughout this chapter.

Figure 15-2   *Frame Relay Terminology, Part I*

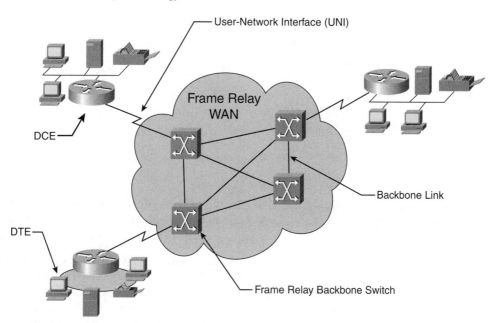

Frame Relay Components

Frame Relay WAN service comprises four primary functional components:

- Customer premise Frame Relay access device (FRAD)
- Local access loop to the service provider network
- Frame Relay switch access port

  Link Management Interface parameters are defined here

- Frame Relay VC parameters to each end site

Customer Premise FRAD

This device is either a dedicated FRAD, such as a Cisco *XXX*; or a router, such as a Cisco 26xx Series Router. Figure 15-3 illustrates a typical FRAD implementation.

NOTE   A router with an integrated CSU/DSU acts as a FRAD/Router.

Figure 15-3 *Frame Relay Access Device*

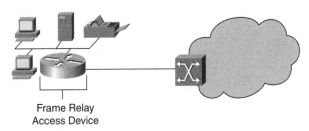

Frame Relay
Access Device

Local Access Loop to the Service Provider Network

Local access loop is the physical wiring that interconnects the customer premise FRAD and the service provider network's Frame Relay switch access port. This local loop is typically a DS0, DS1, NxDS1, DS3 service, or some fraction of DS1/DS3 service (such as Frac-T1).

In telephony, a local loop is the wired connection from a telephone company's central office (CO) in a locality to its customers' telephones at homes and businesses. This connection is usually on a pair of copper wires called twisted pair. The local loop system was originally designed for voice transmission only using analog transmission technology on a single voice channel. A modem is used to handle the conversion between analog and digital signals. With the advent of ISDN or digital subscriber line (DSL), the local loop can carry digital signals directly and at a much higher bandwidth than for voice only.

The local loop requires termination into a network interface unit (NIU) at the customer premise, and subsequent connection to the customer DCE device, usually a CSU/DSU. The DTE port of this CSU/DSU provides connectivity to the FRAD/Router. Figure 15-4 illustrates a typical local loop configuration.

Figure 15-4 *Frame Relay Local Access Loop*

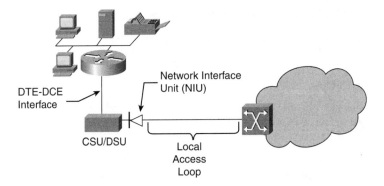

Frame Relay Virtual Circuits

Frame Relay is a connection-oriented service, operating at the data link layer (Layer 2) of the OSI model. A DLCI is used to identify this dedicated communication path between two end nodes: origination and termination. This path, or VC, is a bidirectional logical connection across the wide-area network between two end node DTE devices.

Figure 15-5 illustrates a fully meshed (all sites with connectivity to each other) Frame Relay WAN, with DLCI assignments for each location.

NOTE   Sometimes the originating node of a VC will be annotated as Site A and the terminating node of a VC will be annotated as Site B or Site Z.

Figure 15-5   *Frame Relay WAN with Virtual Circuit and DLCI*

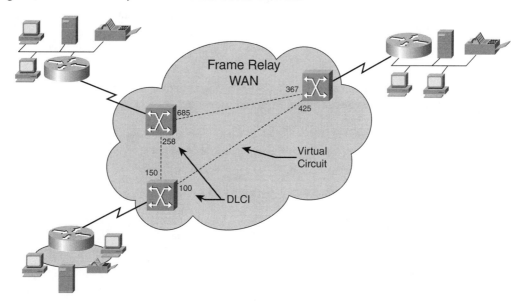

DLCIs

DLCIs are used to identify the PVC that is provisioned to transport data traffic. DLCIs are of local significance, unless an agreement has been made with the network service provider to deploy global DLCIs. Local significance means that DLCIs are of use only to the local Frame Relay network device. Frame Relay DLCIs are analogous to an organization's telephone network that is utilizing speed-dial functions. The most common Frame Relay

WAN deployment involves the use of local DLCIs because a network size limitation exists for the use of global DLCIs.

NOTE   Global DLCI addresses are assigned so that each DLCI has universal significance, meaning that the DLCI number is pointed to the same destination (termination point) regardless of the origination point.

The concept behind global DLCI addressing is to simplify Frame Relay network addressing administration; however, global addressing has an inherent limitation in that no more than 992 DLCIs (1024 DLCIs less the 32 reserved DLCIs) can be used. In a Frame Relay network of more than 992 sites, global addressing will not work.

The use of global DLCIs requires that they each be preassigned. (Typically, the assignments are negotiated between the customer and the network service provider.) In addition, each DLCI can be used only once throughout the network. (If two sites had the same DLCI, the network would not know which termination site was the intended destination.) The Frame Relay switch within the network service provider's network will have tables that route the traffic between each origination and termination pair.

Suppose that an organization has deployed the speed-dialing scheme illustrated for reference in Figure 15-6 and detailed in the following list:

- The CEO speed-dials 1 to talk with the COO.
- The CEO speed-dials 2 to talk with the VP of Marketing.
- The COO speed-dials 1 to talk with the VP of Marketing.
- The COO speed-dials 5 to talk with the CEO.
- The VP of Marketing speed-dials 7 to talk with the CEO.
- The VP of Marketing speed-dials 9 to talk with the COO.

Figure 15-6 *Telephone Speed-Dial Network*

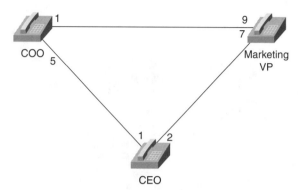

Table 15-2 provides another view of the Telephone Speed-Dial Network.

Table 15-2 *Telephone Speed-Dial Configuration Table*

Site A	Site B	A ➠ B Speed Dial	B ➠ A Speed Dial
COO	Marketing VP	1	9
COO	CEO	5	1
CEO	Marketing VP	2	7
CEO	COO	1	5
Marketing VP	CEO	7	5
Marketing VP	COO	9	1

For the CEO to speak with the COO, the CEO will press speed-dial 1 on the telephone set. However, the COO will see speed-dial 5 on the telephone because that is the local speed-dial assignment given to the CEO, as the speed-dial 1 local assignment on the COO's telephone set is assigned to the VP of Marketing.

If the COO presses speed-dial 1, the VP of Marketing will answer the phone and speed-dial 9 will show on the Marketing VP's phone because that is the local assignment given to the COO.

This same concept applies to Frame Relay DLCIs; the DLCI assignment is locally significant. The distant-end of the VC is unaware of this number because it has its own local DLCI assignment to identify the distant-end node. This is illustrated in Figure 15-7.

Figure 15-7 *Frame Relay Network with DLCI Assignment*

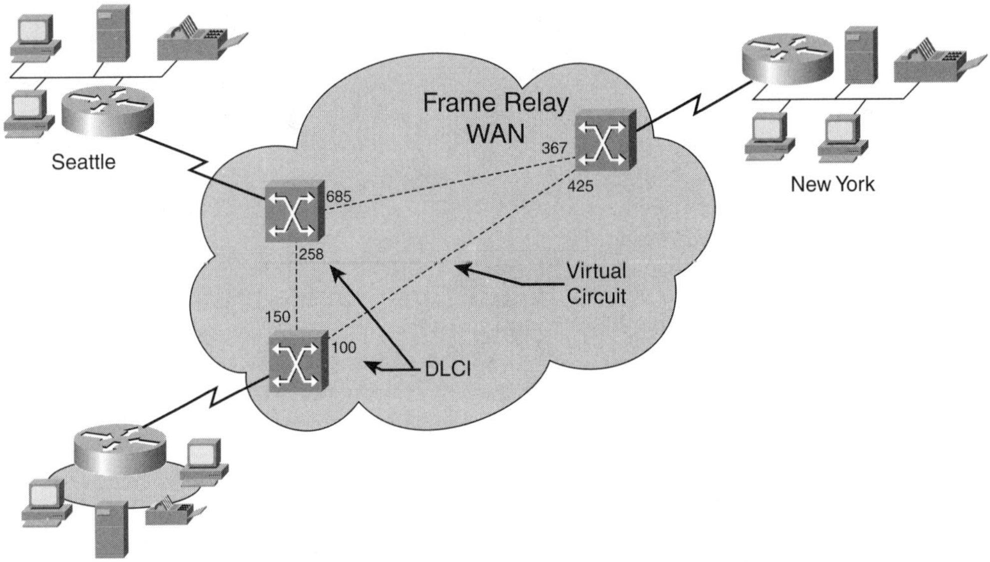

In this example, for Los Angeles to send traffic to New York, the FRAD will map the network layer information, such as IP address, to the DLCI. In this case, the DLCI is 100. New York will see traffic arrive on DLCI 425 and will be able to identify within its Frame Relay mapping tables that this traffic has arrived from Los Angeles.

Table 15-3 provides a view of the Frame Relay network shown in Figure 15-7.

Table 15-3 *Frame Relay DLCI Table for Figure 15-7*

Site A	Site B	A ➡ B DLCI	B ➡ A DLCI
Los Angeles	New York	100	425
Los Angeles	Seattle	150	258
Seattle	New York	685	367
Seattle	Los Angeles	258	150
New York	Seattle	367	685
New York	Los Angeles	425	100

NOTE   The **show frame-relay map** command can be used in Privileged Exec mode to view the mapping of network addressing to a DLCI.

NOTE	To define the mapping between a destination protocol address and the DLCI used to connect to the destination address, use the **frame-relay map** interface configuration command. Use the **no** form of this command to delete the map entry.

```
frame-relay map protocol protocol-address dlci [broadcast] [ietf ¦ cisco]
[payload-compress {packet-by-packet ¦ frf9 stac [hardware-options]}]
no frame-relay map protocol protocol-address
```

Table 15-4 provides details of the **frame-relay map** interface configuration command.

Table 15-4   *frame-relay map Command Field Descriptions*

Field	Description
Protocol	Supported protocol, bridging, or logical link control keywords: **appletalk**, **decnet**, **dlsw**, **ip**, **ipx**, **llc2**, **rsrb**, **vines** and **xns**.
protocol-address	Destination protocol address.
Dlci	DLCI number used to connect to the specified protocol address on the interface.
Broadcast	(Optional) Forwards broadcasts to this address when multicast is not enabled (see the **frame-relay multicast-dlci** command for more information about multicasts). This keyword also simplifies the configuration of Open Shortest Path First (OSPF).
Ietf	(Optional) Internet Engineering Task Force (IETF) form of Frame Relay encapsulation. Used when the router or access server is connected to another vendor's equipment across a Frame Relay network.
Cisco	(Optional) Cisco encapsulation method.
payload-compress packet-by-packet	(Optional) Packet-by-packet payload compression using the Stacker method.
payload-compress frf9 stac	(Optional) Enables FRF.9 compression using the Stacker method. If the router contains a compression service adapter (CSA), compression is performed in the CSA hardware (hardware compression). If the CSA is not available, compression is performed in the software installed on the VIP2 (distributed compression). If the VIP2 is not available, compression is performed in the router's main processor (software compression).

(continues)

Table 15-4 *frame-relay map* Command Field Descriptions (Continued)

Field	Description
hardware-options	**distributed** (Optional)—Specifies that compression is implemented in the software that is installed in a VIP2. If the VIP2 is not available, compression is performed in the router's main processor (software compression). This option applies only to the Cisco 7500 series.
	software (Optional)—Specifies that compression is implemented in the Cisco IOS software installed in the router's main processor.
	csa csa_number (Optional)—Specifies the CSA to use for a particular interface. This option applies only to Cisco 7200 series routers.

PVCs

PVCs are Frame Relay VC connections that are permanently established. PVCs are used for frequent communication between end nodes, such as file sharing, file transfer, and CAD/CAM imaging.

Frame Relay PVCs use DLCIs for Layer 2 addressing.

PVCs operate in one of two modes:

- Idle—The connection between end nodes is active albeit with no data transfer occurring. PVCs are not terminated or "taken-down" when in an idle state.

- Data Transfer—Data traffic is being transmitted between end nodes over the VC.

Even though PVCs are generally discussed as being full-duplex, PVCs are simplex connections, each with its own DLCI/CIR assignment.

The three duplex modes are as follows:

- Full-duplex communication involves origination and termination points transmitting and receiving at the same time; this is two-way communication full-time.

- Half-duplex communication is origination and termination points transmitting and receiving, but not at the same time. Only one flow of traffic is allowed across the connection; this is two-way communication, one-way at a time.

- Simplex communication is origination or termination points transmitting or receiving; this is one-way communication only.

SVCs

Unlike PVCs, which are permanently established connections, SVCs require a call setup process. SVCs are temporary connections that are traditionally used when communication between end nodes is infrequent or sporadic, such as in Voice over Frame Relay (VoFr) situations.

NOTE   Frame Relay SVCs use E.164 or X.121 addresses for Layer 2 addressing.

Whereas PVCs are permanently established, SVCs require a call setup and termination process, defined by the following process and functions:

1 Call setup—Establishes the VC between Frame Relay end nodes. This includes negotiation of VC parameters, such as CIR.

2 Data transfer—Data traffic is transmitted between end nodes (originating and terminating) across the VC.

3 Idle—Like PVCs, when the VC is idle (no data traffic) the connection between end nodes remains active and available for communication. However, unlike PVCs, which do not terminate the connection, an SVC will terminate the connection if it is in an idle state for a configured time period.

4 Call termination—The VC between Frame Relay end nodes is terminated, or "taken down."

NOTE   In bidirectional mode, both ends of a VC send and respond to keepalive requests. If one end of the VC is configured in the bidirectional mode, the other end must also be configured in the bidirectional mode.

In request mode, the router sends keepalive requests and expects replies from the other end of the VC. If one end of a VC is configured in the request mode, the other end must be configured in the reply or passive-reply mode.

In reply mode, the router does not send keepalive requests, but waits for keepalive requests from the other end of the VC and replies to them. If no keepalive request has arrived within the timer interval, the router times out and increments the error counter by 1. If one end of a VC is configured in the reply mode, the other end must be configured in the request mode.

In passive-reply mode, the router does not send keepalive requests, but waits for keepalive requests from the other end of the VC and replies to them. No timer is set when in this mode, and the error counter is not incremented. If one end of a VC is configured in the passive-reply mode, the other end must be configured in the request mode.

The command to configure end-to-end keepalive (Cisco IOS 12.0.5(T) or greater) is frame-relay end-to-end keepalive mode {bidirectional | request | reply | passive-reply}.

X.121 is a hierarchical addressing scheme that was originally designed to number X.25 nodes. E.164 is a hierarchical global telecommunications numbering plan, similar to the North American Number Plan (NANP, 1-NPA-NXX-XXXX).

As one would expect, determining the number of Virtual Circuits required for a network configuration is based on the number of end nodes, and the communication requirements, such as fully meshed (all-to-all), partial meshed (some-to-all), or hub-and-spoke (all-to-one), as illustrated by Figure 15-8.

Figure 15-8 *Fully Meshed, Partially Meshed, and Hub-and-Spoke Networks*

In a fully meshed network environment, the number of VCs required can be represented by the following formula:

$$[(N \times (N-1)) / 2]$$

where N is the number of end nodes in the network. This formula is sometimes referred to as the "N^2 Formula" because it is derived from $((N^2-N) / 2)$.

In a partial meshed network environment, the number of VCs required is not easily represented by a mathematical formula. You must consider many variables, the least of which is based on the determination of which end nodes require communication with which other end nodes. It is a fair assumption to estimate that the number of VCs required would fall between those of a fully meshed and those of a hub-and-spoke environment:

$$[((N \times (N-1)) / 2) \geq X \geq (N-1)]$$

where N is the number of end nodes in the network and X is the number of VCs required to support a partially meshed configuration. The following formula can be used as an approximation to determine the number of VCs necessary to support a partial mesh configuration: $[N^2 / \sqrt{(N-1)}]$, where N is the number of network nodes. This formula is useful from a network planning and cost-determination standpoint; however, because partial mesh connectivity is determined by application and user requirements at the end node, an exact number of partial-mesh VCs is almost impossible to determine.

In a hub-and-spoke network environment, the number of VCs required can be represented by the formula $[N-1]$, where N is the number of end nodes in the network.

Figure 15-9 illustrates the number of VCs necessary to support fully meshed $[(N \times (N–1))\,/\,2]$, partially meshed approximation $[N^2\,/\,\sqrt{(N–1)}]$, and hub-and-spoke $(N–1)$ Frame Relay network configurations.

Figure 15-9   *Graph of Approximate VCs Required by Network Topology*

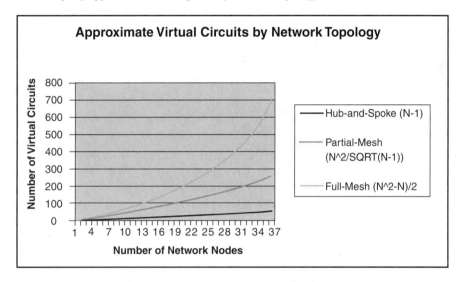

VCs often incur a financial obligation to the service provider. As Figure 15-9 illustrates, even relatively small networks can become quite costly very quickly based on the number of VCs alone. For this reason, hub-and-spoke network configurations are fairly common. As illustrated here, a 30-node network would require approximately 450 VCs in a fully meshed configuration, compared to the 29 VCs necessary to support a hub-and-spoke configuration.

To illustrate the potential cost savings of deploying a hub-and-spoke network over a fully meshed network environment, see Figure 15-10. As is reflected here, a difference of nearly 500 VCs exists between a fully meshed and a hub-and-spoke configuration. If it is not mandated that a fully meshed network be used, it is certainly more cost effective to design and implement a hub-and-spoke or partial-mesh configuration.

Figure 15-10 *Difference Between Fully Meshed (N^2) and Hub-and-Spoke (N-1) Network Configuration*

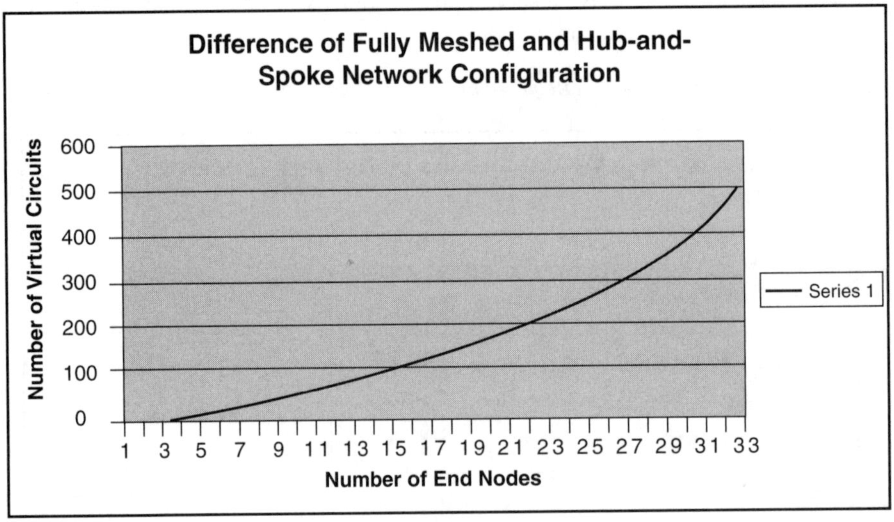

FECN and BECN

Congestion is inherent in any packet-switched network. Frame Relay networks are no exception. Frame Relay network implementations use a simple congestion-notification method rather than explicit flow control (such as the Transmission Control Protocol, or TCP) for each PVC or SVC; effectively reducing network overhead.

Two types of congestion-notification mechanisms are supported by Frame Relay:

- FECN
- BECN

FECN and BECN are each controlled by a single bit in the Frame Relay frame header.

NOTE   A Frame Relay frame is defined as a variable-length unit of data, in frame-relay format, that is transmitted through a Frame Relay network as pure data. Frames are found at Layer 2 of the OSI model, whereas packets are found at Layer 3.

The FECN bit is set by a Frame Relay network device, usually a switch, to inform the Frame Relay networking device that is receiving the frame that congestion was experienced in the path from origination to destination. The Frame Relay networking device that is receiving frames with the FECN bit will act as directed by the upper-layer protocols in operation. Depending on which upper-layer protocols are implemented, they will initiate flow-control operations. This flow-control action is typically the throttling back of data transmission, although some implementations can be designed to ignore the FECN bit and take no action.

Much like the FECN bit, a Frame Relay network device sets the BECN bit, usually a switch, to inform the Frame Relay networking device that is receiving the frame that congestion was experienced in the path traveling in the opposite direction of frames encountering a congested path. The upper-layer protocols (such as TCP) will initiate flow-control operations, dependent on which protocols are implemented. This flow-control action, illustrated in Figure 15-11, is typically the throttling back of data transmission, although some implementations can be designed to ignore the BECN bit and take no action.

Figure 15-11 *Frame Relay with FECN and BECN*

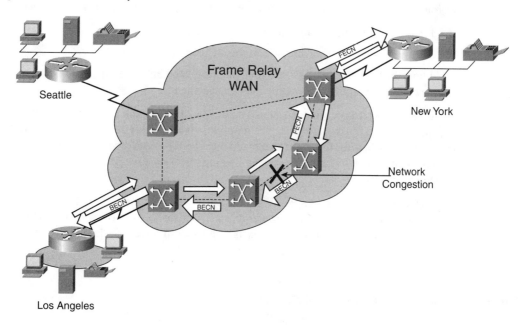

NOTE   The Cisco IOS can be configured for Frame Relay Traffic Shaping, which will act upon FECN and BECN indications. Enabling Frame Relay traffic shaping on an interface enables both traffic shaping and per-VC queuing on the interface's PVCs and SVCs. Traffic shaping enables the router to control the circuit's output rate and react to congestion notification information if it is also configured. To enable Frame-Relay Traffic shaping within the Cisco IOS on a per-VC basis, use the **frame-relay traffic-shaping** command.

Cisco also implements a traffic control mechanism called ForeSight. ForeSight is the network traffic control software used in some Cisco switches. The Cisco Frame Relay switch can extend ForeSight messages over a UNI, passing the backward congestion notification for VCs.

ForeSight allows Cisco Frame Relay routers to process and react to ForeSight messages and adjust VC level traffic shaping in a timely manner. ForeSight must be configured explicitly on both the Cisco router and the Cisco switch. ForeSight is enabled on the Cisco router when Frame Relay traffic shaping is configured. The router's response to ForeSight is not applied to any VC until the **frame-relay adaptive-shaping foresight** command is added to the VC's map-class. When ForeSight is enabled on the switch, the switch will periodically send out a ForeSight message based on the time value configured. The time interval can range from 40 to 5,000 milliseconds (ms).

For router ForeSight to work, the following conditions must exist on the Cisco router:

- Frame Relay traffic shaping must be enabled on the interface.
- The traffic shaping for a circuit must be adapted to ForeSight.

In addition, the UNI connecting to the router consolidated link layer management (CLLM) must be enabled, with the proper time interval specified.

Frame Relay Router ForeSight is enabled automatically when the **frame-relay traffic-shaping** command is used. However, the **map-class frame-relay** command and the **frame-relay adaptive-shaping foresight** command must both be issued before the router will respond to ForeSight and apply the traffic shaping effect on a specific interface, subinterface, or VC.

When a Cisco router receives a ForeSight message indicating that certain DLCIs are experiencing congestion, the Cisco router reacts by activating its traffic shaping function to slow down the output rate. The router reacts as it would if it were to detect the congestion by receiving a frame with the BECN bit set.

Frame Relay Virtual Circuit (VC) Parameters

Frame Relay VCs, both permanent (PVC) and switched (SVC), have three configurable parameters that must be agreed upon between each end node (origination and termination) and the Frame Relay network service provider.

These parameters are as follows:

- CIR
- DE
- VC identifiers
  - DLCIs for PVCs
  - X.121/E.164 addresses for SVCs

Frame Relay CIR

The CIR is the amount of bandwidth that will be delivered as "best-effort" across the Frame Relay backbone network. Network providers typically have provisions in their tariffs guaranteeing delivery of CIR traffic at some percentage. For example, a tariff might state a guarantee such as guaranteeing delivery of 99.9% CIR marked traffic.

CIR is measured in bytes over a periodic interval of time, expressed as T_C. B_C is the committed burst rate across the VC for that period of time. B_c can be represented by the formula $B_c = CIR \times T_c$.

B_c is the negotiated maximum amount of bits that a Frame Relay internetwork is committed to accept and transmit at the CIR. Excess of CIR is measured as B_e.

B_E is the number of bits that a Frame Relay internetwork will attempt to transfer after B_c is accommodated and is marked as DE.

T_C is the periodic interval of time over which B_C and B_E are measured. The T_C interval counter starts when data begins to enter into the Frame Relay network, and ends when data is no longer entering the network. When a new data stream enters the network, the T_C counter starts over.

Frame Relay PVCs are simplex connections. Each VC is configured with its own CIR, meaning an A ➧ B PVC could be configured for 64 kbps CIR, and a B ➧ A PVC could be configured with a 32 kbps CIR. It is up to the network designer/engineer to determine the proper amount of CIR required, generally based on user and application traffic.

Frame Relay Discard Eligibility (DE)

Frame Relay uses a bit in the frame header to indicate whether that frame can be discarded if congestion is encountered during transmission. The DE bit is part of the Frame Relay frame header's address field.

The DE bit can be set by the transmitting Frame Relay networking device to prioritize the frame because it has a lower priority than other outgoing frames. If the network becomes congested, frames with the DE bit marked will be discarded prior to frames that do not have the DE bit marked to relieve this congestion.

Figure 15-12 illustrates the process that each Frame Relay switch runs upon receipt of a frame for transmission.

Figure 15-12   *Frame Relay Data Frame Transmission Flowchart*

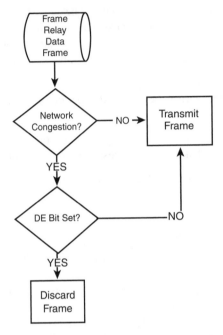

DE requires that the Frame Relay network interpret, and in some cases act on, the DE bit. Some networks take no action when the DE bit is set, and other networks will use the DE bit to determine which frames to discard. Often the DE bit is used to determine which frames should be dropped first or which frames have lower time sensitivity.

DE lists can be created within the Cisco routing device to identify the characteristics of frames eligible for discarding. DE groups can be specified to identify the DLCI that is affected.

When a DE frame is discarded, it is up to the upper-layer protocols, such as TCP, to determine the loss and effect corrective actions as determined by the protocol's data correction and retransmission algorithms.

NOTE   Within the Cisco IOS, the command used to define a DE list specifying the frames that can be dropped when the Frame Relay switch is congested is as follows (this command is entered in global configuration mode):

```
frame-relay de-list list-number {protocol protocol |
interface type number} characteristic
```

For example, the following command specifies that IP packets larger than 512 bytes (including the 4 byte Frame Relay encapsulation) will have the DE bit set:

```
frame-relay de-list 1 protocol ip gt 512
```

DE lists can be created based on the protocol or the interface, and on characteristics such as fragmentation of the frame, a specific TCP or User Datagram Protocol (UDP) port, an access list number, or a packet size (Layer 3 maximum transmission unit (MTU).

To define a DE group that is specifying the DE list and is DLCI-affected, the following command is used in interface configuration mode:

```
frame-relay de-group group-number dlci
```

For example, the following command specifies that group number 3 will be used for DLCI 170:

```
frame-relay de-group 3 170
```

PVC DLCIs

Although DLCI values can be 10, 16, or 23 bits in length, 10-bit DLCIs have become the *de facto* standard for Frame Relay WAN implementations.

The 10-bit DLCI values, as recommended by the Frame Relay Forum, are allocated as Table 15-5 indicates.

Table 15-5   *Frame Relay Forum 10 Bit DLCI Recommendations*

DLCI Value	Function
0	FRF—In-channel signaling
1 to 15	Reserved
16 to 1007	Available for VC endpoint assignment
1008 to 1022	Reserved
1023	LMI

The 10-bit DLCI values, as recommended by both the ANSI (T1.618) and the ITU-T (Q.922), are allocated as Table 15-6 indicates.

Table 15-6   *ANSI (T1.618) and ITU-T (Q.922) 10-Bit DLCI Recommendations*

DLCI Value	Function
0	In-channel signaling and management (LMI)
1 to 15	Reserved
16 to 991	Available for VC endpoint assignment
992 to 1007	Frame Relay bearer service Layer 2 management
1008 to 1022	Reserved
1023	Reserved for in-channel layer management

NOTE	The number of DLCIs configurable per port varies depending on the traffic level. All 1,000 DLCIs can be used. However, 200 to 300 is a common maximum. If the DLCIs are used for broadcast traffic, 30 to 50 is a more realistic number due to CPU overhead in generating broadcasts.

Within the Cisco IOS, the number of PVCs that is configurable per interface is limited to 255; this means that a Frame Relay serial interface is limited to 255 subinterfaces. The 255 subinterface limit is dependent on how they are configured; however, no more than 255 point-to-point subinterfaces with one DLCI each can exist.

You must consider and deal with some practical performance issues on an individual case basis. The higher the CIR on the DLCIs, the more impact that the individual interface's ability will have on supporting the traffic flow.

A T1 could certainly be expected to handle 24 56 K DLCIs with little problem. However, substantial broadcast traffic could affect the performance. If, for example, 50 56 K DLCIs are configured into a T1 interface, traffic issues, such as congestion and dropped traffic, will arise. This configuration is referred to as *oversubscription*. For example, consider the following two scenarios:

A network configuration that consists of 24 (DLCIs/PVCs) × 56 kbps (CIR per PVC) = 1.344 Mbps is well within the T1 bandwidth limitation of 1.344/1.536 Mbps (depending on physical line coding; AMI = 1.344 Mbps, B8ZS = 1.536 Mbps).

This configuration is not oversubscribing the interface because available bandwidth is sufficient to support the traffic requirement: 1.344 Mbps ≤ 1.344/1.536 Mbps.

A network configuration of 50 (DLCIs/PVCs) × 56 kbps (CIR per PVC) = 2.800 Mbps far exceeds the maximum bandwidth supported by a T1 limitation of 1.344/1.536 Mbps (depending on physical line coding; AMI = 1.344 Mbps, B8ZS = 1.536 Mbps).

This configuration is oversubscribing the interface because the bandwidth available is not sufficient to support the traffic requirement: 2.800 Mbps ≥ 1.344/1.536 Mbps.

SVC X.121/E.164 Addressing

X.121 is a hierarchical addressing scheme that was originally designed to number X.25 nodes. X.121 addresses are up to 14 digits in length and are structured as follows:

- Country Code: 3 digits

  The first digit is a zone number that identifies a part of the world. For example, Zone 2 covers Europe and Zone 3 includes North America). The zone numbers can be found in Appendix C, "List of ITU-TX.121 Data Country or Geographical Codes." These codes can also be found in ITU-T Recommendation X.121.

    — Service Provider: 1 digit

    — Terminal Number: Up to 10 digits

- E.164 is a hierarchical global telecommunications numbering plan, similar to the North American Number Plan (NANP). E.164 addresses are up to 15 digits in length and are structured as follows:

- Country Code: 1, 2, or 3 digits

  This code is based on the international telephony numbering plan and can be found in Appendix D, "International Country Codes." These codes can also be found in any phone book.

- National Destination Code and Subscriber Number: Up to 14 digits in length (maximum length is dependent on the length of the Country Code).

  Subaddress: Up to 40 digits

Frame Relay Status Polling

The Frame Relay Customer Premises Equipment (CPE) polls the switch at set intervals to determine the status of both the network and DLCI connections. A Link Integrity Verification (LIV) packet exchange takes place about every 10 seconds, verifying that the connection is still good. The LIV also provides information to the network that the CPE is active, and this status is exported at the other end. Approximately every minute, a Full Status (FS) exchange occurs, passing information regarding which DLCIs are configured and active. Until the first FS exchange occurs, the CPE does not know which DLCIs are active, and as such, no data transfer can take place.

Frame Relay Error Handling

Frame Relay uses the Cyclic Redundancy Check (CRC) method for error detection. Frame Relay services perform error detection rather than error checking; error detection is based on the premise that the underlying network media is reliable. Frame Relay error detection uses the CRC checksum to determine if the frame is received by the Frame Relay networking device (router or switch) with, or without, error. Error correction is left to the upper-layer protocols, such as the TCP (of the TCP/IP protocol suite).

NOTE	Error detection detects errors, but does not make attempts to correct the condition. Error correction detects errors and attempts to correct the condition, usually under control or direction of a higher-layer protocol. The termination node performs error detection.

Frame Relay Frame Format

Figure 15-13 illustrates the standard Frame Relay frame format.

Figure 15-13 *Frame Relay Standard Frame Format*

Flags (8 Bytes)	Address (16 Bytes)	Data (Variable up to 4096 or 8192 Bytes)	FCS (16 Bytes)	Flags (8 Bytes)

Table 15-7 presents a description of each of the Frame Relay standard frame fields.

Table 15-7 *Frame Relay Standard Frame Field Descriptions*

Field	Description
Flags	Delimits the beginning and end of the frame. The value of this field is always the same and is represented as hexadecimal 7E or as binary 0111110.
Address	Contains the following information: • DLCI—The 10-bit DLCI is the most significant part of the Frame Relay header. This value identifies and represents the VC[*] between the FRAD and the Frame Relay [network service provider] switch. Each VC that is multiplexed onto a physical channel will be represented by a unique DLCI. The DLCI values have local significance only, meaning they are only significant to the physical channel on which they reside. Devices on each end of a VC can use different DLCIs to identify the same VC. • Extended Address (EA)—Used to indicate whether the byte in which the EA value is 1 is the last addressing field. If the value is 1, then the current byte is determined to be the last DLCI byte. Although current Frame Relay implementations all use a two-byte DLCI, this capability does allow for the use of longer DLCIs in the future. The eighth bit of each byte of the Address field is used to indicate the EA.

Table 15-7 *Frame Relay Standard Frame Field Descriptions*

Field	Description
	MPLS labels use the extended address field of the Frame Relay frame header.
	• C/R—The C/R (Command/Response) bit that follows is the most significant DLCI byte in the Address field. The C/R bit is not currently defined.
	• Congestion Control—Consists of the 3 bits that control the Frame Relay congestion-notification mechanism. These are the FECN, BECN, and DE bits; they are the last 3 bits in the Address field.
	• Forward-Explicit Congestion Notification (FECN)—A single-bit field that can be set to a value of 1 by a switch to indicate to an end DTE device (router) that congestion was encountered in the direction of the frame transmission from source to destination. The primary benefit of both the FECN and BECN fields is the capability of higher-layer protocols to react intelligently to these congestion indicators. Currently, DECnet and OSI are the only higher-layer protocols that implement these capabilities.
	• Backward-Explicit Congestion Notification (BECN)—A single-bit field that, when set to a value of 1 by a switch, indicates that congestion was encountered in the network in the direction opposite of the frame transmission from source to destination. Explicit congestion notification is proposed as the congestion avoidance policy. It tries to keep the network operating at its desired equilibrium point so that a certain quality of service (QOS) for the network can be met. To do so, special congestion control bits have been incorporated into the address field of the Frame Relay: FECN and BECN. The basic idea is to avoid data accumulation inside the network.
	• Discard Eligibility (DE)—Set by the Frame Relay networking device (router) to indicate that the marked frame is of lesser importance relative to other frames being transmitted. Frames that are marked as "DE" should be discarded before other frames in a congested network. This allows for basic prioritization in Frame Relay networks.
Data	Contains encapsulated upper-layer data. Each frame in this variable-length field includes a user data or payload field that will vary in length up to 4096 bytes. This field serves to transport the higher-layer protocol data unit (PDU) through a Frame Relay network.

(continues)

Table 15-7   *Frame Relay Standard Frame Field Descriptions (Continued)*

Field	Description
Frame Check Sequence (FCS)	Ensures the integrity of transmitted data. This value is computed by the source device and is verified by the receiver to ensure integrity of the data transmission.

*Note: Physical channel = serial interface; VC = sub-interface.

Frame Relay LMI

The Frame Relay LMI is a set of Frame Relay specification enhancements. The original LMI was developed in 1990 by the Gang of Four (Cisco, DEC, Nortel, and StrataCom). LMI includes support for the following:

- Keepalive mechanisms—Verify the flow of data

- Multicast mechanisms—Provide the network server with local and multicast DLCI information

- Global addressing—Give DLCIs global rather than local significance

- Status mechanisms—Provide ongoing status reports on the switch-known DLCIs

Figure 15-14 illustrates the endpoints for LMI status messages.

Figure 15-14   *LMI Status Message Endpoints*

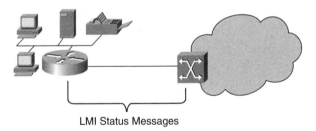

LMI Status Messages

The original LMI supports a number of features, or enhancements, to the original Frame Relay protocol, for managing Frame Relay internetworks. The most notable Frame Relay LMI extensions include support for the following:

- Global addressing—The LMI global addressing extension gives Frame Relay DLCI values a global, rather than local, significance. These global DLCI values become Frame Relay networking device addresses that are unique in the Frame Relay WAN.

NOTE   As discussed earlier in this chapter, global addressing has an inherent limitation in that no more than 992 DLCIs (1024 DLCIs less the 32 reserved DLCIs) can be used. In a Frame Relay network of more than 992 sites, global addressing will not work. Apart from global addressing of DLCIs, the LMI status message presents an inherent limitation on the number of DLCIs that can be supported by an interface. Cisco has published a brief detailing these limitations at http://www.cisco.com/warp/public/125/lmidlci.html.

- Virtual circuit status messages—Provide communication and synchronization between Frame Relay network access devices (FRADs) and the network provider devices (switches). These messages report (in a regular interval) the status of PVCs, which prevents data from being pointed to a PVC that does not exist.

- Multicasting—Supports the assignment management of multicast groups. Multicasting preserves bandwidth by enabling routing updates and address-resolution (such as ARP, RARP) messages to be sent only to specific groups of routers.

LMI VC status messages provide communication and synchronization between Frame Relay DTE and DCE devices. These messages are used to periodically report on the status of PVCs, which prevents data from being sent into black holes (over PVCs that no longer exist).

LMI Types

Three types of LMI are found in Frame Relay network implementations:

- ANSI T1.617 (Annex D)—Maximum number of connections (PVCs) supported is limited to 976. LMI type ANSI T1.627 (Annex D) uses DLCI 0 to carry local (link) management information.

- ITU-T Q.933 (Annex A)—Like LMI type Annex D, the maximum number of connections (PVCs) supported is limited to 976. LMI type ITU-T Q.933 (Annex A) also uses DLCI 0 to carry local (link) management information.

- LMI (Original)—Maximum number of connections (PVCs) supported is limited to 992. LMI type LMI uses DLCI 1023 to carry local (link) management information.

NOTE   LMI Type LMI (Original) is annotated as LMI type Cisco within the Cisco IOS.

NOTE	The frame MTU setting impacts LMI messages. If PVCs appear to be "bouncing," (that is, repeated up/down indications), it might be because of the MTU size of the Frame Relay frame. If the MTU size is too small, not all PVC status messages will be communicated between the service provider edge and the Frame Relay access router. If this condition is suspected, the next step is to contact the network service provider to troubleshoot.

LMI Frame Format

Figure 15-15 illustrates the LMI frame format to which Frame Relay LMI frames must conform, as deemed by the LMI specification.

Figure 15-15 *LMI Frame Format*

Flag (1 Byte)	LMI DLCI (2 Bytes)	Unnumbered Information Indicator (1 Byte)	Protocol Discriminator (1Byte)	Call Reference (1 Byte)	Message Type (1 Byte)	Information Elements (Variable)	FCS (2 Bytes)	Flag (1 Byte)

Table 15-8 presents a description of each LMI field.

Table 15-8 *LMI Frame Format Field Description*

Field	Description
Flag	Delimits the start and end of the LMI frame.
LMI DLCI	Identifies the frame as an LMI frame rather than a Frame Relay data frame. The DLCI value is dependent on the LMI specification used; LMI (original) uses DLCI 1023, LMI (Annex A) and LMI (Annex D) use DLCI 0.
Unnumbered Information Indicator	Sets the poll/final bit to zero (0).
Protocol Discriminator	Always contains a value indicating that the frame is an LMI frame.
Call Reference	Always contains zeros. This field is currently not used for any purpose.
Message Type	Labels the frame as one of the following message types: • Status-inquiry message—Allows a user device to inquire about the status of the network. • Status message—Responds to status-inquiry messages. Status messages include keepalive and PVC status messages.

Table 15-8   *LMI Frame Format Field Description*

Field	Description
Information Elements	Contains a variable number of individual information elements (IEs). IEs consist of the following fields: • IE Identifier—Uniquely identifies the IE. • IE Length—Indicates the length of the IE. • Data—Consists of one or more bytes containing encapsulated upper-layer data.
Frame Check Sequence (FCS)	Ensures the integrity of transmitted data.

LMI Extensions

The LMI global addressing extension gives Frame Relay DLCI values global rather than local significance. DLCI values become DTE addresses that are unique in the Frame Relay WAN. The global addressing extension adds functionality and manageability to Frame Relay internetworks. Individual network interfaces and the end nodes attached to them can be identified by using standard address-resolution and discovery techniques. Additionally, the entire Frame Relay WAN appears as a LAN to routers on the periphery.

The LMI multicasting extension allows multicast groups to be assigned. Multicasting saves bandwidth by allowing routing updates and address-resolution messages to be sent only to specific groups of routers. The extension also transmits reports on the status of multicast groups in update messages.

Frame Relay Applications

Traditionally, four networking suites are deployed using Frame Relay as the Layer 2 transport mechanism:

• TCP/IP Suite
• Novell IPX Suite
• IBM Systems Network Architecture (SNA) Suite
• VoFr

The following sections will discuss the application of these protocol suites across Frame Relay WANs and some of the special issues, challenges, and solutions that have been developed.

Frame Relay and the TCP/IP Suite

The TCP/IP Suite comprises two components: the IP operating at Layer 3 (Network) and the Transmission Control Protocol (TCP) operating at Layer 4. IP is a best-effort delivery protocol, relying on the transmission control mechanisms (that is, packet acknowledgement, sequencing) supported by TCP. IP datagrams, or *packets*, are routed from source to destination based on the address information found in the packet header. IP traffic is typically bursty in nature, making it an ideal network-layer protocol for Frame Relay WANs.

Figure 15-16 illustrates the correlation between the OSI model and an IP-over-Frame Relay implementation.

Figure 15-16   *OSI Reference Model with IP/Frame Relay*

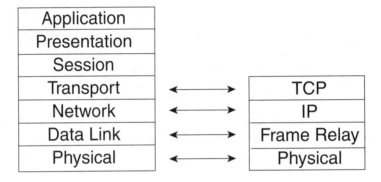

Virtual LANs (VLANs) and IP Subnets

Multiple IP FRADs or routers can be interconnected via a Frame Relay WAN in a configuration behaving like a Virtual LAN (VLAN), or an IP subnet.

NOTE   An IP subnet is a set of systems, or nodes/hosts, that share certain characteristics, such as the following:

- Their IP addressing starts with the same network and subnet numbers.

- Any system, or node/host, can communicate directly with any other system in the subnet. Data traffic in the same subnet will not flow through an intermediate router.

Figure 15-17 illustrates three routers that are interconnected by Frame Relay PVCs in a fully meshed configuration.

Figure 15-17 *Frame Relay with IP Subnet*

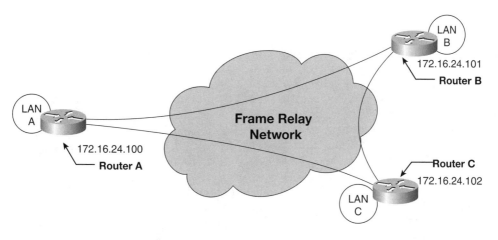

NOTE   Fully meshed configurations enable every device in the system to directly communicate with every other device in the same system. Partially meshed configurations, generally known as hub-and-spoke, enable communication between devices with a central hub point providing the interconnection between end nodes.

A fully meshed Frame Relay network can be treated as a VLAN or a single IP subnet. As illustrated in Figure 15-17, three end nodes, each with an IP address assigned, are interconnected across the Frame Relay network via the Frame Relay interface on each FRAD/router. Each of these addresses shares the same network and subnet numbers, with only the host portion of the address differing.

It is worth noting that in this configuration, each Frame Relay interface is supporting multiple VCs with only a single IP address assigned to that interface, in a broadcast configuration. Another common Frame Relay configuration would have an IP address for each VC on the Frame Relay interface. This is enabled by the use of subinterfaces and will be discussed in more detail later in this chapter.

Figure 15-18 reflects the addition of a fourth router (Router D) with a different IP address from the rest of the subnet assigned to the Frame Relay interface. Router D is not part of the full mesh because it is only connected to Router B. Because Router D is part of a different subnet, new IP addresses are assigned to each endpoint of the permanent virtual circuit (PVC).

Figure 15-18 *Frame Relay with Two IP Subnets*

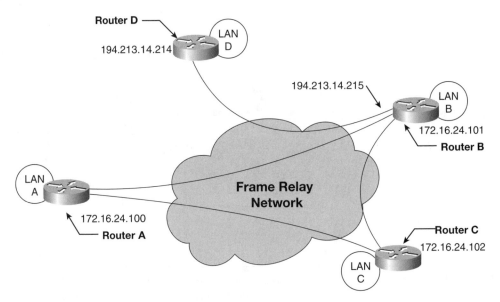

In summary, the following rules apply when dealing with Frame Relay implementations using virtual IP subnets:

- A single IP address can be assigned to the entire Frame Relay interface
- When one or more DLCIs are used requiring the use of subinterfaces, each subinterface is assigned an IP address.

Address Resolution Protocol (ARP)

LAN systems transmit data to one another by wrapping, or encapsulating, the payload in a LAN frame whose header contains the Media Access Control (MAC) address of the destination's LAN host network interface card (NIC). A LAN system cannot communicate with a neighbor until it has discovered this neighbor's MAC address. The discovery method used is set by the procedures outlined in the Address Resolution Protocol (ARP).

To send an IP datagram to a particular IP address, the network driver must have a method to find out whether the IP address belongs to a computer on the network. If the IP address does belong to a computer on the network, the driver must know the hardware address of the computer to transmit the packet over the network. This is accomplished in Ethernet-type devices using an Internet protocol called the Address Resolution Protocol (ARP). This protocol is described in detail in RFC 826.

Figure 15-19 illustrates how ARP operates in an IP network. Host A, with an IP address of 198.24.5.1, wants to establish a connection with Server A, with an IP address of

198.24.5.100. Host A will broadcast an ARP query message across the medium asking the system, or host, with IP address 198.24.5.100 to respond. Server A replies to the ARP query providing its Layer 2 MAC address. In this example, the MAC address is 00-60-08-BF-4C-3E.

Figure 15-19 *Host A ARP Discovery of Server A MAC Address*

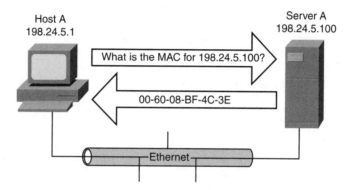

Host A maintains an Ethernet MAC table that records the Layer 3 Network (IP) address with its associated Layer 2 (MAC) address. In this example, Host A's ARP table would look something similar to Table 15-9.

Table 15-9 *Host A ARP Table*

IP Address	MAC Address
192.24.5.100	00-60-08-BF-4C-3E

NOTE   The ARP table can be viewed from any host by entering the command **arp** at a DOS prompt:

```
C:\>arp
```

then it displays and modifies the IP-to-Physical address translation tables used by ARP:

```
ARP -s inet_addr eth_addr [if_addr]
ARP -d inet_addr [if_addr]
ARP -a [inet_addr] [-N if_addr]
```

-a   Displays current ARP entries by interrogating the current protocol data. If inet_addr is specified, the IP and Physical addresses for only the specified computer are displayed. If more than one network interface uses ARP, entries for each ARP table are displayed.

-g   Same as -a.

inet_addr   Specifies an Internet address.

-N if_addr Displays the ARP entries for the network interface specified by if_addr.

-d	Deletes the host specified by inet_addr. inet_addr can be wildcarded with * to delete all hosts.
-s	Adds the host and associates the Internet address inet_addr with the physical address eth_addr. The physical address is given as six hexadecimal bytes separated by hyphens. The entry is permanent.
eth_addr	Specifies a physical address.
if_addr	If present, this specifies the Internet address of the interface whose address translation table should be modified. If not present, the first applicable interface will be used.

Example:

> arp -s 157.55.85.212 00-aa-00-62-c6-09   .... Adds a static entry.

> arp -a   .... Displays the arp table.

Server A, upon receipt of the ARP query, will place the MAC address of Host A into its ARP table.

Inverse ARP

Inverse ARP will be discussed here as it applies to IP networking and address discovery. Inverse ARP operates in a similar fashion for Frame Relay DLCI discovery for AppleTalk, Banyan VINES, DECnet, Novell IPX, and Xerox Network Services (XNS).

The motivation for the development of Inverse ARP is a result of the desire to make dynamic address resolution within Frame Relay both possible and efficient. PVCs and, eventually, SVCs are identified by a DLCI. These DLCIs define a single virtual connection through the WAN and are the Frame Relay equivalent to a hardware address.

Periodically, through the exchange of signaling messages, a network might announce a new VC with its corresponding DLCI. Unfortunately, protocol addressing is not included in the announcement. The station receiving such an indication will learn of the new connection, but will not be able to address the other side. Without a new configuration or mechanism for discovering the protocol address of the other side, this new VC is unusable. RFC 1293 defines Inverse ARP in more detail.

Whereas ARP enables a system to build a table mapping the LAN system's IP address to the Layer 2 MAC address, Inverse ARP is used to build a similar table mapping the connected system's IP address (by Frame Relay Virtual Circuit) to the Layer 2 DLCI on the connected system.

Figure 15-20 illustrates a four-node Frame Relay WAN, each site interconnected by a Frame Relay PVC.

Figure 15-20 *Four-Node Frame Relay WAN with DLCI Assignments*

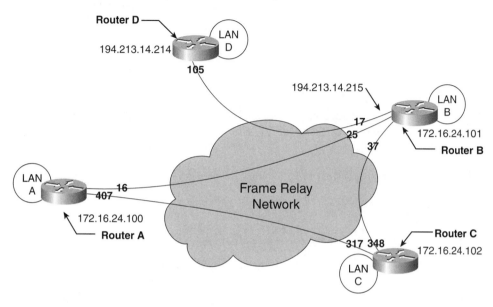

Router B needs to determine the IP address of its neighbors prior to the forwarding of traffic across the interconnection. Router B also needs to map each neighbor's IP address to the DLCI that will be used to reach that neighbor. Router B essentially needs a table similar to Table 15-10.

Table 15-10 *Router B's Inverse ARP Table*

IP Address	DLCI
172.16.24.102	37
172.16.24.100	25
194.213.14.214	17

The IP Address column identifies the IP address of Router B's neighbor; the associated right column identifies the corresponding DLCI assignment.

Although this table could be built manually, it is far more efficient to let the Inverse ARP mechanism build it. Each router uses a simple two-step procedure to build this table. These steps include the following:

1 Each router sends a message across each connected VC asking for the IP address of the distant end.

2 The sending router then records the IP address and the corresponding DLCI into its tables.

ARP is used when the Layer 3 address is known but the corresponding Layer 2 address is
unknown, typically the MAC address. Inverse ARP is used when the Layer 2 address is
known, typically the DLCI, but the corresponding Layer 3 address is unknown.

Inverse ARP and Routing Tables

The information learned via Inverse ARP is of significant use to IP routers. Using the
network represented by Figure 15-21, suppose that Router D has message traffic to forward
to Router A.

Figure 15-21   *Four-Node Frame Relay WAN with IP Address and DLCI Assignments*

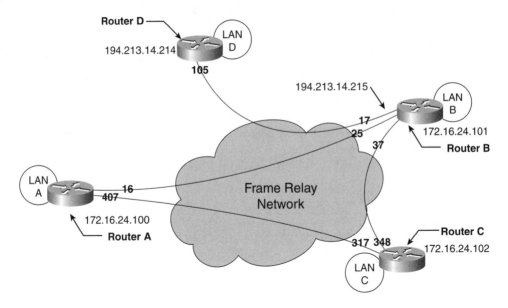

Router D's routing table would look something like Table 15-11.

Table 15-11   *Router D's Routing Table*

Destination IP Address	Forwarding IP Address	Via DLCI
172.16.24.100	194.213.14.215	105
172.16.24.102	194.213.14.215	105
172.16.24.101	194.213.14.215	105

Router B's routing table would look something like Table 15-12.

Table 15-12 *Router B's Routing Table*

Destination IP Address	Forwarding IP Address	Via DLCI
194.213.14.214	194.213.14.214*	17
172.16.24.100	172.16.24.100*	25
172.16.24.102	172.16.24.102*	37

*This would be identified as a directly connected route in the routing table, identified by "C" when using the **show ip route** command from the IOS command prompt.

Router C's routing table would look something like Table 15-13.

Table 15-13 *Router C's Routing Table*

Destination IP Address	Forwarding IP Address	Via DLCI
172.16.24.100	172.16.24.100*	317
194.213.14.214	172.16.24.101	348
172.16.24.101	172.16.24.101*	348

*This would be identified as a directly connected route in the routing table, identified by "C" when using the **show ip route** command from the IOS command prompt.

Frame Relay and the Novell IPX Suite

Novell IPX implementations over Frame Relay are similar to IP network implementation. Whereas a TCP/IP implementation would require the mapping of Layer 3 IP addresses to a DLCI, Novell IPX implementations require the mapping of the Layer 3 IPX address to a DLCI. Special consideration needs to be made with IPX over Frame Relay implementations regarding the impact of Novell RIP (distance-vector algorithm) or NLSP (NetWare Link Services Protocol, link-state algorithm) and SAP (Service Advertising Protocol) message traffic to a Frame Relay internetwork.

Frame Relay IPX Bandwidth Guidelines

IPX can consume large amounts of bandwidth very quickly by virtue of its broadcast announcement-based design. Following are some considerations that demonstrate some methods to consider to manage the IPX traffic and minimize its impact on a Frame Relay WAN.

To reduce overhead in a Frame Relay network, implement the Burst Mode NetWare Loadable Module (NLM). Burst Mode opens the IPX window to avoid waiting for one acknowledgement (ACK) per IPX packet, and allows a maximum window of 128.

Another consideration is the implementation of the Large Internet Packet EXchange (LIPX) NLM if not version 4.X or higher. LIPX will allow for larger-sized packets between client and server. (Often in the case of Frame Relay WANs, the client and server will be connected via Frame Relay VC.) Native IPX without LIPX allows for a maximum payload frame size of 512 bytes; LIPX extends the packet size to 1000 to 4000 bytes. The larger packet size consumes less processing power from the Frame Relay access devices, in turn increasing throughput.

NOTE   Because Ethernet and Token Ring LANs support higher frame sizes, the native IPX 512 byte frame limitation has an adverse effect on network throughput across WAN routers.

If you are working with an older version of Novell NetWare (v3.11), implement the NLSP NLM for network routing. NLSP only sends routing information when an event happens (link failure) or every two hours. The standard RIP [routing] protocol sends its entire routing table to all other routers every 30 seconds. NLSP uses less bandwidth over the WAN, ensuring more bandwidth is available for user data traffic.

NOTE   SAP utilizes IPX packets to broadcast or advertise available services on a NetWare LAN. NetWare servers use these SAP packets to advertise their address, services available, and name to all clients every 60 seconds. All servers on a NetWare LAN listen for these SAP messages and store them in their own server information table. Because most Novell clients utilize local resources, the resources should be advertised on a local basis and not broadcast across the Frame Relay WAN.

Novell SAP

Novell SAP traffic can consume an adverse amount of WAN bandwidth. The router will send, without delay, a SAP update when a change is detected. It is recommended that you modify the SAP delay timer to "slow down" these delays, enabling more user traffic to get through the WAN.

The Cisco IOS command **ipx output-sap-delay 55** will send SAP packets with a 55 ms delay between packets. Without a delay, all packets in the update are sent immediately, and the Frame Relay router consumes all available buffer space. With no bandwidth or buffer space available, user traffic will be dropped, requiring retransmission.

The **ipx output-sap-delay** command causes the router to grab only one buffer a time, leaving the remaining buffer space available to queue user traffic for transmission across the WAN.

The **ipx sap-interval** and **ipx update-interval** IOS commands can be used to change the frequency of the updates between IPX-enabled devices. All IPX-enabled devices (routers) interconnected across the Frame Relay WAN must be set to the same update interval. Otherwise, updates will not be synchronized, resulting in *phantom routes*—routes that appear and disappear with each update.

In a multipoint Frame Relay "broadcast" environment, in which message traffic is propagated to all sites and subinterfaces are not employed, SAP advertisements will be propagated to all sites as well.

NOTE   The absence of the **broadcast** parameter in the Frame Relay map configuration will prevent both IPX RIP and SAP advertisements from being propagated.

Whereas point-to-point Frame Relay WAN links do not employ a map statement, IPX RIP and SAP updates will be propagated at will between each site. It is recommended that you use IPX RIP and SAP filters in this configuration to minimize the Frame Relay WAN traffic.

Frame Relay and the IBM SNA Suite

IBM mainframes and SNA were the *de facto* standard of the networking community for many years, predominantly in the 1970s and 1980s. IP has since replaced SNA as the dominant internetworking protocol suite. SNA is still very much "at large," especially in large legacy networking systems, such as those found within the banking and financial industries.

These IBM SNA networking environments were ideally suited to the internetworking environment enabled by Frame Relay network implementations due to the lower-cost and cleaner architecture, compared to that of traditional point-to-point private line interconnections. Whereas point-to-point network architecture requires several lines and interfaces, Frame Relay networks enable a single line (serial interface) and multiple subinterfaces, one for each SNA communication session (Frame Relay VC).

Migration of a legacy SNA network from a point-to-point infrastructure to a more economical and manageable Frame Relay infrastructure is attractive; however, some challenges exist when SNA traffic is sent across Frame Relay connections. IBM SNA was designed to operate across reliable communication links that supported predictable response times. The challenge that arises with Frame Relay network implementations is that Frame Relay service tends to have unpredictable and variable response times, for which SNA was not designed to interoperate or able to manage within its traditional design.

Migration from SDLC to Frame Relay networking environments will require an upgrade to the communications software packages in both the FEPs and SNA controllers.

Typically, SNA controllers, routers, and FRADs encapsulate SNA traffic as multiprotocol data, as described in the Frame Relay Forum's FRF 3.1 Implementation Agreement.

Traditional IBM SNA Network Configuration

Figure 15-22 illustrates a traditional IBM SNA network configuration.

Figure 15-22 *Traditional IBM SNA Network Configuration*

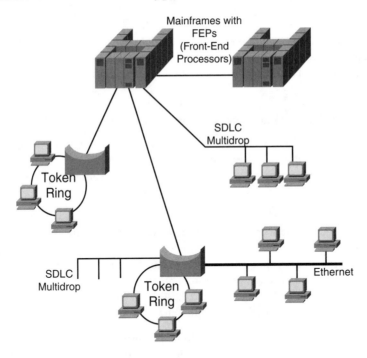

An SNA network has two primary components:

- Front-end processors (FEPs)—FEPs offload the coordination effort required to enable and support communication between IBM hosts and (potentially) thousands of remote devices.

- Remote controllers—Remote controllers are located at remote locations and are used to interconnect LANs and low-bandwidth (typically 9.6 kbps or 56 kbps) leased lines. Remote controllers concentrate several sources of remote traffic onto one high bandwidth connection to the front-end processor.

IBM's SNA environment supports the implementation of multidrop technology, making multipoint leased line configurations more cost effective versus each SNA drop possessing its own leased line. In the multidrop environment, several devices share the same leased line with the front-end processor or remote controller, polling these devices and allowing each device a turn to communicate with the mainframe.

The IBM SNA environment relies heavily upon the FEP's polling mechanisms because the FEP controls when each of its connected remote devices can send and receive data. The SNA infrastructure is based on this polling methodology.

When the FEP polls the remote device, it expects to see a response within a preconfigured timeout period. This timeout threshold is typically a fairly small period of time, generally a few seconds. If the timeout period expires, the poll is retransmitted. Frame discards and late frame arrivals (usually caused by network congestion) can disrupt SNA communication.

Figure 15-23 illustrates a Frame Relay implementation, replacing point-to-point leased lines, supporting an IBM SNA infrastructure.

Figure 15-23 *IBM SNA Implementation over Frame Relay*

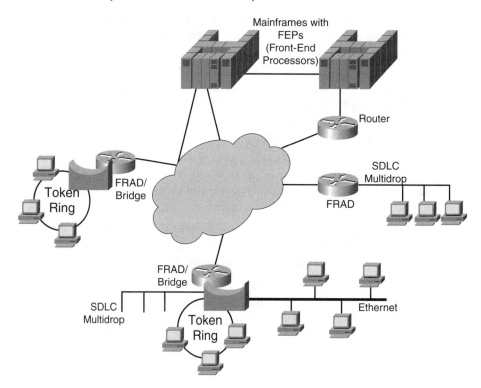

SNA Data Link Protocols

Two reliable data link protocols are used for FEP/controller communication in the IBM SNA environment: Synchronous Data Link Control (SDLC) and Logical Link Control, type 2 (LLC2).

Modern SNA networks also support end-to-end sessions set up by the Advanced Peer-to-Peer Networking (APPN) protocol. Figure 15-24 illustrates an APPN infrastructure supporting communication between a mainframe, AS/400 hosts, and LAN systems.

NOTE   APPN relies on LLC2 links.

IBM offers an extension to APPN that can optionally operate without LLC2: High Performance Routing (HPR). HPR can operate without an underlying [reliable] data link protocol. Retransmission and flow control is performed end-to-end by a higher layer protocol, similar to TCP within the TCP/IP protocol suite.

HPR traffic that does not operate on top of an LLC2 link can support transmission across Frame Relay links without encountering the issues associated with reliable links, such as SDLC or LLC2. An example of reliable link issues not found with HPR is an SDLC or LLC2 poll timeout.

Figure 15-24 *APPN Network*

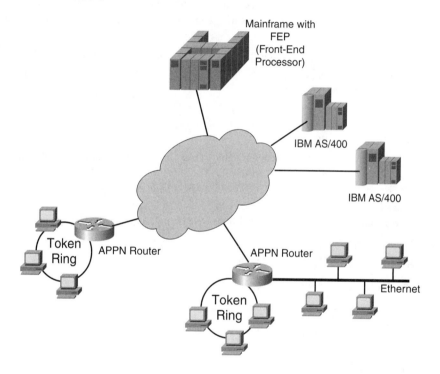

Mainframe with FEP (Front-End Processor)

IBM AS/400

IBM AS/400

Token Ring

APPN Router

APPN Router

Ethernet

Token Ring

SDLC and LLC2

The IBM SDLC protocol was designed for SNA-based networks and has a number of features that must be addressed when leased-lines are replaced by Frame Relay circuits. These features include the following:

- SDLC is a master/slave polling protocol—An FEP or controller polls remote devices to ascertain whether they have data to be sent or received. SDLC polling traffic is heavy and consumes bandwidth. In addition, the FEP or controller must receive poll responses within a strictly predictable time limit, usually measured in a few seconds.

- SDLC makes liberal use of control frames for flow control—A Frame Relay circuit that is carrying raw SDLC traffic will be congested with frequent SDLC polls and other control traffic.

- Each SDLC information frame is numbered in sequence and contains frame acknowledgements—After a preset number of frames have been sent, data transmission will not proceed unless the sender receives an acknowledgement from the terminating partner (receiver).

- SDLC is not used for LAN peer-to-peer communications—SNA LAN frames contain an LLC2 header that contains both the frame sequence and the acknowledgement numbers.

- LLC2 does not have the polling overhead attributed to SDLC—LLC2 does have the overhead associated with reliable, ordered, flow-controlled delivery of data across a communications link.

Data-Link Switching (DLSw)

Data-link switching (DLSw) is a means of transporting SNA and NetBIOS traffic across a network using many different protocols. The original RFC 1434 described DLSw, but that RFC has been superceded by RFC 1795, which describes DLSw version 1. More recently, scalability enhancements have been introduced in DLSw version 2. Cisco has introduced some enhancements in its DLSw+ implementation that are backward compatible with both version 1 and version 2.

DLSw has the following advantages over SRB:

- DLSw gets around the SRB 7-hop limit.
- DLSw allows multiple connections across a network.
- DLSw increases session response times.
- DLSw provides flow control.
- DLSw reroutes traffic around broken links.
- DLSw removes the SRB heavy broadcast traffic.

Additionally, DLSw implementations provide SDLC to LLC2 conversion, eliminating the need for many Front End Processor (FEP) ports. DLSw supports RFC 1490, enabling LLC2 over Frame Relay and DLSw prioritization.

DLSw uses the Switch-to-Switch Protocol (SSP) in place of source route bridging (SRB) between routers. SSP is used to create DLSw peer connections, locate resources, forward data, and handle flow control and error recovery. TCP is used for DLSw encapsulation. A newer, standard version of DLSw is not restricted to TCP for encapsulation services.

The routers are called data-link switches. The data-link connections (DLCs) are terminated at the router, or data-link switch, so that the Routing Information Field (RIF) ends at a virtual ring within the router. Because DLCs are locally terminated, they can be locally acknowledged. This local acknowledgement means that the necessity for link layer acknowledgements or keeping alive messages to run across the WAN do not exist, minimizing session timeouts. Because the RIF ends at the peer router at each end, six hops can be added on each side of the virtual ring, thereby extending the network. With remote source-route bridging (RSRB), the RIF is carried all the way through the virtual ring, thereby limiting the number of hops. With DLSw, the virtual ring can be different in each peer because of the RIF termination.

Frame relay circuits that are carrying reliable link traffic incur a substantial amount of increased overhead. One Frame Relay circuit has the potential to carry several separate reliable links. Each link requires acknowledgement and flow control messages, which in turn require available bandwidth to carry the additional traffic.

The carrying of LLC2 links across a frame circuit can be avoided with the use of DLSw, as illustrated in Figure 15-25.

Figure 15-25 *Data Link Switching (DLSw)*

When DLSw is implemented, the LLC2 links are terminated at each router. Incoming data is transmitted across the Frame Relay WAN via a TCP session and is then forwarded across a new LLC2 link.

NOTE   DLSw is not constrained to Frame Relay WANs; DLSw interoperates with any WAN technology.

The SNA traffic is preserved by the TCP sessions that support reliable data transfer. The TCP protocol, by its nature and design, adjusts well to sporadic transmission delays, efficiently manages acknowledgements, and carries out flow control without adding overhead to the communications flow.

Implementing DLSw has a disadvantage in that the TCP/IP headers add extra overhead to the transmitted data. This is generally worth the tradeoff compared to the overhead involved with the management of multiple independent LLC2 links.

SNA and DLSw Traffic Management

Following is an example of an access list enabling SNA traffic to be passed across a DLSw link:

```
access-list 200 permit 0x0d0d 0x0101
access-list 200 deny 0x0000 0xffff
dlsw remote-peer 0 tcp 1.1.1.1 lsap-output-list 200
```

If non-SNA traffic is to be blocked, it is recommended that you prevent the traffic from coming into the router and being classified. After traffic is classified, the router's resources begin to be consumed.

```
source-bridge input-lsap-list 200
```

Custom Versus Priority Queuing

To ensure that SNA traffic is managed (that is, sessions do not time out), Cisco recommends the use of either custom or priority queuing.

Priority-queuing is easier to configure than custom-queuing, but priority-queuing can potentially "break" the Frame Relay network. Priority queuing *always* checks the higher priority queues before checking the lower priority ones. Therefore, if IP is configured in a high priority queue and IPX in a normal priority queue, the possibility exists to completely choke out IPX traffic if an IP packet is always ready in the high queue (such as infinite preemption). This results in lost IPX sessions, which creates problems for network users. If known low bandwidth protocols are placed on the high queue, this possibility can be eliminated. For example, small numbers of SNA users who are running interactive 3270 traffic on a LAN, or SNA users residing off a slow SDLC line, would not be able to keep the high queues full constantly. This would also apply to other protocols that are bandwidth constrained on the in-bound side. This is the ideal situation in which to use priority queuing.

Custom-queuing removes the possibility of infinite preemption by permitting the administrator to customize how the various queues are serviced.

The following example demonstrates the process of queue servicing:

- For example, if starting with 10 possible queues, the router polls all queues all the time.

- If queue 1 is configured to contain IP traffic and queue 2 to contain IPX traffic, the router services X number of bytes on queue 1, then moves on to queue 2 and services X number of bytes there. (The router administrator can configure the value for X.)

- After servicing queue 1, if queue 2 has no packets, the router immediately moves on to the next queue, which in this case will be queue 1, allowing traffic on queue 1 to use all available bandwidth, if no other protocols require it.

NOTE   Custom-queuing and priority-queuing will be discussed in more detail in Chapter 17, "Frame Relay WAN Analysis."

When the serial line [interface] is saturated, queues can be configured to the proper byte count values (Q) if the average size of the packets is known. This essentially configures bandwidth allocation on a per-protocol basis. In this scenario, some "tweaking" will likely be required.

NOTE   As described here, per-protocol bandwidth allocation is a powerful feature that is not easy to implement. Care should be taken to review all configurations prior to implementing this strategy.

Voice over Frame Relay (VoFr)

Voice over Frame Relay (VoFr) has been recently enjoying the general acceptance of any efficient and cost-effective technology. In the traditional plain old telephone service (POTS) network, a conventional (with no compression) voice call is encoded, as defined by the ITU pulse code modulation (PCM) standard, and utilizes 64 kbps of bandwidth. Several compression methods have been developed and deployed that reduce the bandwidth required by a voice call down to as little as 4 kbps, thereby allowing more voice calls to be carried over a single Frame Relay serial interface (or subinterface PVC). Table 15-14 demonstrates these different compression algorithms and the bandwidth utilized per algorithm.

Table 15-14 *Voice Compression Algorithms with Bandwidth Utilization*

Encoding/Compression	Bit Rate (Bandwidth Required)
G.711 PCM (A-Law/U-Law)	64 kbps (DS0)
G.726 ADPCM	16, 24, 32, 40 kbps
G.729 CS-ACELP	8 kbps
G.728 LD-CELP	16 kbps
G.723.1 CELP	6.3/5.3 kbps variable

NOTE   A common concern regarding VoFR is keeping latency and jitter within acceptable limits. This can be a challenge in a network that is built around applications that can tolerate both; however, it is possible to pull a "trick or two" within the network.

One approach is to increase the CIR over each Frame Relay PVC that will carry voice traffic and not mark the voice traffic as DE.

Another approach is to implement separate PVCs for voice and data applications, segregating the traffic prior to transmission from the router.

A third approach is to work with a network service provider that offers PVC of different levels of delay/priority. Some providers offer as many as three PVC levels, or priorities:

- Top priority for delay-sensitive traffic (such as voice and SDLC)

- No (or middle) priority for traffic that can tolerate some level of delay (such as LAN traffic)

- Low priority for applications that can tolerate significant levels of delay (such as Internet access and e-mail)

Voice Coders-Decoders (Codecs)

The issue with packetized voice is the ability of the sending and receiving voice codecs (coders-decoders) to be able to clock against each other to ensure the synchronization of the data flow. Two of the more common Voice over X (VoX) implementations are Voice over Frame Relay (VoFr) and Voice over ATM (VoATM). The reason for ATM's popularity in the VoX arena is that ATM utilizes fixed cell lengths of 53 bytes, enabling the sending and receiving codecs to clock against each other in synchronicity, ensuring the seamless flow of the voice traffic.

NOTE   VoIP recently has come to the forefront of Voice over X (VoX) and will be discussed in detail in Chapter 20, "Voice Technology."

Frame Relay frames operate in a similar fashion to ATM (packet-switching versus cell-switching). However, one of the significant differences with regard to voice traffic is that Frame Relay frames are of variable length, up to 4096 bytes, making it difficult for the sending and receiving codecs to clock against each other because the "start" and "stop" flags appear at seemingly random intervals.

Several VoFr, or Voice FRAD (VFRAD), vendors are on the market today, each with its own workaround to the variable frame length issue. Each workaround is similar in that the sending codec limits the payload size of the transmitted frame, usually to 2000 bytes, or 2 kilobytes (KB). By utilizing this fixed length, the sending and receiving codecs can now clock against each other because the receiving codec now knows when the "stop" flag will appear, enabling a more seamless voice conversation.

VoFr Quality

A direct correlation exists between the quality of voice and the compression algorithm used. This quality is measured with something called the mean opinion score (MOS). Table 15-15 compares these different compression algorithms and their respective MOS.

Table 15-15 *Voice Compression Mean Opinion Scores*

Encoding Compression	Mean Opinion Score	Native Bit Rate kbps	Voice Quality	BW	DTMF	Dual	Comp	CPU Music on Hold
G.711 PCM	4.1	64	A	D	A	A	A	A
G.726 ADPCM	3.85	32	B	C	B	B	B	B
G.728 LD-CELP	3.61	16	C	B	B	C	C	C
G.729 CS-ACELP	3.92	8	A	A	B	B	C	C
G.729a CS-ACELP	3.7	8	B	A	C	C	B	D
G.723.1	3.65	5.3	C	A	C	D	C	D

It is considered efficient to send compressed voice over data circuits, initially over point-to-point leased lines and more recently over Frame Relay. Because of this, it is natural for enterprise users to consider supporting voice service across an existing, or planned, Frame Relay WAN.

Generally, VoFr implementations utilize CIR/DE to prioritize voice over data traffic across the VC. To do this effectively, the proper amount of CIR bandwidth needs to be determined prior to implementation. The formula used to determine this is as follows:

$$FRL_{CIR} = ((VOX_{MODULE} \times MODULE_{BANDWIDTH}) + VOX_{BUFFER})$$

$$VOX_{BUFFER} = ((VOX_{MODULE} \times MODULE_{BANDWIDTH}) \times 20\%)$$

where VOX_{MODULE} is the number of VoFr modules; $MODULE_{BANDWIDTH}$ is the amount of bandwidth per voice module, and VOX_{BUFFER} is the amount of additional buffer space on the VC for the voice traffic.

For example, assume a FRAD with a 4-port voice module, utilizing G.728 compression (16 kbps). The CIR required to support the VoFr service is determined by the previous formulae:

$$FRL_{CIR} = ((4 \times 16) + 12.8) = 76.8 \text{ kbps}$$

$$VOX_{BUFFER} = ((4 \times 16 \text{ kbps}) \times 20\%) = 12.8 \text{ kbps}$$

The minimum amount of CIR required to support this configuration is 76.8 kbps. Typically, a network provider provisions CIR in multiples of 16 kbps or 64 kbps; therefore, the minimum CIR to support the voice traffic here would be 80 kbps. This is for voice traffic only; it is reasonable to expect to add incremental CIR to support data traffic requirements as well across the VC.

VoFR, as with all VoX, is subjected to and unforgiving of quality issues, most notably delay and jitter. These and other concerns will be discussed in greater detail in Chapter 20.

VFRADs

Voice over Frame Relay service is enabled by the use of Frame Relay communications devices, such as routers or FRADs, configured with voice modules. These devices are sometimes referred to as Voice FRADs, or VFRADs.

Although VoFR implementations are efficient and cost effective for intra-enterprise or intra-corporate communication, there are considerations, such as quality, to be made regarding the use of packetized voice when dealing with non-Frame Relay WAN, or off-net, users.

Figure 15-26 illustrates how a typical Voice over Frame Relay implementation might look, supporting simultaneously both on-net (VoFr) and off-net (POTS) implementations.

Figure 15-26 *On-Net (VoFr) and Off-Net (POTS) Voice Implementation*

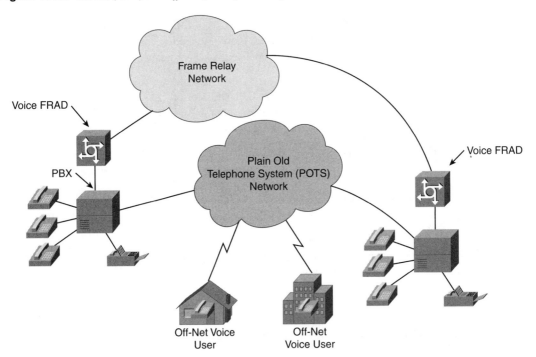

Figure 15-27 illustrates how voice and data can be merged to more effectively utilize WAN resources by the addition of a router to support data communication between enterprise sites.

Figure 15-27 *Frame Relay with Voice, Data, and Fax Communications*

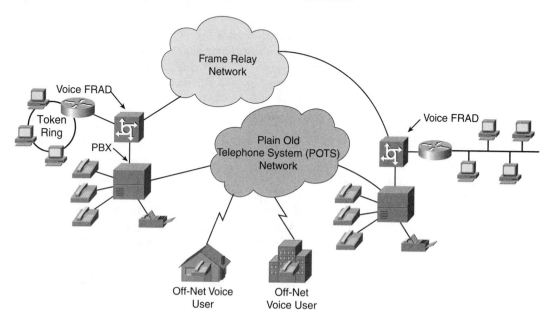

Frame Relay Traffic Shaping

Traffic shaping supports the controlling of the traffic going out of an interface. This control matches the flow of traffic to the speed of the remote destination (or target) interface and ensures that the traffic conforms to policies contracted for the interface. Traffic adhering to a particular profile can be shaped to meet downstream requirements, eliminating bottlenecks in topologies with data-rate mismatches.

The primary reasons for using traffic shaping are to control access to available bandwidth, to ensure that traffic conforms to the policies established for the available bandwidth, and to regulate the flow of traffic to avoid congestion. Congestion can occur when the sent traffic exceeds the access speed of its destination (target) interface across a VC.

Following are some examples of when to use traffic shaping:

- To control access to bandwidth when policy dictates that the rate of a given interface should not, on the average, exceed a certain rate, even though the access rate exceeds the speed.

- To configure traffic shaping on an interface if you have a network with differing access rates. Suppose that one end of the link in a Frame Relay network runs at 256 kbps and the other end of the link runs at 128 kbps. Sending packets at 256 kbps could cause failure of the applications that are using the link.

NOTE   Regarding a similar, more complicated case, a link-layer network giving indications of congestion that has differing access rates on different attached DTE; the network might be able to deliver more transit speed to a given DTE device at one time than another. (This scenario warrants that the token bucket be derived, and then its rate maintained.)

- To partition the T1 or T3 links into smaller channels in a subrate service scenario.

Traffic shaping prevents packet loss. The use of traffic shaping is especially important in Frame Relay networks because the switch cannot determine which frames take precedence and therefore which frames should be dropped when congestion occurs. It is important for real-time traffic, such as VoFR, that latency be bounded, thereby bounding the amount of traffic and traffic loss in the data link network at any given time by keeping the data in the router that is making the guarantees. Retaining the data in the router allows the router to prioritize traffic according to the guarantees that the router is making.

Traffic shaping limits the rate of transmission of data, limiting the data transfer to one of the following:

- A specific configured rate
- A derived rate based on the level of congestion

The transfer rate depends on three components that constitute the token bucket: burst size, mean rate, measurement (time) interval.

The mean rate is equal to the burst size divided by the interval, as demonstrated by the following equation:

Mean rate = Burst Size $(B_C + B_E)$ / Time Interval (T_C)

When traffic shaping is enabled, a maximum burst size can be sent during every time interval. However, within the interval, the bit rate might be faster than the mean rate at any given time.

B_E size is an additional variable that applies to traffic shaping. The excess burst size corresponds to the number of noncommitted bits—those bits outside the CIR—that are still accepted by the Frame Relay switch but marked as DE.

The B_E size allows more than the burst size to be sent during a time interval. The switch will allow the frames that belong to the excess burst to go through, but it will mark them by setting the DE bit. The switch configuration determines whether the frames are sent.

When B_E size equals 0 ($B_E = 0$) the interface sends no more than the burst size every interval, realizing an average rate no higher than the mean rate. When B_E size is greater than 0 ($B_E > 0$) the interface can send as many as $B_C + B_E$ bits in a burst, if the maximum amount was not sent in a previous time period. When less than the burst size is sent during an interval, the remaining number of bits, up to the B_E size, can be used to send more than the burst size in a later interval.

Frame Relay DE Bit

Frame Relay frames can be specified regarding which have low priority or low time sensitivity. These frames will be the first to be dropped when a Frame Relay switch is congested.

The DE bit is the mechanism that allows a Frame Relay switch to identify such frames to be dropped or discarded.

DE lists and groups can be managed in the following manner:

- DE lists can be specified that identify the characteristics of frames to be eligible for discarding.

- DE groups can be specified to identify the affected DLCI.

- DE lists can also be specified based on the protocol or the interface, and on characteristics such as fragmentation of the packet, a specific TCP or User Datagram Protocol (UDP) port, an access list number, or a packet size.

Differences Between Traffic-Shaping Mechanisms

Generic traffic shaping (GTS), class-based shaping, distributed traffic shaping (DTS), and Frame Relay traffic shaping (FRTS) are similar in implementation, share the same code and data structures, differ in regard to their CLIs, and differ in the queue types used.

Following are some examples in which these mechanisms differ:

- For GTS, the shaping queue is a weighted fair queue. For FRTS, the queue can be a weighted fair queue (configured by the **frame-relay fair-queue** command), a strict priority queue with WFQ (configured by the **frame-relay ip rtp priority** command in addition to the **frame-relay fair-queue** command), custom queuing (CQ), priority queuing (PQ), or first-in, first-out (FIFO). See Table 15-16 for detailed differences.

- For class-based shaping, GTS can be configured on a class, rather than only on an access control list (ACL). To do so, you must first define traffic classes based on match criteria including protocols, access control lists (ACLs), and input interfaces. Traffic shaping can be applied to each defined class.

- FRTS supports shaping on a per-DLCI basis; GTS and DTS are configurable per interface or subinterface.

- DTS supports traffic shaping based on a variety of match criteria, including user-defined classes, and DSCP.

Table 15-16 *Differences Between Shaping Mechanisms*

Mechanism	GTS	Class-Based	DTS	FRTS
Command-Line Interface	Applies parameters per subinterface Traffic group command supported	Applies parameters per interface or per class	Applies parameters per interface or subinterface	Classes of parameters Applies parameters to all VCs on an interface through inheritance mechanism No traffic group command
Queues Supported	Weighted fair queuing (WFQ) per subinterface	Class-based weighted fair queuing (CBWFQ) inside GTS	WFQ, strict priority queue with WFQ, CQ, PQ, first come, first served (FCFS) per VC	WFQ, strict priority queue with WFQ, CQ, PQ, FCFS per VC

GTS can be configured to behave the same as FRTS by allocating one DLCI per subinterface and using GTS plus BECN support. The behavior of the two is then the same with the exception of the different shaping queues used.

FRTS, like GTS, can eliminate bottlenecks in Frame Relay networks that have high-speed connections at the central site and low-speed connections at branch sites. Rate enforcement can be configured as a peak rate configured to limit outbound traffic to limit the rate at which data is sent on the VC at the central site.

FRTS can be used to configure rate enforcement to either the CIR or some other defined value, such as the excess information rate, on a per-VC basis. The ability to allow the transmission speed that the router uses to be controlled by criteria other than line speed—the CIR or excess information rate—provides a mechanism for sharing media by multiple VCs. Bandwidth can be allocated to each VC, creating a virtual time-division multiplexing (TDM) network.

PQ, CQ, and WFQ can be defined at the VC or subinterface level. These queuing methods allow for finer granularity in the prioritization and queuing of traffic, providing more control over the traffic flow on an individual VC. If CQ is combined with the per-VC queuing and rate enforcement capabilities, Frame Relay VCs can carry multiple traffic types such as IP, SNA, and IPX with bandwidth guaranteed for each traffic type.

FRTS can dynamically throttle traffic by using information that is contained in the BECN-tagged frames that are received from the network. With BECN-based throttling, frames are held in the router buffers to reduce the data flow from the router into the Frame Relay network. Throttling is done on a per-VC basis, and the transmission rate is adjusted based on the number of BECN-tagged frames received.

Derived Rates

FECNs and BECNs indicate congestion in a Frame Relay WAN and are specified by bits within a Frame Relay frame. FECN and BECN operation is as follows:

- FECNs—These are generated when data is sent out of a congested interface. FECNs indicate to a Frame Relay device that congestion was encountered along the transmission path to the destination. Traffic is marked with BECN if the queue for the opposite direction is full enough to trigger FECNs at the current time.

- BECNs—These notify the sending Frame Relay device to decrease the transmission rate. If the traffic is one-way only (such as multicast traffic), there is no reverse traffic with BECNs to notify the sending device to slow down. When a Frame Relay device receives a FECN, it first determines whether it is sending data. If the Frame Relay device is sending data along the return path of the FECN, this data will be marked with a BECN on its way to the other Frame Relay device. If the Frame Relay device is not sending data, it can send a Q.922 "TEST RESPONSE" message with the BECN bit set.

When an interface that is configured with traffic shaping receives a BECN, it immediately decreases, or throttles down, its maximum rate by a significant amount. If, after several intervals, the [throttled] interface has not received another BECN and traffic is waiting in the queue, the maximum rate slightly increases. This dynamically adjusted maximum rate is called the *derived rate*, which will always be between the upper bound and the lower bound that is configured on the interface.

Traffic Shaping Restrictions

FRTS applies only to Frame Relay PVCs and SVCs.

Figure 15-28 represents the traffic shaping process flow upon receipt of a frame for transmission.

Figure 15-28 *Traffic Shaping Flowchart*

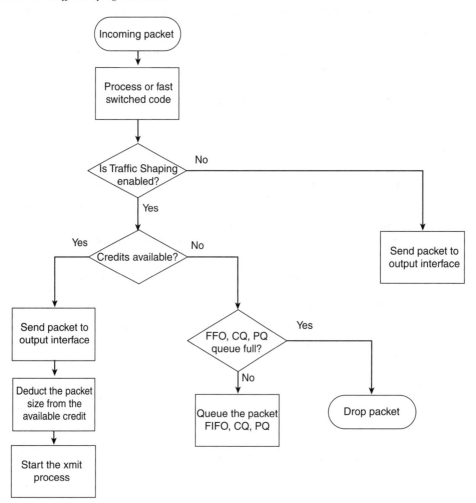

Traffic Policing and Shaping

Cisco IOS QoS offers two types of traffic regulation mechanisms: policing and shaping.

The rate-limiting features of committed access rate (CAR) and the traffic policing feature provide the functionality for policing traffic.

The features of GTS, class-based shaping, DTS, and FRTS provide the functionality for shaping traffic.

These features can be deployed throughout the network to ensure that a frame, packet, or other data source adheres to a stipulated contract. These features can also be used to determine the QoS with which to render the packet. Both policing and shaping mechanisms use the traffic descriptor for a packet—indicated by the classification of the packet—to ensure adherence and service.

Traffic policers and shapers identify traffic descriptor violations in an identical manner. These policers and shapers differ in how they respond to violations, for example:

- A policer drops traffic. For example, the CAR rate-limiting policer will either drop the packet or rewrite its IP precedence, resetting the type of service bits in the packet header.

- A shaper delays excess traffic using a buffer, or queuing mechanism, to hold packets and shape the flow when the data rate of the source is higher than expected. For example, GTS and class-based shaping use a weighted fair queue to delay packets to shape the flow. DTS and FRTS use either a priority queue, a custom queue, or a FIFO queue for the same, depending on how the queue is configured.

Traffic shaping and policing can work in tandem. For example, a good traffic-shaping scheme should make it easy for nodes that are inside the network to detect misbehaving flows. This activity is sometimes called "policing the traffic of the flow."

Because policing and shaping each use the token bucket mechanism, token buckets will be discussed in the next section.

Token Bucket

A token bucket is a formal definition of a rate of transfer with three components: burst size, mean rate, and a time interval (T_C). The mean rate is generally represented as bits per second, and any two values can be derived from the third, as shown by the following formula:

mean rate = burst size / time interval

where

- Mean rate—Also called the CIR. The mean rate specifies how much data can be sent or forwarded per unit time on average.

- Burst size—Also called the committed burst (B_c) size. The burst size specifies in bits (or bytes) per burst how much traffic can be sent within a given unit of time without creating scheduling concerns. For a shaper, such as GTS, burst size specifies bits per burst; for a policer, such as CAR, burst size specifies bytes per burst.

- Time interval (TC)—Also called the measurement interval. The time interval specifies the time in seconds per burst. By definition, over any integral multiple of the interval, the bit rate of the interface will not exceed the mean rate. The bit rate, however, might be arbitrarily fast within the interval.

A token bucket is used to manage a device that regulates the data in a flow. For example, the regulator might be a traffic policer, such as CAR, or a traffic shaper, such as FRTS or GTS. A token bucket has no discard or priority policy. Rather, a token bucket discards tokens and leaves to the flow the problem of managing its transmission queue if the flow overdrives the regulator. (CAR, FRTS, and GTS do not implement either a true token bucket or a true leaky bucket.)

In the token bucket metaphor, the following occurs:

- Tokens are put into the bucket at a certain rate. The bucket has a specified capacity.

- If the bucket fills to capacity, newly arriving tokens are discarded.

- Each token has permission for the source to send a certain number of bits into the network.

- To send a packet, the regulator must remove from the bucket a number of tokens equal in representation to the packet size.

- If not enough tokens are in the bucket to send a packet, the packet either waits until the bucket has enough tokens (in the case of GTS), or the packet is discarded or marked down (in the case of CAR).

- If the bucket is already full of tokens, incoming tokens overflow and are not available to future packets. Thus, at any time, the largest burst that a source can send into the network is roughly proportional to the size of the bucket.

The token bucket mechanism used for traffic shaping has both a token bucket and a data buffer, or queue. If the token bucket mechanism for traffic shaping did not have a data buffer, it would be a traffic policer.

The following applies for traffic shaping:

- Packets that arrive that cannot be sent immediately are delayed in the data buffer.

- A token bucket permits burstiness, but also bounds it.

- Traffic shaping guarantees that the burstiness is bounded so that the flow will never send more quickly than the capacity of the token bucket plus the time interval multiplied by the established rate at which tokens are placed in the bucket.

- Traffic shaping guarantees that the long-term transmission rate will not exceed the established rate at which tokens are placed in the bucket.

Traffic Policing with CAR

CAR is a rate-limiting feature for policing traffic, in addition to its packet classification feature. The rate-limiting feature of CAR manages the access bandwidth policy for a network by ensuring that traffic that falls within specified rate parameters is sent, while dropping packets that exceed the acceptable amount of traffic or sending them with a different priority. CAR's exceed action is to either drop or mark down the packet's priority.

The CAR rate-limiting function performs the following:

- Controls the maximum rate of traffic sent or received on an interface.
- Defines Layer 3 aggregate or granular incoming or outgoing (ingress or egress) bandwidth rate limits and specifies traffic-handling policies when the traffic either conforms to or exceeds the specified rate limits.

CAR bandwidth rate limits perform one of two functions:

- Aggregate—Aggregate bandwidth rate limits match all of the packets on an interface or subinterface.
- Granular—Granular bandwidth rate limits match a particular type of traffic based on precedence, MAC address, or other parameters.

CAR is often configured on interfaces at the edge of a network to limit traffic into or out of a network.

CAR Operation

CAR examines traffic received on an interface or a subset of that traffic selected by access list criteria. CAR compares the rate of the traffic to a configured token bucket and takes action based on the result. For example, CAR will drop the packet or rewrite the IP precedence by resetting the type of service (ToS) bits.

CAR can be configured to send, drop, or set precedence.

Aspects of CAR rate limiting include the following:

- Matching criteria
- Rate limits
- Conform and exceed actions
- Multiple rate policies

CAR utilizes a token bucket measurement, operating as follows:

- Tokens are inserted into the bucket at the committed rate.
- The depth of the bucket is the burst size.
- Traffic arriving at the bucket when sufficient tokens are available is said to conform, and the corresponding number of tokens is removed from the bucket.
- If a sufficient number of tokens is not available, then the traffic is said to exceed.

CAR Traffic-Matching Criteria   Traffic matching involves the identification of interesting traffic for rate limiting, precedence setting, or both. Rate policies can be associated with one of the following qualities:

- Incoming interface
- All IP traffic
- IP precedence (defined by a rate-limit access list)
- MAC address (defined by a rate-limit access list)
- IP access list (standard and extended)

CAR provides configurable actions, such as send, drop, or set precedence when traffic conforms to or exceeds the rate limit.

NOTE   Matching to IP access lists is more processor intensive than matching based on other criteria.

Rate Limits   CAR propagates bursts and performs no smoothing or shaping of traffic; therefore, it performs no buffering and adds no delay. CAR is optimized (but not limited) to run on high-speed links, such as DS3 or higher, and in distributed mode on Versatile Interface Processors (VIPs) on the Cisco 7500 series.

CAR rate limits can be implemented either on input or output interfaces or subinterfaces, including those found with Frame Relay and ATM implementations.

Rate limits define which packets conform to or exceed the defined rate based on the following three parameters:

- Average rate—Determines the long-term average transmission rate. Traffic that falls under this rate will always conform.
- Normal burst size—Determines how large traffic bursts can be before some traffic exceeds the rate limit.
- Excess Burst size (BE)—Determines how large traffic bursts can be before all traffic exceeds the rate limit. Traffic that falls between the normal burst size and the Excess Burst size exceeds the rate limit with a probability that increases as the burst size increases.

The tokens in a token bucket are replenished at regular intervals, in accordance with the configured committed rate. The maximum number of tokens that a bucket can contain is determined by the token bucket's normal burst size configuration.

When the CAR rate limit is applied to a packet, CAR removes from the bucket tokens that are equivalent in number to the byte size of the packet. If a packet arrives and the byte size of the packet is greater than the number of tokens available in the token bucket, extended burst capability is engaged (if it is configured).

Setting the extended burst value greater than the normal burst value configures extended burst. Setting the extended burst value equal to the normal burst value excludes the extended burst capability. If extended burst is not configured, the CAR exceed action takes effect because a sufficient number of tokens are not available.

When extended burst is configured, the flow is allowed to borrow the needed tokens to allow the packet to be sent. This capability exists to avoid tail-drop behavior, and, instead, engage behavior like that of random early detection (RED).

Extended burst operates in the following fashion:

- If a packet arrives and needs to borrow n number of tokens because the token bucket contains fewer tokens than its packet size requires, then CAR compares the following two values:

  — Extended burst parameter value

  — Compounded debt, which is computed as the sum over all ai:

  a indicates the actual debt value of the flow after packet i is sent. Actual debt is simply a count of how many tokens the flow has currently borrowed.

  i indicates the packet that attempts to borrow tokens since the last time a packet was dropped.

- If the compounded debt is greater than the extended burst value, the exceed action of CAR takes effect. After a packet is dropped, the compounded debt is effectively set to 0. CAR computes a new compounded debt value equal to the actual debt for the next packet that needs to borrow tokens.

- If the actual debt is greater than the extended limit, all packets are dropped until the actual debt is reduced through accumulation of tokens in the token bucket.

Dropped packets do not count against a rate or burst limit. In other words, when a packet is dropped, no tokens are removed from the token bucket.

NOTE   Although the entire compounded debt is forgiven when a packet is dropped, the actual debt is not forgiven, and the next packet to arrive to insufficient tokens is immediately assigned a new compounded debt value equal to the current actual debt. In this way, actual debt can continue to grow until it is so large that no compounding is needed to cause a packet to be dropped. In effect, the compounded debt is not really forgiven. This scenario leads to excessive drops on streams that continually exceed normal burst.

Cisco recommends the following values for the normal and extended burst parameters:

normal burst = configured rate × (1 byte)/(8 bits) × 1.5 seconds

extended burst = 2 × normal burst

Now look at an example that shows how the compounded debt is forgiven, but the actual debt accumulates.

In this example, the following parameters are assumed:

- Token rate is 1 data unit per time unit
- Normal burst size is 2 data units
- Extended burst size is 4 data units
- 2 data units arrive per time unit

After two time units, the stream has used up its normal burst and must begin borrowing one data unit per time unit, beginning at time unit 3:

```
Time   DU arrivals    Actual Debt      Compounded Debt
- - - - - - - - - - - - - - - - - - - - - - - - - - - - - - - - - - - - - - -
1       2              0                0
2       2              0                0
3       2              1                1
4       2              2                3
5       2              3 (temporary)    6 (temporary)
```

The following actions occur at this time:

- A packet is dropped because the new compounded debt (6) would exceed the extended burst limit (4).

- When the packet is dropped, the compounded debt effectively becomes 0, and the actual debt is 2. (The values 3 and 6 were only temporary and do not remain valid if a packet is dropped.)

- The final values for time unit 5 follow. The stream begins borrowing again at time unit 6.

```
Time   DU arrivals    Actual Debt      Compounded Debt
- - - - - - - - - - - - - - - - - - - - - - - - - - - - - - - - - - - - - - -
5       2              2                0
6       2              3                3
7       2              4 (temporary)    7 (temporary)
```

```
At time unit 6, another packet is dropped and the debt values are
 adjusted accordingly.
Time   DU arrivals    Actual Debt      Compounded Debt
- - - - - - - - - - - - - - - - - - - - - - - - - - - - - - - - - - - - - - -
7       2              3                0
```

Conform and Exceed Actions   Because CAR utilizes a token bucket, CAR can pass temporary bursts that exceed the rate limit as long as tokens are available.

After a packet has been classified as conforming to or exceeding a particular rate limit, the router performs one of the following actions:

- Transmit—The packet is sent.

- Drop—The packet is discarded.

- Set precedence and transmit—The IP precedence (ToS) bits in the packet header are rewritten. The packet is then sent. You can use this action to either color (set precedence) or recolor (modify existing packet precedence) the packet.

- Continue—The packet is evaluated using the next rate policy in a chain of rate limits. If another rate policy does not exist, the packet is sent.

- Set precedence and continue—Set the IP precedence bits to a specified value and then evaluate the next rate policy in the chain of rate limits.

For VIP-based platforms, two more actions are possible:

- Set QoS group and transmit—The packet is assigned to a QoS group and sent.

- Set QoS group and continue—The packet is assigned to a QoS group and then evaluated using the next rate policy. If another rate policy does not exist, the packet is sent.

Multiple Rate Policies   A single CAR rate policy includes information about the rate limit, conform actions, and exceed actions. Each interface can have multiple CAR rate policies corresponding to different types of traffic. For example, low-priority traffic might be limited to a lower rate than high-priority traffic. When multiple rate policies exist, the router examines each policy in the order entered until the packet matches. If no match is found, the default action is to send.

Rate policies can be independent or cascading:

- Independent—Each rate policy deals with a different type of traffic.

- Cascading—A packet might be compared to multiple different rate policies in succession.

Cascading of rate policies supports a series of rate limits to be applied to packets to specify more granular policies. For example, total traffic could be rate limited on an access link to a specified subrate bandwidth and then rate limit World Wide Web traffic on the same link to a given proportion of the subrate limit.

Match packets could be rate limited against an ordered sequence of policies until an applicable rate limit is encountered. For example, as the sequence of policies is applied, the rate limiting of several MAC addresses with different bandwidth allocations can occur at an exchange point.

Up to 100 rate policies can be configured on a subinterface.

CAR Restrictions

CAR and VIP-distributed CAR can only be used with IP traffic. Non-IP traffic is not rate limited.

CAR or VIP-distributed CAR can be configured on an interface or subinterface, with the exception of the following interface types:

- Fast EtherChannel
- Tunnel
- PRI
- Any interface that does not support Cisco Express Forwarding (CEF)

CAR is supported only on ATM subinterfaces with the following encapsulations: aal5snap, aal5mux, and aal5nlpid.

NOTE   CAR provides rate limiting and does not guarantee bandwidth. CAR should be used with other QoS features, such as distributed weighted fair queuing (DWFQ), if premium bandwidth assurances are required.

Summary

Frame Relay is a Layer 2 (data link) wide-area network (WAN) protocol that works at both Layer 1 (physical) and Layer 2 (data link) of the OSI model. Although Frame Relay services were initially designed to operate over ISDN service, the more common deployment today involves dedicated access to WAN resources.

Frame Relay networks are typically deployed as a cost-effective replacement for point-to-point private line, or leased line, services. Whereas point-to-point customers incur a monthly fee for local access and long-haul connections, Frame Relay customers incur the same monthly fee for local access, but only a fraction of the long-haul connection fee associated with point-to-point private line services.

Frame Relay was standardized by two standards bodies—internationally by the International Telecommunication Union Telecommunication Standardization Sector (ITU-T) and domestically by ANSI (American National Standards Institute).

Frame Relay is a packet-switched technology, meaning that each network end user, or end node, will share backbone network resources, such as bandwidth. Connectivity between these end nodes is accomplished with the use of Frame Relay virtual circuits (VCs).

Frame Relay WAN service primarily comprises four functional components:

- Customer premise Frame Relay access device (FRAD).
- Local access loop to the service provider network.
- Frame Relay switch access port. Link Management Interface parameters are defined here.
- Frame Relay VC parameters to each end site.

Frame Relay is a connection-oriented service, operating the data link layer (Layer 2) of the OSI model. A data-link connection identifier (DLCI) is used to identify this dedicated communication path between two end nodes. This path, or VC, is a bidirectional logical connection across the WAN between two end node DTE devices.

DLCIs are of local significance, unless an agreement has been made with the network service provider to deploy global DLCIs. Local significance means that DLCIs are of use only to the local Frame Relay network device. Frame Relay DLCIs are analogous to an organization's telephone network utilizing speed-dial functions.

Two types of Frame Relay VCs exist:

- Permanent virtual circuits (PVCs)—These are permanently established, requiring no call setup, and utilize DLCIs for endpoint addressing.
- Switched virtual circuits (SVCs)—These are established as needed, requiring call setup procedures and utilizing X.121 or E.164 addresses for endpoint addressing.

Two types of congestion-notification mechanisms are implemented with Frame Relay:

- Forward explicit congestion notification (FECN)—The FECN bit is set by a Frame Relay network to inform the Frame Relay networking device receiving the frame that congestion was experienced in the path from origination to destination. Frame relay network devices that receive frames with the FECN bit will act as directed by the upper-layer protocols in operation. The upper-layer protocols will initiate flow-control operations, depending on which upper-layer protocols are implemented. This flow-control action is typically the throttling back of data transmission, although some implementations can be designated to ignore the FECN bit and take no action.
- Backward explicit congestion notification (BECN)—Much like the FECN bit, the BECN bit is set by a Frame Relay network to inform the DTE that is receiving the frame that congestion was experienced in the path traveling in the opposite direction of frames. The upper-layer protocols will initiate flow-control operations, depending on which upper-layer protocols are implemented. This flow-control action is typically the throttling back of data transmission, although some implementations can be designated to ignore the BECN bit and take no action.

Frame Relay VCs, both permanent and switched, have three configurable parameters that must be agreed upon between each end node and the Frame Relay network provider:

- Committed information rate (CIR)—This is the amount of bandwidth that will be delivered as "best-effort" across the Frame Relay backbone network.

- Discard eligibility (DE)—This is a bit in the frame header that indicates whether that frame can be discarded if congestion is encountered during transmission.

- Virtual circuit identifier

  — Data-link connection identifiers (DLCIs) for PVCs—Although DLCI values can be 10, 16, or 23 bits in length, 10-bit DLCIs have become the de facto standard for Frame Relay WAN implementations.

  — X.121/E.164 addressing for SVCs—X.121 is a hierarchical addressing scheme that was originally designed to number X.25 DTEs. E.164 is a hierarchical global telecommunications numbering plan, similar to the North American Number Plan (NANP, 1-NPA-Nxx-xxxx).

The formulae in Table 15-17 can be used to determine the number of VCs required to enable each associated network topology.

Table 15-17 *Summary of Network Topology Formulae*

Network Topology	Formula[*]
Fully meshed	$[(N \times (N-1)) / 2]$
Partial-mesh	(Approximation) $[N^2 / \sqrt{(N-1)}]$
	(Guideline) $[((N \times (N-1)) / 2) \geq X \geq (N-1)]$
Hub-and-Spoke	$[N-1]$

[*]Note: N is the number of locations.

Frame Relay uses the cyclic redundancy check (CRC) method for error detection. Frame Relay has no inherent error correction mechanisms, leaving error correction to the management and control of the upper-layer protocols.

Local Management Interface (LMI) is a set of enhancements to the basic Frame Relay specification. LMI includes support for keepalive mechanisms, verifying the flow of data; multicast mechanisms, providing the network server with local and multicast DLCI information; global addressing, giving DLCIs global rather than local significance; and status mechanisms, providing ongoing status reports on the switch-known DLCIs.

Three types of LMI are found in Frame Relay network implementations:

- ANSI T1.617 (Annex D)—The maximum number of connections (PVCs) supported is limited to 976. LMI type ANSI T1.627 (Annex D) uses DLCI 0 to carry local (link) management information.

- ITU-T Q.933 (Annex A)—Like LMI type Annex-D, the maximum number of connections (PVCs) supported is limited to 976. LMI type ITU-T Q.933 (Annex A) also uses DLCI 0 to carry local (link) management information.

- LMI (Original)—The maximum number of connections (PVCs) supported is limited to 992. LMI type LMI uses DLCI 1023 to carry local (link) management information.

Frame Relay is a versatile transport mechanism, traditionally supporting four networking applications:

- TCP/IP Suite

- Novell IPX Suite

- IBM SNA Suite

- Voice over Frame Relay (VoFr)

Internet Protocol (IP) is a best-effort delivery protocol, relying on the transmission-control mechanisms (packet acknowledgement and sequencing) that are supported by TCP. IP datagrams, or *packets*, are routed from source to destination based on the address information found in the packet header. IP traffic is typically bursty in nature, making it an ideal network-layer protocol for Frame Relay WANs.

Novell IPX implementations over Frame Relay are similar to IP network implementation. Whereas a TCP/IP implementation would require the mapping of Layer 3 IP addresses to a DLCI, Novell IPX implementations require the mapping of the Layer 3 IPX addresses to a DLCI. Special consideration needs to be made with IPX over Frame Relay implementations regarding the impact of Novell RIP and SAP message traffic to a Frame Relay internetwork.

Migration of a legacy SNA network from a point-to-point infrastructure to a more economical and manageable Frame Relay infrastructure is attractive; however, some challenges exist when SNA traffic is sent across Frame Relay connections. IBM SNA was designed to operate across reliable communication links that support predictable response times. The challenge that arises with Frame Relay network implementations is that Frame Relay service tends to have unpredictable and variable response times, for which SNA was not designed to interoperate or able to manage within its traditional design.

Voice over Frame Relay (VoFr) has recently enjoyed the general acceptance of any efficient and cost-effective technology. In the traditional plain old telephone service (POTS) network, a conventional (with no compression) voice call is encoded, as defined by the ITU pulse code modulation (PCM) standard, and utilizes 64 kbps of bandwidth. Several compression methods have been developed and deployed that reduce the bandwidth required by a voice call to as little as 4 kbps, thereby allowing more voice calls to be carried over a single Frame Relay serial interface (or subinterface PVC).

CHAPTER 16

Frame Relay Documentation

Chapter 15, "Frame Relay," discussed the underlying technology for Frame Relay WAN networks and their components. This chapter discusses some recommendations and guidelines to follow to document a Frame Relay wide-area network (WAN).

Most networking discussions today include the topic of documentation at some point, whether the mention is a statement advising that you should document your network assets or a statement advising that network documentation is a good tool to have when troubleshooting a network issue. The challenge here then is to determine what network information should be documented and later reviewed and analyzed for any potential network-related issues.

NOTE Network documentation is a living process and not a single event. The reason to have clear and simple documentation templates to use is so the WAN staff will be committed to maintaining the documentation, preserving its value. Out-of-date documentation, if used and trusted, can be dangerous. It is useless and brings no value to the organization.

Network documentation should be both easy to complete and easy to understand. In an effort to make the network documentation process easier to manage for Frame Relay WAN implementations, templates have been prepared and presented here for use. These templates are preceded by relevant console commands, a case study, and a sample completed template serving as a guide.

NOTE The templates presented here are also available electronically on the Cisco Press Web site (www.ciscopress.com/1587050390).

Frame Relay WAN documentation can be approached from two perspectives: from the individual site or from the overall WAN view. Both perspectives will be demonstrated here with supporting templates.

An introduction or case study network diagram will precede each template with suggestions regarding template completion. These templates are not all encompassing, nor are they designed to be. Rather, these templates are designed to help the consultant, engineer, or anyone involved with a network gather the vital information pertaining to a network and its related segments.

NOTE   Various **show frame-relay** commands will be introduced throughout this chapter, demonstrating how to gather pertinent information.

Case Study: Naming Conventions

A naming convention, or scheme, should be employed in any network for which you are responsible. A naming convention should grow as the network grows. Naming conventions should be developed so that the network documentation is easy to prepare, thus making network maintenance and troubleshooting easier for the user. For example, a network engineer new to the company's operations would be able to easily recognize the function and purpose of a device named HQ_7500Router_WAN rather than the same device referred to as Sprint Router.

NOTE   Some would view such a descriptive naming convention as a security concern. Like so many things, tradeoffs are involved: descriptive naming versus security. These tradeoffs need to be addressed prior to a naming convention. In some instances, internal codes are used, satisfying both network management and security concerns.

A good convention scheme would incorporate the geographic location of the device. A good naming convention would follow the design as follows:

Geographic-location_Network-Device | Division_Network-Device

For example, a Frame Relay WAN edge-router located at an organization's corporate headquarters could be named in one of the following fashions:

Chicago_WANRouter

HQ_WANRouter

This example reflects a Frame Relay WAN Router located at corporate headquarters—in this case located in Chicago, Illinois.

A naming convention should be easy to use; however, one naming convention cannot work with every network. Generic conventions can be useful. The idea behind generic naming conventions is that if someone else looks at your network documentation, that person could easily determine the topology.

This same naming convention can be globally deployed and supported across the organization by the use of a domain name server (DNS). By deploying the naming scheme across the domain with DNS, administration and inventory is simpler to manage. Troubleshooting is also facilitated in a more manageable fashion than without the use of a naming standard.

For example, the following trace route command would not be of much help to an engineer without the names.

```
 1   WashingtonDC.MCIRouter.Engineering [207.69.220.81]
 2   cisco-f0-1-0.norva3.mindspring.net [207.69.220.65]
 3   s10-0-1.vienna1-cr3.bbnplanet.net [4.1.5.237]
 4   p4-2.vienna1-nbr2.bbnplanet.net [4.0.1.133]
 5   p4-0.washdc3-br2.bbnplanet.net [4.0.1.97]
 6   p3-0.washdc3-br1.bbnplanet.net [4.24.4.145]
 7   p2-0.chcgil1-br2.bbnplanet.net [4.24.6.93]
 8   p4-0.chcgil1-br1.bbnplanet.net [4.24.5.225]
 9   so-4-1-0.chcgil2-br1.bbnplanet.net [4.24.9.69]
10   p1-0.chcgil2-cr11.bbnplanet.net [4.24.6.22]
11   p7-1.paloalto-nbr1.bbnplanet.net [4.24.6.98]
12   p1-0.paloalto-cr1.bbnplanet.net [4.0.6.74]
13   h1-0.cisco.bbnplanet.net [4.1.142.238]
14   pigpen.cisco.com [192.31.7.9]
15   www.cisco.com [198.133.219.25]
```

Frame Relay Site View

This template can be used to document a single frame relay site. The site of discussion is not concerned with the WAN as a whole, but rather only its view into the WAN.

NOTE   If the Frame Relay WAN is in a broadcast configuration, subinterfaces will not be implemented. If the Frame Relay WAN is in a multipoint configuration (see Table 16-1), subinterfaces will be implemented on the WAN serial interface.

Table 16-1 *Frame Relay WAN Site Information*

Site Name		Mnemonic	
FRL Access Bandwidth		FRL Access Ckt ID	
Access Carrier		Local Access Ckt ID		Channels	
Local Management Interface (LMI) Type					

DLCI and Interface	Term. Network Address	Term. Site Name	Term. Site Mnemonic	Term. FRL Circuit ID	Term. FRL Access Bandwidth	PVC CIR B/W

Figure 16-1 will be used to complete the associated documentation example.

It should be noted that the example in Figure 16-1 is a somewhat detailed network diagram of a 3-node Frame Relay WAN. Although diagrams like this one are useful in certain situations, the amount of time involved in their construction could be best spent otherwise. A simpler network diagram, shown in Figure 16-2, is just as useful as the previous diagram, without the additional detail that could clutter the representation. The diagram in Figure 16-2 also takes less time to prepare.

Figure 16-1 *Frame Relay WAN Template Example 1*

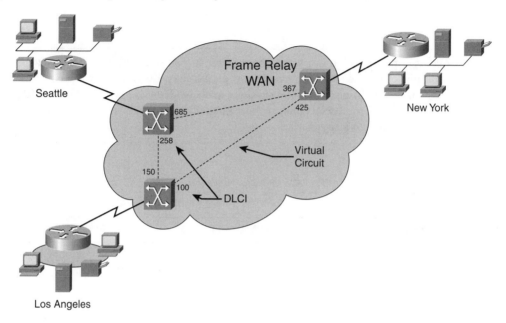

Figure 16-2 *Simpler 3-Node Network Diagram*

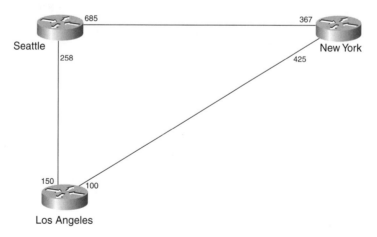

This network would be documented from each site, as shown in Figure 16-2 and detailed in Table 16-2.

NOTE   Access or prioritization lists should be captured as part of the documentation data collection. The Cisco IOS command **show access-lists** is used to show the contents of all access lists. The Cisco IOS command **show ip access-lists** shows the contents of IP access lists only. The Cisco IOS command **show queueing priority** is used to show the contents of the configured priority lists.

Table 16-2   *Frame Relay WAN Template for Example 1 (Los Angeles)*

(Originating) Site Name		Los Angeles	**Mnemonic**		WAN_LA				
FRL Access Bandwidth		128 K	**FRL Access Ckt ID**		ZAC214580001				
Access Carrier	MCI	**Local Access Ckt ID**				**Channels**		1 to 2	
LMI Type									
DLCI and Interface	**Term. Network Address**	**Term. Site Name**	**Term. Site Mnemonic**	**Term. FRL Circuit ID**		**Term. FRL Access Bandwidth**	**PVC CIR B/W**		
100		New York	WAN_NY	ZAV564980001		128 K			
150		Seattle	WAN_SEA	ZAB547810001		128 K			

Table 16-3   *Frame Relay WAN Template for Example 1 (Seattle)*

(Originating) Site Name		Seattle		**Mnemonic**		WAN_SEA	
FRL Access Bandwidth		128 K	**FRL Access Ckt ID**			ZAB547810001	
Access Carrier	MCI	**Local Access Ckt ID**				**Channels**	23 to 24
LMI Type							

DLCI and Interface	Term. Network Address	Term. Site Name	Term. Site Mnemonic	Term. FRL Circuit ID	Term. FRL Access Bandwidth	PVC CIR B/W
258		Los Angeles	WAN_LA	ZAC214580001	128 K	
685		New York	WAN_NY	ZAV564980001	128 K	

Table 16-4   *Frame Relay WAN Template for Example 1 (New York)*

(Originating) Site Name		New York		**Mnemonic**		**WAN_NY**	
FRL Access Bandwidth		128 K	**FRL Access Ckt ID**			ZAV564980001	
Access Carrier	**MCI**	Local Access Ckt ID				**Channels**	12 and 13
LMI Type							

LCI and Interface	Term. Network Address	Term. Site Name	Term. Site Mnemonic	Term. FRL Circuit ID	Term. FRL Access Bandwidth	PVC CIR B/W
367		Seattle	WAN_SEA	ZAB547810001	128 K	
425		Los Angeles	WAN_LA	ZAC214580001	128 K	

These three forms provide each site a view of other sites to which they are directly interconnected. For example, the New York form does not reflect the interconnection between Los Angeles and Seattle because New York is not concerned with this interconnection; it is not in its "view" of the WAN.

Table 16-5 *Frame Relay WAN Template*

(Originating) Site Name			Mnemonic	
FRL Access Bandwidth		FRL Access Ckt ID		
FRL Service Provider		Local Access Ckt ID		Channels
LMI Type				

DLCI and Interface	Term. Network Address	Term. Site Name	Term. Site Mnemonic	Term. FRL Circuit ID	Term. FRL Access Bandwidth	PVC CIR B/W	Comments

Figures 16-3 and 16-4 will be used to complete the associated documentation example. Both figures represent the same network topology previously discussed, albeit with differing methods and additional information.

Figure 16-3 *Frame Relay WAN Template Example 2*

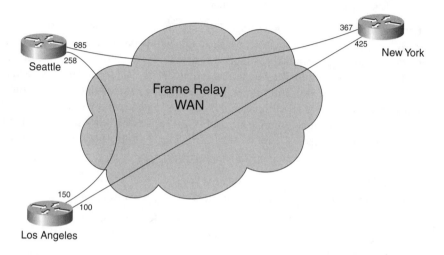

Figure 16-4 *Frame Relay WAN Template Example 2 (Simple Diagram)*

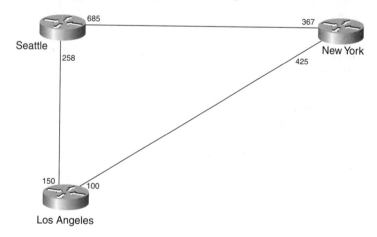

NOTE   Regarding network diagrams, two methods are generally used to illustrate a network topology:

- Topology with the WAN cloud

- End nodes and virtual circuits only

Each method has a distinct advantage. The first method, topology with the WAN cloud, is useful for illustrative purposes, such as inclusion within presentations. However, it becomes cluttered and illegible quickly as more end nodes are added to the WAN, especially if multiple fully or partially meshed virtual circuits exist. The second method, end nodes and virtual circuits only, is useful from a network topology standpoint and is useful for illustrating client network components (such as end nodes and virtual circuits). Both methods of network diagramming are useful. Take care when choosing which methodology to use. For the purposes of the following templates, both methods will be illustrated.

This network would be documented from each site in the following way.

The Cisco IOS command **show frame-relay map** is useful in collecting a view of the Frame Relay WAN from the router's point of view. The following demonstrates the displayed output from this command.

```
Barker#show frame-relay map
Serial0.1 (up): point-to-point dlci, dlci 140(0x8C,0x20C0), broadcast
  status defined, active
  Priority DLCI Group 1, DLCI 140 (HIGH), DLCI 180 (MEDIUM)
  DLCI 190 (NORMAL), DLCI 200 (LOW)
```

When completing a Frame Relay network document, it is important to identify the Layer 2 Addressing (DLCI) from the Layer 3 Network Addressing (IP, IPX, and so on) (see Table 16-5).

When documenting IP network addressing, it is important to include the subnet mask with the network address space. The subnet mask is a 32-bit address mask used in IP to indicate the bits of an IP address that are being used for the subnet address.

Table 16-6   *Frame Relay WAN Template for Example 2 (Seattle)*

(Originating) Site Name		Seattle		**Mnemonic**		WAN_SEA	
FRL Access Bandwidth		128 K		**FRL Access Ckt ID**		ZAB547810001	
FRL Service Provider	MCI	**Local Access Ckt ID**				**Channels**	23 to 24
LMI Type	Cisco						

DLCI and Interface	Term. Network Address	Term. Site Name	Term. Site Mnemonic	Term. FRL Circuit ID	Term. FRL Access Bandwidth	PVC CIR B/W
685/S0.2	192.24.176.34/24	New York	WAN_NY	ZAV564980001	128 K	64 K
258/S0.1	183.127.163.20/24	Los Angeles	WAN_LA	ZAC214580001	128 K	64 K

Table 16-7   *Frame Relay WAN Template for Example 2 (Los Angeles)*

(Originating) Site Name		Los Angeles	**Mnemonic**		WAN_LA	
FRL Access Bandwidth		128 K	**FRL Access Ckt ID**		ZAC214580001	
FRL Service Provider	MCI	**Local Access Ckt ID**			**Channels**	1 to 2
LMI Type	Annex-D					

DLCI and Interface	Term. Network Address	Term. Site Name	Term. Site Mnemonic	Term. FRL Circuit ID	Term. FRL Access Bandwidth	PVC CIR B/W
100/S1.1	192.24.176.38/24	New York	WAN_NY	ZAV564980001	128 K	64 K
150/S1.2	214.68.207.163/24	Seattle	WAN_SEA	ZAB547810001	128 K	64 K

Table 16-8   *Frame Relay WAN Template for Example 2 (New York)*

(Originating) Site Name		New York		**Mnemonic**		WAN_NY	
FRL Access Bandwidth		128 K		**FRL Access Ckt ID**		ZAV564980001	
Access Carrier	MCI		**Local Access Ckt ID**			**Channels**	1 to 2
LMI Type	Cisco						

DLCI and Interface	Term. Network Address	Term. Site Name	Term. Site Mnemonic	Term. FRL Circuit ID	Term. FRL Access Bandwidth	PVC CIR B/W
367/S0.1	214.68.207.124/24	Seattle	WAN_SEA	ZAB547810001	128 K	64 K
425/S0.2	183.127.163.18/24	Los Angeles	WAN_LA	ZAC214580001	128 K	64 K

NOTE   The LMI type does not need to be the same for each node. They do not have to "match" because LMI traffic is between each node and the network service provider's Frame Relay access switch.

IOS Commands

The following Cisco IOS commands can be used to collect the necessary Frame Relay WAN information for the completion of a network document.

show frame-relay map

The **show frame-relay map** command is used (in EXEC mode) to display the current map entries and information about the connections.

The following example demonstrates the **show frame-relay map** command and its displayed output, and Table 16-9 describes the output:

```
Router# show frame-relay map
Serial 1 (administratively down): ip 131.108.177.177
dlci 177 (0xB1,0x2C10), static,
broadcast,
CISCO
TCP/IP Header Compression (inherited), passive (inherited)
```

Table 16-9   *show frame-relay map Field Descriptions*

Field	Description
Serial 1 (administratively down)	A Frame Relay interface and its status (up or down). In this example, the interface was taken down manually.
ip 131.108.177.177	A destination IP address.
dlci 177 (0xB1,0x2C10)	A DLCI that identifies the logical connection being used to reach this interface. This value is displayed in three ways: its decimal value (177), its hexadecimal value (0xB1), and its value as it would appear on the wire (0x2C10).
Static	An indication of whether this entry is static or dynamic. Static entries are manually configured; dynamic entries are learned by the router.
CISCO	An indication of the encapsulation type for this map; either CISCO or IETF.
TCP/IP Header Compression (inherited), passive (inherited)	An indication of whether the TCP/IP header compression characteristics are inherited from the interface or are explicitly configured for the IP map.

Command-Based Documentation

Figures 16-5 and 16-6 and corresponding output will be used to complete the following documentation templates. The network depicted here has not implemented subinterfaces. Instead, it is using frame relay in a broadcast configuration as the command output reflects.

Figure 16-5   *show frame-relay map Network Example*

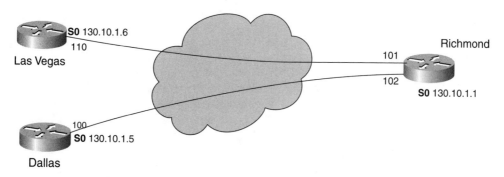

Figure 16-6 *show frame-relay map Network Example (Simple)*

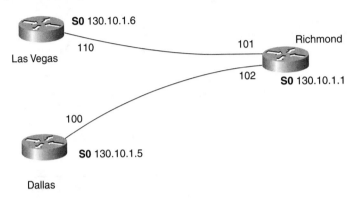

Example 16-1 *Richmond show frame-relay map Output for Figure 16-6*

```
Richmond#show frame-relay map
Serial0 (up): ip 130.10.1.5 dlci 102(0x66,0x1860), static,
              Broadcast,
              Cisco, status defined
Serial0 (up): ip 130.10.1.6 dlci 101(0x66,0x1860), static,
              Broadcast,
              Cisco, status defined
Richmond#
```

The following template will be used to document the network as seen from the Richmond site.

Table 16-10 *Richmond Document for Figure 16-6*

(Originating) Site Name		Richmond		**Mnemonic**		WAN_Richmond		
FRL Access Bandwidth				**FRL Access Ckt ID**				
Access Carrier			**Local Access Ckt ID**				**Channels**	
DLCI and Interface	**Term. Network Address**	**Term. Site Name**		**Term. Site Mnemonic**	**Term. FRL Circuit ID**	**Term. FRL Access Bandwidth**		**PVC CIR B/W**
101/S0	130.10.1.6/24	Las Vegas		WAN_LV				
102/S0	130.10.1.5/24	Dallas		WAN_Dallas				

show frame-relay pvc

The **show frame-relay pvc** command is useful for gathering statistics and measurements for individual virtual circuit interconnections between sites. From a documentation standpoint, only the following information is required from this command's output:

- DLCI—Data Link Connection Identifier
- CIR—Committed Information Rate

The **show frame-relay pvc** command is used (in EXEC mode) to display statistics about permanent virtual circuits (PVCs) for Frame Relay interfaces.

```
show frame-relay pvc [interface interface [dlci]]
```

Table 16-11 *Description of show frame-relay pvc Command*

Syntax	Description
Interface	(Optional) A specific interface for which PVC information will be displayed.
Interface	(Optional) Interface number containing the DLCI(s) for which you want to display PVC information.
Dlci	(Optional) A specific DLCI number used on the interface. Statistics for the specified PVC display when a DLCI is also specified.

NOTE   Use **show frame-relay pvc** to monitor the PPP (Point-to-Point Protocol) link control protocol (LCP) state as being open with an "up" state or closed with a "down" state.

When "vofr" or "vofr cisco" has been configured on the PVC and voice bandwidth has been allocated to the class associated with this same PVC, configured voice bandwidth and used voice bandwidth are both displayed.

Statistics Reporting

To obtain statistics about PVCs on all Frame Relay interfaces, use this command with no arguments.

Per VC counters do not increment when either autonomous or SSE switching is configured; therefore, PVC values will be inaccurate if either switching method is used.

NOTE   Autonomous and SSE switching are only supported on the 7000 series (not family), and that series is at EOL (End of Life). The surviving members of the 7000 family (7200 and 7500) do not support these fast switching types.

Traffic Shaping

Congestion-control mechanisms are currently not supported. However, the switch passes forward explicit congestion notification (FECN) bits, backward explicit congestion notification (BECN) bits, and discard eligibility (DE) bits unchanged from entry to exit points in the network.

LMI Status Inquiries

If an LMI status report indicates that a PVC is not active, then it is marked as inactive. A PVC is marked as deleted if it is not listed in a periodic LMI status message.

Example

Following are various displays demonstrating sample output for a variety of PVCs in different configurations. Some PVCs shown here carry data only, whereas others carry a combination of voice and data.

Table 16-12 provides definitions/explanations for each field that can be viewed with the **show frame-relay pvc** command.

Table 16-12 *show frame-relay pvc Field Descriptions*

Field	Description
DLCI	The data link connection identifier (DLCI) number for the PVC.
DLCI Usage	This lists Switched when the router or access server is used as a switch or Local when the router or access server is used as a Frame Relay DTE.

(continues)

Table 16-12 *show frame-relay pvc Field Descriptions (Continued)*

Field	Description
PVC Status	The status of the PVC:
	Active—PVC is configured and active in both the Frame Relay router (customer) and the Frame Relay switch (service provider).
	Inactive—PVC is configured but not active (down), requiring troubleshooting.
	Deleted—PVC at one time was configured and active but has now been removed from the configuration based on LMI status inquiries from the service provider.
Interface	The specific subinterface associated with this DLCI.
input pkts	The number of packets received on this PVC.
output pkts	The number of packets sent on this PVC.
in bytes	The number of bytes received on this PVC.
out bytes	The number of bytes sent on this PVC.
dropped pkts	The number of incoming and outgoing packets dropped by the router at the Frame Relay (OSI Layer 2) level.
in FECN pkts	The number of packets received with the FECN bit set.
in BECN pkts	The number of packets received with the BECN bit set.
out FECN pkts	The number of packets sent with the FECN bit set.
out BECN pkts	The number of packets sent with the BECN bit set.
in DE pkts	The number of DE packets received.
out DE pkts	The number of DE packets sent.
out bcast pkts	The number of output broadcast packets.
out bcast bytes	The number of output broadcast bytes.
pvc create time	The time the PVC was created.
last time pvc status changed	The time that the PVC changed status (active to inactive or inactive to active).
Service-type	The type of service performed by this PVC. Can be VoFR or VoFR-cisco.
configured voice bandwidth	The amount of bandwidth in bits per second reserved for voice traffic on this PVC.
used voice bandwidth	The amount of bandwidth in bits per second currently being used for voice traffic.

Table 16-12 *show frame-relay pvc Field Descriptions*

Field	Description
voice reserved queues	The queue numbers reserved for voice traffic on this PVC. (This field was removed in Cisco IOS Release 12.0(5)T).
fragment type	The type of fragmentation configured for this PVC. Possible types include the following: VoFR-cisco—Fragmented packets contain the Cisco proprietary header. VoFR—Fragmented packets contain the FRF.11 Annex C header. End-to-end—Fragmented packets contain the standard FRF.12 header.
fragment size	The size of the fragment payload in bytes.
Cir	The current committed information rate (CIR), in bits per second.
Bc	The current committed burst size (B_C), in bits.
Be	The current excess burst size (B_E), in bits.
Limit	The maximum number of bytes transmitted per internal interval (excess plus sustained), where sustained is CIR and excess is burst.
Interval	The interval being used internally (might be smaller than the interval derived from B_C/CIR; this situation occurs when the router determines that traffic flow will be more stable with a smaller configured interval).
Mincir	The minimum committed information rate (CIR) for the PVC.
byte increment	The number of bytes that will be sustained per internal interval.
BECN response	Frame Relay has BECN Adaptation configured.
Pkts	The number of packets associated with this PVC that have gone through the traffic-shaping system.
Bytes	The number of bytes associated with this PVC that have gone through the traffic-shaping system.
pkts delayed	The number of packets associated with this PVC that have been delayed by the traffic-shaping system.
bytes delayed	The number of bytes associated with this PVC that have been delayed by the traffic-shaping system.
Shaping	Traffic shaping will be active for all PVCs that are fragmenting data; otherwise, shaping will be active if the traffic being sent exceeds the CIR for this circuit.
shaping drops	The number of packets dropped by the traffic-shaping process.

(continues)

Table 16-12 *show frame-relay pvc Field Descriptions (Continued)*

Field	Description
Voice Queueing Stats	The statistics showing the size of packets, the maximum number of packets, and the number of packets dropped in the special voice queue created using the **frame-relay voice bandwidth** command **queue** keyword.
Discard threshold	The maximum number of packets that can be stored in each packet queue. If additional packets are received after a queue is full, they will be discarded.
Dynamic queue count	The number of packet queues reserved for best-effort traffic.
Reserved queue count	The number of packet queues reserved for voice traffic.
Output queue size	The size in bytes of each output queue.
max total	The maximum number of packets of all types that can be queued in all queues.
Drops	The number of frames dropped by all output queues.

NOTE   Although the *Oxford English Dictionary* spells "queuing" without the "e," Cisco IOS spells the same word as "queueing."

The following is sample output from the **show frame-relay pvc** command. It shows the PVC statistics for serial interface 3, slot 1, during a PPP session over Frame Relay:

```
Router# show frame-relay pvc 138

PVC Statistics for interface Serial 1/3 (Frame Relay DTE)

DLCI = 138, DLCI USAGE = LOCAL, PVC STATUS = ACTIVE, INTERFACE = Serial5/1.1
        input pkts 9              output pkts 16           in bytes 154
        out bytes 338            dropped pkts 6           in FECN pkts 0
        in BECN pkts 0           out FECN pkts 0          out BECN pkts 0
        in DE pkts 0             out DE pkts 0
        out bcast pkts 0         out bcast bytes 0
        pvc create time 00:35:11, last time pvc status changed 00:00:22
```

Shown here is a sample terminal output from the **show frame-relay pvc** command for a PVC carrying voice over Frame Relay (VoFr) configured via the **vofr cisco** command. The **frame-relay voice bandwidth** command has been configured here on the class associated with this PVC (**vofr-class**), as has fragmentation.

NOTE   The VoFr fragmentation employed is Cisco proprietary.

A sample configuration for this scenario is shown here first, followed by the output for the **show frame-relay pvc** command:

```
interface serial 0
    encapsulation frame-relay
    frame-relay traffic-shaping
    frame-relay interface-dlci 482
      vofr cisco
      class vofr-class
  map-class frame-relay vofr-class
    frame-relay fragment 100
    frame-relay fair-queue
    frame-relay cir 64000
    frame-relay voice bandwidth 25000
```

```
Router# show frame-relay pvc 482
PVC Statistics for interface Serial0 (Frame Relay DTE)
DLCI = 482, DLCI USAGE = LOCAL, PVC STATUS = STATIC, INTERFACE = Serial0
  input pkts 1260        output pkts 1271       in bytes 95671
  out bytes 98604        dropped pkts 0         in FECN pkts 0
  in BECN pkts 0         out FECN pkts 0        out BECN pkts 0
  in DE pkts 0           out DE pkts 0
  out bcast pkts 1271    out bcast bytes 98604
  pvc create time 09:43:17, last time pvc status changed 09:43:17
  Service type VoFR-cisco
  configured voice bandwidth 25000, used voice bandwidth 0
  voice reserved queues 24, 25
  fragment type VoFR-cisco     fragment size 100
  cir 64000      bc 64000     be 0         limit 1000    interval 125
  mincir 32000     byte increment 1000  BECN response no
  pkts 2592      bytes 205140    pkts delayed 1296      bytes delayed 102570
  shaping inactive
  shaping drops 0
  Current fair queue configuration:
   Discard     Dynamic      Reserved
   threshold   queue count  queue count
      64          16            2
  Output queue size 0/max total 600/drops 0
```

Note that the fragment type field in the **show frame-relay pvc** display can have the following entries:

VoFR-cisco	Indicates that fragmented packets will contain the Cisco proprietary header
VoFR	Indicates that fragmented packets will contain the FRF.11 Annex C header
end-to-end	Indicates that pure FRF.12 fragmentation is carried on this virtual circuit

Following is sample terminal output from the **show frame-relay pvc** command for an application that employs pure FRF.12 fragmentation. A sample configuration for this scenario is shown here first, followed by the output from the **show frame-relay pvc** command:

```
interface serial 0
    encapsulation frame-relay
    frame-relay traffic-shaping
    frame-relay interface-dlci 249
      class frag
```

```
      map-class frame-relay frag
        frame-relay fragment 100
        frame-relay fair-queue
        frame-relay cir 64000
Router# show frame-relay pvc 249
PVC Statistics for interface Serial0 (Frame Relay DTE)
DLCI = 249, DLCI USAGE = LOCAL, PVC STATUS = STATIC, INTERFACE = Serial0
  input pkts 0              output pkts 243        in bytes 0
  out bytes 7290            dropped pkts 0         in FECN pkts 0
  in BECN pkts 0            out FECN pkts 0        out BECN pkts 0
  in DE pkts 0              out DE pkts 0
  out bcast pkts 243        out bcast bytes 7290
  pvc create time 04:03:17, last time pvc status changed 04:03:18
  fragment type end-to-end          fragment size 100
  cir 64000      bc 64000      be 0          limit 1000    interval 125
  mincir 32000      byte increment 1000  BECN response no
  pkts 486       bytes 14580      pkts delayed 243        bytes delayed 7290
  shaping inactive
  shaping drops 0
  Current fair queue configuration:
  Discard      Dynamic      Reserved
   threshold    queue count  queue count
   64           16           2
  Output queue size 0/max total 600/drops 0
```

NOTE   When voice is not configured, voice bandwidth output is not displayed.

Shown next is sample terminal output from the **show frame-relay pvc** command for multipoint subinterfaces carrying data only. The output displays both the subinterface number and the DLCI. This display is the same whether the PVC is configured for static or dynamic addressing. Neither fragmentation nor voice is configured on this PVC.

This command will display DLCIs only; CIR information is available when a specified PVC is queried.

Example 16-2   *show frame-relay pvc*

```
Router# show frame-relay pvc
DLCI = 300, DLCI USAGE = LOCAL, PVC STATUS = ACTIVE, INTERFACE = Serial0.103
input pkts 10   output pkts 7   in bytes 6222
out bytes 6034   dropped pkts 0   in FECN pkts 0
in BECN pkts 0   out FECN pkts 0   out BECN pkts 0
in DE pkts 0   out DE pkts 0
outbcast pkts 0   outbcast bytes 0
pvc create time 0:13:11   last time pvc status changed 0:11:46
DLCI = 400, DLCI USAGE = LOCAL, PVC STATUS = ACTIVE, INTERFACE = Serial0.104
input pkts 20   output pkts 8   in bytes 5624
out bytes 5222   dropped pkts 0   in FECN pkts 0
in BECN pkts 0   out FECN pkts 0   out BECN pkts 0
in DE pkts 0   out DE pkts 0
outbcast pkts 0   outbcast bytes 0
pvc create time 0:03:57   last time pvc status changed 0:03:48
```

Shown next is sample terminal output from the **show frame-relay pvc** command for a PVC carrying voice and data traffic with a special queue specifically for voice traffic created using the **frame-relay voice bandwidth** command **queue** keyword:

```
Router# show frame-relay pvc interface serial 1 45

PVC Statistics for interface Serial1 (Frame Relay DTE)

DLCI = 45, DLCI USAGE = LOCAL, PVC STATUS = STATIC, INTERFACE = Serial1

    input pkts 85          output pkts 289      in bytes 1730
    out bytes 6580         dropped pkts 11      in FECN pkts 0
    in BECN pkts 0         out FECN pkts 0      out BECN pkts 0
    in DE pkts 0           out DE pkts 0
    out bcast pkts 0        out bcast bytes 0
    pvc create time 00:02:09, last time pvc status changed 00:02:09
    Service type VoFR
    configured voice bandwidth 25000, used voice bandwidth 22000
    fragment type VoFR        fragment size 100
    cir 20000     bc   1000     be 0          limit 125    interval 50
    mincir 20000     byte increment 125    BECN response no
    fragments 290     bytes 6613      fragments delayed 1      bytes delayed 33
    shaping inactive
    traffic shaping drops 0
     Voice Queueing Stats: 0/100/0 (size/max/dropped)
    ~~~~~~~~~~~~~~~~~~~~~~~~~~~~~~~~~~~~~~~~~~~~~~~~~~~
    Current fair queue configuration:
     Discard     Dynamic      Reserved
     threshold   queue count  queue count
     64          16           2
    Output queue size 0/max total 600/drops 0
```

debug frame-relay lmi

The **debug frame-relay lmi** command is used to display information on the LMI packets exchanged by the router and the Frame Relay service provider. The **no** form of this command disables debugging output.

```
[no] debug frame-relay lmi [interface name]
```

debug frame-relay lmi might be used to determine whether the router and the [network service provider] Frame Relay switch are sending and receiving LMI packets properly. This command is also useful for verifying and validating network documentation.

NOTE   Because the **debug frame-relay lmi** command does not generate much output, it can be used at any time, even during periods of heavy traffic, without adversely affecting other users on the system.

The following is sample output from the **debug frame-relay lmi** command.

```
router #   debug frame-relay lmi
```

LMI
Exchange——

```
Seriall [out]; StEnq, clock 2021760, myseq 206, mineseen 205, yourseen 136, DTE up
Seriall '[in]; Status, clock 20212764, myseq 206
RT IE 1, length 1, type 1
KA IE 3, length 2, yourseq 138, myseq 206

Seriall [out]; StEnq, clock 20222760, myseq 207, mineseen 206, yourseen 138,
                                 DTE up
                                 Seriall [in]; Status, clock 20222764,
                                 myseq 207
                                 RT IE 1, length 1, type 1
                                 KA IE 3, length 2, yourseq 140,
                                 myseq 207
                                 Seriall [out]; clock 20232760,
                                 myseq 208, mineseen 207,
                                 yourseen 140, line up
                                 RT IE 1, length 1, type 1
                                 KA IE 3, length 2, yoursq 142,
```

Full LMI
Status
message

```
                                 myseq 208
Seriall [out]; StEnq, clock 20252760, myseq 210, mineseen 209, yourseen 144, DTE up
Seriall [in]; Status, clock 20252764,
RT IE 1, length 1, type 0
KA IE 3, length 2, youseq 146, myseq 210
PVC IE 0x7, length 0x6, dlci 400, status 0, bw 56000
PVC IE 0x7, length 0x6, dlci 401, status 0, bw 56000
```

The first four lines describe an LMI exchange. The detail of each line is as follows:

- The first line describes the LMI request that the router has sent to the switch.
- The second line describes the LMI reply that the router has received from the switch.
- The third and fourth lines describe the response to this request from the switch.

This LMI exchange is followed by two similar LMI exchanges. The last six lines consist of a full LMI status message that includes a description of the router's two permanent virtual circuits (PVCs).

Table 16-13 describes significant fields in the first line of the **debug frame-relay lmi** output.

Table 16-13 *debug frame-relay lmi Field Description: Part I*

Field	Description
Serial1(out)	An indication that the LMI request was sent out on the Serial1 interface.
StEnq	The command mode of message: StEnq—Status inquiry Status—Status reply
clock 20212760	The system clock (in milliseconds). Useful for determining whether an appropriate amount of time has transpired between events.
myseq 206	The myseq counter that maps to the router's CURRENT SEQ counter.

Table 16-13 *debug frame-relay lmi Field Description: Part I*

Field	Description
yourseen 136	The yourseen counter that maps to the LAST RCVD SEQ counter of the switch.
DTE up	The line protocol up/down state for the DTE (user) port.

Table 16-14 describes significant fields in the third and fourth lines of **debug frame-relay lmi** output.

Table 16-14 *debug frame-relay lmi Field Description: Part II*

Field	Description
RT IE 1	The value of the report type information element.
length 1	The length of the report type information element (in bytes).
type 1	The report type in RT IE.
KA IE 3	The value of the keepalive information element.
length 2	The length of the keepalive information element (in bytes).
yourseq 138	The yourseq counter that maps to the CURRENT SEQ counter of the switch.
myseq 206	The myseq counter that maps to the router's CURRENT SEQ counter.

Table 16-15 describes significant fields in the last line of **debug frame-relay lmi** output.

Table 16-15 *debug frame-relay lmi Output: Part III*

Field	Description
PVC IE 0x7	The value of the permanent virtual circuit information element type.
length 0x6	The length of the PVC IE (in bytes).
dlci 401	The DLCI decimal value for this PVC.
status 0	The status value. Possible values include the following: 0x00—Added/inactive 0x02—Added/active 0x04—Deleted 0x08—New/inactive 0x0a—New/active
bw 56000	The committed information rate (CIR), in decimal, for the DLCI.

show frame-relay route

The **show frame-relay route** command (in EXEC mode) is used to display all configured Frame Relay routes, along with their respective status.

```
show frame-relay route
```

Following is sample terminal output from the **show frame-relay route** command from a router in NNI configuration:

```
Router# show frame-relay route

Input Intf     Input Dlci     Output Intf     Output Dlci   Status
Serial1        100            Serial2         200           active
Serial1        101            Serial2         201           active
Serial1        102            Serial2         202           active
Serial1        103            Serial3         203           inactive
Serial2        200            Serial1         100           active
Serial2        201            Serial1         101           active
Serial2        202            Serial1         102           active
Serial3        203            Serial1         103           inactive
```

Table 16-16 describes the **show frame-relay route** field descriptions.

Table 16-16 *show frame-relay route Field Descriptions*

Field	Description
Input Intf	The input interface and unit
Input Dlci	The input DLCI number
Output Intf	The output interface and unit
Output Dlci	The output DLCI number
Status	The status of the connection: active or inactive

Global Frame Relay WAN Documentation

A global Frame Relay WAN document is one that provides an overall, or global, view of the Frame Relay WAN. This document provides information regarding interconnectivity between each node of the wide-area network. A global document can be used to represent just Layer 2 (DLCI) information, Layer 3 Network (Addressing) information, or some combination of the two. The decision rests with the individual, or organization, for which the document is intended.

The following three-node network (Figures 16-7 and 16-8) will be used to demonstrate how a Layer 2 and Layer 3 global template can be completed (see Tables 16-17 and 16-18). Provided here are both a network diagram and the **show frame-relay map** output from the head-end node—in this case, Richmond.

Figure 16-7 *Global Template **show frame-relay map** Network Example*

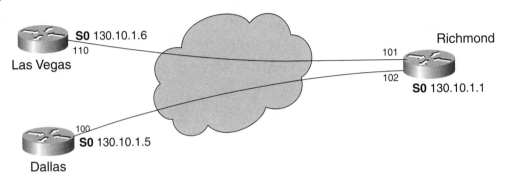

Figure 16-8 *Global Frame Relay WAN Template Diagram (Simple)*

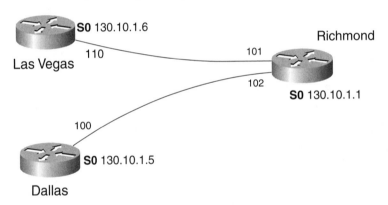

Example 16-3 *Richmond **show frame-relay map** Output for Figure 16-7*

```
Richmond#show frame-relay map
Serial0 (up): ip 130.10.1.5 dlci 102(0x66,0x1860), static,
              Broadcast,
              Cisco, status defined
              TCP/IP Header Compression (inherited), passive (inherited)
Serial0 (up): ip 130.10.1.6 dlci 101(0x66,0x1860), static,
              Broadcast,
              Cisco, status defined
              TCP/IP Header Compression (inherited), passive (inherited)
Richmond#
```

Table 16-17 *Frame Relay [Layer-2] Documentation Example*

Origination (Site A)					Termination (Site B)					
Site Name	Site Ckt ID	Site Location	FRL Port Speed	A⟹B DLCI	Site Name	Site Ckt ID	FRL Port Speed	A⟹B CIR	Comments
Richmond	FRL-Rich001	Richmond	128 K	101	Las Vegas	FRL-Lasv0001	64 K	64 K	
				102	Dallas	FRL-DalT0001	64 K	64 K	
Las Vegas	FRL-Lasv0001	Las Vegas	64 K	110	Richmond	FRL-Rich0001	128 K	64 K	
Dallas	FRL-DalT0001	Dallas	64 K	100	Richmond	FRL-Rich0001	128 K	64 K	

Table 16-18 *Frame Relay [Layer-2] Documentation Template*

| Origination (Site A) | | | | | Termination (Site B) | | | | |
Site Name	Site Ckt ID	Site Location	FRL Port Speed	A→B DLCI	Site Name	Site Ckt ID	FRL Port Speed	A→B CIR	Comments

Frame Relay DLCI Table

The Frame Relay DLCI documentation template might be used as a DLCI Quick Reference. A quick reference sheet like this could be attached to the router for use during troubleshooting of Layer-2 (PVC) connectivity issues, especially if coordinating troubleshooting activities with the network service provider.

Figure 16-9 will be used to complete the Frame Relay DLCI table (see Tables 16-19 and 16-20).

Figure 16-9 *DLCI Table Network Diagram*

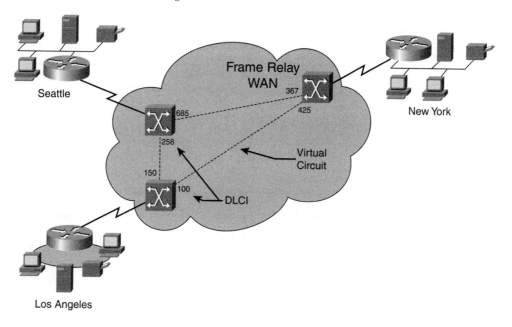

Table 16-19 *Frame Relay DLCI Table Example*

Site A (Origination)	Site B (Termination)	A ➡ B DLCI	B ➡ A DLCI
Los Angeles	New York	100	425
Los Angeles	Seattle	150	258
Seattle	New York	685	367
Seattle	Los Angeles	258	150
New York	Seattle	367	685
New York	Los Angeles	425	100

Table 16-20 *Frame Relay DLCI Table Template*

Site A (Origination)	Site B (Termination)	A ⟹ B DLCI	B ⟹ A DLCI

Summary

The following Cisco IOS commands were used to gather pertinent Frame Relay WAN information and to complete network documentation templates.

The **show frame-relay map** command is used (in EXEC mode) to display the current map entries and information about the connections.

Many DLCIs can be known by a router that can send data to many different places, but they are all multiplexed over one physical link. The Frame Relay map tells the router how to get from a specific protocol and address pair to the correct DLCI.

The optional **ietf** and **cisco** keywords allow flexibility in the configuration. If no keywords are specified in the configuration, the map inherits the attributes set with the **encapsulation frame-relay** command. You can also use the encapsulation options to specify that, for example, all interfaces use IETF encapsulation except one, which needs the original Cisco encapsulation method, and it can be defined using the **cisco** keyword with the **frame-relay map** command.

The **broadcast** keyword provides two functions: It forwards broadcasts when multicasting is not enabled, and it simplifies the configuration of OSPF for nonbroadcast networks that will use Frame Relay.

OSPF treats a nonbroadcast, multiaccess network such as Frame Relay much the same way it treats a broadcast network—it requires selection of a designated router. In previous releases, this required manual assignment in the OSPF configuration using the **neighbor interface** router command. When the **frame-relay map** command is included in the configuration with the **broadcast**, and the **ip ospf network** command (with the **broadcast** keyword) is configured, you don't need to configure neighbors manually. OSPF will now automatically run over the Frame Relay network as a broadcast network.

The **show frame-relay pvc** command is useful for gathering statistics and measurements for individual virtual circuit interconnections between sites. From a documentation standpoint, only the following information is required from this command's output:

When the interface is configured as a DCE and the DLCI usage is Switched, the value displayed in the PVC Status field is determined by the status of outgoing interfaces (up or down) and the status of the outgoing PVC (updated in the local management interface (LMI) message exchange). PVCs terminated on a DCE interface use the status of the interface to set the PVC STATUS.

If the outgoing interface is a tunnel, the PVC status is determined by what is learned from the tunnel.

If an LMI status report indicates that a PVC is not active, then it is marked as inactive. A PVC is marked as deleted if it is not listed in a periodic LMI status message.

In the case of a hybrid DTE switch, the PVC status on the DTE side is determined by the PVC status reported by the external Frame Relay network through the LMI.

Congestion-control mechanisms are currently not supported, but the switch passes FECN, BECN, and DE bits unchanged from ingress to egress points in the network.

The **show frame-relay route** command (in EXEC mode) is used to display all configured Frame Relay routes, along with their respective status.

CHAPTER 17

Frame Relay WAN Analysis

This chapter will discuss frame relay WAN analysis including traffic shaping, SLAs, and basic analysis.

Frame Relay Traffic Shaping

Traffic shaping is required for Frame Relay networks for three reasons:

- Oversubscription of sites is part of the nature of Frame-Relay networks.
- It is common for configurations to allow bursts that exceed the committed information rate (CIR).
- The default interval for Cisco Frame Relay devices can add unnecessary delay.

Some of the aspects of traffic shaping for Frame-Relay networks include the following:

- CIR
- Committed burst rate (Bc)
- Excess burst rate (Be)
- Minimum CIR

The Cisco IOS command that is used to collect Frame Relay PVC information, such as CIR, is **show frame-relay pvc**. The syntax for this command is as follows:

```
show frame-relay pvc [interface interface [dlci]]
```

The optional variables for **show frame-relay pvc** are as follows:

- interface—Interface number containing the DLCI(s) for which PVC information is requested.
- dlci—A specific DLCI number used on the interface. Statistics for the specified PVC display when a DLCI is also specified.

The following example is displayed output from the **show frame-relay pvc** command.

```
TanFerCo_Router# show frame-relay pvc 464

PVC Statistics for interface Serial3/1 (Frame Relay DTE)
DLCI = 464, DLCI USAGE = LOCAL, PVC STATUS = ACTIVE, INTERFACE = Serial3/1.1
        input pkts 9            output pkts 16          in bytes 154
        out bytes 338           dropped pkts 6          in FECN pkts 0
        in BECN pkts 0          out FECN pkts 0         out BECN pkts 0
        in DE pkts 0            out DE pkts 0
        out bcast pkts 0        out bcast bytes 0
        pvc create time 00:35:11, last time pvc status changed 00:00:22
        Bound to Virtual-Access1 (up, cloned from Virtual-Template5)
```

For Pure FRF.12 implementations, the **show frame-relay pvc** output will look like the following:

```
TanFerCo_Router # show frame-relay pvc 110
PVC Statistics for interface Serial0 (Frame Relay DTE)
DLCI = 110, DLCI USAGE = LOCAL, PVC STATUS = STATIC, INTERFACE = Serial0
   input pkts 0             output pkts 243         in bytes 0
   out bytes 7290          dropped pkts 0          in FECN pkts 0
   in BECN pkts 0          out FECN pkts 0         out BECN pkts 0
   in DE pkts 0            out DE pkts 0
   out bcast pkts 243       out bcast bytes 7290
   pvc create time 04:03:17, last time pvc status changed 04:03:18
   fragment type end-to-end        fragment size 100
   cir 64000      bc 64000      be 0        limit 1000    interval 125
   mincir 32000      byte increment 1000  BECN response no
   pkts 486        bytes 14580     pkts delayed 243      bytes delayed 7290
   shaping inactive
   shaping drops 0
   Current fair queue configuration:
   Discard      Dynamic       Reserved
   threshold    queue count   queue count
   64           16            2
   Output queue size 0/max total 600/drops 0
```

The fragment type reflecting "end-to-end" is indicated by FRF.12 implementations.

NOTE

FRF.12 is an implementation agreement defined to help support voice and other real-time (delay-sensitive) data on lower-speed links, supporting frame size variations in a manner enabling the mixture of real-time and near-real-time data through the process of fragmentation. FRF.12 fragmentation provides for a transmitting Frame Relay device to fragment long frames into a sequence of shorter frames that the receiving device can then reassemble. Each of the smaller pieces can then be transmitted separately through the network, allowing better control over delay and delay variation.

Fragmentation also allows the end station to interleave delay-sensitive traffic from one stream with fragments of a longer frame to another stream on the same physical link.

CIR

CIR is measured in bits per second. This is the rate at which the ingress interface accesses the trunk and the egress interface accesses a Frame Relay network and transfers information to the destination frame relay end system (under normal, non-congestive conditions). This transfer rate is averaged over a minimum time interval, T_C, and is illustrated in Figure 17-1.

Figure 17-1 *Frame Relay Data Transfer*

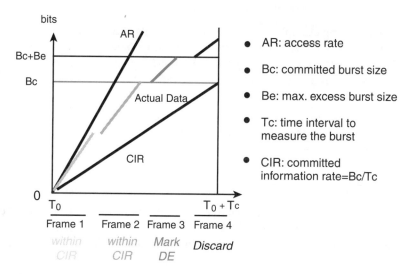

In most Frame Relay networks, a central site uses a high-speed link (T1, NxT1, T3) to terminate WAN connections from many remote offices. The central site sends data out at broadband rates [typically], usually Nx64/T1, whereas a remote site might have only a narrowband (56 kbps) or a smaller broadband access (Nx64) circuit. A typical Frame Relay WAN design deploys a many-to-one ratio of remote offices to central hubs. It is possible for all the remote sites to send traffic at a rate that can overwhelm the T1 at the hub. Both of these scenarios can cause frame buffering in the provider network that induces delay, jitter, and drops. The only solution to these issues is to use traffic shaping at both the central and remote routers.

Committed Burst Rate

Another problem with Frame Relay WANs is the amount of data traffic that a node can transmit at any time interval (T). The problem is that too much data is transmitted for the interface to handle. A 56 kbps Permanent Virtual Circuit (PVC) can transmit a maximum of 56 KB of traffic in 1 second. The interval is how this second is divided. The amount of traffic that a node can transmit during this interval is called the *committed burst (B_C) rate*.

By default, all Cisco routers set B_C to CIR/8; B_C is measured in total bits, not bits per second.

The formula for calculating the interval is as follows:

$$\text{Interval} = B_C / \text{CIR}$$

For example, with a CIR of 56 kbps:

$$\text{Interval} = 7,000 / 56,000 = 125 \text{ milliseconds (ms)}$$

In the preceding example, after a router transmits its allocated 7,000 bits, it must wait 125 ms before sending its next traffic. Although this value is a good default value for data, it is a poor choice for voice. By setting the B_C value to a much lower number, the interval will decrease, meaning the router will send traffic more frequently.

NOTE   An optimal configured value for B_C is 1,000.

Excess Burst Rate

If the router does not have enough traffic to send all of its B_C (1,000 bits, for example), it can "credit" its account and send more traffic during a later interval. The excess burst (B_E) rate defines the maximum amount that can be credited to the router's traffic account.

CAUTION   The issue with B_E in Cisco VoX networks creates a potential for buffering delays within a Frame Relay network because the receiving node can "pull" the traffic from a circuit only at the rate of B_C, not $B_C + B_E$.

Minimum CIR

Cisco IOS defaults to a minimum CIR (mincir) value of CIR/2. Minimum CIR is the transmit value that a Frame-Relay router will "rate down" to when BECNs are received.

Frame Relay Oversubscription

Frame Relay is a nonbroadcast WAN that uses oversubscription to realize cost savings over dedicated private-line networks. Oversubscription occurs when the sum of the services supported by an interface is greater than the interface's configured bandwidth.

Oversubscribing a Frame Relay service is not necessarily bad. For example, in a hub-and-spoke network topology, oversubscription prevents the likelihood of several remote sites sending or receiving from the head-end site at the same time interval.

Figure 17-2 illustrates the Frame Relay oversubscription analysis.

Figure 17-2 *TanFerCo Frame Relay WAN (Oversubscribed)*

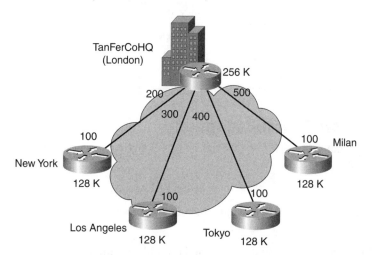

TanFerCo has deployed a five-node Frame Relay WAN, headquartered in London, UK with remote sites located in New York, Los Angeles, Tokyo, and Milan. Data traffic is primarily e-mail, file-sharing, and corporate intranet-related applications. The configuration of this WAN is shown in Table 17-1

Table 17-1 *TanFerCo Case Study Frame Relay Network*

Site Name	TanFerCo HQ			Mnemonic		London
FRL Access Bandwidth	256 K			FRL Access Ckt ID		
Access Carrier		Local Access Ckt ID		Channels		1 to 4
LMI Type	Annex-D					

DLCI and Interface	Term. Network Address	Term. Site Name	Term. Site Mnemonic	Term. FRL Circuit ID	Term. FRL Access Bandwidth	PVC CIR Bandwidth
200		New York	New York		128 K	64 K
300		Los Angeles	Los Angeles		128 K	64 K
400		Tokyo	Tokyo		128 K	64 K
500		Milan	Milan		128 K	64 K

Frame Relay Port Oversubscription

To determine the port oversubscription percentage for this network, use the following formula:

$$[((N_1 + N_2 + N_3...N_X)/N_H) \times 100 = FRL_{PORTOVER}]$$

where N is the access bandwidth provisioned at each remote site and N_H is the access bandwidth at the head-end site.

In the TanFerCo case study, the formula would be applied as such:

$$((128+128+128+128)/256) \times 100 = 200\% \text{ Frame Relay Port Oversubscription}$$

Therefore, the TanFerCo Frame Relay WAN has been implemented with a 200%, or 2:1 Port oversubscription rate. This oversubscription is not necessarily bad given that the data traffic comprises bursty applications. Unless these locations are open 24 hours, it is unlikely that the New York and Tokyo offices will be accessing the HQ office at the same time interval.

Frame Relay PVC/CIR Oversubscription

To determine the PVC/CIR oversubscription percentage for this network, the following formula is used:

$$[((P_1 + P_2 + P_3...P_X)/N_H) \times 100 = FRL_{PORTOVER}]$$

where P is the PVC/CIR of each Permanent Virtual Circuit provisioned to the head-end Frame Relay Port, and N_H is the access bandwidth at the head-end site.

In the TanFerCo case study, the formula would be applied as such:

$$((64+64+64+64)/256) \times 100 = 100\% \text{ PVC/CIR Oversubscription}$$

Therefore, the TanFerCo Frame Relay WAN has been implemented with a 100%, or 1:1 PVC/CIR to Port oversubscription rate. This Frame Relay WAN is designed with no CIR traffic at risk of being discarded due to oversubscription.

NOTE   Most network service providers will not enable a customer network to oversubscribe PVC/CIR to the head-end port because the network service provider's service-level agreement (SLA) would typically be rendered invalid.

If each PVC/CIR were provisioned at 32 K, the formula would reflect the following:

$$((32+32+32+32)/256 \times 100 = 50\% \text{ PVC/CIR Oversubscription}$$

This means that no CIR traffic is at risk of being discarded, and 128 Kbps of DE traffic will be delivered reliably because 128 K of bandwidth remains available for non-CIR traffic.

Frame Relay Data Delivery Ratio (DDR)

The **show frame-relay pvc** command is used to display information that determines the data delivery ratio (DDR) of a Frame Relay PVC. The following output will be used to complete the Frame Relay Frame Delivery Ratio Template example.

```
Router# show frame-relay pvc
DLCI = 154, DLCI USAGE = LOCAL, PVC STATUS = ACTIVE, INTERFACE = Serial0.103
input pkts 21514   output pkts 31452   in bytes 172212
out bytes 251616   dropped pkts 325   in FECN pkts 0
in BECN pkts 0   out FECN pkts 0   out BECN pkts 0
in DE pkts 0   out DE pkts 0
outbcast pkts 0   outbcast bytes 0
pvc create time 0:13:11   last time pvc status changed 0:11:46
DLCI = 329, DLCI USAGE = LOCAL, PVC STATUS = ACTIVE, INTERFACE = Serial0.104
input pkts 3020   output pkts 214   in bytes 15624
out bytes 25222   dropped pkts 13   in FECN pkts 0
in BECN pkts 0   out FECN pkts 0   out BECN pkts 0
in DE pkts 0   out DE pkts 0
outbcast pkts 0   outbcast bytes 0
pvc create time 0:03:57   last time pvc status changed 0:03:48
```

You can determine the Frame Relay frame delivery ratio (FDR) by taking the total number of input and output packets (as displayed by the **show frame-relay pvc** command output), minus the dropped packets, and then dividing that number by the original sum of input and output packets. The formula to determine the FDR is as follows:

$$((INPUT_{PACKETS} + OUTPUT_{PACKETS}) - DROPPED_{PACKETS} / (INPUT_{PACKETS} + OUTPUT_{PACKETS})) \times 100 = FDR \%$$

Table 17-2 *Frame Relay Frame Delivery Ratio Template Example*

Date/Time	Site Name (DLCI)	(Input pkts) + (Output pkts)	Dropped pkts	FDR	Comments
6/30/2001	Tampa (154)	(21514+31452) = 52966	325	98.38%	
6/30/2001	Miami (329)	(3020+214) = 3234	13	99.60%	

Table 17-3 *Frame Relay Frame Delivery Ratio Template*

Date/Time	Site Name	(Input pkts) + (Output pkts)	Dropped pkts	FDR	Comments

Measuring the FDR is a good indication of frame relay network performance; however, network service providers generally measure their service-level agreements (SLAs) against the DDR (percentage of bits/bytes sent/received by an end-node pair).

To measure the DDR accurately, you must enter a **show frame-relay pvc** command on both devices at the same time because the data counters will continue to increase over time and could distort the measurement. If this method is not feasible, you can take an approximate measurement as long as the interface statistics are gathered within a reasonable amount of time of each other.

Figure 17-3 and output from a **show frame-relay pvc** command from a PVC between Dallas and Chicago are used to complete the following FDR template.

Figure 17-3 *Dallas and Chicago WAN*

```
Router# show frame-relay pvc
DLCI = 254, DLCI USAGE = LOCAL, PVC STATUS = ACTIVE, INTERFACE = Serial0.103
input pkts 21514   output pkts 31452   in bytes 172212
out bytes 251616   dropped pkts 12   in FECN pkts 0
in BECN pkts 0   out FECN pkts 0   out BECN pkts 0
in DE pkts 0   out DE pkts 0
outbcast pkts 0   outbcast bytes 0
pvc create time 0:13:11   last time pvc status changed 0:11:46

DLCI = 561, DLCI USAGE = LOCAL, PVC STATUS = ACTIVE, INTERFACE = Serial0.104
input pkts 31420   output pkts 21534   in bytes 251204
out bytes 172300   dropped pkts 12   in FECN pkts 0
in BECN pkts 0   out FECN pkts 0   out BECN pkts 0
in DE pkts 0   out DE pkts 0
outbcast pkts 0   outbcast bytes 0
pvc create time 0:03:57   last time pvc status changed 0:03:48
```

To determine the Frame Relay DDR, use the following formula:

$$(\text{Site A}_{\text{INPUTBYTES}} \,/\, \text{Site B}_{\text{OUTPUTBYTES}}) \times 100 = \text{DDR} \%$$

The number of bytes that Site A receives is divided by the number of bytes that Site B sends; this result is then multiplied by 100 to determine a percentage.

Table 17-4   *Frame Relay DDR Template Example*

Date/Time	Site A (DLCI)	Site B (DLCI)	Site A Bytes Input	Site B Bytes Output	DDR%
6/30/2001	Dallas (254)	Miami (329)	172212	172300	99.95%
6/30/2001	Miami (329)	Dallas (254)	31420	31452	99.90%

NOTE   The FDR and DDR templates can also be found on the Cisco Press Web site (www.ciscopress.com/1587050390) as Microsoft Excel spreadsheets, with the necessary formulae configured.

Table 17-5   *Frame Relay DDR Template*

Date/Time	Site A (DLCI)	Site B (DLCI)	Site A Bytes Input	Site B Bytes Output	DDR%

Frame Relay SLAs

Reliable measurements for network service provider SLA verification cannot be obtained by customer routers alone; the network service provider must provide data from the network edge devices.

Network service provider SLAs typically guarantee CIR-marked traffic from network edge ingress (customer site A) to network edge egress (customer site B), guaranteeing traffic delivery across the service provider's backbone.

Network service providers should provide their Frame Relay WAN customers with Frame Relay usage reports, raw usage data, or both, depending on the arrangement between the service provider and the customer. These reports generally will provide a percentage of the egress CIR marked and delivered data to the ingress CIR marked data, as illustrated by Figure 17-4.

Figure 17-4 *Service Provider Reporting Points*

Measurements are taken at points A and B, with the following formula applied:

$(CIR_B/CIR_A) \times 100 = \%$ delivered of CIR marked traffic

Summary

You can determine some basic Frame Relay WAN traffic delivery analysis by using the information provided by the **show frame-relay pvc** command output.

The amount of traffic that a node can transmit during a time interval is called the committed burst (B_C) rate. By default, all Cisco routers set B_C to CIR/8; B_C is measured in total bits, not bits per second.

The formula for calculating the interval is as follows:

Interval = B_C /CIR

For example, with a CIR of 56 kbps:

Interval = 7,000 / 56,000 = 125 ms

To determine the port oversubscription percentage for this network, the following formula is used:

$$[((N_1 + N_2 + N_3 ... N_X)/N_H) \times 100 = FRL_{PORTOVER}]$$

where N is the access bandwidth provisioned at each remote site and N_H is the access bandwidth at the head-end site.

The Frame Relay frame delivery ratio (FDR) is determined by taking the total number of input and output packets (as displayed by the **show frame-relay pvc** command output), minus the dropped packets, and then dividing that number by the original sum of input and output packets. The formula to determine the FDR is as follows:

$$((INPUT_{PACKETS} + OUTPUT_{PACKETS}) - DROPPED_{PACKETS} /$$
$$(INPUT_{PACKETS} + OUTPUT_{PACKETS})) \times 100 = FDR \%$$

To determine the Frame Relay data delivery ratio (DDR), use the following formula:

$$(Site\ A_{INPUTBYTES} / Site\ B_{OUTPUTBYTES}) \times 100 = DDR \%$$

The number of bytes that Site A receives is divided by the number of bytes that Site B sent; this result is then multiplied by 100 to determine a percentage.

Reliable measurements for network service provider service-level agreement (SLA) verification cannot be obtained by customer routers alone; the network service provider must provide data from the network edge devices.

Network service provider SLAs typically guarantee CIR-marked traffic from network edge ingress (customer site A) to network edge egress (customer site B), guaranteeing traffic delivery across the service provider's backbone.

CHAPTER 18

ATM Wide-Area Networking (WAN) and MPOA

Asynchronous Transfer Mode (ATM) is the most widely implemented backbone technology, especially in the network service provider market. ATM is a standards-based transport medium and is widely used within the core and the access edge to enable data, video, and voice communication at high [broadband] speeds. Although ATM wide-area networks (WANs) are generally found in service provider backbones, with the rise in converged voice and data broadband applications, ATM is making its way into the large enterprise space.

Several standards bodies have been involved with the development of broadband-ISDN (B-ISDN) and ATM. The Telecommunications Standardization Sector of the International Telecommunications Union (ITU-T) is the standards body for B-ISDN and started publishing documents about B-ISDN in 1988. Working groups under the American National Standards Institute (ANSI) and the European Telecommunications Standards Institute (ETSI) have made significant contributions to the ITU-T efforts.

The ATM Forum was established in 1991, enabling ATM equipment vendors and network service providers to cooperate in the development of ATM internetworking products and services. Since its inception, the ATM Forum has worked to define the specifications for ATM-based networks, including the backward compatibility of future standards.

The Internet Engineering Task Force (IETF) defined the encapsulation methods for multiprotocol over ATM (MPOA), as well as standards for ATM network management.

NOTE   The impact of increased user demand on the existing Internet infrastructure has been well documented. A tremendous strain has been placed on the traditional voice and data networks, often resulting in poor performance and costly outages. The networking industry is responding to the challenge by increasing the performance and scalability of routed packet networks. Performance is commonly measured twofold, in terms of transit delay and packet loss, with the addition of throughput (bps) to provide a clearer performance picture.

In typical routed networks, packet level processing must be performed at each hop. As routed networks grow, the number of hops increases. Ultimately, the hop-by-hop processing results in an incremental increase in delay, and network performance begins to suffer.

ATM Forum's MPOA specification is the industry's first standards-based solution that enables routed networks to take advantage of the benefits of the ATM network, such as lower latency, better performance, and scalability. MPOA expands on schemes such as LAN Emulation (LANE), Classical IP/ATM (RFC 1577) and the IETF Next Hop Resolution Protocol (NHRP) to create a standardized notion of a virtual router, or routing functionality integrated within a high-speed, dynamically switched ATM network. Conceptually, MPOA reduces the cumulative latency in a multiprotocol routed network by reducing the number of intermediate points where packet processing must be performed (that is, hop-by-hop processing). MPOA allows traffic to be forwarded to its destination over an ATM virtual circuit, which incurs the net delay of a single router "hop."

MPOA splits the traditional role of the router into two functions. The first, the host functional group, deals with direct communication to the end user devices. The second, the edge device functional group, deals with the network services, such as route determination, virtual channel (VC) mapping, and cut-through packet forwarding. The ability to separate packet forwarding from other router functions allows a more efficient implementation of the two components. Through a new protocol called Next Hop Routing Protocol (NHRP), routing entities within a switching infrastructure can communicate with one another to determine unknown IP-to-ATM address mappings. This enables the host or edge device to establish a shortcut path to the destination, limiting hop-by-hop processing.

NOTE   The ability to expedite forwarding of packets is what is known as *cut-through routing*. It is a distinguishing characteristic of MPOA.

The MPOA switched-routing methodology consists of three components:

- Route servers—These integrate routing (Layer 3) intelligence into an inherently switched (Layer 2) transport infrastructure. To existing routers, the route server looks like a traditional router. The router server performs the "routing" function for the hosts and edge devices in an MPOA network. Cut-through forwarding between edge devices and hosts leverages the underlying ATM connectivity.

- Edge devices—These connect traditional LANs to the MPOA-capable network. In this manner, Ethernet, Fast Ethernet, Token Ring, FDDI, and other LAN traffic enter and exit the ATM network.

- ATM hosts—These are MPOA-enhanced LANE hosts directly attached to the MPOA, usually via ATM network interface cards (NICs).

ATM is best known for its ease of integration with other technologies and its sophisticated management features that allow carriers to guarantee quality of service. These management features are built into the different layers of ATM.

Sometimes referred to as *cell relay*, ATM uses short, fixed-length packets called *cells* for transport. Information is divided among these cells, transmitted, and then reassembled at their destination.

ATM Network Architecture

ATM WANs combine features of both voice and data internetworking. Public or private ATM WANs are made up of a set of ATM switches under control by the same administration. ATM switches on the edge of the network provide backbone communication services to networking devices attached to the network backbone.

Figure 18-1 illustrates an ATM WAN supporting direct access by routers, private branch exchanges, or PBXs (with VoATM modules), file servers (with ATM LANE modules), and a video server (with a LANE module).

Figure 18-1   *ATM WAN*

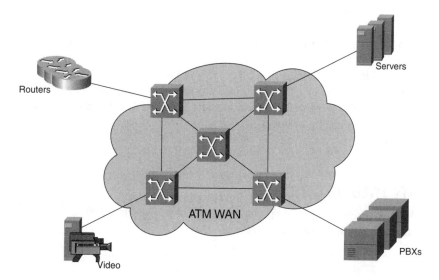

ATM is connection-oriented, meaning that a communication path must be provisioned between endpoints prior to the exchange of traffic across the circuit.

ATM WANs can also be set up as a connectionless service, with the network service provider implementing a VLAN configuration in the WAN cloud. A permanent virtual circuit (PVC) is provisioned from each customer's router into the ATM VLAN switch, as Figure 18-2 illustrates.

Figure 18-2 *ATM WAN VLAN Configuration*

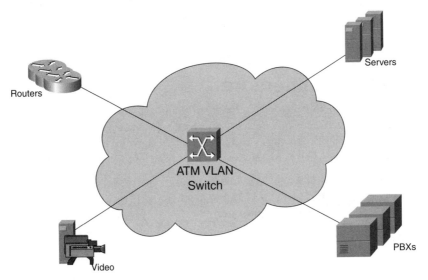

ATM via switched virtual circuits (SVCs) support connectionless architectures, such as those supporting voice or videoconferencing applications. SVCs are similar to PVCs in that they are a logical circuit connection across a WAN. Whereas PVCs use data-link connection identifiers (DLCIs) or virtual path indicators/virtual channel indicators (VPIs/VCIs) for addressing, SVCs use X.121 or E.164 addressing. ATM SVC service operates in a similar fashion to switched multimegabit data service (SMDS) and is enabled by AAL3/4. (ATM adaptation layers are discussed later in this chapter.)

ATM WAN Interfaces

ATM WAN architecture supports the following five interface types, which are discussed in greater detail in the following sections:

- ATM user-network interface (UNI)—This interface defines the interaction among the following:

  — An ATM endpoint device and a private network switch

  — An ATM endpoint device and a public network switch

  — A private network switch and a public network switch

- ATM Network-Network Interface (NNI)—This interface supports signaling between ATM switches across NNI links.

- ATM data-exchange interface (DXI)—This interface supports communication with a DXI-enabled router via the router's serial interface.

- ATM private network node interface or private network-to-network interface (PNNI)—This interface enables differing switch vendors to interoperate across an ATM WAN. Vendors can opt to implement proprietary ATM signaling between their own switches. Cisco Systems, Inc. implements PNNI 1.0.

NOTE   The ATM Forum released the full PNNI 1.0 specification in May 1996. PNNI 1.0 enables scalable, full function, dynamic, multivendor ATM networks by providing both PNNI routing and PNNI signaling. PNNI is based on UNI 3.0 signaling and static routes.

- ATM broadband ISDN (B-ISDN) intercarrier interface (B-ICI)—This interface describes public network-to-network interface points. For a global telecommunications network to exist, public ATM networks must be interconnected.

ATM UNI

UNI signaling in ATM defines the protocol by which the ATM devices in the network dynamically set up SVCs.

The UNI specifications include physical layer, integrated local management interface (ILMI), traffic management, and signaling.

ATM NNI

NNI signaling is part of the PNNI specification, which includes both signaling and routing.

ATM DXI

The ATM Forum developed a standard known as the ATM DXI to make ATM features and functionality immediately available to the networking community. DXI can be used to enable UNI support between Cisco routers and ATM networks, as illustrated in Figure 18-3.

Figure 18-3 *ATM DXI*

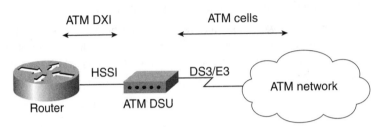

The ATM data service unit (ADSU) receives data from the router in ATM DXI format over a high-speed serial interface (HSSI). The DSU converts the data into ATM cells and transfers them to the ATM network over a DS-3/E3 line.

ATM DXI is available in several modes for DXI header format:

- Mode 1a—Supports AAL5 only, a 9,232 octet maximum, a 2-byte DXI header, and a 2-byte frame check sequence (FCS). Mode 1a supports up to 1,023 virtual circuits.

- Mode 1b—Supports AAL3/4 and AAL5, a 9,224 octet maximum, a 2-byte DXI header, and a 2-byte FCS. Mode 1b AAL5 support is the same as Mode 1a. AAL3/4 is supported on one virtual circuit. Mode 1b supports up to 1,023 virtual circuits.

- Mode 2—Supports AAL3/4 and AAL5, a 65,535-octet maximum, a 4-byte DXI header, and a 4-byte FCS. DXI Mode 2 double-encapsulates AAL5 frames and supports up to 16,777,215 virtual circuits.

NOTE   Cisco uses Mode 1a for the DXI header format.

On the router, data from upper-layer protocols is encapsulated into ATM DXI frame format, as illustrated in Figure 18-4.

Figure 18-4 *DXI Frame Format*

Flag	Header	SDU	FCS	Flag

Field size in octets   1   2   0-9232   2   1

Illustrated in Figure 18-5 is a router configured as a data terminal equipment (DTE) device connected to an ADSU (configured as a data communications equipment, or DCE, device). The router sends ATM DXI frames to the ADSU, which converts the frames to ATM cells, attaches the header, and sends them out the ATM UNI interface.

Figure 18-5   *ATM DXI Mode 1a and 1b Protocol Architecture (for AAL5)*

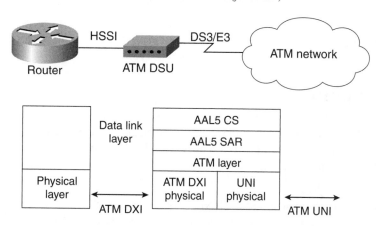

ATM DXI addressing consists of a DXI Frame Address (DFA), essentially the equivalent to a Frame Relay DLCI. As illustrated in Figure 18-6, the ADSU maps the DFA into appropriate VPI and VCI values in the ATM cell.

Figure 18-6   *ATM DXI Address Mapping*

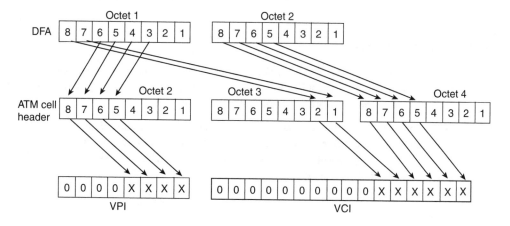

ATM PNNI

ATM PNNI provides mechanisms, which enable scalable, QoS-based ATM routing and switch-to-switch switched virtual connection (SVC) interoperability.

The PNNI specification addresses the following two issues:

- Signaling
- Routing

PNNI Signaling

PNNI signaling is an extension of UNI signaling for use across NNI links. The UNI signaling request, carried on the same virtual channel (VCI=5) used for UNI, is mapped into NNI signaling at the source (ingress) switch. The NNI signaling is remapped back into UNI signaling at the destination (egress) switch. The data is subsequently transmitted on the same path as the signaling request.

The routing component of the PNNI protocol specifies how the signaling request and subsequent data connection are routed through the ATM network.

The PNNI acronym has two interpretations of the PNNI, each suggesting a different application:

- Private network node interface—Routing between ATM switches in a private network
- Private network-network interface—Routing between private ATM networks

ATM Connections

ATM is a connection-oriented technology that supports point-to-point (unicast) and point-to-multipoint (multicast) application connections. Regardless of the application, ATM cells are received in the same order in which they are sent.

ATM does not guarantee delivery of data across the WAN because data might encounter congestion in a backbone switch. ATM determines the handling of such congestion issues based on the class of service to which it is subscribed. (ATM classes of service will be discussed later in this chapter).

Virtual Paths

ATM virtual path connections comprise a bundle of virtual channel connections. The bundling of virtual channels having the same endpoints into a single virtual path simplifies the provisioning and implementation of a large number of virtual channels (VCs) having common endpoints. This provisioning and implementation is simplified as the VCs are multiplexed onto a single virtual path (VP). Virtual paths also simplify the task of switching data from source to destination because all the virtual channels are switched as a single virtual path.

Figure 18-7 illustrates an end-to-end ATM virtual path, with two virtual channels.

Figure 18-7   *ATM end-to-end virtual path*

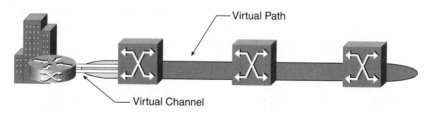

ATM Virtual Channels

ATM point-to-point connections are actually a pair of simplex connections—a simplex connection from end node A ➧ end node B, and a simplex connection from end node B ➧ end node A. Each connection pair comprises a virtual channel connection (VCC).

ATM Cells and Cell Relay

ATM cell relay can occur between two points:

- ATM switch and end point
- ATM switch and ATM switch

ATM cells are fixed 53 bytes in length, 5 byte of header, and a 48-byte payload. Figure 18-8 shows an ATM cell.

Figure 18-8   *ATM Cell*

Header (5 Bytes)	Payload 48 Bytes

NOTE   The 48-byte payload size is a compromise between working groups, some wanting 32 bytes and others wanting 64 bytes.

The ATM cell header carries both the VPI and the VCI of the cell payload being carried.

Cell Transmission

Prior to data transmission, an end-to-end path needs to be established through the ATM WAN. After this path has been provisioned, either on a permanent (PVC) or switched (SVC) basis, the following steps are performed:

1 At the source endpoint, the data is broken down into small, fixed-sized cell payloads for transmission. Each cell header provides the VPI/VCI values for the destination endpoint. VPI/VCI values share the same significance as Frame Relay DLCIs in that they are of local significance.

2 Each ATM switch along the path examines the cell header to determine the appropriate egress interface.

3 Cell payloads are extracted at the destination endpoint, and data contained within is passed on to upper-layer protocols or applications.

Figure 18-9 illustrates four ATM nodes using virtual path and virtual channels to communicate across the ATM WAN. The ATM network service provider is switching the virtual channels based on the VPI/VCI pairs in the ATM cell header.

Figure 18-9   *ATM WAN with Virtual Paths and Virtual Switching*

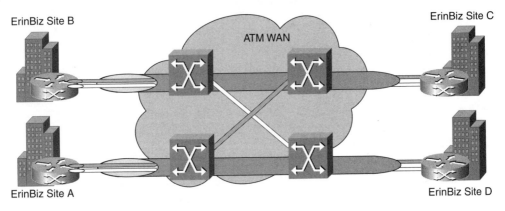

ATM Service Classes

In an effort to reach a unified approach to the definition of ATM-layer services in the ATM Forum and in ITU-T, Table 18-1 correlates the ATM Forum's and ITU-T's definitions of ATM service classes.

Table 18-1   *Correlation of ATM Forum and ITU-T ATM Services*

ATM Forum TM4.0 "ATM Service Category"	ITU-T I.371 "ATM Transfer Capability"	Typical Use
Constant Bit Rate (CBR)	**Deterministic Bit Rate (DBR)**	**Real-Time, QoS Guarantees**
Real-time variable bit rate (rt-VBR)	For further study	Statistical mux, real-time
Near-real-time variable bit rate (nrt-VBR)	Statistical bit rate (SBR)	Statistical mux
Available bit rate (ABR)	Available bit rate (ABR)	Resource exploitation, feedback control
Unspecified bit rate (UBR)	No equivalent	Best effort, no guarantees
No equivalent	ATM block transfer (ABT)	Burst level feedback control

An ATM service category (ATM Forum name) or ATM-layer transfer capability (ITU-T name) is intended to represent a class of ATM connections that have homogeneous characteristics in terms of traffic pattern, QoS requirements, and possible use of control mechanisms, making it suitable for a given type of resource allocation.

ATM Service Architecture

The ATM service architecture makes use of parameters and mechanisms for traffic control and congestion control whose primary role is to protect the network and the end-system to achieve network performance objectives. An additional role is to optimize the use of network resources. The design of these functions is also aimed at reducing network and end-system complexity while maximizing network utilization. To meet these objectives, the set of functions forming the framework for managing and controlling traffic and congestion can be used in appropriate combinations.

ATM service category, or transfer capability, relates quality requirements and traffic characteristics to network behavior parameters and mechanisms. ATM service categories are intended to specify a combination of QoS commitment and traffic parameters that are suitable for a given set of applications (user interpretation) and that allow for specific multiplexing schemes at the ATM layer (network interpretation).

A service category used on an ATM connection must be implicitly or explicitly declared at connection setup. All service categories apply to both virtual channel connections (VCC) and virtual path connections (VPC).

Service functions such as connection admission control (CAC), usage parameter control (UPC), feedback controls, and resource allocation are available within the ATM node equipment and are structured differently for each service category.

The network-specific service functions are as follows:

- CAC
- UPC

CAC

CAC is the set of processes that the network takes during the call (virtual connection) setup phase or renegotiation phase to determine whether a connection request can be accepted or rejected. Network resources (port bandwidth and buffer space) are reserved for the incoming connection at each switching element traversed, if so required, by the service category.

UPC

UPC or policing is the set of processes that the network takes to monitor and control the traffic offered and the validity of the ATM connection at the User Network Interface (UNI). It is an essential requirement for any network that is supporting multiple services. The main purpose of UPC is to protect network resources from malicious and unintentional misbehavior, which can affect the QoS of other already-established connections. Procedures based on a generic cell-rate algorithm (GCRA) can be applied to each cell arrival to assess conformance with respect to the traffic contract for the connection. Violations of negotiated parameters are detected and appropriate actions can be taken, such as cell tagging or discard. *Feedback controls* are defined as the set of procedures that the network and the end systems (possibly cooperating) take to regulate the traffic submitted on ATM connections according to the state of network elements. Specific feedback control procedures can be associated with a service category.

ATM Traffic Parameters

A source traffic parameter describes an inherent characteristic of a source. A set of these parameters constitutes a source traffic descriptor, which, along with cell delay variation tolerance (CDVT) and a conformance definition, characterize an ATM connection.

The following parameters are considered for defining ATM service categories:

- Peak cell rate (PCR)—Maximum bit rate that can be transmitted from the source
- Sustainable cell rate (SCR)—Upper limit for the average cell rate that can be transmitted from the source
- Maximum burst size (MBS) / Burst Tolerance (BT)—Maximum time or number of cells for which the source can transmit the PCR
- Minimum cell rate (MCR)—Minimum cell rate guaranteed by the network (for ABR)
- Cell delay variation tolerance (CDVT)—Tolerance in cell delay variation, referred to as the *peak cell rate*

The QoS parameters selected to correspond to a network performance objective can be negotiated between the end systems and the network—such as via signaling procedures— or can be taken as default. One or more values of the QoS parameters can be offered on a per connection basis.

- Cell delay variation (CDV)—The distortion caused by change in inter-arrival times between cells, also known as *jitter*. Measured in microseconds, this metric represents the worst case for a path.
- Maximum cell transfer delay (Max CTD)—The sum of the fixed-delay component across the link or node and the cell delay variation (CDV). MCTD is a required topology metric for the CBR and VBR-RT service categories; it is an optional metric for VBR-NRT.
- Cell loss ratio (CLR)—The ratio of the number of lost cells to the total number of cells transmitted on a link or node. Two CLR attributes are calculated: CLR0 and CLR0+1. The cell loss priority (CLP) portion of CLR0 considers only CLP=0 traffic. For CLR0+1, both CLP=0 and CLP=1 traffic are considered in the calculation.

CLR_0 and CLR_{0+1} are required parameters for CBR, VBR-rt, and VBR-nrt traffic classes.

The cell loss ratio for CLP_0 traffic is the maximum cell loss ratio for CLP_0 traffic over a link or node.

The cell loss ratio for CLP_{0+1} traffic is the maximum cell loss ratio for CLP_{0+1} traffic over a link or node.

ATM Traffic Contract and Negotiation

A traffic contract specifies the negotiated characteristics of a VPI/VCI connection at an ATM UNI (either private or public). The traffic contract at the public UNI shall consist of a connection traffic descriptor and a set of QoS parameters for each direction of the ATM layer connection and should include the definition of a compliant connection. The values of the traffic contract parameters can be specified either explicitly or implicitly. A parameter value is explicitly specified in the initial call establishment message. This can be accomplished via signaling for SVCs (switched virtual connections), via the network management system (NMS) for permanent virtual connections (PVCs), or at subscription time. A parameter value is implicitly specified when the network assigns its value using default rules.

ATM Service Categories Description

These names are used by the ATM Forum and are the more commonly used names for these classes of service.

CoS	Description
Constant bit rate (CBR)	This provides constant bandwidth across the virtual connection. It is typically used for private line emulated services, such as multimedia, CAD/CAM, or medical imaging.
Variable bit rate real-time (VBR-rt)	This provides a specified average bandwidth across the virtual connection. It is used to support delay-sensitive applications, such as voice or video.
Variable bit rate near-real-time (VBR-nrt)	Provides a specified average bandwidth across the virtual connection. Used to support non-delay-sensitive applications, such as data information.
Unspecified bit rate (UBR)	This is a best-effort service, meaning no bandwidth is specified across the connection, nor is delivery of service guaranteed.
Available bit rate (ABR)	This is a best-effort service implemented in a different fashion from UBR. This service provides continuing feedback indicating how much bandwidth is available for use. By throttling back as necessary, sending hosts avoid network congestion, preventing traffic from being sent, but thrown away before it reaches its intended destination. Typically, this is used to support data applications in which delivery is important, but not necessarily in a near-real-time environment.

CBR

The CBR service category is used by connections that request a fixed (static) amount of bandwidth, characterized by a peak cell rate (PCR) value that is continuously available during the connection lifetime. The source emits cells at or below the PCR at any time and for any duration (or is silent).

This category is intended for real-time applications—that is, those requiring tightly constrained cell transfer delay (CTD) and cell delay variation (CDV), but is not restricted to these applications. It would be appropriate for voice and video applications, as well as for circuit emulation services (CES).

The basic commitment that the network makes is that after the connection is established, the negotiated QoS is assured to all cells.

A CBR port provides a circuit emulation service (CES) for constant bit rate traffic, such as voice and video.

CBR traffic enters and exits the ATM network through a CBR port. The traffic arriving at the CBR port is segmented into ATM cells and introduced to the cell bus. Traffic exiting the CBR port is reassembled from cells back into a raw bit stream. This adaptation utilizes AAL1.

Input Path

When the CBR traffic enters the CBR port, it is segmented into cells. The segmented cells are put in a buffer from which they are placed on the AAC cell bus. Each CBR port is guaranteed enough bandwidth on the cell bus to service the traffic generated by the line connected to the port. The cells are loaded onto the bus without delay and are evenly scheduled to access the bus. The even scheduling helps ensure that the AAC does not clump CBR cells or make them too sparse. This minimizes cell-delay variation.

Output Path

Traffic that is exiting a CBR port is at an endpoint in the ATM network; therefore, it is converted from ATM cells back to a CBR bit stream.

As cells leave the cell bus, the cell header is stripped off and the cell payload is placed in the output buffer. The buffer emits cell payloads to the AAL function at the appropriate rate for the CBR connection. The AAL function checks for errors and replaces any errored payload with all ones. Then the AAL function reassembles the information into the original bit stream.

The buffer does not begin emitting cells to the AAL function until six cells have accumulated. This ensures that the CBR traffic can be reintroduced to the CBR link continuously in the presence of cell delay variation that does not exceed the limits defined in the standard. Under normal operation, the number of cells in the output buffer should remain around six.

Extreme cell delay variation might exist, however, in outbound CBR traffic. Typically, traffic exiting the CBR port enters the AAC from a cell port. The CBR traffic traverses an ATM network as cells. It might have passed through any number of nodes, some of which might have introduced cell delay variation. Although the AAC does not introduce cell delay variation, it does pass existing cell delay variation across the cell bus to the output port.

For this reason, the output buffer at the CBR port is designed to cope with cell delay variation. You can configure the output buffer to a maximum size of between 12 and 21 cells. If the buffer accumulates more than the maximum, an alarm is issued and cells are discarded until the buffer has space for them. You select a higher or lower number depending on the delay variation that is acceptable before an alarm is issued.

If you select the upper limit of 21, the buffer might accumulate up to 21 cells without raising an alarm or causing skips in the continuous flow of bits into the CBR link. If you select a lower number, the AAC will be less tolerant of cell delay variation and will be more likely to discard traffic when it occurs.

Two alarms are associated with the output buffer: overflow and underflow. Cell delay variation could cause either alarm. An intermittent alarm that clears and sets as the traffic fluctuates is an indication of severe cell delay variation or clock fluctuation in the ATM network delivering the traffic.

A persistent alarm is an indication that the connection feeding the port is set at a different rate from the port. In this case, service through the port would be halted.

Real-Time Variable Bit Rate (rt-VBR)

The real-time VBR service category is intended for time-sensitive applications (those requiring tightly constrained delay and delay variation), as would be appropriate for voice and video applications. Sources are expected to transmit at a rate that varies with time. Equivalently, the source can be described as "bursty."

Traffic parameters are PCR, sustainable cell rate (SCR) and maximum burst size (MBS). Cells, which are delayed beyond the value that the CTD specifies, are assumed to be of significantly less value to the application. Real-time VBR service can support statistical multiplexing of real-time sources.

Near-Real-Time (nrt-VBR)

The near-real-time VBR service category is intended for applications that have bursty traffic characteristics and do not have tight constraints on delay and delay variation. As for rt-VBR, traffic parameters are PCR, SCR, and MBS. For those cells that are transferred within the traffic contract, the application expects a low CLR. For all cells, it expects a bound on the CTD. Near-real-time VBR service can support statistical multiplexing of connections.

Available Bit Rate (ABR)

The available bit rate (ABR) is a service category intended for sources that have the ability to reduce or increase their information rate if the network requires them to do so. This allows them to exploit the changes in the ATM layer transfer characteristics (that is, bandwidth availability) subsequent to connection establishment.

NOTE   VBR—ATM FRE2 ILI pairs use VBR to determine bandwidth allocation. VBR allows the VC to accumulate credits whenever it does not use bandwidth within its specified average. When this VC does use bandwidth, the accumulated credits allow it to transmit using the PCR.

ABR—ATM ARE ILI pairs use ABR to determine bandwidth allocation. ABR is a method by which the bandwidth is separated into a guaranteed portion (for PVCs and control VCs) and an available portion (for data SVCs).

Many applications have vague requirements for throughput. They can be expressed as ranges of acceptable values, such as a maximum and a minimum, rather than as an average value, which is typical for the VBR category. To meet this requirement on the establishment of an ABR connection, the end system should specify a maximum required bandwidth and a minimum usable bandwidth. These are designated as the PCR and the minimum cell rate (MCR), respectively. The MCR can be specified as zero. The bandwidth, available from the network, can vary, because it is the sum of an MCR and a variable cell rate, which results from sharing the available capacity among all the active ABR connections via a defined and fair policy. A flow control mechanism is specified that supports several types of feedback to control the source rate. In particular, a closed-loop feedback control protocol using Resource Management (RM) cells has been specified in a rate-based framework.

Although no specific QoS parameter is negotiated with the ABR, it is expected that an end system that adapts its traffic in accordance with the feedback will experience a low CLR and obtain a fair share of the available bandwidth according to a network-specific allocation policy. CDV is not controlled in this service, although admitted cells are not delayed unnecessarily. ABR service is not, as specified at present, intended to support real-time applications.

The ATM Forum specifies a source, destination, and network switch behavior along with details of the rate-based flow control mechanism.

Unspecified Bit Rate (UBR)

The unspecified bit rate (UBR) service category is a "best effort" service intended for non-critical applications, which do not require tightly constrained delay and delay variation, nor a specified quality of service. UBR sources are expected to transmit non-continuous bursts of cells. UBR service supports a high degree of statistical multiplexing among sources.

UBR service does not specify traffic-related service guarantees. Specifically, UBR does not include the notion of a per-connection negotiated bandwidth. Numerical commitments might not be made to the cell loss ratio experienced by a UBR connection or to the cell transfer delay experienced by cells on the connection. Table 18-2 shows the ATM Service Category attributes and guarantees.

NOTE   UBR is the default PVC type in Cisco Router ATM implementations.

Table 18-2   *ATM Service Category Attributes and Guarantees*

Service Category	Traffic Description	Guarantees			
		Min Loss (CLR)	Delay/ Variance	Bandwidth	Use of Feedback Control
CBR	PCR	X	X	X	No
rt-VBR	PCR, SCR, MBS	X	X	X	No
nrt-VBR	PRC, SCR, MBS	X	No	X	No
ABR	PCR, MCR+ behavior parameters	X	No	X	X
UBR	(PCR)	No	No	No	No

NOTE   Previously, only ABR utilized traffic shaping. Traffic shaping involves passing CBR, VBR, or UBR traffic streams through VC queues for scheduled rate shaping.

Traffic shaping is performed on a per-port basis. When traffic shaping is enabled, all traffic exiting the port (out to the network) is subject to virtual channel (VC) scheduling based on the parameters configured for the connection.

ATM Functional Layers

Just as the OSI reference model describes how two computers communicate over a network, the ATM protocol model describes how ATM end systems communicate.

The ATM protocol model consists of the following three functional layers:

- ATM physical layer
- ATM layer
- ATM adaptation layer

As Figure 18-10 illustrates, these three layers correspond roughly to Layer 1 and parts of Layer 2 (such as error control and data framing) of the OSI reference model.

Figure 18-10 *OSI and ATM Layers*

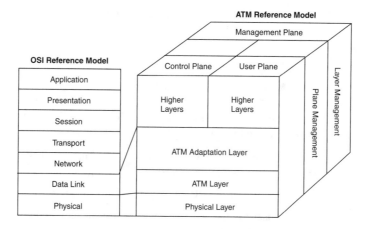

Physical Layer

The ATM physical layer performs the following functions:

- It controls transmission and receipt of bits on the physical medium.
- It keeps track of ATM cell boundaries.
- It packages cells into the appropriate, physical medium- dependent frame.

The ATM physical layer is divided into two parts:

- Physical medium sublayer—This layer is responsible for sending and receiving a continuous flow of bits with associated timing information to synchronize transmission and reception. Because it includes only physical medium-dependent functions, its specification depends on the physical medium used. ATM can use any physical medium capable of carrying ATM cells, such as Synchronous Optical

Network (SONET)/SDH, DS-3/E3, 100-Mbps local fiber (Fiber Distributed Data Interface, or FDDI, physical layer), and 155 Mbps local fiber (Fiber Channel physical layer).

- Transmission convergence sublayer—This layer is responsible for the following:
  - Cell delineation—Maintains ATM cell boundaries
  - Header error control sequence generation and verification—Generates and checks the header error control code to ensure valid data
  - Cell rate decoupling—Inserts or suppresses idle (unassigned) ATM cells to adapt the rate of valid ATM cells to the payload capacity of the transmission system
  - Transmission frame adaptation—Packages ATM cells into frames acceptable to the particular physical-layer implementation
  - Transmission frame generation and recovery—Generates and maintains the appropriate physical-layer frame structure

ATM Layer

The ATM layer establishes virtual connections (VCs) and passes ATM cells through the ATM network using the information contained in the ATM cell header. The ATM layer is responsible for performing the following functions:

- Multiplexing and demultiplexing the cells of different virtual connections. These connections are identified by their VPI and VCI values.
- Translating the values of the VPI and VCI at the ATM switch cross connects.
- Extracting and inserting the header before or after the cell is delivered to or from the higher ATM adaptation layer.
- Handling the implementation of UNI flow-control mechanisms.

ATM Adaptation Layer (AAL)

The AAL translates between the larger service data units (SDUs) (for example, video streams and data packets) of upper-layer processes and ATM cells. Specifically, the AAL receives packets from upper-level protocols (such as AppleTalk, Internet Protocols [IPs], and NetWare) and breaks them into the 48-byte segments that form the payload field of an

ATM cell. Several ATM adaptation layers are currently specified. Table 18-3 summarizes the characteristics of each AAL.

Table 18-3   *ATM Adaptation Layers*

Characteristics	AAL1	AAL3/4	AAL4	AAL5
Requires timing between source and destination	Yes	No	No	No
Data rate	Constant	Variable	Variable	Variable
Connection mode	Connection-oriented	Connection-oriented	Connectionless	Connection-oriented
Traffic types	Voice and circuit emulation	Data	Data	Data

AAL1

AAL1 prepares a cell for transmission. The payload data consists of a synchronous sample (for example, one byte of data generated at a sampling rate of 125 microseconds). The sequence number field (SN) and sequence number protection (SNP) fields provide the information that the receiving AAL1 needs to verify that it has received the cells in the correct order. The rest of the payload field is filled with enough single bytes to equal 48 bytes.

AAL1 is appropriate for transporting telephone traffic and uncompressed video traffic. It requires timing synchronization between the source and destination and, for that reason, depends on a media that supports clocking, such as SONET. The standards for supporting clock recovery are currently being defined.

AAL3/4

AAL3/4 is designed for network service providers and is aligned with Switched Multimegabit Data Service (SMDS) because AAL3/4 is used to transmit SMDS packets over an ATM network. The convergence sublayer (CS) creates a protocol data unit (PDU) by pre-pending a beginning/end tag header to the frame and appending a length field as a trailer.

AAL5

AAL5 is the adaptation layer used to transfer most non-SMDS data, such as classical IP over ATM and LANE.

NOTE	Service classes enable ATM to statistically multiplex varied traffic types. Based on the requirements of each type of stream (its burstiness, tolerance to delay, and so on), packet and circuit traffic are converted to the appropriate cell structure dictated by the AAL. The ATM endpoint equipment performs this conversion, but the equipment within the core of the WAN does not perform or use the conversion.

Several ATM adaptation layers are available:

- ATM adaptation layer type 1 (AAL1)—This layer is designed for CBR, time-dependent traffic, such as voice and video.

- ATM adaptation layer type 2 (AAL2)—This layer is designed for VBR traffic, such as compressed voice.

- ATM adaptation layer type 3/4 (AAL3/4)—This layer is intended for VBR, delay-tolerant data traffic requiring some sequencing or error-detection support.

- ATM adaptation layer type 5 (AAL5)—This layer is used for VBR, delay-tolerant connection-oriented data traffic requiring minimal sequencing or error-detection support. LAN traffic is typically encapsulated with AAL5, and many compressed voice implementations use AAL5 as well.

Traffic Classes

Several traffic classes are in common use:

- CBR service supports a constant or guaranteed rate to transport services such as video or voice. It is also used for CES, which offers services designed to act like existing TDM services. CBR is reliable, with rigorous timing control and performance, but it is less efficient than other traffic classes.

- VBR service provides connection-oriented services, using peak and average traffic parameters to support variable traffic. It is broken down into two sub-classes:

  — VBR-rt is used when controlled delay is essential, such as real-time compressed voice or video.

  — VBR-nrt does not offer delay controls.

- ABR service supports connectionless protocols such as IP, and provides explicit rate control feedback. ABR does not specify delay explicitly.

- UBR service is for best-effort delivery of low-priority traffic.

If public ATM service is to be used, it is important to note that not all carriers offer every traffic class, and the design parameters used by each carrier might be different. You should understand the way the service provider interprets the definition of each class. The presence or absence of a service class offering might not be a problem. For example, a carrier's published latency and jitter specifications for VBR-nrt service might be perfectly adequate to handle compressed voice and video.

Permanent Virtual Circuits Versus Switched Virtual Circuits

Virtual circuits are the logical transport pipes across the ATM backbone. When using permanent virtual circuits (PVCs), the VC is administratively defined, specifying the complete path across the network. This can be an arduous process in large networks, and does not offer the extensive, dynamic rerouting capabilities found with switched virtual circuits (SVCs).

Using SVCs, the circuit is brought up dynamically using ATM signaling. The principal benefit of using SVCs in your network design is to allow direct connection between sites where permanent PVCs would be too expensive to provision. For example, intelligent access devices can set up SVCs based on the digits dialed from a voice handset. This eliminates tandem hops in your voice network and saves PBX ports and access circuit congestion, while simultaneously reducing call setup time. Likewise, delay-sensitive packet-based traffic such as SNA or Voice over IP (VoIP) can benefit from using SVCs.

Few network service providers offer SVC services to customers, although many use SVCs in their backbones to deploy soft PVCs (SPVCs), launching SVCs based on traffic at the customer PVCs. Many of these same carriers offer SVCs on an individual case basis, or can tunnel private SVC signaling traffic over PVCs in hybrid public/private networks. The ATM UNI specification defines the interface point between ATM endpoints and a private ATM switch, or between a private ATM switch and a carrier ATM network. UNI is the most frequent interface type used to connect a router, switch, or other CPE device and a carrier's ATM switch. However, two alternatives to UNI can be used to access the carrier network: ATM DXI and ATM FUNI. Both protocols are designed to use existing, low-cost, frame-based equipment, such as routers, that might not have affordable ATM interfaces.

The principal advantage of FUNI over DXI is that frame traffic remains intact over the access loop, resulting in lower overhead. In addition, DXI does not support management of the access interface via the Integrated Local Management Interface (ILMI) protocol, and is more prone to link failures.

ATM Addressing

The ATM Forum has adapted the subnet model of addressing, in which the ATM layer is responsible for mapping network-layer addresses to ATM addresses.

Several ATM address formats have been developed. Public ATM networks typically use E.164 numbers, which are also used by narrowband ISDN (N-ISDN) networks. Figure 18-11 illustrates the frame format of private network ATM addresses.

Figure 18-11 *ATM Address Formats*

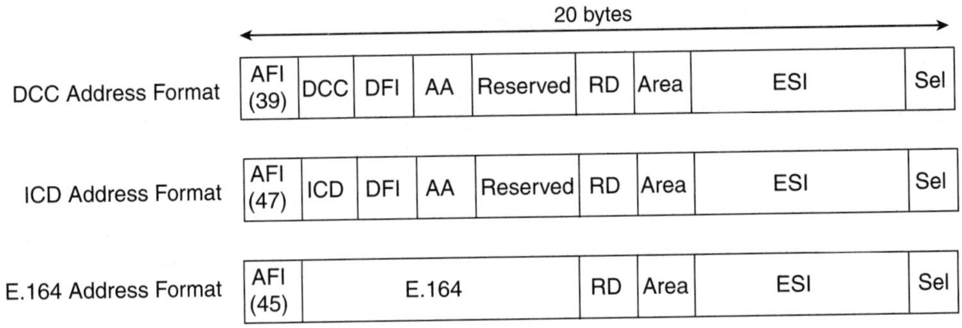

The three frame formats are as follows:

- Data country code (DCC)
- International code designator (ICD)
- Network service access point (NSAP) encapsulated E.164 addresses

The address fields are as follows:

- AFI—One byte of authority and format identifier. The AFI field identifies the type of address. The defined values are 45 (E.164), 47 (ICD), and 39 (DCC).
- DCC—Two bytes of data country code.
- DFI—One byte of domain-specific part (DSP) format identifier.
- AA—Three bytes of administrative authority.
- RD—Two bytes of routing domain.
- Area—Two bytes of area identifier.
- ESI—Six bytes of end system identifier, which is an IEEE 802 Media Access Control (MAC) address.
- Sel—One byte of network service access point (NSAP) selector.
- ICD—Two bytes of international code designator.
- E.164—Eight bytes of Integrated Services Digital Network (ISDN) telephone number.

The ATM address format is modeled after ISO NSAP addresses, with the addition of identifying subnet point of attachment (SNPA) addresses.

Further detailed information regarding ATM addressing can be found in Chapter 10, "ATM LAN Emulation (LANE)."

ATM Applications

The following examples are provided here solely to convey possible use of service categories and how they can relate to internetworked applications.

CBR Applications

CBR applications are any data/text/image transfer applications that contain smooth traffic or for which the end-system's response time requirements justify occupying a fully reserved CBR channel.

CBR application examples include the following:

- Videoconferencing
- Interactive audio (for example, telephony)
- Audio/video distribution (for example, television, distance learning, and pay-per-view)
- Audio/video retrieval (for example, video-on-demand and audio library)

For telephony and voiceband services over ATM, such as 64 kbps N-ISDN-compatible services, the access solution based on AAL1 requires CBR support for taking advantage of delay and variance bounds.

In the multimedia area, a near-term solution for residential services foresees Voice over X (VoX, where X is an alternative voice technology, such as ATM, Frame Relay, or IP). This is based on MPEG2 (transport stream, CBR mode) over AAL5 (ATM adaptation Layer 5), with transportation being provided by the ATM layer with CBR service.

VBR Applications

VBR is suitable for any application for which the end system can benefit from statistical multiplexing by sending information at a variable rate. In addition, the application must be able to tolerate or recover from a potentially small random loss ratio. VBR is the recommendation for any constant bit rate source for which variable rate transmission allows more efficient use of network resources without sensible performance impairment.

Real-time VBR can be used by native ATM voice with bandwidth compression and silence suppression. Some classes of multimedia communications might find real-time VBR appropriate.

Near-real-time VBR can be used for data transfer. For example, it can be used frame relay interworking and for response-time critical transaction processing applications, such as airline reservations, banking transactions, and process monitoring.

ABR Applications

Any non-time-critical application that is running over an end-system capable of varying its emission rate can exploit the ABR service. This category provides an economical support to those applications that show vague requirements for throughput, delay, and low CLR, such as LAN interconnection/internetworking services or LANE services. These are typically run over router-based protocol stacks, such as TCP/IP, which can vary their emission rate as required by the ABR rate control policy. The support through ABR results in an increased end-to-end performance.

Other application examples are critical data transfer (defense information, banking services), super computer applications, and data communications (remote procedure call, or RPC, distributed file services, and computer process swapping/paging).

UBR Applications

UBR can provide a suitable solution for less demanding applications. Most data applications are tolerant to delay and cell loss. In fact, store and forward networks are widely used for these applications. Examples of UBR applications might include the following:

- Text/data/image transfer
- Messaging
- Distribution
- Retrieval
- Remote terminal (telecommuting)

These services can take advantage of any spare bandwidth and profit from the resultant reduced tariffs ("cheap" services).

ATM Applications Summary

Table 18-4 scores applications against service categories. The association and score assignment are based on a subjective perception, shared among a number of people working on the subject of scoring ATM service categories. Although these scores are not based on specific formulae, they are based on the collected opinion of those individuals who have been heavily involved with ATM services and development.

Table 18-4   *Application Areas for ATM Service Categories*

Application Area	CBR	rt-VBR	nrt-VBR	ABR	UBR
Critical data	**	*	***	*	n/s
LAN Interconnect LANE	*	*	**	***	**
Data transport/ interworking (IP-FR-SMDS)	*	*	**	***	**
Circuit emulation PABX	***	**	n/s	n/s	n/s
POTS/ISDN—video conference	***			n/s	n/s
Compressed audio	*	***	**	**	*
Video distribution	***	**	*	n/s	n/s
Interactive multimedia	***	***	**	**	*

Score to indicate the advantage:

Optimum: ***

Good: **

Fair : *

n/s = not suitable.

Multiprotocol Over ATM (MPOA)

The ATM Forum has worked in cooperation with the IETF to develop MPOA, a network layer routing solution that integrates and leverages existing protocols and standards to provide routing functionality over switched ATM networks. MPOA introduces the concept of a virtual router. The virtual router emulates the functionality of traditional routed networks, eliminating the performance limitations of hop-by-hop routing. Shortcut connections are set up over the ATM fabric from any MPOA-capable host or edge device to any other, regardless of their subnet membership. In essence, MPOA identifies data flows and maps them directly to ATM virtual channels. This technique of establishing shortcuts directly across the ATM network is sometimes referred to as *cut-through* or *zero-hop* routing. Figure 18-12 illustrates MPOA zero-hop routing.

Figure 18-12 *MPOA Zero-Hop Routing*

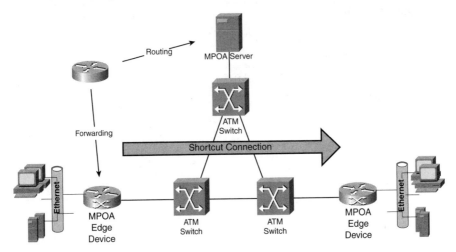

The establishment of a shortcut connection over the ATM fabric provides a significant improvement in performance over pure router-based inter-subnet solutions. Packets transported over the shortcut connection are no longer subjected to the hop-by-hop router processing in traditional networks. Besides improvement in performance, the end-to-end delay between end stations also becomes more deterministic.

The MPOA framework provides a unified model for overlaying inter-networking layer protocols onto ATM. Although vendors will implement different flavors of physical implementations of the MPOA framework, the specifications ensure interoperability among vendors. The general concept involves splitting forwarding and routing functions that are traditionally supported within conventional multiprotocol routers between MPOA clients and MPOA servers. The MPOA server (MPS) performs, for example, address management and topology discovery. MPOA clients (MPCs) provide traffic forwarding via the ATM switch fabric. The MPS typically resides in an ATM switch-router or a stand-alone ATM attached route server, whereas MPCs reside in edge devices and ATM attached hosts. This provides a physical separation between the devices that calculate the internetwork route and those that forward the data. As a result, traditional routers are limited by the speed of their proprietary back-planes. However, an MPOA-based routing system leverages products—such as standards-based ATM switches—that result in a multi-gigabit routing infrastructure. This is ideally suited to meet the demands associated with routed LAN and WAN internetworks.

Furthermore, transport services are provided over a standards-based ATM infrastructure by mapping network layer protocols such as IP and IPX directly to ATM. This enables QoS mechanisms that are being developed for IP, such as RSVP, to be exposed to the underlying ATM fabric. The end result is that time-sensitive traffic can utilize QoS capabilities of an ATM infrastructure while leveraging low-cost installed technologies, such as Ethernet and

TCP/IP at the desktops. This allows for affordable, high-performance multimedia applications such as video conferencing, video distribution, and distance learning.

Illustrated in Figure 18-13, the MPOA servers run the full routing stack, which results in a consolidated configuration for the entire network. The switches are standards-based ATM switches, which results in a highly scalable, low cost, high performance network infrastructure. Edge devices are optimized for forwarding network layer and Layer 2 traffic, resulting in network-wide virtual networks and zero-hop routing across the ATM network.

Figure 18-13 *MPOA Control and Data Planes*

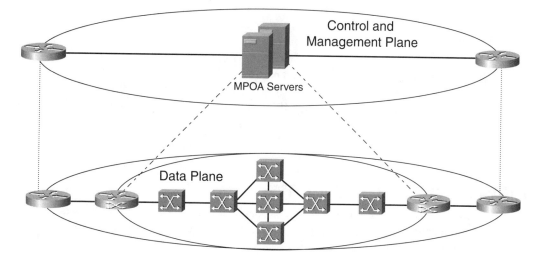

Three Elements of MPOA

MPOA uses three complementary techniques to form its fundamental capability:

- ATM Forum's LANE—LANE supports native LAN environments over ATM in a transparent manner.

- IETF's Next Hop Resolution Protocol (NHRP)—NHRP provides a mechanism to establish a shortcut over the ATM backbone based on network layer addressing.

- Virtual router concept—This provides the ability to separate functions among various elements of the network, which reduces cost and improves efficiency.

LANE

LANE is used for communications within subnets, whereas the MPOA virtual router provides communications between subnets.

NHRP

The IETF has defined NHRP, which, among other capabilities, allows the packet forwarding function of intermediate routers on the data path to be bypassed. NHRP provides an extended address resolution protocol that permits next hop clients (NHCs) to send queries among different logical IP subnets (LISs), sometimes referred to as local address groups (LAGs). Queries are propagated using next hop servers (NHSs) along paths that are discovered by standard routing protocols, such as RIP and OSPF. This enables the establishment of ATM SVCs across subnet boundaries, allowing inter-subnet communications without using intermediate routers for qualified data flows.

Virtual Router

A *virtual router* is a set of devices operating over a network that collectively provide the functionality of multiprotocol routed networks. In the case of MPOA, the edge devices are analogous to router interface cards; the ATM switching fabric can be seen as the "backplane" of the router; and the MPOA server is analogous to the control processor. The MPOA framework defines the protocols between the MPOA server and the edge devices that enable the virtual router behavior.

MPOA Logical Components

MPOA defines logical components that can be implemented in various hardware configurations. The separation of function allows vendors to package their unique solutions to meet the particular needs of their customers.

Edge devices are inexpensive. They forward packets between legacy LAN segments and ATM interfaces based on the destination network layer address and MAC layer address.

MPOA Client: MPC

MPCs reside in the edge device or ATM attached hosts. MPCs' primary function is to act as a point of entry and exit for traffic using internetwork shortcuts. An MPC looks for traffic flows, and when found, it requests its serving MPS to provide information on the destination and check that a shortcut is acceptable. If it is, the MPC sets up an SVC and forwards data to the destination across the path. The MPC and MPS communicate with each other using NHRP. The MPC caches the shortcut information that it derives from its interaction with the MPS. SVCs with no activity are inactivated upon the expiration of a variable time-out.

MPOA Router

The MPOA router is a collection of functions that allow the mapping of network layer subnets to ATM. The MPOA router can be implemented as a standalone product, or it can be built into existing routers or switches. It maintains local network layer, MAC-layer, and ATM address information in addition to routing tables. MPOA routers communicate via NHRP to resolve destination addresses so that MPCs can establish shortcuts. The routing engine runs routing protocols (such as RIP and OSPF) to exchange routing information with traditional routers. This exchange enables interoperability with existing routed LAN and WAN internetworks.

MPOA Server: MPS

An MPS is a logical component of the MPOA router that provides Layer 3 forwarding information to MPCs. It also includes an NHRP server (NHS) function. The MPS interacts with its associated routing function and its NHS to identify a path represented by the destination ATM address and Layer 2 encapsulation information, which it returns in response to a query from the MPC.

Caching

It is commonplace for users in a routed internetwork to have repetitive and habitual external addresses to which they need to be connected, such as particular file servers or remote corporate destinations. For this reason, the edge device can save ("cache") this virtual channel information to be reused without having to issue address resolution requests for every flow. This is a valuable aspect of the MPOA concept. A design goal of MPOA is to minimize the number of times the edge device must visit the route server to retrieve this information. To that end, the MPC maintains its own address cache. Much of the MPOA effort is devoted to devising effective cache-management techniques, including ensuring cache coherency between MPCs and MPSs.

Virtual Subnets

MPOA uses network layer constructs in defining virtual subnetworks. Network layer constructs denote both a Layer 3 protocol and an address range. In the case of IP, network layer constructs can be thought of as virtual subnets. The MPOA model supports all existing LAN internetwork data flows, including both intra-subnet and inter-subnet.

The MPOA model distributes routing among edge devices and ATM attached hosts with MPOA clients, which forward packets. It also attaches hosts with MPOA servers, which supply routing information. MPCs examine the destination address of packets received on legacy LAN segments to make the correct forwarding decision. If the packet is to be routed, it contains the destination MAC address of the MPOA router interface. If so, the MPC looks at the destination network layer address of the packet, and resolves this to the correct ATM address based on information received from the MPOA server or information in its cache. The MPC then establishes a direct virtual channel connection to the appropriate destination. If the packet is destined to a host in the same subnet so that it can be bridged, the MPC uses LANE to resolve the ATM address and establish a virtual channel connection to the destination. If the local MPOA server does not know the appropriate ATM address, it can propagate the query to other MPOA servers or routers using NHRP functionality. The destination ATM address from the MPOA server can be the address of the host (if the host is ATM-attached), or the address of the appropriate edge device to which the packets should be forwarded.

Network Layer Mapping

MPOA works at network Layer 3 to recognize the beginning of a data transfer and respond with a network route destination address. The shortcut SVC is then used to forward traffic using standard Layer 2 switching. With both Layer 3 and Layer 2 capabilities, the MPOA model encompasses routing and switching. The MPOA model can route and switch network layer traffic, and it can also bridge non-routable traffic.

The network layer mapping enables network applications to use the QoS properties of ATM.

For example, the IETF's RSVP Protocol operates at the network layer and provides mechanisms for applications to reserve a particular quality of service. The MPOA framework allows the Layer 3 reservations to be mapped onto the underlying ATM fabric.

Taking a Shortcut: The Basic Concept

The fundamental concept behind the use of MPOA to support multiprotocol LAN-LAN traffic is based on the fact that, in most cases, data transfer usually occurs in a relatively steady flow. That is, a file or message being sent usually consists of multiple frames. For example, a 45 K file, using a typical Ethernet frame size of 1,500 octets, would require about 30 frames. Because all 30 frames would travel to the same destination, it is possible to identify the destination and establish an SVC based on the information contained in the first frame. Then all 30 frames could be broken into approximately 900 ATM cells and transmitted over the virtual channel that the SVC establishes. This could be considered a shortcut in that the entire flow of data follows a pre-established path, avoiding the default path followed by routed traffic, and greatly improving performance. In the case of steady stream transmissions such as video, this is highly efficient and superior to simple router-to-router operation.

Figure 18-14 describes the interaction of the MPCs with the MPS, illustrating the basic operation of MPOA.

Figure 18-14 *MPOA Basic Operation*

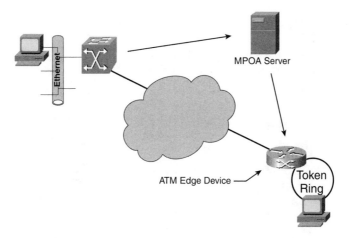

The first time that traffic needs to be forwarded from an ATM host with an IP address of Ipaddr1, the traffic is forwarded to an MPOA server. While forwarding this traffic, the MPOA server learns both the IP-to-MAC address and the MAC-to-ATM address mappings.

Figure 18-15 illustrates a direct shortcut connection.

Figure 18-15 *Direct Shortcut Connection Between ATM Edge Devices*

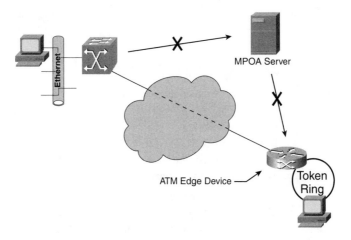

The MPCs obtain the ATM address of the exit point to which the destination host is connected. The destination host is a host with a network layer address that is either connected to a legacy LAN or is ATM attached. If it is a host connected to a legacy LAN such as Ethernet or Token Ring, the MPS returns the ATM address of the edge device that connects to the host on the legacy LAN. If the host is ATM attached, the MPS returns the ATM address of the host that corresponds to its network layer address.

MPOA Packet Flow

Figure 18-16 describes the events that allow a packet to be sent across an MPOA network using the shortcut capabilities of the MPOA system.

Figure 18-16 *MPOA Packet Flow*

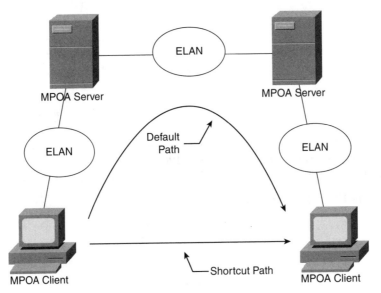

The following list details what is taking place in Figure 18-16:

- A packet enters the MPOA system at the ingress (entry) MPC (MPOA client 1 in Figure 18-16). By default, the packet is bridged via LANE to the default router (co-located with MPS 2). From there, it is forwarded via the router in MPS 2 to the destination edge device or host. However, if this packet is part of a flow for which a shortcut has been established, the ingress MPC strips off the Layer 2 encapsulation from the packet and sends it via the shortcut.

- If no data flow is detected, each packet being sent to an MPS is tallied by its Layer 3 destination address as LANE is forwarding it. When the threshold is exceeded (N packets to a specific Layer 3 address within X time), the MPC sends an MPOA resolution request to the MPS to obtain the ATM address to be used for establishing a shortcut to the Egress (exit) MPC.

- On arriving via a shortcut at the Egress MPC, the packet is examined. Either a matching Egress Cache Entry is found, or the packet is dropped. If a match is found, the packet is re-encapsulated using the cache information, and it is forwarded via a LAN interface to its destination.

- The shortcut is an ATM SVC established for the specific data flow.

Migration and Coexistence

The MPS communicates with external routers via standard routing protocols, such as RIP and OSPF. This allows a seamless integration with non-MPOA systems and with non-shortcut qualified traffic. It is important to note that the routing devices in the MPOA architecture provide all of the ordinary and valuable functions of a router, including connectionless internetworking across WANs, integrity verification, and route prioritization. Figure 18-17 shows MPOA with routing protocols.

Figure 18-17 *MPOA with Routing Protocols*

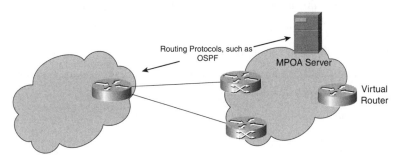

LANE and MPOA

Although MPOA specifications are implemented to overcome some of the performance and scalability limitations of LANE specifications, LANE Version 2 is an integral component of MPOA. The default operation for an MPOA device is the standard LANE connectivity.

NHRP and MPOA

Because NHRP is an integral component of the MPOA server, an MPOA-based network can interact with routers that support NHRP functionality to propagate ATM address resolution requests.

Inverse Multiplexing for ATM (IMA)

The ATM Forum approved the inverse multiplexing for ATM (IMA) specification in July 1997. This specification defines a new physical layer protocol to access ATM services. The significant benefit of the IMA is supporting the introduction of new ATM link rates between traditional lower rates such as DS1 (1.544 Mbps) and E1 (2.048 Mbps) and higher rates such as DS3 (44.736 Mbps) and E3 (34.368 Mbps).

A typical IMA configuration involves the implementation of NxT1/NxE1 access lines with a single virtual link. This virtual link is configured to provide a link rate equal to the sum of the physical links interconnecting two nodes that support IMA.

The IMA protocol inverse multiplexes ATM cells over several physical links. These physical links interconnect two nodes that support the IMA protocol. In the transmit direction, the ATM cell stream received from the ATM layer is distributed on a cell-by-cell basis, across the multiple links within the IMA. At the receiving end, the receiving IMA recombines the cells from each link, on a cell-by-cell, or round-robin, basis, re-creating the original ATM cell stream. The transmit IMA periodically transmits special cells that contain information permitting reconstruction of the ATM cell stream at the receiving IMA.

Advantages of IMA include the following:

- It can support to private UNIs and NNIs.
- It simplifies the addition of bandwidth to existing transport facilities.
- It is compatible with existing ATM and physical layers.
- It handles communication links with different or varying propagation delay.
- It handles links with non-synchronized clocks.
- It preserves service upon dynamic bandwidth adjustment.

Because the IMA interface is implemented over a number of physical links, service interruptions can be minimized. This is the key reason that the protocol has been defined: to maintain communications during circumstances in which the IMA virtual link has been reduced by one or more of the physical links that interconnect the IMA nodes.

Cisco's IMA implementation supports the following:

- Up to eight T1 or E1 ports with IMA (ATM Forum Version 1.0)
- T1 and E1 ATM UNI
- Up to 4,096 total virtual connections (open VCs)
- IMA mixed-mode operation (IMA groups + T1/E1 ATM UNI ports combined on the same interface)
- ATM adaptation Layer 5 (AAL5) for data traffic
- Traffic shaping on a per-VC basis

- nrt-VBR, UBR, and ABR quality of service (QoS)
- Operation, administration, and maintenance (OAM) cells
- UNI signaling
- ILMI
- RFC 1483, RFC 1577

Summary

The increased level of flexibility that is achievable through the introduction of the ATM service categories can be exploited in different ways and in a variety of combinations, in association with any VPI or VCI connection. With this choice of ATM services, the matching of real user needs can be approached in a completely new way. It is expected that the appropriate choice is influenced by a number of factors, including the following:

- Availability of a set of service categories offered by the network
- Actual attainable QoS in the network, dependent on the adopted resource management policy
- Traffic engineering
- Number of nodes crossed and distance
- Capability of the application to cope with some degradation of the ATM-layer transfer characteristics (such as bandwidth availability)
- Tariff strategy adopted for each service category and levels of quality offered

ATM internetworking supports several classes of service (CoS). The following table revisits these CoS.

CoS	Description
Constant bit rate (CBR)	This provides constant bandwidth across the virtual connection. It is typically used for private line emulated services, such as multimedia, CAD/CAM, or medical imaging.
Variable bit rate real-time (VBR-rt)	This provides a specified average bandwidth across the virtual connection. It is used to support delay-sensitive applications, such as voice or video.
Variable bit rate near-real-time (VBR-nrt)	This provides a specified average bandwidth across the virtual connection. It is used to support non-delay-sensitive applications, such as data information.
Unspecified bit rate (UBR)	This is a best-effort service, meaning that no bandwidth is specified across the connection, nor is delivery of service guaranteed.

CoS	Description
Available bit rate (ABR)	This is a best-effort service implemented in a different fashion from UBR. This service provides continuing feedback indicating how much bandwidth is available for use. By throttling back as necessary, sending hosts avoid network congestion. This prevents traffic from being sent, but instead thrown away, before it reaches its intended destination. Typically, this is used to support data applications in which delivery is important, but not necessarily in a near-real-time environment.

The ATM Forum approved the inverse multiplexing for ATM (IMA) specification in July 1997. This specification defines a new physical layer protocol to access ATM services. The significant benefit of the IMA is supporting the introduction of new ATM link rates between traditional lower rates, such as DS1 (1.544 Mbps) and E1 (2.048 Mbps), and higher rates, such as DS3(44.736 Mbps) and E3 (34.368 Mbps).

CHAPTER 19

ATM WAN Documentation

Chapter 18, "ATM Wide-Area Networking (WAN) and MPOA," discussed the underlying technology for ATM WAN networks and their underlying components. This chapter will discuss some recommendations and guidelines to follow to document an ATM wide-area network (WAN).

Most networking discussions today include the topic of documentation at some point, whether the mention is a statement advising that you should document your network assets or a statement advising that network documentation is a good tool to have when troubleshooting a network issue. The challenge is what network information should be documented, reviewed, and analyzed for potential network-related issues.

Network documentation should be both easy to complete and easy to understand. In an effort to make the network documentation process easier to manage for ATM WAN implementations, templates have been prepared and presented here for use. These templates are preceded by relevant console commands, a case study, and a sample completed template serving as a guide.

NOTE

Network documentation is a living process and not a single event. It is important to have clear and simple documentation templates so that the WAN staff will be committed to maintaining the documentation, preserving its value. Out-of-date documentation, if used and trusted, can be dangerous. Documentation that is not trusted is useless and brings no value to the organization.

The templates presented here are also available electronically on the Cisco Press Web site (www.ciscopress.com/1587050390).

You can approach ATM WAN documentation from two perspectives: from the individual site or from the overall WAN view. Both perspectives will be demonstrated here with supporting templates.

An introduction or case study network diagram will precede each template with suggestions regarding template completion. These templates are not all encompassing, nor are they designed to be. Rather, these templates are designed to help the consultant, engineer, or anyone involved with a network, gather the vital information pertaining to a network and its related segments.

Case Study: Naming Conventions

A naming convention, or scheme, should be employed in any network for which you are responsible. A naming convention should grow as the network grows. Naming conventions should be developed so that the network documentation is easy to prepare, thus making network maintenance and troubleshooting easier for the user. For example, a network engineer new to the company's operations would be more able to recognize the function and purpose of a device named HQ_7500Router_WAN than the same device referred to as Sprint Router.

NOTE   Some would view such a descriptive naming convention as a security concern. Like so many things, tradeoffs are involved: descriptive naming versus security. These tradeoffs need to be addressed prior to a naming convention. In some instances, the use of internal codes is used, satisfying both network management and security concerns.

A good convention scheme would incorporate the geographic location of the device. A naming convention following this scheme would be designed as follows:

Geographic-location_Network-Device | Division_Network-Device

For example, an ATM WAN edge-router located at an organization's corporate headquarters could be named in one of the following fashions:

Chicago_WANRouter

HQ_WANRouter

This example reflects an ATM WAN router located at corporate headquarters, in this case, located in Chicago, Illinois.

A naming convention should be easy to use; however, one naming convention cannot work with every network. Generic conventions can be useful. The idea behind generic naming conventions is that if someone else looks at your network documentation, that person can easily determine the topology.

This same naming convention can be globally deployed and supported across the organization by the use of a domain name server (DNS). By deploying the naming scheme across the domain with DNS, administration and inventory is simpler to manage. Troubleshooting is also facilitated in a more manageable fashion than without the use of a naming standard.

For example, the following trace route command would not be of much help to an engineer without the names.

```
1   WashingtonDC.MCIRouter.Engineering [207.69.220.81]
2   cisco-f0-1-0.norva3.mindspring.net [207.69.220.65]
3   s10-0-1.vienna1-cr3.bbnplanet.net [4.1.5.237]
4   p4-2.vienna1-nbr2.bbnplanet.net [4.0.1.133]
5   p4-0.washdc3-br2.bbnplanet.net [4.0.1.97]
6   p3-0.washdc3-br1.bbnplanet.net [4.24.4.145]
7   p2-0.chcgil1-br2.bbnplanet.net [4.24.6.93]
8   p4-0.chcgil1-br1.bbnplanet.net [4.24.5.225]
9   so-4-1-0.chcgil2-br1.bbnplanet.net [4.24.9.69]
10  p1-0.chcgil2-cr11.bbnplanet.net [4.24.6.22]
11  p7-1.paloalto-nbr1.bbnplanet.net [4.24.6.98]
12  p1-0.paloalto-cr1.bbnplanet.net [4.0.6.74]
13  h1-0.cisco.bbnplanet.net [4.1.142.238]
14  pigpen.cisco.com [192.31.7.9]
15  www.cisco.com [198.133.219.25]
```

ATM Site View

Table 19-1 can be used to document a single ATM site, where the site of discussion is not concerned with the WAN as a whole, but rather its view into the WAN.

Table 19-1   *ATM WAN Site Information*

Site Name		Mnemonic						
ATM Access Bandwidth		ATM Access Ckt ID						
Access Carrier		Local Access Ckt ID				Channels		
Intfc/ VPI/VCI	Term. Network Address	Term. Site Name	Term. Site Mnemonic	Term. ATM Circuit ID	Term. ATM Access Bandwidth	SCR	PCR	CoS

Figure 19-1 will be used to complete the associated documentation example. Only the virtual path identifiers (VPIs) are indicated within the drawing because the accompanying form will reflect multiple virtual channel identifiers (VCIs).

Figure 19-1 *ATM WAN Template Example 1*

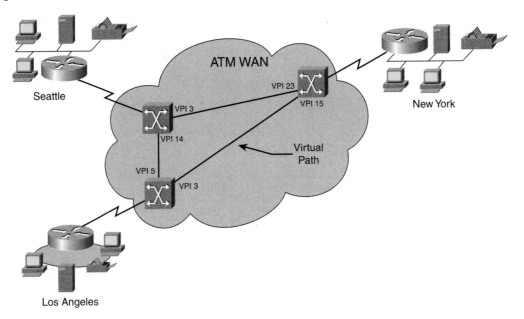

Figure 19-1 is a somewhat detailed network diagram of a 3-node ATM WAN. Although diagrams like this are useful in certain situations, the amount of time involved in their construction could be best spent otherwise. A simpler network diagram (Figure 19-2) is just as useful as the previous diagram, without the additional detail that could clutter the representation. The simpler form also takes less time to prepare.

Figure 19-2 *ATM 3-Node WAN*

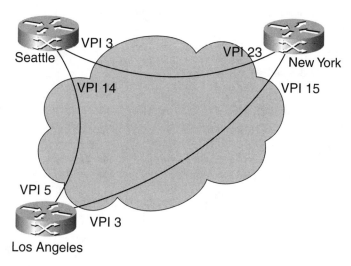

The previous diagram can also be illustrated as shown in Figure 19-3.

Figure 19-3 *Simpler 3-Node Network Diagram*

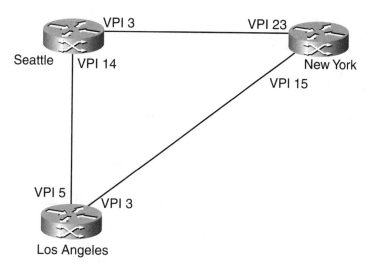

NOTE   Regarding network diagrams, two methods are generally used to illustrate a network topology:

- Topology with the WAN cloud

- End nodes and virtual circuits only

Each method has a distinct advantage. The first method, topology with the WAN cloud, is useful for illustrative purposes, such as inclusion within presentations. However, the WAN cloud becomes cluttered and illegible quickly as more end nodes are added to the WAN. This is especially true if multiple fully or partially meshed virtual circuits are available. The second method, end nodes and virtual circuits only, is useful from a network topology standpoint and is useful for illustrating client network components (such as end nodes and virtual circuits). Both methods of network diagramming are useful, and care should be taken when choosing which methodology will be used. For the purposes of the following templates, both methods will be illustrated.

This network would be documented from each site in Tables 19-2, 19-3, and 19-4.

Table 19-2   *ATM WAN Template for Example 1 (Seattle)*

Site Name		Seattle		**Mnemonic**		SEA_WAN			
ATM Access Bandwidth			1536	**ATM Access Ckt ID**					
Access Carrier			**Local Access Ckt ID**				**Channels**		1 to 24
Intfc/ VPI/VCI	**Term. Network Address**	**Term. Site Name**	**Term. Site Mnemonic**	**Term. ATM Circuit ID**	**Term. ATM Access Bandwidth**		**SCR**	**PCR**	**CoS**
2/14/1		L.A.	WAN_LA		1536		768	768	CBR
2/3/1		N.Y.	WAN_NY		1536		384	384	CBR
2/3/2		N.Y.	WAN_NY		1536		768		VBRnrt

Table 19-3 *ATM WAN Template for Example 1 (New York)*

Site Name		New York		Mnemonic		WAN_NY			
ATM Access Bandwidth			1536	ATM Access Ckt ID					
Access Carrier			Local Access Ckt ID				Channels		1 to 24
Intfc/ VPI/VCI	Term. Network Address	Term. Site Name	Term. Site Mnemonic	Term. ATM Circuit ID	Term. ATM Access Bandwidth		SCR	PCR	CoS
2/23/1		Seattle	WAN_SEA		1536		384	384	CBR
2/15/1		L.A.	WAN_LA		1536		384	384	VBRnrt
2/15/5		L.A.	WAN_LA		1536		768		UBR

Table 19-4 *ATM WAN Template for Example 1 (Los Angeles)*

Site Name		Los Angeles		Mnemonic		WAN_LA			
ATM Access Bandwidth			1536	ATM Access Ckt ID					
Access Carrier			Local Access Ckt ID				Channels		1 to 24
Intfc/ VPI/VCI	Term. Network Address	Term. Site Name	Term. Site Mnemonic	Term. ATM Circuit ID	Term. ATM Access Bandwidth		SCR	PCR	CoS
3/5/2		Seattle	WAN_Sea		1536		768	768	CBR
3/3/17		N.Y.	WAN_NY		1536		384	384	VBRnrt

These three forms provide each site a view of other sites to which they are directly interconnected. For example, the New York form does not reflect the interconnection between Los Angeles and Seattle because New York is not concerned with this interconnection; it is not in its view of the WAN.

Table 19-5   *ATM WAN Template*

(Originating) Site Name			Mnemonic		

ATM Access Bandwidth		ATM Access Ckt ID	

ATM Service Provider		Local Access Ckt ID		Channels	

Intfc/ VPI/ VCI	Term. Nwk Add	Term. Site Name	Term. Site Mnemonic	Term. ATM Circuit ID	Term. ATM Access Bandwidth	SCR	PCR	CoS	Comments

IOS Command Based

Three Cisco IOS commands can be primarily used to collect ATM WAN topology information:

- **show atm vp**
- **show atm vc**
- **show atm map**

The **show atm map** IOS command will be discussed in the next section, "Global ATM WAN Documentation."

show atm vp

The **show atm vp** command is used to display the ATM layer connection information about the virtual path:

```
show atm vp

show atm vp interface {atm ¦ atm-p} card/subcard/port [.vpt#] [vpi vci]

show atm vp [cast-type cast-type] [conn-type conn-type]
[interface {atm ¦ atm-p} card/subcard/port[.vpt#]]

show atm vp traffic [interface {atm ¦ atm-p} card/subcard/port [.vpt#] [vpi vci]]
```

Table 19-6   *show atm vp Syntax and Description*

Syntax	Description
Card/subcard/port	Card, subcard, and port number for the interface
.vpt#	Virtual path tunnel identifier
vpi vci	Virtual path identifier and virtual channel identifier to display
cast-type	Cast type as point-to-multipoint (p2mp) or point-to-point (p2p)
conn-type	Connection type as pvc, soft-vc, or svc
traffic	Virtual channel cell traffic

show atm vp Examples

The following code is displayed from **show atm vp** output:

```
JLBalSwitch# show atm vp

Interface    VPI    Type     X-Interface   X-VPI    Status
ATM3/1/1     1      SVP      ATM3/1/2      200      UP
ATM3/1/1     2      SVP      ATM3/1/2      201      UP
ATM3/1/1     3      SVP      ATM3/1/2      202      UP
ATM3/1/2     200    SoftVP   ATM3/1/1      1        UP
ATM3/1/2     201    SoftVP   ATM3/1/1      2        UP
ATM3/1/2     202    SoftVP   ATM3/1/1      3        UP
ATM3/1/2     255    SoftVP   NOT CONNECTED
```

The following code is displayed from **show atm vp** output for ATM 3/1/1:

```
JLBalSwitch# show atm vp interface atm 3/1/1

Interface    VPI    Type   X-Interface    X-VPI    Status
ATM3/1/1      1     SVP     ATM3/1/2       200      UP
ATM3/1/1      2     SVP     ATM3/1/2       201      UP
ATM3/1/1      3     SVP     ATM3/1/2       202      UP
```

The following table describes the fields shown in the **show atm vp** output display.

Table 19-7 *show atm vp Interface ATM Field Descriptions*

Field	Description
Interface	Displays the card, subcard, and port number of the ATM interface
VPI/VCI	Displays the number of the virtual path identifier and the virtual channel identifier
Status	Displays the type of interface for the specified ATM interface
Time-since-last-status-change	Displays the time elapsed since the last status change
Connection-type	Displays the type of connection for the specified ATM interface
Cast-type	Displays the type of cast for the specified ATM interface
Usage-Parameter-Control (UPC)	Displays the state of the UPC
Number of OAM-configured connections	Displays the number of connections configured by OAM
OAM-configuration	Displays the state of the OAM configuration: enabled or disabled
OAM-states	Displays the status of the OAM state: applicable or not applicable
OAM Loopback-Tx-Interval	Displays the OAM loopback transmit interval
Cross-connect-interface	Displays the cross-connect interface number
Cross-connect-VPI	Displays the cross-connect VPI number
Cross-connect-UPC	Displays the cross-connect UPC status
Cross-connect OAM-configuration	Displays the configuration of the OAM in the cross-connect half-leg
Cross-connect OAM-state	Displays the state of the OAM cross-connect half-leg
OAM-Loopback-Tx-Interval	Displays the OAM loopback transmit interval
Rx cells/Tx cells	Displays the number of cells transmitted and received

Table 19-7   *Frame Relay Standard Frame Field Descriptions*

Field	Description
Rx connection-traffic-table-index	Displays the receive connection-traffic-table-index
Rx service-category	Displays the receive service category
Rx pcr-clp01	Displays the receive peak cell rate for clp01 cells (kbps)
Rx scr-clp01	Displays the receive sustained cell rate for clp01 cells (kbps)
Rx mcr-clp01	Displays the receive minimum cell rate for clp01 cells (kbps)
Rx cdvt	Displays the receive cell delay variation tolerance
Rx mbs	Displays the receive maximum burst size
Tx connection-traffic-table-index	Displays the transmit connection-traffic-table-index
Tx service-category	Displays the transmit service category
Tx pcr-clp01	Displays the transmit peak cell rate for clp01 cells (kbps)
Tx scr-clp01	Displays the transmit sustained cell rate for clp01 cells (kbps)
Tx mcr-clp01	Displays the transmit minimum cell rate for clp01 cells (kbps)
Tx cdvt	Displays the transmit cell delay variation tolerance
Tx mbs	Displays the transmit maximum burst size

show atm vc

The **show atm vc** command is used to display the ATM layer connection information:

```
show atm vc

show atm vc interface {atm ¦ atm-p} card/subcard/port [.vpt#] [vpi vci]

show atm vc [cast-type cast-type] [conn-type conn-type]
[interface {atm ¦ atm-p} card/subcard/port[.vpt#]]

show atm vc traffic [interface {atm ¦ atm-p} card/subcard/port [.vpt#] [vpi vci]]
```

Table 19-8   *show atm vc Syntax and Description*

Syntax	Description
card/subcard/port	Displays the card, subcard, and port number for the interface
.vpt#	Specifies the virtual path tunnel identifier to display
vpi vci	Specifies the virtual path identifier and virtual channel identifier to display
Detail	Displays the Rx cell drops and queued-cells for all VCs on a given interface
cast-type	Specifies the cast type as multipoint-to-point (mp2p), point-to-multipoint (p2mp), or point-to-point (p2p)

(continues)

Table 19-8 *show atm vc Syntax and Description (Continued)*

Syntax	Description
conn-type	Specifies the connection type as pvc, soft-vc, svc, or pvc
traffic	Displays the virtual channel cell traffic

show atm vc Examples

The following code is displayed from **show atm vc** output:

```
JLBalSwitch# show atm vc
Switch# show atm vc
Interface     VPI   VCI    Type    X-Interface   X-VPI   X-VCI   Encap   Status
ATM0/1/0      0     5      PVC     ATM0          0       52      QSAAL   UP
ATM0/1/0      0     16     PVC     ATM0          0       32      ILMI    UP
ATM0/1/0      0     18     PVC     ATM0          0       73      PNNI    UP
ATM0/1/1      0     5      PVC     ATM0          0       53      QSAAL   DOWN
ATM0/1/1      0     16     PVC     ATM0          0       33      ILMI    DOWN
ATM0/1/2      0     5      PVC     ATM0          0       54      QSAAL   DOWN
ATM0/1/2      0     16     PVC     ATM0          0       34      ILMI    DOWN
ATM0/1/3      0     5      PVC     ATM0          0       55      QSAAL   UP
ATM0/1/3      0     16     PVC     ATM0          0       35      ILMI    UP
ATM1/0/0      0     5      PVC     ATM0          0       56      QSAAL   UP
ATM1/0/0      0     16     PVC     ATM0          0       36      ILMI    UP
ATM1/0/1      0     5      PVC     ATM0          0       57      QSAAL   DOWN
ATM1/0/1      0     16     PVC     ATM0          0       37      ILMI    DOWN
ATM1/0/2      0     5      PVC     ATM0          0       58      QSAAL   DOWN
ATM1/0/2      0     16     PVC     ATM0          0       38      ILMI    DOWN
ATM1/0/3      0     5      PVC     ATM0          0       59      QSAAL   UP
ATM1/0/3      0     16     PVC     ATM0          0       39      ILMI    UP
ATM1/0/3      0     18     PVC     ATM0          0       72      PNNI    UP
ATM1/1/0      0     5      PVC     ATM0          0       60      QSAAL   DOWN
ATM1/1/0      0     16     PVC     ATM0          0       40      ILMI    DOWN
ATM1/1/1      0     5      PVC     ATM0          0       61      QSAAL   DOWN
ATM1/1/1      0     16     PVC     ATM0          0       41      ILMI    DOWN
```

Table 19-9 *show atm vc Field Descriptions*

Field	Description
Interface	Displays the card, subcard, and port number of the specified ATM interface
VPI	Displays the number of the virtual path identifier
VCI	Displays the number of the virtual channel identifier
Type	Displays the type of interface for the specified ATM interface
X-Interface	Displays the card, subcard, and port number of the cross-connected value for the ATM interface
X-VPI	Displays the number of the cross-connected value of the virtual path identifier
X-VCI	Displays the number of the cross-connected value of the virtual channel identifier
Encap	Displays the type of connection on the interface
Status	Displays the current state of the specified ATM interface

The following table describes the fields shown in the **show atm vc** output display.

Table 19-10 *show atm vc Interface ATM Field Descriptions*

Field	Description
Interface	Displays the card, subcard, and port number of the ATM interface
VPI/VCI	Displays the number of the virtual path identifier and the virtual channel identifier
Status	Displays the type of interface for the specified ATM interface
Time-since-last-status-change	Displays the time elapsed since the previous status change
Connection-type	Displays the type of connection for the specified ATM interface
Cast-type	Displays the type of cast for the specified ATM interface
Packet-discard-option	Displays the state of the packet-discard option: enabled or disabled
Usage-Parameter-Control (UPC)	Displays the state of the UPC
Wrr weight	Weighted round-robin weight
Number of OAM-configured connections	Displays the number of connections configured by OAM
OAM-configuration	Displays the state of the OAM configuration: enabled or disabled
OAM-states	Displays the status of the OAM state: applicable or not applicable
Cross-connect-interface	Displays the card, subcard, and port number of the cross-connected ATM
Cross-connect-VPI	Displays the number of the cross-connected virtual path identifier
Cross-connect-VCI	Displays the number of the cross-connected virtual channel identifier
Cross-connect-UPC	Displays the state of the cross-connected UPC: pass or not pass
Cross-connect OAM-configuration	Displays the state of the cross-connected OAM configuration: enabled or disabled
Cross-connect OAM-state	Displays the status of the cross-connected OAM state: applicable or not applicable
Encapsulation	Displays the encapsulation type
Threshold Group/Cells queued	Displays the threshold group number and number of cells queued

(continues)

Table 19-10 *show atm vc Interface ATM Field Descriptions (Continued)*

Field	Description
Rx cells/Tx cells	Displays the number of cells transmitted and received
Tx Clp0/Tx Clp1	Displays the number of CLP=0 and CLP=1 cells transmitted
Rx Clp0/Rx Clp1	Displays the number of CLP=0 and CLP=1 cells received
Rx Upc Violations	Displays the number of UPC violations detected in the receive cell stream
Rx cell drops	Displays the number of cells received and then dropped
Rx pkts	Displays the number of packets received
Rx pkt drops	Displays the number of packets dropped
RxClp0q full drops	Displays the number of CLP=0 cells received and then dropped for exceeding the input queue size
Rx Clp1 qthresh drops	Displays the number of CLP=1 cells received and then dropped for exceeding the discard threshold of the input queue
Rx connection-traffic-table-index	Displays the receive connection-traffic-table-index
Rx service-category	Displays the receive service category
Rx pcr-clp01	Displays the receive peak cell rate for clp01 cells (kbps)
Rx scr-clp01	Displays the receive sustained cell rate for clp01 cells (kbps)
Rx mcr-clp01	Displays the receive minimum cell rate for clp01 cells (kbps)
Rx cdvt	Displays the receive cell delay variation tolerance
Rx mbs	Displays the receive minimum burst size
Tx connection-traffic-table-index	Displays the transmit connection-traffic-table-index
Tx service-category	Displays the transmit service category
Tx pcr-clp01	Displays the transmit peak cell rate for clp01 cells (kbps)
Tx scr-clp01	Displays the transmit sustained cell rate for clp01 cells (kbps)
Tx mcr-clp01	Displays the transmit minimum cell rate for clp01 cells (kbps)
Tx cdvt	Displays the transmit cell delay variation tolerance
Tx mbs	Displays the transmit minimum burst size
Crc error	Displays the number of cyclic redundancy check errors
Sar Timeouts	Displays the number of segmentation and reassembly timeouts
OverSizedSDUs	Displays the number of oversized service data units
BufSzOvfl	Displays the number of buffer size overflows

The following code shows the output display for interface ATM 1/0/0 with and without the detail keyword, showing the Rx-cel-drops and the Rx-queued-cells:

```
JLBalSwitch# show atm vc traffic interface atm 1/0/0

Interface       VPI  VCI  Type    rx-cell-cnts     tx-cell-cnts
ATM-P1/0/0       0   32   PVC          1                0
ATM-P1/0/0       0   33   PVC          0                0
ATM-P1/0/0       0   34   PVC          0                0
ATM-P1/0/0       0   35   PVC          0                0
ATM-P1/0/0       0   37   PVC          0                0
ATM-P1/0/0       0   39   PVC          0                0
ATM-P1/0/0       0   48   PVC          0                0

JLBalSwitch# show atm vc traffic interface atm 1/0/0 detail

Interface       VPI  VCI  Type   rx-cell   tx-cell rx-cell-drop rx-cell-qued
ATM-P1/0/0       0   32   PVC       1          0          0           0
ATM-P1/0/0       0   33   PVC       0          0          0           0
ATM-P1/0/0       0   34   PVC       0          0          0           0
ATM-P1/0/0       0   35   PVC       0          0          0           0
ATM-P1/0/0       0   37   PVC       0          0          0           0
ATM-P1/0/0       0   39   PVC       0          0          0           0
ATM-P1/0/0       0   48   PVC       0          0          0           0
```

Global ATM WAN Documentation

A global ATM WAN document is one that provides an overall, or global, view of the ATM WAN. This document provides information regarding interconnectivity between each node of the wide-area network. A global document can be used to represent just Layer 2 (VPI/ VCI) information, Layer 3 network [addressing] information, or some combination of the two. The decision rests with the individual, or organization, for which the document is intended. The goal is for network documentation to be useful, not a burden.

The following three-node network (Figures 19-4 and 19-5) will be used to demonstrate how a Layer 2 and Layer 3 global template (Tables 19-12 and 19-13) can be completed. Provided here are both a network diagram and the **show atm map** output from the head-end node—in this case, Richmond.

The **show atm map** command is used to display the list of all configured ATM static maps to remote hosts on an ATM network.

Figure 19-4 *Global Template **show atm map** Network Example*

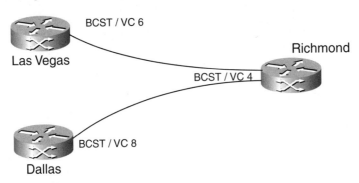

Figure 19-5 *Global ATM WAN Template Diagram (Simple)*

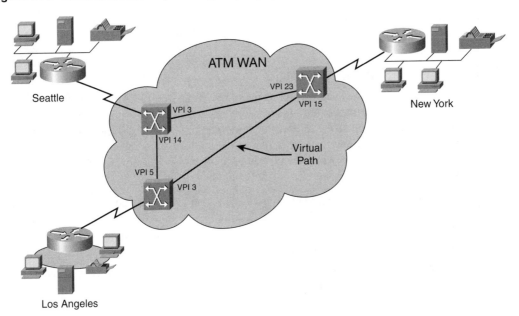

The following code is sample output from the **show atm map** command for a multipoint connection:

```
JLBalSwitch# show atm map

Map list atm_pri: PERMANENT
ip 4.4.4.4 maps to NSAP CD.CDEF.01.234567.890A.BCDE.
  F012.3456.7890.1234.12, broadcast,
Aal5mux, multipoint connection up, VC 6
ip 4.4.4.6 maps to NSAP DE.CDEF.01.234567.890A.BCDE.
  F012.3456.7890.1234.12, broadcast,
Aal5mux, connection up, VC 15, multipoint connection up, VC 6

Map list atm_ipx: PERMANENT
ipx 1004.dddd.dddd.dddd maps to NSAP DE.CDEF.01.234567.890A.
  BCDE.F012.3456.7890.1234.12,
broadcast, aal5mux, multipoint connection up, VC 8
ipx 1004.cccc.cccc.cccc maps to NSAP CD.CDEF.01.234567.890A.
  BCDE.F012.3456.7890.1234.12,
Broadcast, aal5mux, multipoint connection up, VC 8

Map list atm_apple: PERMANENT
AppleTalk 62000.5 maps to NSAP CD.CDEF.01.234567.890A.BCDE.F012.
  3456.7890.1234.12,
Broadcast, aal5mux, multipoint connection up, VC 4
appletalk 62000.6 maps to NSAP DE.CDEF.01.234567.890A.BCDE.F012.
  3456.7890.1234.12,
broadcast, aal5mux, multipoint connection up, VC 4
```

Table 19-11 describes the fields shown in the **show atm map** output display.

Table 19-11 *show atm map Multipoint Field Descriptions*

Field	Description
Map list	Name of map list
PERMANENT	Map entry that was entered from configuration; it was not entered automatically by a process
Protocol address maps to VC x or protocol address maps to NSAP	Name of protocol, the protocol address, and the virtual circuit descriptor (VCD) or NSAP to which the address is mapped
Broadcast	Indication of pseudo-broadcasting
aal5mux	Indication of the encapsulation used, a multipoint or point-to-point virtual connection, and the number of the virtual connection
Multipoint connection up	Indication that this is a multipoint virtual connection
VC 6	Number of the virtual connection
Connection up	Indication a point-to-point virtual connection

Table 19-12 *ATM (Layer 2) Documentation*

Origination (Site A)					Termination (Site B)					
Site Name	Site Ckt ID	Site Location	ATM Intfc and Port Speed	A→B VPI/VCI	Site Name	Site Ckt ID	ATM Intfc and Port Speed	A→B VPI/VCI	Comments	
Richmond	ATM-Rich001	Richmond	ATM3 1536 K	BCST VC4	Las Vegas	ATM-Lasv0001	ATM3 1536 K	BCST VC6		
				BCST VC4	Dallas	ATM-DalT0001		BCST VC8		
Las Vegas	ATM-Lasv0001	Las Vegas	ATM2 1536 K	BCST VC6	Richmond	ATM-Rich0001	ATM2 1536 K	BCST VC4		
Dallas	ATM-DalT0001	Dallas	ATM2 1536L	BCST VC8	Richmond	ATM-Rich0001	ATM2 1536L	BCST VC4		

Table 19-13 *ATM (Layer 2) Documentation Template*

Origination (Site A)					Termination (Site B)					
Site Name	Site Ckt ID	Site Location	ATM Intfc and Port Speed	A→B VPI/VCI	Site Name	Site Ckt ID	ATM Intfc and Port Speed	A→B VPI/VCI	Comments	

ATM VPI/VCI Table

The ATM VPI/VCI documentation template (See Tables 19-14 and 19-15) can be used as a VPI/VCI Quick Reference. A quick reference sheet like this one could be attached to the router for use during troubleshooting of Layer 2 connectivity issues, especially if coordinating troubleshooting activities with the network service provider.

Figure 19-6 will be used to complete the Frame Relay DLCI Table.

Table 19-14 *ATM VPI/VCI Table Example*

Site A (Origination)	Site B (Termination)	A ➡ B VPI/VCI	B ➡ A VPI/VCI
Los Angeles	New York	VPI 3 / BCST[*]	VPI 15 / BCST
Los Angeles	Seattle	VPI 5 / BCST	VPI 14 / BCST
Seattle	New York	VPI 3 / BCST	VPI 23 / BCST
Seattle	Los Angeles	VPI 14 / BCST	VPI 5 / BCST
New York	Seattle	VPI 23 / BCST	VPI 3 / BCST
New York	Los Angeles	VPI 15 / BCST	VPI 3 / BCST

[*]BCST indicates that all traffic sent on this virtual path is broadcast to all configured virtual channels (VCs).

Figure 19-6 *VPI/VCI Table Network Diagram*

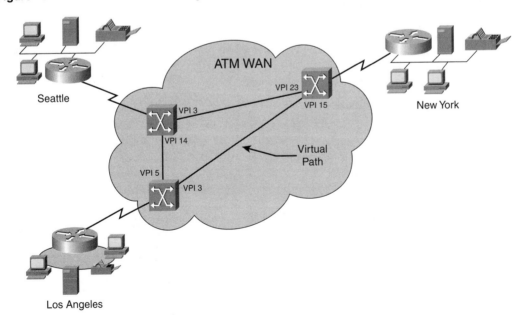

Table 19-15 *ATM VPI/VCI Table Template*

Site A (Origination)	Site B (Termination)	A ➡ B VPI/VCI	B ➡ A VPI/VCI

Summary

The following Cisco IOS commands are used to gather pertinent ATM WAN information and in turn used to complete network documentation templates:

- The **show atm vp** command is used to display the ATM layer connection information concerning the virtual path.

- The **show atm vc** command is used to display the ATM layer connection information.

- The **show atm map** command is used to display the list of all configured ATM static maps to remote hosts on an ATM network.

CHAPTER 20

Voice Technology

The transmission of voice traffic over packet networks, such as Voice over Frame Relay (VoFr), Voice over ATM (VoATM), and especially voice over IP (VoIP), is rapidly gaining acceptance. Collectively, these methodologies are known as Voice over X (VoX). Voice over packet transfer can significantly reduce the per-minute cost, resulting in reduced long-distance bills. Many dial-around-calling schemes available today rely on VoIP backbones to transfer voice, passing some of the cost savings to the customer. These high-speed backbones take advantage of the convergence of Internet and voice traffic to form a single managed network.

The convergence of voice and data networks opens the door to innovative applications. Interactive shopping, such as Web pages supporting "click to talk" buttons, are just one example. Streaming audio, electronic white-boarding, and CD-quality conference calls in stereo are other applications that are being deployed in a more distributed environment.

Concerns abound regarding voice quality when carried over packet networks. These concerns are based typically on experience with the early Internet telephony applications, or on an understanding of the nature of packet networks. Regardless of the foundation, voice quality is a critical parameter in acceptance of VoX services. As such, it is crucial to understand the factors affecting voice over packet transmission, as well as to obtain the tools to measure and optimize them.

VoIP Network Elements

VoIP services need to be able to connect to traditional circuit-switched voice networks. The ITU-T addressed this by defining the H.323 set of standards for packet-based multimedia networks. The basic elements of the H.323 network are shown in Figure 20-1, where H.323 terminals, such as PC-based phones, connect to existing Integrated Services Digital Network (ISDN), public switched telephone network (PSTN), and wireless devices.

Figure 20-1 *Typical H.323 Network*

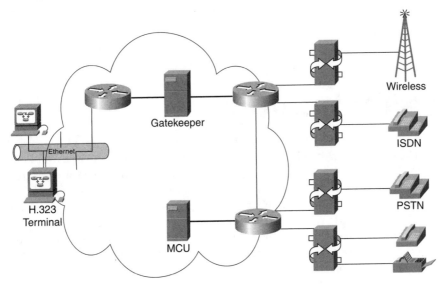

The H.323 components shown here include the following:

- H.323 terminals (LAN endpoints)
- Gateways interfacing between the LAN and switched circuit network
- A gatekeeper performing admission control functions and other related activities
- Multipoint Control Unit (MCU) enabling conferences between three or more endpoints.

H.323 Terminals

H.323 terminals are LAN-based endpoints for voice transmission. Examples of H.323 terminals are PCs running Microsoft NetMeeting software, an Ethernet-enabled phone, or a router such as the Cisco 2600/3600. H.323 terminals support real-time, 2-way communications with other H.323 entities.

H.323 terminals implement voice transmission functions and include at least one voice codec (coder/decoder) that sends and receives packetized voice. Common codecs include the following:

- ITU-T G.711 (PCM)
- G.723 (MP-MLQ)
- G.729

- G.729A (CA-ACELP)
- GSM

Codecs differ in their CPU requirements, in their resultant voice quality, and in their inherent processing delay.

H.323 terminals need to support signaling functions used for call setup, teardown, and so on. The applicable call setup standards used for H.323 include the following:

- H.225.0—Is a subset of ISDN's Q.931 signaling
- H.245—Exchanges capabilities, such as compression standards, between H.323 entities
- RAS (Registration, Admission, Status)—Connects a terminal to a gatekeeper.

H.323 terminals can also enable video and data communication capabilities, depending on the hardware and software configuration.

A functional block diagram of an H.323 terminal is shown in Figure 20-2.

Figure 20-2   *Functional Diagram of an H.323 Terminal*

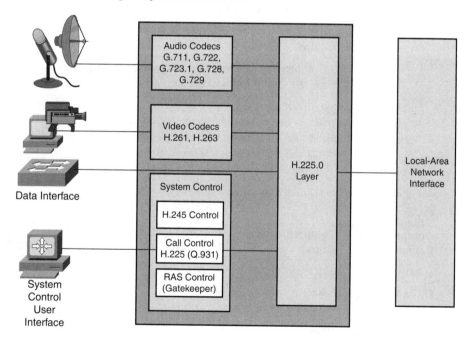

Audio Codecs

When carried over T1 TDM links, voice channels occupy 64 kilobits per second (kbps) using pulse code modulation (PCM) coding. As the telecommunications industry and associated technology have evolved, compression techniques were developed that reduced the required bandwidth while preserving voice quality. These techniques are implemented as codecs.

Many proprietary compression algorithms exist. Most H.323 devices today implement codecs that were standardized by standards bodies, such as ANSI and ITU-T enabling vendor interoperability. Applications such as NetMeeting use the H.245 protocol to negotiate which codec to use according to user preferences and the client installed codecs.

Different compression schemes can be compared using four parameters:

- Compressed voice rate—The codec compresses voice from 64 kbps down to a certain bit rate. Some network designs have a preference for low-bit-rate codecs. Most codecs can accommodate different target compression rates such as 8, 6.4 and even 5.3 kbps. Note that this bit rate is for audio only. When transmitting packetized voice over the network, protocol overhead (such as RTP/UDP/IP/Ethernet) is added on top of this bit rate, resulting in a higher actual data rate.

- Complexity—The higher the complexity of implementing the codec, the more CPU resources are required.

- Voice quality—Compressing voice in some codecs results in good voice quality, whereas others cause a significant degradation.

- Digitizing delay—Each algorithm requires that different amounts of speech be buffered prior to the compression. This delay adds to the overall end-to-end delay (see discussion that follows). A network with excessive end-to-end delay often causes people to revert to a half-duplex conversation ("How are you today? over . . .") instead of the normal full-duplex phone call.

Table 20-1 compares popular codecs according to these parameters.

Table 20-1 *Codec Comparison*

Compression Scheme	Compressed Rate (kbps)	Required CPU Resources	Resultant Voice Quality	Added Delay
G.711 PCM	64 (no compression)	Not required	Excellent	N/A
G.723 MP-MLQ	6.4/5.3	Moderate	Good (6.4) Fair (5.3)	High
G.726 ADPCM	40/32/24	Low	Good (40) Fair (24)	Very low
G.728 LD-CELP	16	Very high	Good	Low
G.729 CS-ACELP	8	High	Good	Low

A "right codec" does not exist. The choice of what compression scheme to use depends on what parameters are more important for a specific installation. In practice, G.723 and G.729 are more popular that G.726 and G.728.

Codec Complexity

Some codec compression techniques require more processing power than others. Codec complexity is broken into two categories: medium complexity and high complexity (see Table 20-2).

- Medium complexity—Allows the digital signal processors (DSPs) to process up to four voice/fax-relay calls per DSP.

- High complexity—Allows the DSPs to process up to two voice/fax-relay calls per DSP.

Table 20-2 *Medium/High Complexity Calls*

Medium Complexity (4 Calls / DSP)	High Complexity (2 Calls / DSP)
G.711 (A-law and M-law)	G.728
G.726 (all versions)	G.723 (all versions)
G.729a, G.729ab (G.729a AnnexB)	G.729, G.729b (G.729-AnnexB)
Fax-relay	Fax-relay
	Medium Complexity codecs[*]

[*]Note: Fax-relay (2,400 bps, 4,800 bps, 7,200 bps, 9,600 bps, 12 kbps, and 14.4 kbps) can use medium or high complexity codecs.

The difference between medium and high complexity codecs is the amount of CPU utilization necessary to process the codec algorithm. The codec algorithm determines the number of voice channels that can be supported by a single DSP. All medium complexity codecs can be run in high complexity mode, but fewer (usually half) of the channels are available per DSP.

Analog (Voice) Waveform Coding Techniques

Humans are well equipped for analog communications. When analog signals become weak because of transmission loss, it is difficult to separate the complex analog structure from the structure of random transmission noise. Amplifying analog signals also amplifies noise, and eventually analog connections become too noisy to use. Digital signals, having only one-bit and zero-bit states, are more easily separated from noise and can be amplified without corruption. Over time, it has become obvious that digital coding is more immune to noise corruption on long-distance connections, and the world's communications systems have converted to a PCM digital transmission format. PCM is a type of coding that is called "waveform" coding because it creates a coded form of the original voice waveform. This document describes at a high level the conversion process of analog voice signals to digital signals.

PCM

PCM is a waveform coding method defined in the ITU-T G.711 specification.

The steps involved with PCM are as follows:

1 Filtering

2 Sampling

3 Digitization

4 Quantization

Filtering

The first step in converting the signal from analog to digital is filtering out the higher frequency component of the signal, mainly because it is going to make things easier downstream for converting this signal. Most of the energy of spoken language is somewhere between 200 or 300 hertz and about 2,700 or 2,800 hertz. Roughly, a 3,000 hertz bandwidth has been established for standard speech. The bandwidth from an equipment point of view is 4,000 hertz.

This bandlimiting filter is used to prevent aliasing (anti-aliasing), which happens when the input analog voice signal is undersampled.

Undersampling, according to the Nyquist criterion, is defined as follows:

$$Fs < 2(BW)$$

where Fs = Sampling frequency and BW = Bandwidth of original analog voice signal.

The sampling frequency is less than the highest frequency of the input analog signal, creating an overlap between the frequency spectrum of the samples and the input analog signal. The low-pass output filter, used to reconstruct the original input signal, is not smart enough to detect this overlap, so it creates a new signal that did not originate from the source. The creation of a false signal during the sampling process is called *aliasing*.

Sampling

The second step in converting an analog voice signal to a digital voice signal is sampling the filtered input signal at a constant sampling frequency. Accomplished by using a process called pulse amplitude modulation (PAM), this step uses the original analog signal to modulate the amplitude of a pulse train that has a constant amplitude and frequency.

The pulse signal is moving at a constant frequency, called the *sampling frequency.* A theoretical limit exists for the number of times this analog (voice) signal can be sampled per second. A scientist named Harry Nyquist discovered that the original analog signal could be reconstructed if enough samples were taken. Nyquist determined that if the sampling frequency is at least twice the highest frequency of the original input analog voice signal, a low-pass filter at the destination could reconstruct this signal.

The Nyquist criterion can be stated as follows:

$$Fs > 2(BW)$$

where Fs = Sampling frequency and BW = Bandwidth of original analog voice signal.

Voice Digitization

After the PAM filtering and sampling of an input analog voice signal, the next step is to digitize these samples in preparation for transmission over a telephony network. The only difference between PAM and PCM is that PCM takes the process one step further by encoding each analog sample using binary code words. Basically, PCM has an analog-to-digital converter on the source side and a digital-to-analog converter on the destination side. PCM encodes these samples by using a technique called quantization.

Quantization

Quantization is the process of converting each analog sample value into a discrete value that can be assigned a unique digital code word.

As the input signal samples enter the quantization phase, they are assigned a quantization interval. All quantization intervals are equally spaced (uniform quantization) throughout the range of the input analog signal. Each quantization interval is assigned a discrete value in the form of a binary code word. The standard word size is 8 bits.

If an input analog signal is sampled 8,000 times per second and each sample is given a code word that is 8 bits long, then the maximum transmission bit rate for telephony systems using PCM is 64,000 bits per second.

Each input sample is assigned a quantization interval that is closest to its amplitude height. If an input sample is not assigned a quantization interval that matches its actual height, an error, or quantization noise, is introduced into the PCM process. Quantization noise is essentially the random noise that impacts the signal-to-noise ratio (SNR) of a voice signal, measured in decibels (dB), and can reduce the signal-to-noise ratio of a signal. An increase in quantization noise degrades the quality of a voice signal; conversely, the higher the signal-to-noise ratio, the better the voice quality.

NOTE   For coding purpose, an ^{N} bit word yields 2^N quantization labels.

The common method to reduce quantization noise is to increase the amount of quantization intervals. The difference between the input signal amplitude height and the quantization interval decreases as the quantization intervals are increased. (Increases in the intervals decrease the quantization noise.) However, the amount of code words would also have to be increased in proportion to the increase in quantization intervals. This process introduces additional problems dealing with the capacity of a PCM system to handle more code words.

Signal-to-noise ratio (SNR), including quantization noise, is the single most important factor affecting voice quality in uniform quantization. As stated earlier, uniform quantization uses equal quantization levels throughout the entire dynamic range of an input analog signal. Thus, low signals have a small low signal-level voice quality SNR, and high signals have a large high signal-level voice quality SNR. Considering that most voice signals generated are of the low kind, having better voice quality at higher signal levels is an inefficient way of digitizing voice signals. To improve voice quality at lower signal levels, a nonuniform quantization process called companding replaced uniform quantization (uniform PCM).

Companding

Companding refers to the process of first compressing an analog signal at the source, and expanding the signal back to its original size when it reaches the destination. The term companding combines two terms, compressing and expanding, into one word.

During the companding process, input analog signal samples are compressed into logarithmic segments, and then each segment is quantized and coded using uniform quantization. The compression process is logarithmic, where the compression increases as the sample signals increase. In other words, the larger sample signals are compressed more than the smaller sample signals, causing the quantization noise to increase as the sample signal increases. A logarithmic increase in quantization noise throughout the range of an input sample signal keeps the signal-to-noise ratio constant throughout.

The ITU-T standards for companding are called A-law and U-law, and they are implemented in the following parts of the world as listed here:

- A-law: Europe and the rest of the world
- U-law: North America and Japan (standardized as 64 kbps codec in ITU-T G.711.

A-Law and U-Law Companding

Similarities between A-law and U-law are as follows:

- A-law and U-law are linear approximations of logarithmic input/output relationship.
- A-law and U-law are implemented using 8-bit code words (256 levels, one for each quantization interval). Eight-bit code words allow for a bit rate of 64 kbps, calculated by multiplying the sampling rate (twice the input frequency) by the size of the code word (2×4 kHz $\times 8$ bits = 64 kbps).
- A-law and U-law break a dynamic range into a total of 16 segments:
  - Within each segment are eight positive and eight negative segments.
  - Each segment is twice the length of the preceding one.
  - Uniform quantization is used within each segment.
- A-law and U-law use a similar approach to coding the 8-bit word:
  - The first MSB identifies polarity.
  - Bits 2, 3, and 4 identify the segment.
  - The final 4 bits quantize the segment and have lower signal levels than A-law.

Differences between A-law and U-law are as follows:

- Different linear approximations load to different lengths and slopes.
- The numerical assignment of the bit positions in the 8-bit code word to segments and to quantization levels within segments are different.
- A-law provides a greater dynamic range than U-law.
- U-law provides better signal/distortion performance for low-level signals than A-law.
- A-law requires 13 bits for a uniform PCM equivalent. U-law requires 14 bits for a uniform PCM equivalent.
- An international connection should use A-law. U-law to A-law (u-to-A) conversion is the responsibility of the U-law country.

Differential Pulse Code Modulation

During the PCM process, the differences between input sample signals are minimal. Differential PCM (DPCM) was designed to calculate the difference between input signals and then transmit this small difference signal instead of the entire input sample signal. Because the difference between input samples is less than an entire input sample, the number of bits required for transmission is reduced, allowing for a reduction in the throughput required to transmit voice signals.

NOTE	DPCM can reduce the bit rate of voice transmission down to 48 kbps.

The difference between the current DPCM sample and the previous DPCM sample is calculated as follows:

- The first part of DPCM works exactly like PCM. (That is why it is called differential PCM.)

- The input signal is sampled at a constant sampling frequency (twice the input frequency). These samples are modulated using the PAM process.

- At this point, the DPCM process takes over.

- The sampled input signal is stored in what is called a predictor.

- The predictor takes the stored sample signal and sends it through a differentiator.

- The differentiator compares the previous sample signal with the current sample signal and sends this difference to the quantizing and coding phase of PCM. (This phase could be uniform quantizing or companding with A-law or U-law.)

- After quantizing and coding, the difference signal is transmitted to its final destination.

- At the receiving end of the network, everything is reversed:
  - First the difference signal is dequantized.
  - This difference signal is added to a sample signal stored in a predictor and sent to a low-pass filter that reconstructs the original input signal.

DPCM is good for reducing the bit rate for voice transmission, but it causes some other problems dealing with voice quality. DPCM quantizes and encodes the difference between a previous sample input signal and a current sample input signal. DPCM quantizes this difference signal using uniform quantization.

As with PCM, uniform quantization generates a signal-to-noise ratio that is small for small input sample signals and large for large input sample signals, resulting in voice quality that is better at higher signals. This scenario is inefficient, considering that most of the signals generated by the human voice are small. To solve the problem of inefficient signal generation due to these small (voice) signals, adaptive DPCM was developed.

Adaptive DPCM (ADPCM)

Adaptive DPCM (ADPCM) is a waveform coding method defined in the ITU-T G.726 specification.

ADPCM adapts the quantization levels of the difference signal that generated during the DPCM process. ADPCM adapts these quantization levels in one of the following methods:

- If the difference signal is low, ADPCM lowers the size of the quantization levels.
- If the difference signal is high, ADPCM decreases the size of the quantization levels.

ADPCM adapts the quantization level to the size of the input difference signal, generating a signal-to-noise ratio that is uniform throughout the dynamic range of the difference signal. ADPCM can reduce the bit rate of voice transmission down to 32 kbps, half the bit rate of A-law or U-law PCM.

ADPCM produces "toll quality" voice just like A-law or U-law PCM. The coder must have a feedback loop, using encoder output bits to recalibrate the quantizer.

Specific 32 Kbps Steps

The following steps are applicable as ITU Standards G.726:

1 Turn A-law or U-law PCM samples into a linear PCM sample.

2 Calculate the predicted value of the next sample.

3 Measure the difference between actual sample and predicted value.

4 Code difference as 4 bits, and send those bits.

5 Feed back 4 bits to the predictor.

6 Feed back 4 bits to the quantizer.

Gateways

The gateway interfaces between the H.323 and non-H.323 network. On one side, the gateway connects to the traditional voice world, and on the other side, the gateway connects to packet-based devices. As the interface, the gateway translates signaling messages in both directions as well as the coding (compression) and decoding (decompression) of the voice signal. A prime example of a gateway is the PSTN/IP gateway, connecting an H.323 terminal with the SCN (Switched Circuit Network, the PSTN).

Gatekeeper

The gatekeeper is not necessary in an H.323 network. If a gatekeeper is present, it must perform the following functions:

- Gatekeepers manage H.323 zones (a logical collection of devices, such as H.323 devices within an IP subnet).
- Multiple gatekeepers can be used for load-balancing or hot-swap backup capabilities.

The purpose of the gatekeeper is to allow H.323 networks to separate gateway processing from intelligent network-control functions. A typical gatekeeper is implemented on a PC, whereas gateways are often based on proprietary hardware platforms, such as the Cisco VG200.

Gatekeepers provide address translation, or routing, for devices in their zone; such as the translation between internal and external numbering systems. Gatekeepers also provide admission control, specifying what devices can call what numbers.

Gatekeepers provide SNMP management information, offering directory and bandwidth management services as an optional function.

A gatekeeper can participate in a variety of signaling models. Signaling models determine what signaling messages pass through the gatekeeper and what can be passed directly between entities, such as the terminal and the gateway.

Figures 20-3 and 20-4 illustrate two (2) signaling models. A direct signaling model (Figure 20-3) calls for exchange of signaling messages without involving the gatekeeper, whereas in a gatekeeper-routed call signaling model (Figure 20-4), all signaling passes through the gatekeeper, and only multimedia streams can pass directly between the stations.

Figure 20-3   *Figure X: Gatekeeper Direct Signaling Model*

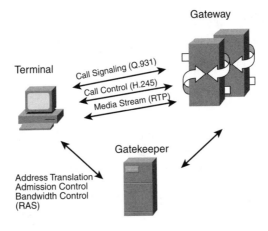

Figure 20-4   *Figure Y: Gatekeeper-Routed Signaling Model*

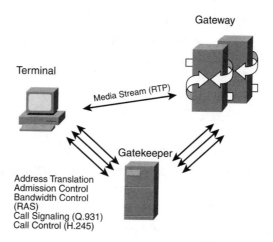

MCU

MCUs allow for conferencing functions between three or more terminals. Logically, an MCU contains two parts:

- Multipoint controller (MC)—Handles signaling and control messages necessary to set up and manage conferences.

- Multipoint processor (MP)—Accepts streams from endpoints, replicates them, and forwards them to the correct participating endpoints.

A centralized MCU implements both MC and MP functions, whereas a decentralized MCU implements only MC functions, leaving the endpoints to support the MP functions.

The definition of all H.323 network entities is logical. No specification has been made on the physical division of the units. For example, MCUs can be standalone devices, or integrated into a terminal, a gateway, or a gatekeeper.

H.323 Protocol Stack

The H.323 protocol stack is shown in Figure 20-5.

Figure 20-5   *H.323 Protocol Stack*

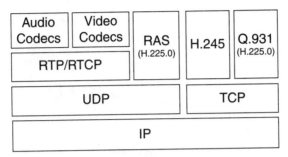

Control messages (Q.931 signaling, H.245 capability exchange, and the RAS protocol) are carried over the TCP layer, ensuring retransmission if necessary. Media traffic is transported over the UDP layer and includes two protocols as defined in IETF RFC 1889:

- RTP (Real-Time Protocol)—Carries the actual media
- RTCP (Real-Time Control Protocol)—Carries periodic status and control messages

Media is carried over UDP because it would not make sense for it to be retransmitted; should a lost sound fragment be retransmitted, it would most likely arrive too late to be useful in voice/video reconstruction. RTP messages are typically carried on even-numbered UDP ports, whereas RTCP messages are carried on the adjacent odd-numbered ports.

In the traditional circuit-switched (TDM) network, each voice channel occupied a unique T1 timeslot with fixed 64 kbps bandwidth. When traveling over the packet network, voice packets must contend with new phenomena that can affect the overall quality as perceived by the end customer. The premier factors that determine voice quality are choice of codec, latency, jitter, and packet loss.

NOTE   The codecs can usually recover loss of a single packet in a VoX stream; however, loss of two consecutive packets can have adverse affects on the data stream because the codecs are not able to recover from such a broad spectrum.

Figure 20-6 illustrates a complete PCM sample (broken down into eight packets).

Figure 20-6   *Complete PCM Sample*

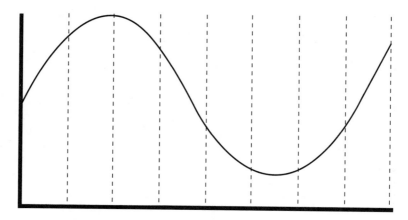

Figure 20-7 illustrates a PCM sample with a dropped packet.

Figure 20-7   *PCM Sample with One Dropped Packet*

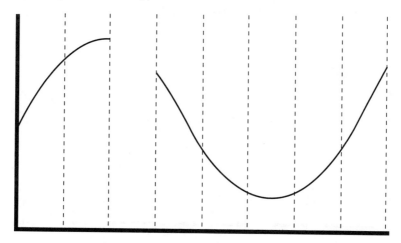

Figure 20-8 illustrates a PCM sample with a dropped packet filled by PCM interpolation.

Figure 20-8   *PCM Sample with Interpolated Packet*

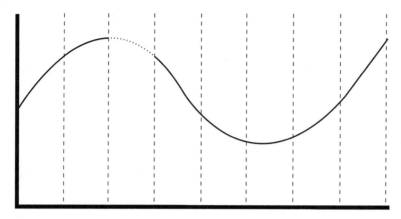

Figure 20-9 illustrates a PCM sample with two dropped packets. Interpolation here is not possible because the spread is too large to compensate.

Figure 20-9   *PCM Sample with Two Dropped Packets*

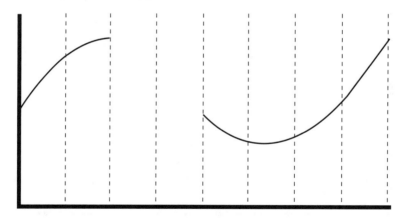

Latency

In contrast to broadcast-type media transmission (such as RealAudio), a two-way phone conversation over the PSTN is quite sensitive to latency. Most PSTN users notice round-trip delays when exceeding 250 milliseconds (ms), loosely calculated to a one-way latency budget of 150 ms.

In the ITU-T G.114 recommendation, 150 ms is specified as the maximum preferred one-way latency to achieve high-quality voice. Beyond that round-trip latency, users start feeling uneasy holding a two-way conversation and usually end up talking over each other.

At 500 ms round-trip delays and beyond, phone calls are impractical. In comparison, the typical delay when speaking through a geo-stationary satellite is 150 to 500 ms.

Data networks are not affected by delay because the receiving network device reassembles out of order packets, in accordance with sequence numbers, such as TCP sequencing. An additional delay of 200 ms on an e-mail or Web page mostly goes unnoticed. However, when sharing the same network, voice callers notice this delay. When considering the one-way delay of voice traffic, you must take into account the delay added by the different network segments and processes.

Components in the delay budget are separated into fixed and variable delay. The backbone transmission delay is a constant, dictated by the distance, whereas networking conditions add a variable delay to the total delay budget.

The significant components of latency are as follows:

- Backbone (network) latency—Delay incurred when traversing the VoIP backbone. To minimize this delay, it is best to try to minimize the router hops between endpoints. Network service providers can sometimes provide an end-to-end delay limit over their managed backbones. Some network service providers negotiate with customers to identify and provision priority connections for voice traffic than for delay-insensitive data.

NOTE   The **traceroute** utility can run from either the Cisco IOS CLI or from any client-PC command prompt to determine the number of hops between endpoints.

- Codec latency—Compression algorithms have some built-in delay costs, such as G.723 adding a fixed 30 ms delay. When this additional overhead is added to the total delay budget, it is possible to end up paying 32 to 35 ms for passing through the gateway. Different codec implementations can reduce the latency; however, this reduced latency might be at the cost of reduced quality or greater bandwidth consumption.

- Jitter buffer depth—Compensating for fluctuating network conditions, many vendors implement a jitter buffer in their voice gateway product suites. The jitter buffer is a packet buffer that holds incoming packets for a specified amount of time before forwarding them to the codec for decompression. Jitter buffers have the effect of smoothing the packet flow, increasing the resiliency of the codec to packet loss, delayed packets, and other transmission effects. Using the jitter buffer has one disadvantage: It can add significant delay. The jitter buffer size is configurable and can be optimized for given network conditions. The jitter buffer size is usually set to be an integral multiple of the expected packet inter-arrival time to buffer an integral number of packets.

NOTE	It is not uncommon to see jitter buffer settings approaching 80 ms for each direction.

When designing or optimizing a VoX network, it is often useful to construct a table showing the one-way delay budget, as demonstrated in Table 20-3.

Table 20-3   *Sample VoIP Delay Budget*

Parameter	Fixed Delay	Variable Delay
Codec (G.729)	25 ms	
Packetization	Included in codec	
Queuing delay		Depends on uplink. In the order of a few milliseconds.
Network delay	50 ms	Depends on network load.
Jitter buffer	50 ms	
Total	125 ms	

Measuring Latency

Three configurations exist for measuring latency:

- Latency of a device
- Round-trip delay
- One-way delay

Measuring latency of a device is important to understand how the delay budget is spent over the network, particularly the latency of data going through a gateway because several parameters are user-configurable, such as jitter-buffer.

Jitter

Network latency impacts the amount of time that a voice packet spends traversing a network. Jitter controls the regularity in which voice packets arrive at the intended destination.

Voice sources generate voice packets at a constant rate, and the voice decompression algorithms expect incoming voice packets to arrive at a similar constant rate. However, the packet-by-packet delay induced by the network can be different for each packet, even if that difference is measurable in milliseconds. This results in packets that are sent in equal intervals from the source gateway arriving at irregular intervals at the destination gateway, as illustrated in Figure 20-10.

Figure 20-10 *Packet Jitter*

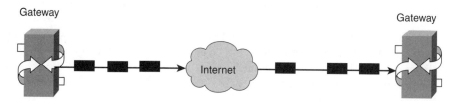

Because the receiving decompression algorithm requires a fixed interval between packets, a solution would be to implement a jitter buffer within the gateway. The jitter buffer deliberately delays incoming packets to present them to the decompression algorithm at fixed intervals. The jitter buffer also corrects any out-of-order errors by looking at the sequence number in the RTP frames. While the voice decompression engine receives packets, the individual packets are delayed further in transit, increasing the overall latency.

Measuring Jitter

Jitter is calculated based on the inter-arrival time of successive packets.

Frequently, two numbers are presented:

- Average inter-arrival time—Inter-arrival time of the emitted packets
- Standard deviation—Low pointing at a consistent inter-arrival time

When correct jitter measurements are measured for audio streams, it is important to take into account the following three phenomena:

- Silence suppression
- Packet loss
- Out of sequence errors

Codecs take advantage of silent periods in the conversation transmission to reduce the number of packets being sent. Generally, up to a 50 percent bandwidth savings can be realized in this fashion. After a period of silence, the RTP packet is immediately marked with the silence suppression bit. Jitter calculations look at the silence suppression bit and disregard the long gap between the packet right before the silence and the packet right after the silence period.

When a packet is lost during transmission, the inter-arrival time between two successive packets appear excessive. For example, if three packets were sent at a time of 0, 20, and 40 ms, and the second packet was lost in transit, the inter-arrival time would appear to be 40 ms even if the network induced no jitter. Correct jitter measurements would discover these cases by looking at the packet sequence number and compensate for packet loss in the jitter calculation.

Out of sequence packets can skew jitter measurements when they are not taken into account. For example, packet 1 was sent at time 0 and arrived at time 100, packet 2 was sent at time 20 and arrived at time 140, and packet 3 was sent at time 40 and arrived at time 120. Packets arrived to the receiver at times 100, 120, and 140, so no jitter would be detected unless the analysis examined the sequence numbers. This examination would show the jitter calculated based on a 40 ms inter-arrival between packets 1 and 2, as well as a –20 ms inter-arrival time between packets 2 and 3.

Packet Loss

Packet loss is a normal occurrence during transmission on packet networks. Packet loss can be caused by many different factors:

- Overloaded links
- Excessive collisions on a LAN
- Physical media errors

Transport layer protocols, such as TCP of the TCP/IP protocol suite, account and adjust for such packet loss and enable packet recovery.

Audio codecs take into account the possibility, or even probability, of packet loss, especially because RTP data is transferred over the UDP layer of the TCP/IP protocol suite. The typical codec performs one of several functions, ensuring that an occasional lost packet is unnoticeable to the users. For example, a codec could elect to use the packet received just before the lost packet instead of the lost one, essentially "replaying" the last received packet. The codec could also interpolate based on the last received packet and the next received packet to fill in the "hole" in the audio stream.

NOTE   TCP is reliable; UDP is not.

Packet loss becomes a severe issue when the percentage of the lost packets exceeds a certain threshold (roughly 5 percent of the packets), or when lost packets are grouped together in large transmission bursts. In these situations, the best codecs are unable to hide the packet loss from the users, resulting in degraded voice quality, such as clicking, static, or dropped calls.

VoX Network Parameters

The total network load is a significant factor affecting voice quality. When load on the network is high, and for networks with statistical access such as Ethernet, jitter and frame loss generally increases; for example, with Ethernet, higher load leads to more collisions.

It does not matter if the collided frames are eventually transmitted across the network; they were not sent when they were intended to, resulting in excess jitter. Beyond a certain collision threshold, significant frame loss occurs and renders voice communication ineffective.

In congested networks, it is sometimes possible to employ packet prioritization schemes based on TCP/UDP port numbers, IP subnets, or the IP precedence field. These methods enable timing-sensitive frames such as voice to be given priority over data frames. Often, no perceived degradation in the quality of data service exists; however, voice quality improves to a usable and clear state.

Another alternative to packet prioritization is the implementation of bandwidth resource reservation protocols, such as Resource Reservation Protocol (RSVP). RSVP ensures that the chosen class of service is available with regards to the specific stream.

Session Initiation Protocol (SIP)

Session Initiation Protocol (SIP) is the Internet Engineering Task Force's (IETF's) standard for multimedia conferencing over IP. SIP is an ASCII-based, application layer control protocol that can be used to establish, maintain, and terminate calls between two or more endpoints.

SIP is detailed in RFC 2543:

> 2543 SIP: Session Initiation Protocol. M. Handley, H. Schulzrinne, E. Schooler, J. Rosenberg. March 1999. Format: TXT=338861 bytes. Status: Proposed Standard.

Like other VoIP protocols, SIP is designed to address the functions of signaling and session management within a packet telephony network. *Signaling* allows call information to be carried across network boundaries. *Session management* provides the ability to control the attributes of an end-to-end call.

SIP provides the following capabilities:

- Ability to determine the location of the target endpoint. SIP supports address resolution, name mapping, and call redirection.

- Ability to determine the media capabilities of the target endpoint, via Session Description Protocol (SDP). SIP determines the "lowest level" of common services between the endpoints. Conferences are established using only the media capabilities that can be supported by all endpoints.

- Ability to determine the availability of the target endpoint. If a call cannot be completed because the target endpoint is unavailable, SIP determines whether the called party is already on the phone or did not answer in the allotted number of rings. SIP then returns a message indicating why the target endpoint was unavailable.

- Ability to establish a session between the originating and target endpoint. If the call can be completed, SIP establishes a session between the endpoints. SIP also supports mid-call changes, such as the addition of another endpoint to the conference or the changing of a media characteristic or codec.

- Ability to handle the transfer and termination of calls. SIP supports the transfer of calls from one endpoint to another. During a call transfer, SIP simply establishes a session between the transferee and a new endpoint (specified by the transferring party) and terminates the session between the transferee and the transferring party. At the end of a call, SIP terminates the sessions between all parties.

Conferences can consist of two or more users and can be established using multicast or multiple unicast sessions.

SIP Protocol Operation

SIP is a peer-to-peer protocol. The peers in a session are called user agents (UAs). A user agent can function in one of the following roles:

- User agent client (UAC)—A client application that initiates the SIP request.

- User agent server (UAS)—A server application that contacts the user when a SIP request is received and that returns a response on behalf of the user.

A SIP endpoint is capable of functioning as both a UAC and a UAS, but functions only as one or the other per transaction. The UA that initiated the request determines whether the endpoint functions as a UAC or a UAS.

The physical components of a SIP network architecture can be grouped into two categories: clients and servers. Figure 20-11 illustrates the architecture of a SIP network.

In addition, the SIP servers can interact with other application services, such as Lightweight Directory Access Protocol (LDAP) servers, location servers, a database application, RADIUS server, or an extensible markup language (XML) application. These application services provide back-end services such as directory, authentication, and billing services.

Figure 20-11 *SIP Architecture*

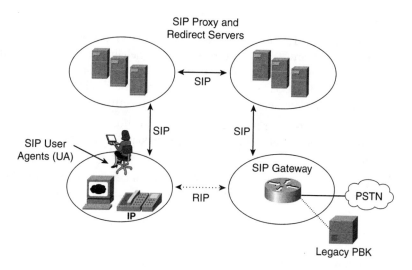

SIP Clients

SIP clients are one of the following components:

- Phones—Act as either a UAS or a UAC. Softphones (PCs that have phone capabilities installed) and Cisco SIP IP phones can initiate SIP requests and respond to requests.

- Gateways—Provide call control. Gateways provide many services, the most common being a translation function between SIP conferencing endpoints and other terminal types. This function includes translation between transmission formats and communications procedures. In addition, the gateway translates between audio and video codecs and performs call setup and clearing on both the LAN side and the switched-circuit network side.

SIP Servers

SIP servers are one of the following components:

- Proxy server—This is an intermediate device that receives SIP requests from a client and then forwards the requests on the client's behalf. Basically, proxy servers receive SIP messages and forward them to the next SIP server in the network. Proxy servers can provide functions such as authentication, authorization, network access control, routing, reliable request retransmission, and security.

- Redirect server—This provides the client with information about the next hop or hops that a message should take. Then the client contacts the next hop server or UAS directly.

- Registrar server—This processes requests from UACs for registration of their current location. Registrar servers are often co-located with a redirect or proxy server.

SIP Operation

SIP is an ASCII-based protocol, using requests and responses to establish communication among various components in the network to establish a conference between two or more endpoints.

SIP network users are identified by a unique SIP address. A SIP address is similar to an e-mail address and is formatted as sip:*userID@gateway*.com. The SIP user ID can be either a username or an E.164 address.

SIP users register with a registrar server using their assigned SIP addresses. The registrar server provides this registration information to the location server upon request.

When a user initiates a call, a SIP request is sent to a SIP server (either a proxy or a redirect server). The request includes the address of the caller (origination) in the From header field, and the address of the intended recipient (destination) in the To header field.

Table 20-4 reviews comparisons between SIP and H.323.

Table 20-4   *SIP/H.323 Comparison*

Aspect	SIP	H.323
Clients	Intelligent	Intelligent
Network intelligence and services	Provided by servers (Proxy, Redirect, Registrar)	Provided by gatekeepers
Model used	Internet/WWW	Telephony/Q.SIG
Signaling protocol	UDP or TCP	TCP (UDP is optional in Version 3)
Media protocol	RTP	RTP
Code basis	ASCII	Binary (ASN.1 encoding)

Table 20-4   *SIP/H.323 Comparison*

Aspect	SIP	H.323
Other protocols used	IETF/IP protocols, such as SDP, HTTP/1.1, IPmc, and MIME	ITU / ISDN protocols, such as H.225, H.245, and H.450
Vendor interoperability	Widespread	Limited

Although SIP messages are not directly compatible with H.323, both protocols can coexist in the same packet telephony network if a device that supports the interoperability is available.

VoIP Equipment Adjustment

VoIP equipment uses several mechanisms to manage the voice transmission:

- Jitter buffers
- Packet size
- Silence suppression

Jitter Buffers

The jitter buffer can be configured in most VoIP gear. The jitter buffer size must be balanced between delay and quality. If the jitter buffer is too small, network anomalies, such as packet loss and jitter, cause adverse audible effects in the received voice. If the jitter buffer is too large, voice quality does not suffer; however, the two-way conversation might turn into a half-duplex one.

A jitter buffer policy that specifies a certain percentage of packets should fit into the jitter buffer. Because the utilization of the jitter buffer depends on the arrival times of the packets, it is useful to look at the jitter buffer problem using a few calculations.

As a general rule, the jitter buffer is set to twice the coder delay. For example, G.729 compression algorithms have a fixed delay of 5 ms (for network look-ahead) and 10 ms per sample (two samples per packet). The total coder delay here is 25 ms; therefore, the jitter buffer delay would be configured at 50 ms.

```
CoderDelay_TOTAL = CoderDelay_LOOKAHEAD + CoderDelay_SAMPLE*

JitterBuffer = ((CoderDelay_TOTAL) ∞ 2)
```

*Some coder algorithms take two samples per voice packet; in this case, both samples need to be counted.

Packet Size

Packet size selection is also about balance between too small and too large a packet size. Larger packet sizes reduce the overall bandwidth but add to the packet creation delay because the sender needs to wait longer to fill up the payload.

Overhead in VoIP communications is quite high. Consider a scenario where 8 kbps is being compressed and frames are being sent every 20 ms. This results in voice payloads of 20 bytes for each packet. To transmit these voice payloads over RTP, the following must be added:

- An Ethernet header of 14 bytes
- An IP header of 20 bytes
- A UDP header of 8 bytes
- An additional 12 bytes for RTP

This brings the total to 54 bytes overhead to transmit a 20-byte payload.

In some cases, such an overhead is manageable with minimal impact on the network. In other cases, the problem has two solutions:

- Increase packet size—Deciding to send packets every 40 ms makes it possible to increase the payload efficiency. Before the inter-arrival time is increased, it should be verified that the delay budget can support the packet size increase.

- Implement header compression—Header compression is popular with some vendor's equipment, especially on slow links that implement such Layer 2 protocols as Point-to-Point Protocol (PPP), Frame Relay, or ISDN. VoX Header compression is commonly referred to as Compressed RTP (CRTP). CRTP compresses the header to a few bytes on a hop-by-hop basis. This is possible because the Frame Relay DLCI determines the logical channel, making some header information redundant.

RTP header compression compresses the IP/UDP/RTP header in an RTP data packet from 40 bytes to approximately 2 to 4 bytes (most of the time), as shown in Figure 20-12.

Figure 20-12 *RTP Header Compression*

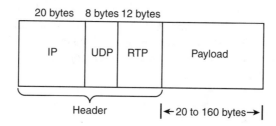

Before RTP Header Compression:

After RTP Header Compression:

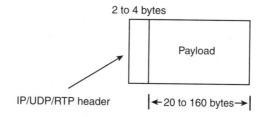

Silence Suppression

Silence suppression takes advantage of prolonged periods of silence in conversations to reduce the number of packets. In a normal interactive conversation, each speaker generally listens for approximately half the time; therefore, it is not necessary to transmit "silent" packets. Cisco, like many vendors, takes advantage of this to reduce the bandwidth and number of packets on a link.

VoX Call Establishment

The call establishment process presents a performance challenge; therefore, the following concerns should be addressed:

- Call setup time—The time required from the initial dialing of digits to establishing a connection. Customers are accustomed to fast call setup times in the PSTN world, and expect to get similar performance in the new VoIP network environment.

- Call success ratio—The ratio of successful connects to dial attempts.

- Call setup rate—The number of calls per second that can be set up through the network. The call setup rate determines the upper performance limit of the current VoX network devices.

Testing and measuring these parameters involves looking deeply into Q.931 messages and analyzing the message sequences. Q.931 messages have a field called Call Reference that allows you to distinguish one setup procedure from the other. These messages are interleaved with the normal data transfer, so it is sometimes difficult to fish for the Q.931 information in the total packet.

Measuring Voice Quality

Standards bodies such as ITU-T and ANSI are continuously addressing the issue of measuring voice quality, trying to take the subjectiveness out of the measurements. ITU-T and ANSI have derived two recommendations:

- P.800 (MOS)—Deals with defining a method to derive a mean opinion score of voice quality. The test involves recording several preselected voice samples over a preferred or specified transmission media and then playing them back to a mixed group of men and women under controlled conditions. The scores given by this group are then weighed to give a single MOS score ranging between 1 (worst) and 5 (best). A MOS of 4 is considered "toll-quality" voice.

- P.861 (PSQM)—Perceptual Speech Quality Measurement (PSQM) tries to automate the P.800 process by defining an algorithm through which a computer can derive scores that have a close correlation to the MOS scores. Although PSQM is useful, many have voiced concerns over the suitability of this recommendation to packetized voice networks. PSQM was designed for the circuit-switched network; it does not take into account parameters such as jitter and frame loss that are relevant to VoIP.

As a result of PSQM limitations, researchers are trying to come up with an alternative objective methodology to measure voice quality. One such proposal is the Perceptual Analysis/Measurement system (PAMS) developed by British Telecom (BT). Tests conducted by BT have shown good correlation between automated PAMS scoring and manual MOS results.

VoX Summary

Voice over X services offer lucrative advantages to customers and service providers; however, as with any new technology, VoX brings its own sets of network design and optimization issues.

Voice over ATM (VoATM)

Asynchronous Transfer Mode (ATM) enables the statistical multiplexing of traffic over any network resource. Statistical multiplexing avoids the need to preallocate resources for a user, but allocates resources on-demand, providing bandwidth to users only when they need it. This allows the network to support more users (typically twice as many as a simple TDM network).

However, to succeed, an ATM network must be able to integrate traffic of all types into this single, integrated, statistically multiplexed stream. This means handling that most testing of traffic—voice. The transport of voice presents the network with a number of technical challenges; these must be successfully managed if the network is to provide an effective voice transport mechanism.

Today, through the work of the ATM Forum and its members, these issues have been addressed and it is possible to build and operate an ATM network to meet the needs of many types of voice application.

It is possible to build an ATM network to meet the VPN voice needs of an enterprise or the backbone transmission needs of national voice network. An ATM network can also be built to support a national cellular network or provide international voice transport.

VoATM Issues

Any packetized approach to the transmission of voice faces a number of technical challenges. These challenges are the same for any packetized technology, be it ATM, Frame Relay, IP, or X.25.

These challenges stem from the real-time and interactive nature of voice traffic:

- Delay
- Signaling support
- Synchronization

Delay

To hold an interactive conversation end-to-end, network-induced delay must be kept to a minimum to ensure that subscribers receive an acceptable quality of service.

Two significant issues must be addressed as network delay increases:

- Telephony phenomenon
- Signaling support

Telephony Phenomenon

The first issue is a direct result of an electrical quirk of the PSTN. Telephone handsets use four wires to connect to the network. However, the PSTN long-distance network uses a single pair of lines to carry a telephone call. This transition from 2-wire to 4-wire operation is accomplished by the use of a device known as a "hybrid" at each end of the network.

Hybrids cause a reflection of signal due to an unavoidable impedance mismatch. The effect of this is that some of the speech signal is reflected back toward the sender by each hybrid, and arrives in the earpiece of each sender's handset. Normally, this is not noticeable because it is just like hearing your own voice through the air of the room. However, if the network experiences a significant delay, the reflected signal from the far-side hybrid arrives back in the sender's earpiece as an echo. The effect of this echo is more pronounced as the delay increases.

At about 30 ms of network delay, the echo is significant enough to make normal conversation difficult. Therefore, after a voice circuit delay exceeds 30 ms, echo cancellers must be deployed in the network. These devices can be costly and operate at a peak when the delay over a circuit is constant. However, in a packetized voice network, delay is not always a constant; therefore, delay is difficult to cancel out on a regular and reliable basis.

Echo cancellation systems allow network delay to reach approximately 150 ms before further voice quality degradation is experienced.

At about 150 ms of delay, a second issue arises. At this level of delay, significant problems in carrying on a normal conversation begin. Normal conversation patterns demand that some responses from the listener are received within less than 200 ms, and delays of this order result in stilted conversations and "clashing" (where both parties try to talk at once).

NOTE   Delay in excess of 150 ms is typically encountered over satellite links.

For these reasons, toll quality networks require that the end-to-end network delay for voice traffic is less than 25 ms in national networks and less than 100 ms in international networks.

ATM Telephony Delay

Despite the broadband applications and speed enabled by ATM internetworking, ATM networks are susceptible to delay. ATM delay is broken into three concerns:

- Packetization delay
- Buffering delay
- Encoding delay

ATM Packetization Delay (Cell Construction Delay)

Packetization delay is the delay caused by the necessity to fill a packet or cell before it is transmitted.

Voice samples are received at a rate corresponding to the compression level of the voice traffic; for example, uncompressed (normal) PCM encoded voice arrives at a rate of 64 kbps. Compressed voice arrives at lower rates (32 kbps, 16 kbps, and 8 kbps). Delay is incurred while sufficient encoded data is received to allow the packet or cell to be filled for transmission.

The minimum packet length that can be transmitted and the encoding rate define this delay. With some packet schemes, it is possible to send small packets; this is unattractive from a networking point of view because the efficiency of any packetized scheme falls as the ratio between payload and header length falls. ATM's fixed cell length means that delay is just proportional to the level of voice compression employed. Greater compression results in greater delay.

For example, if you are using 8 kbps LD-CELP compression and filling ATM AAL1 cells, one cell is filled every 47 ms. Because the cell cannot be transmitted until it is full, the first delay threshold has been exceeded prior to transmission of the first ATM cell.

You can address this problem either with partially filled cells or by multiplexing several voice calls into a single ATM VCC.

VoATM Buffering (Build-Out) Delay

Another area of delay stems from the requirement to maintain real-time delivery of voice traffic across the network. When traffic is transmitted across an ATM internetwork, it must first be broken down into (53-byte) cells for transmission. At the transmission's destination, these cells must be reassembled into the original voice call (via the emulated circuit). In the case of voice, the traffic must be reassembled in real-time with no significant time delay, or latency.

The reassembly mechanism of any ATM constant bit rate (CBR) data stream requires the reconstruction of the carried traffic at the destination at the correct moment in time. If an

ATM cell is delayed during transmission, the segment assembly/reassembly (SAR) function might "under-run" (having no data to process), resulting in gaps in conversation.

To prevent this under-run from happening, the receiving SAR function accumulates a buffer of information prior to commencing the reconstruction of the traffic from received cells. The depth of this buffer must exceed the maximum predicted delay propagated by the network to ensure that no under-runs occur. However, the buffer depth directly translates into delay because each cell must progress through the buffer on arrival at the emulated circuit's line rate.

This buffer delay means that the cell delay variation within the ATM network needs to be controlled, allowing the minimum depth of reassembly buffer to be configured, minimizing the network delay.

VoATM Encoding Delay

The third source of delay occurs in the encoding of the analog signal into a digital form.

The compression of voice traffic, while maintaining quality, results in processing delay. This becomes more significant at lower bit rates. The low delay code excited linear prediction (LD-CELP) encoding algorithm family is now widely used and enables toll-quality encoding to be achieved at bit rates as low as 16 kbps and encoding delays of less than 10 ms.

NOTE   The LD-CELP family can result in as much as 50 percent of the total delay budget.

VoATM Signaling Support

ATM signaling support addresses resource utilization and the transfer of signaling and support information.

A voice call consists of two parts: the voice samples and the signaling information. The signaling information includes the dialed number, the on-hook/off-hook status of the call, and other routing and control information (if so configured). Signaling can be encoded in a number of ways, and can be sent as common channel, channel associated, or DTMF dialed digits.

In a TDM networking environment, multiple voice channels are combined into a single circuit. For example, a North American T1 (1.536 Mbps) carries 24 64 kbps voice channels, and a European E1 (2.048 Mbps) carries 30 discrete 64 kbps voice channels. Signaling information can be embedded within each discrete voice channel (known as *channel associated signaling*) or aggregated into a single signaling channel, containing signaling information for all the channels on the circuit (*common channel signaling*).

When voice traffic is being carried across an ATM network in a single voice trunk, you might want the signaling to carry end to end. However, when using common channel signaling, where traffic from one site must be switched and delivered to two or more endpoints, the trunk-based approach might not work. In these cases, the signaling channels must be terminated and interpreted at the ATM switch so the correct information can be passed to the correct endpoint. Given that many signaling mechanisms (both proprietary and standardized) exist, the ATM network might need to understand several types of signaling protocol.

The on-hook/off-hook signals can be used to allocate active voice channels to active virtual channel connections (VCCs) within the network. An ATM network can ensure that valuable bandwidth is allocated to only active calls, and a large community of users can contend for available resources because only active circuits are transmitted.

Synchronization

ATM is asynchronous in nature; however, the transport of voice traffic demands that the data be synchronized to maintain the time-based relationship between speaker and listener.

With point-to-point applications, the two endpoints can be synchronized by two standardized mechanisms, adjusting the clock rate on one end of the circuit based on the clock rate of the other end. These two mechanisms are as follows:

- Adaptive clocking—Adaptive clocking does this by monitoring the depths of the SAR receive buffers. It then adjusts the clock rate of the "slave" end to maintain an appropriate buffer depth.

- Synchronous residual time stamping (SRTS)—SRTS monitors the rate of the line clock at the "master" end of the circuit, with respect to a standard clock. The difference between the two clocks ("master" and "slave") is then encoded and transmitted as part of the data stream. The slave (receiving) end examines the difference in the signal retrieved and uses the received signal to adjust the slave clock by reference to the differing signal and the standard clock.

Neither adaptive nor SRTS clocking can function with regard to multipoint services. For example, with adaptive clocking, a slave can adjust its line clock in response to changes in the buffer depth, resulting in two different data sources adversely affecting one of them. With SRTS, it is not possible for a slave site "A" to adjust its clock in response to two different signals being received from two different master sites.

For multipoint services to occur, an externally synchronized clocking model must be adopted in which each node in the network is synchronized to some external source. This is relatively easy to do given the availability of global timing standards.

VoATM Applications

Many applications exist for voice transport over an ATM network. These encompass both the enterprise network builder and the public network service provider. Each application has differing requirements; this section considers the applications and the requirements they have for voice transport.

For this discussion, three classes of network operator are clearly defined:

- National or international operators—These organizations typically have an extensive PSTN service in place operating over existing PDH or SDH/SONET infrastructure. They also have data networking services supporting business and residential users with multiple, discrete networks supporting these applications.

  Where bandwidth is limited, a strong requirement exists to integrate voice and data traffic into a single ATM network for reasons of efficiency. This is particularly true within the international segment of a carrier's network where the cost of leased international bandwidth demands top levels of efficiency.

  Within the local loop, ATM might be a valuable solution for the carriage of voice and data to business premises, where copper-enhanced (xDSL) or fiber-to-the-curb (FTTC) architectures are in place.

- Alternate carriers or value-added network suppliers—These companies are typically taking up licenses to provide communications services in competition with the incumbent national operators. They do not own their transmission infrastructure. They must, therefore, either buy bandwidth from the primary operator or form alliances or joint ventures with companies who have rights-of-way, or have deployed bandwidth.

  In these cases, cost and limited availability of bandwidth demand ATM's efficiency as well as integration of voice and data services. Many cell phone companies are in this situation where they must build a fixed voice network to interconnect their cell sites and message-switching centers. The efficiencies that ATM can provide result in major improvements in the cost performance of their network.

- Enterprise (private) networks—Most private, enterprise networks are buying bandwidth at commercial (retail) rates and must achieve the most they can with the resources on hand. In any corporation, a significant proportion of the traffic in the network is voice, so integration of voice and data under ATM becomes an obvious goal.

  In many cases, such organizations have already deployed a TDM network that utilizes T1, E1, or J1 (Asia-Pacific) links. They want to integrate these solutions into a new ATM network, and gain improvements in network performance and efficiency by moving from TDM to statistical multiplexing.

Two Basic VoATM Models

Two fundamental models for the transport of voice emerge: voice trunking and voice switching.

- Voice trunking—Involves the tunneling of voice traffic across a network between two fixed endpoints.

  This is an appropriate mechanism for the connecting of voice switch sites, PBXs, or message-switching centers. The network does not have a requirement to be able to process or terminate signaling other than the opportunity to use the signaling to detect idle channels.

  However, the large scale of these networks often allows efficient configurations to be achieved just by the analysis and use of traditional PSTN traffic engineering mechanisms.

- Voice switching—Involves the ATM network in the interpretation of voice signaling information and the routing of a call across the network.

  The ATM switch, which receives the voice call, routes it to the appropriate destination. This type of functionality is most appropriate for VPN network.

  For a voice switching network solution to operate, the ATM network must be able to interpret the signaling provided from the voice network.

  In the past, this has presented a major challenge; many types of voice signaling existed, but many of them were proprietary.

Network Requirements

Regardless of the network model deployed—voice trunking or voice switching—a common set of network requirements emerges. To implement voice trunking, you must meet the minimum requirements, as outlined in Table 20-5.

Table 20-5   *ATM Voice Trunk Minimum Requirements*

Requirement	Description
Adaption	Encode voice samples into ATM cells while meeting delay and real-time constraints of voice traffic.
Signaling	Enable the end-to-end transport of voice signaling (common channel or channel associated) with the voice traffic.
Low cross network delay (Latency)	Minimize delay issues, and enable normal interactive conversation. (This is not a requirement for broadcast applications.)
Limited variation in delay	Minimize delays and allow effective echo cancellation.

Beyond these basic demands, a more extensive set of requirements is necessary to support a complete voice-switched solution, or statistical multiplexing in a voice trunk environment. Table 20-6 lists the requirements for supporting voice-switched solutions.

Table 20-6   *Requirements to Support Voice-Switched Solutions*

Requirement	Necessity
Signaling analysis	Enable call setup and tear-down of circuits on demand (or allocation and release of resources).
Call switching and routing mechanisms	Enable configuration of "real-world" VPN applications.
Silence suppression or VBR encoding	Realize statistical gains (provides at least a doubling in performance).
Call admission control (CAC)	Ensure that quality of service is preserved.
Network resource allocation	Enable statistical overbooking of network resources.

VoATM Expectations

Any ATM solution is measured against the current generation of deployed TDM solutions that have been deployed. The ATM Forum has developed a solution set that enables direct commercial or operational benefits to any user. These solution sets allow voice traffic to be carried over an ATM network more efficiently than when carried over traditional TDM or packet-based network infrastructures.

ATM's ability to statistically allocate network resources and to accept variable bit rate (VBR) voice results in a much higher level of resource utilization. Idle channels across an ATM path do not consume bandwidth, and resources can be allocated on-demand to voice and data traffic presented to the network.

ATM's ability to transport real-time traffic over heavily loaded links results in an ATM solution that is able to maintain call quality under all circumstances.

ATM solutions are measured against the following two characteristics:

- Voice traffic must arrive unimpaired by its transport across the network.
- Valuable network bandwidth must be managed to provide a cost-efficient solution.

VoATM Solutions

The ATM Forum has defined three principal approaches to deploying a VoATM network solution, with a fourth "workaround" approach. These principals are as follows:

- Circuit Emulation Service (CES). This carries full or fractional rate E1/T1 circuits between endpoints.

- Dynamic bandwidth circuit emulation service (DBCES).
- ATM trunking of narrowband services using AAL2 (under development).

The fourth approach is the transport of voice traffic that has previously been encapsulated in another protocol, such as Voice over IP (VoIP) or Voice over Frame Relay (VoFR).

CES

The ATM forum defined CES in January 1997 as af-vtoa-0078.000. Today, Circuit Emulation represents a stable and reliable standard, widely implemented by ATM equipment suppliers.

When using circuit emulation, the ATM network provides a transparent transport mechanism for structured G.703/4 links. Voice is encoded into these links as in a normal TDM network using PCM, ADPCM, or other encoding and compression mechanisms.

The network ensures that the delivered circuit is reconstructed exactly as received. CES is a full duplex mechanism, and it presents the voice equipment with an apparent leased circuit. This approach is valuable because no change to an existing TDM or PBX network is required. A circuit-emulated link can carry any type or mixture of data/voice/video traffic.

CES uses the ATM AAL1 adaptation mechanism to segment the incoming E1 or T1 traffic into ATM cells with the necessary timing information to ensure that the circuit can be correctly reassembled at the destination.

The advantage to CES is the simplicity of implementation; the ATM network is used to provide virtual replacements for physical links in an existing network. CES also provides an ideal stepping-stone from legacy TDM networks to full ATM-enabled broadband solutions.

However, CES exhibits two limitations:

- CES is unable to provide statistical multiplexing—The ATM network does not differentiate between idle and active timeslots; idle traffic/time-slots are carried. CES voice transport consumes about 10 percent more bandwidth than would be required to transfer the same voice traffic over leased circuits.
- CES is often implemented as a point-to-point service—CES provides the transport of the contents of one network physical interface to a single other physical network interface. This can prevent the implementation of some network topologies, and can result in increased network cost. This is because a physical interface must be provided for traffic destined to each remote destination.

DBCES

The restrictions of simple CES resulted in the development of a new standard by the ATM Forum: DBCES.

This standard was ratified in July 1997 as af-vtoa-0085.000, and is implemented by many member companies in their equipment.

The objective of this standard is to enable dynamic bandwidth utilization by detecting which time slots of a TDM trunk are active and which are inactive.

When an inactive state is detected in a specific time slot, the time slot is dropped from the next ATM CES data structure and the bandwidth is reused for other services.

DBCES can use any method of time slot activity detection. The specific implementation and method(s) chosen by individual vendors for activity detection is not defined, and various companies adopt differing strategies.

NOTE   Cisco implements DBCES with the dynamic rate queue mechanism. A rate queue defines the speed at which individual virtual circuits transmit data to the remote end. Rate queues can be configured as permanent, dynamic (allow the software to set up rate queues), or some combination of permanent and dynamic. The software dynamically creates rate queues when a virtual circuit (VC) is created with a peak rate that does not match a user-configured rate queue. The Cisco IOS software automatically creates rate queues as necessary when you create a VC. If traffic shaping is not configured on the VC, the peak rate of the VC is set to the UBR at the maximum peak rate that the physical layer interface module (PLIM) allows. A rate queue is then dynamically created for the peak rate of that VC.

The most common implementation mechanisms are the monitoring of A and B (on-hook/off-hook) bits in the channel associated signaling, and the detection of idle codes within the payload of the voice channel.

DBCES can operate in either PVC or SVC ATM network configurations. The active time slots are transmitted using the standardized CES service.

In operation, the transmitting system assigns sufficient bandwidth to support the DBCES function when all the provisioned time slots are active. When some of the time slots become inactive, the transmitting system dynamically stops transmitting the inactive time slots, resulting in fewer queued cells for transmission.

The queuing system in the ATM switch can then take the bandwidth not used by the DBCES function and temporarily assign it to another service. This capability provides bandwidth for unspecified bit rate (UBR)-type services during times of lighter voice load, increasing the effective bandwidth utilization of the network.

VBR Voice Solutions Using AAL2 Adaption

CES treats voice as being a constant stream of information encoded as a CBR stream. In reality, voice is not like this at all; there are silences in conversation where one party speaks and the other listens.

It is unnecessary to occupy bandwidth by transmitting this silence.

These mechanisms typically minimize the problems of cell construction delay by transmitting the voice as an uncompressed 64 kbps stream. This approach ultimately relates to wasted bandwidth, not enabling the enterprise network to realize the cost savings of implementing voice compression algorithms, which in turn is wasted money.

To address these limitations, the ATM forum defined a more advanced mechanism for the transport of voice as a variable bit rate compressed stream. This mechanism is described in the specification af-vtoa-0113.000, completed in February 1999, entitled "ATM Trunking Using AAL2 for Narrowband Services." This approach combines the suppression of silence in the conversation with compression and the ability to multiplex multiple voice channels into a single VCC. This multiplexing of multiple voice channels overcomes the packetization delay issues resulting from the use of low-bit-rate voice encoding.

This standard also provides for the inclusion of network switching mechanisms based on the interpretation of the voice signaling channels. This enables the building of switched private or public voice networks.

The AAL-2 adaptation layer provides for the real-time delivery of variable bit rate (real time) traffic in an ATM network. This is perfectly matched to the needs of VBR compressed voice traffic.

The standard describes how data is collected from several TDM interfaces and compressed using one of a selection of compression algorithms. The resulting data streams are then merged into a single sequence of cells so that they can be transmitted over a single ATM virtual circuit. Each ATM cell potentially contains data from several voice calls. The packetization delay is reduced because the data rate perceived by the SAR function is the sum of the data rates of all the calls included in the multiplexed stream.

The interworking function defined in this standard can route incoming traffic into various virtual circuits based on a variety of parameters, enabling calls to be routed on called-address, incoming interface, time slot, priority, or other signaling mechanisms.

For equipment supporting switched trunking mechanisms, fully routed VPN networks can be built and significant reductions in network complexity can be achieved.

VoATM Switching

In a point-to-point network, it is necessary to provide a virtual circuit (and sometimes physical port) for each destination in the network. This results in an N^2 scaling problem, where network complexity and the number of VCCs required grows geometrically with network size, as illustrated in Figure 20-13.

Figure 20-13 *ATM Fully Meshed, Non-Switched, Voice Network*

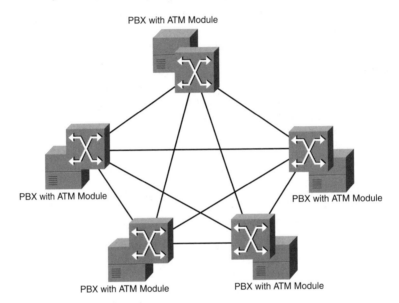

If the ATM switched network can route calls by interpretation of the signaling, the network topology becomes more manageable and the number of access ports is reduced. If the access lines are being purchased, this cost savings is even greater. Additionally, the statistics of network provisioning mean that more traffic per access port can be handled.

Interpretation of call signaling enables the network designer to utilize the switching capability of the underlying network topology to avoid the N^2 virtual circuit requirement. Figure 20-14 illustrates this topology.

Figure 20-14 *ATM Non-Fully Meshed, Switched Voice, Network Topology*

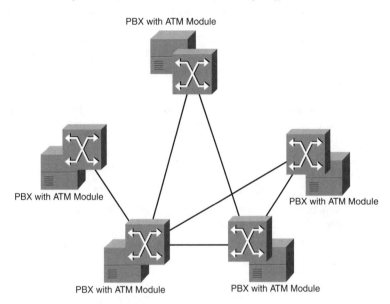

PBX with ATM Module

PBX with ATM Module

PBX with ATM Module

PBX with ATM Module

PBX with ATM Module

Encapsulation Techniques

The fourth methodology enabled by the ATM voice network is the transport of encapsulated voice over the ATM network, such as VoIP or VoFR encapsulation with ATM transport. VoIP and VoFR are technologies become more and more prevalent in today's networking environment, and an ATM network can be used to transport this traffic between endpoints. Although this is not a "Voice over ATM" solution by definition of VoATM, it should be viewed as the support of real-time data services.

This is a simple implementation in as much as the network is being configured to carry simple data traffic. Delay is a concern, which must be met by the equipment and ATM transport network. However, these are no worse than the criteria, which must be met to enable voice over CES to operate.

The second benefit of the encapsulated Voice over ATM approach is that it is a statistical VBR mechanism. When the conversation stops, most Voice FRADS or VoIP devices stop generating frames or packets. This directly translates into savings at the ATM layer because no cells are generated for transport during periods of silence.

Architecturally, this is a complex solution because the ATM network is unaware that voice is being transported. As a result of this lack of awareness, the network is unaware of the application requirements. This causes inefficiency in the system, which must be taken into account during design and implementation. For example, the overlay Frame Relay or IP network negotiates virtual connections between its own nodes to cover its peak traffic demands; the ATM network must allocate resources to support these virtual links.

Because the ATM network is unaware of the voice signaling, it is unable to release resources as calls terminate. The network works off the assumption that a short period of silence is in progress; therefore, it cannot reallocate its capacity to other applications, except on a "best efforts" or UBR basis.

This leads to underutilization of the ATM network because the CAC applications are deprived of information on the actual state of the voice network.

VoATM Comparison

Table 20-7 summarizes the benefits of the different VoATM trunking specifications; it shows the capabilities of the new standards defined in this area during the past two years. It is clear that the AAL2-based mechanisms are able to address all the principal areas of efficient voice transport.

Table 20-7   *VoATM Comparison*

	Voice Compression	Silence Removal	Idle Channel Suppression	Switched Concentration
CES	No	No	No	No
DB-CES	No	No	Yes	No
ATM trunking using AAL1 for narrowband services	No	No	Yes	Yes
ATM trunking using AAL2 for narrowband services	Yes	Yes	Yes	Yes
VoIP or VoFR over ATM	Yes	Yes	No	No

VoATM Summary

ATM is capable of transporting voice in an efficient and flexible manner.

The network designer can use a number of available approaches. Some of these are well established and have been proven over several years, whereas other new approaches offer significant sophistication, and provide a highly efficient voice transportation mechanism.

The range of standards now available allows a variety of applications and topologies of voice networking to be effectively addressed.

By including ATM in the design of the modern multiservice network, it is possible to integrate a complete range of voice and data services into a single network. This can translate into major savings in bandwidth and network complexity with the associated reductions in operational costs and improvements in reliability.

The vendors of the ATM Forum have pooled their knowledge to provide solutions that are both robust and flexible.

Voice over Frame Relay (VoFR)

Frame Relay is the most widely deployed of the three popular packet/cell technologies. Frame Relay is commonly used in enterprise data networks due to its flexible bandwidth, widespread accessibility, support of a diverse traffic mix and technological maturity.

Frame Relay service is based on permanent virtual connections (PVCs). Frame Relay is appropriate for closed user groups. It is also recommended for star topologies and when performance needs to be predictable. VoFR is a logical progression for corporations already running data over Frame Relay.

VoFR access devices (VFRADs), such as Cisco's 36x0 Series integrated bandwidth manager, integrate voice into the data network by connecting the router (or using the integrated router available on certain Cisco's 36x0 Series models), SNA controller, and PBX at each site in the corporate network to the Frame Relay network.

Many VFRADs, such as Cisco's 36x0 Series, employ sophisticated techniques to overcome the limitations of transporting voice over the Frame Relay network without adding costly bandwidth.

VoFR Prioritization

The VFRAD's prioritization schemes "tag" different applications according to their sensitivity to delay, assigning higher priority to voice and other time-sensitive data such as SNA. The VFRADs queue the data frames/packets so that higher priority voice frames/packets are transmitted first. The data traffic is not affected in this scheme because the transmission of voice frames/packets is relatively short and (if compressed) requires small amounts of network bandwidth.

Some Frame Relay network service providers have begun to offer and support quality of service (QoS). Users can generally negotiate for the following QoS:

- Real-time variable frame rate—Highest QoS for voice and SNA traffic
- Non-real time variable frame rate—Typically purchased for LAN-to-LAN and business class Internet and intranet traffic
- Available/unspecified frame rate—Lowest QoS that is used for e-mail, file transfer, and residential Internet traffic

In addition to the Frame Relay QoS offerings, the VFRAD can be configured to assign less sensitive traffic with a discard eligibility (DE) bit, dropping these frames first in case of network congestion.

NOTE   Prior to Frame Relay QoS offerings, most VoFR users had to implement their own QoS. This was accomplished by the VFRAD, marking traffic as CIR or DE prior to transmission. The concern here was ensuring that enough CIR was provisioned across the PVC to carry the CIR-marked traffic.

VoFR Fragmentation

The Cisco 36x0 series and other vendor VFRADs incorporate fragmentation schemes to improve performance. Data packets are divided into small fragments, allowing higher priority voice packets to receive the right-of-way without waiting for the end of long data transmissions. The remaining data packets in the data stream are momentarily buffered until the voice transmission gets through.

Fragmentation increases the number of data frames, in turn increasing the number of flags and headers, which in turn increases overhead and reduces bandwidth efficiency. One method of working around fragmentation issues for data transmission is to increase the size of the MTU. There are some drawbacks in that changing the MTU of the data packets prior to frame encapsulation can have adverse effects on the applications. It is best to open a case with the Cisco TAC for assistance if this is the course of action being considered.

VoFR Variable Delay

Variation in the arrival times between packets, called *jitter*, causes unnatural-sounding voice instead of a smooth voice stream. If a voice packet does not arrive in time to fit into the voice stream, the previous packet is replayed, detracting from the quality of the voice call. To avoid the effect of jitter, VFRADs detain each packet in a jitter buffer, giving subsequent packets time to arrive and still fit into a natural voice flow. Because the jitter buffer adds to the overall delay of voice transmissions, the optimal jitter buffer should fit the differential delay of the network.

The Cisco AS 5300/5400/5800 series devices employ adaptive jitter buffering, which continuously monitors the network delay and adjusts the queuing period accordingly.

Voice Compression

Voice compression allows the packet-switching network to carry a combination of voice and data sessions without compromising voice quality. Because traditional Frame Relay access is usually at data rates of Nx56/64 kbps, where N is the number of DS0s, low bit-rate voice compression algorithms such as ITU G.723.1 and G.729A permit the greatest number of simultaneous multiple calls while maintaining high-quality voice.

Cisco has implemented the following voice compression algorithms in its AS 5x00 series gateways:

- G.711
- G.723.1 (5.3 K and 6.3 K)
- G.729a
- G.729ab

Silence Suppression

In a telephone conversation, about 50 percent of the full duplex connection is used at any given time because generally, only one person talks while the other person listens. Voice packets are not sent during conversational pauses and pauses between words in the conversation, reducing the required bandwidth by another 10 percent. Silence suppression frees this 60 percent of bandwidth on the full duplex link for other voice or data transmissions.

Echo Cancellation

Echo cancellation improves the quality of voice transmissions. It eliminates the echo that results from the reflection of the telephony signal back to the caller, which can occur in a 4-wire to 2-wire hybrid connection between the VFRAD and the telephone sets or PBX. The longer it takes the signals to return to the caller, the more perceptible the echo.

You need to address the following concerns in any VoFR network:

- Compression—VoFR equipment should compress a voice signal from 64 kbps to at least 32 kbps to conserve bandwidth. In most cases, compression to 16 or 8 kbps is possible and preferred.

- Fragmentation—VoFR equipment must segment data and voice packets into small ones. This fragmentation algorithm allows the voice quality to remain high. If fragmentation is not performed, large data packets can block or delay voice packets behind it. Fragmenting the voice and data packets has a more constant delay and a reduced possibility of being temporarily blocked by a large data packet.

- Prioritization—Real-time voice traffic is sensitive to delay, whereas many data applications such as e-mail are more delay tolerant. If you are running delay-sensitive data applications and voice, it is necessary to ensure that voice and data applications perform as needed or a new prioritization scheme might need to be developed.

- Echo cancellation—Due to the delay introduced by compression, decompression, packetization, and transmission processes, users can hear their own voice (an echo) across the Frame Relay network. This problem is not limited to VoFR because PSTN service providers have had to address this issue as well. VoFR equipment should have echo cancellation capabilities to prevent a noticeable or interfering echo.

- Jitter buffer—Public frame relay networks are shared among many customers. No matter how much control is exerted over traffic prioritization and fragmentation, no customer can control any other customers' traffic. This can lead to some packets experiencing 50 ms network delay, whereas others might be delayed during times of congestion. The jitter buffer temporarily holds incoming packets to assemble them in the correct order and re-create a high-quality voice signal. Like dynamic compression, some jitter buffers are also dynamic. This allows them to sense variable delay and provide a higher quality voice signal.

VoIP

VoIP is the ability to make telephone calls and send faxes over IP-based data networks with a suitable quality of service (QoS) and superior cost/benefit. Internet service providers are deploying VoIP services to compete with the PSTN; users are integrating voice and data applications to realize the cost savings.

VoIP technology has not been developed to the point where it can replace the services and quality provided by the PSTN. To compete with today's PSTN, the total cost of operation must be significantly lower.

Applications for IP telephony include real-time facsimile transmission, PC conferences (such as Microsoft NetMeeting), or integrated voice/data mailboxes.

IP is a connectionless protocol in which packets can take different paths between the endpoints and packets from different transmissions share all paths. This enables efficient allocation of network resources because packets are routed on the paths with the least congestion. Header information makes sure that the packets reach their intended destinations and helps reconstruct the messages at the receiving end. To ensure QoS, however, all packets should use the same path. IP headers are large (20 bytes) as compared to the headers of Frame Relay frames (2 bytes) and of ATM cells (5 bytes). Therefore, headers add significant overhead to IP traffic.

IP networks implement the same bandwidth-saving schemes as the Frame Relay network, including prioritization, fragmentation, voice compression, jitter buffering, silence suppression, and echo canceling:

- Prioritization—Techniques used for VoIP are different from those employed by Frame Relay access devices. Prioritization is directly related to QoS. The key IP QoS protocol is RSVP, which allows the sender to request a certain set of traffic-handling characteristics for traffic flow, but is not widely adopted. The Differentiated Services

(DiffServ) model uses the type of service (ToS) octet field of the IP header to classify traffic at the borders between the customer and service provider or Internet service providers (ISPs).

- IP fragmentation—This is performed in a similar fashion to Frame Relay fragmentation. Fragmentation, although required to reduce the overall delay of voice traffic, adds overhead to IP transmissions due to the large size of IP headers. Therefore, IP voice traffic consumes 50 percent more WAN bandwidth than Frame Relay voice traffic. However, as IP matures, header compression and improved routers eliminate these shortcomings.

- Voice compression—This is crucial in Voice over IP because traffic is usually carried over low-speed links; for example, some connections can be connected at 28.8 kbps. Microsoft NetMeeting is a popular voice application for PCs and laptops and supports ITU G.723.1 voice compression for transmission over dial-up modems. The ITU G.723.1 standard for voice compression over IP ensures toll quality voice.

- Jitter buffer, silence suppression and echo cancellation—These are similar to those employed in VoFR. Echo cancellation, a significant component in VoIP infrastructures, often suffers from long network delays.

Further information regarding VoIP can be found at the beginning of this chapter.

VoX Circuit Sizing

The sizing of a VoX circuit is critical in ensuring that all voice traffic is being carried across the network and is being handled efficiently by the origination and termination endpoints.

The following formula is useful in determining the amount of network bandwidth needed to support a VoX call.

$$\text{Voice}_{\text{BANDWIDTH}} = ((N \times B) + 20\%)$$

where N = Number of VoX channels (module ports) and B = Bandwidth per channel. (Generally this is the same as the compression algorithm.) The additional 20 percent is used to calculate the amount of buffer-related overhead that is necessary.

For example, given 16 VoX channels using G.729 CS-ACELP compression (8 kbps), the total network bandwidth calculates to be N=16, B=8; therefore, $(16 \times 8) = 128 + (25.6) = 153.6$ kbps. Because network service providers provision bandwidth in an Nx64 configuration, the minimum amount of provisioned bandwidth would be 192 kbps (Nx64, where N=3).

VoX Erlangs

Erlang measurements are the most common measurements used to measure telephone traffic. One erlang is equal to one full hour of use: $60 \times 60 = 3,600$ seconds of telephone traffic (conversation). When traffic on a trunk group is measured in erlangs, the measure in erlangs equals the average number of trunks in use during the hour under review. For example, if the average number of trunks used during the "review hour" carries 12.35 erlangs, then on average, a little more than 12 trunks were in use.

Table 20-8 demonstrates the number of voice channels necessary to sustain a P01 reliability. (P01 indicates that .01 percent of the incoming calls receive a busy signal.)

Table 20-8   *Erlang Table for 100,000 Minutes/Month*

Traffic		Hours	Minutes	Assumptions	
Monthly		1,666.67	100,000		
Daily		75.76	4,545.5	22	Days Per Month
Busy Hour		12.88	772.7	17 percent	Busy Hour
		Busy Hour	Carried/ Circuit		
		Uncarried Load			GOS
# CKTS		(Hours)	(Hours)		(Blockage)
0		12.878788	1.000000		1
1		11.950840	0.927948		92.795 percent
2		11.032478	0.918362		85.664 percent
3		10.125435	0.907043		78.621 percent
4		9.231810	0.893625		71.682 percent
5		8.354139	0.877671		64.867 percent
6		7.495482	0.858658		58.200 percent
7		6.659504	0.835978		51.709 percent
8		5.850562	0.808942		45.428 percent
9		5.073757	0.776805		39.396 percent
10		4.334941	0.738817		33.660 percent
11		3.640626	0.694315		28.268 percent
12		2.997760	0.642866		23.277 percent
13		2.413308	0.584453		18.739 percent

Table 20-8 *Erlang Table for 100,000 Minutes/Month*

14		1.893615	0.519693		14.703 percent
15		1.443590	0.450024		11.209 percent
16		1.065818	0.377772		8.276 percent
17		0.759802	0.306016		5.900 percent
18		0.521612	0.238191		4.050 percent
19		0.344117	0.177494		2.672 percent
20		0.217843	0.126275		1.691 percent
21		0.132226	0.085617		1.027 percent
22	<<<P01	0.076943	0.055283		0.597 percent
23		0.042940	0.034002		0.333 percent
24		0.023001	0.019939		0.179 percent

Summary

The transmission of voice traffic over packet networks, such as Voice over Frame Relay (VoFr), Voice over ATM (VoATM) and especially voice over IP (VoIP), is rapidly gaining acceptance. Collectively, these methodologies are known as Voice over X (VoX). Voice over packet transfer can significantly reduce the per-minute cost, resulting in reduced long-distance bills. Many dial-around-calling schemes available today rely on VoIP backbones to transfer voice, passing some of the cost savings to the customer. These high-speed backbones take advantage of the convergence of Internet and voice traffic to form a single managed network.

VoIP services need to be able to connect to traditional circuit-switched voice networks. The ITU-T addressed this by defining the H.323 set of standards for packet-based multimedia networks.

ATM enables the statistical multiplexing of traffic over any network resource. Statistical multiplexing avoids the need to pre-allocate resources for a user, but allocates resources on-demand, providing bandwidth to users only when they need it. This allows the network to support more users (typically twice as many as a simple TDM network).

Frame Relay is the most widely deployed of the three popular packet/cell technologies: Frame Relay, IP, and ATM. Frame Relay is commonly used in enterprise data networks due to its flexible bandwidth, widespread accessibility, support of a diverse traffic mix, and technological maturity.

Frame Relay service is based on permanent virtual connections (PVCs). Frame Relay is appropriate for closed user groups and is also recommended for star topologies and when performance needs to be predictable. VoFR is a logical progression for corporations that are already running data over Frame Relay.

VoIP is the ability to make telephone calls and send faxes over IP-based data networks with a suitable quality of service (QoS) and superior cost/benefit. Internet service providers are deploying VoIP services to compete with the PSTN; users are integrating voice and data applications to realize the cost savings.

The sizing of a VoX circuit is critical in ensuring that all voice traffic is being carried across the network and being handled efficiently by the origination and termination endpoints.

The following formula is useful in determining the amount of network bandwidth needed to support a VoX call.

$$\text{Voice}_{\text{BANDWIDTH}} = ((N \times B) + 20\%)$$

Erlang measurements are the most common measurements used to measure telephone traffic. One erlang is equal to one full hour of use: $60 \times 60 = 3{,}600$ seconds of telephone traffic (conversation). When traffic on a trunk group is measured in erlangs, the measure in erlangs equals the average number of trunks in use during the hour under review. For example, if the average number of trunks used during the "review hour" carries 12.35 erlangs, then on average, a little more than 12 trunks were in use.

CHAPTER 21

Remote Access and VPNs

Discussed in this chapter are remote access options and alternatives, including traditional remote access and virtual private networking (VPN) architectures.

Remote Access

Remote access can be defined as providing access to fixed site resources to those users who are not at a fixed workstation at that location's local-area network (LAN). Remote access connectivity can be provided via the plain old telephone system (POTS), leased lines, T-carriers, fractional-T1 systems, X.25 (public switched data network, or PSDN system), Integrated Services Digital Network (ISDN), or Frame Relay system. Traditional remote access systems involve users dialing into a dedicated modem pool, maintained either by a corporate IS/IT staff, or by an IntereXchange Carrier (IXC), such as AT&T, MCIWorldCom, or Sprint. Some IXC offerings involve users dialing into IXC maintained modem pools, and then traversing a dedicated path to a client's office. (Not all IXC carriers offer this option). Traditional modem-pool remote access options can be costly. As the number of remote access users grow, so must the number of modems in the modem-pool, access lines, and long-distance or 800 number charges. Applications such as Remote Access Server (RAS) or pcAnywhere are supported by these modem-pool access infrastructures.

A cost-effective and secure alternative to traditional remote access is Virtual Private Networking (VPN). With VPNs, all phone calls that access corporate networks are local calls tunneled from the remote site to a local Internet service provider (ISP), over the Internet, and to the corporate VPN gateway.

VPNs

A VPN session is an authenticated and encrypted communications channel, or tunnel, across some form of public network, such as the Internet. Because the network is considered insecure, encryption and authentication are used to protect the data while it is in transit. Typically, a VPN service is independent, meaning that nearly all client operation is transparent to the user and that all information exchanged between the two hosts (WWW, FTP, e-mail, and so on) is transmitted across the encrypted channel.

VPN Basics

Before a VPN is established, each network must verify certain requirements. Each site must be set up with a VPN-capable device (router, firewall, or some other VPN dedicated device) on the network perimeter. Each site must know the IP addressing scheme (host, network, and network mask) in use by the other side of the intended connection. Both ends of the tunnel must agree on the authentication method, and if required, exchange digital certificates. Both sides must also agree on the encryption method and exchange the keys required.

VPNs are frequently used to replace both dial-in modem pools or dedicated WAN links. A VPN solution for remote dial-in users can dramatically reduce support costs because no phone lines or 800-number charges must be paid. Hardware does not need to be upgraded as new modem standards are released. A VPN solution also offers advantages over a dedicated WAN environment when most sites are geographically diverse or mobile, saving the cost of dedicated facilities and hardware.

VPNs provide security, at the cost of additional overhead, to what would otherwise be an insecure connection through a private network. A VPN is basically composed of three technologies that, when used together, form the secure connection. These three technologies are authentication, tunneling, and encryption.

Tunneling Protocols

Tunneling is used to encapsulate network protocols (TCP/IP, IPX/SPX, AppleTalk, and NetBEUI) into an IP packet that can travel across the Internet. TCP/IP can travel across the Internet on its own, but then it would not be a part of the tunnel or the VPN.

Before the tunnel can be created, it must be verified that the two endpoints are who they say they are. After these endpoints are authenticated, the tunnel is created and information between the two ends is exchanged. Figure 21-1 illustrates a tunnel established across a network service provider's (NSP's) backbone.

Figure 21-1   *Tunneling Protocol*

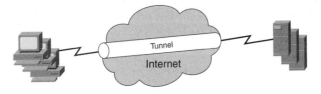

The two protocols in Windows 2000 that are responsible for creating the VPN tunnels are Point-to-Point Tunneling Protocol (PPTP) and Layer 2 Tunneling Protocol (L2TP). L2TP is an advancement over the PPTP tunneling protocol, and it uses the IP Security (IPSec) authentication and encryption protocol.

Table 21-1 reflects Microsoft clients and the tunneling protocols they support.

Table 21-1   *Microsoft Clients and Supported Tunneling Protocols*

VPN Client	Tunneling Protocols Supported
Windows 2000	PPTP, L2TP, (IPSec with NTFS)
Windows NT version 4	PPTP
Windows 98	PPTP
Windows 95	PPTP with Windows Dial-Up Networking 1.3

PPP

Tunneling protocols do not function without an underlying infrastructure protocol, typically PPP. PPP is one of the most common access protocols in use today and is the default for most desktop operating systems (Windows 2000/NT, 9x).

PPP is actually a suite of standardized protocols, much like TCP/IP, that work together to provide a multitude of services used to establish and maintain point-to-point connections.

PPP provides many features, including encapsulation (tunneling) of data, compression of data, multiplexing (multilink) to combine two or more WAN links, reliability by using the high-level data link control (HDLC) protocol to configure data framing, and network configuration negotiation.

NOTE   PPP functions over several media types, such as copper or fiber-optic facilities.

PPP uses two other protocols, Link Control Protocol (LCP) and Network Control Protocol (NCP), to establish and maintain the point-to-point connections. LCP is primarily used to establish the connection and maintain the link parameters such as frame size. NCP is primarily responsible for negotiating network configuration parameters, such as encapsulation and compression, for the network protocols (AppleTalk, TCP/IP, IPX.SPX, and NetBEUI) on the wide-area network (WAN) link.

PPTP

PPP was designed to allow remote users to dial into their local ISPs and then tunnel their way to the corporate server, such as a Windows 9x PPTP client tunneling to a PPTP server on the corporate network. PPTP uses the existing infrastructure protocols to allow for dial-up connection, namely PPP. PPTP then takes these PPP packets and encapsulates them inside a generic routing encapsulation (GRE) header. Because of the reliance on PPP, PPTP uses encryption algorithms such as Password Authentication Protocol (PAP) and Challenge

Handshake Authentication Protocol (CHAP) to provide the encryption. PPTP also uses Microsoft point-to-point encryption (MPPE) to provide for encryption. Due to the availability of PPTP on NT stations and the installed user base, PPTP is a VPN protocol. PPTP comes in two configurations: compulsory mode and voluntary mode.

- A compulsory mode PPTP session uses the services of an ISP with a PPTP front-end processor. Compulsory modes are made with the help of a network access server (NAS). No PPTP software is needed on the client. Any communication problems in a dial-up connection to the ISP are handled by the PPP protocol; therefore, any troubleshooting on the laptop/desktop would be dial-up networking configurations. Compulsory modes also restrict users from accessing other parts of the Internet.

- Voluntary mode is where the clients establish the PPTP connection straight to the PPTP server on the other side of the network to create the tunnel. In this instance, the ISP is out of the picture.

PPTP is a combination of the PPP and TCP/IP protocol suites. PPTP combines the features of PPP such as multiprotocol, user authentication, and privacy with the compression of data packets, and TCP/IP offers the routing capabilities of these packets over the Internet.

PPTP is an RFC draft standard (draft-ietf-pppext-pptp-06.txt). As quoted from the draft, PPTP was meant to be able to encapsulate PPP packets and forward them to their destination.

PPTP can take packets such as IP, IPX, NetBIOS, and Systems Network Architecture (SNA) and wrap them in a new IP packet for transport. PPTP uses the GRE to transport PPP packets. It uses encryption for encapsulated data and provides for authentication.

PPTP and IPSec can be thought of as the same: You can have an IPSec client establish a secure session to a firewall and create a VPN or have a PPTP client establish a session to the firewall.

PPTP consists of three types of communications:

- PPTP connection—This is just where a client establishes a PPP or ISDN link to its ISP.

- PPTP control connection—Using the Internet, a user creates a PPTP connection to the VPN server and sets up the PPTP tunnel characteristics.

- PPTP data tunnel—The client and server send communications back to each other inside this encrypted tunnel.

A PPTP connection is typically encrypted with either RC4 or Data Encryption Standard (DES) 40-bit encryption schemes, but a 128-bit encryption version can also be obtained if it is kept within the United States.

L2TP

L2TP promises to replacement replace PPTP as the tunneling protocol of choice. Vendors such as Cisco, Microsoft, 3Com and others support L2TP. L2TP is based on PPTP and the L2F (Layer 2 Forwarding) Protocol. Cisco designed L2F as is a more robust tunneling protocol that supports the encapsulation of many more protocols than PPTP, including AppleTalk and SNA.

L2TP is basically the same as PPTP. L2TP relies on PPP to establish a dial-up connection, but unlike PPTP, it defines its own tunneling protocol. L2TP uses the PPP (PAP and CHAP) for user authentication, and because it is a Layer 2 protocol, it allows for transportation of non-IP protocols.

L2TP merges PPTP (developed by vendors such as Microsoft, Ascend, and 3Com) with L2F (developed by Cisco) as a single standard (draft-ietf-pppext-l2tp-12.txt). These vendors agreed on a new IETF draft specification that they named L2TP.

L2TP is frequently used for dial-up connections because its design is optimized for dial-up connections rather than site-to-site implementations.

An L2TP VPN setup is similar to the PPTP setup. The data packets include the initial PPP communications, and PPP can be used for the encrypted packets. L2TP is media independent, meaning it can be used over Asynchronous Transfer Mode (ATM), Frame Relay, or IP. An L2TP server replaces the PPTP servers, and an L2TP Access Concentrator replaces the ISP PPTP FEP (Front End Processor). The L2TP VPN allows for multiple connections inside the tunnel and assigns a unique Call ID for each session inside the tunnel. Like PPTP, L2TP defines message types: control and data.

- The control messages are responsible for such things as setup, teardown, session management, and tunnel status. Control messages are also used to maintain characteristics inside the tunnel, such as maintaining flow control and determining transmission rates and buffering parameters for the PPP packets for individual sessions.

- The data messages are the PPP packet without the framing information.

L2TP uses the same modes as PPTP: compulsory and voluntary.

PPTP and L2TP offer software-based compression, which shrinks user packets. Compression techniques also add a layer of encryption, although it is a small amount. L2TP uses two functions: a client-like line server function referred to as LAC (an L2TP access concentrator) and a server-side network server function called LNS.

L2F

Cisco Systems developed L2F to be used in combination with PPTP. With the growth of dial-up services and the availability of many different protocols, it was necessary to find a way to create a virtual dial-up scenario, where any of these non-IP protocols could enjoy the benefit of the Internet. Cisco defined the concept of *tunneling*, meaning encapsulation of non-IP packets. Users make a PPP, SLIP connection to a dial-up ISP provider, and by the use of L2F, connect to their corporate machines. This tunneling takes place at the border points of the Internet, which are routers with tunneling software called tunnel interfaces.

L2F supports the following:

- Protocol independence (IPX, SNA)
- Authentication (PPP, CHAP, TACACS)
- Address management (assigned by destination)
- Dynamic and secure tunnels
- Accounting
- Media independence (L2F over ATM, Frame Relay, X.25)
- Both L2F tunneling and local Internet access

LAN-to-LAN VPN

LAN-to-LAN VPN is the next common VPN configuration. The LAN-to-LAN VPN is closely tied to the IPSec standard. Whereas the remote dial-up user VPN uses protocols such as PPTP, L2F, and L2TP, IPSec concentrates on LAN-to-LAN.

In a typical LAN-to-LAN design, not all traffic is encrypted. Two types of communication are possible:

- Web server access—When a user wants to connect to the Web server on another network, it is simply unencrypted HTTP traffic. The VPN device should not encrypt this traffic; it should flow untouched.

- VPN server access—When a user wants to connect to the VPN server on another network, the VPN device should recognize that it is a VPN request and encrypt the packets.

The DES supports 56-bit encryption and can also be used for LAN-to-LAN encryption. DES is the most popular symmetric-key system and cannot be used for export. Symmetric-key systems are simpler and faster, but their main drawback is that the two parties must somehow exchange the key in a secure way. Public-key encryption avoids this problem because the public key can be distributed in a non-secure way, and the private key is never transmitted.

The customer could use DES or Triple-DES (168-bit encryption) to support cryptographic requirements between routers for intranet communication, as long as both cryptographic endpoints are in the United States.

Authentication

Authentication is the process of positively identifying the entity (user, router, network device) that requires access. This authentication is usually done by means of a cryptographic function.

The primary reason for authentication with VPNs is to have a method of ensuring that the client and server are who they say they are before the VPN session is established.

Throughout the customers' infrastructure, several password-protected servers and applications are likely to exist. Users can have multiple passwords, such as different ones for different servers. Users are always advised never to write down their passwords or tell anyone else. However, if these users are like the rest of the general computing population, they do one of two things: write it down anyway or choose a password that is easy to recall.

This is the inherent problem with password protection and one of the reasons that passwords are easily guessed. One such attack on this type of security is called a "dictionary attack," a simple guessing type of attack. These attacks continue to be successful. User authentication scenarios, sometimes described as 2-factor or 3-factor authentication, eliminate this type of guessing attack.

PPTP-PAP/CHAP

PAP is actually a misnomer because it is the most insecure authentication method available today. Both the username and password are sent across the link in clear text. Anyone snooping the connection could easily grab and use the information to gain access to the network. As a result, using PAP for authentication is not advisable.

The PPTP uses GRE (Microsoft Generic Routing Encapsulation) to tunnel PPP. It adds a connections setup and control protocol.

The PPTP authentication implementation supports three types of user authentication. The two that are concerned with security are the hashed method and challenge response method. Hashed password authentication is based on two one-way hashing functions. During the first hashing function, all passwords entered are converted to uppercase, which reduces the data space. Second, the hashing functions produce the same hash output, given the same password. Unfortunately, no salt or added bits are added to the hashed output, which eliminate duplicate hash outputs from the same hash input. In this authentication model, PPTP is open to dictionary attacks. Additionally, both hash outputs are sent together in the communications string. An attacker can attack the first hash function to compromise the second hash function.

The second security authentication method uses CHAP. CHAP works by the client contacting the server and the server sending back a challenge. The client then performs a hash function, adds some extra information, and sends this back to the server. The server looks in its own database and computes the hash with the challenge. If they are the same, authentication succeeds. Although this method eliminates the dictionary attack, the hashing functions could still be attacked. CHAP also supports the (user transparent) periodic challenge of the client username/password during the session to protect against wire-tapping.

The PPTP framework calls for MPPE, in which the encryption is based on the user's password. After the initial communication is set up, only certain PPP packets are encrypted.

Microsoft Windows 2000 supports three versions of CHAP:

- CHAP, an industry standard, is a challenge-response authentication protocol that supports one-way encryption of responses to challenges. The authentication process uses three steps to completion. First, the server challenges the client to prove its identity. Then the client sends an encrypted CHAP message in response to the challenge. The server then verifies the response, and if it is correct, grants the client access.

- MS-CHAP is a modified, proprietary version of CHAP. The major difference between MS-CHAP and CHAP in Windows 2000 is that the user's password is in a reversibly encrypted form in MS-CHAP.

- MS-CHAPv2 is a stronger, more secure authentication method than previous implementations. It no longer supports Microsoft NT LAN Manager, or NTLM (it can be used only with Windows 2000), it provides mutual authentication, and its separate cryptographic keys are used to send and receive data.

Digital Certificates

Digital certificates include information about the owner of the certificate; therefore, when users visit the (secured) Web site, their Web browser check information on the certificate to see if it matches the site information included in the URL. A digital certificate could be likened to a "security" driver's license. Sometimes a box appears warning that someone might be trying to intercept your communications. This could be true; however, the problem usually is more likely that the site name is incorrect or the domain name is wrong.

Certificates are issued by Certificate Authorities (CAs) and are priced differently depending on the type of certificate required. Some of the certificates available are as follows:

- Class A, 1, Premium, High. These are digital certificates with high-level assurance. Usually used for SSL and SOCKS-enabled sites, they offer high-level security for S/MIME applications, financial transactions, enhanced e-commerce, and other secure applications.

- Class B, 2, Medium, Basic. These are the digital certificates with medium-level assurance. Used for access to SSL-enabled sites, they provide medium-level security for S/MIME applications, enhanced e-commerce, online shopping, newspapers, and so on.

- Class C, 3, Basic, Freemail. These are the digital certificates with basic security. Used for simple electronic ordering and personal secure mail.

- Class D or 4 (chained). This type is used for multipurpose organizations, very much like a multi-user license.

The reason that different names exist is because different CAs name their certificates differently, and some overlap.

Pricing for certificates varies considerably. Variables include the CA and the certificate type requested. Pricing ranges from free to $175 to $200 each, with most CAs offering price breaks for volume.

CAs are actual third-party companies, not concepts or software algorithms. This means that CAs can be broken into and hacked just like any other site. The stronger the CA infrastructure, the stronger the protection that is assured.

The contents of a digital certificate are as follows:

- The certificate holder's identity
- The certificate's serial number
- A valid, unchangeable date for the transaction
- The certificate's expiration dates
- A copy of the certificate holder's public key for encryption or signature
- The group name
- The city and state

Digital certificates are based on the International Telecommunications Union, Series X recommendations, ITUX.509 standards, and RSA's "PKCS #7, Cryptographic Message Syntax Standard."

X.509 digital certificates have been revised to the current proposed version X.509v3. Some modifications to the X.509 standards have been:

With the acceptance of X.509v3 and the public key infrastructure (PKI), businesses are able to conduct business using digital certificates in the PKI framework from their workstations by using a Web-browser and an LDAP-aware application, such as a database.

Some hardware vendors support digital certificates as an IOS feature. This relieves the pressure of each user owning a digital certificate; they "borrow" the certificate from the VPN device when the tunnel connection is made.

Figure 21-2 *Digital Certificate (X.509)*

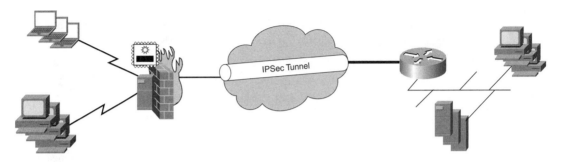

Smart Cards

Smart cards are similar to credit cards. Smart cards are credit card-sized plastic cards with small chips embedded in them. Smart cards provide data portability, security, and convenience. Three terms used in conjunction with smart cards are as follows:

- An IC card with an ISO 7816 interface
- A processor IC card
- A personal identity token containing IC-s

A smart card is an access control device that supports different applications; it allows users to access personal and business data.

Hardware Tokens/PKCS #11

Hardware tokens are tamper-resistant, credit-card sized or smaller devices (a type of smart card) that a user holds in his possession. An LCD on the card consists of six to eight digits, which usually change every 60 seconds. In user-authorization, the LCD is usually combined with a personal identification number (PIN). Only the user knows both the digits and the PIN, and together they serve as the password. For convenience, however, you can limit the password to just the LCD display.

The term *software token* is just an application on a machine that emulates a hardware token device.

The Public-Key Cryptography Standards (PKCS), developed by RSA in conjunction with a consortium of others, are a set of standards that are being developed for public-key cryptography. PKCS are compatible with the ITU-T X.509 digital certificate standards. The PKCS standard includes some defined algorithm standards such as RSA and Diffie-Hellman. PKCS also defines independent standards that can be used for digital certificates, digital envelopes, and extended digital certificates.

The current list of PKCS standards is available from RSA Laboratories at http://www.rsa.com/rsalabs/pubs/PKCS/.

Lightweight Directory Access Protocol (LDAP)

The Lightweight Directory Access Protocol (LDAP) is an extensible network protocol for accessing information inside a directory. However, the directory structure inside LDAP is not the same as a regular directory. A regular directory usually offers a static view of the contents in that directory—where its contents are created, modified, and deleted over time. An LDAP directory is more dynamic with all types of data that can be stored, such as URLs, certificates, and so on.

LDAP was born out of the X.500 Directory Access Protocol (DAP). X.500 DAP defined a set of protocols in an open system that provided for users and machines to access directory system agents (DSAs), each having a portion of the total directory service in a company.

Some of the LDAP standards define the following:

*   The network protocol for accessing this information
*   A namespace defining how information is referenced
*   How information is organized inside the directory
*   A distributed model (in LDAPv3)

RADIUS Servers

Remote Authentication Dial-In User Service (RADIUS) is a system of distributed security that secures remote access to networks and network resources against unauthorized access by using the User Datagram Protocol (UDP).

RADIUS authentication includes two components: an authentication server and client protocols. The server is installed on a machine at the customer's site. All user authentication and network service access information is located on the RADIUS server. RADIUS allows for multiple formats that can be suited to an individual customer's requirements. A RADIUS server authenticates users against a UNIX password file, Sun Microsystems Network Information Service (NIS), or in a separately maintained RADIUS database. The RADIUS model works on the client sending authentication requests to the RADIUS server, and acts on acknowledgements sent back by the server.

RADIUS authenticates users through a series of communications between the client and the server.

RADIUS service is not limited to dial-up service. Many firewall vendors support the use of a RADIUS server. Dial-in and VPN users could authenticate using the RADIUS server.

TACACS+ (Terminal Access Controller Access Control System Plus)

Cisco Systems developed the Terminal Access Controller Access Control System Plus (TACACS+) protocol. It is a TCP-based access-control protocol using reserved Port 49.

With TACACS+, when the user attempts to log in, the network access server asks the security server what to do, instead of merely forwarding the name/password to a central server. The security server tells the network access server to initiate a command, such as prompt for the username/password. After the username/password combination has been entered, the security server then sends a permit or denies packet to the NAS.

Encryption Alternatives

Encryption is the third major component of a VPN. Encryption is an extra precautionary measure that protects the data through the tunnel. Data is encrypted before it is encapsulated to reduce the risk that someone might tamper with it if the tunnel is breached.

Microsoft Windows 2000 supports two encryption technologies: MPPE and IPSec. Both methods use an encryption key to encrypt and decrypt information at the sender and receiver ends.

Pretty Good Privacy (PGP)

Philip Zimmerman's Pretty Good Privacy (PGP) has been used worldwide. PGP is a hybrid cryptosystem, enabling the best of both worlds. It combines both a public-key algorithm and a private-key algorithm. This gives PGP both the speed of a symmetric cryptosystem and the advantages of an asymmetric system. From a user standpoint, PGP acts like any other public-key cryptosystem. PGP uses the Rivest, Shamir, and Adelman (RSA) public-key algorithm and International Data Encryption Algorithm (IDEA) for encryption. A single IDEA key is used to encrypt the message, and the same key is used to decrypt the message (symmetric encryption). Then RSA is used to encrypt the IDEA key used for encryption with the recipient public key (asymmetric). The receiver uses the private key to decrypt the RSA-encrypted IDEA key. Then the decrypted IDEA key is used to decrypt the rest of the message. Along with PGP, Zimmerman created a set of utilities to manage a public key ring, where users can manage multiple keys.

PGP is available free worldwide in versions that run on a variety of platforms, including DOS/Windows, UNIX, and Macintosh. PGP was not developed, nor controlled by, any government or standards organization.

PGP supports the use of digital signatures, message encryption, compression, e-mail compatibility, and segmentation (to accommodate protocol message size limitations).

PKI

PKI is a system of digital certificates, certificate authorities (both commercial and governmental), certificate management services, and directory services (LDAP, X.500) that verify the identity and authority of each party involved in any transaction over the Internet. PKI is the framework that provides for privacy and digital signature services in support of international commerce, balancing the needs of government and ensuring privacy.

Currently, several PKI standards are available, including RSA Data Security's PKCS and the digital certificates that X.509 provides. Certificates formats differ: there are X.509 identity certificates, X.509 SET (Secure Electronic Transaction) certificates, PGP signed keys, and SPKI certificates.

Some uses of PKI are for authentication and authorization, privacy and confidentiality, data integrity, and non-repudiation. PKI offers an alternative to plain-text passwords, and supports the client/server requirement for information exchange to be private. PKI offers the ability to protect the tampering of data and offers both the client and server non-repudiation.

Non-repudiation is the ability to prove that one party actually agreed to a transaction. A method must exist to ensure for one party that the other party has indeed sent the message. Without such guarantee, financial house, banking, and sales transactions could not occur. Non-repudiation, in the form of digital signatures, prevents a sending party from "denying" that any transmission actually occurred, hence the guarantee.

MD5 (Message Digest 5)

Developed by Ron Rivest of RSA Labs, MD5 is a hash function that takes a string of arbitrary length and produces a fixed length output of 128 bits.

IPSec

The Internet Engineering Task Force (IETF) has a working group called IPSec, which is responsible for defining standards and protocols relating to Internet security. IPSec development efforts came from the Automotive Network Exchange (ANX) requirements. (The goal of the ANX was to connect multiple vendors, suppliers, and customers so that they could exchange data safely). VPNs use these standards as part of their security measures. The IPSec working group is defining the structure of the IP packet and implementing a security association that is used in VPN communications.

IPSec defines protocols for authentication, confidentiality, and data integrity. However, it does not describe access control other than in its packet filtering abilities. This is seen as a major drawback. In addition, the IPSec protocol has not been finalized concerning its key management standards. IP packets have no inherent security. It is relatively easy to forge the source and destination addresses of IP packets, modify the contents of IP packets, replay old packets, and inspect the contents of IP packets in transit. It is not guaranteed that IP datagrams received (1) are from the sender (the source address in the IP header); (2) contain the original data that the sender placed in them; or (3) were not inspected and/or copied by a third party while the packet was in transit. IPSec is a method of protecting IP datagrams. This protection takes the form of data origin authentication, connectionless data integrity authentication, data content confidentiality, anti-replay protection, and limited traffic flow confidentiality.

IPSec is a collection of cryptography-based services and protocols. It provides authentication as well as encryption to a VPN connection that uses L2TP. However, L2TP still uses authentication methods, such as EAP and MS-CHAP.

IPSec currently supports Simple Key Management for Internet Protocol (SKIP) and Internet Security Association Key Management Protocol (ISAKMP). Yet another drawback of IPSec is that it is not compliant with IPv4, so it requires the use of IPv6. This incompatibility is causing much discussion among IETF officials, resulting in the delay with the release of the protocol.

IPSec states that before any communication can take place, a security association (SA) is negotiated between the two VPN nodes or gateways. The SA sets up all the information needed to ensure secure communications. Aspects such as transport and application layer services, authentication, and payload encryption are set up during this SA communication. The SA is responsible for setting up several items in establishing the future secure communication between end hosts, including whether the packet is encrypted, authenticated, or both. IPSec specifies both the endpoint encryption and authentication protocols, such as DES for encryption and MD5 for authentication.

The basic function of IPSec is to encapsulate packets in two optional headers. The authentication header supports authentication and data integrity while the encapsulating security payload ensures privacy. These two headers can be used separately or together, but, for most applications, one header is sufficient.

IPSec provides two modes of operation: transport and tunneled. In transport mode, IPSec encrypts only the IP payload, not the original IP headers. In tunneled mode, the entire packet is encrypted and encapsulated in a new IP packet, which results in significant overhead, but is highly secure.

IPSec has a few problems associated with it. One is that the keys are static; over the duration of the communication, no mechanism allows for exchanging these keys. Scalability has also been hard with IPSec due to the difficulty in managing enormous amounts of encryption keys in large networks. The Certificate Enrollment Protocol (CEP), developed by Cisco Systems and VeriSign, has described a specific way of communicating with a CA to allow the exchange of keys for large numbers of keys.

Another problem with the encapsulation approach of IPSec is that it makes each IP packet bigger after the encryption process takes place. On some LANs, the MTU size would force the fragmentation of these packets, which would increase the network burden network devices, such as routers. The other alternative is encrypting tunnels. Encrypt in Place, for instance, does not increase the size of the packet, but the trade-off is that most tunnels are proprietary. That means that vendor interoperation might be difficult to implement if not impossible.

IPSec does not currently support dynamic addressing. This is one of the many changes proposed to the original IPSec standard. With dial-up users, IPSec needs to know how to handle dynamic addresses within the tunnel.

IPSec provides an IP-only tunnel (not multiprotocol without L2TP or PPTP) or straight IP connection between two endpoints.

Despite these issues and challenges, IPSec is projected to be the standard for future VPN solutions because it combines several security technologies to provide the complete system:

- Diffie-Hellman key-exchange is used for deriving key material between peers on a public network.

- Public-key cryptography is used for signing the Diffie-Hellman exchanges to guarantee the identity of the two parties.

- Encryption algorithms, such as DES, Triple DES, and IDEA, are used for the encryption of the data.

- Keyed hash algorithms, such as HMAC, combined with traditional hash algorithms such as MD5 or SHA, are used to provide packet authentication.

- Digital certificates signed by a certificate authority allow the exchange of keys for large numbers of keys.

Internet Key Exchange (IKE)

IKE is a good general-purpose security exchange protocol. It can be used for policy negotiation and establishment of authenticated keying material for a variety of needs. The specification of what IKE is being used for is done in a domain of interpretation (DOI). The IPSec DOI exists in RFC2407, which defines how IKE negotiates IPSec SA.

Security associations are used with IPSec to define the processing done on a specific IP packet.

VPN Products: Gateways, Clients, and Applications

Customers usually evaluate multiple vendor product suites. The National Information Assurance Partnership (NIAP) between the National Institute of Standards and Technology (NSIT) and the National Security Agency (NSA) has established a common criteria evaluation methodology for the testing and evaluation of vendors' firewall products. The focus of this evaluation is to establish an evaluation assurance level (EAL) that can be used to measure the products' IT security assurances.

IT security is defined as the protection of information from unauthorized disclosure, modification, or loss of use by countering threats to that information arising from human or systems-generated activities, malicious or otherwise. Countering threats to an IT product and mitigating risk helps to protect the confidentiality and integrity of information and ensure its availability.

The Common Criteria Scheme overcomes the limitations of the customer having to test each product directly and enables the customer to obtain an impartial assessment of an IT product by an independent entity. This impartial assessment, or *security evaluation,* includes an analysis of the IT product and the testing of the product for conformance to a set of security requirements. The specific IT product being evaluated is referred to as the *target of evaluation (TOE).* The security requirements for that product are described in its *security target (ST).* IT security evaluations are composed of analysis and testing, distinguishing these activities from the more traditional forms of conformance testing in other areas.

Common Criteria (CC) for Information Technology Security

The common criteria (CC) document, also known as ISO 15408, combines the best features of three sets of heavy-duty international guidelines for effective network security. The CC provides a common language and structure to express IT security requirements. Using the CC framework, users and developers of IT security products create *protection profiles (PPs).* PPs are implementation-independent collections of objectives and requirements that a given category of products or systems *must* meet (as with VPN gateways and firewalls). PPs are used to support defining functional standards; they aid in specifying needs for procurement purposes.

PPs serve as a generic description of product and environment requirements; TOEs are specific products or systems that are evaluated against an existing PP. The sets of evidence about a TOE and the TOE itself form the inputs to an ST.

Security requirements come in two forms: functional and assurance. *Functional requirements* describe what a product needs to do. *Assurance requirements* describe how well it meets the functional requirements.

CC Protection Profiles

As cited from ISO 15408, a PP is a vigorous overview of a potential candidates system. PPs are organized as follows:

- Introduction provides the descriptive information needed to identify, catalog, register, and cross-reference the PP. The overview provides a summary of the PP as a narrative.

- TOE clarifies the TOE's security requirements. It also provides a context for the evaluation by addressing the product type and general features of the TOE.

- Security environment consists of three subsections that describe and specify the security aspects of the environment in which the TOE is used.

- Assumptions about the system include intended usage, aspects of the intended applications, potential asset value, and possible limitations of use.

- Threats that require specific protection within the TOE or its environment.

- Organizational security policies that govern the TOE or its operating environment.

- Security objectives address all aspects of the security environment, as identified in earlier sections of the PP. These objectives define the intent of the TOE to counter identified threats, conform to the organizational security policies, and meet the assumptions.

- Security requirements describe what supporting evidence is needed to satisfy security objectives, whether for the TOE or its environment. Two types of requirements are relevant here:

   — Functional requirements stating what the system has to do to actually fulfill its mission.

   — Assurance requirements stated as one of the evaluation assurance levels (EALs) from the CC Part III assurance components.

Rationale presents the evidence used by a PP evaluation. This evidence supports the claims that the PP is a complete and cohesive set of requirements and that a compliant TOE provides an effective set of IT security countermeasures within the security environment.

Enterprise Assurance Levels

Assurance levels define a scale for measuring the criteria contained in PPs and STs. EALs provide an increasing scale that balances the levels of assurance claimed with the cost and feasibility of acquiring such assurance.

Seven EAL levels exist, ranging from EAL1 (Minimal Protection) to EAL7 (Verified Design).

- EAL levels 1 to 4 are considered adequate for most commercially available security devices and systems.

- EAL levels 5 to 7 are for government agencies that might need additional assurances that the equipment they have procured or developed actually meets tighter security requirements than would otherwise normally be found in the marketplace.

EAL1, corresponding to Orange Book Criteria Assurance Level D (Minimal Protection), applies where some confidence in correct operation is required, but the threats to security are not considered serious. If independent assurance is required to support a contention that due care has been exercised in protecting personal or similar sensitive information, EAL1 often fits the bill.

EAL2, corresponding to Orange Book Criteria Assurance Level C1 (Discretionary Security Protection), requires the cooperation of the developer so that design information and test results can be obtained, but no further effort is demanded from the developer than is consistent with good commercial practice. EAL2 is applicable where developers or users require independently assured security at a low-to-moderate level, in case the complete development record is not readily available. Such a situation can arise when trying to secure a legacy system (the original documentation might have been discarded), or where access to the developer might be limited.

EAL3, corresponding to Orange Book Criteria Assurance Level C2 (Controlled Access Protection), permits a conscientious developer to gain maximum assurance from positive security engineering at the design stage—without substantial alteration to existing development practices. EAL3 applies when developers or users require a moderate level of independently assured security.

EAL4, corresponding to Orange Book Criteria Assurance Level B1 (Labeled Security Protection), allows a developer to gain maximum assurance from positive security engineering that is based on good commercial development practices. EAL4 is applicable in circumstances where developers or users require a moderate-to-high level of independently assured security in conventional, off-the-shelf products.

Telecommunications Access Methods to a Local ISP

For a customer office to establish a VPN tunnel, a connection must first be made to the Internet. This Internet access can be to a local or national ISP. The decision of which to use should be based on individual user and site requirements. If a user is known to travel, an ISP that supports national "local" number dialing should be chosen. A fixed location can benefit from dedicated ISP access, such as ISDN, DSL, or cable modem.

The newer broadband access methods, such as DSL and cable modems, do not currently have ubiquitous coverage in the U.S. It is highly recommended that each site manager verify service availability prior to implementation planning and equipment procurement.

POTS Dial-Up

The POTS network is the most familiar communication system in use today. The public switched telephone network (PSTN) is made up of millions of telephone lines in the United States, and various switching systems that connect the voice and data calls. The POTS/PSTN was designed to provide an extremely high level of reliability.

Because POTS was designed for voice communications, it is limited on the rate at which data can be transmitted.

Modems convert digital links to analog signals to be transmitted across the communications link, and convert these signals back again to digital so that the computer can understand them. Modems are categorized by the standards they support—such as V.32, V.32bis, and V.90—and the speed at which they send and receive data. Modems can operate at speeds up to 56 kbps using the V.90 modulation standard. However, the Federal Communication Commission (FCC) power rules limit the ability to send data faster than 33.6 kbps and receive data at 53.3 kbps. The conversion, along with other factors such as noise that are inherent to POTS, chokes the amount of data that can be sent and received over the connection.

ISDN

ISDN is a digital version of the telephone system (POTS). It can transfer data at a rate much higher than the analog phone system because the line is much cleaner (higher clarity, less noise, and so on).

ISDN is an all-digital transmission facility that is designed to replace the analog PSTN on a worldwide basis. ISDN service is available in two forms: BRI and PRI. Basic Rate Interface (BRI), sometimes represented as 2B + D, operates at 144 kbps. Each (B)earer channel operates at 64 kbps, and the (D)ata channel operates at 16 kbps. Primary Rate Interface (PRI), sometimes represented as 23B + D, operates at 1.536 Mbps.

Cable Modems

A cable modem is a modem designed to operate over cable TV lines. Because the coaxial cable used by cable TV provides much greater bandwidth than telephone lines, a cable modem can be used to achieve extremely fast access to the Internet. This, combined with the fact that millions of homes are already wired for cable TV, has made the cable modem something of a holy grail for Internet and cable TV companies.

The cable modem has a number of technical difficulties. One is that the cable TV infrastructure is designed to broadcast TV signals in just one direction—from the cable TV company to people's homes. The Internet, however, is a two-way system where data also needs to flow from the client to the server. In addition, it is still unknown whether the cable TV networks can handle the traffic that would ensue if millions of users began using the system for Internet access.

Cable modem implementations are treated like 10/100-BaseT (Ethernet) LANs. A PC connected via cable modem is on a shared Ethernet segment with other homes/offices. A PC connected via cable modem must meet minimum system and hardware requirements, including support for an Ethernet LAN card. Cable modems act as transparent Ethernet bridges connecting to an NSP. Cable modems modulate data into an analog signal (QAM, QPSK) and perform both frequency-division multiplexing (FDM) and time-division multiplexing (TDM).

Despite these problems, cable modems that offer speeds up to 2 Mbps are already available in many areas. The bandwidth speeds supported by cable modems are dependent on many factors: available bandwidth in the FDM network, number of active users, and usage.

Digital Subscriber Line (DSL)

Digital subscriber line is a digital WAN technology that brings high-speed digital networking to homes and businesses over POTS. DSL has many types, including high-speed DSL (HDSL), very high bit-rate DSL (VDSL), and asymmetric DSL (ADSL). ADSL is the most common application because the uplink and downlink bandwidths are not symmetrical, meaning they are not of the same link speed.

ADSL provides high-speed data connections using the same copper phone lines that are used in POTS.

Although ADSL promises high bandwidth, the upstream is slower than the downstream data rate. Typically, the upstream transfer rate ranges from 64 kbps to 256 kbps, whereas downstream rates approach 1.544 Mbps.

Microsoft Windows 9x/NT/2000/XP can support ADSL connections with the installation of a DSL modem/adapter. When an ADSL network adapter is installed in Windows 2000, the adapter appears as either an Ethernet or dial-up interface. If ADSL appears as an Ethernet interface, the connection operates just as it would with an Ethernet connection, but if it appears as a dial-up interface, ADSL uses ATM.

When a customer is too far (beyond 18,000 feet) from an LEC central office (CO), DSL or single-line digital subscriber line (SDSL) offerings are usually deployed. IDSL is essentially the DSL "flavor" of ISDN-BRI, offering 144 kbps of bandwidth. Table 21-2 details the available bandwidth as determined by the distance from the CO.

Table 21-2   *SDSL Distance/Bandwidth Chart*

Distance (Feet)	Distance (Meters)	Data Rate
22,700	6,920	160 kbps
20,000	6,097	208 kbps
19,000	5,793	320 kbps
17,900	5,457	416 kbps
14,900	4,543	784 kbps
12,500	3,811	1.04 Mbps
9,500	2,896	1.568 Mbps

Policy and Administrative Management

The following discussion focuses on the policy and administration management of an enterprise organization, including discussions regarding security policies and key management.

Centralized Security Management

At any time in client/server architecture, different applications are running on different servers that support different clients on different networks. If a security application is upgraded or modified, it can affect the entire organization, and it might take days for the IT department to isolate the cause of trouble.

Some vendors support a centralized management feature in their VPN products. This is both a strong security feature and a great troubleshooting mechanism. For example, multiple sites are connected to the Internet and are protected by a firewall/VPN combination or some other VPN device. A central security manager can resolve any problems that might arise connecting an application from a client machine in one department to a server in another department through the VPN. The difficulties arise when trying to get multiple IT staffs involved and coordinating some sort of troubleshooting process to resolve the issue in a timely manner.

Some vendors support the total outsourcing of VPN network security management. This is especially beneficial to those users where maintaining IT infrastructure is not considered a core competency, much less maintaining a security infrastructure. If outsourcing security management is considered, at a minimum, certain requirements should be met.

These minimum requirements include the following:

- The vendor should make centralized security management available. This prevents the multiple database updates from being managed, which could lead to inconsistencies in the security platform.

- The security management platform of the vendor should be scalable to support multiple thousands of users and change requests.

- The vendor should be able to support user administration, authentication, password synchronization, and access control across the entire enterprise network (LAN and WAN).

- The vendor should be in a position that it can enforce customer's security standards, policies, and practices. Some vendors can also assist in drafting these security documents.

- The vendor should maintain defined backup/restore procedures as agreed upon between the customer and the central security manager.

Worst-Case Scenario

Sometimes even though a solution to a particular issue works on paper, it does not work in application. When one solution is tried and does not work, another solution is tried. Then it is decided to contact the vendor, so a meeting with the vendor and the entire original IT staff working the issue is called. This process continues on and on, and each time meetings need to be arranged with several people to try to correct one issue. The IT staff, vendor, and possibly users are trying to troubleshoot over the telephone, which can lead to further confusion and time delays due to miscommunication or misinterpretation of the original problem.

A centralized security management process can eliminate these coordination issues. Only the end user and the VPN technician need to be online, and by monitoring both VPN ends, the issue can easily be isolated.

This centralized management feature greatly simplifies the maintenance and troubleshooting processes of the VPN infrastructure. Centralized management eliminates the need for multiple diverse IT staffs and lessens the administrative burdens. If a VPN infrastructure is installed without route-management capabilities, another method needs to be figured out to manage these devices. One method is to put a modem on every VPN device's console port. If this route is chosen, it is best to ensure that the modems have encryption software. This prevents someone from accidentally dialing into the modem because encryption modems communicate only with other encryption modems.

Backup/Restore Procedures

Backup and restore procedures are usually designed for servers and user home directories. The keys of a VPN device are what make the VPN technology safe. If the VPN device experiences problems, it is necessary to have backup configurations so that the device can be reinstalled. Other parties with whom the VPN service has been set up know the keys in the VPN device. If the keys cannot be restored, communication with other parties is unable to be reestablished.

Security Policy

A clearly stated security policy document is a valuable tool. If a third-party central security manager is deployed, the customer and this respective third party should jointly draft this policy.

This security policy should clearly state the following:

- The basic security approach (optimistic or pessimistic) for the organization and the portions of the network that are exceptions to the rule
- Details of all aspects of security, including physical and human security
- The access that is required for each employee or group of employees

There are generally two schools of thought with regards to security policy:

- That which is not expressly prohibited is permitted.
- That which is not expressly permitted is prohibited.

Windows NT includes several options called *policies* that are configurable for basic rules to secure the network. The Account Policy dialog box includes options for password requirements, minimum password length, and other items related to user accounts. The policy documentation for an organization should include values for each of the policy options for Windows NT.

Many organizations implement their rule-based firewall policy in accordance with the second item—that which is not expressly permitted is prohibited. The first item, although flexible, can be a security risk to implement. The second item is a secure way to implement a rule policy that continues to allow users to access the Internet.

Any user needs only a standard set of network services to conduct his work: SMTP, HTTP, HTTPS, NNTP, and DNS. These five services cover 90 to 95 percent of necessary user access; any other necessary services can be added for individuals and restricted to specific workstations.

Additional services such as Internet Relay Chat (IRC), Telnet, Trivial File Transfer Protocol (TFTP), and File Transfer Protocol (FTP) can be added on an as-needed basis and restricted to certain individuals who need them.

A firewall or other network boundary device is designed to block all incoming traffic. By allowing incoming services to pass through the firewall, the basic design is circumvented. However, if these incoming services are not allowed, users are unable to perform day-to-day, mission-critical tasks. Creating these holes in the firewall is a necessity, but it is a necessity that needs to be carefully managed and maintained. This approach can be further refined with a demilitarized zone (DMZ). The requested services are first directed to a DMZ, which in turn directs traffic internally.

Figure 21-3 illustrates a good policy to implement. Any traffic coming in from the Internet is first routed to a DMZ. This accomplishes two things. First, it allows an organization to direct traffic to the DMZ, and only that traffic that is necessary is then redirected to the internal networks. Second, this process allows all incoming traffic to be examined first, by placing antivirus software on the DMZ servers; the packets can be examined first and cleaned if necessary. Because of the processing power required, a separate server for this function can be decided upon.

Figure 21-3   *Firewall with DMZ*

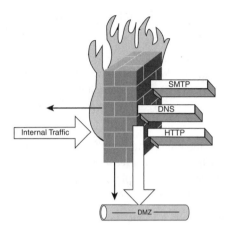

Key Management

In any of the ISP VPN offerings or in any of the VPN architectures, key safety is an important issue. Just as any backup/restore procedure should be maintained, so must the VPN keys be part of a routine procedure. This is not the generation and management of keys, but where to get them if duplicates are needed. In all VPN architectures, the keys that are generated and managed must be stored in a safe, secure place, not only for security purposes but also for recovery of those keys. These include the public keys, device keys, and any certificates that are published. The encryption keys for the tunnel must also be able to be reproduced in case the VPN device fails and a replacement is needed. The old keys and certificates are still available on the server. This is important because the original keys are needed for revocation.

VPN Network Requirements

The following sections discuss network requirements for a VPN implementation.

Network Architecture

The following remote access VPN network architectures are discussed:

- Firewall based
- "Black-box" based

- Router based
- Remote-access based

Firewall-Based VPNs

The most popular VPN solution is firewall integration. It is a safe assumption that a firewall is placed at the network perimeter; therefore, it is a natural extension to let this device support the VPN connections as well. This provides a central point of management as well as direct cohesion between firewall security policy and traffic let through the tunnel.

A drawback to this method is performance. A busy Internet circuit with multiple VPNs (running strong encryption on each tunnel) could overload the system if all these services are consolidated on a single box. Some firewalls, such as Firewall-1, do support encryption cards to reduce processor load. The encryption card fits in a standard PCI expansion slot and takes care of all traffic encryption and decryption.

Firewall-based VPNs are probably the most common form of VPN implementation today (see Figure 21-4). Many vendors offer firewall-based VPN solutions, each also including its proprietary encryption technology.

Figure 21-4   *Firewall-Based VPN*

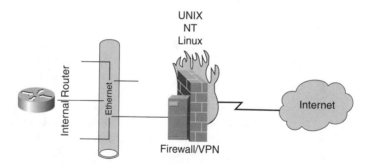

Regardless of the vendor hardware/software package used, a VPN standard must still be chosen; PPTP, L2TP, and the IPSec standard are currently being developed. IPSec is a framework so that DES encryption can be used in an IPSec setting.

VPN technology runs on the lower levels of the Open System Interconnection (OSI) stack. A proxy server runs at Layer 7, the application layer of the OSI model, and the packet filtering firewall must examine the complete packet every time it goes by. A stateful-inspection firewall runs at Layers 2 and 3. Because of the processing requirement, VPN technology should only be added to a stateful-inspection firewall.

Black-Box-Based VPNs

In the black-box scenario, a vendor offers exactly that—a black box. A black box is a device that is loaded with encryption software to create a VPN tunnel. Some black boxes come with software that runs on a desktop client to help manage that device, and some can be configured via a Web browser. It is generally believed that these hardware encryption devices are faster than the software types. The hardware devices create faster tunnels on demand and perform encryption processes more quickly. However, not all offer or support centralized management or logging. In this scenario, logs need to be sent to external databases for queries. Another server is needed if authentication is a requirement.

Vendors should be supporting all three tunneling protocols (PPTP, L2TP, and IPSec). However, specific vendors need to be thoroughly researched.

The black box VPN sits behind a firewall. It can, however, sit on the side of the firewall. The firewall provides security to the organization, not to the data. Likewise, the VPN device provides security to the data, but not the organization.

Figure 21-5 illustrates a typical black box VPN implementation.

Figure 21-5 *Black-Box Based VPN*

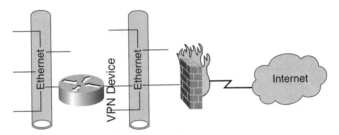

The firewall is in front of the VPN device, and most likely, a rule-based policy on the firewall needs to be installed. In the firewall configuration, ensure that encrypted packets can be passed. The firewall is there for protection. If the firewall is filtering on the TCP ports and the packets come in encrypted, the firewall tries to examine the packet, realizes it cannot, and drops the packet.

Router-Based VPNs

Router-based VPNs are possible for an organization that has a large capital investment in routers and an experienced IT staff. Many router vendors support this configuration. Two types of router-based VPNs exist. The first method is where software is added to the router to allow an encryption process to occur. The second method is where an external card from a third-party vendor is inserted into the router chassis. This method is designed to off-load the encryption process from the router CPU to the additional card.

Some vendors support hot swapping and redundancy, which are built into their router-based VPN products. This is certainly a requirement for organizations that cannot tolerate downtime. It is also worth noting that performance can be an issue with router-based VPNs. Due to the addition of an encryption process to the routing process, a heavier burden can be added to the router CPU. This is especially true if the router is handling a large number of routes or implementing an intensive routing algorithm.

Figure 21-6 represents a typical router-based VPN, where packets are encrypted from source to destination.

Figure 21-6   *Router-Based VPN*

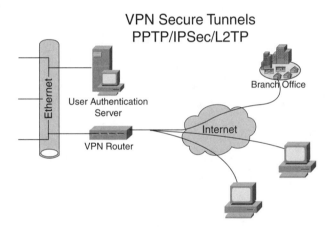

The two concerns with router-based VPNs are as follows:

- Interoperability—If a connection to the VPN of a supplier is required, will both the site router and the router of the supplier operate with one another and create the VPN?

- Encapsulation—Will non-IP protocols, such as IPX or SNA, be transported? Some router manufacturers only encrypt; they do not encapsulate.

Terminating the VPN at the border router allows the traffic stream to be decrypted before it reaches the firewall. Although process load is still a concern, many routers now use application-specific integrated circuit (ASIC) hardware. This allows the router to dedicate certain processors for specific tasks, thus preventing any one activity from overloading the router.

The drawback to a router-based VPN is security. Routers are (typically) extremely poor at providing perimeter security compared to the average firewall. It is possible that an attacker would be able to spoof traffic past the router, which the firewall would interpret as originating from the other side of the VPN tunnel. This means that the attacker might be able to gain access to services that are typically not visible from other locations on the Internet.

Remote Access-Based VPNs

Remote access, as the term applies, means that a remote user is trying to access the resources of an organization by creating an encrypted packet stream. The term might appropriately apply to the software running on a user's machine, which is trying to create the tunnel to the organization, and to a device on the network allowing the connection. This tunnel could be coming in from the Internet, but it also could be coming in from a dedicated, dial-up, or ISDN line.

Figure 21-7 illustrates a typical remote access VPN implementation.

Figure 21-7   *Remote Access-Based VPN*

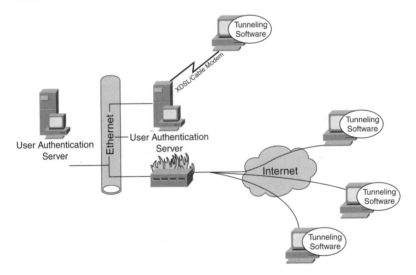

This scenario reflects software running on remote machines, and those machines establish a connection via an encrypted tunnel to the internal server, or from a dial-up access line, to an authentication server. An access server on the network, router, firewall, black box, or stand-alone authentication server grants the access. This remote access device minimizes the amount of costly leased-line equipment and remote dial-up access equipment.

Remote Access VPN Network Design

Common VPN components of any network are as follows:

- Gateway devices (routers, dedicated servers, firewalls)
- Client software
- PKI and associated key management strategies
- Hardware-based encryption accelerators

- X.509 digital certificates
    - CAs
    - A customer-entrusted CA, if utilized, should maintain the digital certificates for that customer. This CA can be internal to the customer or a trusted third-party vendor or security manager.
- Directory services
    - LDAP is the recommended protocol for secure certificate services (that is, certificate storage and lookup).
- Servers with load balancing, fail-over, redundancy
- VPN gateway product(s) feature requirements:
    - X.509 digital-certificate support.
    - LDAP support.
    - IPSec compliant.
    - Encryption types supported.
    - Performance (Mbps) [This is negotiable with a service level agreement, or SLA.]
    - Maximum number of interfaces.
    - Maximum number of connections.
    - Quality of service (QoS) support [This is negotiable with an SLA.]
    - Clustering support.
    - Custom-application support.
    - Support of high-availability (HA) features.
- Compliance with EAL/TISEC/TCSEC laws
- Network transport

Network Access Points

VPN access points are dependent on the ISP used. This should be a factor when choosing an ISP because local access numbers should be available nationwide to support traveling users.

Dynamic Protocol Support

This requirement is relative only when non-IP protocols are being used. Any customer application that is using IPX, AppleTalk, and so on needs to have those protocols tunneled by the VPN client and server.

IP Service Requirements

TCP/IP is the underlying protocol suite for all VPN services. All VPN clients and network devices must be configured to support TCP/IP.

Existing Routers, Firewalls, and Proxy Servers

The existing Cisco PIX and Checkpoint FireWall-1 firewalls can support a VPN infrastructure. Some vendor firewalls and clients can exchange keys using IKE, such as Cisco network devices and Cisco PIX firewall. However, inter-vendor options require the firewall to be configured for manual IPSec. Manual IPSec requires the security manager to manually configure the IPSec keys on the firewall. Existing authentication technologies include the following:

- UserID/Password only
- Hardware or software token support, such as SecureID
- PKI support

Types of Applications That Cross VPN Boundaries

These applications are typically e-mail services, intranet HTTP services, and possibly batch data transfers.

Bandwidth Requirements

The bandwidth requirement is determined by three factors:

- Number of users at each remote access point
- Type and nature of data traffic that is generated/received by each remote access user/ site
- Frequency of traffic

Cryptographic Processing Requirements on Servers and Desktops

The VPN server and client must be configured to support the same tunneling protocol, such as IPSec or PPTP.

Support Personnel Requirements

It is advisable that the customer designates an internal or external organization that can be available on a 24-7 basis to respond to major security issues, such as breaches.

Administrative-related security issues, such as password resets, can be handled on a Monday through Friday, 9 a.m. to 5 p.m. basis.

Future Network Plans

The VPN architecture needs to scale to meet the anticipated growth that the customer sees in the number of users of the network architecture. As the number of users and required resources grow, the VPN infrastructure—including server farms and access devices—should be reviewed to ensure that maximum network availability is maintained.

Scalability of Critical Devices

This is directly related to the future network plans that the customer has for his network and the related remote access/VPN infrastructure. The critical devices that must be scalable are authentication server(s), database servers, and Web servers.

Security Policy

The customer should publish a standard security document, made available to all users and internetworked vendors. This document should include a basic overview of the security approach supported by the customer, and clearly identify any authorized exceptions. The customer security document should also include details of all security aspects, levels of security authorized for defined user groups, and procedures for users to request changes be made to their security profiles/access rights.

The security policy document should also include VPN management responsibilities, such as the following:

- Who administers and enforces the VPN and security systems?
- Who performs Registration Authority (RA) activities?
- Who administers the desktop systems for the users?

    This is important because the systems should be consistent for users across all platforms, including drivers, plug-ins, dynamic link libraries (DLLs), application programs, and any network operating systems (NOS) client components.

    Desktop systems are also points of vulnerability and should have up-to-date virus protection installed. Rogue software that could support a security breach needs to be accounted for, and auto-answer modems should be disabled because they allow an intruder with a "wardialer" to penetrate the VPN by "piggybacking" off the machine of a legitimate user.

VPN User-Access Requirements

The following sections address VPN requirements around remote user access requirements.

Remote Office Locations

Remote user-access requirements are simply stated; connect to a local ISP by whatever option is preferred and supported. Access options were previously discussed under the Telecommunications category, but simply revisited, these options are: Analog Dial-up (POTS), ISDN, xDSL, Cable Modem, or dedicated (private) access lines.

NSP or ISP Requirements

It is recommended that a single, nationwide ISP be chosen to provide access services. Most nationwide ISPs support POTS dial-up, ISDN and xDSL. However, sometimes the ISP is unable to support a preferred access method, such as a cable modem. These cases should be handled on an individual basis.

For traveling/mobile users, a nationwide ISP would be preferred because it is almost assured that local access numbers from every major city are available, precluding any additional long-distance charges.

VPN Performance Requirements

The following sections discuss performance requirements for a VPN implementation.

Cryptographic Hardware Accelerator Support

Cryptographic hardware accelerator support is not a mandated requirement, but any VPN equipment considered for procurement should support this function in support of potential future growth.

Clustering of Servers for Scalability

The clustering of servers, or a server farm, is important to maintaining near-100 percent availability. If one (or multiple) servers fail or are taken down for maintenance, it should be transparent to the remote office/end user. Server farms are scalable as long as they can share databases. No server should be an "information island."

QoS is a process whereby switches and routers set up resources to move data quickly and reliably. Often ISPs cannot support true QoS because they do not control the entire connection, including local access and backbone interconnects.

The IETF published a standard called Diff-Serv, which is intended to allow ISPs to deploy different QoS levels on the Internet's backbone. This is accomplished by allowing users to mark data packets so that routers can forward them appropriately.

Diff-Serv has all but replaced Resource Reservation Protocol (RSVP) in an effort to implement QoS. RSVP relied on a type of signaling mechanism between devices on the Internet—specifically routers. This signaling setup was done on a per-connection basis, and it required that all routers on the Internet agree to a specific level of service.

SLAs

SLAs are contractual agreements between the organization for a user (in this case the customer) and the ISP. Some of the aspects that are spelled out in these contracts are data rates, types of service, and performance statistics. The objective of an SLA is to quantify specific objectives and metrics that are used as a benchmark to ensure adherence to the agreement.

In an SLA, the following three areas should be addressed: network uptime, bandwidth, and latency. The network provider can usually provide some sort of guarantee for network uptime and bandwidth, but latency continues to be a major obstacle for any kind of performance guarantee.

Network Uptime

This is the actual time that the network is up and available to pass traffic. It is important to consider both *up* and *pass*. The network could be up but unable to pass traffic. For example, if monitoring on the data link level (such as Frame Relay), a device could report as being up, but the network layer (such as IP) of that device—the actual layer that forwards the traffic—could be down.

Bandwidth

Bandwidth could mean the bandwidth of the access pipe to the provider, or the available bandwidth over the backbone of the provider. Although most service providers are deploying Synchronous Optical Network (SONET) technology in their backbones, with terabit per second (Tbps) service, the available bandwidth is still only the least of the access pipes on either side of the connection.

In most SLAs, the provider can easily document and verify bandwidth statistics.

Latency

Latency is the concept that explains the time delay in setting up the initial communication link between points. A network connection can traverse two, three, or multiple ISP backbones. This makes it difficult for an ISP to guarantee latency between two endpoints because it does not always have control over the middle. Because of this, most ISPs only offer a latency guarantee across their own backbone. This is about the best kind of latency guarantee that can be expected.

Failover to Redundant Devices

The customer should have either hot-standby VPN devices interconnected with the VPN network, or spares that are physically available to meet a 4 hour mean time to repair (MTTR).

As previously discussed, the VPN infrastructure should scale as the number of users, and subsequently the amount of bandwidth required, grows. An ISP's ability to support user-required bandwidth growth within a minimal turnaround time (usually 30 days) should be a factor in the selection process.

VPN Client Essentials, Security Guidelines, and Vulnerabilities

The following sections discuss VPN client requirements, guidelines, and vulnerabilities.

Windows 9x (95/98)

The Windows 95 operating system does not fully lend itself to immediate secure communications. Microsoft has issued several patches to resolve security issues within the operating system, related applications, and dial-up networking. The Windows 95 operating system is limited to the FAT file system, which does not include security features. When Windows 95 files are shared across the network, they use a simple password scheme with limited security. The Windows 98 operating system is limited to the FAT or FAT32 file system, which does not include security features. Like Windows 95, when Windows 98 files are shared across the network, they use a simple password scheme with limited security.

Windows 98 can be used for client workstations in a Windows NT network environment with little security risk. This is provided that the users save their files on the server rather than a local hard drive, log out whenever they leave the console, and do not log in as a member of the administrators group over the network.

It is recommended that the customer deploy Windows 98 Second Edition, Windows NT Workstation, or Windows 2000/XP Professional to the remote users of the VPN. These platforms are not immune to security vulnerabilities, but they are more secure than Windows 95 or the first edition of Windows 98. These security vulnerabilities are discussed next.

Windows 9x Security Guidelines

A good place to start regarding Windows 9x would be at the Microsoft Security Advisor Page at http://www.microsoft.com/security/default.asp. Some general guidelines are listed next:

- Do not enable file sharing! Windows 9x does not understand the security behind file security. When logged on to a 9x system, the user is usually asked for a username/password. This is just identification to other machines; it is not intended to protect the machine. What this does is tell everybody on the network that a new user is on the network and that person can read and copy any files on the network. This accessible data could include any public/private keys used for encryption. If others need access to the machine of a specific user, make sure that machine is password protected and restricted to only those necessary resources.

- Ensure that virus software is installed and is up to date. Although a virus attack might have no direct impact on VPN security, a virus could attack the PPTP stack, preventing PPTP session establishment with the VPN server.

Windows 9x Vulnerabilities

Windows 9x has a list of known vulnerabilities, along with available patches to correct these problems. These vulnerabilities are most likely to compromise only a local machine, but it is a compromise nonetheless. The following is a list of Windows 9x vulnerabilities:

- Back office vulnerability allows a user to remotely manage another machine. It gives the remote user more control than the person sitting at the console. Back office vulnerability can be done over a LAN or the Internet.

- The Internet Explorer vulnerability might allow a malicious Web page to crash Internet Explorer and possibly execute arbitrary code on the browser's machine. As certificates are added to the VPN infrastructure, this becomes particularly worrisome. An attacker could use the certificate on the browser for another user, creating a situation of compromised certificates.

- Teardrop vulnerability occurs when an attacker sends an overlapping, fragmented IP data stream to the intended victim. Windows 9x cannot handle this, and the system hangs, forcing the need for a reboot to be able to recover. A WinSock 2 update is recommended.

- ICMP vulnerability is exploited when an attacker sends a ping packet to the intended victim and specifies in the header an incorrect packet length. The only recourse here is a reboot.

- Out-of-band (OOB) vulnerability occurs if IP packets are sent to a Windows 9x machine that has an out-of-band data flag set. A common port is 139, although others can be used. A reboot is needed in this situation to recover.

- Windows 9x stores passwords to network resources in a file (designated with a .PWL extension) that is encrypted using an RC4 encryption algorithm. The problem is that the PWL files are too predictable, making a plaintext attack viable, and possibly resulting in the revealing of passwords on the network.

- When using the file and print services for the NetWare system, any user who has remote administration software can view files on other hard drives on the network without authorization.

- It might be possible to obtain the clear-text Windows 9x login password from a Windows 9x machine on a network connected directly to the Internet. There is vulnerability when using a Samba server on Ports 137 and 139, a malicious Web page, and an NT server that tries to log in with the Windows 9x username/password in clear text.

UNIX

Like Windows NT, UNIX was plagued with security problems in its early days. UNIX was not really developed with security in mind. In fact, the creators of UNIX initially developed it so that they would have a platform on which to play games.

UNIX is considered more secure than Windows NT because it has been around longer. UNIX was created in 1969 and since then has been the preferred victim for hackers everywhere. Because of this, UNIX developers have rushed to keep up, plugging security holes as hackers find them.

Despite its maturity, UNIX still has security problems. Although it is possible to make an extremely secure UNIX system by carefully configuring features and installing security fixes, many administrators do not have the time or budget to maintain a completely secure system.

A breakdown of security vulnerabilities with UNIX is not discussed here because they are beyond the scope of this customer report.

Windows NT

Although Windows NT was originally intended to replace Windows, it has evolved into a platform for reliable network servers. Although Windows NT was designed with security in mind, it was not widely used for networking at first, and was plagued with security problems. Microsoft has improved its security significantly, but security holes still exist. Nevertheless, it is possible to run a secure system using Windows NT; all it takes are the latest security fixes from Microsoft.

Microsoft publishes updates called "hot fixes" on its Web site at http://support.microsoft.com/support/.

Windows NT Security Guidelines

Some guidelines are associated with the implementation of the Windows NT operating system. Windows NT was designed with networking in mind and requires some extra care when deployed in a secure environment. Windows NT can be used as a main server, file server, Web server, application firewall, and PPTP VPN server. The following is a list of guidelines:

- Running unneeded networking protocols increases the risk of system break-in. Most organizations need TCP/IP networking, along with NetWare resources. However, it is usually not recommended that the NetBEUI protocol be enabled. It is best to ensure that whatever services are turned on are operationally needed. A common approach taken by many is to shut down everything except the basic ports needed to communicate, and then add them back in one-by-one as necessary (such as TCP Port 25, UDP Port 53). A detailed and continuously updated list of all TCP/UDP ports can be found at http://www.iana.org/assignments/port-numbers.

- It is recommended that a false administrator account be set up with minimal or no privileges. The real administrator privileges should then be established using a different account name. Because NT uses the administrator as the super-user, an attacker can try to break into the administrator account. If someone breaks into this account, he will not realize it is a fake one. He will think it is just a dead machine with nothing interesting.

- If NetBIOS service is not needed, block ports 137, 138, and 139. By blocking these ports, most attacks can be prevented, including red buttons and OOB data packets that can crash the system.

- To prevent against certain types of guessing attacks against passwords, it is a good idea to periodically check that users have chosen strong passwords. L0phtcrack 2.0 is a utility that can be used with password dictionaries to check this (http://www.l0pht.com).

- Ensure that virus software is installed and is up to date. Although a virus attack might have no direct impact on VPN security, a virus could attack the PPTP stack, preventing PPTP session establishment with the VPN server.

- The Windows NT Resource Kit provides Windows NT the C2 Configuration Manager (C2CONFIG.EXE). This program compares the security of the NT machine configuration against the C2-level security standards of the federal government's National Computer Security Center. It then presents the options required to bring the machine up to C2 standards.

Windows NT Vulnerabilities

Like Windows 9x and UNIX, Windows NT has its share of vulnerabilities, including the following:

- A denial of service can occur if an attacker uses the Windows NT 4 named pipes. The way that NT handles pipes over a remote procedure call (RPC) is the cause of this problem.

- The NT ICMP vulnerability is similar to the one in the Windows 9x operating system. A ping packet is sent to the victim, and the packet size does not match the actual size of the packet. A reboot is needed to correct this problem. A fix for this is available from Microsoft.

- An attacker can exploit the Internet Explorer vulnerability and use malicious code on a Web page to crash and execute a teardrop denial of service on a machine. By executing this code, the NT machine hangs after receiving corrupted UDP data packets, and a reboot is necessary.

- Another vulnerability exists where an attacker can spoof the remote procedure call (RPC) vulnerability and send spoofed RPC datagrams to Port 135 of the victim. The server would then send reject packets to the spoofed machine. This would continue, and a loop would occur. In addition, if multiple machines were targeted, network bandwidth would be wasted.

- Windows NT, like Windows 9x, is subject to OOB vulnerability.

- Anonymous login vulnerability exists within Windows NT. NT Explorer and ACL use account names for various functions. Explorer uses account names to decide whether to grant access to an object, and the NT ACL uses it to decide whether to grant access rights to specific objects. However, because of this functionality, anonymous logon users can list domain usernames and identify share names. For enhanced security, this functionality should be restricted.

DHCP Support

DHCP is supported by the local ISP-dial platform. The client obtains a registered IP address space from the DHCP server upon IP session negotiation. After a registered space is given, the user is then required to initiate a VPN session to the host server to access any protected services.

This VPN session needs to be established with a dedicated customer VPN server. As multiple ISP DHCP servers support the remote client, a username/password scheme is best used here so that authorized users are not inadvertently blocked.

Security Policy

The customer should publish a standard security document, made available to all customer members. This document should include a basic overview of the customer's security approach, and clearly identify any authorized exceptions. The customer security document should also include details of all security aspects, levels of security authorized for defined user groups, and procedures for users to request that changes be made to their security profiles/access rights.

The security policy document should also include VPN management responsibilities:

- Who administers and enforces the VPN and security systems?
- Who performs RA activities?
- Who administers the desktop systems for the users?

  This is important because systems should be consistent for all users across all platforms, including drivers, plug-ins, DLLs, application programs, and any NOS client components.

  Desktop systems are also points of vulnerability and should have up-to-date virus protection installed. Rogue software that could support a security breach needs to be accounted for, and auto-answer modems should be disabled because they allow an intruder with a "wardialer" to penetrate the VPN by "piggybacking" off the machine of a legitimate user.

Summary

This chapter discussed remote access options and alternatives, including traditional remote access and Virtual Private Network (VPN) architectures.

Remote access is defined as providing access to fixed site resources to those users who are not at a fixed workstation at that location's local-area network (LAN).

A cost-effective and secure alternative to traditional remote access is VPN. With VPNs, all phone calls that access corporate networks are local calls tunneled from the remote site to a local Internet service provider (ISP), over the Internet, and to the corporate VPN gateway.

VPN has three major components:

- LAN-to-LAN VPN is the next common VPN configuration. The LAN-to-LAN VPN is closely tied to the IPSec standard. Whereas the remote dial-up user VPN uses protocols such as PPTP, L2F, and L2TP, IPSec concentrates on LAN-to-LAN.

- Authentication is the process of positively identifying the entity (user, router, network device) that requires access. This authentication is usually done by means of a cryptographic function.

- Encryption is an extra precautionary measure that protects the data through the tunnel. Data is encrypted before it is encapsulated to reduce the risk that someone might tamper with it if the tunnel is breached.

CHAPTER 22

Network Management Introduction

Network management is a service that is needed to control and optimize network operations and respond to changes in user requirements or network conditions. With the implementation of the Simple Network Management Protocol (SNMP), local-area network (LAN) and wide-area network (WAN) components can be monitored and "managed," typically from a central facility. Network management is an integrated platform, or suite, of functions that can be on one machine but span thousands of miles, different support organizations, and many machines and databases.

Network Management Architecture

Network management architecture comprises a common set of relationships and the same basic structure:

- Network element (end stations)—Computer systems and network devices that are running software called *agents*, enabling the sending of alerts to management entities when network issues are identified.

- Management entities—Programmed to react to end-station alerts by executing a defined set of actions, such as the following:
  - Event logging
  - System shutdown
  - Console notification
  - Automatic (attempts) to repair the system, such as reload or reboot

The elements of a management system are network manager applications and agents. Agents are software modules that compile information about the network devices, platforms, or applications within which they reside.

Network Management Agents

Agents collect management information and report problems to a manager. The manager controls a set of agents and ensures that they collect the appropriate information. Agents within managed objects will respond to all polls, whether automatic or manual, and information is conveyed to the management entity within the network management system (NMS) via a network management protocol.

Network Management Protocols

The following lists the network management protocols as defined by various IETF standards:

- Simple Network Management Protocol (SNMP)—SNMP is used to communicate with a management "agent" in a network device. A remote manager can obtain status information and control the device through the agent. SNMP depends on IP and other protocols.

  — SNMPv1—Reports only whether a device is functioning properly.

  — SNMPv2—Provides enhancements including security and a Remote Monitoring (RMON) Management Information Base (MIB). The RMON MIB provides continuous feedback without having to be queried by the SNMP console.

  — SNMPv3—Provides message level security. SNMPv3 also includes an MIB for remotely monitoring/managing the configuration parameters for this security model.

- Management Information Base (MIB)—MIB is the other part of the SNMP standard. The agent delivers information from the MIB or changes it under the direction of a remote manager. Each type of managed resource has an MIB, which contains information detailing what can be known about it and what can be done to it. For example, an MIB for a router contains information about each interface—its speed, protocols supported, and current status. A server MIB has information about CPUs, operating system, memory, and disk.

- RMON—The Remote Monitoring MIB controls an agent monitoring a single LAN segment. It collects information as instructed about traffic levels, which systems are talking, and specific conversations between two parties. RMON covers Layers 1 and 2 of the OSI model. Additionally, basic RMON functionality is built into the application-specific integrated software (ASIC) for many switch ports.

- RMON2—This is an MIB for controlling agents that monitor traffic across the network. It measures traffic flows between different parts of the network and identifies which protocols and applications are being used by each system. RMON2 covers Layers 1 through 7 of the OSI model.

- MIB2—This is a standard MIB that defines basic interface information such as speed, numbers of packets sent and received, numbers of broadcast and unicast packets, and errors. Usually every network device and interface card has one.

- Common Management Interface Protocol (CMIP)—This is an OSI standard protocol used with the Common Management Information Services. (CMIS defines a system of network management information services.) CMIP was proposed as a replacement for the less sophisticated SNMP, but it has not been widely adopted. CMIP provides improved security and better reporting of unusual network conditions.

Network Management Model

The ISO FCAPS model has been a major contributor to network management. The FCAPS model is not unlike the OSI model used for internetworking.

The FCAPS model is made up of the following components:

- Fault management
- Configuration management
- Accounting management
- Performance management
- Security management

Fault Management

Fault management is designed to detect, log, notify users of, and (if possible) automatically fix network issues. Most systems poll the managed objects for error conditions and present this information to the network manager.

NOTE   Fault management deals primarily with events and traps as they occur on the network. Fault management is reactive by nature.

Fault management involves identifying and isolating network issues, resolving problems, and logging the issues and associated effective resolution. (Testing on non-production systems should be performed prior to deployment of any "fixes.")

Fault management elements include the following:

- Events
- Alarms
- Problem identification

- Troubleshooting
- Problem resolution
- Fault logging

Configuration Management

Configuration management is designed to monitor network and system configuration information so that the impact on network operation of various hardware and software elements can be tracked and managed. Changes, additions, and deletions from the network need to be coordinated with the network management personnel, usually in a network operations center (NOC).

Configuration management elements include the following:

- Hardware inventory
- Software inventory
- Inventory software
- Other software
- Configuration information
- Change control

Accounting Management

Accounting management is designed to measure network utilization parameters so that individual or group users on a network can be regulated or charged back to the user's department.

Accounting management processes share the following similarities to those of performance management:

- Measure network resource utilization
- Analyze current usage patterns
- Measure network resources, which can yield billing information and resource utilization

Performance Management

Performance management is designed to measure and make available various aspects of network performance so that they can be maintained at acceptable thresholds.

NOTE   Performance management deals primarily with metrics and measures maintaining a network. Performance management is proactive by nature.

The main processes involved with performance management include the following:

- Interesting performance data is gathered.
- Data is analyzed to determine baselines.
- Performance thresholds for each variable are established.

Aside from reactive-based processes, such as a rapid increase in network congestion, performance management enables proactive monitoring and management in the form of network simulation or trend analysis.

The following are performance-management elements:

- Network-capacity planning
- Availability
- Response time
- Accuracy
- Throughput
- Utilization

Security Management

Security management is designed to control access to network resources, as established by organizational security guidelines.

Most network-management systems address security regarding network hardware, such as when someone is logging into a router or bridge.

Security management systems perform several functions:

- Identify sensitive network resources
- Establish mappings between sensitive network resources and user sets
- Monitor access points to sensitive network resources and logging of inappropriate or failed access to these resources

The following are security management elements:

- Policy
- Authority
- Access level

- Exceptions
- Logging

Network Management Categories

Network management can be grouped into two categories:

- Tactical—Relates to proactive and reactive situations such as failures, congestion, and unacceptable service quality. These tasks include troubleshooting, configuration, and adjusting traffic flows.
- Strategic—Long-term perspective, oriented toward adequate planning to avoid shortages as the network grows. Strategic tasks use information to adjust operations, optimize quality, and manage facilities to reduce overall operational costs.

Network Management Components

Network management applications use collected and historical information for tactical and strategic purposes. Network management applications are generally classified into one of the following categories:

- Element managers
- Network management platforms
- Network management probes
- Performance reporting and analysis

Element Managers

Element managers are network management software packages that are usually provided by a manufacturer for managing a vendor-specific device, or element, within a system or application. Element managers are primarily used for configuration and troubleshooting. Element managers can be either stand-alone applications or part of a network management platform.

Network Management Platforms

Network management platforms are designed to serve as integration points for a set of network management tools. They provide some limited underpinnings for activation and use of third-party tools.

Platforms provide automated discovery, using the network to discover LANs, WANs, links, and the devices attached to them. Network management platforms typically feature network maps with varying levels of detail for the network manager.

Network management platforms typically poll for network device availability, using attributes as defined by the MIB variables.

Network management platforms provide event management, receiving and processing SNMP traps in accordance with filtering rules that determine their severity.

Network Management Probes

Network management probes are agents designed to collect information directly from a network. Different types of probes rely on different information sources, such as device MIBs, statistics, system logs, and DSU/CSUs.

Generally, LAN switches have embedded RMON probes that collect statistics and send alarms on each port's activity to a specific network management station. RMON probes function in one of three ways:

- Roving—Pointing a probe from port to port
- Mirroring—Copying traffic to a probe-monitored port
- Steering—Directing traffic to a remote monitor

Combinations of portable and embedded probes are used for more complete network traffic coverage.

Remote Monitoring (RMON)

Remote Monitoring, or RMON, is a standard SNMP MIB that controls remote monitoring agents.

RMON is a standard monitoring specification that enables various network monitors and console systems to exchange network-monitoring data. RMON provides network administrators with more freedom in selecting network-monitoring probes and consoles with features that meet their particular networking needs. This chapter provides a brief overview of the RMON specification, focusing on RMON groups.

The RMON specification defines a set of statistics and functions that can be exchanged between RMON-compliant console managers and network probes. As such, RMON provides network administrators with comprehensive network-fault diagnosis, planning, and performance-tuning information.

The user community, with the help of the Internet Engineering Task Force (IETF), defined RMON. RMON became a proposed standard in 1992 as RFC 1271 (for Ethernet). RMON then became a draft standard in 1995 as RFC 1757, effectively obsoleting RFC 1271.

RMON covers Layers 1 and 2 of the OSI model.

RMON2

RMON2 is an extension of RMON that collects an enhanced set of information about the content of network traffic showing end-to-end volume and applications.

RMON covers Layers 1 through 7 of the OSI model.

Protocol Analyzers

Protocol analyzers also collect statistics and packets from the network. They overlap with RMON probes.

Performance Reporting/Analysis

Reporting/analysis tools organize large volumes of management data into information and insight needed to make effective investment decisions. Reporting/analysis tools provide an enterprise-wide view of network operations, enabling an understanding that element managers alone cannot offer. Sophisticated network analysis identifies trends and evaluates the health of the enterprise network.

Network performance relates to the speed of the network.

Application performance relates to the speed of the applications as seen by the end user and depends on the network, server, client, and application. Network performance is a key concern because it is usually blamed for most performance problems. A network that delivers traffic quickly might be seen as "slow" if the server is underpowered or supporting too many users. Conversely, a finely tuned server might have no impact if excessive network delays exist.

Performance-Related Terms

The following terminology is associated with network performance management:

- Availability—Measure of network usability for service. Availability is measured as a percentage of the day, week, or month that the resource could be used.

- Bandwidth—Measure of the capacity of a communications link, or a service across a communications link. For example, a T1 link has a bandwidth of 1.544 Mbps, or can carry a streaming media feed of 256 Kbps bandwidth.

- Baseline—Measure of "normal" behavior. Many networks experience "traffic spikes" at various times related to core business operations, such as e-mail or bulk database updates. A baseline separates a "bad" day or one-day anomaly from "normal" days.

- Congestion—Congestion occurs at higher loads and is an indication that the network, or network devices, have reached, or are reaching, their capacity. Congestion generally leads to rapidly increasing latency and ultimately loss of data if the situation is not corrected. Queuing delays are one indication of possible congestion or latency problems.

- Latency—Delay measurement from one end of a network, link, or device to another; a high latency indicates long delay. Latency can never be eliminated in a network and is used as a measurement of network performance. Like utilization, latency might vary based on loads. Network service providers can change network latency by reprovisioning virtual circuits so that they use lower-speed links or incorporate more hops, making it a necessary to monitor network latency.

- Threshold—Value that is set for warning the management system when utilization, latency, or congestion exceeds critical limits. Network managers in management agents that measure the actual behavior of networks and links typically set the threshold.

- Utilization—A measure of how much the capacity (of the total) is being used at any point in time. For example, if a T1 link carries 924 Kbps, it has a utilization of 60% at that particular time interval. Utilization varies according to the actual traffic loads and the time from over which it is averaged. Utilization also measures CPU load in servers and clients.

Service-Level Agreements (SLAs)

Service-level agreements, or SLAs, are contracts between network service providers and customers detailing what the customer expects from the provider. A good SLA has the following components:

- Specific descriptions of services being delivered, including the criteria used to evaluate the service

- Reporting requirements

- Escalation agreements (what to do when serious interruptions occur)

- Service provider penalties for failing to meet the contract terms, usually in the form of revenue (billing) credit

SLA Service-Level Metrics

The following are metrics and measurements typically found in a network service provider's SLA:

- Availability—Measure of the network availability for customer activity. Availability is usually measured as mean time between failures (MTBF) and mean time to repair (MTTR). For example, a MTBF of 99.5% every day means downtime cannot exceed 7.2 minutes every 24 hours.

    Most implementations use a network availability formula similar to the formula shown in Equation 22-1.

Equation 22-1   *Availability Calculation*

$$1 - \frac{\text{\# minutes of outage}}{(10{,}080 \text{ minutes in one week} - \text{\# minutes of block time})} =$$

$$\text{Availability} \ * \ 100 \ = \ \% \text{ Availability}$$

For each device, then averaged among themselves.

This formula is usually geared toward specific devices on the network or the availability of a trunk. Notice that the more devices that are added into the overall calculation, the more obscure the calculation becomes. One considers all the devices on the same level as the others. Furthermore, the more devices that are added into the overall average, the more hidden they become.

This calculation is accomplished for each device, then averaged as a group.

Availability can also be accomplished by doing the following:

- Gathering a list of services provided on the network by priority.

- Reporting on the availability of each of the services on a monthly basis. (Use a modifier or weighting on those services that are considered more important to the organization.)

- Telling management the truth about the availability of services. This provides an avenue to correct those problems and provides better services to the end user community.

In Equation 22-2, specific services can be weighed according to the importance to the business units.

Equation 22-2 *Method Reported by Service*

$$1 - \frac{\text{\# minutes of outage * Weighting Factor}}{\text{(10,080 minutes in one week - \# minutes of block time)}} =$$

$$\text{Availability * } 100 \; = \; \text{\% Availability}$$

These services include the following:

- Response time—Measures the time to complete a request for a client, group of clients, or network.

- Throughput—Measures the amount of data (or volume) sent in a given period of time. For example, videoconferencing generally requires 384 Kbps to provide satisfactory quality.

Network Management Functional Architecture

Network management systems have four basic levels of functionality. Each level has a set of tasks defined to provide, format, or collect data necessary to manage the objects. The levels are as follows:

- Managed Objects
- Element Management Systems (EMS)
- Manager of Managers Systems (MoM)
- User Interface

Managed Objects

Managed objects are the devices and systems requiring monitoring and management.

Examples of managed objects include routers, concentrators, hosts, servers, and applications, such as Oracle, Microsoft SMS, Lotus Notes, and Microsoft Mail. The managed object is not necessarily a piece of hardware, but rather a network function.

EMS

EMS manages specific portions of the network. For example, an SNMP management application is used to manage SNMP manageable elements.

MoM

MoM integrates the information associated with several element management systems, usually performing alarm correlation between EMSs. The data by the EMS systems typically comes from the managed object. The EMS then consolidates the data in a database for processing and retrieval.

User Interface

The user interface for the collected information is the principal piece to deploying a successful system.

Network Operation Centers (NOCs)

Most fault detection, isolation, and troubleshooting is accomplished in the Network Operations Center (NOC). Technicians are dispatched when issues have been analyzed. Several company locations might be involved in the overall network, spanning thousands of miles around the globe. Sometimes, network service providers or enterprise network customers will implement follow-the-sun support. *Follow-the-sun support* occurs when each NOC takes ownership of the network at the beginning of the day and hands it off to the next NOC in line at the end of the day, but the beginning of the day for the next NOC.

Four levels of activity occur within any NOC:

* Inactive—No monitoring is being done. If an alarm is received in this area, it is generally ignored.

* Reactive—NOC engineers react to a problem after it has occurred, although no monitoring has been applied.

* Interactive—Monitoring of components occurs, but troubleshooting is interactive to isolate and eliminate the side effect alarms and to isolate to a root cause.

* Proactive—Monitoring of components occurs and the system provides a root cause alarm for the problem at hand. Automatic restore processes are in place where possible to minimize downtime.

Network Utilization Reporting

Network utilization can be measured from SNMP-based managed objects using the MIBv2 Interface Input (ifinput) and Interface Output (ifoutput) tables of a network device. These types of interfaces are considered promiscuous, meaning that they listen for all packets in the attached subnet, regardless of destination.

Alarms and Alerts

Alarm and alert displays need to be simple to read and easy to understand, providing useful information with regard to the reported condition. Alarms need to be correlated prior to further action, meaning that if an alarm is detected, it needs to be verified against other network elements that could be indicative of larger issues.

Alarm Correlation

Alarm correlation is the process by which several alarms are narrowed from a mass of problems to a root cause and side effects. Alarm correlation narrows the possible issues to a root common denominator. For example, if a T1 link fails, it is more effective to isolate and troubleshoot the T1, not the systems behind the T1 that are also reporting down.

Alarm correlation incorporates some artificial intelligence into the network management platform. Artificial intelligence applications are broken down into two categories:

- Rules based—Information that can be used to depict entity relationships and how those entities interact with each other. As such, most rules tables are static in nature in that one inputs the information associated with the relationships.

- Heuristic—Dynamic information derived from previous conditions that have occurred.

These same relationships can also be accomplished in a database solution, identifying root and side effect alarms.

Root alarms are alarms that indicate that something has actually gone wrong. A side effect alarm is one in which the alarm is caused by a failure external to the managed object.

For example, in the event of a DS3 failing, the DS3 link failure is reported as the root alarm, whereas the T1 links, and subsequent services being carried, are reported as side effect alarms.

MIB

An MIB is a formal description of a set of network objects that can be managed using the SNMP. The format of the MIB is defined as part of the SNMP. All other MIBs are extensions of this basic MIB. MIB-I refers to the initial MIB definition. MIB-II is the current definition. SNMPv2 includes MIB-II and adds some new objects.

MIBs (or more accurately, MIB extensions) exist for each set of related network entities that can be managed. For example, some MIB definitions are in the form of Requests for Comments (RFCs) for AppleTalk, DNS server, FDDI, and RS-232C network objects. Product developers can create and register new MIB extensions. Companies that have created MIB extensions for their sets of products include Cisco, Fore, IBM, Novell, QMS, and Onramp. New MIB extension numbers can be requested by contacting the Internet Assigned Numbers Authority (IANA) at 310-822-1511, extension 239.

All managed objects are contained in the MIB, a database of the managed objects. The managed objects, or variables, can be set or read to provide information on network devices and interfaces. A network management system can control a managed device by sending a message to a managed agent of a network device, requiring a change to the value of one or more of its variables.

Table 22-1 is a partial list of MIBs and their referenced IETF RFCs.

Table 22-1 *MIB RFCs*

IETF RFC	MIB Description
1212	Concise definitions
1213	MIB II
1315	Frame Relay DTE
1406	DS1
1407	DS3
1573	MIBv2 extensions
1595	SONET
1604	Frame Relay service
1695	ATM
2064	FlowMeter v1
2115	Frame Relay DTE v2
2233	MIB2 extensions
2515	ATM
2662	ADSL
2667	IP tunnel
2863	ifMIB update
2864	ifMIB update
2925	Ping and TraceRoute

NOTE   The Cisco MIB for Cisco IOS is provided with all Cisco software releases and with CiscoWorks router management software.

NOTE   The Cisco MIB is a set of variables that are private extensions to the Internet standard
                  MIB II. The MIB II is documented in RFC 1213, Management Information Base for
                  Network Management of TCP/IP-based Internets: MIB-II.

MIB Hierarchy

A tree hierarchy logically represents the MIB structure, as illustrated in Figure 22-1.

Figure 22-1 *MIB Hierarchy*

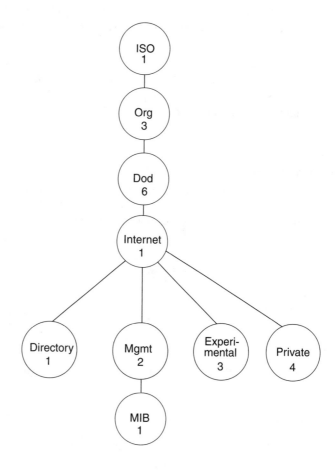

The *root* of the tree is unnamed and splits into three main branches:

- Consultative Committee for International Telegraph and Telephone (CCITT)
- International Organization for Standardization (ISO)
- Joint ISO/CCITT

These branches and those that fall below each category have short text strings and integers to identify them. Text strings describe *object names*, whereas integers allow computer software to create compact, encoded representations of the names. For example, the Cisco MIB variable *authAddr* is an object name and is denoted by number 5, which is listed at the end of its object identifier number *1.3.6.1.4.1.9.2.1.5*.

The object identifier 1.3.6.1.2.1 represents the Internet standard MIB. It also can be expressed as *iso.org.dod.internet.mgmt.mib* (as illustrated in Figure 22-1).

NOTE   The object identifier *1.3.6.1.4.1.9*, or *iso.org.dod.internet.private.enterprise.cisco*, represents the Cisco Workgroup MIB. The Cisco Workgroup MIB splits into two main areas: Workgroup Products and Cisco Management.

Cisco MIB Hierarchy

For all MIBs relevant to a Cisco Systems device, please refer to the www.cisco.com Web site. The MIB hierarchies for the Catalyst 5000 and the LS1010 switches are presented in Figures 22-2 and 22-3 for example purposes.

Figure 22-2 *Catalyst 5000 MIB Hierarchy*

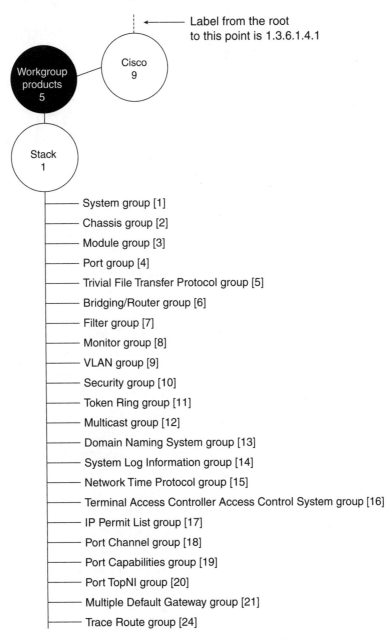

Label from the root
to this point is 1.3.6.1.4.1

Cisco
9

Workgroup
products
5

Stack
1

System group [1]

Chassis group [2]

Module group [3]

Port group [4]

Trivial File Transfer Protocol group [5]

Bridging/Router group [6]

Filter group [7]

Monitor group [8]

VLAN group [9]

Security group [10]

Token Ring group [11]

Multicast group [12]

Domain Naming System group [13]

System Log Information group [14]

Network Time Protocol group [15]

Terminal Access Controller Access Control System group [16]

IP Permit List group [17]

Port Channel group [18]

Port Capabilities group [19]

Port TopNI group [20]

Multiple Default Gateway group [21]

Trace Route group [24]

Figure 22-3 *LS-1010 MIB Hierarchy*

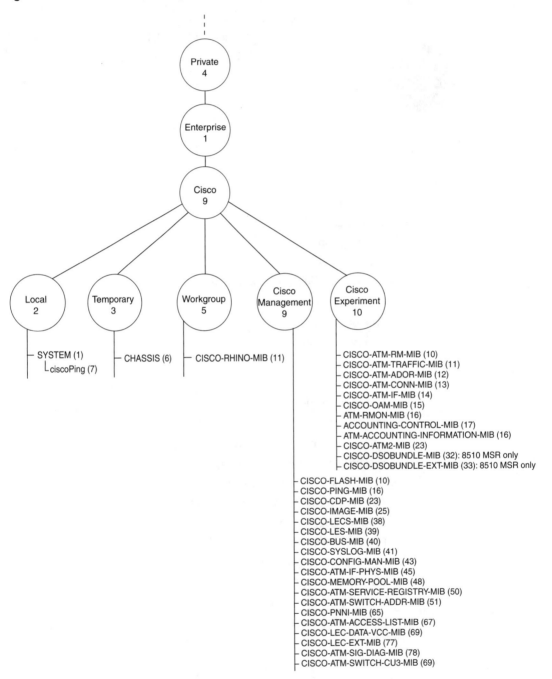

Summary

Several volumes have been published that focus on network management, discussing in far greater detail the elements, MIB definitions, enterprise, and personnel management aspects.

Network management is a service that is needed to control and optimize network operations, respond to changes in user requirements, and respond to changes in network conditions. With the implementation of SNMP, local-area network (LAN), and wide-area network (WAN), components can be monitored and "managed," typically from a central facility. Network management is an integrated platform, or suite, of functions that can be on one machine but span thousands of miles, different support organizations, many machines, and databases.

The ISO FCAPS model has been a major contributor to network management. The FCAPS model is not unlike the OSI model used for internetworking.

The FCAPS model is made up of the following components:

- Fault management
- Configuration management
- Accounting management
- Performance management
- Security management

It is important to delineate between fault management and performance management. Fault management is a reactive methodology, and performance management is a proactive one.

Alarm correlation based on some form of artificial intelligence applications is broken down into two categories:

- Rules based—Information that can be used to depict entity relationships and how those entities interact with each other. As such, most rules tables are static in nature in that one inputs the information associated with the relationships.
- Heuristic—Dynamic information derived from previous conditions that have occurred.

Several protocols are exclusive to network management:

- Simple Network Management Protocol (SNMP) is used to communicate with a management "agent" in a network device.
  - SNMPv1—Reports only whether a device is functioning properly
  - SNMPv2—Provides enhancements, including security and a Remote Monitoring (RMON) Management Information Base (MIB)
  - SNMPv3—Provides message-level security

- Management Information Base (MIB)—The other part of the SNMP standard. The agent delivers information from the MIB or changes it under the direction of a remote manager.

- Remote Monitoring (RMON)—MIB that controls an agent monitoring a single LAN segment. RMON covers Layers 1 and 2 of the OSI model.

- RMON2—An MIB for controlling agents that monitor traffic across the network. RMON2 covers Layers 1 through 7 of the OSI model.

- MIB2—A standard MIB that defines basic interface information such as speed, numbers of packets sent and received, numbers of broadcast and unicast packets, and errors.

- Common Management Interface Protocol (CMIP)—An OSI standard protocol used with the Common Management Information Services. (CMIS defines a system of network management information services.)

Network management targets the monitoring of service-level agreements (SLAs). SLAs are contracts between network service providers and customers detailing what the customer expects from the provider.

Most fault detection, isolation, and troubleshooting are accomplished in the Network Operations Center (NOC). Technicians are dispatched when issues have been analyzed.

Four levels of activity occur within any NOC:

- Inactive—No monitoring is being done. If an alarm is received in this area, it is generally ignored.

- Reactive—NOC engineers react to a problem after it has occurred although no monitoring has been applied.

- Interactive—Monitoring of components occurs, but troubleshooting is interactive to isolate and eliminate the side effect alarms and to isolate to a root cause.

- Proactive—Monitoring of components occurs and the system provides a root cause alarm for the problem at hand. Automatic restoration processes are in place where possible to minimize downtime.

All managed objects are contained in the MIB, which is a database of the managed objects. The managed objects, or variables, can be set or read to provide information on network devices and interfaces. A network management system can control a managed device by sending a message to a managed agent of a network device that requires a change to the value of one or more of its variables.

CHAPTER 23

IP VPN WAN Documentation

Chapter 21, "Remote Access and VPNs," discussed the underlying technology for IP WAN networks and their underlying components. This chapter will discuss some recommendations and guidelines to follow to document an IP Multiprotocol Label Switching (MPLS) wide-area network (WAN).

Most networking discussions today include the topic of documentation at some point, whether the mention is a statement advising that you should document your network assets or a statement advising that network documentation is a good tool to have when troubleshooting a network issue. The challenge is what network information should be documented, reviewed, and analyzed for any potential network-related issues.

Network documentation should be both easy to complete and easy to understand. In an effort to make the network documentation process easier to manage for IP WAN implementations, templates have been prepared and presented for use. These templates are preceded by relevant console commands, a case study, and a sample completed template serving as a guide.

NOTE	The templates presented here are also available electronically on the Cisco Press Web site at www.ciscopress.com/1587050390.

IP WAN documentation can be approached from two perspectives: from the individual site or from the overall WAN view. Both perspectives will be demonstrated here with supporting templates.

Two types of VPN documentation templates will be presented: one for remote access VPNs and one for IP WAN VPNs.

Remote Access Documentation Template

Figure 23-1 will be used as a reference to support the remote access documentation template (see Tables 23-1 and 23-2).

Figure 23-1 *Remote Access Network Topology*

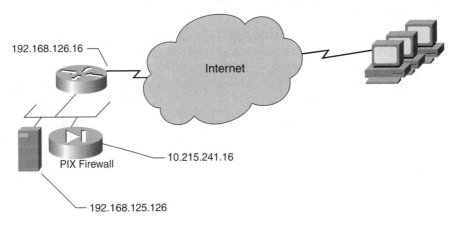

Table 23-1 *Remote Access Network Topology Documentation Template (Example)*

Network Service Provider				
IP Dedicated Access ID				
Access Bandwidth	1536 K		T1 Channels	1 to 24
WAN Router Serial Interface	S1		Firewall Hardware and Version	Cisco PIX v5.1
WAN Router Serial Interface Address	192.168.125.16		Firewall Network Address	10.215.241.16
VPN Server Network Address	10.215.241.16		Authentication Server Address	192.168.125.126
End-Node Username	End-Node Password	End-Node Tunnel Protocol	End-Node Encryption	
User1	Password1	PPTP	3DES	
User2	Password2	PPTP	3DES	
User3	Password3	L2TP	3DES	

Table 23-2 *Remote Access Network Topology Documentation Template*

Network Service Provider				
IP Dedicated Access ID				
Access Bandwidth		T1 Channels		
WAN Router Serial Interface		Firewall Hardware and Version		
WAN Router Serial Interface Address		Firewall Network Address		
VPN Server Network Address		Authentication Server Address		
End-Node Username	End-Node Password	End-Node Tunnel Protocol		End-Node Encryption

IP WAN VPN Documentation

Figure 23-2 will be used as a reference to support the remote access documentation template (see Tables 23-3 and 23-4).

Figure 23-2 *IP VPN WAN*

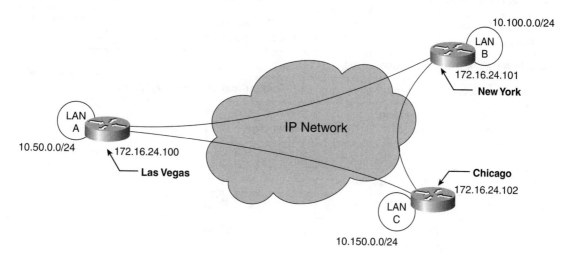

As with ATM and Frame Relay, you can document IP VPN WANS using two methods: single-node view and global view. Both network views will be documented here (see Tables 23-3, 23-4, 23-5, and 23-6).

Table 23-3 *IP VPN WAN Template: Las Vegas (Site View Example)*

Site Name		Las Vegas	Site Mnemonic			IP_WAN_LVS
Network Service Provider			IP Dedicated Access ID			
Access Bandwidth		1536	T1 Channels			1 to 24
VPN WAN Router Serial Interface		S0	VPN WAN Router Serial Interface Address			172.16.24.100
Inside Network Address Space		10.50.0.0/24				
VPN Server Network Address			Authentication Server Address			
Sub-Interface and Address	Destination Address	QoS	B/W Percentage	CAR Policy	Comments	
S0.1	172.16.24.101	Gold	50	Recolor/Silver	Streaming Video	
S0.2	172.16.24.101	Silver	50	Drop		
S0.3	172.16.24.102	Silver	80	Drop	Database Updates	
S0.4	172.16.24.102	Bronze	20	Drop		

Table 23-4   *IP VPN Document Template: Site View*

Site Name		Site Mnemonic	
Network Service Provider		IP Dedicated Access ID	
Access Bandwidth		T1 Channels	
VPN WAN Router Serial Interface		VPN WAN Router Serial Interface Address	
Inside Network Address Space			
VPN Server Network Address		Authentication Server Address	

Sub-Interface and Address	Destination Address	QoS	B/W Percentage	CAR Policy	Comments

Table 23-5 *IP VPN WAN: Global View Example*

Organization Name		SpringCo		
Originating Node	**Originating IP Address**	**Terminating Node**	**Terminating IP Address**	**QoS**
Las Vegas	172.16.24.100	New York	172.1.24.101	Gold, Silver
Las Vegas	172.16.24.100	Chicago	172.16.24.102	Silver, Bronze
New York	172.1.24.101	Chicago	172.16.102	Platinum, Bronze

Table 23-6   *IP VPN WAN: Global View Example*

Organization Name				
Originating Node	Originating IP Address	Terminating Node	Terminating IP Address	QoS

IOS Commands

Primarily, two Cisco IOS commands can be used to collect information regarding IP (MPLS) VPNs:

- **show ip vrf**
- **show ip route vrf**

show ip route vrf

The **show ip route vrf** command is used to display the IP routing table associated with a VPN routing/forwarding instance (VRF) See Table 23-7 for the **show ip route vrf** output description.

```
show ip route vrf vrf-name [connected] [protocol [as-number] [tag]
[output-modifiers]] [list number [output-modifiers]] [profile]
[static [output-modifiers]]
[summary [output-modifiers]] [supernets-only [output-modifiers]]
[traffic-engineering [output-modifiers]]
```

Table 23-7   *show ip route vrf Syntax and Description*

Syntax	Description
vrf-name	This is the name assigned to the VRF.
connected	This displays all connected routes in a VRF.
protocol	To specify a routing protocol, use one of the following keywords: bgp, egp, eigrp, hello, igrp, isis, ospf, or rip.
as-number	This is the autonomous system number.
tag	This is the IOS routing area label.
output-modifiers	(Optional) For a list of associated keywords and arguments, use context-sensitive help.
list number	This specifies the IP access list to display.
profile	This displays the IP routing table profile.
static	This displays static routes.
summary	This displays a summary of routes.
supernets-only	This displays supernet entries only.
traffic-engineering	This displays only traffic-engineered routes.

Example

This following code shows the IP routing table associated with the VRF called vrf1:

```
Router#show ip route vrf vrf1
Codes: C - connected, S - static, I - IGRP, R - RIP, M - mobile, B - BGP
       D - EIGRP, EX - EIGRP external, O - OSPF, IA - OSPF inter area
       N1 - OSPF NSSA external type 1, N2 - OSPF NSSA external type 2
       E1 - OSPF external type 1, E2 - OSPF external type 2, E - EGP
       i - IS-IS, L1 - IS-IS level-1, L2 - IS-IS level-2, * - candidate default
       U - per-user static route, o - ODR
       T - traffic engineered route

Gateway of last resort is not set

B    51.0.0.0/8 [200/0] via 13.13.13.13, 00:24:19
C    50.0.0.0/8 is directly connected, Ethernet1/3
B    11.0.0.0/8 [20/0] via 50.0.0.1, 02:10:22
B    12.0.0.0/8 [200/0] via 13.13.13.13, 00:24:20
```

The following code shows BGP entries in the IP routing table associated with the VRF called vrf1:

```
Router#show ip route vrf vrf1 bgp
B   51.0.0.0/8 [200/0] via 13.13.13.13, 03:44:14
B   11.0.0.0/8 [20/0] via 51.0.0.1, 03:44:12
B   12.0.0.0/8 [200/0] via 13.13.13.13, 03:43:14
```

show ip vrf

The **show ip vrf** command is used to display the set of defined VRFs (VPN routing/forwarding instances) and associated interfaces. See Table 23-8 for a **show ip vrf** description.

```
show ip vrf [{brief ¦ detail ¦ interfaces}] [vrf-name] [output-modifiers]
```

Table 23-8   *show ip vrf Syntax and Description*

Syntax	Description
brief	(Optional) This displays concise information on the VRF(s) and associated interfaces.
detail	(Optional) This displays detailed information on the VRF(s) and associated interfaces.
interfaces	(Optional) This displays detailed information about all interfaces bound to a particular VRF, or any VRF.
vrf-name	This is the name assigned to a VRF.
output-modifiers	(Optional) For a list of associated keywords and arguments, use context-sensitive help.

The **show ip vrf** command is used to display information about VRFs. Two levels of detail are available: use the brief keyword or no keyword to display concise information, or use the detail keyword to display all information. To display information about all interfaces bound to a particular VRF or to any VRF, use the **interfaces** keyword.

Example

The following code shows brief information for the VRFs currently configured (see Table 23-9 for the field descriptions):

```
Router#show ip vrf
  Name              Default RD        Interfaces
  vrf1              100:1             Ethernet1/3
  vrf2              100:2             Ethernet0/3
```

Table 23-9 *show vrf Field Descriptions*

Field	Description
Name	Specifies the VRF name.
Default RD	Specifies the default route distinguisher.
Interfaces	Specifies the network interfaces.

The following code shows the interfaces that are bound to a particular VRF:

```
router#show ip vrf interfaces
Interface      IP-Address      VRF                Protocol
Ethernet2      130.22.0.33     blue_vrf           up
Ethernet4      130.77.0.33     hub                up
router#
```

Summary

Primarily, two Cisco IOS commands can be used to collect information regarding IP (MPLS) VPNs:

- **show ip vrf**
- **show ip route vrf**

Three VPN variations were discussed, with topology document templates for each:

- Remote Access VPN
- IP VPN WAN Local View
- IP VPN WAN Global View

CHAPTER 24

Routing Protocols, Part I

The purpose of this chapter is to provide a summary of IP, and where noted, IPX, routing protocols.

The routing protocols that are discussed in this chapter include the following:

- Routing Information Protocol (RIP) and RIPv2 (RFC 2453)
- Interior Gateway Routing Protocol (IGRP)
- Enhanced Interior Gateway Routing Protocol (EIGRP)
- Open Shortest Path First (OSPF)

Prior to discussion of these routing protocols, it is recommended that you review some basic routing methodologies and mechanics of routing protocols.

Border Gateway Protocol (BGP), specifically BGP version 4, and Intermediate System-to-Intermediate System (IS-IS) is discussed in Chapter 25, "Routing Protocols, Part II."

Routing: Static Versus Dynamic

A router can learn of a network route in two ways; the route is either statically configured or dynamically learned and calculated.

- Static—Static routes are manually configured. Static routes have no mechanism to calculate or exchange routing information. Routers with routes that are statically configured can only forward packets that are defined by these routes. Static routes are generally used in small networks, or routers with only one WAN interface connection, such as a point-to-point link.

- Dynamic—Dynamic routes are learned, or discovered, by the router. Dynamic routes adjust to conditions affected by network topology changes. Routers with routes that are dynamically learned can forward packets over any available discovered route. Three categories of dynamic routing protocols exist:

  — Distance vector

  — Link state

  — Hybrid

NOTE	Dynamic routing protocols have a distinct advantage over static routing protocols because dynamic protocols can adapt to changes in network topologies, such as those caused by outages, automatically, whereas static routing protocols cannot.

Administrative Distance

The administrative distance is used to determine which route, if multiple routes are present, is the preferred route. The *administrative distance* is the distance that a neighbor router states, or advertises, is the distance to a destination. This is the deciding factor in electing a feasible successor, or backup route, for any routing protocol. The lower the administrative distance the better because the route is considered to be more believable.

Administrative distance is a measure of reliability (see Table 24-1). It is the deciding factor among routes, if routing information has more than one source. An example of this would be if both a static route and a dynamically learned route exist for a destination, or if multiple-routing protocols are in use for a routed protocol.

NOTE	The administrative distance values can be changed with the **distance** command.

Table 24-1   *Routing Protocol Administrative Distance Values*

Protocol	Distance Value
Connected Interface	0
Static routes	1
EIGRP Summary routes	5
Exterior Border Gateway Protocol (EBGP)	20
Internal EIGRP	90
IGRP	100
OSPF	110
IS-IS	115
RIP	120
Exterior Gateway Protocol (EGP)	140
External EIGRP	170
Internal BGP	200
Unknown	255

Distance-Vector Routing

Distance-vector–based routing protocols periodically forward copies of their routing tables to their respective (immediate) network neighbors. Each recipient of this table adds its own distance value (distance vector) to the table and then forwards it on to its immediate neighbors, including the router from which the table was just received.

Each router uses this "completed table" to update its own routing tables. Each router, in possession of this "completed" table, has only learned distances, or hops, to other routes. The router has learned nothing about the distant routers or the network topology beyond hop counts, such as bandwidth of each link, transmission relay, reliability of the links, or the load on each link.

NOTE   Distance-vector algorithms are also known as Bellman-Ford algorithms.

The following routing protocols are classified as distance-vector routing protocols:

- RIP / RIPv2
- IGRP
- EIGRP (Distance-Vector/Link-State Hybrid)

Distance-Vector Routing Concerns

Distance-vector routing protocols can create routing issues in certain situations. A change to the network topology, such as one caused by a network link outage, requires a certain amount of time for each router to converge on, or learn, a new network topology. It is during this convergence process that the network is vulnerable to inconsistent, or "faulty," routing. This vulnerability might result in, but is not limited to, routing "black holes" or infinite loops.

Link-State, or Shortest Path First, Routing

Link-state, or shortest path first (SPF), routing algorithms create and maintain complex routing table databases of the network topology. Link-state protocols possess a full knowledge of the network topology and its routers. This information is conveyed via link-state advertisements (LSAs).

NOTE   For the math oriented, SPF algorithms are based on graph theory.

LSAs are used to build the topological database that the SPF algorithm is run against to determine network destination reachability. The results of these SPF calculations are then used to update each individual router's routing table. This methodology enables each router to dynamically adapt to changes in the network topology, such as those caused by outages or reconfigurations (due to the addition of network nodes). Some LSAs are triggered by changes in network topology rather than sending periodic updates.

NOTE   The SPF algorithm is also called Dijkstra's algorithm, after its creator.

The following routing protocols are classified as link-state routing protocols (Interior Gateway Protocols, or IGPs):

- OSPF
- Open System Interconnection (OSI) IS-IS
- Novell's NetWare Link Services Protocol (NLSP)

Link-State Routing Concerns

Link-state routing protocols can flood a network during the initial route discovery process. This flooding consumes network bandwidth that might otherwise be used for data traffic. Although this degradation of network performance is temporary, possibly lasting only a few seconds, it can be noticeable to network users. Flooding on large networks with low-bandwidth connections, such as Frame Relay WAN PVCs with low committed information rate (CIR) configurations, causes more noticeable congestion than similar networks with large bandwidth connections, such as PVCs with high CIR configurations.

Link-state routing protocols are both router memory and processor intensive. This requirement can lead to a capital expenditure to add additional memory to existing routers. If the network is large, adding memory might not be enough and upgrading of the routers becomes a consideration, which can also be costly.

Hybrid Routing

Hybrid routing protocols are a combination of distance-vector and link-state routing protocols. Hybrid routing protocols use weighted distance-vector metrics with the more rapid convergence found with link-state protocols, without the additional overhead of the LSA.

NOTE	*Convergence* is the concept of all routers in a network understanding and adapting to a change in the network's topology, agreeing on a consistent view of the network topology.

Cisco Systems, Inc. is credited with the creation of the hybrid routing-protocol with the advent of its proprietary routing protocol, EIGRP. EIGRP was engineered to combine the "best of both worlds"—distance-vector and link-state algorithms—without the adverse effects, such as network performance, of each.

The EIGRP routing protocol is classified as a hybrid routing protocol.

NOTE	EIGRP is sometimes classified as a distance-vector protocol because the hybrid classification has only recently been introduced.

Hybrid Routing Concerns

Although hybrid routing, such as EIGRP, certainly appears to be the best routing protocol, one important concern must be taken into consideration. EIGRP was developed by Cisco and is proprietary to Cisco Systems routers, meaning that direct interoperability with another vendor is not possible with EIGRP. EIGRP interoperability with another (non-Cisco) network is only possible if EIGRP redistributes its routes into the routing protocol being run by the other network, such as RIP or BGP. If non-Cisco devices are being deployed, the EIGRP tables should be redistributed into the non-EIGRP routed network. The other option is selecting a routing protocol that is supported by all devices within the internetwork.

NOTE	Redistribution is the process by which routes learned via one routing protocol are distributed into another routing protocol.

Figure 24-1 illustrates two disparate networks with the following routing protocols:

- A, B, C—EIGRP
- A, E, D—OSPF

Figure 24-1 *Routing Protocol Redistribution*

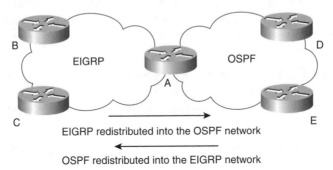

Router A is configured to redistribute EIGRP routes into the OSPF cloud so that Routers D and E have visibility into the EIGRP cloud and can connect, or exchange routing information, with Routers B and C. Router A is also configured to redistribute OSPF routes into the EIGRP cloud so that Routers B and C can connect with Routers D and E.

Routing Metrics

Metrics are a key component in how a routing protocol operates. Some routing protocols require only one or two metrics, whereas others require upwards of five or more metrics. It is a general rule that the more metrics that are involved, the more varied and specific they are, resulting in a more "tailored" network.

Distance-vector routing protocols use a single metric, distance, to calculate their routing tables, whereas link-state routing protocols use several factors to calculate their tables. These factors used by link-state routing protocols include the following:

- Propagation delay
- Reliability of the link
- Bandwidth of the link (both available and total)
- Traffic load on the link
- Hop count
- Maximum transmission unit (MTU)
- Cost

As these values change throughout the course of operation, the dynamic routing protocol metrics also change in correlation and adapt to the new topology environment.

Routing Information Protocol (RIP)

RIP has been around since before the Advanced Research Projects Agency Network (ARPANET) came into existence in 1969. RIP was standardized as an open standard routing protocol with RFC 1058. RIP has endured several updates, as the following timeline demonstrates:

June 1988 / RFC 1058 Routing Information Protocol. C.L. Hedrick. Jun-01-1988. Format: TXT=93285 bytes. Updated by RFC 1388, RFC 1723.

RIP was designed and engineered to be a simple distance-vector routing protocol, and because RIP is an open standard, it is a safe assumption that any network routing device is capable of supporting RIP. RIP is an IGP that was designed for use in small, simple networks. RIP was designed and engineered to support only classful routing and has no support for classless routing, such as classless interdomain routing (CIDR).

NOTE   IGPs are designed to convey routing updates within their own routing domain, or autonomous system. EGPs are designed to convey routing updates between routing domains, or autonomous systems.

RIP-configured routers construct a routing table, calculated from the information shared by the exchanging of routing information with each router's immediate neighbors. This routing table consists of one entry for each known (and reachable) destination. This entry is the lowest-cost path to that destination.

NOTE   The term *cost*, when applied to routing tables and metrics, is a value that describes the total value of that route. This cost is compared with the cost of other routes to determine the ideal path for traffic. The lower the cost value (closer to zero), the better the path.

RIP Routing Table

Each RIP routing table contains an entry for the destination IP network, a specific network host (address), a subnet, or an optional default route.

NOTE   A default route is used when no other route is available to the specified destination. In most cases, the default route points to the Internet service provider (ISP) and is configured within the Cisco IOS as follows:

```
Router(config)# ip route 0.0.0.0 0.0.0.0 network_address
```

There is no difference in the following configuration commands:

```
Router(config)# ip route 0.0.0.0 0.0.0.0 network_address
```

and

```
Router(config)# ip route 0.0.0.0 255.255.255.255 network_address
```

The RIP routing table has five fields, as detailed in Table 24-2.

Table 24-2 *RIP Routing Field Descriptions*

Field	Description
Destination IP Network Address	This is the destination of any data packet that the RIP router receives. The RIP router looks up the destination network or host address of the packet in its routing table to determine where to send the packet.
Metric	This is the total cost of carrying the packet from origination to destination. This field contains the sum of the costs associated with the network links comprising the end-to-end path across the network from the router. RIP link costs are equal to 1 per link, with a total cost, or metric, of 16 (an unreachable destination).
Next Hop IP Address	This is the IP address of the next router interface in the network path to the ultimate destination. This field is populated in the router's table if the destination IP address is on a network that is not otherwise directly connected to the router.
Route Change	Specified in RFC 1058, this field is not always implemented by router vendors. This field is used to identify changes in routes to specific destination entries.
Route Timers	Three timers are associated with each route: • Update timer—Timer that initiates routing updates • Route timeout—Amount of time (default is 180 seconds) without a route update before the route is marked as invalid • Route-flush—Amount of time (default is 90 seconds) after the route timeout timer has expired before the route is flushed, or purged, from the routing table.

The network topology shown in Figure 24-2 is used to demonstrate the abbreviated contents of a RIP routing table, focusing on hop count (distance-vector metric).

NOTE	The default cost for each hop is 1; however, the network administrator can manually adjust the cost so that links with less bandwidth, such as 56 kbps, could have a cost of 10, giving weight to those links with more bandwidth, such as T1 links.

Figure 24-2 *Five-Node RIP-Routed Network*

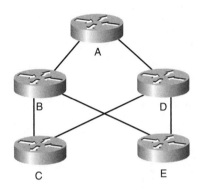

Table 24-3 shows the routing table for each router prior to the network failure.

Table 24-3   *RIP Routing Table for Five-Node Network (Figure 24-2)*

Router Name	Destination Host	Next Hop	Number of Hops	Via Network Path
A	Any B Network	B	1	Directly Connected
	Any C Network	B	2	B-C
		D	2	D-C
		D	4	D-E-B-C
	Any D Network	D	1	Directly Connected
	Any E Network	B	2	B-E
		D	2	D-E
		B	4	B-C-D-E
B	Any A Network	A	1	Directly Connected
		C	3	C-D-A
		E	3	E-D-A
	Any C Network	C	1	Directly Connected
		A	3	A-D-C
	Any D Network	A	2	A-D
		C	2	C-D

(continues)

Table 24-3 *RIP Routing Table for Five-Node Network (Figure 24-2) (Continued)*

Router Name	Destination Host	Next Hop	Number of Hops	Via Network Path
		E	2	E-D
	Any E Network	E	1	Directly Connected
		A	3	A-D-E
		C	3	C-D-E
C	Any A Network	B	2	B-A
		D	2	D-A
		B	4	B-E-D-A
		D	4	D-E-B-A
	Any B Network	B	1	Directly Connected
		D	3	D-A-B
	Any D Network	D	1	Directly Connected
		B	3	B-A-D
	Any E Network	B	2	B-E
		D	2	D-E
		B	4	B-A-D-E
		D	4	D-A-B-E
D	Any A Network	A	1	Directly Connected
		C	3	C-B-A
		E	3	E-B-A
	Any B Network	A	2	A-B
		C	2	C-B
		E	2	E-B
	Any C Network	C	1	Directly Connected
		A	3	A-B-C
		E	3	E-B-C
	Any E Network	E	1	Directly Connected
		A	3	A-B-E
		C	3	C-B-E
E	Any A Network	B	2	B-A
		D	2	D-A

Table 24-3 *RIP Routing Table for Five-Node Network (Figure 24-2)*

Router Name	Destination Host	Next Hop	Number of Hops	Via Network Path
		B	4	B-C-D-A
		D	4	D-C-B-A
	Any B Network	B	1	Directly Connected
		D	3	D-A-B
		D	3	D-C-B
	Any C Network	B	2	B-C
		D	2	D-C
		B	4	B-A-D-C
		D	4	D-A-B-C
	Any D Network	D	1	Directly Connected
		B	3	B-A-D
		B	3	B-C-D

RIP Routing Convergence

Any time the network topology changes, each router must converge on the change. The most significant change is to an immediate neighbor. Simply stated, *convergence* is the mechanism by which each router agrees with each other on what the new network topology looks like.

In Figure 24-2, if the link between Router C and Router D fails, each interconnected router converges and updates its routing tables as a consequence. If Router B fails, the same process occurs, whereby Routers A, C, D, and E will update their tables and mark any path that involves Router B as unavailable.

Several mechanisms are in place that affect the convergence of RIP routers:

- Count to infinity
- Split horizon
- Poison reverse
- Triggered updates
- Hold-down timers

Count to Infinity

The three-node network shown in Figure 24-3 has experienced a link failure between Router A and Router C.

Figure 24-3 *RIP Network with Failed Link*

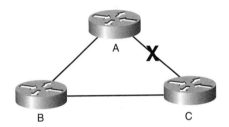

Table 24-4 shows the routing table for each router prior to the network failure.

Table 24-4 *RIP Routing Table for Three-Node Network (Figure 24-3)*

Router Name	Destination Host	Next Hop	Number of Hops	Via Network Path
A	Any B Network	B	1	Directly Connected
		C	2	C-B
	Any C Network	C	1	Directly Connected
		B	2	B-C
B	Any A Network	A	1	Directly Connected
		C	2	C-A
	Any C Network	C	1	Directly Connected
		A	2	A-C
C	Any A Network	A	1	Directly Connected
		B	2	B-A
	Any B Network	B	1	Directly Connected
		A	2	A-B

However, something unique starts to happen when Routers A and C detect the failed link. Router A is trying to connect to Router C, but has no direct connection. Router A learns that Router B has a connection to Router C; however, Router B advertises that it can also get to Router C directly or through Router A. Router A in turn advertises that it can get to Router C through Router B. This goes back and forth, adding 1 to the hop count, between the two routes until the next routing update (180 seconds) takes place.

Table 24-5 shows how the routing table looks after each router has counted to infinity to determine the reachability of each node after the network link failure.

Table 24-5   *RIP Routing Table Node Status*

Router Name	Destination Host	Next Hop	Number of Hops	Via Network Path
A	Any B Network	B	1	Directly Connected
		C	2	C-B
	Any C Network	C	1	Directly Connected
		B	2	B-C
B	Any A Network	A	1	Directly Connected
		C	16	Unreachable
	Any C Network	C	1	Directly Connected
		A	16	Unreachable
C	Any A Network	A	16	Unreachable
		B	2	B-A
	Any B Network	B	1	Directly Connected
		A	2	A-B

The issue here is the amount of time taken for the 16-hop count (unreachable) to be achieved. During this time, datagram traffic is circling around between the two nodes, never reaching its ultimate destination until the network converges upon the next routing update.

Two methods are used to help avoid the count to infinity problem: split horizon and triggered updates.

Split Horizon

Split horizon is based on a simple premise: The router does not advertise a route over the same interface from which it was learned.

NOTE   If you are operating a Frame Relay internetwork with multiple subinterfaces, be sure to disable split horizon on the interface if it is desired for the remote sites to see each other across the network. Use the **no ip split-horizon** command in the Cisco IOS, as follows:

```
Router(config)#no ip split-horizon
```

However, just implementing split horizon has a drawback. Each router must wait for the destination to be marked as unreachable after a route has timed out and been flushed from the table. This process takes six update messages 30 seconds each, totaling upwards of 3 minutes before each routing table is updated with the inactive link. During this time, five update intervals can pass where each router can misinform another as to the reachability of certain destinations. Split horizon with poison reverse addresses and solves this problem.

RIP Split Horizon with Poison Reverse

Whereas split horizon is designed to prevent routing loops in an internetwork, split horizon with poison reverse makes this a bit more effective in that six update cycles do not have to pass to stop a routing loop (see "Count to Infinity" and "Split Horizon"). Split horizon with poison reverse takes a more proactive stance in managing and updating the routing tables. Upon detection of an inactive link, RIP with poison reverse sets the metric for that destination to infinity for the next routing update.

NOTE	The specification of poison reverse states that reverse routes are always advertised at a cost of 16. The negative here is the increased routing table size. However, the RFC also states: "It is also permissible to implement hybrid schemes that advertise some reverse routes with a metric of 16 and omit others. An example of such a scheme would be to use a metric of 16 for reverse routes for a certain period of time after routing changes involving them, and thereafter omitting them from updates." Cisco uses this approach in its IGRP implementation.

Although split horizon with poison reverse is the preference over [standalone] split horizon, larger internetworks with multiple paths are still a concern because RIP is still subject to the counting to infinity problem of routing updates. Triggered updates were introduced to solve the problem of routing loops caused by the "counting to infinity" operations.

RIP Triggered Updates

Triggered updates are used to speed up convergence of a RIP-routed network. Triggered updates are rules in the routing protocol that require routers to immediately broadcast an update message whenever the route metric changes, without waiting for the next 30-second regular update interval to pass.

Triggered updates are designed to overcome the time issues that are still involved when dealing with split horizon or split horizon with poison reverse.

RIP Hold-Down Timers

Although triggered updates are a significant improvement over split horizon and poison reverse, time is still an issue. The question is whether each router in the internetwork receives and updates its tables in a reasonable amount of time (an interval that passes before traffic is to be transmitted).

Hold-down timers solve this potential problem by working in conjunction with triggered updates. Essentially, when a triggered update has been sent, a clock starts counting down (to zero). Until this hold-down timer hits zero, the router does not accept neighbor updates for the route in question.

The use of a hold-down timer prevents a RIP router from accepting and converging on updates for a route that has been invalidated over a period of time. Hold-down timers prevent a router from believing that another router might have a path to an invalid destination.

RIP Concerns

Although RIP has been a mainstay of internetwork routing for quite a long time, it still has some concerns and limitations that need to be addressed. These concerns and limitations are as follows:

- Inability to support paths with more than 15 hops
- (Static) Fixed metrics for route calculation
- Network bandwidth consumption for routing table updates
- Slow convergence
- No dynamic load balancing support

RIP Hop Count Limit

RIP was designed for use in supporting networks of relatively small diameter, enforcing a strict hop count of 15 hops maximum, with 16 hops being marked as unreachable.

NOTE The network diameter is categorized as the longest path, measured in hops, between two end nodes.

As data packets are forwarded across a RIP router, their hop counters are incremented by the cost of the link over which they traverse. One is the default. If the data packet's hop counter hits 15 and the packet is not at its intended destination, it is dropped and the destination is considered unreachable because the next hop would be 16.

RIP Fixed Metrics

RIP cannot update its cost metrics in a real-time environment to adapt to changes in the network topology. RIP metrics can only be changed manually and are static for the duration. It is because of these fixed, static metrics that RIP is not ideal in supporting real-time applications.

RIP Network Bandwidth Consumption for Routing Table Updates

RIP routers broadcast their entire routing table, with the exception of split-horizon routes, out every RIP-enabled interface every 30 seconds, rather than sending an update of the affected route. In large internetworks, this can consume a fair amount of network bandwidth that would otherwise be used to carry data traffic.

RIP Slow Convergence

RIP routing updates are sent every 30 seconds. This is near eternity in "network time" because several things could happen during this 30-second timeframe, such as data traffic being transmitted, or another change in the network topology. Additionally, a single RIP router takes up to 180 seconds (3 minutes) to invalidate a route. As the network topology grows, this convergence time also grows to a near unmanageable state.

This convergence time inadequately supports real-time networked applications.

RIP's Lack of Dynamic Load Balancing

RIP does not have the capability to dynamically load-balance across two or more links. If RIP learns of a 56 kilobits per second (kbps) path to a destination first, and learns of a T1 megabits per second (Mbps) path to the same destination in a later update, RIP continues to use the 56 kbps path because that was the first one learned. A RIP router only uses the T1 path if the 56 Kbps path is marked as *unreachable* (due to a link failure or the like).

NOTE   Cisco IOS supports dynamic load balancing across a default of four equal-cost paths, with a maximum setting of six equal-cost paths.

RIP Routing Protocol Summary

RIP was designed for use with small networks, with both static configurations and stable links. Because of issues with no dynamic load balancing, slow convergence, bandwidth consumption by routing updates, fixed cost metrics, and hop count limit, RIP is not well suited to large internetworks, or to internetworks that support real-time networked applications.

RIP Version 2 (RIPv2)

RIPv2 was created in January 1993 and is backward compatible with RIPv1, with some feature-based exceptions that are detailed after the following list.

RIPv2 can trace its lineage by the following RFCs:

- January 1993 / 1388 RIP Version 2 Carrying Additional Information. G. Malkin. January 1993. Format: TXT=16227 bytes. Obsoleted by RFC 1723. Updates RFC 1058. Status: Proposed Standard.

- November 1994 / 1723 RIP Version 2—Carrying Additional Information. G. Malkin. November 1994. Format: TXT=18597 bytes. Obsoletes RFC1388. Obsoleted by RFC 2453. Updates RFC 1058. Also STD0056) Status: Standard.

- November 1998 / 2453 RIP Version 2. G. Malkin. November 1998. Format: TXT=98462 bytes. Obsoletes RFC 1723. Also STD0056. Status: Standard.

RIPv2 added four features to those found with RIP:

- RIPv2 authentication
- Subnet mask support (CIDR)
- Next hop IP addresses
- RIPv2 message multicasting

RIPv2 Authentication

RIPv2 authentication is used to authenticate routing response messages that are propagated throughout the network. Authentication of these routing response messages prevents the routing tables from being corrupted by routes from fraudulent sources.

Authentication is achieved with a 16-octet maximum password with no encryption. Consequently, RIPv2 authentication messages are susceptible to attack by anyone with direct access to the network.

RIPv2 Subnet Mask Support

RIPv2 added a 4-octet field behind the packet's IP address to carry the subnet mask of a destination IP address. The implementation of subnet mask support enables RIPv2 to route to a specific subnet, whether fixed or variable length.

RIPv2 Next Hop Identification

The inclusion of a next hop identification field helps make RIPv2 more efficient than RIP. The next hop identification prevents unnecessary hops between endpoints in a network. In a RIPv2 only network, the identification of the next hop does not add significant value. However, when RIPv2 is implemented with other (dissimilar) routing protocols, without the next hop identification, it is possible that some routes would never be discovered.

RIPv2 Multicasting

RIPv2 multicasting enables the simultaneous delivery of routing table updates to multiple neighbors rather than repeatedly unicasting the routing update to each neighbor on an individual basis. RIPv2 multicasting can also implement filters to prevent RIPv2 routing updates from being received by RIPv1 routers.

RIPv2 Concerns

Although RIPv2 provides significant improvements over its predecessor, RIPv1, some concerns regarding operation remain:

- Maximum hop count (15)
- Count to infinity
- (Static) Fixed metrics for route calculation
- Lack of alternative routing support

RIPv2 Maximum Hop Count (15)

RIPv2 inherited the maximum hop count limit of 15 from RIPv1. This inheritance was preserved so that RIPv2 could maintain its backward compatibility with RIPv1.

RIPv2 Count to Infinity

RIPv2, like its predecessor RIPv1, relies on the count to infinity mechanism to resolve certain network error conditions. Counting to infinity becomes problematic because routing loops are permitted for potentially lengthy periods of time before the "loop" is detected by the hop count and the route is marked as unreachable.

RIPv2 (Static) Fixed Metrics for Route Calculation

RIPv2, like RIPv1, selects routes based on a fixed cost metric—hop count. The network administrator can manually adjust this cost metric, but the metric remains static until it is manually changed again.

RIPv2 Lack of Alternative Routing Support

RIPv2, like RIPv1, maintains only a single route to a specific destination in its routing tables, providing no support for dynamic load balancing. If the "known" route fails, RIPv2 must wait for another routing update to determine the next optimal path to a destination.

NOTE   Cisco IOS supports dynamic load balancing across a default of 4 equal-cost paths, with a maximum setting of 6 equal-cost paths.

RIPv2 Summary

RIPv2 is a more modern, updated version of RIP. RIPv2 was designed as an update to RIP that enables its legacy base of internetworking devices a smooth transition to RIPv2, with its added networking features.

IGRP

Cisco System's developed IGRP in the early 1980s as an answer to the limitations of RIPv1, while preserving its ease of implementation.

IGRP Metrics

IGRP is a distance-vector routing protocol designed for use within autonomous systems. IGRP, like other distance-vector routing protocols (such as RIP and RIPv2), forwards its entire routing table, with the exception of split-horizon routes, on a regular basis. IGRP, unlike most other distance-vector protocols, uses a series of metrics rather than a single hop-count metric. These metrics are as follows:

- Hop count
- Packet size (MTU)
- Link bandwidth
- Delay

- Load
- Reliability

IGRP supports multipath routing, load balancing across two, three or four links, with automatic link recovery from a failed link.

NOTE   IGRP supports unequal-cost paths for load balancing. As with RIP, the default is 4, with a maximum of 6 and the default variance of 1, which is equal-cost paths.

Like RIP, IGRP is a classful routing protocol, with no support for variable-length subnet mask (VLSM) or CIDR.

IGRP Hop Count

IGRP supports incrementing hop count as one method of determining the distance to a specific destination. Unlike RIP, which has a maximum hop count of 16, IGRP has a default maximum hop count of 100, which can be further increased to 255.

IGRP does not use the hop counter as a metric to determine optimal paths to a destination, but rather as a means to detect routing loops in the network. Any route with a hop count in excess of the stated, or configured, maximum is automatically invalidated.

IGRP Packet Size (MTU)

The MTU identifies the largest-sized datagram that an IGRP router accepts for transmission. IGRP neither uses the MTU to calculate a route nor as a factor in its metrics. IGRP routers exchange MTU information with each other identifying the maximum datagram size they can support. Datagrams larger than the MTU size are broken down into manageable "pieces" by the router.

NOTE   Large MTU sizes can result in what is called a *performance penalty*. Routers buffer these incoming datagrams for transmission until it can be determined where they are to be forwarded. The performance penalty lies in the delay to determine the next hop and the amount of router buffer (memory) space that is consumed waiting for the entire datagram to be received for transmission.

IGRP Link Bandwidth

By default, IGRP uses the link bandwidth as one of the metrics to calculate the total cost of a network path. The default bandwidth statement is 1.544 Mbps (T1), but can range from 1,200 bits per second (bps) to 10 gibabits per second (Gbps).

IGRP looks at the defined bandwidth on each outbound interface router port for a given route and selects the smallest bandwidth statement, which is the bandwidth limit for that route. To determine the bandwidth, measurable in kilobits per second (kbps), the bandwidth number is divided by 10^7 (100,000,000).

IGRP Delay

Also used by default, the delay metric measures the approximate amount of time needed to traverse a network link, based on no other link usage at the time. The aggregated delay metric of a route is the sum of all delays attributed to each outbound router interface in the path. To express the delay result in microseconds, the delay sum is divided by 10. The metric value for delay ranges from 1 to 16,777,215 ($2^{24} - 1$).

IGRP Load

The IGRP load metric measures the amount of bandwidth currently available across a given link. The heavier the link utilization, the more time required for data traffic to traverse that link. This metric enables IGRP to factor current link utilization levels into the network's optimal route calculation.

This metric can be configured manually to any value between 1 and 255, although it is not recommended to do so.

IGRP Reliability

The reliability metric keeps track of the current error rate per transmission facility. The error rate is a ratio of packets received by a destination without error.

This metric is between the range of 1 and 255; the higher the metric value, the more reliable the link. For example, 255/255 represents complete (100 percent) reliability, and 0/255 represents 0 percent reliability.

Metric Calculation

IGRP calculates and uses a composite metric of the previous values (bandwidth and delay, by default) to calculate the route optimization. The metric value ranges from 1 to 16,277,215 ($2^{24} - 1$), and for purposes of route calculation, the lower the number (closer to zero), the better the route.

This composite metric reflects the various weights of each of the previously listed metrics. The general formula for this composite metric is as follows:

$$\text{Metric} = (K1 \times \text{Bandwidth}) + (K2 \times \text{Bandwidth})/(256 - \text{Load}) + (K3 \times \text{Delay})$$

K1, K2, and K3 are constants used to weigh the effect of these routing metrics. The default values for K1 and K3 is 1, and the default for K2 is 0.

Two other constant values exist: K4 and K5. They both default to 0 and are not used if they are left at the default value. The network administrator can change these values because they are not changed dynamically by IGRP operation.

The mathematical simplification of the composite metric, provided all values remain at their defaults, is as follows:

$$\text{Metric} = \text{Bandwidth} + \text{Delay}$$

The reliability metric, K5, is a constant and is used only if the reliability metric is greater than the default of 0. The composite operation used to determine the metric for K5 (Reliability) > 0 is as follows:

$$\text{Metric} = \text{Metric} \times [K5/(\text{Reliability} + K4)]$$

Delay is in units of 10 microseconds. This gives a range of 10 microseconds to 168 seconds.

Bandwidth is inverse minimum bandwidth of the path in bits per second scaled by a factor of 10e10. The range is from a 1,200 bps line to 10 Gbps.

Table 24-6 outlines the default values used for the following media types.

Table 24-6   *(E)IGRP Default Delay Values*

	Delay	**Bandwidth**
Satellite	200,000 (2 seconds)	20 (500 Mb)
Ethernet	100 (1 ms)	1,000
1.544 Mb	2000 (20 ms)	6,476
64 Kb	2000 (20 ms)	156,250
56 Kb	2000 (20 ms)	178,571
10 Kb	2000 (20 ms)	1,000,000
1 Kb	2000 (20 ms)	10,000,000

IGRP Timers

The default IGRP timer intervals are as follows:

- Update timer—90 seconds. This is how often the router is to initiate routing table updates.

- Hold timer—280 seconds (3 × update timer + 10 seconds). This is the amount of time that the IGRP routing table holds down routing updates.
- Route invalid timer—270 seconds (3 × update timer). This is the amount of time that a router waits, in the absence of routing update messages about a specific route, before declaring the route invalid.
- Route-flush timer—630 seconds (7 × update timer). This is the amount of time before a route is flushed from the routing table.

IGRP Convergence Mechanisms

IGRP uses similar convergence mechanisms to that of RIP. The convergence mechanisms used by IGRP include the following:

- Triggered, or flash, update
- Hold-downs
- Split horizon
- Poison reverse update

IGRP Flash Update

Rather than wait for the update timer to elapse before sending a routing update, IGRP uses flash updates to send a routing change immediately to its routing neighbors. This mechanism results in significantly reduced convergence time compared to other distance-vector routing protocols, such as RIP or RIPv2.

IGRP Hold-Downs

Although IGRP flash-updates are a significant improvement over "traditional" routing table updates (timer-based versus event-based updates), the issue of time remains. Does each router in the internetwork receive changes and update its tables in a reasonable amount of time (the time interval that passes before traffic is to be transmitted).

Hold-down timers solve this potential problem by working in conjunction with triggered updates. Essentially, when a triggered update has been sent, a clock starts counting down to zero. Until this hold-down timer hits zero, the router does not accept neighbor updates for the route in question unless it is a better route, advertising an administrative distance lower (closer to 0) than the route in hold-down.

The use of a hold-down timer prevents an IGRP router from accepting and converging on updates for a route that has been invalidated over a period of time. Hold-down timers prevent a router from believing that another router might have a path to an invalid destination.

IGRP Split Horizon

Like RIP, the IGRP split horizon is based on a simple premise: The router does not advertise a route over the same interface from which it was learned.

NOTE   If you are operating a Frame Relay internetwork with multiple subinterfaces, be sure to disable split horizon on the interface if it is desired for the remote sites to see each other across the network. Use the **no ip split-horizon** command in the Cisco IOS, as follows:

```
Router(config)#no ip split-horizon
```

However, just implementing split horizon has a drawback: each router must wait for the destination to be marked as unreachable. After a route has timed out and been flushed from the table, each routing table is updated with the inactive link. This flushing process takes six update messages 90 seconds each (flushed on the 7th update interval), totaling upwards of 9 minutes. During this time, five update intervals can pass, where each router can misinform another as to the reachability of certain destinations. IGRP uses hold-down timers, in conjunction with split horizon, to prevent routing instability caused by the misinformation traded between neighboring routers.

IGRP Poison Reverse

IGRP uses poison reverse updates to invalidate a route that is learned from a neighbor if that router believes the route to be looping. When an IGRP node receives a routing table update from a neighbor, it then compares the learned information with the routing table information currently in memory. If the learned, or updated, information includes a routing metric whose value has increased 10 percent or more since the last routing update, that route is assumed to be invalid. This assumption is based on the generalization that increases in routing metrics are caused by routing loops.

IGRP Load Balancing

IGRP has the capability to perform multipath routing—up to four different routes to a given destination. This multipath routing enables IGRP to perform load balancing of both an equal-cost and unequal-cost nature.

NOTE   Cisco IOS supports dynamic load balancing across a default of four equal-cost paths, with a maximum setting of six equal-cost paths.

IGRP Equal-Cost Load Balancing

Equal-cost load balancing is the balancing of traffic across redundant, or multiple, links of equal cost. Equal-cost load balancing can be achieved on a per-packet or a per-destination basis.

Per-packet load balancing means that sequential packets in a data stream, bound for the same destination, can be transmitted out different interfaces. The drawback to this type of operation is that data packets might be received late, or out of sequence, causing possible application performance issues.

Per-destination load balancing means that packets in a data stream bound for the same destination are forwarded via the same route, alleviating the potential for issues caused by per-packet load balancing. However, per-destination load balancing can result in a less than ideal equal-cost traffic distribution.

IGRP makes the determination regarding which of these approaches to use based on its ability to perform route caching, a technique used to keep a route cached in memory. Route caching is per-destination–based load balancing and can be memory intensive. If route caching is disabled, per-packet load balancing is automatically performed.

IGRP Unequal-Cost Load Balancing

Unequal-cost load balancing sends traffic across up to four paths of unequal cost, with the lowest cost link being the primary path. Paths with higher cost are used as alternatives, providing redundant link connectivity to a single, or multiple, destination(s).

NOTE   Cisco IOS supports dynamic load balancing across a default of four equal-cost paths, with a maximum setting of six equal-cost paths.

IGRP Feasibility and Feasible Successors

IGRP feasibility means that each network path conforms to three basic principles:

- Alternative path metrics must be within the specified variance range of the local best metric.

- The best local metric must be greater than the metric for the same destination that is learned from the next router. Simply stated, the next hop must be closer to the destination than the current router.

- The variance value, multiplied against the best local metric for a destination, must be greater than or equal to the cost metric for that destination on the next router.

- IGRP can be used to establish a hierarchy of feasible successors in a multipath routing environment. Feasible successors are routes whose costs are greater than the specified variance from the optimal route to a given destination. As such, the successors are not feasible for unequal-cost load balancing, but are feasible routes in the event that the primary route becomes unavailable.

IGRP Summary

Interior Gateway Routing Protocol (IGRP) is a proprietary routing protocol developed by Cisco Systems, Inc. in the early 1990s and was built with functional similarity to RIP, but with the additional features of weighted metrics.

Cisco Systems developed an enhancement to IGRP, aptly named the Enhanced Interior Gateway Routing Protocol (EIGRP).

The composite IGRP metric is computed according to the following formula:

Metric = (K1 × Bandwidth) + (K2 × Bandwidth)/(256 − Load) + (K3 × Delay) × [K5/(Reliability + K4)]

If K5 = 0, then there is no reliability term.

The default K Values are as follows:

K1 = 1

K2 = 0

K3 = 1

K4 = 0

K5 = 0

EIGRP

Cisco Systems, Inc. developed EIGRP, and like its predecessor IGRP, EIGRP is Cisco proprietary. EIGRP is considered a hybrid routing protocol. Although it shares the distance-vector mechanisms found in IGRP, it differs greatly in the mechanics of operation. EIGRP introduces several features:

- Neighbor discovery and recovery
- Reliable transport protocol
- DUAL finite-state machine
- Protocol-specific modules

EIGRP also introduces a new route determination and update algorithm, the Diffusing Update Algorithm (DUAL). DUAL enables EIGRP routers to determine whether a path advertised by a neighbor is looped or loop free and allows an EIGRP router to find alternative routes to destinations without waiting for routing updates from neighboring routers.

EIGRP, unlike IGRP, supports both VLSM and CIDR.

EIGRP was designed to be completely compatible with IGRP. EIGRP uses the same composite metrics as IGRP, as well as the same distance vectors and their respective mathematical weights. EIGRP and IGRP metrics are directly comparable and can be used interchangeably after translation.

NOTE   The only difference between the IGRP and EIGRP algorithms is in the calculation of the composite metric. IGRP is 20 bits long and EIGRP is 32 bits long, resulting in the EIGRP metric being 256 times larger than a comparable IGRP metric. The larger EIGRP metric enables a better and finer mathematical comparison of potential routes.

EIGRP Features

EIGRP implements the following features, improving its operating efficiencies across the internetwork:

- Neighbor discovery and recovery
- Reliable transport protocol
- DUAL finite-state machine
- Protocol-specific modules

Neighbor Discovery and Recovery

EIGRP does not rely exclusively on the use of timers for routing table maintenance; rather EIGRP uses periodic communication to perform the following:

- Dynamically learn of new routers that can join the network.
- Identify routers that become either unreachable or inoperable.
- Rediscover routers that had previously been unreachable.

The initial exchange of routing tables is accomplished with the EIGRP *hello* packet between neighbors.

Reliable Transport Protocol

EIGRP can provide guaranteed and reliable delivery of its various packets, whereas other routing protocols rely on other mechanisms, such as time, to determine if a packet needs to be retransmitted. EIGRP uses the Reliable Transport Protocol (RTP) to provide reliable delivery of its own packets.

RTP is a transport layer (OSI Layer 4) protocol that correlates to the functions found in TCP and UDP; however, RTP is not an open protocol standard.

RTP is used to transport all EIGRP messages through an internetwork and supports both unicasting and multicasting, even simultaneously for different peers.

DUAL Finite-State Machine

The DUAL finite-state machine engine contains all the logic used to calculate and compare EIGRP routes in an internetwork. DUAL tracks all routes advertised by neighbors and uses the composite metric of each route to compare them. Selected route paths must be both loop free and have the lowest cost. The DUAL engine then inserts these route paths into the routing table.

Routes selected for routing table insertion are also evaluated by the feasible successor process, as described for use by IGRP. Feasible successors are routes to a destination where the neighbor router is the next hop in a least cost path.

Protocol-Specific Modules

EIGRP was developed to be completely independent from routed protocols, such as IP, IPX, and AppleTalk. As such, EIGRP has implemented a modular approach to supporting these routed protocols.

The modular support of EIGRP provides for the following:

- AppleTalk (AT-EIGRP)—EIGRP can redistribute routes learned from Routing Table Maintenance Protocol (RTMP).
- Novell IPX (IPX-EIGRP)—EIGRP can redistribute routes learned from the proprietary RIP as well as Service Advertising Protocol (SAP) and Novell or NLSP.
- IP (IP-EIGRP)—EIGRP can redistribute routes learned from OSPF, RIP, IS-IS, EGP, and BGP.

EIGRP Tables

EIGRP stores routing-related information in three tables, each one dedicated to the organization and storage of network data. These tables are as follows:

- Neighbor table—Neighbor relationships are tracked in this table and are the basis for all of the EIGRP routing update and convergence activities.

- Routing table—Contains least-cost routes that DUAL calculated for all known destinations. EIGRP tracks up to six routes to each destination.

- Topology table—Stores all information needed to calculate a set of distances and vectors to all known and reachable destinations. This information includes the following:

  - Bandwidth—The bandwidth of the slowest interface in the path to a destination.

  - Total delay—The sum total of delay expected in that route.

  - Reliability—The path reliability identical to the IGRP Reliability metric.

  - Load—The load of the path

  - MTU—The size of the smallest MTU supported by the router interfaces in the path. EIGRP notifies all routers in advance of the MTU on each path to a given destination.

  - Reported distance—The distance reported by an adjacent neighbor to a specific destination. This metric does not include the distance between this router and the adjacent neighbor.

  - Feasible distance—The lowest calculated metric to each destination.

  - Route source—The identification number of the router that originally advertised that route. This field is only populated for routes learned from outside the EIGRP network.

NOTE   The Cisco IOS command **show ip eigrp topology all** can be used to view the entire contents of the EIGRP topology table.

Topology table entries are in one of two states:

- Active—This is a route that is currently being recomputed (the process of recalculating routes in search of new successors). This recalculating process is time and resource intensive. DUAL is designed to use any and all available feasible successors before recomputing routes. Recomputing occurs only when no successors, feasible or otherwise, are available to a route.

- Passive—This is a route currently stable and available for use.

CAUTION   If, upon executing the **show ip eigrp topology all** command, several routes continue to appear to be in ACTIVE states, this in an indication of an unstable network and should be investigated immediately.

EIGRP Packet Types

EIGRP uses five specialized packets for routing table maintenance:

- Hello—Used to rediscover and track other network EIGRP routers. Neighbor rediscovery sometimes occurs during the convergence process.

  — The [fixed] hello interval is 60 seconds for serial interfaces less than T1. For multipoint, such as Frame Relay, ATM, or X.25, these can be configured.

  — Serial interfaces with links over T1 or greater have a hello interval of 5 seconds.

  — The hold-timer is defaulted to three times the hello interval, either 15 or 180 seconds, depending on the interface.

- Acknowledgement—Used to acknowledge receipt of any EIGRP packet that requires reliable delivery.

- Update—Used to convey routing information to known destinations. Update packets are used to either provide a complete topological data dump to a new EIGRP router or to provide an update to a topological change in the network, such as a downed link or change in link cost.

- Query—Used whenever a router needs specific information from one or all of its neighbors. Queries are sent only when a destination becomes active. When the network is stable, all routes in the topology table are marked as PASSIVE, making it unnecessary (and a waste of bandwidth) to send EIGRP query packets.

- Reply—Sent in reply to EIGRP query packets.

NOTE   EIGRP can consume up to 50 percent of a link's bandwidth during the Hello interval. Use the **ip bandwidth-percent eigrp** interface configuration command to properly configure the bandwidth statement on each WAN interface.

EIGRP Convergence

EIGRP convergence occurs rapidly in an internetwork, due in no small part to EIGRP supporting up to six parallel paths to all destinations in the network.

EIGRP convergence time is low, based on both the Reliable Transport Protocol and EIGRP update packets. Rapid convergence is based on the feasible successors, which are determined by the DUAL engine.

The DUAL finite-state machine uses distance information to select efficient, loop-free paths and selects routes for insertion into a routing table based on feasible successors. The *feasible successor* is a neighboring router used for packet forwarding that is a least-cost path to a destination that is guaranteed not to be part of a routing loop. When a neighbor changes a metric, or when a topology change occurs, DUAL tests for feasible successors. If one is found, DUAL uses it to avoid recomputing the route unnecessarily. When no feasible successors exist but neighbors still advertise the destination, a recomputation (also known as a *diffusing computation*) must occur to determine a new successor. Although recomputation is not processor intensive, it does affect convergence time; therefore, it is advantageous to avoid unnecessary recomputations.

Due to the combination of the DUAL finite-state machine and the EIGRP topology table packets, EIGRP convergence can occur within a few seconds, making it the premier choice for [Cisco only] internetworks.

EIGRP Summary

EIGRP is Cisco Systems, Inc. proprietary and is one of the most feature-rich and vigorous routing protocols developed and used today. EIGRP is considered to be a hybrid by some because it combines the best features and attributes of both distance-vector and link-state protocols.

EIGRP is easy to configure, enabling efficient operation in the support of IP(v4), AppleTalk, and Internetwork Packet Exchange (IPX) routed protocol traffic.

NOTE   As of this writing, Cisco plans to implement EIGRP IPv6 support in CY 2002.

OSPF

OSPF is an open version of the link-state or SPF class of routing protocols. OSPF was designed for use in large, heterogeneous IP networks. OSPF, like all SPF routing protocols, is based on the Dijkstra algorithm. The Dijkstra algorithm enables route selection based on link-state versus distance vectors.

NOTE   OSPF is based on the mathematical concept known as Graph Theory.

OSPF has endured several updates, as the following timeline demonstrates:

- October 1989 / 1131 OSPF specification. J. Moy. Oct-01-1989. Format: TXT=268, PS=857280, PDF=398863 bytes. Obsoleted by RFC 1247. Status: Proposed Standard.

- July 1991 / 1247 OSPF Version 2. J. Moy. Jul-01-1991. Format: TXT=433332, PS=989724, PDF=490300 bytes. Obsoletes RFC 1131. Obsoleted by RFC 1583. Also RFC 1246, RFC 1245. Status: Draft Standard.

- March 1994 / 1583 OSPF Version 2. J. Moy. March 1994. Format: TXT=532636, PS=990794, PDF=465711 bytes. Obsoletes RFC 1247. Obsoleted by RFC 2178. Status: Draft Standard.

- July 1997 / 2178 OSPF Version 2. J. Moy. July 1997. Format: TXT=495866 bytes. Obsoletes RFC 1583. Obsoleted by RFC 2328. Status: Draft Standard.

- April 1998 / 2328 OSPF Version 2. J. Moy. April 1998. Format: TXT=447367 bytes. Obsoletes RFC 2178. Also STD0054. Status: Standard.

OSPF, and later OSPFv2, calculates routes based on the destination IP address found in IP datagram headers, with no provisions made for route calculation to non-IP destinations. OSPF was designed to quickly detect and adapt to changes in the network topology within an autonomous system. OSPF routing decisions are based on the state of the router interconnecting links within the autonomous system. Each OSPF router maintains a database of network link states, including information regarding its usable interfaces, known-reachable neighbors, and link-state information.

Routing table updates, known as LSAs, are transmitted, or flooded, to all other neighbors within a router's area. *Areas* are defined as a logical set of network segments and their attached devices. Areas are usually connected to other areas via routers, making up a single autonomous system.

OSPF was introduced to overcome some of the limitations found with RIP and RIPv2, such as the following:

- RIP and RIPv2 both have a limit of 15 hops. A RIP network that spans more than 15 hops (15 routers) is considered unreachable.

- RIP cannot handle VLSM; however, RIPv2 can. Given the shortage of IP addresses and the flexibility that VLSM gives in the efficient assignment of IP addresses, this is considered a major flaw.

- Periodic broadcasts of the full routing table, without common network and split horizon route statements, consume a large amount of bandwidth. This is a major issue with large networks, especially on slow links and WAN clouds.

- RIP and RIPv2 both converge more slowly than OSPF. In large networks, convergence can be on the order of minutes. RIP routers go through a period of a hold-down and slowly timing-out information that has not been received recently. This is inappropriate in large environments and could cause routing inconsistencies.

- RIP and RIPv2 both have no concept of network delays and link costs. Routing decisions are based on hop counts. The path with the lowest hop count to the destination is always preferred even if the longer path has a better aggregate link bandwidth and lower delays.

- RIP and RIPv2 networks are flat networks without areas or boundaries. With the introduction of classless routing and the use of network aggregation and summarization, RIP networks struggle to provide a coherent networking infrastructure.

  Although RIPv2 supports address summarization with the use of VLSM, the concept of areas is not supported.

Link-state protocols, such as OSPF, provide several networking features that enable a more robust and flexible internetworking environment. These OSPF-enabled features are as follows:

- No hop-count limitation exists.

- VLSM support is useful in IP address allocation.

- OSPF uses IP multicast to send link-state updates. This ensures less processing on routers that are not listening for OSPF packets.

- OSPF updates are "event triggered." This means they are sent only in the case of routing changes occurring within the network instead of periodically.

- OSPF allows for better load balancing.

- OSPF allows for a logical definition of networks in a hierarchical network structure where routers can be divided into areas. This limits the explosion of link-state updates over the entire network. This also provides a mechanism for aggregating routes and cutting down on the unnecessary propagation of subnet information.

- OSPF allows for the transfer and tagging of external routes injected into an autonomous system (AS). This keeps track of external routes that are injected by exterior protocols, such as BGP.

OSPF uses a link-state algorithm to build and calculate the shortest path to all known destinations. The algorithm alone is quite complicated. The following is a high-level, simplified way of looking at the various steps of the algorithm:

- Upon initialization or due to any change in routing information, a router will generate an LSA. This advertisement will represent the collection of all link-states on that router.

- All routers will exchange link states by means of flooding. Each router that receives a link-state update should store a copy in its link-state database and then propagate the update to other routers.

- After the database of each router is completed, the router will calculate a Shortest Path Tree to all destinations. The router uses the Dijkstra algorithm to calculate the shortest path tree. The destinations, the associated cost, and the next hop to reach those destinations form the IP routing table.

- If no changes in the OSPF network occur, such as cost of a link or a network being added or deleted, OSPF should be quiet. Any changes that occur are communicated via link-state packets, and the Dijkstra algorithm is recalculated to find the shortest path.

OSPF Areas

OSPF's rapid convergence is due to its use of areas. OSPF area numbers are 32 bits in length. Area IDs range from 1 to 4,294,967,295 (the theoretical maximum number of OSPF supported areas).

OSPF Area Router Types

Based on area membership, three types of routers exist within an OSPF network (see Figure 24-4):

- Internal routers—All router interfaces are defined in the same area, but not Area 0 (Backbone Area).
- Area border routers—These interconnect the backbone and its area members.
- Backbone routers—At least one defined interface belongs to Area 0 (Backbone Area).

Figure 24-4 *OSPF Areas*

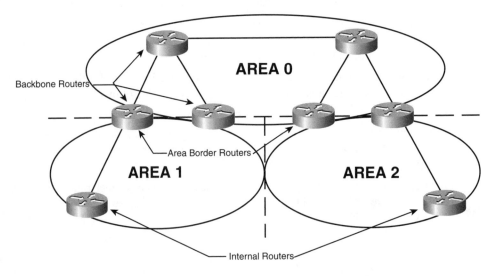

OSPF Routing Types

OSPF supports two different types of routing:

- Inter-area—Exchanges data between different areas. All inter-area routing must traverse through Area 0. Nonzero OSPF areas are not permitted to communicate directly with each other.

- Intra-area—Routing is self-contained and is limited to the routers internal to a single area.

OSPF Area Types

The area types, listed next, determine what LSAs the area receives. Following are the different area types:

- Stub area—Does not accept external LSAs. LSA Type 5s are rejected. Can accept route summaries.

- Totally stubby areas—Do not accept LSAs with external or summaries.

- Internal routers—Exchange LSAs 1 and 2. They share the same routing database and all interfaces are within the same area.

- Backbone routers (BBR)—Exchange LSAs 1 and 2. Share at least on interface in Area 0.

- Area border router (ABR)—Shares an interface with another OSPF area. This router keeps a database for each area.

- Autonomous system boundary router (ASBR)—Has at least one interface in a non-OSPF network; uses LSA 5s to distribute this routing information into the OSPF network.

OSPF Packets

OSPF uses five different packet types, each designed to support a different specific network function. The packet types include the following:

- Hello packets (Type 1)—Used to establish and maintain relationships, or adjacencies, between neighboring nodes.

- Database description packets (Type 2)—Exchanged between two OSPF routers as they initialize an adjacency. They are used to describe the content of an OSPF router's link-state database. (An adjacency is best defined as the relationship formed between selected neighboring routers and end nodes for the purpose of exchanging routing information. Adjacencies are based on the use of a common media segment.)

- Link-state request packets (Type 3)—Used to request specific pieces of a neighboring router's link-state database.

- Link-state update packets (Type 4)—Used to transport LSAs to neighboring nodes. Eleven types of LSAs exist:

  — LSA1—Router Links LSA. Sends information about the routers links.

  — LSA2—Network Link LSA. Sent by the designated router (DR) to all routers in the AS containing a list of routers in the segment.

  — LSA3—Summary Link LSA. Sent by ABRs that contain a list of networks available outside the area.

  — LSA4—Summary Link LSA. Sent by autonomous system boundary routers (ASBRs) that contain a list of networks available outside the area.

  — LSA5—External Link LSA. Sent by ASBRs containing a list of external network routes.

  — LSA6—Group Membership LSA. Part of Multicast OSPF (MOSPF), which routes multicast packets. As of this writing, Cisco does not support MOSPF, but it does support Protocol Independent Multicast (PIM).

  — LSA7—Not-so-stubby area (NSSA) External LSA. Originated by ASBRs in NSSAs. LSA7s operate in the same fashion as LSA5s, with the exception that LSA7s are limited to NSSAs.

  — LSA8—External Attributes LSA

  — LSA9—Opaque LSA (link-local scope)

  — LSA10—Opaque LSA (area-local scope)

  — LSA11—Opaque LSA (AS scope)

  LSA types 8, 9, 10, and 11 have been proposed, but are not currently implemented.

- Link-state acknowledgement packets (Type 5)—OSPF features a reliable distribution of LSA packets. This reliable distribution means that packet receipt must be acknowledged otherwise source nodes would have no mechanism to determine actual receipt of the LSA.

OSPF Convergence

Regardless of which two methods of route calculation that OSPF uses, the cost of any given route path is the sum of the costs of all interfaces encountered along the path.

OSPF calculates route costs in one of two ways:

- A non-bandwidth–sensitive default value can be used for each OSPF interface.

- OSPF can automatically calculate the cost of using individual router interfaces.

At a minimum, OSPF uses bandwidth to calculate the cost of a route, using the formula (10^8/Bandwidth). Table 24-7 demonstrates some of these default calculated costs.

Table 24-7   *OSPF Link Costs*

Interface	OSPF Cost
100 Mbps FDDI/Ethernet	1
45 Mbps T3	2
10 Mbps Ethernet	10
1.544 Mbps T1	~64 (64.7)
56 kbps	1,768

OSPF convergence is based on the adjacency mechanism.

OSPF Adjacencies

Adjacency is the next step after the OSPF neighboring process. Adjacent routers are routers that go beyond the simple Hello protocol exchange and proceed into the database exchange process. To minimize the amount of information exchange on a particular segment, OSPF elects one router to be a DR, and one router to be a backup designated router (BDR), on each multiaccess segment. The BDR is elected as a backup mechanism in case the DR goes down. The idea behind this is that routers have a central point of contact for information exchange. Instead of each router exchanging updates with every other router on the segment, every router exchanges information with the DR and BDR. The DR and BDR relay the information to everybody else.

NOTE   OSPF uses LSAs to become adjacent with each other.

OSPF routers become adjacent when each router has the same link-state database. Following is a brief summary of the states an interface passes through before the router becomes adjacent to another router on that interface:

- Down: No information has been received from anyone on the segment.

- Attempt: On non-broadcast multiaccess clouds such as Frame Relay, this state indicates that no recent information has been received from the neighbor. An effort should be made to contact the neighbor by sending Hello packets at the reduced rate poll interval.

- Init: The interface has detected a Hello packet coming from a neighbor, but bi-directional communication has not yet been established.

- Two-way: Bi-directional communication exists with a neighbor. The router has seen itself in the Hello packets coming from a neighbor. At the end of this stage, the DR and BDR election would have been done. At the end of the two-way stage, routers decide whether to proceed in building an adjacency or not. The decision is based on whether one of the routers is a DR or BDR or the link is a point-to-point or a virtual link.

NOTE   Area 0 is the backbone area that is connected to each OSPF area in the internetwork. In some rare instances, it is impossible to have an area physically connected to the backbone. In this case, a virtual link is used. The virtual link provides the disconnected area a logical path to the backbone.

- Exstart: Routers are trying to establish the initial sequence number that is going to be used in the information exchange packets. The sequence number ensures that routers always get the most recent information. After two OSPF neighboring routers establish bi-directional communication and complete DR/BDR election (on multiaccess networks), the routers transition to the exstart state. In this state, the neighboring routers establish a master/slave relationship and determine the initial database descriptor (DBD) sequence number to use when exchanging DBD packets. The primary router then polls the secondary for information.

- Exchange: Routers describe their entire link-state database by sending database description packets. At this state, packets could be flooded to other interfaces on the router.

- Loading: At this state, routers are finalizing the information exchange. Routers have built a link-state request list and a link-state retransmission list. Any information that looks incomplete or outdated is put on the request list. Any update that is sent is put on the retransmission list until it is acknowledged.

- Full: At this state, the adjacency is complete. The neighboring routers are fully adjacent. Adjacent routers have an identical link-state database.

OSPF Route Summarization

Route summarization is the consolidation of multiple routes in a single route advertisement. Route summarization is normally performed at the area boundaries by the ABRs. It is recommended that you summarize directly into the backbone (Area 0), although summarization can be configured between any two areas. By summarizing routes directly into the backbone, the backbone then turns around and injects these routes into other areas as part of the normal LSA.

Summarization is of two types:

- Inter-area route summarization—Inter-area route summarization is done on ABRs, and it applies to routes from within the AS. It does not apply to external routes injected into OSPF via redistribution.

- External route summarization—External route summarization is specific to external routes that are injected into OSPF via redistribution. It is imperative to ensure that external address ranges being summarized are contiguous. The summarization of overlapping ranges from two different routers could cause packets to be sent to the wrong destination. It is also imperative to ensure that all subnets being summarized are in use within the network; otherwise, routing "black holes" might be created, which leads to dropped traffic.

OSPF Authentication

OSPF provides for link security in the form of routing update authentication. OSPF packets can be authenticated so that routers can participate in routing domains based on predefined passwords. By default, a router uses a Null authentication, which means that routing exchanges over a network are not authenticated. Two other authentication methods exist:

- Simple password authentication—Simple password authentication allows a password (key) to be configured per area. Routers in the same area that want to participate in the routing domain must be configured with the same key.

  The drawback of this method is that it is vulnerable to passive attacks. Anyone with a link analyzer could easily get the password off the wire.

- Message Digest authentication (MD5)—Message Digest authentication is a cryptographic authentication. A key (password) and key-id are configured on each router. The router uses an algorithm based on the OSPF packet, the key, and the key-id to generate a "message digest" that is appended to the packet. Unlike the simple authentication, the key is not exchanged over the wire. A non-decreasing sequence number is also included in each OSPF packet to protect against replay attacks.

OSPF Security

OSPF configurations can be secured by the following method:

The first step in securing an OSPF routing environment is to configure all participating devices as non-broadcast devices. In non-broadcast, or directed, mode, OSPF devices need to be explicitly configured to communicate with valid OSPF neighbors. This configuration provides a basic layer of security against misconfiguration because valid OSPF devices will only communicate with the OSPF devices with which they have been configured to interoperate. In a broadcast (actually, OSPF is a multicast protocol) OSPF environment, any

OSPF devices with the correct configuration parameters for the network will be able to participate in OSPF routing.

On Cisco routers, interfaces will use broadcast OSPF by default. To turn on directed OSPF, use the following interface configuration statement:

```
ip ospf network non-broadcast
```

This command would be issued while at the interface configuration prompt. Under the specific OSPF process configuration, the router's OSPF neighbors must be explicitly named.

OSPF Authentication

By definition, all OSPF protocol exchanges are authenticated; however, one method of authentication is "none." OSPF authentication can be either none, simple, or MD5.

With simple authentication, the password goes in clear-text over the network. Anyone with a sniffer on the OSPF network segment could pull the OSPF password, and the attacker would be one step closer to compromising the OSPF environment.

With MD5 authentication, the key does not pass over the network. MD5 is a message-digest algorithm specified in RFC 1321. MD5 should be considered the most secure OSPF authentication mode.

To turn on MD5 OSPF authentication on a Cisco router, use the following configuration statement:

```
ip ospf message-digest-key 5 md5 peanutbuttercups
```

This statement should be entered at the interface configuration prompt. In this example, 5 is the key ID and peanutbuttercups is the MD5 key.

Authentication must be turned on for the specific OSPF process ID. This is done with the following statement, at the OSPF process configuration prompt:

```
area 0 authentication message-digest
```

This command turns on MD5 authentication for the OSPF backbone area.

Testing and Troubleshooting

To verify proper OSPF configuration, the following commands might be used:

- **show ip route**—This verifies the routing table.
- **show ip ospf neighbors**—This to verifies the router's OSPF neighbors.
- **debug ip ospf ?**—This turns on OSPF debugging. (Warning: A lot of output can be generated depending on the ? selection.)

OSPF Summary

OSPF is a powerful and feature-rich routing protocol due to its flexibility. OSPF provides a high functionality open protocol standard enabling inter-vendor networking with the TCP/IP protocol suite. Some of the benefits of OSPF include faster convergence than standard distance-vector routing protocols (such as RIP and RIPv2), VLSM support, authentication, hierarchical segmentation, route summarization, and aggregation, which is needed to handle large and complicated networks.

Summary

A router can learn of a network route using two methods: the route is either statically configured or dynamically learned and calculated.

- Static—Routes that are manually configured. Static routes have no mechanism to calculate or exchange routing information. Routers with routes that are statically configured can only forward packets defined by these routes. Static routes are generally used in small networks, or routers with only one WAN interface connection, such as a point-to-point link.

- Dynamic—Routes that are learned, or discovered, by the router. Dynamic routes adjust to conditions affected by network topology changes. Routers with routes that are dynamically learned can forward packets over any available discovered route. Three categories of dynamic routing protocols exist:

    — Distance-vector

    — Link-state

    — Hybrid

The administrative distance (see Table 24-8) is used to determine which route, if multiple routes are present, is preferred. Administrative distance is the distance that a neighbor router states, or advertises, is the distance to a destination. This could be the deciding factor in electing a feasible successor, or backup route, for any routing protocol. A route with a low administrative distance is considered to be more believable than one with a high administrative distance.

NOTE   The administrative distance values can be changed with the **distance** command.

Table 24-8 *Routing Protocol Administrative Distance Values*

Protocol	Distance Value
Connected Interface	0
Static Routes	1
EIGRP Summary Routes	5
EBGP	20
Internal EIGRP	90
IGRP	100
OSPF	110
IS-IS	115
RIP	120
EGP	140
External EIGRP	170
Internal BGP	200
Unknown	255

Distance-vector–based routing protocols periodically forward copies of their routing tables to their respective (immediate) network neighbors. Each recipient of this table adds its own distance value (distance vector) to the table and then forwards it on to its immediate neighbors, including (without split horizon) the router from which the table was just received.

The following routing protocols are classified as distance-vector routing protocols:

- RIP / RIPv2
- IGRP
- EIGRP (Distance-Vector/Link-State Hybrid)

Link-state, or shortest path first (SPF), routing algorithms create and maintain complex routing table databases of the network topology. Link-state protocols possess a full knowledge of the network topology and its routers. This information is conveyed via link-state advertisements (LSAs).

OSPF is classified as a link-state routing protocol.

RIP was designed for use with small networks, with both static configurations and stable links. Because of issues with no dynamic load balancing, slow convergence, bandwidth consumption of routing updates, fixed cost metrics, and hop count limit, RIP is not well suited to large internetworks, or to internetworks supporting real-time networked applications.

RIPv2 is a more modern, updated version of RIP. RIPv2 was designed as an update to RIP that enables its legacy base of internetworking devices a smooth transition to RIPv2, with its added networking features.

IGRP is a proprietary routing protocol developed by Cisco Systems, Inc. in the early 1990s. It was built with functional similarity to RIP, but with the additional features, including weighted metrics.

Cisco Systems developed an enhancement to IGRP, aptly named the Enhanced Interior Gateway Routing Protocol (EIGRP).

The composite IGRP metric is computed according to the following formula:

Metric = (K1 × Bandwidth) + (K2 × Bandwidth)/(256 – Load) + (K3 × Delay) × [K5/(Reliability + K4)]

If K5 = 0, then there is no reliability term.

The default K values are as follows:

K1 = 1

K2 = 0

K3 = 1

K4 = 0

K5 = 0

EIGRP is Cisco Systems, Inc. proprietary and is one of the most feature-rich and vigorous routing protocols developed and used today. EIGRP is considered to be a hybrid because it combines the best features and attributes of both distance-vector and link-state protocols.

EIGRP is easy to configure, enabling efficient operation in the support of IP(v4), AppleTalk, and IPX routed protocol traffic.

OSPF is a powerful and feature-rich link-state routing protocol due to its flexibility. OSPF provides a high functionality open protocol standard enabling intervendor networking with the TCP/IP protocol suite. Some of the benefits of OSPF include faster convergence than standard distance-vector routing protocols (such as RIP and RIPv2), VLSM support, authentication, hierarchical segmentation, route summarization, and aggregation, which is needed to handle large and complicated networks.

CHAPTER 25

Routing Protocols, Part II

This chapter will focus on Intermediate System to Intermediate System (IS-IS), which supports the OSI Layer 3, and Border Gateway Protocol (BGP), which is a distributed-backbone, autonomous system-based topology.

Intermediate System to Intermediate System (IS-IS)

IS-IS is defined by ISO/IEC 10589 and was initially developed by the International Organization for Standardization (ISO) in 1992. This development was at the same time that the Internet Architecture Board was developing Open Shortest Path First (OSPF), defined by the Internet Engineering Task Force (IETF) in RFC 1131. IS-IS was initially developed to support the OSI Layer 3 Routing Protocol Connectionless Mode Network Service (CLNS). Integrated IS-IS was developed as an extension to the original IS-IS specification to support IP routing.

NOTE   Typically, IS-IS is the term used when discussing Integrated IS-IS (IP extension).

In many ways, IS-IS is similar to OSPF; however, they are different in some significant ways.

IS-IS is similar to OSPF in the following ways:

- IS-IS is a link-state protocol, with each router maintaining a link-state database by using the shortest path first algorithm for route calculation.

- IS-IS uses areas to divide the routed network into more manageable pieces, which reduces route resource requirements.

- IS-IS uses a two-layer hierarchy to route between areas.

- IS-IS routers use Hello packets to maintain neighbor adjacencies with other IS-IS routers.

- IS-IS supports variable length subnet masking (VLSM) and network summarization area boundaries.

NOTE	Because of its multiprotocol design, IS-IS is suitable for IPv6 transport with only the modification of an address family definition for IPv6.

IS-IS is different from OSPF in the following ways:

- IS-IS routers are part of a single area, and area boundaries fall *between* routers. In OSPF, area boundaries fall *within* routers.
- The IS-IS backbone is defined by router types versus a particular area ID, such as area 0.
- IS-IS information is passed between routers using CLNS versus IP. Rather than use IP packets, IS-IS uses protocol data units (PDUs) to communicate information.

IS-IS Operation

IS-IS dictates how routers, known as independent systems, communicate routing information with each other. ES-IS specifies communications between end systems (hosts) and routers.

Similar to OSPF, IS-IS divides the network into smaller parts, called *areas*. The IS-IS definition of an area is the part of the network about which a router must have complete knowledge.

IS-IS uses ISO-defined PDUs to communicate between routers. Following are the three most prominent PDUs:

- Hello PDUs—Enable IS-IS routers to form neighbor relationships (adjacencies), discover new routes, and determine route availability and reachability.
- Sequence Number PDUs (SNPs)—Two types of SNPs exist:
  — Complete SNPs (CSNPs)—Include all link state PDUs (LSPs) in the link state database.
  — Partial SNPs (PSNPs)—Include some LSPs in the link state database.
- LSPs—IS-IS routers use LSPs to exchange routing information, building and maintaining a link-state database in each router.

Also similar to OSPF, IS-IS uses Dijkstra's Shortest Path First (SPF) algorithm to calculate routes. This algorithm is run whenever the network topology changes.

IS-IS Areas

IS-IS routers are part of one area only. This is in contrast to OSPF routers, which might be part of several areas. IS-IS area boundaries fall on the links between routers, whereas OSPF area boundaries are assigned to differing interfaces on the router.

Figure 25-1 illustrates IS-IS area boundaries.

Figure 25-1   *IS-IS Areas and Area Boundaries*

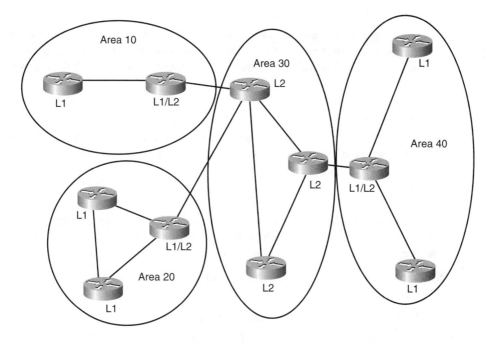

IS-IS defines three types of routers:

- Layer 1 (L1) router—This is within a non-backbone area that will only share updates with other L1 routers and L1/L2 routers in its area. L1 routers never receive routing updates about networks outside of their area.

- Layer 2 (L2) router—This shares updates with other L2 routers and L1/L2 routers. An L2 router shares information with L2 and L1/L2 routers regardless of the area. L2 routers comprise the backbone of the IS-IS routing domain.

- Layer 1/Layer 2 (L1/L2) router—This router is at an IS-IS boundary and shares updates with all router types, including L1, L2, and L1/L2. L1/L2 routers are responsible for exchanging routing information between their area and the backbone.

IS-IS routing information does not cross area boundaries, unlike OSPF. In OSPF parlance, IS-IS areas behave in a similar fashion to OSPF Totally Stubby Areas.

IS-IS Metrics

IS-IS uses the following four metrics:

- Cost / Default—Must be supported by all IS-IS routers. This metric is the cost of an IS-IS router interface. The value ranges from 0 to 63; the Cisco default value is 10.

- Delay—(Optional) Not used.

- Expense—(Optional) Not used.

- Error—(Optional) Not used.

The delay, expense, and error metrics are not used because IS-IS requires that the SPF algorithm be run against each of these metrics. The only metric used by Cisco and other vendors is cost, which is why this metric is often referred to as the IS-IS default metric.

IS-IS Network Types

IS-IS supports two network types: broadcast and point-to-point. The essential difference between these two network types is in the operation of adjacencies (with Hello PDUs).

IS-IS Adjacencies

IS-IS routers use Hello PDUs to build and maintain neighboring relationships. The Hello PDUs carry information that identifies the sending router and indicates that router's behavior, such as the Hello interval and hold-time.

IS-IS routers establish separate adjacencies at L1 and L2. These routing adjacencies are as follows:

- L1 routers form adjacencies with L1 and L2/L2 neighbors.

- L2 routers form adjacencies with L2 and L1/L2 neighbors.

- L1/L2 routers form separate adjacencies: one for L1 neighbors, and one for L2 neighbors. If both neighbors are L1/L2 routers, two independent adjacencies are formed: one for L1, and the other for L2.

    L1 and L2 routers can never become adjacent.

IS-IS routers use separate L1 and L2 Hello PDUs on broadcast networks to establish and maintain neighboring adjacencies. L1/L2 routers send two Hello PDUs: one for L1, and the other for L2.

Designated IS (DIS)

IS-IS uses the designated IS (DIS) on broadcast networks to reduce network traffic and to flood LSPs into the routing domain. The DIS behaves in a similar fashion to the designated router (DR) of OSPF. The DIS is responsible for advertising the broadcast network to which all routers are attached.

The DIS advertises a pseudonode, which represents the network, and each IS-IS router advertises only one adjacency to the pseudonode. The pseudonode is actually a network; it appears as a single router in the IS-IS link-state database.

The DIS is elected based on router priority. The DIS router priority is a configurable parameter on each interface and is separate for L1 and L2 adjacencies.

The DIS router priority value ranges from 0 to 127; the Cisco default value is 64. If the DIS priority value is zero, that particular router is ineligible to become the DIS on that network. Choosing the highest system ID breaks priority value ties.

NOTE	IS-IS System IDs are typically the MAC address of the router interface.

NOTE	IS-IS routers on point-to-point links do not elect a DIS; therefore, the priority will always be zero.

IS-IS LSPs

Each IS-IS autonomous system router generates LSPs, similar to OSPF LSPs. IS-IS LSPs are maintained in IS-IS link state databases on each router in the system and are used to calculate routes using the SPF algorithm.

IS-IS point-to-point configured routers send unicast LSPs directly to each other. IS-IS broadcast network routers multicast the LSPs with separate addressing for L1 and L2 LSPs.

Frame Relay subinterfaces are configured as multiple point-to-point configurations on an IS-IS router.

NOTE	IS-IS L1 LSPs are multicasted to the MAC address 0180.C200.0015, known as AllL2ISs.

The IS-IS remaining lifetime (hold time) timer is 1,200 seconds (20 minutes). When the remaining lifetime counter reaches zero, the router will hold the route for 60 seconds before flushing it from the link state database. To prevent this route flushing, IS-IS routers refresh their LSPs every 900 seconds (15 minutes) by default. The LSP hold time is known as the remaining lifetime, similar to OSPF Link State Advertisement's (LSA's) age parameter.

NOTE   The remaining lifetime time interval can be manually reconfigured using the **max-lsp-lifetime [seconds]** command in router EXEC mode, "(config-router)#". The range for this value is from 1 to 65,535 seconds (~18 hours).

The LSP distribution time interval can be manually reconfigured using the **lsp-refresh-interval [seconds]** command in router EXEC mode, "(config-router)#". The range for this value is from 1 to 65,535 seconds (~18 hours).

Sometimes MTU limitations can affect the routes that the LSP update announces. Generally, this is not an issue; however, if different LSP routes appear to be "flapping" for no apparent reason, MTU size might be suspect. Use the **lsp-mtu [range]** command in router EXEC mode, "(config-router)#" to change the LSP MTU size. The MTU range, in bytes, is 128 to 4,352.

LSP Flooding

LSPs are flooded through the network by sequence number PDUs (SNPs). The number sequencing ensures that the LSP flooding is performed in a reliable fashion by each IS-IS router. As mentioned at the beginning of this chapter, SNPs come in two types:

- CSNPs—Include all LSPs in the link state database.
- PSNPs—Include some LSPs in the link state database.

On point-to-point IS-IS networks, PSNPs are used to acknowledge CSNPs. The default configuration on Cisco routers for LSP transmission is 5 seconds; however, this interval can be changed manually. The range for this value is from 0 to 65,535.

On broadcast IS-IS networks, routers receive multicast LSPs from each neighbor. As opposed to having each router on the network acknowledge each received LSP, the DIS sends CSNPs in response, containing its link state database. CSNPs are multicasted every 10 seconds by default; however, this interval can be changed manually. The range for this value is from 0 to 65,535.

L1 CSNPs are sent to the multicast address AllL1ISs; L2 CSNPs are sent to AllL2ISs.

Upon receipt of the CSNP, each router in the broadcast network compares the CSNP against its link state database. If a router is missing an LSP that is contained within the CSNP, that same router multicasts a PSNP containing the missing LSP. The DIS responds with the requested LSPs to any PSNPs.

IS-IS Authentication

IS-IS uses three types of password-based authentication:

- Neighbor password—Router interfaces on the same network can share a common password. The Hello PDUs contain the password and can prevent adjacencies from being formed. L1 and L2 neighbors use separate passwords.

- Area password—L1 and L1/L2 routers in the same area can share a common password. All routers in the area must support authentication and be configured with the same password. L1 LSPs and SNPs carry the password and can prevent L1 LSPs from being accepted by or from all routers within the area.

- Domain password—L2 and L1/L2 routers in the same IS-IS routing domain can share a common password. The same password must be configured on all L2 routers. L2 LSPs and SNPs carry the password and can prevent L2 LSPs from being accepted by or from all routers within the domain.

NOTE   To configure passwords for each of these three types, use the following command set:

- Neighbor Password

```
Router(config)#interface serial 0
Router(config-if)#isis password password [level-1/level-1-2/level-2-only]
```

NOTE   The default configuration is L1/L2.

- Area Password

```
Router(config)#router isis
Router(config-router)#area-password password
```

- Domain Password

```
Router(config)#router isis
Router(config-router)#domain-password password
```

IS-IS Summary

IS-IS is a link state protocol that is similar to OSPF in its operation. Whereas OSPF was defined by the Internet Engineering Task Force (IETF) in RFC 1131 and later updated by RFC 2328, IS-IS was defined by ISO/IEC 10589.

IS-IS is a simpler SPF algorithm—based on link-state routing protocols—than OSPF. IS-IS is a good choice for internetworks that use areas to limit the propagation of routing information. The simplicity of IS-IS roughly translates to a limitation in flexibility when compared to OSPF.

IS-IS is similar to OSPF in the following ways:

- IS-IS is a link-state protocol, with each router maintaining a link-state database by using the shortest path first algorithm for route calculation.

- IS-IS uses areas to divide the routed network into more manageable pieces, which reduces route resource requirements.

- IS-IS uses a two-layer hierarchy to route between areas.

- IS-IS routers use Hello packets to maintain neighbor adjacencies with other IS-IS routers.

- IS-IS supports variable length subnet masking (VLSM) and network summarization area boundaries.

IS-IS is different from OSPF in the following ways:

- IS-IS routers are part of a single area, and area boundaries fall *between* routers. In OSPF, area boundaries fall *within* routers.

- The IS-IS backbone is defined by router types versus a particular area ID, such as area 0.

- IS-IS information is passed between routers using CLNS versus IP. Rather than use IP packets, IS-IS uses protocol data units (PDUs) to communicate information.

IS-IS is currently under review for improvement by the IS-IS Working Group of the IETF. One possibility for improvement is transporting IS-IS directly over IP without having to use CLNP encapsulation. The group is also considering including a stricter security mechanism, such as the MD-5-based algorithms used in RIP and OSPF.

Border Gateway Protocol, Version 4 (BGP4)

BGP was initially developed in June 1989 and was published as RFC 1105. BGP was born out of the requirement to move away from a backbone-centered tree-topology and into a more distributed-backbone, autonomous-system based topology. BGP has endured several updates as the following timeline demonstrates:

- June 1989 / 1105 Border Gateway Protocol (BGP). K. Lougheed, Y. Rekhter. Jun-01-1989. Format: TXT=37644 bytes. Obsoleted by RFC 1163. Status: Experimental.

- June 1990 / 1163 Border Gateway Protocol (BGP). K. Lougheed, Y. Rekhter. Jun-01-1990. Format: TXT=69404 bytes. Obsoletes RFC 1105. Obsoleted by RFC 1267. Status: Historic.

- October 1991 / 1267 Border Gateway Protocol 3 (BGP-3). K. Lougheed, Y. Rekhter. Oct-01-1991. Format: TXT=80724 bytes. Obsoletes RFC 1163. Status: Historic.

- July 1994 / 1654 A Border Gateway Protocol 4 (BGP-4). Y. Rekhter, T. Li, Editors. July 1994. Format: TXT=130118 bytes. Obsoleted by RFC 1771. Status: Proposed Standard.

- March 1995 / 1771 A Border Gateway Protocol 4 (BGP-4). Y. Rekhter, T. Li. March 1995. Format: TXT=131903 bytes. Obsoletes RFC 1654. Status: Draft Standard.

BGP is an Exterior Gateway Protocol (EGP) and is used to pass routing information between autonomous systems (ASs). BGP is still a routing protocol and, like other routing protocols, it passes routing information and uses metrics for route determination. BGP advertises which networks can be reached and can act in either an interior (IBGP) or exterior (EBGP) mode. IBGP or EBGP configurations mean that BGP can be configured to advertise networks within an AS or between different ASs. The key to BGP operation is in the configuration of which networks to advertise and whether they are directly connected.

NOTE	BGP uses TCP (port 179) to communicate with other routers.

The primary purpose of BGP4 is to exchange network reachability information with other BGP (autonomous) systems. This network layer reachability information (NLRI) includes information about each AS in the list of ASs that reachability information traverses. NLRI updates carry a network number, a list of the ASs through which the NLRI has passed (called the AS path), and a list of other path attributes that is used to construct a graph of network connectivity to remove routing loops.

Figure 25-2 illustrates how the Internet is constructed with multiple BGP autonomous systems.

Figure 25-2 *Internet Connectivity Example with Random ASNs*

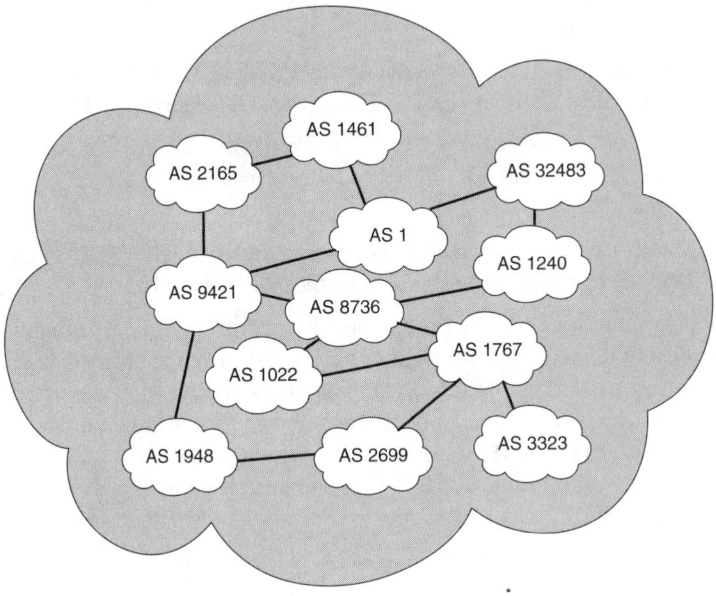

NOTE

A macroscopic visualization of the Internet can be found at the following Web site: http://www.caida.org/analysis/topology/as_core_network/.

The visualization on the Web site reflects 626,773 IP addresses and 1,007,723 IP links (immediately adjacent addresses in a traceroute-like path) of skitter data. This data was collected from 16 monitors probing approximately 400,000 destinations spread across more than 48,302 (52%) globally routable network prefixes. The Cooperative Association for Internet Data Analysis (CAIDA) then aggregates the network view into a topology of autonomous systems (ASs), each of which approximately maps to an Internet service provider (ISP). CAIDA maps each IP address to the AS responsible for routing it. The abstracted graph consists of 7,624 AS nodes and 25,126 peering sessions. (Geographical location could not be provided for 61 ASs). The resulting graph contains 7,563 ASs (81 percent of all ASs present in the Oregon BGP table of Oct. 15, 2000) and 25,005 peering sessions.

CAIDA is a collaborative undertaking among organizations with a strong interest in keeping primary Internet capacity and usage efficiency in line with demand. Participants come from the commercial, government, and research sectors. CAIDA's members use their organization as a focal point for promoting greater cooperation in the engineering and maintenance of a robust, scalable, global Internet infrastructure. Cisco Systems is a CAIDA sponsor. CAIDA provides the world with a neutral framework to support cooperative technical endeavors that have the potential to be critical in meeting the demands of an exponentially growing system of networks.

BGP is classified as a path-vector routing protocol. A path vector routing protocol is used to select a path across the network. Path vector protocols are similar to distance vector routing protocols. The primary difference between path and distance vector routing protocols is that distance vector routing protocols use hop count to calculate the best path to a destination, whereas path vector routing protocols advertise the reachable destinations to their neighbors. The border router (BR) advertises these destinations, as well as the attributes of the path to the destination. These path vector attributes include the number of hops and the administrative distance of each hop. Interior (IBGP-based) learned routes are given more preference than those learned from an Exterior BGP (EBGP) advertisement.

BGP Multihoming

The popularity of BGP stems from its ability to add redundancy in support of critical networks and their connections for two-way traffic (inbound and outbound). BGP also can be used to load balance, or load share, traffic across multiple links. Load balancing of BGP traffic is possible when a BGP AS speaker (router) learns of two EBGP paths for an IP prefix from a neighboring autonomous system. By default, the BGP routing process selects the path with the lowest router ID to enter into its routing table. BGP multipath must be enabled for BGP to take advantage of multiple paths to a destination.

BGP can support up to eight paths to a destination, either load balancing or load sharing across each path.

NOTE   Load balancing is an equal distribution of the traffic load across all available links. Load sharing is the shared distribution of traffic load across all available links, but not necessarily equal. Load-balanced traffic is load shared; load-shared traffic is not always load balanced.

Interior BGP (IBGP) Versus Exterior BGP (EBGP)

Internal BGP neighbors are in the same autonomous system; external BGP neighbors are in different autonomous systems. In general, external neighbors are adjacent to each other and share a common subnet, whereas internal neighbors can be anywhere in the same autonomous system. Figures 25-3 and 25-4 illustrate both an external BGP (EBGP) peering session and an internal BGP (IBGP) peering session between two peers.

Figure 25-3   *External BGP Session Between Two BGP Peers*

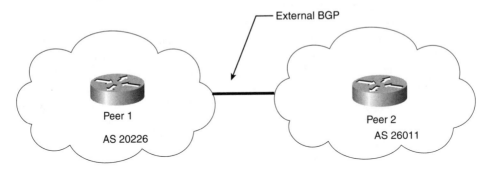

Figure 25-4   *Internal BGP Session Between Two Peers*

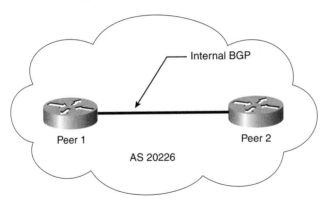

Figure 25-5 illustrates routers exchanging both internal and external BGP sessions.

Figure 25-5   *Internal (IBGP) and External (EBGP) Peering Sessions*

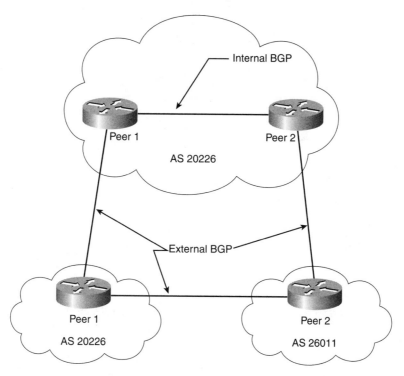

Common BGP Implementation

From a customer standpoint, BGP is generally implemented in a multihomed environment for backup purposes. Figure 25-6 illustrates a customer WAN, MichelleCo, with dual Internet connections: a T1 each to ISP 1 and ISP 2. MichelleCo will announce the private autonomous system number (ASN) of 65162 to both ISPs, and will receive route updates from ISP 1 (ASN 4276) and ISP 2 (ASN 174).

Figure 25-6 *MichelleCo Dual, Multihomed BGP Implementation*

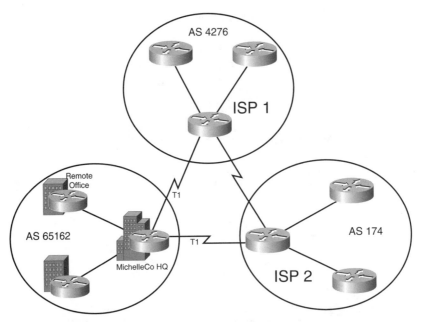

As with OSPF, a BGP-configured router first exchanges the entire routing table. After a peering relationship has been established, only changes are sent. BGP routers send keepalives to ensure that connections are still active and available. Like OSPF and EIGRP, BGP uses AS numbers. BGP uses a single metric for path selections, which can be manually configured to fine-tune the network to meet determined design needs.

BGP4 uses ASNs to identify to which system a router belongs. The Internet Administration Numbering Authority (IANA) allocates these ASNs to the national registries. The ASNs range from 1 to 64,511; ARIN assigns ASNs 64512 to 65535 for private use. They will only be seen by the upstream service provider and are not propagated into other ASNs.

BGP Autonomous System Numbers

The ARIN national registries are at ARIN (hostmaster@ARIN.net), RIPE-NCC (ncc@ripe.net), and the AP-NIC (admin@apnic.net). The following list details the allocated blocks to the regional registries:

Number	Description
0	Reserved. Can be use to identify non-routed networks
1,877 to 1,901	Allocated by RIPE NCC
1,902 to 2,042	Allocated by ARIN
2,043	Allocated by RIPE NCC

2,044 to 2,046	Allocated by ARIN
2,047	Allocated by RIPE NCC
2,048 to 2,106	Allocated by ARIN
2,107 to 2,136	Allocated by RIPE NCC
2,137 to 2,584	Allocated by ARIN
2,585 to 2,614	Allocated by RIPE NCC
2,615 to 2,772	Allocated by ARIN
2,773 to 2,822	Allocated by RIPE NCC
2,823 to 2,829	Allocated by ARIN
2,830 to 2,879	Allocated by RIPE NCC
2,880 to 3,153	Allocated by ARIN
3,154 to 3,353	Allocated by RIPE NCC
3,354 to 4,607	Allocated by ARIN
4,608 to 4,864	Allocated by AP NIC
4,865 to 5,376	Allocated by ARIN
5,377 to 5,631	Allocated by RIPE NCC
5,632 to 6,655	Allocated by ARIN
6,656 to 6,911	Allocated by RIPE NCC
6,912 to 7,466	Allocated by ARIN
7,467 to 7,722	Allocated by AP NIC
7,723 to 8,191	Allocated by ARIN
8,192 to 9,215	Allocated by RIPE NCC
9,216 to 10,239	Allocated by AP NIC
10,240 to 11,263	Allocated by ARIN
11,264 to 12,287	Allocated by ARIN
12,288 to 13,311	Allocated by RIPE NCC
13,312 to 14,335	Allocated by ARIN
14,336 to 15,359	Allocated by ARIN
15,360 to 16,383	Allocated by RIPE NCC
16,384 to 17,407	Allocated by ARIN
17,408 to 18,431	Allocated by AP NIC
18,432 to 19,455	Allocated by ARIN
19,456 to 20,479	Allocated by ARIN
20,480 to 21,503	Allocated by RIPE NCC
21,504 to 22,527	Allocated by ARIN
22,528 to 32,767	Held by the IANA
32,768 to 64,511	Reserved by the IANA
64,512 to 65,534	Designated for private use (Allocated to the IANA)
6,5535	Reserved

BGP Attributes

BGP's flexibility comes from configurable parameters called *attributes*, which can be adjusted manually in the Cisco IOS. BGP attributes are classified into four categories:

- Well-known—This attribute must be implemented in all BGP routers.

- Mandatory—This attribute must be present in all BGP update messages; otherwise, the BGP connection is incompatible and will fail.

- Discretionary—This attribute might or might not be present in all BGP update messages; however, if discretionary attributes are present, they must be recognized by all BGP implementations.

- Optional—This attribute does not have to be recognized by all BGP implementations. The type of optional attribute determines whether the information is passed on to other peers if the option is unrecognized. The types of optional attributes are as follows:

  - Transitive optional attributes—These are passed on to other peers.

  - Non-transitive optional attributes—If unrecognized, these are ignored and not passed on to other BGP peers.

NOTE	Communities are a way to group destinations into a logical unit to make the application of routing processes a bit easier to manage. The grouping of routing processes is easier to manage because it is easier to apply routing policies to a single community than to each destination individually. A community is a group of BGP networks that share common properties, or attributes. This grouping of communities crosses AS boundaries so that other ASs can use the community values. Community values are the means for sending non-transitive attributes between ASs. Community values are implemented with the use of route maps. With route maps in place, you can match the non-transitive attribute value and set the community value. After the community value is set, you can configure the EBGP peer router to send the community values. Route maps that receive community values then set the proper attribute value.

NOTE	By default, all destinations belong to the general Internet community.

BGP attributes are translated into community values by the Route Map, which is in turn translated back into a BGP attribute by the receiving EBGP peer.

The initial BGP specification (RFC 1771) defines seven attributes, as detailed in Table 25-1.

Table 25-1   *RFC 1771 BGP Attributes*

Attribute	Type	Flags	Value
ORIGIN	1	Well known	IGP (0)
			EGP (1)
			Incomplete (2)
AS_PATH	2	Well known	ASNs in the path
NEXT_HOP	3	Well known	Address of the next router
MULTI_EXIT_DESC (MED)	4	Optional, local	32 bit metric
LOCAL_PREF	5	Well known	32 bit metric
ATROMIC_AGGREGATE	6	Well known	Flags certain aggregations
AGGREGATOR	7	Operational, transitive	AS number and router ID

AS Path Attribute

The AS-path attribute is a list of all the autonomous systems (ASs) of which a routing update has traversed. When an update passes through an AS, BGP prepends its AS number onto the existing AS path in the update.

Origin Attribute

The origin attribute indicates how reachability information through the path was obtained from the source, or origin, of the BGP update. This attribute has three values:

- IGP (Internal)—Indicates that the route originated within the AS of the advertising router.

- EGP (External)—Indicates that the route was learned via another router using an EBGP.

- Incomplete—Indicates that the origin of the route has been learned by some means other than EGP or redistributed from an IGP.

NOTE   Always use a route-map to override the origin attribute. In making the origin of all routes of an equal value, other criterion can be used to choose the best route. The Cisco IOS commands are "SteelRouter(config-route-map)#**match** *attribute attribute_value*" and "SteelRouter(config-route-map)#**set** *attribute attribute_value*".

Next Hop Attribute

For a BGP peer to be told what next hop is to be used to reach a particular AS, the router that sends the updates adjusts the value of the next hop attributes. For EBGP, this attribute is usually the IP address. For IBGP, this attribute is usually the address of the EBGP peer in the neighboring AS.

The next hop attribute is generally used to optimize BGP routing.

Weight Attribute

This is a Cisco proprietary BGP attribute that was added to assist in the BGP path selection process. Adjustments to the weight attribute can affect which route is preferred when multiple paths to the same destination exist. The weight attribute is only present on the local router and is not propagated to other BGP peers. Routes originated by the router are assigned a default weight of 32,768. The range for this attribute is 0 to 65,535. The larger the weight, the greater the preference of that path. Other paths learned by the router are assigned a value of 0.

Multiexit Discriminator (MED) Attribute

The multiexit discriminator (MED) attribute is non-transitive. It is defined as a metric that is used to convey the relative preference of entry points into an AS. The MED is assigned a value of zero by default when an update is generated. Lower MED values are the preferred values in an update. The MED is used to calculate the cost of using a particular router for reaching the next group in the AS.

Unlike the local preference attribute, the MED attribute is exchanged between ASs. However, the MED attribute is non-transitive; therefore, the MED value for a destination is reset to zero when it leaves the neighboring AS, unless the AS is explicitly configured to propagate MED information into other ASs.

A set of path exchanges by BGP routers (internal to an AS) can include several nearly identical paths to destination, with the MED value and the next-hop attributes being the only differentiators. The router should not aggregate, or sum, these paths. Instead, these paths should use the MED value to select the preferred—or best—exit point from the AS.

MED values received for the same destination from multiple ASs are usable only if the receiving router has the **bgp always-compare-med** configured. If the MED comparison is not configured, the MED value of the routing updates will not be used in the path selection process.

Local Preference Attribute

The local preference attribute is another way (from the weight attribute) to affect the path selection process. Unlike the weight attribute, the local preference attribute is propagated via routing updates to other routers in the AS. The values for this attribute range from 0 to 255, with a default local preference value of 100. The path with the highest preference is preferred.

The various AS border routers can learn several paths that lead to the same routing prefixes. These paths will be propagated inside the AS; however, the BGP border gateways will each select the path with the lowest local preference value.

Atomic Aggregate Attribute

This atomic aggregate attribute does not have content; its length is always 0. This attribute indicates that the router chose to pass an aggregated prefix—a prefix that is the aggregate, or summarization, of several short prefixes. More specific routes might be available for longer network prefixes, but the BGP router chose to hide them to reduce the size of the AS path parameters.

Aggregator Attribute

The AS that made the decision to aggregate the network prefix inserts the aggregator attribute. This value is 6 octets in length and consists of the 16-bit ASN and the 32-bit IP address of the router that is performing the aggregation.

Additional Attributes

BGP supports additional attributes, developed in later RFCs, beyond the scope of this book. Table 25-2 presents a complete list of these attributes and their respective RFC specification.

Table 25-2   *BGP Full Attribute Values (as of April 30, 2001)*[*]

Attribute Value	Description	Reference
1	ORIGIN	RFC 1771
2	AS_PATH	RFC 1771
3	NEXT_HOP	RFC 1771
4	MULTI_EXIT_DISC	RFC 1771
5	LOCAL_PREF	RFC 1771
6	ATOMIC_AGGREGATE	RFC 1771
7	AGGREGATOR	RFC 1771

(continues)

Table 25-2   *BGP Full Attribute Values (as of April 30, 2001)*[*] *(Continued)*

Attribute Value	Description	Reference
8	COMMUNITY	RFC 1997
9	ORIGINATOR ID	RFC 1998
10	CLUSTER_LIST	RFC 1998
11	DPA	Chen
12	ADVERTISER	RFC 1863
13	RCID_PATH / CLUSTER_ID	RFC 1863
14	MP_REACH_NLRI	RFC 2283
15	MP_UNREACH_NLRI	RFC 2283
16	EXTENDED COMMUNITIES	Rosen
17 -> 255	Reserved for future development	-----

[*]References:

[RFC 1771] Rekhter, Y., and Li, T., "A Border Gateway Protocol 4 (BGP-4)," RFC 1771, March 1995.

[RFC 1863] Haskin, D., "A BGP/IDRP Route Server Alternative to a Full Mesh Routing," RFC 1863, October 1995.

[RFC 1997] Chandra, R., Traina, P., and T. Li, "BGP Communities Attribute," RFC 1997, August 1996.

[RFC 1998] Bates, T., Chandra, R., "BGP Route Reflection: An Alternative to Full Mesh IBGP," RFC 1998, June 1996.

[RFC 2283] Bates, T., et al., "Multiprotocol Extensions for BGP-4," RFC 2283, February 1998.

[Chen] Chen, E., Bates, T., "Destination Preference Attribute for BGP," Work in progress, March 1996.

[Rosen] Eric Rosen <erosen@cisco.com>, March 1999.

draft-ramachandra-bgp-ext-communities-00.txt.

BGP Route Selection

Following are the steps that a BGP router takes when determining which path is the preferred to a destination. After a BGP path criterion has been selected, the path selection process ends for that session.

1 Verify that the next hop is accessible.

2 (Internal Paths Only) If synchronization is enabled, the route must exist in the IGP to be selected.

3 (Cisco Proprietary) Use the path with the largest weight because the weight gives the path preference.

4 If routes have identical weights, use the route with the highest local preference.

5 If routes have identical local preference, use the route that the local router originated.

6 If no route was originated, use the shorter AS path.

7 If AS paths are the identical length, choose the external path over an internal path.

8 If all routes are external, use the route with the lowest origin code.

9 If the origin codes are the same and the paths came from the same AS, use the path with the lowest MULTI_EXIT_DISC (MED) attribute.

10 The EBGP path holds preference over the IBGP path.

11 Select the shortest path within the AS (the lowest IGP metric).

12 If multipath (Cisco IOS "maximum-path") is enabled, then multiple paths can be inserted into the routing table, if both (or all) paths are external routes and originated from the same autonomous system.

13 Use the route with the lowest IP address value for the BGP Router ID (RID).

14 If IGP is disabled and only internal paths are left, use the path through the closest neighbor.

BGP Peering

BGP mandates that each external router establish an internal BGP connection with each other external router in the same AS. These external peered routers will be linked by a fully meshed graph of route paths. The internal interconnections are used to propagate external routing information, independently of whatever Interior Gateway Protocol (IGP) might be running, such as OSPF or EIGRP.

These internal interconnections are also used among BGP routers to reach an agreement on the best route to an external destination network. This ensures that only the router that is managing the best path inserts information into the AS internal routing tables through the IGP in use.

Two types of BGP peers exist:

- Internal—BGP peers that are connected within the same AS (with intra-AS links)

- External—BGP peers that are interconnected between two ASs (with inter-AS links)

Figure 25-7 illustrates internal and external BGP peers, with respective inter- and intra-AS links.

Figure 25-7 *Internal and External BGP Peers*

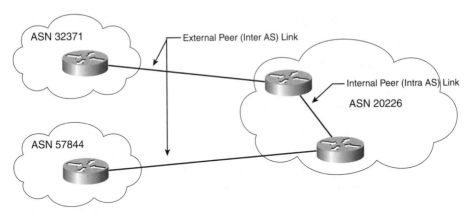

BGP Route Reflectors

To help reduce the amount of peers that a router will have in an AS, BGP employs the use of route reflectors. The routers peer with another router or concentration router. These peers are then known as clients. They receive updates from and send updates to the route reflector.

The use of route reflectors, illustrated in Figure 25-8, is one way to reduce the size of the IBGP routing mesh. The issue with meshed IBGP routes is scalability. Routing meshes are subject to the *N-squared* algorithm, N^2-N/2, also represented as N(N-1)/2, where N is the number of nodes in the network. As internetworks and autonomous systems grow, so will the size of each BGP router's routing table at the rate of N(N-1)/2 for each additional node (N).

Figure 25-8 *BGP Route Reflector Topology*

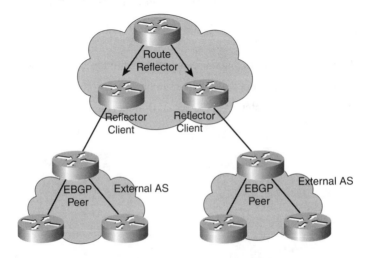

In a BGP AS, several routers can exchange route information. To reduce the amount of peers that a router has to establish, a concentration router and or route reflector router can be configured. Reflect clients are configured to exchange information with a central concentration router (route reflector). Reflect clients (client peers) only peer with the central concentration router instead of every router in the AS. The central router (route reflector) is responsible for sending updates to the reflector clients. The reflector clients are responsible for sending updates to the central concentration router instead of every router in the AS. Routers that are not configured as route reflector clients are known as *non-client peers*. The route reflector "reflects" routes between client peers and non-client peers.

As Figure 25-9 illustrates, IBGP peers do not have to be fully meshed with each other to receive full-mesh routing updates.

Figure 25-9   *BGP With and Without Route Reflectors*

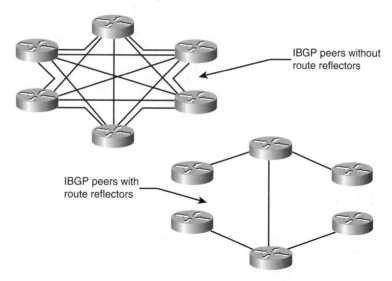

The sole requirement is for each IBGP client peer to have a session that is established with the route reflector. Non-client peers will require full mesh connectivity with other non-client peers, and those must be configured as route reflectors. Router reflector clients can only communicate with the route reflector, not with non-client peers.

NOTE   It is a good networking practice to have the router reflector topology mirror the physical network topology.

BGP Confederations

BGP confederations is another method used to manage the number of IBGP mesh routes in an AS. To help reduce the amount of peers a router will have in an AS, BGP employs the use of route reflectors. The routers peer with another router, or concentration router. These peers are then known as clients. They receive updates from and send updates to the route reflector.

The other networks see the confederation as a single AS, as illustrated by Figure 25-10. The sub-ASs, or mini-ASs, are transparent to the outside world. Similar to using route reflectors, this method reduces the number of IBGP mesh paths.

Figure 25-10 *BGP Confederation*

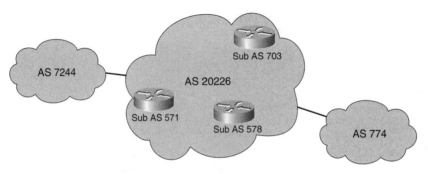

BGP Administrative Distances

Administrative distance is a way to set the preference of different routing protocols. Routers use administrative distances as tiebreakers, with the lower administrative distance being the winner and subsequently entered into the router's routing table. BGP does not use administrative distances during the route selection process. BGP uses administrative distances to select which routes are placed in the routing table.

Three administrative distances are associated with BGP:

- Internal (IBGP)—Routes are learned from IBGP peers. The default administrative distance is 200.
- External (EBGP)—Routes are learned from EBGP peers. The default administrative distance is 20.
- Local—Routes are generated locally. The default administrative distance is 20.

BGP Timers

BGP uses two timers to manage protocol functions:

- Keepalive—The default is 60 seconds. The keepalive timer is the maximum amount of time that a BGP router will let pass between routing updates.

- Hold-down—The default is 180 seconds. The hold-down timer is the maximum amount of time that a BGP route will hold the route in its table after the keepalive timer has passed with no update.

The amount of time for routing updates, keepalive, and hold-down is negotiated among BGP peers upon session initialization. In the absence of a timer, the defaults are used. These timers can be manually configured; however, the BGP router will use the lower value discovered during session negotiation.

BGP Summary

BGP was initially developed in June 1989 and was published as RFC 1105. BGP was born out of the need to move away from a backbone-centered tree-topology and into a more distributed-backbone, autonomous system-based topology. BGP version 4 (BGP4) makes it possible to ensure reliable routing, enabling route aggregation, multihoming, and policy-based routing.

The primary purpose of BGP4 is to exchange network reachability information with other BGP (autonomous) systems. This NLRI includes information about each AS in the list of ASs that reachability information traverses. NLRI updates carry a network number, a list of the ASs that the NLRI has passed through (called the AS path), and a list of other path attributes that is used to construct a graph of network connectivity to remove routing loops.

BGP provides support for multihoming across u to eight (8) paths to a destination.

BGP's flexibility and complexity lies in its use of attributes (carried by community values) in route maps to "customize" a network topology. The attributes as defined by RFC 1771 are as follows:

- ORIGIN
- AS_PATH
- NEXT_HOP
- MULTI_EXIT_DESC (MED)
- LOCAL_PREF
- ATROMIC_AGGREGATE
- AGGREGATOR

BGP enables internal and external peering within and between ASs. These peers exchange routing updates every 60 seconds, with a default hold time of 180 seconds.

To help reduce the amount of peers a router will have in an AS, BGP employs the use of either route reflectors or confederations. Route reflector client routers peer with another router or concentration router. These peers are then known as clients. They receive updates from and send updates to the route reflector.

BGP does not use administrative distances during the route selection process. BGP uses administrative distances to select which routes are placed in the routing table.

Three administrative distances are associated with BGP:

- Internal (IBGP)—Routes are learned from IBGP peers. The default administrative distance is 200.

- External (EBGP)—Routes are learned from EBGP peers. The default administrative distance is 20.

- Local—Routes are generated locally. The default administrative distance is 20.

The following list contains the rules that BGP uses to determine the best path to a destination network:

1 Prefer the path with the largest weight. Note: Weight is a Cisco-specific parameter, local to the router on which it is configured.

2 Prefer the path with the largest LOCAL_PREF.

3 Prefer the path that was locally originated via a **network** or **aggregate** BGP subcommand, or through redistribution from an IGP. Local paths sourced by **network/redistribute** commands are preferred over local aggregates sourced by the **aggregate-address** command.

4 Prefer the path with the shortest AS_PATH. Note the following:

   — This step is skipped if **bgp bestpath as-path ignore** is configured.

   — An AS_SET counts as 1, no matter how many ASs are in the set.

   — The AS_CONFED_SEQUENCE is not included in the AS_PATH length.

5 Prefer the path with the lowest origin type. IGP is lower than EGP, and EGP is lower than INCOMPLETE.

6 Prefer the path with the lowest MED. Note the following:

   — This comparison is only done if the first (neighboring) AS is the same in the two paths; any confederation sub-ASs are ignored. In other words, MEDs are compared only if the first AS in the AS_SEQUENCE is the same for multiple paths. Any preceding AS_CONFED_SEQUENCE is ignored.

   — If **bgp always-compare-med** is enabled, MEDs are compared for all paths. This option needs to be enabled over the entire AS; otherwise, routing loops can occur.

— If **bgp bestpath med-confed** is enabled, MEDs are compared for all paths that consist only of AS_CONFED_SEQUENCE (paths originated within the local confederation).

— Paths received from a neighbor with a MED of 4,294,967,295 will have the MED changed to 4,294,967,294 before insertion into the BGP table.

— Paths received with no MED are assigned a MED of 0, unless **bgp bestpath missing-as-worst** is enabled, in which case they are assigned a MED of 4,294,967,294.

— The **bgp deterministic med** command can also influence this step.

7 Prefer external (eBGP) over internal (iBGP) paths. Note: Paths containing AS_CONFED_SEQUENCE are local to the confederation; therefore, they are treated as internal paths. No distinction is made between confederation external and confederation internal.

8 Prefer the path with the lowest IGP metric to the BGP next hop.

9 If **maximum-paths n** is enabled, and multiple external or confederation-external paths exist from the same neighboring AS or sub-AS, BGP inserts up to *n* most recently received paths in the IP routing table. This allows eBGP multipath load sharing. The maximum value of *n* is currently 6. The default value, when this option is disabled, is 1. The oldest received path is marked as the best path in the output of **show ip bgp <longer-prefixes>**, and the equivalent of **next-hop-self** is performed before forwarding this best path to internal peers.

10 If both paths are external, prefer the path that was received first (the oldest one). This step minimizes route-flap because a newer path will not displace an older one, even if it was the preferred route based on the additional decision criteria listed next. It is better practice to apply the additional decision steps to iBGP paths only to ensure a consistent best-path decision within the network, and thereby avoid loops. Note: This step is skipped if any of the following is true:

— The **bgp best path compare-routerid** command is enabled. Note: This command was introduced in IOS releases 12.0.11S, 12.0.11SC, 12.0.11S3, 12.1.3, 12.1.3AA, 12.1.3.T, and 12.1.3.E.

— The router ID is the same for multiple paths. The routes were received from the same router.

— No current best path exists. An example of losing the current best path occurs when the neighbor offering the path goes down.

11 Prefer the route coming from the BGP router with the lowest router ID. The router ID is the highest IP address on the router, with preference given to loopback addresses. It can also be set manually using the **bgp router-id** command. Note: If a path contains route-reflector (RR) attributes, the originator ID is substituted for the router ID in the path selection process.

12 If the originator or router ID is the same for multiple paths, prefer the path with the minimum cluster ID length. This will only be present in BGP route-reflector environments. It allows clients to peer with RRs or clients in other clusters. In this scenario, the client must be aware of the RR-specific BGP attribute.

13 Prefer the path coming from the lowest neighbor address. This is the IP address used in the BGP **neighbor** configuration, and corresponds to the remote peer used in the TCP connection with the local router.

BGP is a complex routing protocol, the intricacies of which have commanded volumes of books to be published. Following is some recommended reading to learn more about BGP:

- *Internet Routing Architectures: Second Edition*, Sam Halabi, ISBN 1-57870-233-X, Cisco Press, Indianapolis, Indiana, 2000

- *Cisco BGP-4 Command and Configuration Handbook*, William Parkhurst, ISBN 1-58705-017-X, Cisco Press, Indianapolis, Indiana, 2001.

- *Routing in the Internet: Second Edition*, Christian Huitema, ISBN 0-13022-647-5, Prentice Hall PTR, Upper Saddle River, New Jersey, 2000.

- RFC 1771 A Border Gateway Protocol 4 (BGP-4). Y. Rekhter, T. Li. March 1995.

EGP

EGP is an Exterior Routing Protocol used for exchanging routing information with gateways in other autonomous systems. Unlike interior protocols, EGP propagates only reachability indications, not true metrics. EGP updates contain metrics, called *distances*, which range from 0 to 255. The EGP communications server will only compare EGP distances learned from the same AS.

EGP is defined by the following RFCs:

0827 Exterior Gateway Protocol (EGP). E.C. Rosen. Oct-01-1982. Format: TXT=68436 bytes. Updated by RFC0904. Status: Unknown.

0904 Exterior Gateway Protocol formal specification. D.L. Mills. Apr-01-1984. Format: TXT=65226 bytes. Updates RFC0827, RFC0888. Status: Historic.

Before EGP sends routing information to a remote router, it must establish an adjacency with that router. This is accomplished by an exchange of "Hello" (not to be confused with the HELLO protocol, or OSPF HELLO messages) and "I Heard You" (I-H-U) messages with that router. Computers communicating via EGP are called EGP *neighbors*, and the exchange of "Hello" and "I-H-U" messages is referred to as *acquiring a neighbor*. After the neighbor is acquired, the system polls the neighbor for routing information. The neighbor responds by sending an update that contains routing information. If the system receives a poll from its neighbor, it responds with its own update packet. When the system receives an update, it includes routes from the update into its routing database. If the neighbor fails to respond to three consecutive polls, the router assumes that the neighbor is down and removes the neighbor's routes from its database.

EGP Configuration

EGP, specified in RFC 904, is an older Exterior Gateway Protocol that is used for communicating with certain communication servers in the defense data network (DDN) that the U.S. Department of Defense designates as *core communication servers*. EGP also was used extensively when attaching to the National Science Foundation Network (NSFnet) and other large backbone networks.

An exterior communication server uses EGP to advertise its knowledge of routes to networks within its autonomous system. It sends these advertisements to the core communication servers, which then readvertise their collected routing information to the exterior communication server. A neighbor or peer communication server is any communication server with which the communication server communicates using EGP.

NOTE   Cisco's implementation of EGP supports three primary functions, as specified in RFC 904:

- Routers that are running EGP establish a set of neighbors, and these neighbors share reachability information.
- EGP communication servers poll their neighbors periodically to see if they are "alive."
- EGP communication servers send update messages that contain information about the reachability of networks within their autonomous systems.

To enable EGP routing on a communication server, complete the following tasks:

1 Enable EGP routing (mandatory).

2 Configure EGP neighbor relationships (mandatory).

3 Adjust EGP timers (optional).

4 Configure third-party EGP support (optional).

5 Configure backup communication servers (optional).

6 Configure default routes (optional).

7 Define a central routing information manager (core gateway) (optional).

EGP Summary

EGP is an older Exterior Gateway Protocol that has not been implemented widely in recent years due to increased feature, functionality, and deployment of BGP.

Summary

Intermediate System to Intermediate System (IS-IS) is defined by ISO/IEC 10589 and was initially developed by the International Organization for Standardization (ISO) in 1992. This occurred at The same time that the Internet Architecture Board was developing Open Shortest Path First (OSPF), defined by the Internet Engineering Task Force (IETF) in RFC 1131). IS-IS was initially developed to support the OSI Layer 3 Routing Protocol Connectionless Network Service (CLNS). Integrated IS-IS was developed as an extension to the original IS-IS specification to support IP routing.

NOTE   Typically, IS-IS is the term used when discussing Integrated IS-IS (IP extension).

In many ways, IS-IS is similar to OSPF; however, some significant differences exist as well.

IS-IS is similar to OSPF in the following ways:

- IS-IS is a link-state protocol, with each router maintaining a link-state database by using the shortest path first algorithm for route calculation.
- IS-IS uses areas to divide the routed network into more manageable pieces, which reduces route resource requirements.
- IS-IS uses a two-layer hierarchy to route between areas.
- IS-IS routers use Hello packets to maintain neighbor adjacencies with other IS-IS routers.
- IS-IS supports variable length subnet masking (VLSM) and network summarization area boundaries.

NOTE   Because of its multiprotocol design, IS-IS is suitable for IPv6 transport, with only the modification of an address family definition for IPv6.

IS-IS is different from OSPF in the following ways:

- IS-IS routers are part of a single area, and area boundaries fall *between* routers. In OSPF, area boundaries fall *within* routers.
- The IS-IS backbone is defined by router types versus a particular area ID, such as area 0.
- IS-IS information is passed between routers using CLNS versus IP. Rather than use IP packets, IS-IS uses protocol data units (PDUs) to communicate information.

BGP is an Exterior Gateway Protocol (EGP) that is used to pass routing information between autonomous systems (ASs). BGP is still a routing protocol and, like other routing protocols, it passes routing information and uses metrics for route determination. BGP advertises which networks can be reached and can act in either an interior (IBGP) or exterior (EBGP) mode. IBGP or EBGP configurations mean that BGP can be configured to advertise networks within an AS or between different ASs. The key to BGP operation is in the configuration of which networks to advertise and whether they are directly connected.

NOTE	BGP uses TCP (port 179) to communicate with other routers.

The primary purpose of BGP4 is to exchange network reachability information with other BGP (autonomous) systems. This network layer reachability information (NLRI) includes information about each AS in the list. NLRI updates carry a network number, a list of the ASs through which the NLRI has passed (called the AS path), and a list of other path attributes that is used to construct a graph of network connectivity to remove routing loops.

CHAPTER 26

IPv6 Introduction

The Internet Engineering Task Force (IETF) has adopted Internet Protocol, version 6 (IPv6) as a replacement for Internet Protocol, version 4 (IPv4), the standard used today. This chapter provides an overview of IPv6, including routing and addressing, address autoconfiguration, neighbor discovery, and transitioning from IPv4 to IPv6.

NOTE   It is worth mentioning that IPv6 is a work in progress; therefore, it is subject to developmental changes.

The developmental efforts regarding IPv6 can be traced through the following RFCs. (This is a partial list of the directly relevant RFCs.)

- December 1995 / 1883 Internet Protocol, Version 6 (IPv6) Specification. S. Deering, R. Hinden. December 1995. Format: TXT=82089 bytes. Obsoleted by RFC 2460. Status: Proposed Standard.

- December 1998 / 2460 Internet Protocol, Version 6 (IPv6) Specification. S. Deering, R. Hinden. December 1998. Format: TXT=85490 bytes. Obsoletes RFC 1883. Status: Draft Standard.

- January 1999 / 2492 IPv6 over ATM Networks. G. Armitage, P. Schulter, M. Jork. January 1999. Format: TXT=21199 bytes. Status: Proposed Standard.

- March 1999 / 2545 Use of BGP-4 Multiprotocol Extensions for IPv6 Inter-Domain Routing. P. Marques, F. Dupont. March 1999. Format: TXT=10209 bytes. Status: Proposed Standard.

- May 1999 / 2590 Transmission of IPv6 Packets over Frame Relay Networks Specification. A. Conta, A. Malis, M. Mueller. May 1999. Format: TXT=41817 bytes. Status: Proposed Standard.

- December 1999 / 2740 OSPF for IPv6. R. Coltun, D. Ferguson, J. Moy. December 1999. Format: TXT=189810 bytes. Status: Proposed Standard.

- June 2001 / 3142 An IPv6-to-IPv4 Transport Relay Translator. J. Hagino, K. Yamamoto. June 2001. Format: TXT=20864 bytes. Status: Informational.

The Internet Protocol (IP) was introduced in the Advanced Research Projects Agency Network (ARPANET) in the mid-1970s. The current version of IP in use today is IP version 4 (IPv4). IPv4 was never intended for the Internet as it is today, specifically with regard to the number of hosts, types of applications, and security concerns.

In the early 1990s, the IETF recognized that the only way to cope with the changes to the Internet, specifically regarding the growth, was to design a new version of IP to become the successor to IPv4. The IETF formed the IP next generation (IPng) working group to define this transitional protocol to ensure long-term compatibility between the current and new IP versions and support for current and emerging IP-based applications.

IPv6 is designed to be an evolution from IPv4 rather than a change. Useful features of IPv4 were carried over in IPv6 and less useful features were dropped. According to the IPv6 specification, the changes from IPv4 to IPv6 fall primarily into the following categories:

- Expanded addressing capabilities

  — The IP address size was increased from 32 bits (2^{32} address) to 128 bits (2^{128} address) in IPv6; supporting a greater number of addressable nodes, more levels of hierarchical addressing, and autoconfiguration of addresses for remote users.

  — The scalability of multicast routing is improved by adding a Scope field to multicast addresses.

  — A new type of address, called anycast, is enabled.

- Header format simplification

  — Certain IPv4 header fields have been dropped, or made optional, reducing the necessary amount of packet processing and limiting the bandwidth cost of the IPv6 header.

- Improved support for extensions and options

  — IPv6 header options are encoded to allow for more efficient forwarding, less stringent limits on the length of options, and increased flexibility for introducing new, but not yet, developed options.

  — Some fields of an IPv4 header have been made optional in IPv6.

- Flow labeling capability

  — A new quality-of-service (QoS) capability has been added to enable the labeling of packets belonging to particular traffic "flows" for which the sender requests special handling, such as real-time service.

- Authentication and privacy capabilities

  — Extensions to support security options, such as authentication, data integrity, and data confidentiality, are available.

One of the deficiencies of IPv4 that the committees identified was the complexity of the IPv4 headers. If these headers were allowed to grow by the same factor that the address space was to be enlarged, things would get rather unwieldy.

The IPv4 header has a total of 10 fields, the two 32-bit address fields (one for the source, and one for the destination), and an options field, which is padded to bring the entire header up to the correct length. With no options in the options field, an IPv4 header is 20 bytes long, so an 80-byte header for IPv6 was not a desirable thing.

The IPv6 header is simplified by allowing headers to be chained together. Six fields are available—the two 128-byte addresses for source and destination, and no options. Variations in the header that would have been contained within the IPv4 header or its options field are now identified using a new field, which specifies that another header is included after the current one but before the data.

The first header defines the minimum needed for an IPv6 packet, including the version, priority, flow label, payload length, and hop limit. It also includes a field to say "and there is another header after this one." The number of headers that can be chained together in this way is unlimited. The next header field is an 8-bit number, so 255 different types of header can exist.

Only seven different header types are presently defined:

- Hop-by-hop options header
- Routing header
- Fragment header
- Authentication header
- Encapsulating security header
- Payload header
- Destination options header

The result of this simplification and improved flexibility is that the simplest IPv6 header is still only 40 bytes long, or double the size of the IPv4 header without options. This is despite the fact that the two addresses it incorporates are four times the size of the IPv4 header. The reduced complexity of the default IPv6 header makes the task of the average router much easier than it otherwise might be.

IPv6 Terms

IPv6 standardizes some terminology that in the IPv4 environment has been defined almost by word-of-mouth.

The standardized terminology is as follows:

- Packet—An IPv6 protocol data unit (PDU), comprising a header and the associated payload. In IPv4, this would have been termed *packet* or *datagram*.
- Node—A device that implements IPv6.
- Router—An IPv6 node that forwards packets, based on the IP address, not explicitly addressed to itself. In former TCP/IP terminology, this device was often referred to as a *gateway*.
- Host—Any node that is not a router, typically end-user systems.
- Link—A medium over which nodes communicate with each other at the data link layer (such as an ATM, frame relay, or SMDS wide-area network, or an Ethernet or Token Ring LAN).
- Neighbors—Nodes that are attached to the same link.

IPv6 Addressing

To accommodate almost unlimited growth and a variety of addressing formats, IPv6 addresses are 128 bits in length (2^{128}).

NOTE 2^{128} addresses provide enough address space to provide every molecule in the solar system with its own address, totaling approximately 3.402823669209384634633746074317e+38 unique addresses.

IPv6 defines three types of addresses:

- Unicast—Address specifies a single host.
- Anycast—Address specifies a set of hosts, such as a set of servers for a given organization's application. A packet sent to an anycast address is delivered to one of the hosts identified by that address, usually the closest one as defined by the routing protocol.
- Multicast—Address identifies a set of hosts. A packet sent to a multicast address is delivered to all of the hosts in the group.

IPv6 has no broadcast address like IPv4 does. That function in IPv6 is provided by multicast addresses.

IPv4 addresses are written in dotted decimal notation, where the decimal value of each of the four address bytes is separated by dots, such as 198.133.219.25.

The regular form of an IPv6 address is the hexadecimal value of the eight 16-bit blocks of the address, separated by colons (:), such as FF04:19:5:ABD4:187:2C:754:2B1. (Leading zeros do not have to be written because each field must have some value).

IPv6 addresses often contain long strings of zeros because of the way in which addresses are allocated. A shorthand, or compressed, address form uses a double colon (::) to indicate multiple 16-bit blocks of zeros; for example, the address FF01:0:0:0:0:0:0:5A could be written as FF01::5A. To avoid ambiguity, the :: can only appear once in an address.

An alternative hybrid address format has been defined to make it more convenient to represent an IPv4 address in an IPv6 environment. In this scheme, the first 96 address bits (six groups of 16) are represented in the regular IPv6 format. The remaining 32 address bits are represented in common IPv4 dotted decimal, such as 0:0:0:0:0:0:199.182.20.17 (or ::199.182.20.17).

Table 26-1 demonstrates the allocation of IPv6 address prefixes, as defined by RFC 1884.

Table 26-1   *Address Prefix Allocation (RFC 1884)*

Allocation	Prefix (Binary)	Fraction of Address Space
Reserved	0000 0000	1/256
Unassigned	0000 0001	1/256
Reserved for NSAP allocation	0000 001	1/128
Reserved for IPX allocation	0000 010	1/128
Unassigned	0000 011	1/128
Unassigned	0000 1	1/32
Unassigned	0001	1/16
Unassigned	001	1/8
Provider-based unicast address	010	1/8
Unassigned	011	1/8
Reserved for geographic-based unicast addresses	100	1/8
Unassigned	101	1/8
Unassigned	110	1/8
Unassigned	1110	1/16
Unassigned	1111 0	1/32
Unassigned	1111 10	1/64
Unassigned	1111 110	1/128
Unassigned	1111 1110 0	1/512
Link local use addresses	1111 1110 10	1/1024

(continues)

Table 26-1   *Address Prefix Allocation (RFC 1884) (Continued)*

Allocation	Prefix (Binary)	Fraction of Address Space
Site local use addresses	1111 1110 11	1/1024
Multicast addresses	1111 1111	1/256

One of the goals of the IPv6 address format is to accommodate many different types of addresses. The beginning of an address contains a three- to ten-bit format prefix that defines the general address type per the previous table. The remaining bits contain the actual host address, in a format specific to the indicated address type.

For example, the provider-based unicast address is an IPv6 address that a network service provider might assign to a customer. The format for this address is illustrated in Figure 26-1.

Figure 26-1   *Provider-Based Unicast Address Format (RFC 1884)*

010 (3 bits)	Registry ID (5 bits)	Provider ID (*N* bits)	Subscriber ID (56 - *N* bits)	Intra-Subscriber ID (64 bits)

The following list describes Figure 26-1, defining the unicast address format in detail.

- Format prefix—Indicates the type of address as provider-based unicast. This is always 3 bits, and it is coded as 010.

- Registry ID—Identifies the Internet address registry from which this ISP obtains addresses. This is a 5-bit value indicating the Internet Assigned Numbers Authority (IANA) or one of the three regional registries, namely the Internet Network Information Center (InterNIC), Rèseaux IP Europèens Network Coordination Center (RIPE NCC), or Asia-Pacific Network Information Center (APNIC). In the future, national registries might also be accommodated.

- Provider ID—Identifies the ISP. This field contains the address block that the address registry authority assigns to the ISP.

- Subscriber ID—Identifies the ISP's subscriber. This field contains the address that the ISP assigns to the subscriber. The ProviderID and SubscriberID fields together are 56 bits in length.

- Intra-Subscriber ID—Contains the portion of the address assigned and managed by the subscriber. The 64-bit value used comprises a 16-bit subnet identifier and a 48-bit interface identifier (such as an IEEE MAC address).

With more than 16 million hosts using 32-bit addresses, the public Internet must continue to accommodate IPv4 addresses as it migrates to IPv6 and IPv6 addressing. IPv4 addresses are carried in a 128-bit IPv6 address that begins with 80 zeros (0:0:0:0:0).

The next 16-bit block contains the compatibility bits, which indicate the way in which the host/router handles IPv4 and IPv6 addresses. If the device can handle either IPv4 or IPv6 addresses, the compatibility bits are all set to zero (0) and termed an IPv4-compatible IPv6 address. If the address represents an IPv4-only node, the compatibility bits are all set to one (0xFFFF), and the address is termed an IPv4-mapped IPv6 address. The final 32 bits contain a 32-bit IPv4 address in dotted decimal form.

IPv6 Multicast

IPv6 multicast addresses provide an identifier for a group of nodes. A node can belong to any number of multicast groups. Multicast addresses cannot be used as source addresses in IPv6 packets or appear in routing headers. Figure 26-2 illustrates the format for multicast addresses.

Figure 26-2 *Multicast Address Format (RFC 1884)*

11111111 (8 bits)	Flag (4 bits)	Scope (4 bits)	Group ID (112 bits)

The following list describes Figure 26-2, defining the multicast address format in detail.

- A multicast address starts with eight ones (0xFF).

- The next four bits are a set of flag bits (flgs) The three high-order bits are set to zero, and the fourth bit (T-bit) indicates a permanently assigned ("well-known") multicast address (T=0) or a nonpermanent assigned ("transient") multicast address (T=1).

- The next four bits indicate the scope of the address (scop), or the part of the network for which this multicast address is relevant. Options include node-local (0x1), link-local (0x2), site-local (0x5), organization-local (0x8), or global (0xE).

- The remaining 112 bits form the Group ID, which identifies the multicast group, either permanent or transient, within the given scope.

The interpretation of a permanently assigned multicast address is independent of the scope value. For example, if the Internet video servers group were assigned a permanent multicast address with a group identifier of 0x77, then the following conditions would exist:

- FF01:0:0:0:0:0:0:77 would refer to all video servers on the same node as the sender.

- FF02:0:0:0:0:0:0:77 would refer to all video servers on the same link as the sender.

- FF05:0:0:0:0:0:0:77 would refer to all video servers at the same site as the sender.

- FF0E:0:0:0:0:0:0:77 would refer to all video servers on the Internet.

A number of well-known multicast addresses are predefined:

- Reserved multicast addresses—These are reserved and are never assigned to a multicast group. These addresses have the form FF0x:0:0:0:0:0:0:0, in which x is any hexadecimal digit.

- All nodes addresses—These identify the group of all IPv6 nodes within the given scope. These addresses are of the form FF0t:0:0:0:0:0:0:1, in which t = 1 (node-local) or 2 (link-local).

- All routers addresses—These identify the group of all IPv6 routers within the given scope. These addresses are of the form FF0t:0:0:0:0:0:0:2, where t = 1 (node-local) or 2 (link-local).

- The DHCP server/relay-agent—This identifies the group of all IPv6 Dynamic Host Configuration Protocol (DHCP) servers and relay agents with the link-local scope. This address is FF02:0:0:0:0:0:0:C.

IPv6 Extension Headers

In IPv6, optional IP layer information is encoded in separate extension headers that are placed between the IPv6 basic header and the higher layer protocol header. An IPv6 packet might carry zero, one, or more such extension headers, each identified by the next header field of the preceding header and each containing an even multiple of 32 bits (see Figure 26-3). A fully compliant implementation of IPv6 includes support for the following extension headers and corresponding options:

- The hop-by-hop options header is used to carry information that must be examined by every node along a packet's path. Three options are included in this category:

  — The Pad1 option is used to insert a single octet of padding into the options area of a header for 64-bit alignment.

  — The PadN option is used to insert two or more octets of padding.

  — The jumbo payload option is used to indicate the length of the packet when the payload portion is longer than 65,535 octets. (This option is employed when the payload length field is set to zero.)

- The routing header is used by an IPv6 source to list one or more intermediate nodes that must be visited as part of the packet's path to the destination. This option is functionally similar to IPv4's loose and strict source route options. The routing header contains a list of addresses and an indication of whether each address is strict or loose. If an address is marked strict, it means that this node must be a neighbor of the previously addressed node. If an address is marked loose, this node does not have to be a neighbor of the previous node.

- The fragment header is used by an IPv6 source to send packets that are larger than the maximum transmission unit (MTU) on the path to the destination. This header will contain a packet identifier, fragment offset, and final fragment indicator. Unlike IPv4, in which fragmentation information is carried in every packet header, IPv6 carries fragmentation/reassembly information only in those packets that are fragmented. In another departure from IPv4, fragmentation in IPv6 is performed only by the source and not by the routers along a packet's path. All IPv6 hosts and routers must support an MTU of 576 octets. It is recommended that path MTU discovery procedures (per RFC 1981) be invoked to discover and take advantage of those paths with a larger MTU.

- The destination options header is used to carry optional information that has to be examined only by a packet's destination node(s). The only destination options defined so far are Pad1 and PadN, as described earlier.

The IP authentication header (AH) and IP encapsulating security payload (ESP) are IPv6 security mechanisms. Figure 26-3 illustrates examples of an IPv6 extension header.

Figure 26-3 *IPv6 Extension Header Examples*

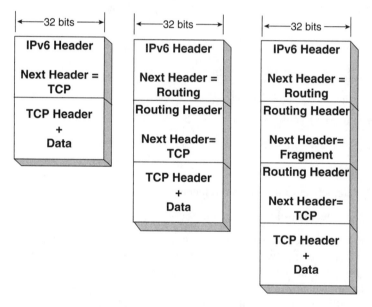

Figure 26-3 is detailed as follows:

- The TCP segment is encapsulated in IP without additional options (left).
- The TCP segment follows a routing header (middle).
- The TCP segment fragment follows a fragment header that follows a routing header (right).

With the exception of the hop-by-hop option, extension headers are only examined or processed by the intended destination node(s). The contents of each extension header determine whether to proceed to the next header; therefore, extension headers must be processed in the order they appear in the packet.

IPv6 Quality of Service (QoS)

The priority and flow label fields in the IPv6 header are used by a source to identify packets that need special handling by network routers. The concept of a flow in IP is a major departure from IPv4 and most other connectionless protocols. Some protocols have called flows a form of connectionless virtual circuit because all packets with the same flow label are treated similarly, and the network views them as associated entities.

Special handling for non-default QoS is an important capability to support applications that require guaranteed throughput, end-to-end delay, or jitter, such as multimedia or real-time communication. These QoS parameters are an extension of IPv4's type of service (TOS) capability.

The priority field allows the source to identify the desired priority of a packet. Values 0 to 7 are used for congestion-controlled traffic, or traffic that backs off in response to network congestion, such as TCP segments. For this type of traffic, the following priority values are recommended:

1 Uncharacterized traffic

2 "Filler" traffic, such as Netnews

3 Unattended data transfer, such as e-mail

4 Reserved

5 Attended bulk transfer, such as FTP, HTTP, and NFS

6 Reserved

7 Interactive traffic, such as Telnet and X

8 Internet control traffic, such as routing protocols and SNMP

Values 8 to 15 are defined for noncongestion-controlled traffic, or traffic that does not back off in response to network congestion, such as real-time packets being sent at a constant rate. For this type of traffic, the lowest priority value (8) should be used for packets that the sender is most willing to have discarded under congestion conditions, such as high-fidelity video traffic. The highest value (15) should be used for those packets that the sender is least willing to have discarded, such as low-fidelity audio traffic.

A source uses the flow label to identify packets that need nondefault QoS. A control protocol might convey the nature of the special handling to the network routers, such as the Resource Reservation Protocol (RSVP). The special handling might also be conveyed by information within the flow packets, such as a hop-by-hop option. Multiple active flows might be present from a source to a destination, as well as traffic that is not associated with a flow (Flow Label = 0). The combination of a source address and a nonzero flow label uniquely identify a flow. This aspect of IPv6 is still in the experimental stage. Future definition is expected.

IPv6 Migration

The transition to IPv6 has already begun, even though most Internet and TCP/IP users have not yet seen new IPv6 software deployed. Before IPv6 can be widely deployed, the network infrastructure must be upgraded to employ software that accommodates the new protocol.

The new IPv6 address format must accommodate every TCP/IP protocol that uses addresses. For example, the Domain Name System (DNS) has defined an AAAA resource record for IPv6 128-bit addresses (IPv4's 32-bit addresses use an A record) and the IP6.INT address domain (IPv4 uses the ARPA address domain).

Other protocols must be modified for IPv6. These protocols include the following:

- Dynamic Host Configuration Protocol (DHCP)
- Address Resolution Protocol (ARP)
- IP routing protocols
    - Routing Information Protocol (RIP)
    - Open Shortest Path First (OSPF)
    - Border Gateway Protocol (BGP)

IPv6 trials started in 1996, and initial rollout of IPv6 in the Internet backbone was completed in 1997. There is no scheduled or desired date of a flash cut from one to the other. Coexistence of IPv4 and IPv6 is anticipated for many years to come. Although IPv6 will appear in the large ISP backbones sooner rather than later, some smaller service providers and local network administrators will not make the conversion quickly unless they perceive some benefit from IPv6.

The coexistence of IPv4 and IPv6 in the network means that different protocols and procedures will need to be accommodated. In one common short-term scenario, IPv6 networks will be interconnected via an IPv4 backbone, as illustrated in Figure 26-4.

Figure 26-4 *Short-Term Scenario with an IPv4 Network Interconnecting IPv6 Networks*

The IPv4/IPv6 tunneling process is detailed as follows:

- The boundary routers will be IPv4-compatible IPv6 nodes, and the interfaces will be given IPv4-compatible IPv6 addresses.

- The IPv6 packet is transported over the IPv4 network by encapsulating the packet in an IPv4 header.

Tunneling can also be performed when an organization has converted a part of its subnet to IPv6. This process can be used on host-host, router-router, or host-router links.

Although the introduction of IPv6 is inevitable, many of the market pressures for its development have been somewhat obviated because of parallel developments that enhance the capabilities of IPv4. The address limitations of IPv4, for example, are minimized by use of classless interdomain routing (CIDR). The DHCP can manage nomadic user address allocation. The Resource Reservation Protocol (RSVP) can manage quality of service. The IP Authentication Header and Encapsulating Security Payload procedures can be applied to IPv4 as well as IPv6.

One of the important proving grounds of IPv6 is the 6bone, a test network spanning North America, Europe, and Japan. The 6bone began operation in 1996 and is a virtual network built on top of portions of today's IPv4-based Internet, designed specifically to route IPv6 packets. The goal of this collaborative trial is to test IPv6 implementations and to define early policies and procedures that will be necessary to support IPv6 in the future. In addition, it will demonstrate IPv6's new capabilities and will provide a basis for user confidence in the new protocol.

The transition from IPv4 to IPv6 will likely occur when host operating system software is updated. In some cases, dual-stacked systems with both versions of IP will be in operation. This dual-stacking supports migration efforts from IPv4 to IPv6. For larger networks, it might make sense to follow the model of the larger global Internet. In particular, pre-design the IPv6 network topology and addressing scheme, build a testbed IPv6 network with routers and a DNS, and then slowly migrate applications, users, and subnets to the new backbone. The lessons learned from the 6bone activity will be useful for individual networks as well as the Internet backbone.

Host Address Autoconfiguration

To minimize the amount of disruption during host renumbering, it is important to take steps that will minimize forceful termination of established communications between the hosts, renumbered or otherwise. TCP/IP communications are bound to a particular IP address of a host. This means you can minimize disruption by avoiding binding new communications to an old address, while allowing the existing communications to use the old address for as long as possible.

NOTE	The binding of new addressing to an old address is an approach adopted by IPv6.

IPv6 address autoconfiguration is supported through two mechanisms:

- Stateful—Based on the DHCP) and appropriately modified for IPv6 [DHCPv6].
- Stateless—Eliminates the need to maintain DHCP servers. Hosts are expected to construct their IPv6 address by concatenating their IEEE MAC address with the subnet prefix that they learn by using neighbor discovery from the routers that are on the same subnet.
  - While the stateful address autoconfiguration does not restrict the type of addresses that it could configure, the stateless address autoconfiguration does not support autoconfiguration of IPv4 compatible IPv6 addresses, potentially limiting the usefulness of the stateless autoconfiguration during transition from IPv4 to IPv6.

IPv6 Renumbering Issues

Renumbering for IPv6 internetworks presents several issues. The more significant issues are as follows:

- DNS databases require updating for all the nodes whose addresses have been changed. Renumbering requires updating destination reachability information regarding DNS server addresses.
- Renumbering requires changing router configurations, such as access lists and destination reachability information (for routing table construction and maintenance).
- Some TCP/IP applications rely on IP address-based configuration databases. Renumbering requires the changing and updating of these databases.
- For various client/server applications, if the clients are configured with the IP addresses of the servers, renumbering a site requires changing client configuration information. This is an issue because some software licensing technologies are based on using IP addresses. Renumbering a site could require changing such a licensing database.

IPv6 Neighbor Discover Protocol (NDP)

NDP is to IPv6 what ARP, ICMP, and ICMP Redirect are to IPv4. IPv6 uses multicast, rather than broadcast (IPv4), for data link layer (MAC) address resolution. This significantly reduces the number of address-resolution interrupts on nodes, or hosts, other than the resolution target.

IPv6 replaces the ICMP redirect message with the ND redirect message. To support multiple IP subnets on a common subnet, IPv6 enables a host to accept redirects regardless of whether the next hop (specified by the redirect) is on the same IP subnet as the host. The target address carried by an IPv6 NDP (ICMP) redirect can either identify a router or the ultimate destination subnet (host).

IPv6 addressing information carries explicit timeouts, set by the information sender to directly control the lifetime of the information.

NOTE   IPv6 explicit timeouts are an important feature in dynamic internetworks, such as with mobile hosts.

NDP provides hosts with such information as the maximum hop count that hosts should use in outgoing packets, as well as some data-link (MAC) layer parameters, such as the maximum transmission unit (MTU), facilitating host autoconfiguration.

NDP controls whether hosts use stateful or stateless address autoconfiguration. Regarding stateless address autoconfiguration, NDP provides all necessary information for hosts to configure their addresses.

IPv4/IPv6 Transition

Graceful transition from IPv4 to IPv6 is crucial for the success of IPv6. During the transition period, it is essential to maintain compatibility with the existing installed base of IPv4 hosts and routers.

IPv6 Host Transition

IPv6 transition is based on the assumption that every IPv6 host will have two IP stacks: IPv6 and IPv4. This same dual host will also have an application programming interface (API) that supports IPv4 and IPv6.

NOTE   The dual-stack API is likely to be an extension of the current (IPv4) API.

Implementing an IPv6 stack on hosts and developing IPv6-capable APIs are essential IPv6 transitions.

IPv6 Routing Transition

The transition to IPv6 routing assumes deployment of routers that support both IPv4 and IPv6 routing protocols and packet forwarding. The routing protocols that are expected to be used with IPv6 (at least initially) are mostly straightforward extensions of the existing IPv4 routing protocols. Tunneling IPv6 over IPv4 will support IPv6 connectivity among hosts in different segments.

IPv4/IPv6 Tunneling

IPv6 transition allows for two types of tunnels:

- Automatic—As the name implies, manual configuration is not required.

    — IPv6 addresses of the reachable hosts through automatic tunnels must be IPv4 compatible. IPv4 addresses that are used to form IPv6 addresses of these hosts (IPv4-compatible addresses) must be routable.

    — Establishing automatic tunnels between any pair of IPv6 hosts whose IPv6 addresses are IPv4-compatible enables these hosts to use IPv6 encapsulated into IPv4 end-to-end, without requiring routers on the path to support IPv6.

- Manually configured—As the name implies, these tunnels are manually configured and established. Manually configured tunnels do not require hosts to have IPv4-compatible IPv6 addresses, eliminating the preconditions associated with using automatic tunnels.

IPv4/IPv6 Network Address Translation (NAT)

An organization changes its network service provider only when an address needs to be changed. The network service provider's globally unique addressing would be "recovered" by the service provider. Because information about these addresses is localized to the NAT device(s), only these same devices require reconfiguring.

NAT devices could also play an important role during the IPv4 to IPv6 transition. They would enable the interconnection of hosts that have IPv6-only addresses (hosts that do not have IPv4-compatible addresses) with hosts that have IPv4-only addresses.

IPv6 Header

The format of an IPv6 header is shown in Figure 26-5. Although IPv6 addresses are four times the size of IPv4 addresses, the basic IPv6 header is only twice the size of an IPv4 header, thus decreasing the impact of the larger address fields.

Figure 26-5 *IPv6 Header Format*

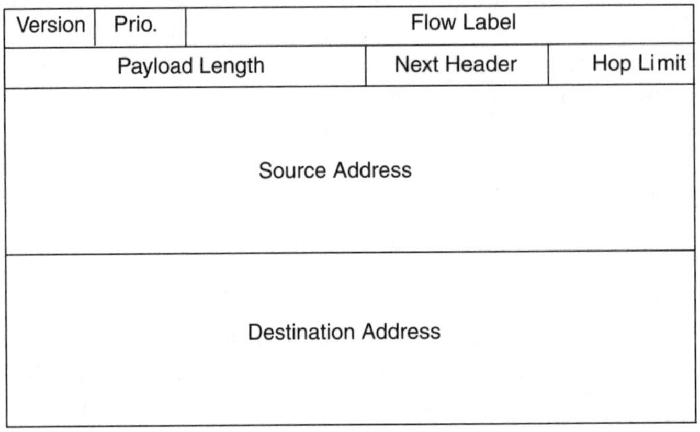

The fields of the IPv6 header are as follows:

- Version—IP version number (4 bits). This field's value is 6 for IPv6 and 4 for IPv4. Note that this field is in the same location as the version field in the IPv4 header, making it simple for an IP node to quickly distinguish an IPv4 packet from an IPv6 packet.

- Priority—This enables a source to identify the desired delivery priority of this packet (4 bits).

- Flow label—A source uses this to identify associated packets that need the same type of special handling, such as a real-time service between a pair of hosts (24 bits).

- Payload length—This is the length of the payload (the portion of the packet following the header) in octets (16 bits). The maximum value in this field is 65,535. If this field contains a zero, the packet contains a payload larger than 64 KB and the actual payload length value is carried in a jumbo payload hop-by-hop option.

- Next header—This identifies the type of header immediately following the IPv6 header. It uses the same values as the IPv4 protocol field, where applicable (8 bits). The next header field can indicate an options header, higher layer protocol, or no protocol above IP. Sample values are listed in Table 26-2.

- Hop limit—This specifies the maximum number of hops that a packet can take before it is discarded (8 bits). This value is set by the source and decremented by 1 by each node that forwards the packet. The packet is discarded if the hop limit reaches zero. The comparable field in IPv4 is the time to live (TTL) field, renamed for IPv6 because the value limits the number of hops, not the amount of time that a packet can stay in the network.

- Source address—This is the IPv6 address of the originator of the packet (128 bits).

- Destination address—This is the IPv6 address of the intended recipient(s) of the packet (128 bits).

Table 26-2 provides next header field values for the IPv6 header.

Table 26-2   *Possible Values for the Next Header Field*

Value	Contents of the Next Header
1	Internet Control Message Protocol (ICMP)
6	Transmission Control Protocol (TCP)
17	User Datagram Protocol (UDP)
43	Routing header
44	Fragment header
58	Internet Control Message Protocol version 6 (ICMPv6)
59	Nothing; this is the final header
60	Destination options header
89	Open Shortest Path First (OSPF)

IPv6/IPv4 Tunneling

IPv6/IPv4, or 6to4, connectivity can be accomplished by configuring tunnels directly with each IPv6 site, or by configuring a tunnel into a larger IPv6 routing infrastructure, as illustrated in Figure 26-6.

Figure 26-6 *IPv6/IPv4 Tunnels*

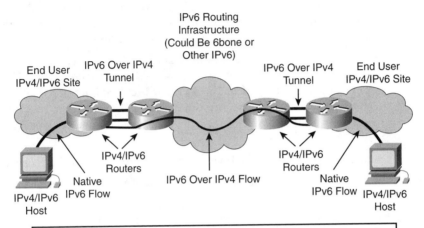

Both example end user site's IPv6 addresses are carried in the global DNS and are based on routable Aggregatable Global Unicast Address Public Topology prefixes (for instance, from the 6bone Testbed 3FFE=/16 TLA or the production allocation 2001::/16 TLAI).

The 6bone IPv6 testbed was the first IPv6 routing infrastructure to provide worldwide IPv6 connectivity (starting in 1996). In late 1999, networks that provided production IPv6 Internet service interconnected to provide this connectivity. In fact, the 6bone and production IPv6 routing infrastructures are well interconnected to guarantee worldwide IPv6 connectivity.

The 6to4 mechanism addresses many of the challenges with manually configured tunneling.

The end-user site IS/IT staff must choose an IPv6 Internet service to which to tunnel, requiring the following three (3) processes:

- Finding candidate networks when the site's choice of IPv4 service does not provide IPv6 service (either tunneling or native).

- Determining which paths are the best IPv4 paths to use so that an IPv6-over-IPv4 tunnel does not inadvertently follow an unreliable or low-performance path.

- Making arrangements with the desired IPv6 service provider for tunneling service. This scenario might be difficult if the selected provider is not willing to provide the service, or if for other administrative/cost reasons, it is difficult to establish a business relationship.

It is generally easier to have the network service provider perform these steps; however, in the early days of an IPv4-to-IPv6 transition, this might not be an option. In this case, an IPv6-over-IPv4 tunnel must be built to the network service provider and a peering relationship must be established with the same network service provider. This requires a technical relationship with the network service provider. It is also necessary to work through the various details of how to configure tunnels between two routers, including answering the following questions:

- Are the site and network service provider routers compatible and interoperable in supporting a 6to4 tunnel?

- What peering protocol will be used? (Generally this will be BGP4; however, it is always a good idea to verify with each other.)

- Have all the technical tunnel configuration issues between the site and network service provider been addressed?

6to4 Tunnel Management

A 6to4 site trying to reach another will discover the 6to4 tunnel endpoint from a DNS name to perform the address lookup and dynamically build a site-to-site tunnel, as illustrated in the Figure 26-7. The tunnels are transient, lasting only as long as a specific transaction uses the path. A 6to4 tunnel bypasses the need to establish a tunnel to a wide-area IPv6 routing infrastructure, such as the 6bone.

Figure 26-7 *6to4 Tunnel Overview*

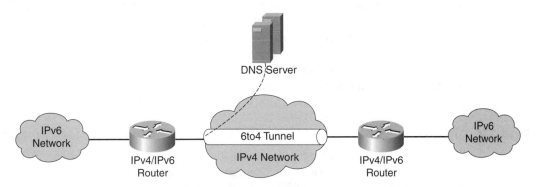

A 48-bit external routing prefix specified in the IPv6 aggregatable global unicast address format (AGGR), illustrated in Figure 26-8, provides just enough space to hold the 32 bits required for the 32-bit IPv4 tunnel endpoint.

Figure 26-8 *6to4 Prefix Format*

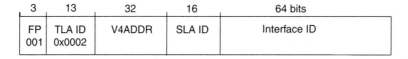

	FP = Format Prefix
	TLA ID = Top Level Aggregation Identifier
	V4ADDR = IPv4 Address of 6to4 Tunnel Endpoint
	SLA ID = Site Level Aggregation Identifier
	Interface ID = Link Level Host Identifier

This prefix has the same format as normal prefixes assigned according to the AGGR.

6to4 Case Study

The simplest 6to4 scenario occurs when several sites start to use IPv6 alongside IPv4, with no native IPv6 ISP service available. Each site identifies a router to run dual stack (that is, IPv4 and IPv6 together) and 6to4 tunneling. This ensures that the router has a globally routable IPv4 address, and that the 6to4 router is reachable by IPv6-capable hosts within the site.

A new 6to4 site advertises the 6to4 prefix to its site via the Neighbor Discovery (ND) protocol, causing IPv6 hosts at this site to have their DNS name/address entries included in the 6to4 prefix.

In operation, when one IPv6-enabled host at a 6to4 site tries to access an IPv6-enabled host by domain name at another 6to4 site, DNS will return both an IPv4 and an IPv6 IP address for that host. This is an indication that the IPv6-enabled host is reachable by both IPv4 and IPv6. The requesting host selects the IPv6 address, which will have a 6to4 prefix, and sends a packet off to its nearest router. The requesting host eventually reaches its site boundary router, assuming that it also has 6to4 service.

6to4 Communication

When the requesting site's 6to4 router sees that it must send a packet to another site (a nonlocal destination), and that the next hop destination prefix contains the special 6to4 top level aggregation (TLA) value of 2002::/16, the IPv6 packet is encapsulated as follows:

- The source IPv4 address will be the one in the requesting site's 6to4 prefix. The 6to4 prefix is the IPv4 address of the outgoing interface to the Internet on the 6to4 router and is contained in the source 6to4 prefix of the IPv6 packet.

- The IPv6 packet also contains the destination IPv4 address and will be the one in the next hop destination 6to4 prefix of the IPv6 packet.

When the destination site of the IPv4 packet, the 6to4 router, recognizes the IPv4 protocol type of 41, IPv4 security checks are made and the IPv4 header is removed, leaving the original IPv6 packet for local forwarding.

NOTE   The 6to4 mechanism is unaffected by the presence of a firewall at the border router.

It is not necessary to operate an exterior routing protocol, such as BGP4+, for 6to4 scenarios. The IPv4 exterior routing protocol handles this function.

NOTE   No new entries in IPv4 routing tables result from the use of 6to4.

6to4 Relay

The most complex 6to4 scenario occurs when sites with only 6to4 connectivity communicate with sites with only native IPv6 connectivity. This communication is accomplished by the use of a 6to4 relay that supports both 6to4 and native IPv6 connectivity, as illustrated in Figure 26-9. The 6to4 relay is accomplished with the use of an IPv4/IPv6 dual-stack router.

Figure 26-9 *6to4 Relay*

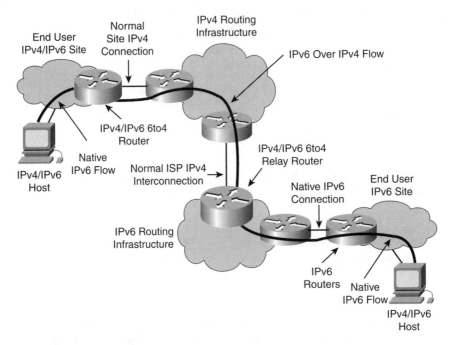

The 6to4 relay advertises a route to 2002::/16 for itself into the attached native IPv6 infrastructure. The native IPv6 network operators must filter out and discard any 6to4 (2002:...) prefix advertisements that are longer than /16. The 6to4 relay can then advertise into its 6to4 connection whatever native IPv6 routes that its policies enable. The 6to4 router at the 6to4-only site picks up these native IPv6 routes either through a BGP4+ peering session or through a default route to the 6to4 relay.

The 6to4-only site sends a packet to the native IPv6-only site by forwarding an encapsulated (tunneled) IPv6 packet to the 6to4 relay. This removes the IPv4 header (de-encapsulates) and forwards the packet to the IPv6-only site.

6to4 Maximum Transmission Unit (MTU) Issues

The IPv6 maximum transmission unit (MTU) size could be too large for some intermediate IPv4 links when a 6to4 tunnel is in use; therefore, IPv4 fragmentation could occur. The IPv4 "Do Not Fragment" bit should not be set in the IPv4 packet that carries the 6to4 tunnel.

NOTE	The following information details Cisco's implementation of IPv6.

Cisco IOS IPv6 is only available on IP Plus, Enterprise, or Service Provider IOS images.

Cisco IOS Software Early Deployment Release was available worldwide June 7, 2001 in the form of IOS 12.2T. With Release 12.2(2)T, Cisco introduced the availability of Internet Protocol Version 6 (IPv6) Phase I, as announced on May 14.

The following Cisco IOS commands are used for IPv6 implementations:

- **address-family ipv6**
- **clear bgp ipv6**
- **clear bgp ipv6 dampening**
- **clear bgp ipv6 external**
- **clear bgp ipv6 flap-statistics**
- **clear ipv6 neighbors**
- **clear ipv6 prefix-list**
- **clear ipv6 route**
- **clear ipv6 traffic**
- **copy**
- **debug bgp ipv6 dampening**
- **debug bgp ipv6 updates**
- **debug ipv6 icmp**
- **debug ipv6 nd**
- **debug ipv6 packet**
- **debug ipv6 rip**
- **debug ipv6 routing**
- **dialer-list protocol**
- **distance (IPv6 RIP)**
- **distribute-list prefix-list (IPv6 RIP)**
- **ipv6 access-class**
- **ipv6 access-list**
- **ipv6 address**

- **ipv6 address eui-64**
- **ipv6 atm-vc**
- **ipv6 enable**
- **ipv6 hop-limit**
- **ipv6 host**
- **ipv6 icmp error-interval**
- **ipv6 mtu**
- **ipv6 nd managed-config-flag**
- **ipv6 nd ns-interval**
- **ipv6 nd other-config-flag**
- **ipv6 nd prefix-advertisement**
- **ipv6 nd ra-interval**
- **ipv6 nd ra-lifetime**
- **ipv6 nd reachable-time**
- **ipv6 nd suppress-ra**
- **ipv6 prefix-list**
- **ipv6 rip default-information**
- **ipv6 rip enable**
- **ipv6 rip metric-offset**
- **ipv6 rip summary-address**
- **ipv6 route**
- **ipv6 router rip**
- **ipv6 traffic-filter**

- ipv6 unicast-routing
- ipv6 unnumbered
- match ipv6 address
- match ipv6 next-hop
- match ipv6 route-source
- neighbor activate
- neighbor override-capability-neg
- ping
- poison-reverse (IPv6 RIP)
- port (IPv6 RIP)
- redistribute (IPv6 RIP)
- show bgp ipv6
- show bgp ipv6 community
- show bgp ipv6 community-list
- show bgp ipv6 dampened-paths
- show bgp ipv6 filter-list
- show bgp ipv6 flap-statistics
- show bgp ipv6 inconsistent-as
- show bgp ipv6 neighbors
- show bgp ipv6 paths

- show bgp ipv6 quote-regexp
- show bgp ipv6 regexp
- show bgp ipv6 summary
- show ip sockets
- show ipv6 access-list
- show ipv6 interface
- show ipv6 mtu
- show ipv6 neighbors
- show ipv6 prefix-list
- show ipv6 rip
- show ipv6 route
- show ipv6 route summary
- show ipv6 routers
- show ipv6 traffic
- show ipv6 tunnel
- split-horizon (IPv6 RIP)
- telnet
- timers (IPv6 RIP)
- traceroute
- tunnel mode ipv6ip

Current Cisco documentation regarding IPv6 development and implementation can be found at http://www.cisco.com/warp/public/732/Tech/ipv6/ipv6_techdoc.shtml.

Summary

The Internet Engineering Task Force (IETF) has adopted Internet Protocol, version 6 (IPv6) as a replacement for IPv4, the standard used today. This chapter provides an overview of IPv6, including routing and addressing, address autoconfiguration, neighbor discovery, and transitioning from IPv4 to IPv6.

The proper implementation of 6to4 has no significant impact to either IPv4 or IPv6 routing table size.

To accommodate almost unlimited growth and a variety of addressing formats, IPv6 addresses are 128 bits in length (2^{128}).

IPv6 defines three types of addresses:

- Unicast—This address specifies a single host.

- Anycast—This address specifies a set of hosts, such as a set of servers for a given organization's application. A packet sent to an anycast address is delivered to one of the hosts that is identified by that address, usually the closest one as defined by the routing protocol.

- Multicast—This address identifies a set of hosts. A packet sent to a multicast address is delivered to all of the hosts in the group.

The 6to4 mechanism assumes unicast capability in the underlying IPv4 network. It is expected that IPv6 multicast packets can be sent to, or sourced from, a 6to4 router. When IPv6 multicast is supported, an IPv6 multicast routing protocol must be used.

The use of IPv6 anycast is compatible with 6to4 prefixes.

6to4 for hosts only, as opposed to sites, is possible and will likely be developed in the future.

When using IPv4 network address translation (NAT), 6to4 mechanisms remain valid because the NAT device includes a fully functional IPv6 router with the 6to4 mechanism included. This method offers the advantages of NAT for IPv4 use along with the additional address space of IPv6.

IPv6/IPv4, or 6to4, connectivity can be accomplished by configuring tunnels directly with each IPv6 site, or by configuring a tunnel into a larger IPv6 routing infrastructure.

CHAPTER 27

Multiprotocol Label Switching (MPLS)

In early 1997, the Internet Engineering Task Force (IETF) established the Multiprotocol Label Switching (MPLS) working group to produce a unified and interoperable multilayer switching standard as each vendor (Cisco Systems, Lucent, and so on) developed a proprietary multilayer switching solution, maintaining the IP control component and label-swapping components in different ways. The majority of these multilayer switching solutions required an ATM transport because they could not operate over mixed media infrastructures, such as Frame Relay, PPP, SONET, and LANs.

This chapter will review some of the history behind MPLS and the fundamental components before discussing MPLS in itself.

MPLS is an IETF-specified framework that provides for the efficient designation, routing, forwarding, and switching of traffic flows through the network.

MPLS performs the following functions:

- It specifies mechanisms to manage traffic flows of various granularities, such as flows among different hardware, machines, or even flows among different applications.

- It remains independent of the Layer 2 and Layer 3 protocols.

- It provides a means to map IP addresses to simple, fixed-length labels used by different packet-forwarding and packet-switching technologies.

- It interfaces to existing routing protocols such as Resource Reservation Protocol (RSVP) and Open Shortest Path First (OSPF).

- It supports the IP, ATM, and frame-relay Layer 2 protocols.

In MPLS, data transmission occurs on label-switched paths (LSPs). LSPs are a sequence of labels at each node along the path from the source to the destination. LSPs are established either prior to data transmission (control driven) or upon detection of a certain flow of data (data driven). The labels, which are underlying protocol-specific identifiers, are distributed using label distribution protocol (LDP) or RSVP. They might also be piggybacked on routing protocols such as Border Gateway Protocol (BGP) and OSPF. Each data packet encapsulates and carries the label(s) during the packet's journey from source to destination. High-speed switching of data is possible because the fixed-length labels are inserted at the beginning of the packet or cell and can be used by hardware to switch packets quickly among links.

Label-Edge Routers (LERs) and Label-Switching Routers (LSRs)

The devices that participate in the MPLS Protocol mechanisms can be classified into label-edge routers (LERs) and label-switching routers (LSRs).

An *LSR* is a high-speed router device in the core of an MPLS network that participates in the establishment of LSPs using the appropriate label signaling protocol and high-speed switching of the data traffic based on the established paths.

An *LER* is a device that operates at the edge of the access network and MPLS network. LERs support multiple ports connected to dissimilar networks (such as frame relay, ATM, and Ethernet) and forward this traffic on to the MPLS network after establishing LSPs. LERs use the label-signaling protocol at the ingress and distribute the traffic back to the access networks at the egress. LERs play an important role in the assignment and removal of labels, as traffic enters or exits an MPLS network.

Forward Equivalence Classes (FECs)

A forward equivalence class (FEC) is a representation of a group of packets that share the same requirements for their transport. All packets in such a group are provided the same treatment en route to the destination. As opposed to conventional IP forwarding, in MPLS, the assignment of a particular packet to a particular FEC is done just once, as the packet enters the network. FECs are based on service requirements for a given set of packets or simply for an address prefix. Each LSR builds a table to specify how a packet must be forwarded. This table, called a label information base (LIB), comprises FEC-to-label bindings.

Labels and Label Bindings

A label, in its simplest form, identifies the path that a packet should traverse. A label is carried or encapsulated in a Layer 2 header along with the packet. The receiving router examines the packet for its label content to determine the next hop. After a packet has been labeled, the rest of the journey of the packet through the backbone is based on label switching. The label values are of local significance only, meaning that they pertain only to hops between LSRs.

After a packet has been classified as a new or existing FEC, a label is assigned to the packet. The label values are derived from the underlying data link layer. These data link layer identifiers, such as Frame Relay DLCIs or ATM VPI/VCIs, can be used directly as labels. The packets are then forwarded based on their label value.

Labels are bound to an FEC as a result of some event or policy that indicates a need for such binding. These events can be either data-driven bindings or control-driven bindings. The latter is preferable because of its advanced scaling properties that can be used in MPLS.

Label assignment decisions can be based on forwarding criteria such as the following:

- Destination unicast routing
- Traffic engineering (TE)
- Multicast
- Virtual private network (VPN)
- Quality of Service (QoS)

MPLS Fundamentals

The fundamental building blocks of MPLS solutions are as follows:

- Control and forwarding components
- Label-swapping forwarding algorithms

Control and Forwarding Components

MPLS, like all multilayer-switching solutions, comprises two distinct functional components, as shown in Figure 27-1:

- Control component—Uses standard routing protocols, such as OSPF, BGP4, and so on, to exchange routing information to build and maintain a forwarding table, which is also known as the *control plane*.
- Forwarding component—Searches the forwarding table, maintained by the control component, to ascertain routing for each packet. The forwarding component examines the packet header, searches the forwarding table for a match, and directs the packet from the input interface to the output interface across the switching fabric.

Figure 27-1 *Control and Forwarding Functional Components*

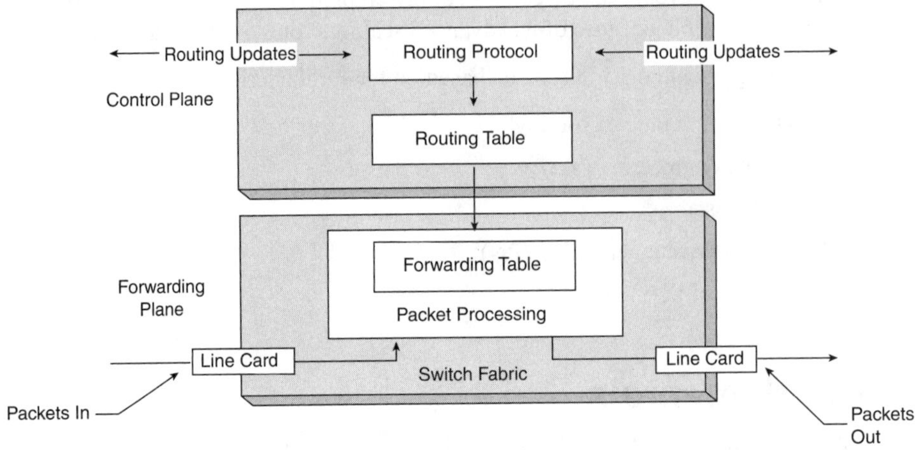

By separating the control component from the forwarding component, individual components can be independently developed and modified, similar to developmental efforts for the OSI model. The only requirement for component developmental efforts is that the control component manages the forwarding table.

Label-Swapping Forwarding Algorithm

MPLS's forwarding component is based on a label-swapping forwarding algorithm—the same algorithm used to forward data in ATM and Frame Relay switches. Signaling and label distribution are fundamental to the label-swapping forwarding algorithm and are discussed later in this chapter.

A *label* is a short, fixed-length value carried in the packet's header to identify a forwarding equivalence class (FEC). A label is analogous to a connection identifier, such as an ATM VPI/VCI or a Frame Relay DLCI, because it has only link-local significance, does not encode information from the network layer header, and maps traffic to a specific FEC. An FEC is a set of packets that is forwarded over the same path through a network even if its ultimate destinations are different. For example, in longest-match IP routing, an FEC would be a set of unicast packets whose destination addresses map to a given IP address prefix.

The label-swapping forwarding algorithm requires packet classification at the ingress edge of the network to assign an initial label to each packet described in the following list. Figure 27-2 illustrates the path of an unlabeled packet with a destination of 192.4.2.1.

   1 The ingress label switch receives an unlabeled packet with a destination address of 192.4.2.1.

2 The label switch performs a longest-match routing table lookup and maps the packet to an FEC—192.4/16.

3 The ingress label switch then assigns a label (with a value of 5) to the packet and forwards it to the next hop in the label-switched path (LSP). This next hop is specified as an outgoing interface on the LSR.

4 This process repeats until the destination interface is reached and the packet is delivered to the intended destination network, via the specified outgoing interface. When the last LSR is reached, the delivered packet has been stripped, or "popped," of its last label.

Figure 27-2 *Packet Traversing a Label-Switched Path*

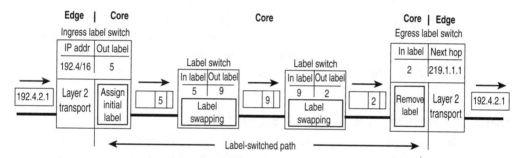

An LSP is equivalent to an ATM or Frame Relay virtual circuit (VC) as it defines an ingress-to-egress path through a network that is followed by all packets assigned to a specific FEC. The first label switch in an LSP is called the *ingress,* or *head end,* label switch. The last label switch in an LSP is called the *egress,* or *tail end,* label switch.

In the network core, label switches ignore the packet's network layer header and forward the packet based on decisions made using the label-swapping algorithm. When a labeled packet arrives at a switch, the forwarding component uses the input port number and label as an index to perform an exact match search of its forwarding table. After the forwarding component finds a match, it retrieves the outgoing label, the outgoing interface, and the next-hop address from the forwarding table. The forwarding component then swaps (or replaces) the incoming label with the outgoing label and directs the packet to the outbound interface for transmission to the next hop in the LSP.

When the labeled packet arrives at the egress label switch, the forwarding component searches its forwarding table. If the next hop is not a label switch, the egress switch discards the label and forwards the packet using conventional longest-match IP forwarding.

Multilayer Switching

As the Internet market grew over time, it became apparent that the only protocol steadily being deployed was the Internet Protocol (IP). IP convergence of voice, data, and multimedia applications rivaled that of ATM. By 1996, a number of vendors were promoting proprietary multilayer-switching solutions that integrated ATM switching and IP routing:

- IP Switching designed by Ipsilon/Nokia
- Tag Switching developed by Cisco Systems
- Aggregate Route-Based IP Switching (ARIS) designed by IBM Corporation
- IP Navigator delivered by Cascade/Ascend/Lucent Technologies
- Cell Switching Router (CSR) developed by Toshiba

Each of these vendor-dependent approaches had a number of characteristics in common. However, they were not interoperable because each relied on different technologies to combine IP routing and ATM switching into an integrated solution.

Multilayer-Switching Solutions Similarities

Although MPLS implementations are supported over different Layer 2 implementations, the discussion here focuses on MPLS over ATM, the most common among network service providers.

Each multilayer-switching solution sought to combine the best properties of IP routing and ATM switching while still maintaining an IP focus. The fundamental approach adopted by these strategies was to take the IP router's control software, integrate it with the ATM switch label-swapping forwarding performance, and create an extremely fast and cost-efficient IP router.

For the control component, each multilayer switch ran standard IP routing software (OSPF, IS-IS, and BGP-4) and a proprietary label-binding mechanism. The routing software permitted multilayer switches to exchange Layer 3 network routing and destination reachability information. The label-binding mechanism mapped Layer 3 routes to labels—that is, to ATM VPI/VCIs—and distributed them to neighbors, establishing LSPs across the core of the network.

Routing protocols run on core systems rather than edge systems. That provides a number of benefits to network operations:

- It eliminates the IP-over-ATM "N2" PVC scaling problem (where full-mesh connectivity between ATM switches reaches a theoretical maximum).
- It reduces Interior Gateway Protocol routes by decreasing the number of peers that each router maintains.

- It permits information about the core's physical topology to be made available to network layer routing algorithms.

NOTE   Some MPLS implementations will run routing protocols on the edge systems, using the core for LSP functions.

Multilayer switches use conventional ATM switching hardware and label swapping to forward cells across the core of the network. The control procedures assign labels to routes, distribute the labels among multilayer switches, and create the forwarding tables that are managed by proprietary IP-based protocols, not ATM Forum protocols.

ATM label swapping in the network core provides a number of benefits:

- Label swapping optimizes network performance by leveraging the benefits of hardware-based forwarding.

- Label swapping makes explicit routing practical. An explicit route is a preconfigured sequence of hops that defines the path that traffic should take across a service provider's network, enabling the construction of a forwarding path that is different from the one typically created by destination-based routing. Explicit paths provide precise control over traffic flows, making it possible to support traffic engineering, QoS, and loop prevention.

- Label swapping provides a mechanism to extend control beyond destination-based routing.

Excluding the ATM Forum's routing and signaling protocols enabled multilayer switching to reduce operational complexity by eliminating the need to coordinate and map between two different protocol architectures: IP and ATM. Although multilayer switching still uses standard ATM VPI/VCIs as labels, they are assigned and distributed using proprietary IP-based protocols versus standard ATM Forum protocols.

Multilayer Switching Solutions Fundamental Differences

Vendor-developed multilayer switching solutions relied on two fundamentally different approaches to initiate the assignment and distribution of label bindings to establish LSPs:

- Data-driven model
- Control-driven model

Data-Driven Model

In the data-driven model, label bindings are created when user data packets arrive into the network. A *flow* is a sequence of packets that have the same source and destination IP addresses and TCP or UDP port numbers. A multilayer switch can create a label binding as soon as it sees the first packet in a traffic flow. The multilayer switch can also wait until it has seen a number of packets in the flow. The benefit of waiting for a number of packets ensures that the flow is long enough to merit the overhead of assigning and distributing a label. Multilayer switching solutions that implemented the data-driven approach included Ipsilon's IP Switching and Toshiba's Cell Switching Router.

NOTE	MPLS does not support the data-driven model.

The advantage of the data-driven model is that a label binding is created only when traffic flow uses the label binding.

The data-driven model has a number of implementation limitations in the core of a large service provider network, where a large number of individual traffic flows exist:

- Each multilayer switch must provide packet classification capabilities to identify traffic flows.

- Latency occurs between the recognition of a flow and the assignment of a label to the recognized flow. Each multilayer switch must also support longest-match IP forwarding during the setup phase so that packets that have not been assigned to a flow can be forwarded and not dropped.

- The amount of control traffic needed to distribute label bindings is directly proportional to the number of traffic flows.

- The presence of a significant number of relatively short-lived flows can impose a heavy burden on network operations.

- The data-driven model does not have the scaling properties required for application in the core of the Internet.

Control-Driven Model

In the control-driven model, label bindings are created when control information arrives. Labels are assigned in response to the normal processing of routing protocol traffic, control traffic (such as RSVP traffic), or static route configuration. Multilayer switching solutions that implement the control-driven model are Cisco Systems Tag Switching, Lucent/Ascend's IP Navigator, and IBM's ARIS.

NOTE	MPLS uses the control-driven model.

The control-driven model has a number of benefits for deployment in the core of a large service provider network:

- Labels are assigned and distributed before the arrival of user data traffic. If a route exists in the IP forwarding table, then a label has already been allocated for the route. Traffic that is arriving at a multilayer switch can be immediately label swapped without having to determine if an IP flow exists or will exist.

- Because the number of label-switched paths is proportional to the number of entries in the IP forwarding table, not to the number of individual traffic flows, control-driven models are more scalable than data-driven models. For traffic engineering in large service provider networks, scaling is proportional to the number of exit points in the network. Label assignment is based on prefixes, rather than individual flows; that permits a single label to represent a highly aggregated FEC.

- In a stable topology, the label assignment and distribution overhead are lower than in the data-driven model. This is because the label-switched paths are established after a topology change or the arrival of control traffic, not with the arrival of each "new" traffic flow.

- Every packet in a flow is label switched, not just the tail end of the flow as in the data-driven model when the switch recognizes a flow.

MPLS Evolution

MPLS is the latest step in the evolution of multilayer switching in the Internet. It is an IETF standards-based approach built on the efforts of the various proprietary multilayer-switching solutions.

The development of MPLS can be traced through the following RFCs:

- 2547 BGP/MPLS VPNs. E. Rosen, Y. Rekhter. March 1999. (Format: TXT=63270 bytes) (Status: Informational)

- 2702 Requirements for Traffic Engineering Over MPLS. D. Awduche, J. Malcolm, J. Agogbua, M. O'Dell, J. McManus. September 1999. (Format: TXT=68386 bytes) (Status: Informational)

- 2917 A Core MPLS IP VPN Architecture. K. Muthukrishnan, A. Malis. September 2000. (Format: TXT=35352 bytes) (Status: Informational)

- 3032 MPLS Label Stack Encoding. E. Rosen, D. Tappan, G. Fedorkow, Y. Rekhter, D. Farinacci, T. Li, A. Conta. January 2001. (Format: TXT=48314 bytes) (Status: Proposed Standard)

- 3035 MPLS using LDP and ATM VC Switching. B. Davie, J. Lawrence, K. McCloghrie, E. Rosen, G. Swallow, Y. Rekhter, P. Doolan. January 2001. (Format: TXT=46463 bytes) (Status: Proposed Standard)

- 3063 MPLS Loop Prevention Mechanism. Y. Ohba, Y. Katsube, E. Rosen, P. Doolan. February 2001. (Format: TXT=93523 bytes) (Status: Experimental)

MPLS Model

MPLS uses the control-driven model to initiate assignment and distribution of label bindings for the establishment of LSPs. LSPs are simple in nature: traffic flows in one direction from the head end toward the tail end. Duplex traffic requires two LSPs—one LSP to carry traffic in each direction. Concatenating one or more label-switched hops creates an LSP, allowing a packet to be forwarded from one LSR to another across the MPLS domain.

The MPLS control component centers around IP functionality, which is similar to proprietary multilayer switching solutions, as illustrated in Figure 27-3.

Figure 27-3 *MPLS*

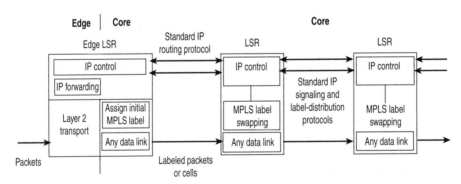

MPLS defines new standards-based IP signaling and label distribution protocols, as well as extensions to existing protocols, supporting multivendor interoperability. MPLS does not implement ATM Forum signaling or routing protocols, simplifying the coordination of different protocol architectures.

The MPLS forwarding component is based on the label-swapping algorithm. If the Layer 2 technology supports a label field (such as the ATM VPI/VCI or the Frame Relay DLCI fields), the native label field encapsulates the MPLS label. However, if the Layer 2 technology does not support a label field, the MPLS label is encapsulated in a standardized MPLS header that is inserted between the Layer 2 and IP headers, as illustrated in Figure 27-4. The MPLS header permits any link layer technology to carry an MPLS label so it can benefit from label swapping across an LSP.

Figure 27-4 *MPLS Header*

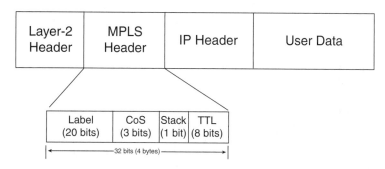

MPLS Header

The 32-bit MPLS header, illustrated in Figure 27-4, contains the following fields:

- Label field (20-bits)—Carries the value of the MPLS label
- Class-of-Service (CoS) field (3-bits)—Affects the queuing and discard algorithms applied to the packet as it is transmitted through the network
- Stack (S) field (1-bit)—Supports a hierarchical label stack (if the labels are concatenated as the packet is carried through the network)
- Time-to-live (TTL) field (8-bits)—Provides IP TTL functionality

MPLS Requirements

The charter of the IETF MPLS working group is to standardize a base technology that combines the use of label swapping in the forwarding component with network layer routing in the control component.

To meet this requirement, the MPLS working group must deliver a solution that satisfies the following requirements:

- MPLS must run over any link layer technology, such as ATM, Frame Relay, or PPP (IP).
- MPLS core technologies must support the forwarding of both unicast and multicast traffic flows.
- MPLS must be compatible with the IETF integrated services model, including RSVP.
- MPLS must scale to support constant Internet growth.
- MPLS must support operations, administration, and maintenance (OAM) facilities, meeting at least what is supported in current IP networks.

MPLS and Layer 3 Forwarding

The following steps must be taken for a data packet to travel through an MPLS domain:

- Label creation and distribution
- Table creation at each router
- Label-switched path creation
- Label insertion/table lookup
- Packet forwarding

The source sends its data to the destination. In an MPLS domain, not all of the source traffic is necessarily transported through the same path. Depending on the traffic characteristics, different LSPs could be created for packets with different CoS requirements.

IP packets transmitted by a host require forwarding to a first-hop Layer 3 device, where the packet header can be examined prior to forwarding it toward its destination. The first-hop router can then either forward the packet using conventional longest-match routing or assign a label and forward the packet over an LSP.

If a Layer 3 device along the path examines the IP header and assigns a label, the label represents an aggregate route because it is impossible to maintain label bindings for every host on the global Internet. This means that at some point along the path, another Layer 3 device must examine the IP header to determine a finer granularity—such as longest match—to continue forwarding the packet. This router can elect to either forward the packet using routing algorithms or assign a label and forward the packet over a new label-switched path.

At the last hop before the destination host, the packet must be forwarded using Layer 3 routing. It is not practical to assign a separate label to every host on the destination subnet.

NOTE   Packet filtering at firewalls and service provider boundaries is a fundamental component of security and administrative policy. Because packet filtering requires a detailed examination of packet headers, Layer 3 forwarding is still required for these applications.

MPLS Operation

Figure 27-5 illustrates a packet traversing an MPLS-enabled network.

Figure 27-5 *MPLS Operation*

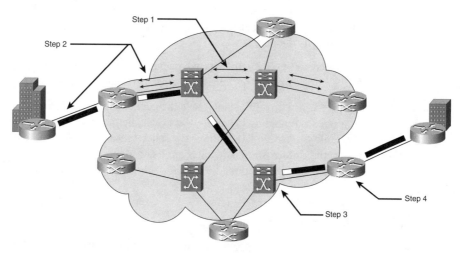

As shown by the dashed blue lines in Figure 27-6, the LSPs are created in the reverse direction to the creation of entries in the LIBs.

Figure 27-6 *MPLS Enhanced Routing*

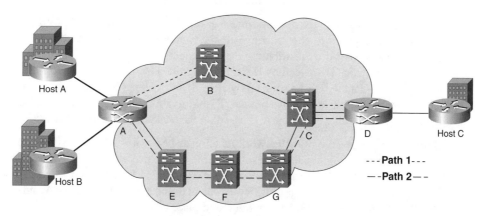

 1 The network automatically builds routing tables as Cisco routers or IP+ATM switches participate in interior gateway protocols, such as OSPF, throughout the service provider network. LDP uses the routing topology in the tables to establish label values between adjacent devices. This operation creates *label-switched paths (LSPs)*, which are preconfigured maps between destination endpoints. Unlike ATM permanent virtual circuits (PVCs), which require manual assignment of VPIs/VCIs, labels are automatically assigned.

2 A packet enters the ingress Edge LSRs, where it is processed to determine which Layer 3 services it requires, such as QoS and bandwidth management. Based on routing and policy requirements, the edge LSR selects and applies a label to the packet header and forwards the packet.

3 The LSR in the core reads the label on each packet, replaces it with a new one as listed in the table, and forwards the packet. This action is repeated at all core "hops."

4 The egress edge LSR strips the label, reads the packet header, and forwards it to its final destination. For enabling business IP services, the most significant benefit of MPLS is its ability to assign labels that have special meanings. Sets of labels distinguish routing information as well as application type or service class, as discussed in the following sections.

MPLS Enhanced Routing

Figure 27-6 illustrates how MPLS provides enhanced routing capabilities by supporting applications that require more than destination-based forwarding. For this example, the routers in the network core perform conventional, longest-match IP forwarding.

If either Host A or Host B transmits a packet to Host C, the packet follows Path 1 across the core of the network because this is the shortest path computed by the IGP.

Further in this example, the network manager has been monitoring traffic statistics and is implementing a policy to control congestion at Router B. The policy would reduce congestion at Router B by distributing the traffic load along different paths across the network. Traffic that is sourced by Host A and destined for Host C would follow the IGP shortest path—Path 1. Traffic sourced by Host B and destined for Host C would follow another path—Path 2. With conventional IP routing, this policy cannot be implemented because all forwarding at Router A is based on the packet's destination address.

If the routers in the core of the network function as LSRs, it is relatively simple to implement a policy to reduce congestion at LSR B. The network administrator configures LSP 1 to follow Path 1. The network manager configures LSP 2 to follow Path 2. The network manager then configures LSR A to put all traffic received from Host A and destined for Host C into LSP 1. LSR A is configured to place all traffic received from Host B and destined for Host C into LSP 2. The ability to assign any forward equivalence class (FEC) to a custom-tailored LSP gives the network manager control of traffic as it flows through the service provider's network.

Packets can be assigned to an FEC based on a combination of the destination subnet and the application type, a combination of the source and destination subnets, a specific QoS requirement, an IP multicast group, or a virtual private network (VPN) identifier.

Network managers can provision LSPs to satisfy specific FEC requirements, such as minimizing the number of hops, adhering to specific bandwidth requirements, and directing traffic across certain links in the network.

MPLS Applications

Currently, three popular applications exist for MPLS in the core of large network service provider networks:

- Traffic engineering
- CoS
- VPNs

MPLS Traffic Engineering (MPLS-TE)

Traffic engineering allows network service providers to move traffic flows away from the shortest path calculated by the IGP and onto potentially less congested physical paths across the network, as illustrated in Figure 27-7.

Figure 27-7 *Traffic Engineering LSP Versus IGP Shortest Path*

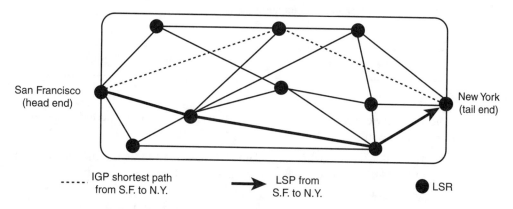

Traffic engineering is currently one of the two primary applications for MPLS because of the unprecedented growth in demand for network resources, the mission-critical nature of IP applications, and the increasingly competitive nature of the service provider marketplace. The other primary application for MPLS is VPN. Traffic engineering solutions can balance a network's aggregate traffic load on various network links, routers, and switches. This traffic load balancing ensures that none of the individual traffic engineering components are over- or under-utilized. This balancing results in a network that is efficiently operated, providing a more predictable service.

MPLS is well suited to provide the foundation to enable traffic engineering in large ISP networks for the following reasons:

- Explicit path support enables network managers to specify the exact physical path that an LSP takes across the service provider's network.

- Per-LSP statistics can be used for network planning and analysis to identify bottlenecks and trunk-utilization planning for future expansion.

- Constraint-based routing provides enhanced capabilities that enable an LSP to meet specific performance requirements before the path is established.

- An MPLS-based solution can run over packet-oriented networks, such as IP, and is not limited to ATM infrastructures.

MPLS Class of Service (MPLS-CoS)

MPLS provides an immediate benefit to network service providers in its support for differentiated services (DiffServ). The differentiated services model defines a variety of mechanisms for classifying traffic into a small number of service classes. With DiffServ, subscribers are motivated to use the Internet as a public transport network for applications ranging from traditional file transfer to delay-sensitive services such as voice and video. To meet customer requirements, network service providers are adopting both MPLS-TE (Traffic Engineering) and CoS technologies.

NOTE   MPLS supports up to eight service classes, the same number as IP precedence.

A network service provider can take one of two approaches to support MPLS-based class of service forwarding:

- Traffic flowing through a particular LSP can be queued for transmission on each LSR's outbound interface based on the setting of the precedence bits carried in the MPLS header.

- Network service providers can provision multiple LSPs between each pair of edge LSRs. Each LSP can be traffic engineered to provide different performance and bandwidth guarantees. The head end LSR places high-priority traffic in one LSP, medium-priority traffic in another LSP, best-effort traffic in a third LSP, and less-than-best-effort traffic in a fourth LSP.

- These traffic priorities are often assigned colors to define their priority. Colorization terminology is often vendor dependant, as the following table shows:

Table 27-1 *Traffic Colorization Assignments*

Priority	Color	(Cisco) Color	Guaranteed
High	Platinum	Gold	Latency, Delivery
Medium	Gold	Silver	Delivery
Low	Silver	Bronze	—
Best-Effort	Bronze	Best-Effort	—

MPLS gives network service providers flexibility in the different types of services that it can provide its customers. The precedence bits are used only to classify packets into one of several classes of service. It is the network service provider that determines the specific type of service that is supported by each service classification.

Cisco IOS Technical Note: MPLS-enabled networks using Cisco IOS QoS elements benefit from the following architectural enhancements:

- IP precedence—Uses three bits in the IP header to indicate the service class of a packet (up to eight classes). This is set at the edge and enforced in the core. In IP+ATM networks, different labels are used to indicate precedence levels.

- Committed access rate (CAR)—Performs two functions: packet classification and bandwidth management. CAR analyzes the packet and assigns a service class based on the packet's header information. Because this is done at Layer 3, a variety of attributes, such as source, destination, protocol, or application, can be used to classify the packets. CAR also manages bandwidth allocation for specified traffic types. To enforce customer network policies, managers can configure multiple Layer 3 thresholds based on the desired parameters, such as application or protocol. If a flow exceeds a given threshold, a variety of responses can be provisioned, such as dropping excess packets or sending them at a lower service class.

- Weighted random early detection (WRED)—Prevents network congestion by detecting and slowing flows (according to service class) before congestion occurs. WRED drops selected packets, which alerts the TCP sender to reduce its transmission rate. Weights are assigned to service classes, resulting in low priority flows being slowed more aggressively than high priority ones.

- Class-based weighted fair queuing (CBWFQ)—Provides the ability to reorder packets and control latency at the edge and in the core. By assigning different weights to different service classes, a switch can manage buffering and bandwidth for each service class. This mechanism constrains delay bounds for time-sensitive traffic, such as voice or video.

- MPLS—Implements both IP and ATM QoS and Layer 3 traffic engineering.

MPLS Virtual Private Networks (MPLS-VPNs)

A VPN simulates the operation of a private WAN over the public Internet. To offer a viable VPN service for its customers, a network service provider must solve the problems of data privacy and support the use of non-unique, private IP addresses within a VPN. MPLS provides a simple and efficient solution to both of these challenges because it makes forwarding decisions based on the value of the label, not the destination address in the packet header.

NOTE   RFC 2547 provides the following definition of a VPN, an intranet, and an extranet: "If all the sites in a VPN are owned by the same enterprise, the VPN is a corporate 'intranet.' If the various sites in a VPN are owned by different enterprises, the VPN is an 'extranet.' A site can be in more than one VPN; e.g., in an intranet and several extranets. We regard both intranets and extranets as VPNs. In general, when we use the term 'VPN,' we will not be distinguishing between intranets and extranets."

VPNs are typically constructed using four fundamental building blocks:

*   Firewalls to protect each customer site and provide a secure interface to the Internet
*   Authentication to verify that each customer site exchanges data with only validated remote sites
*   Encryption to protect data from examination or manipulation as it is transported across the Internet
*   Tunneling encapsulation to provide a multiprotocol transport service and enable the use of the private IP address space within a VPN

MPLS gives network service providers the capability to offer VPN services by providing a simple and flexible VPN tunneling mechanism, as illustrated in Figure 27-8.

Figure 27-8 *MPLS VPN Tunnels*

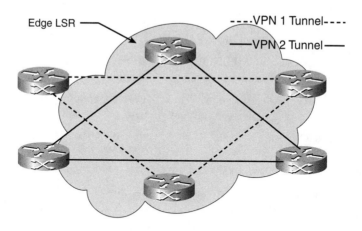

A network service provider can deploy VPNs by provisioning a set of LSPs to provide connectivity among the different sites in the VPN. Each VPN site then advertises to the network service provider a set of prefixes that are reachable within the local site. The network service provider's routing mechanisms distribute this information by piggybacking labels in routing protocol updates or by using a label distribution protocol.

VPN identifiers allow a single routing system to support multiple VPNs whose internal address spaces overlap with each other. Each ingress or the ingress LSR places this VPN-identified traffic into LSPs based on a combination of a packet's destination address and VPN membership information.

IP/MPLS Network

An IP core merges the control planes of both Layer 2 and Layer 3 networks into a single network. This integration eliminates the management burden of coordinating the two distinct networks, permits routing and automated traffic engineering to occur on the same platform, and reduces the operational cost of the network.

IP/MPLS architectures have numerous advantages:

- They support high-speed optical interfaces without the limitations imposed by SAR chips on ATM router interfaces.

- They eliminate the cell tax because ATM is no longer required as the Layer 2 technology. The bandwidth previously consumed with ATM cell overhead—usually 15 to 25 percent of the provisioned bandwidth—is now available to carry additional customer traffic.

- They do not require a specific Layer 2 technology (ATM or Frame Relay) that supports switching and virtual circuits. Traffic engineering can be implemented at Layer 3, providing support over mixed-media networks and reducing the number of layers between IP and fiber.

- IP cores supporting MPLS offer numerous advantages using traffic engineering to maximize the efficient use of bandwidth and reduce congestion.

- IP/MPLS cores do not exhibit ATM's n-squared PVC problem, which stresses the IGP and results in complex configuration issues.

MPLS architectures are based on the combination of IGP extensions, constraint-based Shortest Path First (CSPF) path selection, RSVP signaling, and MPLS forwarding leverages work performed by the IETF without introducing radically new technologies.

- IP/MPLS architectures provide tremendous flexibility in determining how to implement traffic engineering. LSPs can be calculated online or offline, and they can be installed manually or by using RSVP signaling.

- Constraint-based routing provides enhanced capabilities that enable specific performance requirements to be met. Explicit paths enable the network manager to specify the exact physical path that an MPLS LSP takes across the network.

- Per-LSP statistics can be used for network planning and analysis to identify bottlenecks and trunk utilization planning for future expansion.

- MPLS can carry ATM cells, if necessary, by mapping virtual channels onto LSPs using Layer 2 VPN technology.

BGP-Extended Community Attributes

The distribution of VPN routing information is constrained through the use of BGP extended community attributes. Extended community attributes are carried in BGP messages as attributes of the route. They identify the route as belonging to a specific collection of routes, all of which are treated the same with respect to routing policy. Each BGP-extended community must be globally unique and contain either a public IP address or an ASN and can be used by only one VPN. However, a given customer VPN can make use of multiple globally unique BGP-extended communities to help control the distribution of routing information.

BGP/MPLS VPNs use 32-bit BGP extended community attributes instead of conventional 16-bit BGP community attributes. The use of 32-bit extended community attributes enhances scalability because a single service provider can support a maximum of 232 communities. Because each community attribute contains the provider's globally unique autonomous system (AS) number, the service provider can control local assignment while also maintaining the global uniqueness of that assignment.

RFC 2547 BGP/MPLS VPNs can use up to three types of BGP-extended community attributes:

The route target attribute identifies a collection of VPN routing and forwarding tables (VRFs) to which a PE router distributes routes. A provider edge (PE) router uses this attribute to constrain the import of remote routes into its VRFs.

- The VPN-of-origin attribute identifies a collection of sites and establishes the associated route as coming from one of the sites in that set.

- The site-of-origin attribute identifies the specific site from which a PE router learns a route. It is encoded as a route origin extended community attribute, which can be used to prevent routing loops.

MPLS VPN Operational Model

Before distributing local routes to other PE routers, the ingress PE router attaches a route target attribute to each route learned from directly connected sites. The route target attached to the route is based on the value of the VRF's configured export target policy.

The ingress PE router can be configured as follows:

- To assign a single route target attribute to all routes learned from a given site.

- To assign one route target attribute to a set of routes learned from a site and other route target attributes to other sets of routes learned from a site.

- If the customer edge (CE) router communicates with the PE router via EBGP, the CE router can specify one or more route targets for each route. This approach shifts the control of implementing VPN policies from the service provider to the customer.

Before installing remote routes that have been distributed by another PE router, each VRF on an egress PE router is configured with an import target policy. A PE router can only install a VPN-IPv4 route in a VRF if the route target attribute carried with the route matches one of the PE router VRFs import targets.

By careful configuration of export target and import target policies, network service providers can construct different types of VPN topologies. The mechanisms that implement the VPN topologies can be completely restricted to the service provider so that VPN customers are not aware of this process.

VPN Routing Maintenance

When the configuration of a PE router is changed by creating a new VRF or by adding one or more new import target policies to an existing VRF, the PE router might need to obtain VPN-IPv4 routes that it previously discarded. The speed of delivering updated routing information can present a problem with BGP4 because it is a stateful protocol and does not support the exchange of route refresh request messages and the subsequent re-advertisement of routes. After BGP peers synchronize their routing tables, they do not exchange routing information until that routing information changes.

The BGP route refresh capability provides a solution to the issue of routing information exchange. During the establishment of a Multiprotocol Interior Border Gateway Protocol (MP-IBGP) session, a BGP speaker that wants to receive a route refresh message from its peer or route reflector advertises the BGP route refresh capability using a BGP capabilities advertisement. The BGP route refresh capability states that a BGP speaker can send a route refresh message to a peer or route reflector only if it has received a route refresh capabilities advertisement from that peer or route reflector. When the configuration of a PE router changes, the PE router can request the retransmission of routing information from its MP-IBGP peers to obtain routing information that it previously discarded. When the routes are re-advertised, the updated import target policy is applied as the PE router populates its VRFs.

Provider Edge (PE) Router Resources

During the process of populating its VRFs, a BGP speaker often receives and then filters unwanted routes from peers based on each VRF's import target policy. Because the generation, transmission, and processing of routing updates consumes backbone bandwidth and router packet processing resources, eliminating the transmission of unnecessary routing updates can conserve these assets.

Enabling the new BGP cooperative route-filtering capability can reduce the number of BGP routing updates. During the establishment of the MP-IBGP session, a BGP speaker that wants to send or receive outbound route filters (ORFs) to or from its peer or route reflector advertises the cooperative route-filtering capability using a BGP capabilities advertisement. The BGP speaker sends its peer a set of ORFs that are expressed in terms of BGP communities. The ORF entries are carried in BGP route refresh messages. The peer applies the received ORFs in addition to its locally configured export target policy, to constrain and filter outbound routing updates to the BGP speaker. A BGP peer might or might not honor the ORFs received from a BGP speaker. By implementing the outbound route filter mechanism, BGP cooperative route filtering can be used to conserve service provider backbone bandwidth and PE router packet-processing resources.

Customer Edge (CE) Routing

For the CE router to take advantage of the multiple CoS tunnels enabled by MPLS, priority or custom-queues must be configured on the CE device (see Figure 27-9).

Figure 27-9 *MPLS IP-VPN*

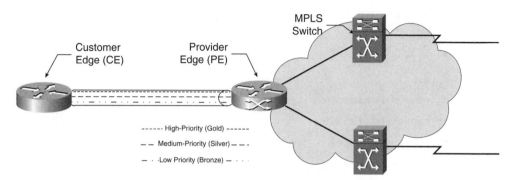

The CE router is configured with three queues: High-priority (Gold), Medium-priority (Silver) and Low-priority (Bronze). Each queue is provisioned with a percentage of the total bandwidth; for example, Gold is 40 percent, Silver is 40 percent, and Bronze is 20 percent. The CE router assigns packets to each queue based on configured access lists, using TCP/UDP port, source IP host/subnet, or destination IP host/subnet.

Cisco IOS enables policing of these queuing policies through the use of committed access rate (CAR) algorithms. CAR policies can be implemented on the CE device or, under agreement, on the network service provider's PE device. CAR policies are used for packet classification and bandwidth management. CAR analyzes the packet and assigns a service class based on the packet's header information. CAR policies use access lists to police against a variety of attributes, such as source, destination, protocol, or application. CAR policies are also used to manage bandwidth allocation for specified traffic types, ensuring, for example, that Gold-classified traffic takes precedence over Silver-classified traffic. To enforce customer network policies, network managers configure Layer 3 thresholds based on the desired parameters, such as application or protocol. If a flow exceeds a given threshold, a variety of responses can be enacted, such as dropping excess packets or sending them at a lower service class (recoloring).

NOTE   To configure an MPLS VPN with Cisco IOS services, the following must be in operation:

- MPLS in provider backbone routers, or GRE tunnel connectivity among all provider edge (PE) routers

- MPLS with VPN code in provider routers with VPN edge service (PE) routers

- BGP in all routers that provide a VPN service

- CEF switching in every MPLS-enabled router

- CoS feature (optional)

The following Cisco IOS commands are used to support MPLS service implementations:

- **append-after**
- **index**
- **ip explicit-path**
- **list**
- **metric-style narrow**
- **metric-style transition**
- **metric-style wide**
- **mpls traffic-eng**
- **mpls traffic-eng area**
- **mpls traffic-eng administrative-weight**
- **mpls traffic-eng attribute-flags**
- **mpls traffic-eng flooding thresholds**
- **mpls traffic-eng link timers bandwidth-hold**
- **mpls traffic-eng link timers periodic-flooding**
- **mpls traffic-eng reoptimize timers frequency**
- **mpls traffic-eng router-id**
- **mpls traffic-eng tunnels**
- **show ip explicit-paths**
- **show ip rsvp host**
- **show isis database verbose**
- **show isis mpls traffic-eng adjacency-log**
- **show isis mpls traffic-eng advertisements**
- **show isis mpls traffic-eng tunnel**
- **show mpls traffic-eng autoroute**
- **show mpls traffic-eng link-management admission-control**
- **show mpls traffic-eng link-management advertisements**
- **show mpls traffic-eng link-management bandwidth-allocation**
- **show mpls traffic-eng link-management igp-neighbors**
- **show mpls traffic-eng link-management interfaces**

- **show mpls traffic-eng link-management summary**
- **show mpls traffic-eng topology**
- **show mpls traffic-eng tunnel**
- **show mpls traffic-eng tunnel summary**
- **tunnel mpls traffic-eng affinity**
- **tunnel mpls traffic-eng autoroute announce**
- **tunnel mpls traffic-eng autoroute metric**
- **tunnel mpls traffic-eng bandwidth**
- **tunnel mpls traffic-eng path-option**
- **tunnel mpls traffic-eng priority**
- **tunnel mode mpls traffic-eng**

Summary

Multiprotocol Label Switching (MPLS), based on Cisco Tag Switching, was designed to address the most significant issues that were facing network service providers, specifically the need for a highly scalable foundation to deliver value-added IP business services.

The label-based forwarding mechanism of MPLS simplifies IP traffic routing in complex networks and enables several scalable value-added IP services.

MPLS enables the provisioning of connectionless-based IP VPNs, offering the same privacy enabled by Frame Relay, without IP tunneling or encryption. MPLS enables multiple IP VPN classes of service (CoS), allowing network service provider customers to guarantee latency and delivery based on customer-defined policies.

Although SP networks run IS-IS, BGP is usually used for the MPLS platform, with routes being injected into the BGP Autonomous System by the IS-IS protocol.

MPLS is a simple protocol, allowing for ease of implementation. MPLS improves network packet-forwarding performance by using Layer 2 switching paradigms. MPLS increases network performance because it enables routing by switching at wireline speeds.

MPLS supports Quality of Service (QoS) and CoS-based applications for service differentiation. MPLS uses traffic-engineered path setup mechanisms and helps achieve service-level guarantees.

MPLS incorporates provisions for constraint-based and explicit path setup supporting network scalability. MPLS can be used to avoid the N^2 overlay problem associated with meshed IP-ATM networks.

MPLS integrates IP and ATM in the network, providing a bridge between access IP and core ATM platforms. MPLS can reuse existing router/ATM switch hardware, effectively joining the two disparate networks and building interoperable networks.

MPLS is a proposed standards-based solution that achieves synergy between IP and ATM networks, facilitating IP-over-synchronous optical network (SONET) integration in optical switching.

LAN/WAN Network Assessment

Following is a network assessment template that can be used for any deliverables. Some of the format here has been previously published in *Designing Cisco Networks* (by Cisco Press).

Introduction

The "Introduction" section of a network assessment document should include a brief overview of the network environment.

Executive Summary of Findings

The "Executive Summary of Findings" section of a network assessment document should include a high-level overview of what was found. The idea here is a one- or two-page summary of what issues (if any) were found. The bulk of the document will be supporting facts for this section.

Current Network Topology and Characterization

The "Current Network Topology" section of a network assessment document should include a description of the network addressing models that is used in the current network design. Current addressing might impact the ability to later modify the network structure. For example, current IP subnet masking might limit the number of nodes in a local-area network (LAN) or virtual LAN (VLAN). Be sure to include a network diagram to reflect the topology. The figure does not have to represent every location if they are mirrors.

NOTE *Mirrors* are multiple locations with similar configurations, sometimes known as "cookie-cutter."

To identify potential network bottlenecks, use a protocol analyzer to determine how much of each network segment's traffic is not local (to that segment). Identify how much of the traffic travels to different network segments, how much comes from different network segments, and how much just passes through this network segment. Use Table A-1 to characterize how much of the traffic is not local. In each column, enter the percentage of traffic that applies.

Table A-1   *Network Traffic Percent Allocation*

	Both Source and Destination Are Local[*]	Source Is Local; Destination Is Not Local	Source Is Not Local; Destination Is Local	Source Is Not Local; Destination Is Not Local
Segment 1				
Segment 2				
Segment 3				
Segment 4				

[*]Source and destination refer to source and destination network hosts.

Characterize Network Applications and Protocols

To help characterize networking applications and protocols, you should first gather the following information:

- Identify any mission-critical data or operations.
- Document what networking policies are in use regarding distributed authority for network design and implementation.

Use Table A-2 to list the network applications and number of users and hosts on the customer's current network. For "Type of Application," write in some text that will help you identify the application, such as database, multimedia, electronic mail, manufacturing support system, and so on. Add any comments relevant to the network design. Include any information you have about corporate directions.

Table A-2   *Network Applications*

Name of Application	Type of Application	Number of Users	Number of Hosts	Comments

List the network protocols (see Table A-3) and the number of users and hosts. Add any comments that are relevant to the network design.

Table A-3   *Network Protocols*

Name of Protocol	Type of Protocol	Number of Users	Number of Hosts	Comments

Characterize Existing Network Availability and Performance

Document the mean-time-between-failure (MTBF) for the internetwork. If possible, determine the cost of downtime by assessing the following (reference Table A-4):

- What is the cost by department for a network outage (per hour)?
- What is the cost to the company or organization for a network outage (per hour)?

Table A-4   *Network Performance (MTBF)*

	MTBF	Date of Last Downtime	Duration of Last Downtime	Cause of Last Downtime
Internetwork				
Segment 1				
Segment 2				
Segment 3				

Perform PING tests to document response time measurements between mission-critical network devices, such as servers, routers, or identified workstations (see Table A-5).

Table A-5 *Network Response Times (Host-to-Host PING)*

	Host A	Host B	Host C	Host D
Host A				
Host B				
Host C				
Host D				

Characterize Existing Network Reliability and Utilization

Gather statistics about each major network segment using a monitoring tool such as a protocol analyzer, network monitor, or network management tool. If possible, monitor each segment for at least a day. At the end of the day, record the following measurements:

- Total megabytes
- Total number of frames
- Total number of CRC errors
- Total number of MAC-layer errors (collisions, Token Ring soft errors, FDDI ring ops)
- Total number of broadcasts/multicast frames
- Network utilization for each hour

Characterize the current network by filling in Table A-6. To calculate average network utilization, add each hourly average and divide by the number of hourly averages, as demonstrated by the following formula:

$Z = (X_1 + X_2 + X_3...X_x)/n$, where Z = Network$_{AVERAGE,}$ x = Hourly Average, and n = Number of Hours

or

Network$_{AVERAGE}$ = (Z Hourly Average / Number of Hours)

Table A-6   *Network Bandwidth Utilization*

	Average Network Utilization	Peak Network Utilization	Average Frame Size	CRC Error Rate	MAC-Layer Error Rate	Broadcasts/ Multicasts Rate
Segment 1						
Segment 2						
Segment 3						
Segment 4						
Segment 5						

For peak network utilization, record the highest hourly average. (If you have more granular data than hourly, record any short-term peaks.) For the average frame size, divide the total number of megabytes (MB) by the total number of frames, as demonstrated by the following formula:

$$\text{Frame}_{AVERAGE} = \text{Total}_{MB} / \text{Total}_{FRAMES}$$

Rate calculations are more complex. The concern here is the amount of errors or broadcasts compared to the amount of normal traffic. To calculate the CRC error rate, divide the total number of CRCs by the total amount of megabytes, as demonstrated by the following formula:

$$\text{CRC}_{ERRORRATE} \% = (\text{CRC}_{TOTAL} / \text{Total}_{MB}) \times 100$$

To determine the MAC-layer error rate, divide the total number of MAC-layer errors by the total number of frames:

$$\text{MAC}_{ERRORRATE} \% = (\text{MAC}_{ERRORS} / \text{Frame}_{TOTAL}) \times 100$$

To determine the broadcasts/multicasts rate, divide the total number of broadcasts/ multicasts by the total number of frames:

$$\text{Broadcast}_{RATE} \% = (\text{Broadcast}_{TOTAL} / \text{Frame}_{TOTAL}) \times 100$$

Characterize how much of the bandwidth on each segment is used by different protocols by filling in Table A-7. Many network monitors let you specify the bandwidth used by protocols as relative or absolute bandwidth (see the following list for explanations).

- Relative usage—How much bandwidth does this protocol use in comparison to the total bandwidth used on this segment?

- Absolute usage—How much bandwidth does this protocol use in comparison to the total capacity of the segment (for example, in comparison to 10 megabits per second (Mbps) on Ethernet)?

Table A-7   *Network Protocol Utilization*

	Relative Network Utilization	Absolute Network Utilization	Average Frame Size	Broadcasts/ Multicasts Rate
IP				
IPX				
AppleTalk				
NetBIOS				
SNA				
Other				

Characterize the Status of the Major Routers

Characterize the status of the major routers in the customer's network by filling out Table A-8. Plan to spend about a day studying the routers. The following Cisco IOS software shows commands that will help with completion of the chart:

- ROUTER>show tech-support
- ROUTER>show interfaces
- ROUTER>show processes
- ROUTER>show buffers

Table A-8   *Router Utilization*

	Router Name	5-minute CPU Utilization	Output Queue Drops Per Hour	Input Queue Drops Per Hour	Missed Packets Per Hour	Ignored Packets Per Hour	Comments
Router 1							
Router 2							
Router 3							
Router 4							
Router 5							

Fill out the table every hour for each interface, averaging the results for each category, using the following formula:

$$Z = [(X_1 + X_2 + X_3...X_x)/n]$$

where

- Z is the mean, or average, measurement
- x is each measurement collected
- X is the operation of summing each x measurement
- n is the number of measurements collected

Recommendations

Document any recommendations, assigning a priority to each one:

- URGENT—Recommendation is mission critical and mission impacting.
- HIGH—Recommendation is mission critical, but not immediately mission impacting.
- IMMEDIATE—Recommendation is not mission critical, but is mission impacting.
- PRIORITY—Recommendation is not mission critical or mission-impacting. Recommendations of this type are generally infrastructure improvements.
- NORMAL—Recommendation is not mission critical or mission impacting. The recommendation should be considered and revisited at a later date to determine if it should be escalated. (Generally, a NORMAL recommendation is used to flag a potential issue.)

Network Health

Based on the network data collected, review the following Network Health Checklist. A healthy network should have all items on the following list checked or removed.

NOTE   These are general guidelines and should not be taken as an exact measurement. As with all network design-related issues, "it depends" is the classic answer to any question or concern.

Network Health Checklist

☐ No shared Ethernet segments are saturated (40% network utilization).

☐ No shared Token Ring segments are saturated (70% network utilization).

☐ No WAN links are saturated (70% network utilization).

☐ The response time is generally less than 100 milliseconds (ms), which is 1/10 of a second.

☐ No segments have more than 20 percent broadcasts/multicasts.

☐ No segments have more than one CRC error per million bytes of data.

☐ On the Ethernet segments, less than 0.1 percent of the packets are collisions.

☐ On the Token Ring segments, less than 0.1 percent of the packets are soft errors that are not related to ring insertion.

☐ On the FDDI segments, not more than one ring operation per hour is related to ring insertion.

☐ The Cisco routers are not over-utilized (5-minute CPU utilization under 75%).

☐ The number of output queue drops has not exceeded more than about 100 per hour on any Cisco router.

☐ The number of input queue drops has not exceeded more than about 50 per hour on any Cisco router.

☐ The number of buffer misses has not exceeded more than about 25 per hour on any Cisco router.

☐ The number of ignored packets has not exceeded more than about 10 per hour on any interface on a Cisco router.

Traffic Overhead

Table A-9 illustrates the amount of traffic overhead that is associated with various protocols. Overhead is a factor to be considered when selecting a networking protocol.

Table A-9   *Traffic Overhead for Various Protocols*

Protocol	Notes	Total Bytes
Ethernet	Preamble = 8 bytes, header = 14 bytes, CRC = 4 bytes, interframe gap (IFG) = 12 bytes	38
802.3 with 802.2	Preamble = 8 bytes, header = 14 bytes, LLC = 3 or 4 bytes, SNAP (if present) = 5 bytes, CRC = 4 bytes, IFG = 12 bytes for 10 Mbps or 1.2 bytes for 100 Mbps	46
802.5 with 802.2	Starting delimiter = 1 byte, header = 14 bytes, LLC = 3 or 4 bytes, SNAP (if present) = 5 bytes, CRC = 4 bytes, ending delimiter = 1 byte, frame status = 1 byte	29
FDDI with 802.2	Preamble = 8 bytes, starting delimiter = 1 byte, header = 13 bytes, LLC = 3 or 4 bytes, SNAP (if present) = 5 bytes, CRC = 4 bytes, ending delimiter and frame status = about 2 bytes	36
HDLC	Flags = 2 bytes, addresses = 2 bytes, control = 1 or 2 bytes, CRC = 4 bytes	10
IP	With no options	20
TCP	With no options	20
IPX	Does not include NCP	30
DDP	Phase 2 (long "extended" header)	13

Traffic Caused by Workstation Initialization

Workstation initialization can cause a load on networks due to the number of unicast, multicast, or broadcast packets.

Packets for NetWare Client Initialization

Table A-10 shows the packets that a Novell NetWare client sends when it boots. The approximate packet size is also shown. On top of the packet size, add the data link layer overhead, such as 802.3 with 802.2, 802.5 with 802.2, and FDDI with 802.2. Network layer and transport layer overhead are already included in these examples. Depending on the version of NetWare, the packets might be slightly different than shown here.

Table A-10 *Packets for NetWare Client Initialization*

Packet	Source	Destination	Packet Size in Bytes	Number of Packets	Total Bytes
GetNearestServer	Client	Broadcast	34	1	34
GetNearestServer response	Server or router	Client	66	Depends on number of servers	66 if 1 server
Find network number	Client	Broadcast	40	1	40
Find network number response	Router	Client	40	1	40
Create connection	Client	Server	37	1	37
Create connection response	Server	Client	38	1	38
Negotiate buffer size	Client	Server	39	1	39
Negotiate buffer size response	Server	Client	40	1	40
Log out old connections	Client	Server	37	1	37
Log out response	Server	Client	38	1	38
Get server's clock	Client	Server	37	1	37
Get server's clock response	Server	Client	38	1	38
Download login.exe requests	Client	Server	50	Hundreds, depending on buffer size	Depends
Download login.exe responses	Server	Client	Depends on buffer size	Hundreds, depending on buffer size	Depends
Login	Client	Server	37	1	37
Login response	Server	Client	38	1	38

Packets for AppleTalk Client Initialization

Table A-11 shows the packets that an AppleTalk station sends when it boots. The approximate packet size is also shown. On top of the packet size, add data link layer overhead. Depending on the version of Macintosh system software, the packets might be slightly different than shown here.

Table A-11 *Packets for AppleTalk Client Initialization*

Packet	Source	Destination	Packet Size in Bytes	Number of Packets	Total Bytes
AARP for ID	Client	Multicast	28	10	280
ZIPGetNetInfo	Client	Multicast	15	1	15
GetNetInfo response	Router(s)	Client	About 44	All routers respond	44 if one router
NBP broadcast request to check uniqueness of name	Client	Router	About 65	3	195
NBP forward request	Router	Other routers	Same	Same	Same
NBP lookup	Router	Multicast	Same	Same	Same
If Chooser started					
GetZoneList	Client	Router	12	1	12
GetZoneList reply	Router	Client	Depends on number and names of zones	1	Depends
NBP broadcast request for servers in zone	Client	Router	About 65	Once a second if Chooser still open; decays after 45 seconds	About 3,000 if Chooser closed after 45 seconds
NBP forward request	Router	Other routers	About 65	Same	Same
NBP lookup	Router	Multicast	About 65	Same	Same
NBP reply	Server(s)	Client	About 65	Depends on number of servers	Depends
ASP open session and AFP login	Client	Server	Depends	4	About 130
ASP and AFP replies	Server	Client	Depends	2	About 90

NOTE	An AppleTalk station that has already been on a network remembers its previous network number and node ID and tries 10 times to verify that the network node combination is unique. If the AppleTalk station has never been on a network or has moved, it sends 20 multicasts—10 multicasts with a provisional network number and 10 multicasts with a network number supplied by a router that responded to the ZIPGetNetInfo request.

Packets for NetBIOS Client Initialization

Table A-12 shows the packets that a NetBIOS station sends when it boots. The approximate packet size is also shown. On top of the packet size, add data link layer overhead. Depending on the version of NetBIOS, the packets might be slightly different than shown here.

Table A-12   *Packets for NetBIOS Client Initialization*

Packet	Source	Destination	Packet Size in Bytes	Number of Packets	Total Bytes
Check name (make sure own name is unique)	Client	Broadcast	44	6	264
Find name for each server	Client	Broadcast	44	Depends on number of servers	44 if 1 server
Find name response	Server(s)	Client	44	Depends	44 if 1 server
Session initialize for each server	Client	Server	14	Depends	14 if 1 server
Session confirm	Server	Client	14	Depends	14 if 1 server

Packets for Traditional TCP/IP Client Initialization

Table A-13 shows the packets that a traditional TCP/IP station sends when it boots.

The approximate packet size is also shown. On top of the packet size, add data link layer overhead. Depending on the implementation of TCP/IP, the packets might be slightly different than shown here.

Table A-13 *Packets for Traditional TCP/IP Client Initialization*

Packet	Source	Destination	Packet Size in Bytes	Number of Packets	Total Bytes
ARP to make sure its own address is unique (optional)	Client	Broadcast	28	1	28
ARP for any servers	Client	Broadcast	28	Depends on number of servers	Depends
ARP for router	Client	Broadcast	28	1	28
ARP response	Server(s) or router	Client	28	1	28

Packets for DHCP Client Initialization

When a server receives a DHCPDISCOVER message from a client, the server chooses a network address for the requesting client. If no address is available, the server can choose to report the problem to the system administrator. If an address is available, the new address should be chosen as follows:

- The client's current address as recorded in the client's current binding, ELSE

- The client's previous address as recorded in the client's (now expired or released) binding, if that address is in the server's pool of available addresses and not already allocated, ELSE

- The address requested in the 'Requested IP Address' option, if that address is valid and not already allocated, ELSE

- A new address allocated from the server's pool of available addresses; the address is selected based on the subnet from which the message was received (if 'giaddr' is 0) or on the address of the relay agent that forwarded the message ('giaddr' when not 0).

Note that, in some network architectures (such as Internets with more than one IP subnet assigned to a physical network segment), it might be the case that the DHCP client should be assigned an address from a different subnet than the address recorded in 'giaddr'. Thus, DHCP does not require that the client be assigned an address from the subnet in 'giaddr'. A server is free to choose some other subnet, and it is beyond the scope of the DHCP specification to describe ways in which the assigned IP address might be chosen.

Although not required for correct operation of DHCP, the server should not reuse the selected network address before the client responds to the server's DHCPOFFER message. The server might choose to record the address as offered to the client.

The server must also choose an expiration time for the lease, as follows (see Tables A-14 and A-15 for field and option descriptions):

- IF the client has not requested a specific lease in the DHCPDISCOVER message and the client already has an assigned network address, the server returns the lease expiration time that was previously assigned to that address (note that the client must explicitly request a specific lease to extend the expiration time on a previously assigned address), ELSE

- IF the client has not requested a specific lease in the DHCPDISCOVER message and the client does not have an assigned network address, the server assigns a locally configured default lease time, ELSE

- IF the client has requested a specific lease in the DHCPDISCOVER message (regardless of whether the client has an assigned network address), the server might choose either to return the requested lease (if the lease is acceptable to local policy) or select another lease.

Table A-14 *Fields Used by DHCP Servers*

Field	DHCPOFFER	DHCPACK	DHCPNAK
'op'	BOOTREPLY	BOOTREPLY	BOOTREPLY
'htype'	(From "Assigned Numbers" RFC)		
'hlen'	(Hardware address length in octets)		
'hops'	0	0	0
'xid'	'xid' from client DHCPDISCOVER message	'xid' from client DHCPREQUEST Message	'xid' from client DHCPREQUEST message
'secs'	0	0	0
'ciaddr'	0	'ciaddr' from DHCPREQUEST or 0	0
'yiaddr'	IP address offered to client	IP address Assigned client	0
'siaddr'	IP address of next bootstrap server	IP address of next Bootstrap server	0
'flags'	'flags' from client DHCPDISCOVER message	'flags' from Client DHCPREQUEST Message	'flags' from client DHCPREQUEST message

Table A-14 *Fields Used by DHCP Servers*

Field	DHCPOFFER	DHCPACK	DHCPNAK
'giaddr'	'giaddr' from client DHCPDISCOVER message	'giaddr' from Client DHCPREQUEST Message	'giaddr' from client DHCPREQUEST message
'chaddr'	'chaddr' from client DHCPDISCOVER message	'chaddr' from Client DHCPREQUEST Message	'chaddr' from client DHCPREQUEST message
'sname'	Server host name or options	Server host name or options	(unused)
'file'	Client boot file name or options	Client boot file name or options	(unused)
'options'	Options	Options	

Table A-15 *Options Used by DHCP Servers*

Option	DHCPOFFER	DHCPACK	DHCPNAK
Requested IP address	MUST NOT	MUST NOT	MUST NOT
IP address lease time	MUST	MUST (DHCPREQUEST) MUST NOT (DHCPINFORM)	MUST NOT
Use 'file'/'sname' fields	MAY	MAY	MUST NOT
DHCP message type	DHCPOFFER	DHCPACK	DHCPNAK
Parameter request list	MUST NOT	MUST NOT	MUST NOT
Message	SHOULD	SHOULD	SHOULD
Client identifier	MUST NOT	MUST NOT	MAY
Vendor class identifier	MAY	MAY	MAY
Server identifier	MUST	MUST	MUST
Maximum message size	MUST NOT	MUST NOT	MUST NOT
All others	MAY	MAY	MUST NOT

After the network address and lease have been determined, the server constructs a DHCPOFFER message with the offered configuration parameters. It is important for all DHCP servers to return the same parameters (with the possible exception of a newly allocated network address) to ensure predictable client behavior regardless of which server the client selects. The configuration parameters MUST be selected by applying the following rules in the order given in the following list. The network administrator is responsible for configuring multiple DHCP servers to ensure uniform responses from those servers. The server MUST return to the client:

- The client's network address, as determined by the rules given earlier in this section.

- The expiration time for the client's lease, as determined by the rules given earlier in this section.

- Parameters requested by the client, according to the following rules:

  — IF the server has been explicitly configured with a default value for the parameter, the server MUST include that value in an appropriate option in the 'option' field, ELSE.

  — IF the server recognizes the parameter as a parameter defined in the Host Requirements Document, the server MUST include the default value for that parameter as given in the Host Requirements document in an appropriate option in the 'option' field, ELSE.

- The server MUST NOT return a value for that parameter.

  The server MUST supply as many of the requested parameters as possible and MUST omit any parameters it cannot provide. The server MUST include each requested parameter only once unless explicitly allowed in the DHCP Options and BOOTP Vendor Extensions document.

- Any parameters from the existing binding that differ from the Host Requirements Document defaults.

- Any parameters specific to this client (as identified by the contents of 'chaddr' or 'client identifier' in the DHCPDISCOVER or DHCPREQUEST message), for example, as configured by the network administrator.

- Any parameters specific to this client's class (as identified by the contents of the 'vendor class identifier' option in the DHCPDISCOVER or DHCPREQUEST message), for example, as configured by the network administrator. The parameters MUST be identified by an exact match between the client's vendor class identifiers and the client's classes identified in the server.

- Parameters with non-default values on the client's subnet.

Table A-16 shows the packets that a TCP/IP station running DHCP sends when it boots. Although a DHCP client sends more packets when initializing, DHCP is still recommended. The benefits of dynamic configuration far outweigh the disadvantages of the extra traffic and extra broadcast packets. (The client and server use broadcast packets until the point that they believe each other's IP addresses.)

The approximate packet size is also shown. On top of the packet size, add data link layer overhead. Depending on the implementation of DHCP, the packets might be slightly different than shown here.

Table A-16 *Packets for DHCP Client Initialization*

Packet	Source	Destination	Packet Size in Bytes	Number of Packets	Total Bytes
DHCP discover	Client	Broadcast	576	Once every few seconds until client hears from a DHCP server	Depends
DHCP offer	Server	Broadcast	328	1	328
DHCP request	Client	Broadcast	576	1	576
DHCP ACK	Server	Broadcast	328	1	328
ARP to make sure its own address is unique	Client	Broadcast	28	3	84
ARP for client	Server	Broadcast	28	1	1
ARP response	Client	Server	28	1	28
DHCP request	Client	Server	576	1	576
DHCP ACK	Server	Client	328	1	328

Provisioning Hardware and Media for the LAN

The most significant design rule (see Table A-17) for Ethernet is the rule that states that "the round-trip propagation delay in one collision domain must not exceed 512 bit times," which is a requirement for collision detection to work correctly. This rule means that the maximum round-trip delay for 10-Mbps Ethernet is 51.2 microseconds. The maximum round-trip delay for 100 Mbps Ethernet is only 5.12 microseconds because the bit time on 100 Mbps Ethernet is 0.01 microseconds as opposed to 0.1 microseconds on 10 Mbps Ethernet.

Table A-17   *Scalability Constraints for IEEE 802.3*

	10Base5	10Base2	10BaseT	100BaseT
Topology	Bus	Bus	Star	Star
Maximum segment length (meters)	500	185	100 from hub to station	100 from hub to station
Maximum number of attachments per segment	100	30	2 (hub and station or hub-hub)	2 (hub and station or hub-hub)
Maximum collision domain	2,500 meters of 5 segments and 4 repeaters; only 3 segments can be populated	2,500 meters of 5 segments and 4 repeaters; only 3 segments can be populated	2,500 meters of 5 segments and 4 repeaters; only 3 segments can be populated	See next discussion

To make 100 Mbps Ethernet work, more severe distance limitations exist than those required for 10 Mbps Ethernet. The general rule is that a 100 Mbps Ethernet has a maximum diameter of 205 meters when UTP cabling is used, whereas 10 Mbps Ethernet has a maximum diameter of 2,500 meters.

This section provides some guidelines to help choose the right media for network designs.

100 Mbps Ethernet Topologies

As in 10 Mbps Ethernet (see Table A-18), the overriding design rule for 100 Mbps Ethernet states that the round-trip collision delay must not exceed 512 bit times. However, the bit time on 100 Mbps Ethernet is 0.01 microseconds as opposed to 0.1 microseconds on 10 Mbps Ethernet. This means that the maximum round-trip delay for 100 Mbps Ethernet is 5.12 microseconds as opposed to the more lenient 51.2 microseconds in 10 Mbps Ethernet.

Table A-18   *Scalability Constraints for 10 Mbps Fiber Ethernet*

	10BaseFP	10BaseFB	10BaseFL	Old FOIRL	New FOIRL
Topology	Passive star	Backbone or repeater fiber system	Link	Link	Link or star
Allows DTE (end-node) connections?	Yes	No	No	No	Yes
Maximum segment length (meters)	500	2,000	1,000 or 2,000	1,000	1,000
Allows cascaded repeaters?	No	Yes	No	No	Yes
Maximum collision domain in meters	2,500	2,500	2,500	2,500	2,500

To make 100 Mbps Ethernet work, distance limitations are imposed. The limitations depend on the type of repeaters that are used.

In the IEEE 100BaseT specification, two types of repeaters are defined:

- Class I repeaters have a latency of 0.7 microseconds or less. Only one repeater hop is allowed.

- Class II repeaters have a latency of 0.46 microseconds or less. One or two repeater hops are allowed.

Table A-19 shows the maximum size of collision domains, depending on the type of repeater(s).

Table A-19   *Maximum Collision Domains for 100BaseT*

	Copper	Mixed Copper and Multimode Fiber	Multimode Fiber
DTE-DTE (or switch-switch)	100 meters	—	412 meters (2,000 if full duplex)
One Class I repeater	200 meters	260 meters	272 meters
One Class II repeater	200 meters	308 meters	320 meters
Two Class II repeaters	205 meters	216 meters	228 meters

To check a path to make sure the path delay value (PDV) does not exceed 512 bit times, add up the following delays:

- All link segment delays
- All repeater delays
- DTE delay
- A safety margin (0 to 5 bit times)

Path Delay Value

The following steps are used to calculate the PDV:

1 Determine the delay for each link segment (link segment delay value, or LSDV), including interrepeater links, using the following formula. (Multiply by two so that it is a round-trip delay.)

LSDV = 2 × segment length × cable delay for this segment.

For end-node segments, the segment length is the cable length between the PHY interface at the repeater and the PHY interface at the DTE. Use your two farthest DTEs for a worst-case calculation. For interrepeater links, the segment length is the cable length between the repeater PHY interfaces.

Cable delay is the delay specified by the manufacturer, if available. When actual cable lengths or propagation delays are not known, use the delay in bit times as specified in Table A-20.

Cable delay must be specified in bit times per meter (bT/m). You can use Table A-20 to convert values specified relative to the speed of light (c) or nanoseconds per meter (ns/m) to bT/m.

2 Sum together the LSDVs for all segments in the path.

3 Determine the delay for each repeater in the path. If model-specific data is not available from the manufacturer, determine the class of repeater (I or II) and use the data in Table A-20.

4 MII cables for 100BaseT should not exceed 0.5 meters each. When evaluating system topology, MII cable lengths need not be accounted for separately. Delays attributable to the MII are incorporated into DTE and repeater delays.

5 Use the DTE delay value shown in Table A-19 unless your equipment manufacturer defines a different value.

6 Decide on an appropriate safety margin between 0 and 5 bit times. Five bit times is a safe value.

7 Insert the values obtained in the calculations described in the following formula for calculating the path delay value (PDV):

PDV = link delays + repeater delays + DTE delay + safety margin

If the PDV is less than 512, the path is qualified in terms of worst-case delay.

Table A-20 shows round-trip delay in bit times for standard cables and maximum round-trip delay in bit times for DTEs, repeaters, and maximum-length cables. (Note that the values have already been doubled to provide a round-trip delay. If these numbers are used, multiplying by two again in the LSDV formula is not necessary.)

Table A-20 *Network Component Delays**

Component	Roundtrip Delay in Bit Times Per Meter	Maximum Roundtrip Delay in Bit Times
Two TX/FX DTEs	—	100
Two T4 DTEs	—	138
One T4 DTE and one TX/FX DTE	—	127
Cat 3 cable segment	1.14	114 (100 meters)
Cat 4 cable segment	1.14	114 (100 meters)
Cat 5 cable segment	1.112	111.2 (100 meters)
STP cable segment	1.112	111.2 (100 meters)
Fiber optic cable segment	1.0	412 (412 meters)
Class I repeater	—	140
Class II repeater with all ports TX or FX	—	92
Class II repeater with any port T4	—	67

*IEEE 802.3 u - 1995, "Media Access Control (MAC) Parameters, Physical Layer, Medium Attachment Units, and Repeater for 100 Mb/s Operation, Type 100BASE-T."

Calculating Cable Delays

Some cable manufacturers specify propagation delays relative to the speed of light (c) or in nanoseconds per meter (ns/m). To convert to bit times per meter (bT/m), use Table A-21.

Table A-21 *Conversion for Cable Delays**

Speed Relative to C	ns/m	bT/m
0.4	8.34	0.834
0.5	6.67	0.667
0.51	6.54	0.654
0.52	6.41	0.641
0.53	6.29	0.629
0.54	6.18	0.618
0.55	6.06	0.606
0.56	5.96	0.596
0.57	5.85	0.585
0.58	5.75	0.575
0.5852	5.70	0.570
0.59	5.65	0.565
0.6	5.56	0.556
0.61	5.47	0.547
0.62	5.38	0.538
0.63	5.29	0.529
0.64	5.21	0.521
0.65	5.13	0.513
0.654	5.10	0.510
0.66	5.05	0.505
0.666	5.01	0.501
0.67	4.98	0.498
0.68	4.91	0.491
0.69	4.83	0.483
0.7	4.77	0.477
0.8	4.17	0.417
0.9	3.71	0.371

*IEEE 802.3 u - 1995, "Media Access Control (MAC) Parameters, Physical Layer, Medium Attachment Units, and Repeater for 100 Mbps Operation, Type 100BASE-T."

Table A-22 lists some scalability concerns when designing token ring segments. IBM Token Ring documentation should be considered the absolute resource for Token Ring implementation concerns and constraints.

Table A-22 *Scalability Constraints for Token Ring*

	IBM Token Ring	**IEEE 802.5**
Topology	Star	Not specified
Maximum segment length (meters)	Depends on type of cable, number of MAUs, and so on	Depends on type of cable, number of MAUs, and so on
Maximum number of attachments per segment	260 for STP, 72 for UTP	250
Maximum network diameter	Depends on type of cable, number of MAUs, and so on	Depends on type of cable, number of MAUs, and so on

FDDI does not actually specify the maximum segment length or network diameter (see Table A-23). It specifies the amount of allowed power loss, which works out to the approximate distances shown.

Table A-23 *Scalability Constraints for FDDI*

	Multimode Fiber	**Single-Mode Fiber**	**UTP**
Topology	Dual ring, tree of concentrators, and others	Dual ring, tree of concentrators, and others	Star
Maximum segment length	2 kilometers (km) between stations	60 km between stations	100 m from hub to station
Maximum number of attachments per segment	1,000 (500 dual attachment stations)	1,000 (500 dual attachment stations)	2 (hub and station or hub-hub)
Maximum network diameter	200 km	200 km	200 km

Network Provisioning

You can calculate the amount of required bandwidth by adding the bandwidth requirements for each major application, such as voice, video, and data. This sum then represents the minimum bandwidth requirement for any given link, and it should not exceed approximately 75 percent of the total available bandwidth for the link. This 75 percent rule assumes that some bandwidth is required for overhead traffic, such as routing and Layer 2 keepalives, as well as for additional applications such as e-mail and Hypertext Transfer Protocol (HTTP) traffic.

A Voice over IP (VoIP) packet consists of the payload, IP header, User Datagram Protocol (UDP) header, Real-time Transport Protocol (RTP) header, and Layer 2 Link header as illustrated in Figure A-1. At the default packetization rate of 20 ms, VoIP packets have a 160-byte payload for G.711 or a 20-byte payload for G.729. The IP header is 40 bytes, the UDP header is 8 bytes, and the RTP header is 12 bytes. The link header varies in size according to media.

Figure A-1 *VoIP Packet*

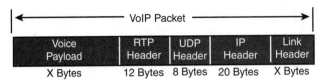

The bandwidth consumed by VoIP streams is calculated by adding the packet payload and all headers (in bits), then multiplying by the packet rate per second (default of 50 packets per second). Table A-24 details the bandwidth per VoIP flow at a default packet rate of 50 packets per second (pps). This does not include Layer 2 header overhead and does not take into account any possible compression schemes, such as compressed Real-time Transport Protocol (cRTP).

Table A-24 *Bandwidth Consumption for Voice Payload-Only Codec*

	Sampling Rate	Voice Payload in Bytes	Packets Per Second	Bandwidth Per Conversation
G.711	20 ms	160	50	80 kbps
G.711	30 ms	240	33	53 kbps
G.729A	20 ms	20	50	24 kbps
G.729A	30 ms	30	33	16 kbps

Table A-25 includes header overhead in the codec bandwidth calculations.

Table A-25 *Bandwidth Consumption with Headers Included Codec*

	Ethernet 14 Bytes of Header	PPP 6 Bytes of Header	ATM 53-Byte Cells with a 48-Byte Payload	Frame-Relay 4 Bytes of Header
G.711 at 50 pps	85.6 kbps	82.4 kbps	106 kbps	81.6 kbps
G.711 at 33 pps	56.5 kbps	54.4 kbps	70 kbps	54 kbps
G.729A at 50 pps	29.6 kbps	26.4 kbps	42.4 kbps	25.6 kbps
G.729A at 33 pps	19.5 kbps	17.4 kbps	28 kbps	17 kbps

Subnet Masks

Table A-26 includes CIDR prefix lengths and related information for subnet masks.

Table A-26 *Subnet Masks*

CIDR Prefix Length	Dotted-Decimal	Binary	Number of Classful INetworks
/1	128.0.0.0	1000 0000 0000 0000 0000 0000 0000 0000	128 ampere (A)
/2	192.0.0.0	1100 0000 0000 0000 0000 0000 0000 0000	64 A
/3	224.0.0.0	1110 0000 0000 0000 0000 0000 0000 0000	32 A
/4	240.0.0.0	1111 0000 0000 0000 0000 0000 0000 0000	16 A
/5	248.0.0.0	1111 1000 0000 0000 0000 0000 0000 0000	8 A
/6	252.0.0.0	1111 1100 0000 0000 0000 0000 0000 0000	4 A
/7	254.0.0.0	1111 1110 0000 0000 0000 0000 0000 0000	2 A
/8	255.0.0.0	1111 1111 0000 0000 0000 0000 0000 0000	1 A or 256 Bs
/9	255.128.0.0	1111 1111 1000 0000 0000 0000 0000 0000	128 Bs
/10	255.192.0.0	1111 1111 1100 0000 0000 0000 0000 0000	64 Bs
/11	255.224.0.0	1111 1111 1110 0000 0000 0000 0000 0000	32 Bs
/12	255.240.0.0	1111 1111 1111 0000 0000 0000 0000 0000	16 Bs
/13	255.248.0.0	1111 1111 1111 1000 0000 0000 0000 0000	8 Bs
/14	255.252.0.0	1111 1111 1111 1100 0000 0000 0000 0000	4 Bs
/15	255.254.0.0	1111 1111 1111 1110 0000 0000 0000 0000	2 Bs
/16	255.255.0.0	1111 1111 1111 1111 0000 0000 0000 0000	1 byte (B) or 256 Cs
/17	255.255.128.0	1111 1111 1111 1111 1000 0000 0000 0000	128 Cs

(continues)

Table A-26   *Subnet Masks (Continued)*

CIDR Prefix Length	Dotted-Decimal	Binary	Number of Classful lNetworks
/18	255.255.192.0	1111 1111 1111 1111 1100 0000 0000 0000	64 Cs
/19	255.255.224.0	1111 1111 1111 1111 1110 0000 0000 0000	32 Cs
/20	255.255.240.0	1111 1111 1111 1111 1111 0000 0000 0000	16 Cs
/21	255.255.248.0	1111 1111 1111 1111 1111 1000 0000 0000	8 Cs
/22	255.255.252.0	1111 1111 1111 1111 1111 1100 0000 0000	4 Cs
/23	255.255.254.0	1111 1111 1111 1111 1111 1110 0000 0000	2 Cs
/24	255.255.255.0	1111 1111 1111 1111 1111 1111 0000 0000	1 C or 256 hosts
/25	255.255.255.128	1111 1111 1111 1111 1111 1111 1000 0000	1/2 C or 128 hosts
/26	255.255.255.192	1111 1111 1111 1111 1111 1111 1100 0000	1/4 C or 64 hosts
/27	255.255.255.224	1111 1111 1111 1111 1111 1111 1110 0000	1/8 C or 32 hosts
/28	255.255.255.240	1111 1111 1111 1111 1111 1111 1111 0000	1/16 C or 16 hosts
/29	255.255.255.248	1111 1111 1111 1111 1111 1111 1111 1000	1/32 C or 8 hosts
/30	255.255.255.252	1111 1111 1111 1111 1111 1111 1111 1100	1/64 C or 4 hosts
/31	255.255.255.254	1111 1111 1111 1111 1111 1111 1111 1110	1/128 C or 2 hosts
/32	255.255.255.255	1111 1111 1111 1111 1111 1111 1111 1111	1/256 C or 1 host

Interface Types by Region/Country

Table A-27 includes interface types for the continent.

Table A-27   *Interface Types by Region/Country*

Continental Region	Country	Interface Type
North America		
	U.S., Canada	RS232 for 9.6 to 19.2 kbps
		V.35 for 56 kbps
		RS422/RS449 > 56 kbps
	Mexico	V.35
		G.703 and G.704

Table A-27   *Interface Types by Region/Country*

Continental Region	Country	Interface Type
South America		
	Colombia	V.35
	Venezuela	V.35
United Kingdom (U.K.)		
	U.K.	X.21
		G703/704
Continental Europe		
	Austria	X.21, V.35 (optional)
	Belgium, Brussels	V.35
		X.21/V.11
		G.703
		G.703/G.704
	Czech Republic	V.35
	Denmark, Copenhagen	X.21
		V.35
		G.703
	France, Paris	V.35
		X.24, V.11
		G.703
		X.21 (where feasible)
	Finland	V.35
	Greece	V.35
	Germany, Frankfurt, Munich	X.21
	Hungary	V.35

(continues)

Table A-27 *Interface Types by Region/Country (Continued)*

Continental Region	Country	Interface Type
	Italy, Milan	V.35
		G.703/G.704
	Ireland, Dublin	X.21 (15-way D-connector)
		G.703/G.704 (delivered as dual 750 hm co-ax)
	Luxembourg	V.35
	Netherlands, Amsterdam	V.35 (V.36, X.21/X.24 on request)
		G.703
		G.703/G.704
	Norway	V.35
	Portugal	V.35
	Russia	V.35, X.21 (most common)
	Spain, Madrid	V.35
		G.703/G.704
	Sweden, Stockholm	V.35, X.21
		V.36/V.11
	Switzerland, Zurich	X.35 (X.21/V.11 also)
		G.703
Middle East		
	Israel	V.35

Table A-27 *Interface Types by Region/Country*

Continental Region	Country	Interface Type
Asian Pacific		
	Australia	V.35/X.21/V11
	Japan	I or Y
	Hong Kong	V.35/V11
	Indonesia	V.35
	Malaysia	V.35
	Singapore	V.35
	New Zealand	V35/X21
	South Africa	X21 (V.35)
	Taiwan	V.35
	Philippines	V.35
	South Korea	V35

Data Transmission Throughput

Tables A-28, A-29, and A-30 demonstrate the amount of time, in seconds, minutes, hours, or days, that it would take to transfer a given amount of data across a private line (minimal overhead), ATM, or Frame Relay connection.

Table A-28 *Raw Data Transmission Rates/Time*

Data Rates

DS0	0.064	Mbps
DS1/T1	1.544	Mbps
DS3/T3	45	Mbps
OC3	155	Mbps
OC12	622	Mbps
OC48	2,500	Mbps (2.5 Gbps)
OC192	10,000	Mbps (10 Gbps)

(Transmission measurement in seconds, excluding any protocol or frame overhead)

Data (MB)	DS0	DS1/T1	DS3/T3	OC3	OC12	OC48	OC192
<1	125	5.18134715	0.0222222	0.0064516	0.0016077	0.0004	0.0001
1	125	5.18134715	0.1777777	0.0516129	0.0128617	0.0032	0.0008
10	1,250	51.8134715	1.7777777	0.5161290	0.1286173	0.032	0.008
100	12,500	518.134715	17.777777	5.1612903	1.2861736	0.32	0.08
1,000	125,000	5,181.34715	177.77777	51.612903	12.861736	3.2	0.8
10,000	1,250,000	51,813.4715	1,777.7777	516.12903	128.61736	32	8
100,000	12,500,000	518,134.715	17,777.777	5,161.2903	1,286.1736	320	80
1,000,000	125,000,000	5,181,347.15	177,777.77	51,612.903	12,861.736	3,200	800

(Transmission measurement in minutes, excluding any protocol or frame overhead)

Data (MB)	DS0	DS1/T1	DS3/T3	OC3	OC12	OC48	OC192
<1	2.083	0.086	0.000	0.000	0.000	0.000	0.000
1	2.083	0.086	0.003	0.001	0.000	0.000	0.000
10	20.833	0.864	0.030	0.009	0.002	0.001	0.000
100	208.333	8.636	0.296	0.086	0.021	0.005	0.001
1,000	2,083.333	86.356	2.963	0.860	0.214	0.053	0.013
10,000	20,833.333	863.558	29.630	8.602	2.144	0.533	0.133
100,000	208,333.333	8,635.579	296.296	86.022	21.436	5.333	1.333
1,000,000	2,083,333.333	86,355.786	2,962.963	860.215	214.362	53.333	13.333

Bytes-to-bits conversion

User Data	MB		Mb
	<1		<8
	1		8
	10		80
	100		800
	1,000 (1 GB)		8,000
	10,000 (10 GB)		80,000
	100,000 (100 GB)		800,000
	1,000,000 (1 TB)		8,000,000

Table A-28 *Raw Data Transmission Rates/Time*

Data (MB)	DS0	DS1/T1	DS3/T3	OC3	OC12	OC48	OC192
(Transmission measurement in hours, excluding any protocol or frame overhead)							
<1	0.035	0.001	0.000	0.000	0.000	0.000	0.000
1	0.035	0.001	0.000	0.000	0.000	0.000	0.000
10	0.347	0.014	0.000	0.000	0.000	0.000	0.000
100	3.472	0.144	0.005	0.001	0.000	0.000	0.000
1,000	34.722	1.439	0.049	0.014	0.004	0.001	0.000
10,000	347.222	14.393	0.494	0.143	0.036	0.009	0.002
100,000	3,472.222	143.926	4.938	1.434	0.357	0.089	0.022
1,000,000	3,4722.222	1,439.263	49.383	14.337	3.573	0.889	0.222
(Transmission measurement in days, excluding any protocol or frame overhead)							
<1	0.001	0.000	0.000	0.000	0.000	0.000	0.000
1	0.001	0.000	0.000	0.000	0.000	0.000	0.000
10	0.014	0.001	0.000	0.000	0.000	0.000	0.000
100	0.145	0.006	0.000	0.000	0.000	0.000	0.000
1,000	1.447	0.060	0.002	0.001	0.000	0.000	0.000
10,000	14.468	0.600	0.021	0.006	0.001	0.000	0.000
100,000	144.676	5.997	0.206	0.060	0.015	0.004	0.001
1,000,000	1,446.759	59.969	2.058	0.597	0.149	0.037	0.009

Table A-29 *ATM Raw Data Transmission Rates/Time*

Data Rates

(Transmission measurement in seconds, excluding any protocol overhead)

			Data (MB)	DS0	DS1/T1	DS3/T3	OC3	OC12	OC48	OC192
DS0	0.064	Mbps	<1	136.7924528	5.67015348	0.0243186	0.0070602	0.0017593	4.37736E-	1.09434E-
DS1/T1	1.544	Mbps	1	136.7924528	5.67015348	0.1945492	0.0564820	0.0140751	0.0035018	8.75472E-
DS3/T3	45	Mbps	10	1,367.924528	56.7015348	1.9954926	0.5648204	0.1407510	0.0350188	0.0087547
OC3	155	Mbps	100	13,679.24528	567.015348	19.454926	5.6482045	1.4075107	0.3501886	0.0875471
OC12	622	Mbps	1,000	136,792.4528	5670.15348	194.54926	56.482045	14.075107	3.5018867	0.8754716
OC48	2,500	Mbps (2.5 Gbps)	10,000	1,367,924.528	56,701.5348	1,945.4926	564.82045	140.75107	35.018867	8.7547169
OC192	10,000	Mbps (10 Gbps)	100,000	13,679,245.28	567,015.348	19,454.926	5,648.2045	1,407.5107	350.18867	87.547169
			1,000,000	136,792,452.8	5,670,153.48	194,549.26	56,482.045	14,075.107	3,501.8867	875.47169

User Data

(Transmission measurement in minutes, excluding any protocol overhead)

Bytes-to-bits conversion			Data (MB)	DS0	DS1/T1	DS3/T3	OC3	OC12	OC48	OC192
<8		Mb	<1	2.280	0.095	0.000	0.000	0.000	0.000	0.000
8			1	2.280	0.095	0.003	0.001	0.000	0.000	0.000
80			10	22.799	0.945	0.032	0.009	0.002	0.001	0.000
800			100	227.987	9.450	0.324	0.094	0.023	0.006	0.001
8,000	(1 GB)		1,000	2,279.874	94.503	3.242	0.941	0.235	0.058	0.015
80,000	(10 GB)		10,000	22,798.742	945.026	32.425	9.414	2.346	0.584	0.146
800,000	(100 GB)		100,000	227,987.421	9,450.256	324.249	94.137	23.459	5.836	1.459
8,000,000	(1 TB)		1,000,000	2,279,874.214	94,502.558	3,242.488	941.367	234.585	58.365	14.591

Table A-29 *ATM Raw Data Transmission Rates/Time*

ATM Overhead (%):	9.433962

(Transmission measurement in hours, excluding any protocol overhead)

< 1	0.038	0.002	0.000	0.000	0.000	0.000	0.000
1	0.038	0.002	0.000	0.000	0.000	0.000	0.000
10	0.380	0.016	0.001	0.000	0.000	0.000	0.000
100	3.800	0.158	0.005	0.002	0.000	0.000	0.000
1,000	37.998	1.575	0.054	0.016	0.004	0.001	0.000
10,000	379.979	15.750	0.540	0.157	0.039	0.010	0.002
100,000	3,799.790	157.504	5.404	1.569	0.391	0.097	0.024
1,000,000	37,997.904	1,575.043	54.041	15.689	3.910	0.973	0.243

(Transmission measurement in days, excluding any protocol overhead)

< 1	0.002	0.000	0.000	0.000	0.000	0.000	0.000
1	0.002	0.000	0.000	0.000	0.000	0.000	0.000
10	0.016	0.001	0.000	0.000	0.000	0.000	0.000
100	0.158	0.007	0.000	0.000	0.000	0.000	0.000
1,000	1.583	0.066	0.002	0.001	0.000	0.000	0.000
10,000	15.832	0.656	0.023	0.007	0.002	0.000	0.000
100,000	158.325	6.563	0.225	0.065	0.016	0.004	0.001
1,000,000	1,583.246	65.627	2.252	0.654	0.163	0.041	0.010

Table A-30 *Frame Relay Raw Data Transmission Rates/Time*

			Data (MB)	DS0	DS1/T1	DS3/T3	OC3	OC12	OC48	OC192
Data Rates			*(Transmission measurement in seconds, excluding any protocol overhead)*							
DS0	0.064	Mbps	< 1	126.4478764	5.24136275	0.0224796	0.0065263	0.0016263	4.04633E-	1.01158E-
DS1/T1	1.544	Mbps	1	126.4478764	5.24136275	0.1798369	0.0522107	0.0130107	0.0032370	8.09266E-
DS3/T3	45	Mbps	10	1,264.478764	52.4136275	1.7983697	0.5221073	0.1301071	0.0323706	0.0080926
OC3	155	Mbps	100	12,644.78764	524.136275	17.983697	5.2210736	1.3010713	0.3237065	0.0809266
OC12	622	Mbps	1,000	126,447.8764	5,241.36275	179.83697	52.210736	13.010713	3.2370656	0.8092664
OC48	2,500	Mbps (2.5 Gbps)	10,000	1,264,478.764	52,413.6275	1,798.3697	522.10736	130.10713	32.370656	8.0926640
OC192	10,000	Mbps (10 Gbps)	100,000	12,644,787.64	524,136.275	17,983.697	5,221.0736	1,301.0713	323.70656	80.926640
			1,000,000	126,447,876.4	5,241,362.75	179,836.97	52,210.736	13,010.713	3,237.0656	809.26640
	MB	Mb								
User Data			*(Transmission measurement in minutes, excluding any protocol overhead)*							
	< 1	< 8	< 1	2.107	0.087	0.000	0.000	0.000	0.000	0.000
		Bytes-to-bits conversion								
	1	8	1	2.107	0.087	0.003	0.001	0.000	0.000	0.000
	10	80	10	21.075	0.874	0.030	0.009	0.002	0.001	0.000
	100	800	100	210.746	8.736	0.300	0.087	0.022	0.005	0.001
	1,000 (1 GB)	8,000	1,000	2,107.465	87.356	2.997	0.870	0.217	0.054	0.013
	10,000 (10 GB)	80,000	10,000	21,074.646	873.560	29.973	8.702	2.168	0.540	0.135
	100,000 (100 GB)	800,000	100,000	210,746.461	8,735.605	299.728	87.018	21.685	5.395	1.349
	100,0000 (1 TB)	800,0000	1,000,000	2,107,464.607	87,356.046	2,997.283	870.179	216.845	53.951	13.488

Table A-30 *Frame Relay Raw Data Transmission Rates/Time*

Data (MB)	Bytes-to-bits conversion	DS0	DS1/T1	DS3/T3	OC3	OC12	OC48	OC192
User Data								
< 1	< 8	2.107	0.087	0.000	0.000	0.000	0.000	0.000
1	8	2.107	0.087	0.003	0.001	0.000	0.000	0.000
10	80	21.075	0.874	0.030	0.009	0.002	0.001	0.000
100	800	210.746	8.736	0.300	0.087	0.022	0.005	0.001
1,000 (1 GB)	8,000	2,107.465	87.356	2.997	0.870	0.217	0.054	0.013
10,000 (10 GB)	80,000	21,074.646	873.560	29.973	8.702	2.168	0.540	0.135
100,000 (100 GB)	800,000	210,746.461	8,735.605	299.728	87.018	21.685	5.395	1.349
100,0000 (1 TB)	8,000,000	2,107,464.607	87,356.046	2,997.283	870.179	216.845	53.951	13.488
(Transmission measurement in hours, excluding any protocol overhead)								
FRL Overhead (%): 1.158301								
< 1		0.035	0.001	0.000	0.000	0.000	0.000	0.000
1		0.035	0.001	0.000	0.000	0.000	0.000	0.000
(based on 4096 byte payload)								
10		0.351	0.015	0.000	0.000	0.000	0.000	0.000
100		3.512	0.146	0.005	0.001	0.000	0.000	0.000
1,000		35.124	1.456	0.050	0.015	0.004	0.001	0.000
10,000		351.244	14.559	0.500	0.145	0.036	0.009	0.002
100,000		3,512.441	145.593	4.995	1.450	0.361	0.090	0.022
1,000,000		35,124.410	1,455.934	49.955	14.503	3.614	0.899	0.225

(continues)

Table A-30 *Frame Relay Raw Data Transmission Rates/Time*

Data (MB)	DS0	DS1/T1	DS3/T3	OC3	OC12	OC48	OC192
	(Transmission measurement in days, excluding any protocol overhead)						
< 1	0.001	0.000	0.000	0.000	0.000	0.000	0.000
1	0.001	0.000	0.000	0.000	0.000	0.000	0.000
10	0.015	0.001	0.000	0.000	0.000	0.000	0.000
100	0.146	0.006	0.000	0.000	0.000	0.000	0.000
1,000	1.464	0.061	0.002	0.001	0.000	0.000	0.000
10,000	14.635	0.607	0.021	0.006	0.002	0.000	0.000
100,000	146.352	6.066	0.208	0.060	0.015	0.004	0.001
1,000,000	1,463.517	60.664	2.081	0.604	0.151	0.037	0.009

Mesh Network Connectivity

Table A-31 demonstrates the number of connections required to meet a hub-and-spoke, partial mesh, or full mesh networking requirement.

Table A-31   *Mesh Network Connectivity Connections*

Number of Nodes	Hub-and-Spoke	Partial Mesh	Full Mesh
	$n-1$	$n^2/\sqrt{(n-1)}$	$n^2-n/2$
1			
2	1	4	
3	2	6	3
4	3	9	6
5	4	13	10
6	5	16	15
7	6	20	21
8	7	24	28
9	8	29	36
10	9	33	45
11	10	38	55
12	11	43	66
13	12	49	78
14	13	54	91
15	14	60	105
16	15	66	120
17	16	72	136
18	17	79	153
19	18	85	171
20	19	92	190
21	20	99	210
22	21	106	231
23	22	113	253

(continues)

Table A-31 *Mesh Network Connectivity Connections (Continued)*

Number of Nodes	Hub-and-Spoke n–1	Partial Mesh $n^2/\sqrt{(n-1)}$	Full Mesh $n^2-n/2$
24	23	120	276
25	24	128	300
26	25	135	325
27	26	143	351
28	27	151	378
29	28	159	406
30	29	167	435
31	30	175	465
32	31	184	496
33	32	193	528
34	33	201	561
35	34	210	595
36	35	219	630
37	36	228	666
38	37	237	703
39	38	247	741
40	39	256	780
41	40	266	820
42	41	275	861
43	42	285	903
44	43	295	946
45	44	305	990
46	45	315	1,035
47	46	326	1,081
48	47	336	1,128
49	48	347	1,176

Table A-31 *Mesh Network Connectivity Connections*

Number of Nodes	Hub-and-Spoke $n-1$	Partial Mesh $n^2/\sqrt{(n-1)}$	Full Mesh $n^2-n/2$
50	49	357	1,225
51	50	368	1,275
52	51	379	1,326
53	52	390	1,378
54	53	401	1,431
55	54	412	1,485
56	55	423	1,540
57	56	434	1,596
58	57	446	1,653
59	58	457	1,711
60	59	469	1,770
61	60	480	1,830
62	61	492	1,891
63	62	504	1,953
64	63	516	2,016
65	64	528	2,080
66	65	540	2,145
67	66	553	2,211
68	67	565	2,278
69	68	577	2,346

Figure A-2 *Approximate Virtual Circuits by Network Topology*

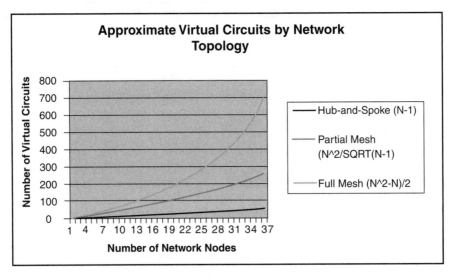

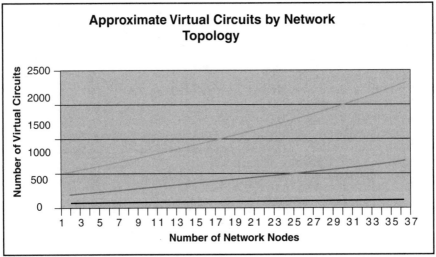

VoIP Bandwidth Consumption

Table A-32 demonstrates the amount of bandwidth consumed, dependent upon the compression algorithm used, across a VoIP network.

Table A-32 *VoIP Bandwidth Consumption Per Channel*

VoIP/Channel Bandwidth Consumption

Algorithm	Voice BW (Kbps)	MOS	Codec Delay (ms)	Frame Size (Bytes)	Cisco Payload (Bytes)	Packets Per Second	IP/UDP/RTP Header (Bytes)	CRTP Header (Bytes)	L2	Layer2 Header (Bytes)	Total Bandwidth Kbps No VAD
Current											
G.729	8	3.9	15	10	20	50	40		Ether	14	29.6	14.8
G.729	8	3.9	15	10	20	50		2	Ether	14	14.4	7.2
G.729	8	3.9	15	10	20	50	40		PPP	6	26.4	13.2
G.729	8	3.9	15	10	20	50		2	PPP	6	11.2	5.6
G.729	8	3.9	15	10	20	50	40		FR	4	25.6	12.8
G.729	8	3.9	15	10	20	50		2	FR	4	10.4	5.2
G.729	8	3.9	15	10	20	50	40		ATM	2 cells	42.4	21.2
G.729	8	3.9	15	10	20	50		2	ATM	1 cell	21.2	10.6
G.711	64	4.1	1.5	160	160	50	40		Ether	14	85.6	42.8
G.711	64	4.1	1.5	160	160	50		2	Ether	14	70.4	35.2
G.711	64	4.1	1.5	160	160	50	40		PPP	6	82.4	41.2
G.711	64	4.1	1.5	160	160	50		2	PPP	6	67.2	33.6
G.711	64	4.1	1.5	160	160	50	40		FR	4	81.6	40.8
G.711	64	4.1	1.5	160	160	50		2	FR	4	66.4	33.2
G.711	64	4.1	1.5	160	160	50	40		ATM	5 cells	106.0	53.0
G.711	64	4.1	1.5	160	160	50		2	ATM	4 cells	84.8	42.4

(continues)

Table A-32 *VoIP Bandwidth Consumption Per Channel (Continued)*

VoIP/Channel Bandwidth Consumption

Algorithm	Voice BW (Kbps)	MOS	Codec Delay (ms)	Frame Size (Bytes)	Cisco Payload (Bytes)	Packets Per Second	IP/UDP/RTP Header (Bytes)	CRTP Header (Bytes)	L2	Layer2 Header (Bytes)	Total Bandwidth Kbps	No VAD
Futures												
G.729	8	3.9	15	10	30	33	40		PPP	6	20.3	10.1
G.729	8	3.9	15	10	30	33		2	PPP	6	10.1	5.1
G.729	8	3.9	15	10	30	33	40		FR	4	19.7	9.9
G.729	8	3.9	15	10	30	33		2	FR	4	9.6	4.8
G.729	8	3.9	15	10	30	33	40		ATM	2 cells	28.3	14.1
G.729	8	3.9	15	10	30	33		2	ATM	1 cell	14.1	7.1
G.723.1	6.3	3.9	37.5	30	30	26	40		PPP	6	16.0	8.0
G.723.1	6.3	3.9	37.5	30	30	26		2	PPP	6	8.0	4.0
G.723.1	6.3	3.9	37.5	30	30	26	40		FR	4	15.5	7.8
G.723.1	6.3	3.9	37.5	30	30	26		2	FR	4	7.6	3.8
G.723.1	6.3	3.9	37.5	30	30	26	40		ATM	2 cells	22.3	11.1
G.723.1	6.3	3.9	37.5	30	30	26		2	ATM	1 cell	11.1	5.6
G.723.1	5.3	3.65	37.5	30	30	22	40		PPP	6	13.4	6.7
G.723.1	5.3	3.65	37.5	30	30	22		2	PPP	6	6.7	3.4
G.723.1	5.3	3.65	37.5	30	30	22	40		FR	4	13.1	6.5
G.723.1	5.3	3.65	37.5	30	30	22		2	FR	4	6.4	3.2
G.723.1	5.3	3.65	37.5	30	30	22	40		ATM	2 cells	18.7	9.4
G.723.1	5.3	3.65	37.5	30	30	22		2	ATM	1 cell	9.4	4.7

Protocol List

The information contained in this Appendix is a collected list of protocols. It details their suites, layers, revision dates, and standards. This information is supplied for reference only. For detailed information on each standard, visit the host's Web site.

Name	Stack Protocol Sub	Protocol Suite	Protocol Layer	Description	Documents and Rev	Standard
AAL1	Protocol	ATM	Data Link	ATM Adaptation Layer 1	ITU-T Recommendation I.363.1 August 1996	ITU
AAL2	Protocol	ATM	Data Link	ATM Adaptation Layer 2	ITU-T Recommendation I.363.2 August 1996	ITU
AAL3/4	Protocol	ATM	Data Link	ATM Adaptation Layer 3/4	ITU-T Recommendation I.363.3 August 1996	ITU
AAL5	Protocol	ATM	Data Link	ATM Adaptation Layer 5	ITU-T Recommendation I.363.5 August 1996	ITU
AARP	Protocol	AppleTalk	Data Link	AppleArp Protocol	Book: *Inside AppleTalk, Second Edition*	Proprietary
ACSE	Protocol	ISO	Application	Association Control Service Element Protocol	x.227 April 1995	ISO

(continues)

(Continued)

Name	Stack Protocol Sub	Protocol Suite	Protocol Layer	Description	Documents and Rev	Standard
AH	Protocol	TCP/IP	Network	Security sub of the IP	RFC 1826 RFC 1827 Drafts IPSec, isakmp	IETF
AppleArp (Intel)	Protocol	AppleTalk	Data Link	AppleArp Protocol	Book: *Inside AppleTalk*, 1989 Book: *AppleTalk Phase 2*, 1989	Proprietary
AppleTalk (Intel)	Protocol	AppleTalk	Transport	AppleTalk Protocol	Book: *Inside AppleTalk*, 1989 Book: *AppleTalk Phase 2*, 1989	Proprietary
ARP/RARP	Protocol	TCP/IP	Network	Address Resolution Protocol, also Inverse ARP	RFC 826 January 1982 RFC 1390 January 1993 RFC 1293 January 1992	IETF
ATCP	Protocol	PPP	Data Link	AppleTalk Control Protocol	RFC 1378 November 1992	IETF
ATM	Protocol	ATM	Physical	Decode RADCOM header information	RADCOM header structure Circuit Emulation System 1995	ATM Forum
ATM/SAR	Protocol	ATM	Data Link	ATM packet formats for various AAL types	I.363 March 1993	ITU
ATM_Cell-NNI	Protocol	ATM	Data Link	ATM Cell NNI	None	ATM Forum
ATM_Cell-UNI	Protocol	ATM	Data Link	ATM Cell UNI	None	ATM Forum

Name	Stack Protocol Sub	Protocol Suite	Protocol Layer	Description	Documents and Rev	Standard
ATM_DXI	Protocol	ATM	Data Link	ATM data exchange interface	ATM Data exchange interface August 1993	ATM Forum
ATM_Signaling	Protocol	ATM	Data Link	ATM Signaling for Connection Control	UNI 4.0 July 1996 UNI 3.0 October 1993 UNI 3.1 October 1993	ATM Forum
ATM_Signaling (PNNI)	Protocol	ATM	Network	Private network-network specification interface v1.0	PNNI 1.0 (af-pnni-0055.000 letter ballot) March 1996	ATM Forum
ATM_Signaling (Q2931)	Protocol	ATM	Network	B-ISDN application protocols for access signaling	Q.2931 February 1995	ITU
ATM_Signaling (UNI30)	Protocol	ATM	Network	ATM user-network interface specification version 3.0	UNI 3.0 October 1993	ATM Forum
ATM_Signaling (UNI31)	Protocol	ATM	Network	ATM user-network interface specification version 3.1	UNI 3.1 October 1993	ATM Forum
ATM_Signaling (UNI40)	Protocol	ATM	Network	ATM user-network interface specification version 4.0	UNI 4.0 July 1996	ATM Forum

(continues)

(Continued)

Name	Stack Protocol Sub	Protocol Suite	Protocol Layer	Description	Documents and Rev	Standard
ATMP	Protocol	TCP/IP	Network	Tunnel-management protocol that allows remote dial-in users to access their home network as if they were directly attached to the home network	RFC-2107 February 1997	IETF
BACP	Protocol	PPP	Data Link	PPP Bandwidth Allocation Control Protocol	Internet draft—BACP.txt March 1996-03 Internet draft—BACP04.txt March 1996	IETF
Banyan (Intel)	Protocol	Banyan	None	Banyan Protocols	None	Banyan
BAP	Protocol	PPP	Data Link	PPP Bandwidth Allocation Protocol	Internet draft—bacp02.txt March 1996	IETF
BCAST	Protocol	Novell NetWare	Network	NetWare Broadcast Message Notification	Novell's NetWare LAN Analysis; N003 1994	Proprietary
BCP	Protocol	PPP	Data Link	Bridging Control Protocol for PPP	RFC 1638 June 1994	IETF
BGP4	Protocol	TCP/IP	Transport	Border Gateway Protocol; the BGP is an inter-Autonomous System Routing Protocol	RFC 1771 RFC 1654 July 1994 RFC 1745 December 1994	IETF
BICI	Protocol	ATM	Data Link	Bearer Inter Carier Interface	B-ICI Specification Version 2.0 (Include Version 1.1) December 1995	ATM Forum

Name	Stack Protocol Sub	Protocol Suite	Protocol Layer	Description	Documents and Rev	Standard
BISUP	Protocol	ATM	Network	B-ISDN signaling system no.7 (B-ISUP)	q.2763 February 1995	ITU
BMP	Protocol	Novell NetWare	Application	Burst Mode Type of NCP; split from IPX	Novell's NetWare LAN Analysis, N003 1994	Proprietary
BPDU	Protocol	IEEE 802	Data Link	Bridging PDU Protocol	IEEE 802.3D July 1993 IEEE 802.1P 1992	IEEE
BSD	Protocol	PPP	Data Link	PPP BSD Compression Protocol	RFC 1977 August 1996	IETF
BSMAP	Protocol	SS7	Transport	BS Management Application Part	TIA/EIA/IS-634-A	ETSI
BSSAP	Protocol	SS7	Transport	Base station system – mobile services switching center (BSS-MSC)	GSM 08.06 / TIA/EIA/IS-634-A	ETSI
BSSAP+	Protocol	Other	Session	BSSAP+ : SGSN—VLR Interface (Gs Layer 3)	GSM 09.18 / TS 101 346 July 1998 6.1.0	ETSI
BSSGP	Protocol	SS7	Network	Base Station System GPRS Protocol	GSM 08.18 ver 6.1.0 July 1998	ETSI
BSSMAP	Protocol	SS7	Transport	Mobile-services Switching Center—Base Station System (MSC-BSS) interface	GSM 08.08 September 1996 4.11.0	ETSI
BTSM	Protocol	SS7	Transport	Base Station Controller-Base Transceiver Station (BSC-BTS) interface Layer 3	GSM 08.58— ETS 300 596 May 1996 4.9.0	ETSI

(continues)

(Continued)

Name	Stack Protocol Sub	Protocol Suite	Protocol Layer	Description	Documents and Rev	Standard
BTSM/LAPD	Stack	Unknown	{UNKNOWN}	None	None	Unknown
BVCP	Protocol	PPP	Network	PPP Banyan Vines Control Protocol	RFC 1763, March 1995	IETF
CC	Protocol	SS7	Transport	Call Control	GSM 04.08 August 1997 4.19.1	ETSI
CCP	Protocol	PPP	Data Link	Compression Control Protocol for PPP	Draft-ietf-pppext-compression-04.txt March 1994 RFC 1962 March 1996	IETF
CDP	Protocol	Routers	Data Link	Cisco Discovery Protocol	Reverse engineering	Proprietary
CHAP	Protocol	PPP	Data Link	Challenge Handshake Authentication Protocol	RFC 1334 October 1992	IETF
CIF	Protocol	ATM	Data Link	Cell in frames	Cells in Frames Version 1.0 21.10.1996 1.0	ATM Forum
Cisco_Router	Protocol	Routers	Data Link	Cisco router	None	Proprietary
Cisco_SRB	Protocol	Routers	Data Link	CISCO Source Routing Bridge	Structure was understood from record	CISCO
CLNP	Protocol	ISO	Network	Connectionless Network Protocol	ISO 8473 December 1988 RFC 1575 February 1994	ISO
COPS	Protocol	TCP/IP	Data Link	COPS-Common Open Policy Service	Internet Draft January 2000	IETF
DCAP	Protocol	TCP/IP	{UNKNOWN}	Data Link Switching Client Access Protocol	RFC 2114 February 1997	No specific Internet standard of any kind

Name	Stack Protocol Sub	Protocol Suite	Protocol Layer	Description	Documents and Rev	Standard
DCP	Protocol	Frame Relay	Transport	Data Compression Over Frame Relay Implementation Agreement FRF-9 (this protocol could be above ATM or Frame Relay)	RFC 1661 January 1996 FRF.9	Frame Relay Forum
DEC_LANBridge (Intel)	Protocol	DECnet IV	Data Link	DEC LANbridge	None	Proprietary
DEC_LAT (Intel)	Protocol	DECnet IV	Application	Local area transport	None	Proprietary
DEC_LAVC (Intel)	Protocol	DECnet IV	Transport	Local area vax cluster port to port communications	None	Proprietary
DEC_MOP_D/L (Intel)	Protocol	DECnet IV	Application	Maintenance Operations Protocol dump/ load	v3.0.0	Proprietary
DEC_MOP_RC (Intel)	Protocol	DECnet IV	Application	Maintenance Operations Protocol remote console	v3.0.0	Proprietary
DEC_Route (Intel)	Protocol	DECnetIV	Network	DECnet Routing Protocol	v2.0.0	Proprietary
DESE	Protocol	PPP	Application	Des Encryption Protocol	RFC 1969 June 1996	ITU
DHCP (BOOTP)	Protocol	TCP/IP	Transport	Dynamic Host Configuration Protocol (DHCP/ BOOTP) provides configuration parameters to Internet hosts	1531 October 1993	IETF

(continues)

(Continued)

Name	Stack Protocol Sub	Protocol Suite	Protocol Layer	Description	Documents and Rev	Standard
DHCPv6	Protocol	TCP/IP	Session	Dynamic_Host_ Configuration_ Protocol_for_ IPv6_(DHCPv6)	Draft-ietf-dhc- dhcpv6-13.txt June 1998 Draft-ietf-dhc- v6exts-10.txt July 1996	IETF
DIAG	Protocol	Novell NetWare	Network	Diagnostics packet (request, response); split from IPX	Novell's NetWare LAN Analysis, N003 1994	Proprietary
DISL	Protocol	Routers	Data Link	Dynamic Inter Switch Link Protocols	Reverse engineering	Proprietary
DLSw	Protocol	SNA	Data Link	Data Link Switching: Switch-to-Switch Protocol	RFC 1434 March 1993 RFC 1795 April 1995 RFC 2166 (Updated Version)	IETF
DNCP	Protocol	PPP	Network	PPP FECnet Phase IV Control Protocol	RFC 1376 Mar 1995	IETF
DNS	Protocol	TCP/IP	Session	Domain name server	RFC 1035 November 1987 RFC 1706 January 1994	IETF
DRiP	Protocol	Routers	Data Link	DRiP	Reverse engineering	Unknown
DSMCC	Protocol	TCP/IP	Session	Digital Storage Media Protocol	13818-6 June 1995	ISO
DTAP	Protocol	SS7	Transport	Direct Transfer Application Part	TIA/EIA/IS-634- A	ETSI
DUP	Protocol	SS7	Application	Data User Part	X.61 {Doc. Date} {Doc. Rev}	ITU

Name	Stack Protocol Sub	Protocol Suite	Protocol Layer	Description	Documents and Rev	Standard
DVB	Protocol	MPEG-2	Network	Digital Video Broadcasting	ETS-300800 December 1998	ETSI
DVMRP	Protocol	TCP/IP	Network	DVMRP provides efficient mechanism for connection	RFC-1075 July 1998 Draft_ietf_idmr_dvmrp-v3-08 March 1998	Unknown
EAP	Protocol	PPP	Data Link	PPP Extensible Authentication Protocol	Draft-ietf-pppext-eap-auth-03.txt December 1997	IETF
ECP	Protocol	PPP	Data Link	PPP Encryption Control Protocol	RFC 1968 June 1996	IETF
EGP	Protocol	TCP/IP	Network	Exterior Gateway Protocol	RFC 904 April 1984 1	IETF
EIGRP	Protocol	TCP/IP	Network	Enhanced Interior Gateway Protocol	Reverse engineering	Proprietary
ESIS	Protocol	ISO	Network	End system to intermediate system routing	ISO 9542 December 1988	ISO
ESP	Protocol	TCP/IP	Network	Security sub of the IP	RFC 1826 RFC 1827 Drafts IPSec, isakmp	IETF
Ethernet	Protocol	IEEE 802	Data Link	IEEE 802.3	ANSI\IEEE Std 802.3 1988	IEEE
Ethernet_	Stack	Other	Physical	None	None	Unknown
EtherTalk (Intel)	Protocol	AppleTalk	Data Link	AppleTalk over Ethernet	Book: *Inside AppleTalk*, 1989	Proprietary
FDDI	Protocol	IEEE 802	Data Link	Fiber distributed data interface	ISO 9314 RFC 1188 October 1990	ISO
FINGER	Protocol	TCP/IP	Application	Protocol for the exchange of user information	RFC 1288, December 1991	IETF
FR/ATM	Stack	Frame Relay	Data Link	None	See framerel.rul	Unknown

(continues)

(Continued)

Name	Stack Protocol Sub	Protocol Suite	Protocol Layer	Description	Documents and Rev	Standard
FR/LAPF	Stack	Frame Relay	Data Link	Frame Relay over LAPF	FRF.10 1994 Q.922 1994	ITU-CCITT
Frame_Relay	Protocol	Frame Relay	Data Link	Frame Relay Protocol	ANSI CCITT	ANSI & CCITT
Frame_Relay (ANSI_T1.617)	Protocol	Frame Relay	Data Link	ANSI variant T1.617 of Frame Relay	ANSI T1.617 1994	ANSI
Frame_Relay (ANSI_T1.618)	Protocol	Frame Relay	Data Link	ANSI variant T1.617 of Frame Relay	ANSI T1.618 1991	ANSI
Frame_Relay (Cascade)	Protocol	Frame Relay	Data Link	Cascade variant of Frame Relay	Cascade Communications Corp. Inc.\ Trunk Header Specification 1.0	Proprietary
Frame_Relay (CCITT_Q.922)	Protocol	Frame Relay	Data Link	CCITT Q.922 variant of Frame Relay	CCITT Q.922 1992	CCITT
Frame_Relay (CCITT_Q.933)	Protocol	Frame Relay	Data Link	CCITT Q.933 variant of Frame Relay	CCITT Q.933 1993	CCITT
Frame_Relay (Manufacturers)	Protocol	Frame Relay	Data Link	Manufacturer's variant of Frame Relay	Manufacturers 001-208966 1990 1.0	ANSI & CCITT
Frame_Relay (Manufacturers)	Protocol	Frame Relay	Data Link	Manufacturer's + Extensions variant of Frame Relay	Manufacturers 001-208966 1990 1.0	ANSI & CCITT
Frame_Relay (Tplx_GTWY)	Protocol	Frame Relay	Data Link	Proprietary Timplx BRE2 GTWY variant of Frame Relay	AscomTimeplex BRE2 frame decoding July 1996	Proprietary
Frame_Relay (Tplx_TRNK)	Protocol	Frame Relay	Data Link	Proprietary Timplx BRE2 TRNK variant of Frame Relay	AscomTimeplex BRE2 frame decoding July 1996	Proprietary
FREther	Stack	Frame Relay	Data Link	None	None	Unknown

Name	Stack Protocol Sub	Protocol Suite	Protocol Layer	Description	Documents and Rev	Standard
FRF.3	Protocol	Frame Relay	Data Link	Frame Relay multiprotocol encapsulation	Book: *FRF's New Member Handbook*: FRF.3, 1995 RFC 2427 (1490)	Frame Relay Forum
FTAM	Protocol	ISO	Application	File Transfer Access and Management	ISO 8571-4 January 1992 x.227 April 1994	ISO
FTP	Protocol	TCP/IP	Application	File Transfer Protocol	RFC 959 October 1985	IETF
FUNI	Protocol	ATM	Data Link	Frame-based user to network interface	Frame-based user to network interface (FUNI), Specifications September 1995	ATM Forum
GARP	Protocol	IEEE 802	Data Link	GARP	IEEE P802.1Q/ D10 March 1998	IEEE
GMM/SM	Protocol	GPRS	Network	GPRS MM/SM	Draft ETSI EN 300 940 v7.1.2	Unknown
GMRP	Protocol	IEEE 802	Data Link	GARP Multicast Registration Protocol (GARP)	IEEE P802.1Q/ D10 March 1998	IEEE
GOPHER	Protocol	TCP/IP	Application	Protocol for burrowing through a TCP/IP Internet	RFC 1436 March 1993	IETF
GPRS_(NS/FR)	Stack	Frame Relay	Data Link	See framerel.rul	None	Unknown
GR303_(IDLC/ LAPD)	Stack	Unknown	{UNKNOWN}	Integrated Digital Loop Carrier (GR-303)	GR-303-ILR	Unknown
GRE	Protocol	TCP/IP	Network	Generic Routing Encapsulation	RFC 1701 October 1994 RFC 1702 October 1994 PPTP Internet Draft July 1997	IETF

(continues)

(Continued)

Name	Stack Protocol Sub	Protocol Suite	Protocol Layer	Description	Documents and Rev	Standard
GSM_L3	Protocol	SS7	Transport	GSM Layer 3 Protocol	GSM 04.08 August 1997 4.19.1	ETSI
GSMP	Protocol	ATM	Network	Ipsilon General Switch Management Protocol	RFC 1987 August 1996	IETF
GTP	Protocol	TCP/IP	Transport	GPRS Tunneling Protocol	GSM 09.60/EN 301 347 August 1998 6.2.0	ETSI
GVRP	Protocol	IEEE 802	Data Link	GARP VLAN Registration Protocol (GARP)	IEEE P802.1Q/ D10 March 1998	IEEE
H.225	Protocol	H.323	Transport	Line Transmission of non telephone signals	H.225.0, version 2, 1997	ITU-T
H.235	Protocol	Other	Transport	Security and encryption for H series (H.323 and other H.245-based) multimedia terminals	H.235 January 1998	ITU
H.245	Protocol	Other	Transport	Control protocol for multimedia communication	H.245 March 1996	ITU
H.261	Protocol	H.323	Transport	Protocol for video stream for transport using real-time	RFC 2032 November 1996	IETF
H.263	Protocol	H.323	Transport	Protocol H263 video streams; the protocol is above RTP	RFC 2429 October 1998	IETF
H.450.1	Protocol	H.323	Transport	H.450	None	ITU
H.450.2	Protocol	Other	None	None	None	Unknown
H.450.3	Protocol	Other	None	None	None	Unknown

Name	Stack Protocol Sub	Protocol Suite	Protocol Layer	Description	Documents and Rev	Standard
H245TPKT	Protocol	TCP/IP	Transport	H245TPKT checks if H245 needs TPKT after the TCP; if it does, H245TPKT serves as one	RFC 1006 May 1987	ISO
HDLC	Protocol	X.25	Data Link	High level data-link control	3309 December 1993	ISO
High_IP_Layers (Intel)	Protocol	TCP/IP	None	Different protocols belong to high IP layers	None	IETF
HSRP	Protocol	TCP/IP	Transport	Hot Standby Router Protocol	RFC 2281 March 1998	IETF
HTTP	Protocol	TCP/IP	Application	HTTP over TCP or UDP	RFC-1945 May 1996	IETF
ICMP	Protocol	TCP/IP	Network	Internet Control Message Protocol	RFC 792 September 1981	IETF
ICMPv6	Protocol	TCP/IP	Network	Internet Control Message Protocol v6	RFC-1885, 1970 December 1995	IETF
IDLC	Protocol	Other	Network	Integrated Digital Loop Carrier (GR-303)	GR-303-ILR	Bellcore
IFMP	Protocol	ATM	Network	Ipsilon Flow-Management Protocol	RFC 1953 May 1996	IETF
IGMPv3	Protocol	TCP/IP	Network	Internet Group Management Protocol	RFC 1112 August 1989	IETF
IGRP	Protocol	TCP/IP	Network	Internet Gateway Routing Protocol	None	Cisco
ILMI	Protocol	ATM	Data Link	Interim local management interface	UNI3.0, UNI3.1, . . . ILMI specification 4.0 1996-0	ATM Forum

(continues)

(Continued)

Name	Stack Protocol Sub	Protocol Suite	Protocol Layer	Description	Documents and Rev	Standard
IMAP4	Protocol	TCP/IP	Application	Internet Message Access Protocol—Version 4	RFC 2060 December 1996	IETF
intelCLNP (Intel)	Protocol	ISO	Network	Connectionless Network Protocol	ISO 8473 December 1988 RFC 1575 January 1994	ISO
intelISO (Intel)	Protocol	ISO	Network	Call Intel decode of ISO	None	ISO
IP	Protocol	TCP/IP	Network	Internet Protocol	RFC 791 September 1981 RFC 1853 January 1995	IETF
IP/ATM	Stack	ATM	None	None	None	Unknown
IP/HDLC	Stack	AppleTalk	{UNKNOWN}	None	None	Unknown
IP/X.25/LAPB	Stack	AppleTalk	{UNKNOWN}	None	None	Unknown
IP/X.25/LAPB/ FR	Stack	Frame Relay	Data Link	None	None	Unknown
IPARSE	Protocol	Other	None	IPARSE character set over X.25	A letter from Singapore December 1996	Proprietary
IPARSE/X.25/ LAPB	Stack	Other	Data Link	None	None	Unknown
IPCP	Protocol	PPP	Data Link	Internet Protocol Control Protocol for PPP	RFC 1332 May 1992 RFC 2290 February 1998	IETF
IPDC	Protocol	TCP/IP	Session	IP_Device_ Control	Draft-taylor-ipdc-00.txt July 1998 Draft-dugan-ipdc-connection-00.txt 08-1998 Draft-eiottipdc-media-00.txt August 1998	IETF

Name	Stack Protocol Sub	Protocol Suite	Protocol Layer	Description	Documents and Rev	Standard
IPHC	Protocol	PPP	Data Link	IP Header Compression over PPP	2509 February 1999	Unknown
Ipsilon	Protocol	TCP/IP	Data Link	Transmission of flow-labeled IPv4 data links	RFC 1954 May 1996 Ipsilon V 1.0	IETF
IPv6	Protocol	TCP/IP	Network	Internet Protocol Version 6	RFC-1883, 1826, 1827 December 1995 Book: *IPv6* by Christian Huitema, 1998	IETF
IPv6CP	Protocol	PPP	Network	IP Version 6 Control Protocol for PPP	RFC 2023 October 1996	IETF
IPX	Protocol	Novell NetWare	Network	Main Protocol of Novell that splits to all others; lies on the Ethernet	Novell's NetWare LAN Analysis. N003 1994	Proprietary
IPXCP	Protocol	PPP	Data Link	IPX Control Protocol for PPP	RFC 1552 December 1993	IETF
ISAKMP	Protocol	TCP/IP	Transport	Internet Security Association and Key Management Protocol	Draft July 1997	IETF
ISDN	Protocol	ISDN	{UNKNOWN}	ISDN main protocol for all variants	SR-NWT-001953 June 1991 ETS 300 102-1 December 1990 AT&T 801-802-100 May 1989	ITU
ISDN(5ESS-AT&T)	Protocol	ISDN	{UNKNOWN}	ISDN variant 5ESS_(AT&T)	AT&T 801-802-100 May 1989 IE of codeset 0 is defined in Q.931.rul	AT&T

(continues)

(Continued)

Name	Stack Protocol Sub	Protocol Suite	Protocol Layer	Description	Documents and Rev	Standard
ISDN(ARINC_att'11)	Protocol	ISDN	Network	ISDN variant ARINC attachment 11	ARINC Characteristic 746-4 April 1996	AEEC
ISDN(ARINC_att'17)	Protocol	ISDN	Network	ISDN variant ARINC attachment 17	ARINC Characteristic 746-4 April 1996	AEEG
ISDN(Australia)	Protocol	ISDN	Network	ISDN variant Australia	AP IX-123-E	ISO
ISDN(DMS-100)	Protocol	ISDN	Network	ISDN variant DMS-100	NIS S208-6 Issue 1.1 August 1992	Northern Telecom
ISDN(ETSIi)	Protocol	ISDN	Network	ISDN variant Euro ISDN(ETSI)	ETS 300 102-1 December 1990	ETSI
					CCITT V.120*******N TT 9/ 1992************** ****1993	
					PTT 840.73.2, PTT 840.73.3 June 1995	
ISDN(H225)	Protocol	ISDN	Network	ISDN variant H225	RFC 1006 (TPKT)	ITU-T
					H.225.0 January 1996	
ISDN(National_ISDN-1)	Protocol	ISDN	Network	ISDN variant National ISDN-1	SR-NWT-001953 June 1991	Bellcore
ISDN(National_ISDN-2)	Protocol	ISDN	Network	ISDN variant National_ISDN-2	SR-NWT-002361 December 1992	Bellcore
					SR-NWT-002120 May 1993	
ISDN(NTT_INS)	Protocol	ISDN	Network	ISDN variant NTT INS	INS-NET Interface and Services March 1993	NTT
ISDN(QSIG)	Protocol	ISDN	Network	ISDN variant QSig	ISO/IEC 11572 1995	ISO

Name	Stack Protocol Sub	Protocol Suite	Protocol Layer	Description	Documents and Rev	Standard
ISDN(Swiss)	Protocol	ISDN	Network	ISDN variant Swiss	PTT 840.73.2 June 1995	Swiss telecom PTT
ISDN(T1.607 (ANSI))	Protocol	ISDN	Network	ISDN variant T1.607 (ANSI)	T1.607 (ANSI)) February 1996	ANSI
ISDN(TS014_ Australia)	Protocol	ISDN	Network	ISDN variant T1.607 (ANSI)	TS014 (austel) 1995	AUSTEL
ISDN(V.120)	Protocol	ISDN	Network	ISDN variant V.120	Recommendation V.120 September 1992	ITU
ISDN/LAPD	Stack	Unknown	{UNKNOWN}	None	None	Unknown
ISDN_ (1TR6-Germanyi)	Protocol	ISDN	Network	ISDN variant 1TR6 (Germany)	1 TR 6 August 1990	FTZ
ISIS	Protocol	ISO	Network	Intermediate system to intermediate system routing	ISO/IEC 10589:1992/ Cor.1:1993 (E) May 1993	ISO
ISL	Protocol	Routers	Physical	Inter-Switch Link	Reverse engineering	IEEE
ISO_PP	Protocol	ISO	Application	Association Control Service Element Protocol	x.227 April 1995	ISO
ISO_SP	Protocol	ISO	Session	ISO Session Protocol	x225 11-1995	ITU
ISO_TP	Protocol	ISO	Transport	ISO Transport Protocol	ISO 8073 December 1992 ISO 8073 Corr.1 1993 ISO 8073 Corr.2 1994-11 1997	

(continues)

(Continued)

Name	Stack Protocol Sub	Protocol Suite	Protocol Layer	Description	Documents and Rev	Standard
ISUP	Protocol	SS7	Network	Signaling connection control part over MTP level 3, SS7	Q.763, ITU-T: Signaling System No. 7 ISDN User Part Formats and Codes March 1993 Book: *SS7 Basics*, Toni Beninger/ S038, 1991 ANSI T1.112	ITU
L2F	Protocol	PPP	Data Link	Layer 2 Forwarding Protocol	Draft-ietf-pppext-l2f-03 December 1996	Proprietary
L2TP	Protocol	TCP/IP	Data Link	Layer 2 Tunneling Protocol	Draft-ietf-pppext-l2tp-08.txt 0397	IETF
LAPB	Protocol	X.25	Data Link	Link access procedure balanced	Recommendation X.25 March 1993	ITU
LAPB_	Stack	Unknown	{UNKNOWN}	None	None	Unknown
LAPD	Protocol	ISDN	Data Link	Link access procedure D-channel	Blue Book: *ITU Q.921* ETS 300 125	ITU
LAPD(ARINC)	Protocol	ISDN	Data Link	LAPD variant ARINC	ARINC Characteristic 746-4 April 1996	AEEC
LAPD(CCITT-I.441)	Protocol	ISDN	Data Link	LAPD variant CCITT-I.441	CCITT I-441	ITU
LAPD(Dass2)	Protocol	ISDN	Data Link	LAPD variant Dass2	BTNR 190 July 1992	ITU
LAPD(DPNSS1)	Protocol	ISDN	Data Link	LAPD variant DPNSS1	BTNR 188 January 1995	ITU
LAPD(V.120)	Protocol	ISDN	Data Link	LAPD variant V.120	Recommendation V.120 September 1992	ITU

Name	Stack Protocol Sub	Protocol Suite	Protocol Layer	Description	Documents and Rev	Standard
LAPF	Protocol	Frame Relay	Physical	Data link layer specification for frame mode bearer services	Q.922 1992	ITU-CCITT
LAPV5	Protocol	V5	Data Link	Data link sublayer of LAPV5 for V5 system	V5.1 G.964 June 1994 Q.921	ITU
LCP	Protocol	PPP	Data Link	Link Control Protocol for PPP	RFC 1570 January 1994 RFC 1661 February 1994	IETF
LDAP	Protocol	TCP/IP	Application	Lightweight Directory Access Protocol	RFC 1777 March 1995	ITU
LDP	Protocol	TCP/IP	Transport	LDP	Draft-ietf-mpls-ldp-06 October 1999	Draft
LE_802.3	Protocol	ATM	Data Link	LAN Emulation 802.3 (Ethernet) over ATM version 1.0	LAN Emulation over ATM version 1.0 January 1995	ATM Forum
LE_802.3_	Stack	ATM	None	None	LAN Emulation over ATM version 1.0 January 1995	ATM Forum
LE_802.5	Protocol	ATM	Data Link	LAN Emulation 802.5 (Token Ring) over ATM version 1.0	LAN Emulation over ATM version 1.0 January 1995	ATM Forum
LE_802.5_	Stack	ATM	None	None	LAN Emulation over ATM version 1.0 January 1995	ATM Forum
LE_CONTROL	Protocol	ATM	Data Link	LAN Emulation control procedures	LAN Emulation over ATM version 1.0 January 1995	ATM Forum

(continues)

(Continued)

Name	Stack Protocol Sub	Protocol Suite	Protocol Layer	Description	Documents and Rev	Standard
LEX	Protocol	PPP	Data Link	PPP Network Control Protocol for LAN extension	RFC 1841 September 1995	IETF
LEXCP	Protocol	PPP	Data Link	PPP Network Control Protocol for LAN extension	RFC 1841 September 1995	IETF
LLC	Protocol	IEEE 802	Data Link	Logical link control	ISO 8802-2 December 1989 RFC 2364 July 1991	ISO
LLC/FR	Stack	Frame Relay	Physical	None	None	Unknown
LQR	Protocol	PPP	Data Link	Link quality monitoring	RFC 1333 1992-05	IETF
LZS	Protocol	PPP	Data Link	Compression Protocol for PPP	Draft-mppc-00.txt July 1996	IETF
MAP	Protocol	SS7	Transport	Mobile Application Part—IS41	EIA/TIA IS41.5 1997 IS41-D	ETSI
MAPOS	Protocol	PPP	Physical	Distance Vector Protocol that establishes and maintains the routing table	RFC 2175 June 1997	Unknown
MARS	Protocol	TCP/IP	Network	Multiaddress Resolution Server	RFC 2022 November 1996	ATM Forum
MDLP	Protocol	CDPD	Data Link	Mobile Data Link Protocol	CDPD	CDPC
MEGACO	Protocol	Other	None	None	None	Unknown
MM	Protocol	SS7	Transport	Mobility management	GSM 04.08 August 1997 4.19.1	ETSI
MNRP	Protocol	CDPD	Transport	Mobile Network Registration Protocol	CDPD	CDPD

Name	Stack Protocol Sub	Protocol Suite	Protocol Layer	Description	Documents and Rev	Standard
MNTv1	Protocol	TCP/IP	None	Mount Protocol version 1 for NFS version 2	RFC 1094 March 1989	SUN
MNTv3	Protocol	TCP/IP	None	Mount Protocol version 3 for NFS version 3	RFC 1813 June 1995	SUN
Mobile_IP	Protocol	TCP/IP	Transport	IP mobility support	RFC 2002 October 1996	IEFT
MPEG-2	Protocol	MPEG	Data Link	Motion Picture Expert Group	13818-1 October 1994	ISO
MPLS	Protocol	TCP/IP	Transport	Multiprotocol label switching	Draft-ietf-mpls-arch-04.txt February 1999 Draft-ietf-mpls-label-encaps-05.txt	IETF
MPPC	Protocol	PPP	Data Link	Microsoft Point-to-Point Compression Protocol	Draft-mppc-00.txt July 1996	IETF
MTP-2	Protocol	SS7	Data Link	MTP level 2 of SS7	Q.703 1994 ANSI T1.111 1995	ITU
MTP-3	Protocol	SS7	Network	SS7 Message transfer part level 3	Q.704 February 1995 T1.111.4 1998	ITU
MultiPPP	Protocol	PPP	Data Link	PPP Multilink Protocol	RFC 1717 November 1994 RFC 1990 March 1996	IETF
NARP	Protocol	TCP/IP	Application	NBMA Address Resolution Protocol (NARP)	RFC 1735 December 1994	IETF
NBFCP	Protocol	PPP	Network	PPP NetBIOS Frames Control Protocol	RFC 2097 January 1997	IETF

(continues)

(Continued)

Name	Stack Protocol Sub	Protocol Suite	Protocol Layer	Description	Documents and Rev	Standard
NCP	Protocol	Novell NetWare	Application	NetWare Core Protocol; all NetWare services, and most popular	Novell's NetWare LAN Analysis, N003 1994	Proprietary
NDS	Protocol	Novell NetWare	Application	NetWare Directory Services; split from NCP	Novell's NetWare LAN Analysis, N003 1994	Proprietary
NetBIOS	Protocol	NetBIOS	Session	Basic NetBIOS; usually over LLC	IBM: *Local-Area Network Technical Reference*, 1990 4th DA-30/31 Protocol Operating Manual 1998	IBM
NetBIOS/IP	Protocol	NetBIOS	Session	NetBIOS over TCP/UDP	DA-30/31 Protocol Operating Manual (D015): NETBIOS Over IP 1992 RFC 1002 1987 Troubleshooting TCP/IP (T015) 1996 2nd	IBM
NFSv2	Protocol	TCP/IP	None	NFS version 2	RFC 1094 March 1989	SUN
NFSv3	Protocol	TCP/IP	None	NFS version 3	RFC 1813 June 1995	SUN
NHDR	Protocol	SNA	Network	Network layer header	12.3—APPN HPR Architecture Reference	IBM

Name	Stack Protocol Sub	Protocol Suite	Protocol Layer	Description	Documents and Rev	Standard
NHRP(MPOA)	Protocol	TCP/IP	Network	NBMA Next Hop Resolution Protocol + Multi Protocol Over ATM	Draft-ietf-rolc-nhrp-11.txt August 1996 STR-MPOA-MPOA-01.00 April 1998	IETF
NLMv4	Protocol	TCP/IP	None	Network Lock Manager Protocol versions 3, 4 for (NFS version 2, 3)	RFC 1813 June 1995 The Open Group (Protocols for interworking) 1996	SUN
NLP	Protocol	SNA	Network	Network layer packet	12.3—APPN HPR Architecture Reference	IBM
NLSP	Protocol	Novell NetWare	Network	NetWare Link Service Protocol	NetWare Link Service Protocol Specification February 1994	Novell
NovelNetBIOS	Protocol	NetBIOS	Session	NetBIOS over IPX (Novell)	Information was taken from Sniffer	Proprietary
NS	Protocol	SS7	Network	GPRS network service	GSM 08.16/TS 101 299 July 1998 6.2.0	ETSI
NSMv1	Protocol	TCP/IP	None	Network Status Monitor Protocol for NFS	The Open Group 1998	Unknown
NSP	Protocol	Other	Data Link	Node Switch Protocol— MAPOS Extension	RFC 2173	IETF
NTP	Protocol	TCP/IP	Application	The Network Time Protocol	RFC 1305 March 1992 RFC 1119 September 1989 RFC 1059 August 1988	IAB

(continues)

(Continued)

Name	Stack Protocol Sub	Protocol Suite	Protocol Layer	Description	Documents and Rev	Standard
OAM_F4	Protocol	ATM	Data Link	OAM F4 cell	Recommendation I.610	ATM Forum
OAM_F5	Protocol	ATM	Data Link	OAM F5 cell	Recommendation I.610	ATM Forum
OSINLCP	Protocol	PPP	Data Link	PPP OSI Network Layer Control Protocol	RFC 1377 November 1992	IETF
OSPF	Protocol	TCP/IP	Network	Open Shortest Path First Protocol	RFC 2328 April 1998	IETF
PAP	Protocol	PPP	Data Link	Printer Access Protocol	RFC 1334 October 1992	IETF
PIM	Protocol	TCP/IP	Network	Protocol-Independent Multicast Sparse Mode	RFC 2362 1/98 <Draft-farinacci-bidir-pim-01.txt> 5/9	IETF
PNNI_routing	Protocol	ATM	Network	Private network-network specification interface v1.0	PNNI 1.0 (af-pnni-0055.000 letter ballot) March 1996	ATM Forum
POP3	Protocol	TCP/IP	Application	Post Office Protocol—Version 3	RFC 1939 May 1996	IETF
PPP	Protocol	PPP	Physical	Point-to-Point Protocol	RFC 1661 July 1994 RFC 1548 December 1993 RFC 1662 July 1994	IETF
PPP/ATM	Stack	ATM	None	None	RFC 2364	Unknown
PPP/LAPB	Stack	Other	Data Link	None	None	Unknown
PPP/LAPF	Stack	Frame Relay	Data Link	Frame Relay, Over LAPF	FRF.10 1994 Q.922 1996	ITU-CCITT
PPP_BPDU	Protocol	PPP	Data Link	PPP Bridging Protocol	RFC 1638 June 1994	IETF
PPPoE	Protocol	PPP	Data Link	PPP over Ethernet	RFC 2516 September 1998	IETF

Name	Stack Protocol Sub	Protocol Suite	Protocol Layer	Description	Documents and Rev	Standard
PPTP	Protocol	TCP/IP	Network	Point to Point Tunneling Protocol	Draft-ietf-pppext-pptp-00.txt June 1996	IETF
PROTEON	Protocol	Other	Data Link	Proprietary Protocol used in Proteon WAN routers	None	Proprietary
Q.SAAL	Protocol	ATM	Data Link	Queue signaling ATM adaptation layer	ATM Forum QSAAL and ITU Q2110	ITU
Q2140	Protocol	ATM	Data Link	SSCF for NNI signaling	Q.2140 February 1995	ITU
QLLC	Protocol	SNA	Data Link	Qualified logical link control	The x.25 interface for attaching SNA nodes to packet-switched data networks; general information manual March 1985	Proprietary
QLLC_	Stack	SNA	Data Link	None	None	Unknown
RADIUS	Protocol	TCP/IP	Transport	Remote Authentication Dial-In User Service (RADIUS)	2138 April 1997 2139 April 1998	IETF
RAS	Protocol	ISO	Application	Association Control Service Element Protocol	x.227 April 1995	ISO
Raw_Cell	Protocol	ATM	Data Link	All kinds of cell formats (OAM, AAL0-5, SMDS)	I.610 1995-11 I.361 1995-1	ITU

(continues)

(Continued)

Name	Stack Protocol Sub	Protocol Suite	Protocol Layer	Description	Documents and Rev	Standard
RIP	Protocol	TCP/IP	Network	Routing Information Protocol (supports RIP versions 1 and 2)	RFC 1058 June 1988 RFC 1723 May 1996 RFC 1528 February 1994	IETF
RIPng	Protocol	TCP/IP	Network	RIPNG—RIP Protocol for IPv6	RFC 2080 January 1997	IETF
RIPX	Protocol	Novell NetWare	Network	Routing Information (Request/Reply); split from IPX	Novell's NetWare LAN Analysis; N003, 1994	IBM
RLP	Protocol	Other	Data Link	gsm	Etsi ts 100 946 v.7.0.1 7/99 V7.0.1	ETSI
RND	Protocol	Routers	Data Link	A layer 2 routing protocol	RND—Layer 2 Router Package Description April 1993 1.00	Proprietary
RPC	Protocol	TCP/IP	{UNKNOWN}	Remote Procedure Call Protocol	1057 June 1988 1831 August 1995 1833, 2203	IETF
RPCBv3	Protocol	TCP/IP	None	Binding Protocol version 3 for RPC	RFC 1833 August 1995	Unknown
RPCBv4	Protocol	TCP/IP	None	Binding Protocol version 4 for RPC	RFC 1833 August 1995	Unknown
RPCgss	Protocol	TCP/IP	None	Security Protocol version 3 for RPC	RFC 2203 September 1997	Unknown
RPCmap	Protocol	TCP/IP	None	Port Mapper Protocol version 2 for RPC	RFC 1833 September 1995	Unknown
RR	Protocol	SS7	Transport	Call Control	GSM 04.08 August 1997 4.19.1	ETSI

Name	Stack Protocol Sub	Protocol Suite	Protocol Layer	Description	Documents and Rev	Standard
RSVP	Protocol	TCP/IP	Network	Resource Reservation Protocol	Draft-ietf-rsvp-spec-13.txt August 1996 Draft-ietf-rsvp-md5-02.txt June 1997	IETF
RTCP	Protocol	TCP/IP	Transport	Transport Real-Time Control Protocol	RFC 1889 January 1996 RFC 1890 January 1996 RFC 2032 October 1996	IETF
RTP	Protocol	TCP/IP	Transport	Real-Time Transport Protocol for Audio and Video Conferences	RFC 1889 January 1996 RFC 1890 January 1996 RFC 2032 October 1996	IETF
RTSP	Protocol	TCP/IP	Application	Real Time Streaming Protocol	RFC 2326 April 1998	IETF
RUDP	Protocol	Other	None	None	None	Unknown
RVP	Protocol	TCP/IP	Transport	MCK Communications Protocol for transporting digital telephony sessions over packet or circuit-based data networks	MCK Communication 17-August 1999	Proprietary
S/MGCP	Protocol	TCP/IP	Session	Protocol for controlling voice over IP gateways from external call control elements	Draft-hutitema-MGCP-v0r1-o1.txt May 1999	ITU

(continues)

(Continued)

Name	Stack Protocol Sub	Protocol Suite	Protocol Layer	Description	Documents and Rev	Standard
SAM	Protocol	X.25	Data Link	Stack : LAPB -> X.25 -> SAM (protocol status)	Telecom-italia fax December 1996	Proprietary
SAM/FREther	Stack	Frame Relay	Data Link	None	None	Unknown
SAM/ISDN/ LAPD	Stack	AppleTalk	{UNKNOWN}	None	None	Unknown
SAM/X.25/LAPB	Stack	Other	Data Link	None	None	Unknown
SAM/X.25/LAPD	Stack	Other	Data Link	None	None	Unknown
SAP	Protocol	Novell NetWare	Session	Service Advertising (Request/Reply/ Broadcast)	Novell's NetWare LAN Analysis; N003 1994	IBM
SAPv2	Protocol	Other	None	Session Announcement Protocol	Draft-ietf- mmusic-sap-v2- 01.txt June 1999	IETF
SCCP	Protocol	SS7	Network	Signaling connection control part over MTP level 3, SS7	Q.713, ITU-T: Signaling System No. 7 SCCP Formats and Codes 03-93 SS7 Basics/ Toni Beninger/ S038 1991 ANSI T1.112	ITU
SCTP	Protocol	TCP/IP	Application	Simple Control Transmission Protocol	Draft-ietf- sigtran-sctp- 03.txt November 1999 3	IETF
SDCP	Protocol	PPP	Data Link	Serial Data Control Protocol	1963 August 1996	IETF
SDLC	Protocol	SNA	Data Link	Synchronous data link control	IBM – SNA FORMATS GA27-3136-10 June 1989	Proprietary
SDP	Protocol	Other	None	Session Description Protocol	None	Unknown

Name	Stack Protocol Sub	Protocol Suite	Protocol Layer	Description	Documents and Rev	Standard
SER	Protocol	Novell NetWare	Network	Serialization packet; split from IPX	Novell's NetWare LAN Analysis. N003 1994	Proprietary
SIP	Protocol	TCP/IP	Application	Protocol for creating, modifying, and terminating sessions over TCP/UDP with one or more participants	RFC 2543 March 1999	IETF
SIP-L3	Protocol	SMDS	Network	SMDS Interface Protocol Layer 3	None	IEEE
SMB	Protocol	TCP/IP	Application	Server Message Block is a protocol for sharing files, printers, serial ports, and communications abstractions such as named pipes and mail slots between computers	Microsoft Networks/ OpenNET File Sharing Protocol— INTEL PN138446 November 1990 2.0 Microsoft Networks SMB File Sharing Protocol Extensions Version 2.0 November 1988 3.3 Microsoft Networks SMB File Sharing Protocol Extension Version 3.0 November 1989 1.09	IBM

(continues)

(Continued)

Name	Stack Protocol Sub	Protocol Suite	Protocol Layer	Description	Documents and Rev	Standard
SMDS/DXI	Protocol	SMDS	Network	Switched Multimegabit Data Service	None	Proprietary
SME	Protocol	CDPD	Data Link	None	None	CDCP
SMS	Protocol	SS7	Transport	Short Message Service	GSM 04.11 September 1997 5.2.1	ETSI
SMT	Protocol	Other	Data Link	Station Management Protocol Data Unit	Interoperability Lab FDDI Tutorials and Resources, 1999	Unknown
SMTP	Protocol	TCP/IP	Application	Simple Mail Transport Protocol	RFC 1939, May 1996	IETF
SNA	Protocol	SNA	Network	Systems Network Architecture Protocol	Look TH2, TH3, TH4	Proprietary
SNA/SDLC	Stack	AppleTalk	{UNKNOWN}	None	None	Unknown
SNA_5250	Protocol	SNA	Network	IBM 5250 information display system	IBM 5250 Information Display System— Functions Reference Manual March 1987	IBM
SNACP	Protocol	PPP	Data Link	PPP SNA Control Protocol	RFC 2043, October 1996	IETF
SNAP	Protocol	TCP/IP	Data Link	Sub-Network Access Protocol	RFC 1042 February 1988	IETF
SNARH	Protocol	SNA	Transport	SNA request/ response header	IBM—SNA Formats (GA27-3136-10)	Proprietary
SNATH0	Protocol	SNA	Network	SNA header 0	APPN_HPR_ Architecture_ Reference	IBM

Name	Stack Protocol Sub	Protocol Suite	Protocol Layer	Description	Documents and Rev	Standard
SNATH1	Protocol	SNA	Network	SNA header 1	APPN_HPR_ Architecture_ Reference	IBM
SNATH2	Protocol	SNA	Network	SNA transmission header type 2	IBM—SNA Formats (GA27-3136-10) June 1989	Proprietary
SNATH3	Protocol	SNA	Network	SNA transmission header type 3	IBM—SNA Format and Protocol Ref. Manual: Architectural Logic (OBS. SC30-3112-1) November 1980	Proprietary
SNATH4	Protocol	SNA	Network	SNA transmission header type 4	IBM—SNA Format and Protocol Ref. Manual: Architectural Logic (OBS. SC30-3112-1) November 1980	Proprietary
SNATH5	Protocol	SNA	Network	FID5 TH	APPN_HPR_ Architecture_ Reference	IBM
SNDCP	Protocol	SS7	Transport	Subnetwork Dependent Convergence Protocol	GSM 04.65/TS 101 297 July 1998 6.2.0 " " August 1999 6.4	ETSI
SNDCP(CDPD)	Protocol	CDPD	Network	Subnetwork Dependent Convergence Protocol	CDPD	CDCP
SNMP	Protocol	TCP/IP	Application	Simple Network Management Protocol	RFC 1157 May 1990	IETF

(continues)

(Continued)

Name	Stack Protocol Sub	Protocol Suite	Protocol Layer	Description	Documents and Rev	Standard
SNMPv1/2	Protocol	Other	None	To distribute between SNMP v1 to SNMP v2	None	Unknown
SNMPv2	Protocol	Other	None	None	None	Unknown
SOCKS	Protocol	TCP/IP	Transport	SOCKS version 5	RFC 1928 March 1996	IETF
SPANS	Protocol	ATM	Network	Fore Proprietary Signaling Protocol	Spans UNI release 2.3 SPANS NNI release 3.0 SPANS UNI release 3.0	Proprietary
SPANS_	Stack	ATM	None	None	None	Unknown
SPX	Protocol	Novell NetWare	Transport	Sequenced packet exchange; guaranteed packet delivery that split from IPX	Novell's NetWare LAN Analysis 1994	Proprietary
SRP	Protocol	Other	Data Link	SRP Spatial Reuse Protocol	<Draft-tsiang-srp-00.txt> January 1999	Draft
SS7	Stack	Unknown	{UNKNOWN}	None	None	Unknown
SS7/ATM	Stack	Unknown	{UNKNOWN}	None	None	Unknown
SSP	Protocol	HDLC	Data Link	Distance Vector Protocol that establishes and maintains the routing table	RFC-2174 June 1997 {Doc. Rev}	Unknown
T125	Protocol	H.323	Transport	T125	None	ITU
T38TCP	Protocol	TCP/IP	Application	Facsimile Communication Over IP Networks	ITU—T.38 June 1998	ITU
T38UDP	Protocol	TCP/IP	Application	Facsimile Communication Over IP Networks	ITU—T.38 June 1998	ITU

Name	Stack Protocol Sub	Protocol Suite	Protocol Layer	Description	Documents and Rev	Standard
TACACS+	Protocol	TCP/IP	Session	TACACS over TCP or UDP provides access control, including separate authentication, authorization, and accounting services for network devices	Draft-grant-tacacs-00.txt October 1996	IETF
TALI	Protocol	TCP/IP	Transport	Transport Adapter Layer Interface	Draft-benedyk-sigtran-tali-00.txt May 1999	IETF
TCAP	Protocol	SS7	Session	Transaction capabilities, SS7	ITU-T Q.773 March 1993 ANSI T1.114 1995	ITU, ANSI
TCP	Protocol	TCP/IP	Transport	Transport Control Protocol	RFC 793 September 1981 RFC 1072 November 1994 RFC 1693 October 1988 RFC 1146 March 1990 RFC 1323 May 1992	IETF
TDP	Protocol	ATM	Data Link	Tag Distribution Protocol	Cisco system draft September 1996	IETF
TELNET	Protocol	TCP/IP	Application	TELNET Protocol provides bi-directional communication	RFC 854-855.txt May 1983	IETF
TeraData	Protocol	Other	Transport	None	None	Proprietary

(continues)

(Continued)

Name	Stack Protocol Sub	Protocol Suite	Protocol Layer	Description	Documents and Rev	Standard
TFTP	Protocol	TCP/IP	Application	Trivial File Transfer Protocol	RFC 1350 July 1992 RFC 783 July 1992	IETF
THDR	Protocol	SNA	Network	RTP Transport Header	12.3—APPN HPR Architecture Reference	IBM
Timeplex	Protocol	Frame Relay	Data Link	Timeplex	None	Proprietary
Timeplex_	Stack	Frame Relay	Data Link	None	None	Unknown
Timplx_BRE2	Protocol	Frame Relay	Network	Ascom Timeplex BRE2	Ascom Timeplex BRE2 Frame Decoding January 1996	Proprietary
Token_Ring	Protocol	IEEE 802	Data Link	Token Ring access method	8802-5 1995 IEEE 802.5 1996	IEEE
TPKT	Protocol	TCP/IP	Transport	ISO transport service on top of the TCP	RFC 1006 May 1987	ISO
TUP	Protocol	SS7	Session	Signaling System No.7: Telephone User Part	ITU-T Q.723 November 1988	ITU
UDP	Protocol	TCP/IP	Transport	User Datagram Protocol	RFC 768 August 1980	IETF
Unix_Rexec	Protocol	TCP/IP	Application	Remote Login for Unix	None	IETF
Unix_Rlogin	Protocol	TCP/IP	Application	Remote Login for Unix	None	IETF
Unix_Rprint	Protocol	TCP/IP	Application	Remote Login for Unix	None	IETF
Unix_Rshell	Protocol	TCP/IP	Application	Remote Login for Unix	None	IETF
Unix_Rwho	Protocol	TCP/IP	{UNKNOWN}	Uxix Rwho Protocol	Taken from Sniffer	IETF

Name	Stack Protocol Sub	Protocol Suite	Protocol Layer	Description	Documents and Rev	Standard
URP	Protocol	Datakit	Network	Universal Receiver Protocol	AT&T: Internal interface specification (700-283) December 1991	Proprietary
V5	Protocol	V5	Physical	Envelope Function Sublayer for V5 System	V5.1 G.964 June 1994	ITU
V5-BCC	Protocol	V5	Network	Bearer Channel Connection (BCC) Protocol for V5 System	V5.2 G.965 March 1995	ITU
V5-CONTROL	Protocol	V5	Network	Control Protocol for V5 System	V5.1 G.964 1994	ITU
V5-LINK_CONTROL	Protocol	V5	Network	V5 Link Control Protocol for V5 System Manager	V5.2 ITU G.965 March 1995	ITU
V5-PROTECTION	Protocol	V5	Network	V5-Protection Protocol for V5 System	V5.2 G.965 March 1995	ITU
V5-PSTN	Protocol	V5	Network	V5-PSTN Protocol for V5 System	V5.1 G.964 June 1994	ITU
Van_Jacobson	Protocol	TCP/IP	Application	TCP/IP header compression	RFC 1144 February 1990	IETF
VB51	Protocol	ATM	Network	Real-Time Management Coordination Protocol	ITU COM 13-999-E December 1997	ITU

(continues)

(Continued)

Name	Stack Protocol Sub	Protocol Suite	Protocol Layer	Description	Documents and Rev	Standard
VIVID	Protocol	ATM	Data Link	Video voice image data	The ATM Host\Router on Vivid Release 2.x Draft Version 1.0 Newbridge Corporation, January 1996	Newbridge Network Corporation
					Vivid System Forwarding and Cache Management for MPOA Partners draft version 1.0 1996	
VIVIDarm	Protocol	ATM	Data Link	VIVID address registration and management	See vivid.rul	Newbridge Network Corporation
VIVIDbme	Protocol	ATM	Data Link	VIVID broadcast multicast and exception	See vivid.rul	Newbridge Network Corporation
VIVIDccp	Protocol	ATM	Data Link	VIVID Configuration Control Protocol	See vivd.rul	Newbridge Network Corporation
VRRP	Protocol	Other	Network	Virtual Router Redundancy Protocol	2338 April 1998	ETSI
VTP	Protocol	Routers	Data Link	Cisco VLAN Trunk Protocol	Reverse engineering	Proprietary
WCCP	Protocol	TCP/IP	Transport	Web Cache Coordination Protocol version 1	Internet Draft January 1999	Cisco Systems
WDOG	Protocol	Novell NetWare	Network	WatchDog; poll inactive station/ session is valid	Novell's NetWare LAN Analysis, N003 1994	IBM

Name	Stack Protocol Sub	Protocol Suite	Protocol Layer	Description	Documents and Rev	Standard
Wellfleet_BOFL	Protocol	Routers	Data Link	Wellfleet Breath of Life	Structure was understood from record	Proprietary
Wellfleet_SRB	Protocol	Routers	Data Link	Wellfleet Source Routing Bridge Protocol	Structure was understood from record	Proprietary
WMTP	Protocol	TCP/IP	Application	Protocol for transferring data among components of a wireless messaging system	Glenaure document—110-0083-IDD40 Version 1.06 June 1998	Glenaure doc
WSP	Protocol	WAP	{UNKNOWN}	Wireless Session Protocol	WAP WSP May 1999	WAP Forum
WTLS	Protocol	WAP	{UNKNOWN}	Wireless Transport Layer Security Protocol	WAP WTLS 14/5 May 1999	WAP Forum
WTP	Protocol	WAP	{UNKNOWN}	Wireless Transaction Protocol	WAP WTP November 1999	WAP Forum
X.25	Protocol	X.25	Network	X.25 Protocol	Recommendation X.25 March 1993	ITU
X.25/FR	Stack	Frame Relay	Data Link	See framerel.rul	None	Unknown
X.25/LAPB	Stack	Other	Data Link	Stack : LAPB -> X.25	None	Unknown
X.25/LAPB/FR	Stack	Frame Relay	Data Link	None	None	Unknown
X.25/LAPB/FR/ LAPF	Stack	Frame Relay	Data Link	X.25 over Frame Relay	T1.618 Q.922 1997	ITU-CCITT
X.75	Protocol	X.25	Network	X.75 Protocol	x.75 March 1993	ITU
X.75/LAPB	Stack	Other	Data Link	Stack : LAPB -> X.75	None	Unknown
X.75/LAPB/FR	Stack	Frame Relay	Data Link	Encapsulation of ITU-T X.75 over Frame Relay (T1.617 Annex G)	T1.617 1994	Unknown

(continues)

(Continued)

Name	Stack Protocol Sub	Protocol Suite	Protocol Layer	Description	Documents and Rev	Standard
XID	Protocol	SNA	Network	DLC exchange identification information fields	IBM—SNA Formats (GA27-3136-10) June 1989	Proprietary
XID1	Protocol	SNA	Data Link	XID I-field Format 1	12.3—APPN HPR Architecture Reference	IBM
XID3	Protocol	SNA	Network	XID Format 3	12.3—APPN HPR Architecture Reference	IBM
XNS (Intel)	Protocol	XNS	None	Xerox Network Systems Protocol	None	Proprietary
XNS_3Com (Intel)	Protocol	XNS	None	Xerox Network Systems Protocol with a small change	None	Proprietary
XOT	Protocol	TCP/IP	Transport	Cisco Systems X.25 over TCP	RFC 1613	IETF

APPENDIX C

List of ITU-T X.121 Data Country or Geographical Area Codes

This annex forms an integral part of the International Telecommunications Union (ITU-T) X.121 Recommendation.

ITU-T Recommendation X.121 was revised by ITU-T Study Group 7 (1993–1996) and was approved under the World Telecommunication Standardization Conference (WTSC), Resolution No. 1 procedure on October 5, 1996.

This listing is of ITU-T country codes only. Further details regarding X.121 addressing can be found in ITU-T Recommendation X.121 (10/96), available from http://www.itu.ch.

The countries or geographical areas shown in this annex include those that already have code assignments in the case of other public telecommunication networks. The information contained in this annex was correct at the time of publication. Changes are published in the ITU Operational Bulletin.

Table C-1   *Zone 2*

Code	Country or Geographical Area
202	Greece
204	Netherlands (Kingdom of the)
205	Netherlands (Kingdom of the)
206	Belgium
208	France
209	France
210	France
211	France
212	Monaco (Principality of)
213	Andorra (Principality of)
214	Spain
215	Spain

(continues)

Table C-1 *Zone 2 (Continued)*

Code	Country or Geographical Area
216	Hungary (Republic of)
218	Bosnia and Herzegovina (Republic of)
219	Croatia (Republic of)
220	Yugoslavia (Federal Republic of)
222	Italy
223	Italy
224	Italy
225	Vatican City State
226	Romania
228	Switzerland (Confederation of)
229	Switzerland (Confederation of)
230	Czech Republic
231	Slovak Republic
232	Austria
233	Austria
234	United Kingdom of Great Britain and Northern Ireland
235	United Kingdom of Great Britain and Northern Ireland
236	United Kingdom of Great Britain and Northern Ireland
237	United Kingdom of Great Britain and Northern Ireland
238	Denmark
239	Denmark
240	Sweden
242	Norway
243	Norway
244	Finland
246	Lithuania (Republic of)
247	Latvia (Republic of)
248	Estonia (Republic of)
250	Russian Federation
251	Russian Federation

Table C-1   *Zone 2*

Code	Country or Geographical Area
255	Ukraine
257	Belarus (Republic of)
259	Moldova (Republic of)
260	Poland (Republic of)
261	Poland (Republic of)
262	Germany (Federal Republic of)
263	Germany (Federal Republic of)
264	Germany (Federal Republic of)
265	Germany (Federal Republic of)
266	Gibraltar
268	Portugal
269	Portugal
270	Luxembourg
272	Ireland
274	Iceland
276	Albania (Republic of)
278	Malta
280	Cyprus (Republic of)
282	Georgia
283	Armenia (Republic of)
284	Bulgaria (Republic of)
286	Turkey
288	Faeroe Islands
290	Greenland
292	San Marino (Republic of)
293	Slovenia (Republic of)
294	The Former Yugoslav Republic of Macedonia
295	Liechtenstein (Principality of)

Zone 2: Spare Codes **30**

Table C-2 *Zone 3*

Code	Country or Geographical Area
302	Canada
303	Canada
308	Saint Pierre and Miquelon (Collectivité Territoriale de la République Française)
310	United States of America
311	United States of America
312	United States of America
313	United States of America
314	United States of America
315	United States of America
316	United States of America
330	Puerto Rico
332	United States Virgin Islands
334	Mexico
335	Mexico
338	Jamaica
340	Guadeloupe (French Department of) and Martinique (French Department of)
342	Barbados
344	Antigua and Barbuda
346	Cayman Islands
348	British Virgin Islands
350	Bermuda
352	Grenada
354	Montserrat
356	Saint Kitts and Nevis
358	Saint Lucia
360	Saint Vincent and the Grenadines
362	Netherlands Antilles
363	Aruba
364	Bahamas (Commonwealth of the)
365	Anguilla

Table C-2   *Zone 3*

Code	Country or Geographical Area
366	Dominica (Commonwealth of)
368	Cuba
370	Dominican Republic
372	Haiti (Republic of)
374	Trinidad and Tobago
376	Turks and Caicos Islands

Zone 3: Spare Codes **64**

Table C-3   *Zone 4*

Code	Country or Geographical Area
400	Azerbaijani Republic
401	Kazakstan (Republic of)
404	India (Republic of)
410	Pakistan (Islamic Republic of)
411	Pakistan (Islamic Republic of)
412	Afghanistan (Islamic State of)
413	Sri Lanka (Democratic Socialist Republic of)
414	Myanmar (Union of)
415	Lebanon
416	Jordan (Hashemite Kingdom of)
417	Syrian Arab Republic
418	Iraq (Republic of)
419	Kuwait (State of)
420	Saudi Arabia (Kingdom of)
421	Yemen (Republic of)
422	Oman (Sultanate of)
424	United Arab Emirates
425	Israel (State of)
426	Bahrain (State of)
427	Qatar (State of)

(continues)

Table C-3   *Zone 4 (Continued)*

Code	Country or Geographical Area
428	Mongolia
429	Nepal
430	United Arab Emirates (Abu Dhabi)
431	United Arab Emirates (Dubai)
432	Iran (Islamic Republic of)
434	Uzbekistan (Republic of)
436	Tajikistan (Republic of)
437	Kyrgyz Republic
438	Turkmenistan
440	Japan
441	Japan
442	Japan
443	Japan
450	Korea (Republic of)
452	Vietnam (Socialist Republic of)
453	Hong Kong
454	Hong Kong
455	Macau
456	Cambodia (Kingdom of)
457	Lao People's Democratic Republic
460	China (People's Republic of)
466	Taiwan, China
467	Democratic People's Republic of Korea
470	Bangladesh (People's Republic of)
472	Maldives (Republic of)
480	Korea (Republic of)
481	Korea (Republic of)

Zone 4: Spare Codes **53**

Table C-4   *Zone 5*

Code	Country or Geographical Area
502	Malaysia
505	Australia
510	Indonesia (Republic of)
515	Philippines (Republic of the)
520	Thailand
525	Singapore (Republic of)
528	Brunei Darussalam
530	New Zealand
534	Northern Mariana Islands (Commonwealth of the)
535	Guam
536	Nauru (Republic of)
537	Papua New Guinea
539	Tonga (Kingdom of)
540	Solomon Islands
541	Vanuatu (Republic of)
542	Fiji (Republic of)
543	Wallis and Futuna (French Overseas Territory)
544	American Samoa
545	Kiribati (Republic of)
546	New Caledonia (French Overseas Territory)
547	French Polynesia (French Overseas Territory)
548	Cook Islands
549	Western Samoa (Independent State of)
550	Micronesia (Federated States of)

Zone 5: Spare Codes **76**

Table C-5   *Zone 6*

Code	Country or Geographical Area
602	Egypt (Arab Republic of)
603	Algeria (People's Democratic Republic of)
604	Morocco (Kingdom of)
605	Tunisia
606	Libya (Socialist People's Libyan Arab Jamahiriya)
607	Gambia (Republic of the)
608	Senegal (Republic of)
609	Mauritania (Islamic Republic of)
610	Mali (Republic of)
611	Guinea (Republic of)
612	Côte d'Ivoire (Republic of)
613	Burkina Faso
614	Niger (Republic of the)
615	Togolese Republic
616	Benin (Republic of)
617	Mauritius (Republic of)
618	Liberia (Republic of)
619	Sierra Leone
620	Ghana
621	Nigeria (Federal Republic of)
622	Chad (Republic of)
623	Central African Republic
624	Cameroon (Republic of)
625	Cape Verde (Republic of)
626	Sao Tome and Principe (Democratic Republic of)
627	Equatorial Guinea (Republic of)
628	Gabonese Republic
629	Congo (Republic of the)

Table C-5   *Zone 6*

Code	Country or Geographical Area
630	Zaire (Republic of)
631	Angola (Republic of)
632	Guinea-Bissau (Republic of)
633	Seychelles (Republic of)
634	Sudan (Republic of the)
635	Rwandese Republic
636	Ethiopia (Federal Democratic Republic of)
637	Somali Democratic Republic
638	Djibouti (Republic of)
639	Kenya (Republic of)
640	Tanzania (United Republic of)
641	Uganda (Republic of)
642	Burundi (Republic of)
643	Mozambique (Republic of)
645	Zambia (Republic of)
646	Madagascar (Republic of)
647	Reunion (French Department of)
648	Zimbabwe (Republic of)
649	Namibia (Republic of)
650	Malawi
651	Lesotho (Kingdom of)
652	Botswana (Republic of)
653	Swaziland (Kingdom of)
654	Comoros (Islamic Federal Republic of the)
655	South Africa (Republic of)

Zone 6: Spare Codes **47**

Table C-6   *Zone 7*

Code	Country or Geographical Area
702	Belize
704	Guatemala (Republic of)
706	El Salvador (Republic of)
708	Honduras (Republic of)
710	Nicaragua
712	Costa Rica
714	Panama (Republic of)
716	Peru
722	Argentine Republic
724	Brazil (Federative Republic of)
725	Brazil (Federative Republic of)
730	Chile
732	Colombia (Republic of)
734	Venezuela (Republic of)
736	Bolivia (Republic of)
738	Guyana
740	Ecuador
742	Guiana (French Department of)
744	Paraguay (Republic of)
746	Suriname (Republic of)
748	Uruguay (Eastern Republic of)

Zone 7: Spare Codes **79**

International Country Codes

The following table lists country codes, international direct dialing (IDD) prefixes, and national direct dialing (NDD) prefixes. The country code is the national prefix to be used when dialing to that particular country from another country. The country codes and prefixes are as follows.

Country	Country Code	IDD International Prefix	NDD National Prefix
Afghanistan	93	00	0
Albania	355	00	0
Algeria	213	00	7
American Samoa	684	00	
Andorra, Principality of	376	00	
Angola, Republic of	244	00	0
Anguilla	1-264*	011	1
Antarctica	672		
Antigua	1-268*	011	1
Argentina	54	00	0
Armenia	374	00	8
Aruba	297	00	
Ascension Island	247	01	
Australia*	61	0011 (voice calls), 0015 (fax calls), 0018 (bulk international access)	0
Austria	43	00	0
Azerbaijan	994	810	8
Bahamas	1-242*	011	1
Bahrain	973	00	

(continues)

(Continued)

Country	Country Code	IDD International Prefix	NDD National Prefix
Bangladesh	880	00	0
Barbados	1-246*	011	1
Barbuda	1-268*	011	1
Belarus	375	8† 10*	8
Belgium	32	00	
Belize	501	00	0
Benin	229	00	
Bermuda	1-441*	011	1
Bhutan	975	00	
Bolivia	591	00	0
Bosnia and Herzegovina	387	00	0
Botswana	267	00	
Brazil	55	0021 (Embratel); 0023 (Intelig)	021 (Embratel); 023 (Intelig); 0 (mobile phones)
British Virgin Islands	1-284*	011	1
Brunei	673	00	0
Bulgaria	359	00	0
Burkina Faso	226	00	
Burundi	257	90	
Cambodia	855	00	0
Cameroon	237	00	
Canada	1	011	1
Cape Verde Islands	238	0	
Cayman Islands	1-345*	011	1
Central African Republic	236	19	
Chad	235	15	
Chatham Island (New Zealand)	64	00	

Country	Country Code	IDD International Prefix	NDD National Prefix
Chile	56	00	0
China, People's Republic of	86	00	0
Christmas Island	61	00	0
Cocos-Keeling Islands	61	0011	0
Colombia	57	009 (Telecom), 007 (ETB/Mundo), or 05 (Orbitel)	09
Comoros	269	10	
Congo	242	00	
Congo, Dem Rep of (Former Zaire)	243	00	
Cook Islands	682	00	00
Costa Rica	506	00	
Croatia	385	00	0
Cuba	53	119	0
Cuba (Guantanamo Bay)	5399	00	0
Curacao	599	00	
Cyprus	357	00	0
Czech Republic	420	00, 52 (discount carrier)	0
Denmark	45	00	
Diego Garcia	246	00	
Djibouti	253	00	
Dominica	1-767*	011	1
Dominican Republic	1-809*	011	1
East Timor	670	00	
Easter Island	56	00	
Ecuador	593	00	0
Egypt	20	00	0
El Salvador	503	0 144+0	
Equatorial Guinea	240	00	
Eritrea	291	00	0

(continues)

(Continued)

Country	Country Code	IDD International Prefix	NDD National Prefix
Estonia	372	00	0
Ethiopia	251	00	0
Faeroe Islands	298	009	
Falkland Island	500	0	
Fiji Islands	679	05	
Finland	358	00, 990, 994, 999	0
France	33	00 (France Telecom), 40 (TELE2), 50 (OMNICOM), 70 (LE 7 CEGETEL), 90 (9 TELECOM)	0
French Antilles	596	00	
French Guiana	594	00	
French Polynesia	689	00	
Gabon	241	00	
Gambia	220	00	
Georgia	995	8~ 10	8
Germany	49	00	0
Ghana	233	00	
Gibraltar	350	00	
Global Mobile Satellite System (GMSS)	881		
Greece	30	00	0
Greenland	299	009	
Grenada	1-473*	011	1
Guadeloupe	590	00	
Guam	1-671*	011	1
Guantanamo Bay	5399	00	0
Guatemala, Republic of	502	00 130+00	0
Guinea, Republic of	224	00	0
Guinea-Bissau	245	00	
Guyana	592	001	0

Country	Country Code	IDD International Prefix	NDD National Prefix
Haiti	509	00	0
Honduras	504	00	0
Hong Kong	852	001-HKCWT (their phone booths are most commonly seen in the street), 0080 – Hutchison, 009 – New World	
Hungary	36	00	06
Iceland	354	00	0
India	91	00	0
Indonesia	62	001, 008	0
Inmarsat (Atlantic Ocean East)	871	00	
Inmarsat (Atlantic Ocean West)	874	00	
Inmarsat (Indian Ocean)	873	00	
Inmarsat (Pacific Ocean)	872	00	
Inmarsat SNAC	870		
Iran	98	00	0
Iraq	964	00	0
Ireland	353	00	0
Iridum	8816, 8817		
Israel	972	00 (default selected carrier, not available from public phones); 012 (Golden Lanes); 013 (Barak LTD); or 014 (Bezeq LTD)	0
Italy	39	00	
Ivory Coast	225	00	0
Jamaica	1-876*	011	1
Japan	81	001 (KDD) 010 0061 (cable and wireless IDC) 0041 (Japan Telecom	0
Jordan	962	00	0

(continues)

(Continued)

Country	Country Code	IDD International Prefix	NDD National Prefix
Kazakhstan	7	8~ 10	8
Kenya	254	000	0
Kiribati	686	00	0
Korea (North)	850	00	0
Korea (South)	82	001, 002	0, 082
Kuwait	965	00	0
Kyrgyz Republic	996	8~ 10	8
Laos	856	14	0
Latvia	371	00	8
Lebanon	961	00	0
Lesotho	266	00	0
Liberia	231	00	22
Libya	218	00	0
Liechtenstein	423	00	
Lithuania	370	8~ 10	8
Luxembourg	352	00	
Macau	853	00	0
Macedonia (former Republic of Yugoslavia)	389	00	0
Madagascar	261	00	0
Malawi	265	101	
Malaysia	60	00	0
Maldives	960	00	0
Mali Republic	223	00	0
Malta	356	00	0
Marshall Islands	692	011	1
Martinique	596	00	0
Mauritania	222	00	0
Mauritius	230	00	0
Mayotte Island	269	10	
Mexico	52	00	01

Country	Country Code	IDD International Prefix	NDD National Prefix
Micronesia, Federal States of	691	011	1
Midway Island	808	00	0
Moldova	373	8~ 10	8
Monaco	377	00	0
Mongolia	976	00	0
Montserrat	1-664*	011	1
Morocco	212	00~	
Mozambique	258	00	0
Myanmar	95	0	
Namibia	264	09	0
Nauru	674	00	0
Nepal	977	00	0
Netherlands Antilles	599	00	0
Netherlands	31	00	0
Nevis	1-869*	011	1
New Caledonia	687	00	0
New Zealand	64	00	0
Nicaragua	505	00	0
Niger	227	00	0
Nigeria	234	009	0
Niue	683	00	0
Norfolk Island	672	00	
Northern Marianas Islands (Saipan, Rota, Tinian)	1-670*	011	1
Norway	47	00	
Oman	968	00	0
Pakistan	92	00	0
Palau	680	011	
Palestine	970	00	0
Panama	507	0	0
Papua New Guinea	675	05	

(continues)

(Continued)

Country	Country Code	IDD International Prefix	NDD National Prefix
Paraguay, Republic of	595	00	0
Peru	51	00	0
Philippines	63	00	0
Poland	48	0~ 0	0
Portugal	351	00	
		882 Rubicon	
Puerto Rico	1-787*	011	1
Qatar	974	0	0
Reunion Island	262	00	0
Romania	40	00	0
Russia	7	8~ 10	8~
Rwanda	250	00	0
St. Helena	290	01	
St. Kitts/Nevis	1-869*	011	1
St. Pierre & Miquelon	508	00	0
St. Vincent and the Grenadines	1-784*	011	1
St. Lucia	1-758*	011	1
San Marino	378	00	0
Sao Tome and Principe	239	00	0
Saudi Arabia	966	00	0
Senegal	221	00	0
Serbia	381	99	0
Seychelles	248	00	0
Sierra Leone	232	00	0
Singapore	65	001 - Singtel IDD 002 - MobileOne IDD 008 - Starhub IDD 012 - Singtel FaxPlus (fax over IP) 013 - Singtel BudgetCall (voice recommended only/fax possible) 018 - Starhub I-Call (voice over IP) 019 - Singtel V019 (voice over IP)	

Country	Country Code	IDD International Prefix	NDD National Prefix
Slovak Republic	421	00	0
Slovenia	386	00	0
Solomon Islands	677	00	
Somalia	252	19	
South Africa	27	09	0
Spain	34	00 or 07	9 (also required after IDD on international calls to Spain)
Sri Lanka	94	00	0
Sudan	249	00	0
Surinam	597	00	
Swaziland	268	00	
Sweden	46	00	0
Switzerland	41	00	0
Syria	963	00	0
Taiwan	886	002	
Tajikistan	992	8~ 10	8
Tanzania	255	000	0
Thailand	66	001 (to call Malaysia from Thailand, dial 007-60 + area code)	0
Togo	228		
Tokelau	690	00	
Tonga	676	00	
Trinidad and Tobago	1-868*	011	1
Tunisia	216	00	0
Turkey	90	00	0
Turkmenistan, Republic of	993	8~ 10	8
Turks and Caicos Island	1-649*	011	1

(continues)

(Continued)

Country	Country Code	IDD International Prefix	NDD National Prefix
Tuvalu	688	00	
Uganda	256	000	0
Ukraine	380	8~ 10	8
United Arab Emirates	971	00	
United Kingdom*	44	00	0
United States of America	1	011	1
Universal Personal Telecommunications	878		
Uruguay	598	00	0
US Virgin Islands	1-340*	011	1
Uzbekistan	998	8~ 10	8
Vanuatu	678	00	
Vatican City	39	00	
Venezuela	58	00	
Vietnam	84	00	
Wake Island	808	00	
Wallis and Futuna	681	19~	
Western Samoa, Independent State of	685	0	
Yemen, Republic of	967	00	0
Yugoslavia, Federal Republic of	381	99	0
Zambia, Republic of	260	00	0
Zanzibar	255	00	
Zimbabwe, Republic of	263	00	0

*These countries are part of the North America Numbering Plan (NANP), although some of them are far removed from North America (and Mexico is not included). The country code for all NANP countries is 1; the numbers that follow function similar to area codes in the U.S. and Canada.
~Await a second tone before dialing the next number.

Source: AT&T International Dialing Guide; Microsoft TechNet Knowledge Base; ITU Documents; personal reports.

APPENDIX E

Bibliography

Black, Uyless D. *IP Routing Protocols: RIP, OSPF, BGP, PNNI, and Cisco Routing Protocols*. Prentice Hall PTR, 2000.

"Cisco SNMP." Cisco Systems. http://www.cisco.com/warp/public/535/3.html.

Cisco Systems, Inc. *Internetworking Technologies Handbook: An Essential Reference for Every Network Professional*. 3rd ed. Cisco Press, 2000.

———. *Internetworking Troubleshooting Handbook (Cisco Press Core Series)*. 2nd ed. Cisco Press, 2001.

Comer, Douglas. *Internetworking with TCP/IP Vol. I: Principles, Protocols, and Architecture*. 4th ed. Vol. 1. Prentice Hall, 2000.

"Configuring Frame Relay." Cisco Systems. http://www.cisco.com/univercd/cc/td/doc/product/software/ios121/121cgcr/wan_c/wcdfrely.htm.

"Configuring Frame Relay and Frame Relay Traffic Shaping." Cisco Systems. http://www.cisco.com/univercd/cc/td/doc/product/software/ios120/12cgcr/qos_c/qcpart4/qcfrts.htm.

"Configuring IP Routing Protocols." Cisco Systems. http://www.cisco.com/univercd/cc/td/doc/product/software/ios11/cbook/ciproute.htm.

Cunningham, David, William G. Lane, and Bill Lane. *Gigabit Ethernet Networking*. Pearson Higher Education, 1999.

Davidson, Jonathan, et al. *Voice over IP Fundamentals*. Cisco Press, 2000.

Davie, Bruce S., Larry L. Peterson, and David Clark. *Computer Networks: A Systems Approach*. 2nd ed. Morgan Kaufmann Publishers, 1999.

Davie, Bruce S. and Yakov Rekhter. *MPLS: Technology and Applications*. Morgan Kaufmann Publishers, 2000.

"Designing ATM Networks." Cisco Systems. http://www.cisco.com/univercd/cc/td/doc/cisintwk/idg4/nd2008.htm.

Doyle, Jeff. *Routing TCP/IP Volume I (CCIE Professional Development)*. Vol. 1. Cisco Press, 1998.

Doyle, Jeff and Jennifer DeHaven Carroll. *Routing TCP/IP, Volume II (CCIE Professional Development).* Vol. 2. Cisco Press, 2001.

Guichard, Jim and Ivan Pepelnjak. *MPLS and VPN Architectures: A Practical Guide to Understanding, Designing, and Deploying MPLS and MPLS-Enabled VPNs.* Cisco Press, 2000.

Halabi, Sam and Danny McPherson (contributor). *Internet Routing Architectures.* 2nd ed. Cisco Press, 2000.

Held, Gilbert. *Enhancing LAN Performance: Issues and Answers.* 3rd ed. John Wiley & Sons, 2000.

————. *Understanding Data Communications.* 6th ed. New Riders Publishing, 1999.

————. *Voice over Data Networks.* 1st ed. McGraw-Hill Publishing, 1998.

Huitema, Christian. *Routing in the Internet.* 2nd ed. Prentice Hall PTR, 2000.

Lee, Donald C. *Enhanced IP Services for CISCO Networks: A Practical Resource for Deploying Quality of Service, Security, IP Routing, and VPN Services.* Cisco Press, 1999.

McDysan, David E. and Darren L. Spohn. *ATM Theory and Application.* McGraw-Hill Series on Computer Communications by Signature edition. McGraw-Hill Professional Publishing, 1998.

McGregor, Mark. *Cisco WAN Quick Start.* Ed. R. W. McCarty. Cisco Systems/Cisco Press, 2000.

McQuerry, Steve and Stephen Foy. *Cisco Voice over Frame Relay, ATM, and IP.* Ed. K. McGrew. Cisco Press, 2001.

"MPLS-Based Layer 2 Virtual Private Networks." Juniper Networks. http://www.juniper.net/techcenter/techpapers/200009.html.

"MPOA." The Applied Technologies Group, 1997. http://www.techguide.com.

Muthukrishnan, K. and A. Malis. RFC 2917, "A Core MPLS IP VPN Architecture." September 2000. http://www.ietf.org/rfc/rfc2917.txt.

"Optical Networks." Alcatel for The International Engineering Consortium. http://www.iec.org.

Paradyne DSL Sourcebook. 3rd Ed. 2001. http://www.paradyne.com/cgi-bin/universal.perl.

Parkhurst, William R., Ph.D. *Cisco BGP-4 Command and Configuration Handbook.* Cisco Press, 2001.

Pildush, Galina Diker. *CISCO ATM Solutions: Master ATM Implementation of Cisco Networks.* Cisco Press, 2000.

"Planning for Quality of Service." Cisco Systems. http://www.cisco.com/univercd/cc/td/doc/product/rtrmgmt/ciscoasu/class/qpm1_1/using_qo/c1plan.htm.

"Policing and Shaping Overview." Cisco Systems. http://www.cisco.com/univercd/cc/td/doc/product/software/ios122/122cgcr/fqos_c/fqcprt4/qcfpolsh.htm.

RFC 2547bis. "BGP/MPLS VPN Fundamentals." Juniper Networks. http://www.juniper.net/techcenter/techpapers/200012.html.

Riley, Sean and Robert A. Breyer. *Switched, Fast, and Gigabit Ethernet (Mtp Network Engineering Series)*. 3rd ed. New Riders Publishing, 1999.

Rosen, E. and Y. Rekhter. RFC 2547, "BGP/MPLS VPNs." March 1999. http://www.ietf.org/rfc/rfc2547.txt.

Rybaczyk, Peter. *Cisco Router Troubleshooting Handbook*. Hungry Minds, Inc., 2000.

Salvagno, Michael. *Cisco Network Design Handbook: The Ultimate Shop Manual*. Hungry Minds, Inc., 2000.

"SDH Pocket Guide." Acterna. http://www.ttc.com/technical_resources/pocket_guides/sdh_guide1.html.

"SONET Pocket Guide." Acterna. http://www.ttc.com/technical_resources/pocket_guides/sonet_guide.html.

Sportack, Mark A. *IP Routing Fundamentals*. Cisco Press, 1999.

Stallings, William. *Cryptography and Network Security: Principles and Practice*. 2nd ed. Prentice Hall, 1998.

———. *Data and Computer Communications*. 6th ed. Prentice Hall, 2000.

Thomas, Thomas M. II, et al. *Interconnecting Cisco Network Devices*. McGraw-Hill Professional Publishing, 2000.

"T1 Basics." Acterna. http://www.ttc.com/downloads/white_papers/t1_tn.pdf.

"Traffic Engineering for the New Public Network." Juniper Networks. http://www.juniper.net/techcenter/techpapers/200004.html.

"Using the Border Gateway Protocol for Interdomain Routing." Cisco Systems. http://www.cisco.com/univercd/cc/td/doc/cisintwk/ics/icsbgp4.htm.

Vegesna, Srinivas. *IP Quality of Service (Cisco Networking Fundamentals*. Cisco Press, 2001.

"Voice over IP (VoIP)." The Applied Technologies Group, Inc., 1998. http://www.techguide.com.

Wright, Robert. *IP Routing Primer*. Cisco Press, 1998.

INDEX

Numerics

B

C

D

E

G

H

M

N

O

T

Train with authorized Cisco Learning Partners.

Discover all that's possible on the Internet.

One of the biggest challenges facing networking professionals is how to stay current with today's ever-changing technologies in the global Internet economy. Nobody understands this better than Cisco Learning Partners, the only companies that deliver training developed by Cisco Systems.

Just go to **www.cisco.com/go/training_ad**. You'll find more than 120 Cisco Learning Partners in over 90 countries worldwide.* Only Cisco Learning Partners have instructors that are certified by Cisco to provide recommended training on Cisco networks and to prepare you for certifications.

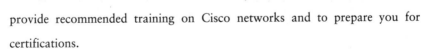

To get ahead in this world, you first have to be able to keep up. Insist on training that is developed and authorized by Cisco, as indicated by the Cisco Learning Partner or Cisco Learning Solutions Partner logo.

Visit **www.cisco.com/go/training_ad** today.

CISCO SYSTEMS

EMPOWERING THE
INTERNET GENERATION™

Cisco Press Solutions

Enhanced IP Services for Cisco Networks
Donald C. Lee, CCIE

1-57870-106-6 • AVAILABLE NOW

This is a guide to improving your network's capabilities by understanding the new enabling and advanced Cisco IOS services that build more scalable, intelligent, and secure networks. Learn the technical details necessary to deploy Quality of Service, VPN technologies, IPsec, the IOS firewall and IOS Intrusion Detection. These services will allow you to extend the network to new frontiers securely, protect your network from attacks, and increase the sophistication of network services.

Developing IP Multicast Networks, Volume I
Beau Williamson, CCIE

1-57870-077-9 • AVAILABLE NOW

This book provides a solid foundation of IP multicast concepts and explains how to design and deploy the networks that will support appplications such as audio and video conferencing, distance-learning, and data replication. Includes an in-depth discussion of the PIM protocol used in Cisco routers and detailed coverage of the rules that control the creation and maintenance of Cisco mroute state entries.

Designing Network Security
Merike Kaeo

1-57870-043-4 • AVAILABLE NOW

Designing Network Security is a practical guide designed to help you understand the fundamentals of securing your corporate infrastructure. This book takes a comprehensive look at underlying security technologies, the process of creating a security policy, and the practical requirements necessary to implement a corporate security policy.

Cisco Press

www.ciscopress.com

Cisco Press Solutions

Residential Broadband, Second Edition
George Abe

1-57870-177-5 • **AVAILABLE NOW**

This book will answer basic questions of residential broadband networks such as: Why do we need high speed networks at home? How will high speed residential services be delivered to the home? How do regulatory or commercial factors affect this technology? Explore such networking topics as xDSL, cable, and wireless.

Internetworking Technologies Handbook, Second Edition
Kevin Downes, CCIE, Merilee Ford, H. Kim Lew, Steve Spanier, Tim Stevenson

1-57870-102-3 • **AVAILABLE NOW**

This comprehensive reference provides a foundation for understanding and implementing contemporary internetworking technologies, providing you with the necessary information needed to make rational networking decisions. Master terms, concepts, technologies, and devices that are used in the internetworking industry today. You also learn how to incorporate networking technologies into a LAN/WAN environment, as well as how to apply the OSI reference model to categorize protocols, technologies, and devices.

OpenCable Architecture
Michael Adams

1-57870-135-X • **AVAILABLE NOW**

Whether you're a television, data communications, or telecommunications professional, or simply an interested business person, this book will help you understand the technical and business issues surrounding interactive television services. It will also provide you with an inside look at the combined efforts of the cable, data, and consumer electronics industries' efforts to develop those new services.

Performance and Fault Management
Paul Della Maggiora, Christopher Elliott, Robert Pavone, Kent Phelps, James Thompson

1-57870-180-5 • **AVAILABLE NOW**

This book is a comprehensive guide to designing and implementing effective strategies for monitoring performance levels and correctng problems in Cisco networks. It provides an overview of router and LAN switch operations to help you understand how to manage such devices, as well as guidance on the essential MIBs, traps, syslog messages, and show commands for managing Cisco routers and switches.

Cisco Press

www.ciscopress.com

Cisco Press Fundamentals

IP Routing Primer

Robert Wright, CCIE

1-57870-108-2 • AVAILABLE NOW

Learn how IP routing behaves in a Cisco router environment. In addition to teaching the core fundamentals, this book enhances your ability to troubleshoot IP routing problems yourself, often eliminating the need to call for additional technical support. The information is presented in an approachable, workbook-type format with dozens of detailed illustrations and real-life scenarios integrated throughout.

Cisco Router Configuration

Allan Leinwand, Bruce Pinsky, Mark Culpepper

1-57870-022-1 • AVAILABLE NOW

An example-oriented and chronological approach helps you implement and administer your internetworking devices. Starting with the configuration devices "out of the box;" this book moves to configuring Cisco IOS for the three most popular networking protocols today: TCP/IP, AppleTalk, and Novell Interwork Packet Exchange (IPX). You also learn basic administrative and management configuration, including access control with TACACS+ and RADIUS, network management with SNMP, logging of messages, and time control with NTP.

IP Routing Fundamentals

Mark A. Sportack

1-57870-071-x • AVAILABLE NOW

This comprehensive guide provides essential background information on routing in IP networks for network professionals who are deploying and maintaining LANs and WANs daily. Explore the mechanics of routers, routing protocols, network interfaces, and operating systems.

Cisco Press

www.ciscopress.com

Cisco Press Solutions

EIGRP Network Design Solutions
Ivan Pepelnjak, CCIE

1-57870-165-1 • AVAILABLE NOW

EIGRP Network Design Solutions uses case studies and real-world configuration examples to help you gain an in-depth understanding of the issues involved in designing, deploying, and managing EIGRP-based networks. This book details proper designs that can be used to build large and scalable EIGRP-based networks and documents possible ways each EIGRP feature can be used in network design, implmentation, troubleshooting, and monitoring.

Top-Down Network Design
Priscilla Oppenheimer

1-57870-069-8 • AVAILABLE NOW

Building reliable, secure, and manageable networks is every network professional's goal. This practical guide teaches you a systematic method for network design that can be applied to campus LANs, remote-access networks, WAN links, and large-scale internetworks. Learn how to analyze business and technical requirements, examine traffic flow and Quality of Service requirements, and select protocols and technologies based on performance goals.

Cisco IOS Releases: The Complete Reference
Mack M. Coulibaly

1-57870-179-1 • AVAILABLE NOW

Cisco IOS Releases: The Complete Reference is the first comprehensive guide to the more than three dozen types of Cisco IOS releases being used today on enterprise and service provider networks. It details the release process and its numbering and naming conventions, as well as when, where, and how to use the various releases. A complete map of Cisco IOS software releases and their relationships to one another, in addition to insights into decoding information contained within the software, make this book an indispensable resource for any network professional.

Cisco Press

Cisco Press Fundamentals

Internet Routing Architectures, Second Edition
Sam Halabi with Danny McPherson
1-57870-233-x • **AVAILABLE NOW**

This book explores the ins and outs of interdomain routing network design with emphasis on BGP-4 (Border Gateway Protocol Version 4)--the de facto interdomain routing protocol. You will have all the information you need to make knowledgeable routing decisions for Internet connectivity in your environment.

Voice over IP Fundamentals
Jonathan Davidson and James Peters
1-57870-168-6 • **AVAILABLE NOW**

Voice over IP (VoIP), which integrates voice and data transmission, is quickly becoming an important factor in network communications. It promises lower operational costs, greater flexibility, and a variety of enhanced applications. This book provides a thorough introduction to this new technology to help experts in both the data and telephone industries plan for the new networks.

For the latest on Cisco Press resources and Certification and

Training guides, or for information on publishing opportunities, visit

www.ciscopress.com

CCIE Professional Development

Cisco LAN Switching

Kennedy Clark, CCIE; Kevin Hamilton, CCIE

1-57870-094-9 • AVAILABLE NOW

This volume provides an in-depth analysis of Cisco LAN switching technologies, architectures, and deployments, including unique coverage of Catalyst network design essentials. Network designs and configuration examples are incorporated throughout to demonstrate the principles and enable easy translation of the material into practice in production networks.

Advanced IP Network Design

Alvaro Retana, CCIE; Don Slice, CCIE; and Russ White, CCIE

1-57870-097-3 • AVAILABLE NOW

Network engineers and managers can use these case studies, which highlight various network design goals, to explore issues including protocol choice, network stability, and growth. This book also includes theoretical discussion on advanced design topics.

Large-Scale IP Network Solutions

Khalid Raza, CCIE; and Mark Turner

1-57870-084-1 • AVAILABLE NOW

Network engineers can find solutions as their IP networks grow in size and complexity. Examine all the major IP protocols in-depth and learn about scalability, migration planning, network management, and security for large-scale networks.

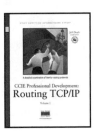

Routing TCP/IP, Volume I

Jeff Doyle, CCIE

1-57870-041-8 • AVAILABLE NOW

This book takes the reader from a basic understanding of routers and routing protocols through a detailed examination of each of the IP interior routing protocols. Learn techniques for designing networks that maximize the efficiency of the protocol being used. Exercises and review questions provide core study for the CCIE Routing and Switching exam.

Cisco Press

www.ciscopress.com

Cisco Career Certifications

Cisco CCNA Exam #640-507 Certification Guide
Wendell Odom, CCIE

0-7357-0971-8 • AVAILABLE NOW

Although it's only the first step in Cisco Career Certification, the Cisco Certified Network Associate (CCNA) exam is a difficult test. Your first attempt at becoming Cisco certified requires a lot of study and confidence in your networking knowledge. When you're ready to test your skills, complete your knowledge of the exam topics, and prepare for exam day, you need the preparation tools found in *Cisco CCNA Exam #640-507 Certification Guide* from Cisco Press.

CCDA Exam Certification Guide
Anthony Bruno, CCIE & Jacqueline Kim

0-7357-0074-5 • AVAILABLE NOW

CCDA Exam Certification Guide is a comprehensive study tool for DCN Exam #640-441. Written by a CCIE and a CCDA, and reviewed by Cisco technical experts, *CCDA Exam Certification Guide* will help you understand and master the exam objectives. In this solid review on the design areas of the DCN exam, you'll learn to design a network that meets a customer's requirements for performance, security, capacity, and scalability.

Interconnecting Cisco Network Devices
Edited by Steve McQuerry

1-57870-111-2 • AVAILABLE NOW

Based on the Cisco course taught worldwide, *Interconnecting Cisco Network Devices* teaches you how to configure Cisco switches and routers in multi-protocol internetworks. ICND is the primary course recommended by Cisco Systems for CCNA #640-507 preparation. If you are pursuing CCNA certification, this book is an excellent starting point for your study.

Designing Cisco Networks
Edited by Diane Teare

1-57870-105-8 • AVAILABLE NOW

Based on the Cisco Systems instructor-led and self-study course available worldwide, *Designing Cisco Networks* will help you understand how to analyze and solve existing network problems while building a framework that supports the functionality, performance, and scalability required from any given environment. Self-assessment through exercises and chapter-ending tests starts you down the path for attaining your CCDA certification.

Cisco Press   www.ciscopress.com

Cisco Press

ciscopress.com

How many computer technology books do you own?
❏ 1   ❏ 2–7   ❏ more than 7

Which best describes your job function? (check all that apply)
❏ Corporate Management	❏ Systems Engineering	❏ IS Management	❏ Cisco Networking
❏ Network Design	❏ Network Support	❏ Webmaster	Academy Program
❏ Marketing/Sales	❏ Consultant	❏ Student	Instuctor
❏ Professor/Teacher	❏ Other _____		

Do you hold any computer certifications? (check all that apply)
❏ MCSE	❏ CCNA	❏ CCDA	
❏ CCNP	❏ CCDP	❏ CCIE	❏ Other _____

Are you currently pursuing a certification? (check all that apply)
❏ MCSE	❏ CCNA	❏ CCDA	
❏ CCNP	❏ CCDP	❏ CCIE	❏ Other _____

On what topics would you like to see more coverage?

_____

_____

Do you have any additional comments or suggestions?

_____

_____

Thank you for completing this survey and registration. Please fold here, seal, and mail to Cisco Press.

Network Consultants Handbook (1-58705-039-0)

Cisco Press
Customer Registration—CP0500227
P.O. Box #781046
Indianapolis, IN 46278-8046

ciscopress.com
Indianapolis, IN 46290
201 West 103rd Street
Cisco Press

Place Stamp Here